# THE INSIDERS' GUIDE® TO

# The Twin Cities

# THE INSIDERS' GUIDE® TO

# The Twin Cities

by
Barbara DeGroot
and
Jack El-Hai

THE INSIDERS' GUIDE®

The Insiders' Guides, Inc.

Co-published and marketed by:
Saint Paul Pioneer Press
Northwest Publications, Inc.
345 Cedar St.
St. Paul, MN 55101
(612) 222-5011

Co-published and distributed by:
The Insiders' Guides, Inc.
P.O. Box 2057 • Highway 64
Manteo, NC 27954
(919) 473-6100

•

FIRST EDITION
1st printing

•

Copyright © 1994
Northwest Publications, Inc.

•

Printed in the
United States of America

•

•

ISBN 0-912367-66-0

## Saint Paul Pioneer Press

Director of New Ventures
**David A. Fryxell**

Advertising Sales Manager
**Lee S. Koch**

Account Executives
**Mary Sue Godfrey, Janice Stober**

Researchers
**Rob Hubbard, Debra Nygren,
Kathleen Rysgaard**

## The Insiders' Guides, Inc.

Publisher/Managing Editor
**Beth P. Storie**

President/General Manager
**Michael McOwen**

Vice President of Advertising
**Murray Kazmenn**

Creative Services Director
**Michael Lay**

Partnership Services Director
**Giles Bissonnette**

Distribution Manager
**Julie Ross**

Fulfillment Coordinator
**Gina Twiford**

Controller
**Claudette Forney**

# Preface

This *Insiders' Guide to the Twin Cities* is for you if you're thinking of visiting Minneapolis-St. Paul, considering relocating there, or simply if you're a current Twin Cities resident who wants to learn more about the rich and complex place in which you live. It's undoubtedly the most complete guide to life in the Twin Cities ever published — and if you use it to its fullest, it will be dog-eared, scribbled upon, highlighted and riddled with bookmarks within a few weeks. You can also use it to introduce others to the area's riches.

The Twin Cities is a changing place, one quite unlike the quiet and homogenous community that existed only a few decades ago. Today it is an artistic center, a healthy business region, a good place to work and a great place to live. Although this guide is not intended to be an encyclopedic, you'll find an incredible amount of information in its pages. If you don't find your own favorite place or event listed here, let us know. We'll undoubtedly be making changes and additions in forthcoming editions.

Although writing this book has been a fun project, using it should prove even more enjoyable. That part of this guide's life is now in your hands.

# About the Authors

## Barbara DeGroot . . .

Barbara DeGroot is a free-lance writer and frequent contributor to the *St. Paul Pioneer Press* newspaper. Her articles also have appeared in local magazines, such as *Mpls.St. Paul* and *Minnesota Parent*.

A graduate of the University of Minnesota, Barbara worked for newspapers in Texas, Nevada and Wisconsin (where she wrote an award-winning column for the *Wausau Daily Herald*) and held a public-relations position in Phoenix, Arizona, before returning home to the "land of loons" in 1985. Last year, she finally came to her senses and got a job in the real world — as a school secretary at Cedar Manor Intermediate Center in St. Louis Park.

A Minneapolis native who grew up in the western suburbs, Barbara fondly remembers a childhood filled with trips to the lake, Aquatennial parades, Lake Harriet band concerts, pickled herring and crackers on Sunday afternoon, family ice-fishing trips and Dayton's sales. Today, she lives in St. Louis Park with her engineer husband, Bob, 12-year-old daughter, Leigh, and a Brittany spaniel puppy named Larry. Her free time is spent playing tennis, volunteering at school, traveling, catching the latest movies and, of course, exploring these ever-fascinating cities.

## Jack El-Hai . . .

Jack El-Hai said farewell to Los Angeles and became a Twin Cities resident in 1980. A freelancer who works from a Minneapolis warehouse-district office, he has written more than 300 articles on the arts, history, business, current events and interesting personalities for such publications as *American Heritage*, *Minnesota Monthly*, *City Pages*, the *Minneapolis Star Tribune* and the *St. Paul Pioneer Press*. He is also a contributing editor of *Mpls.St.Paul Magazine* and *Architecture Minnesota*. The Minnesota Historical Society Press published his book *Minnesota Collects* in 1992.

A writer of fiction as well, he is featured in the forthcoming anthology *25 Minnesota Writers* (Nodin Press) and has published short stories in *Sunday Magazine* of the *Minneapolis Star Tribune*, *Twin Cities Magazine* and *Northern Lit Quarterly*, among other publications. He's a winner of a Loft-McKnight Award, the Loft's Mentor Series and Creative Non-Fiction competitions, the Great Lakes

Regional Writers Competition, and a Travel and Study Grant from the Center for Arts Criticism.

In 1988 the Minnesota Composers Forum staged El-Hai's one-act opera libretto *Scotichronicon*, based upon a tale by Sir Walter Scott. Fond of music in many forms, he plays mandolin, mandola and mando-cello and is the founder of the Minnesota Mandolin Orchestra.

El-Hai can be contacted at jelhai@maroon.tc.umn.edu. via e-mail.

*Minnehaha Falls inspired Longfellow's "The Song of Hiawatha."*

# Acknowledgments

## Jack . . .

Diane Hellekson contributed most of the information in the Restaurants section, and we also thank the people at all of the libraries, government agencies, community organizations and businesses that provided arcane data of all sorts.

## Barbara . . .

wishes to thank Rob Hubbard. The Nightlife chapter was based on information supplied by Rob and we are most grateful. She also thanks Karen Keljik, David Hawley, Larry May, Harris Smith, Judi Mollerus and countless others who supplied important information and advice. Gratitude also to: Beth Storie and David Fryxell, for their editorial assistance; Brad Brinkworth, for the photo; her mother, Betty Lundquist, for her support; and, most importantly, her husband, Bob, and daughter, Leigh, for their love, patience and encouragement throughout this challenging project.

# Minnesota

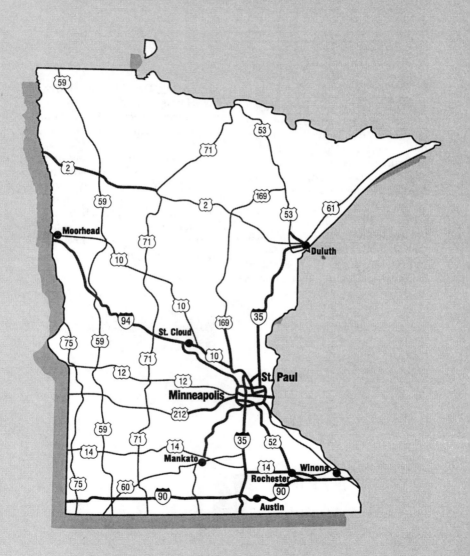

# We don't invite comparison.

## WE INSIST ON IT.

Quality. It's just as important in a diamond as it is in anything else you own. But that's only part of the reason we insist you compare when purchasing a diamond for that special person in your life.

We're convinced that when you do, you'll find R.F. Moeller Jeweler offers the best quality, the best selection and the best price on diamonds — from 25 points up to 4 carats.

So don't feel slighted if we suggest you compare our diamonds with those of other jewelers before you buy. In the end, we'll both be glad you did.

## R.F. MOELLER
### J E W E L E R

**50th & France**
3901 W. 50th St., Edina • 926-6166

**Highland Village**
2073 Ford Pkwy., St. Paul • 698-6321

# Minneapolis

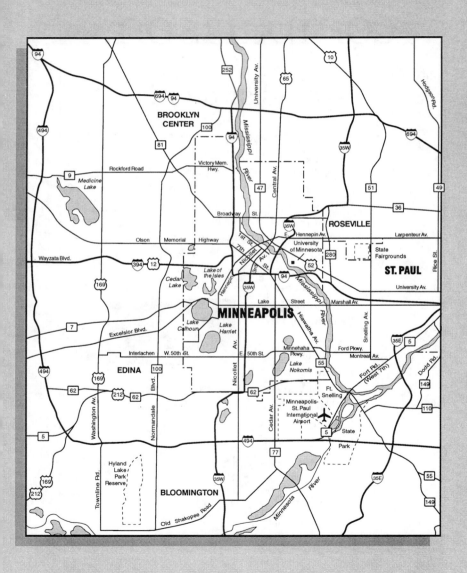

# St. Paul

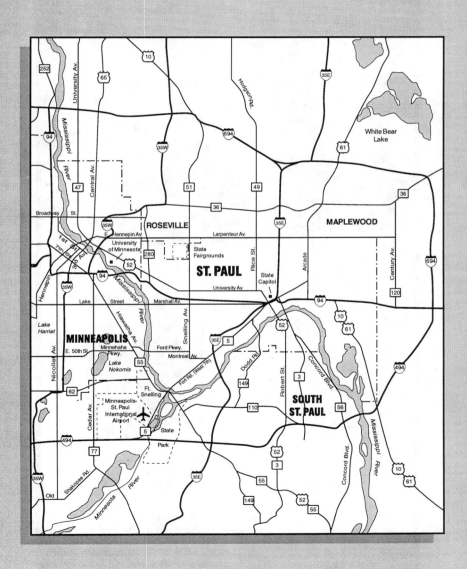

# Table of Contents

# Directory of Maps

Photo: Richard Marshall, Pioneer Press

*This view of the Norwest and IDS buildings is from the Multifoods Tower in downtown Minneapolis.*

# *Inside*
# The Twin Cities

The overhead honking of Canada geese in flight. The hot, sticky scent of the Minnesota State Fair. The head of a parking meter impudently protruding from a pile of snow. A deer gliding across headlight beams on a suburban road. The house lights dimming and the crowd hushing at a Guthrie Theater performance. The clatter of a bicycle careening down Grand Avenue Hill.

Like every other place in the world, the Twin Cities is a unique mixture of sights, smells and sounds — a distinctive coming together of earth, water, sky and people. In our case the earth is fertile, the water plentiful, the sky often cold, and the people generous and friendly (with a deep-down reluctance to draw too close too quickly).

## *The Personality of the Twin Cities*

Can a metropolitan area consisting of more than 2 million souls even have an identifiable personality? You bet it can, because a city's character is built as much from public perception as from truth.

Take a poll of people around the country and you'll discover that certain images and qualities recur when they think about the Twin Cities:

• Cultural richness. There are a lot of facts to back up this perception. Here's a metropolitan area that has four major art museums, two big orchestras, the nation's foremost regional theater, bookstores galore, a wealth of talent in jazz, pop and gospel music, a pair of the finest science and history museums in the country, unusually strong public radio and TV, and a rapidly diversifying ethnic mix that keeps the area's culture in a healthy flux.

• An involved community. It's true — a lot of companies reinvest in the community, an extremely strong group of local foundations feed money to area nonprofits of all kinds, and people are unusually supportive of neighborhood associations and other community organizations.

• Cold. There's no getting around this one. The only cities in the continental United States that can claim a colder climate are Duluth, Bismarck and Great Falls, and they probably won't. To imagine the Twin Cities as a metropolitan Siberia, however, is to forget about the months of May through October, when snow is unlikely.

• Flat. This perception is demonstrably false. Much of St. Paul is actually hilly; try the walk from the riverfront to the State Capitol. Minneapolis is significantly flatter, but the areas near the Mississippi River in both cities (and some suburbs) contain high bluffs.

• Ethnically homogeneous. The image of the Twin Cities as a mini-Scandinavia was never truly accurate. St. Paul, in fact, has drawn most of its population from such places as Ireland, Canada, Germany, Great Britain, Southeast Asia and Mexico. Minneapolis, which always has had a larger number of Norwegians, Finns, Danes and Swedes and their descendants, now boasts increasing numbers of African Americans, Russian Jews, Ethiopians and American Indians. At the same time, the suburbs — particularly those north and south of Minneapolis — are growing richer with residents of varied cultural backgrounds. The Twin Cities, although it remains the least racially mixed of the nation's top 25 metropolitan areas, is white bread no more.

• Crime free. There is actually a division of opinion here, with outsiders perceiving the Twin Cities as a haven free of murders, muggings and carjackings, while residents often believe the crime rate is soaring. Comparative statistics show that the Twin Cities' overall crime rate is lower than that of most of the other largest metropolitan areas, with significantly lower violent crime figures and relatively high property crime figures.

• Nice. See the discussion of "Minnesota nice" later in this chapter.

It is a good mixture of people and qualities we have here, one that keeps the Twin Cities economically and culturally healthy while spurring its people to steadily and painfully leave behind this metropolitan area's origins as a group of isolated settlements perched on the windy plains of the Upper Midwest.

## Looking Through the Mists of Time

Long before those settlements sprouted, perhaps 10,000 years before any European settlers set eyes upon the land that would become the Twin Cities, the first people arrived. It was good food that brought them here. These Paleo-Indians, a big-game hunting people, probably came from the south, following herds of mammoths and bison that roamed plains leveled by earlier advances of ice. The mammoths eventually vanished, and the people that hunted them left the region.

Some time after, another peo-

Insiders' Tips

In its first official census (1850), Minnesota had only 6,077 people.

Photo: Joe Oden, Pioneer Press

*The Mississippi River by downtown St. Paul with the recently replaced High Bridge.*

ple migrated to the area. They ate berries, nuts, fish and small animals. These people — now known as the Late Woodland people — grew in number, becoming some of the first North Americans to fashion tools and weapons out of metal. Other innovations arrived in succeeding years: the atlatl, a hinged pole that gave spear-throwers greater range and speed; the ability to weave baskets and floor mats from plant stalks; techniques of harvesting wild rice, an abundant plant that became an important food source; and the use of clay to produce pots and jars. They fished, decorated their pottery, smoked tobacco, traded with other people to the south, and buried their dead in some 10,000 mounds that once dotted the land of Minnesota. Most of the mounds are now gone.

For reasons not completely understood, the Late Woodland people left the region by about 500 or 1000 A.C.E. (After the Common Era). Over the course of centuries, the Dakota Indians, part of a great community of people who lived throughout much of the Midwest, arrived and occupied the land upon which the Twin Cities now stands. The Dakota were hunters of game, planters of gardens, harvesters of corn and wild rice, and traders. Dakota bands established villages at Lake Calhoun and elsewhere in the area.

To the north and east were the Ojibwa Indians (sometimes called the Chippewa), whose roots lay among the Algonquin tribes of eastern North America. The Ojibwa and Dakota were in frequent conflict over hunting and fishing grounds, and it was the Ojibwa who coined the pejorative name "Nadouessioux" (later shortened to "Sioux"), meaning "little snakes," for the Dakota.

By the middle of the 17th century, Frenchmen had entered the region via Lake Superior and moved as far west as Lake Mille Lacs. These Europeans could more properly be called prospectors than explorers, because their main aim was to investigate and eventually exploit the potential of the fur trade. The year 1680 marked the arrival of the Franciscan missionary Louis Hennepin, who ventured from the south, up the Mississippi River. Held captive for a time by the Dakota, Hennepin became perhaps the first European to view the Mississippi River's Falls of St. Anthony (which are now at the heart of downtown Minneapolis). Hennepin returned to France and wrote a largely fictitious account of his Minnesota sojourn.

The French built stockades in several locations south and west of the Twin Cities, but the English were steadily weakening the French influence in the region. A handful of large English trading companies opened posts and directed the fur trade, including the Hudson Bay Company and the North West Company. In 1763 the French gave up their claim to land in North America, and three years later Jonathan Carver, a native New Englander working for the British government, arrived in Minnesota territory to survey and explore. He scrutinized much of the land in present-day Minneapolis and St. Paul and wrote a best-selling account of his adventures.

The next big-name explorer to set foot in the Twin Cities area was Zebulon Pike, the U.S. Army officer whose name later went to Pike's Peak in Colorado. In 1805, with the territory now supposedly under United States control after the Louisiana Purchase of 1803, he came north from St. Louis to survey the upper reaches of the Mississippi River. He bargained with the Dakota to gain rights to a military site at the confluence of the Mississippi and Minnesota rivers, hoisting the U.S. flag at the future location of Fort Snelling. After Pike's departure, however, the British fur trading concerns refused to recognize any U.S. jurisdiction over the area. Not until the United States and Britain signed the treaty of Ghent in 1814 did the territory become indisputably American.

With all the international jockeying for the territory now completed, the U.S. government moved to strengthen its control. In 1820 Captain Josiah Snelling and a garrison of Army troops began constructing a fort on the land that Pike had acquired for a military post years earlier. Initially called Fort St. Anthony, the military installation became known as Fort Snelling in 1825. Now crowded between freeways, federal buildings and the Minneapolis-St. Paul International Airport, the fort dominated the area in the 19th century in ways that are unimaginable today.

Starting in 1823, for instance, the fort was the docking area for the first steamboats to arrive up the river from St. Louis. Its soldiers constructed the first flour mill and sawmill at the Falls of St. Anthony, thus sparking the birth of Minneapolis. The fort also served as a refuge for some of the region's first farm families, who arrived in 1821.

## Talking Minnesotan

| Minnesotan term | English translation |
| --- | --- |
| dale | shopping center |
| that's interesting | that's stupid |
| cool | freezing |
| hot dish | casserole |
| rusty bucket | rusty car |
| ish | yuk |
| pop | soda |
| rubber binder | rubber band |
| salad | Jell-O |
| Scandahoovian | Scandinavian |
| uff da | oy vey |
| Strib | *Star Tribune* newspaper |
| outstate | Outside the Twin Cities but inside Minnesota ("Greater Minnesota" is a term some outstaters prefer.) |

In 1840, these people were finally evicted from the fort reservation, and they moved across the Mississippi and several miles north to establish a new community.

They found another character already squatting on that land: Pierre Parrant, a French Canadian whisky seller. Parrant's trading post was nicknamed Pig's Eye by the soldiers who proved its most dedicated customers. Only the arrival in 1841 of the French priest Lucian Galtier, who built a humble log chapel at the riverboat landing near Parrant's buildings and consecrated it to Saint Paul, prevented Minnesota's second largest city from the humiliation of having Pig's Eye as its official moniker.

The population of this fledgling city of St. Paul grew rapidly. By 1847, the town had a school, enjoyed the regular visits of steam-boats carrying passengers and freight, and boasted the headquarters of the American Fur Company. Two years later, when the U.S. Congress created the Territory of Minnesota, St. Paul's population stood at 840.

Meanwhile, upriver at the mills the soldiers had built to tap the power of the Mississippi at the Falls of St. Anthony, another settlement (although an initially smaller one) was taking shape. Two men — the merchant Franklin Steele and the eccentric, part-Indian guide Pierre Bottineau — bought land at the east bank of the falls in the late 1830s and early '40s. In 1847 Steele started building his own sawmill there, an undertaking that attracted workers of all kinds, including a sizable number of freed African American slaves. This dusty settlement grew into the village of St.

Anthony, which numbered 250 people by 1850. Five years later illegal squatters on the west bank of the Falls acquired official status as landowners, and they got fancy, joining the Dakota word for "water" with the Greek word for "city" and naming their town Minneapolis.

And so began a unique rivalry and interdependence between burgeoning communities separated from one another by the vast Fort Snelling reservation. At the start, St. Paul, to the east, had the political and commercial power, along with the greater population. Minneapolis, which absorbed St. Anthony in 1872, had the strength of the Falls, industrial smarts and a reckless Western spirit. They both mushroomed, supported armies of land speculators, survived financial panics, and, after Minnesota achieved statehood in 1858, promoted themselves tirelessly as the leading representatives of civilization in a rough-and-tumble state.

Slowly, and with much vicious spilling of ink in the newspapers, Minneapolis began to attain a certain kind of dominance. The rapid growth of the milling industry, spawning such giant businesses as Pillsbury, Cargill and General Mills, gave it a clear industrial lead over St. Paul. And by 1890, after a scandalous U.S. census fiasco in which enumerators from both cities counted dead and imaginary people to boost their figures, Minneapolis claimed an indisputable supremacy in population. Minneapolis boosters also crowed over the placement of the University of Minnesota's main campus in their city.

St. Paul, on the other hand, early on became the state capital and won the Minnesota State Fair, an institution enormously prestigious as a showcase of the state's agricultural and industrial wealth. It also was the home of a genteel class of the rich, people who made their money from such refined enterprises as banking, insurance and commercial transportation, not by chopping down trees and grinding up grain. No residential area in Minneapolis could match St. Paul's elegant Summit Hill neighborhood, where the palatial Cathedral of Saint Paul presided over one of the nation's grandest collections of oversize Victorian-style houses. (Nevermind that during the Prohibition era, St. Paul also was a popular refuge for notorious gangsters!)

Seen through the mists of time, the old rivalry between Minneapolis and St. Paul now seems ridiculous and destructive. A favorite joke from the turn of the century sums up its silliness: A visiting minister, the story goes, was preaching at a church in Minneapolis. He rose to the pulpit and declared that he would draw the text of his sermon from Saint Paul. To his astonishment, the congregation walked out en masse.

One of the reasons why Minneapolis and St. Paul never melded into a "Minneapaul" megacity is that each had a different vision of what a large city should be like. To this day, St. Paul prides itself on its distinct neighborhoods, its small-town atmosphere, and its resistance to pointless glitz. (Drive through certain sections of north St. Paul, for instance, and you'll see stretches of commercial and residential blocks that look virtually unchanged from the 1950s.) Minneapolis, on the other hand, makes a big deal of its glamorous music and film industries, its major-league sports teams (none plays in St. Paul), and its nightlife. It's a cliche, but nonetheless true, to observe that St. Paul is a small town grown large, while Minneapolis is a metropolis on a small scale. (Another oft-repeated cliche maintains that "St. Paul is the westernmost city of the East, while Minneapolis is the easternmost city of the West." What exactly that means, who knows?)

## What Really are "the Twin Cities"?

To focus on the cities' differences, though, is to ignore that Minneapolis and St. Paul grew quite alike as they matured. Both developed outstanding park systems. Both sponsored good public schools. Both became progressive and generally veered to the left politically. And, perhaps most telling, both lost big chunks of their populations to the suburbs during the last half of this century, and that migration created the "metropolitan area" that now constitutes the real Twin Cities.

Nowadays, most people in the Twin Cities live outside the city limits of Minneapolis and St. Paul. Some live far outside — the "toll-free" local telephone calling area, which stretches from New Prague in the southwest to Isanti in the northeast, is reportedly the largest in the world. Officially, the metropolitan area includes seven counties: Hennepin, Ramsey, Anoka, Washington, Dakota, Scott and Carver. Hennepin and Ramsey counties contain Minneapolis and St. Paul, respectively, and they are growing only slowly in population. The other five are exploding.

Much that's worth seeing and experiencing in the Twin Cities, in fact, is outside Minneapolis and St. Paul. Restrict yourself to the big twin towns and you'll miss the Mall of America, the Minnesota Zoo and many of the best restaurants, hotels and historic sites. The reverse side of the coin, of course, is that if you shy away from the urban centers you'll never see the Minnesota State Capitol, the Minneapolis Institute of Arts, the Como Park Zoo and Basilica of St. Mary.

Yes, in the Twin Cities you'll find people from Minneapolis who couldn't think of a reason to go to Coon Rapids, folks from Eagan who don't set foot in Minneapolis, people in Roseville who most contentedly get everything they need from their own community, and residents

When the Civil War erupted, Minnesota was the first state to offer troops to President Abraham Lincoln.

Insiders' Tips

# A Gallery of Famous Twin Citians

**Eddie Albert**: The actor eventually found his green acres in Hollywood.

**Loni Anderson**: That "WKRP" femme fatale grew up in suburban St. Paul.

**Richard Dean Anderson**: TV's "McGyver" also hails from the Twin Cities.

**The Andrews Sisters**: Patty, Maxine and LaVerne sang their way to fame and fortune in the 1930s and '40s.

**Carol Bly**: She's one of the nation's best spinners of stories and promoters of social conscience.

**Robert Bly**: A leading figure of the men's movement, accomplished poet and author of the book *Iron John*. He lives in Minneapolis.

**John Camp/"John Sandford"**: The best-selling author of *The Empress File* and a series of "prey" novels — *Silent Prey, Eyes of Prey*, etc. — lives in St. Paul and was for years a local newspaperman. He won a Pulitzer Prize at the *St. Paul Pioneer Press*.

**Joel and Ethan Coen**: They learned how to direct such films as *Raising Arizona* and *Barton Fink* while growing up with a home movie camera in St. Louis Park.

**Arlene Dahl**: The glamorous Hollywood actress is from Minneapolis.

**William Demarest**: He excelled as Uncle Charley in "My Three Sons" and as a series of irascible characters in many film comedies of the 1940s.

**Amelia Earhart**: The famed aviatrix was a St. Paul schoolgirl.

**F. Scott Fitzgerald**: The writer of *The Great Gatsby*, born in St. Paul, used Minnesota locales for some of his early stories and novels.

**J. Paul Getty**: The billionaire was a native of Minneapolis.

**Peter Graves**: Along with his brother James Arness, the star of "Mission: Impossible" grew up in Minneapolis.

**Judith Guest**: The author of *Ordinary People* is from Edina.

**Kent Hrbek**: The Minnesota Twins' recently retired star first baseman is a hometown boy.

**Hubert Humphrey**: He served as mayor of Minneapolis, U.S. Senator, Vice President, the Democratic nominee for President in 1968, and the embodiment of political progressivism in Minnesota.

**Garrison Keillor**: A humorist par excellence, he's involved in a love-hate relationship with the Twin Cities press.

**Sister Elizabeth Kenny**: For three decades, this native Australian ran a trailblazing polio clinic in Minneapolis.

**Greg LeMond**: The two-time Tour de France-winning bicyclist lived in suburban Medina.

**Meridel Le Sueur**: The writer of fiction, leftist activist and social-justice worker lives in St. Paul.

**Harvey Mackay**: The businessman and book author has spent most of his years swimming with the sharks in the Twin Cities.

**Paul Molitor:** The great Milwaukee Brewers and Toronto Blue Jays baseball player is a St. Paul native.

**Walter Mondale:** U.S. senator, vice president to Jimmy Carter, wager of an unsuccessful campaign for the presidency against Ronald Reagan in 1984, he's now the U.S. ambassador to Japan.

**Jack Morris:** The World Series-winning pitcher (for both the Twins and the Blue Jays) is a St. Paul lad.

**Gordon Parks:** This photographer, author of *The Learning Tree* and film director (*Shaft* is among his credits) grew up in St. Paul.

**Prince:** Except for his own staff, nobody calls him by the unpronounceable graphic symbol he recently adopted as his new name. (His original name was Prince Rogers Nelson.) But forget the name — the rock star, music producer and film director is the most influential popular artist ever to come from these parts.

**Harry Reasoner:** The "60 Minutes" newsman attended West High in Minneapolis.

**Maria Sanford:** The first woman in the United States ever to become a full professor of history (at Swarthmore) later joined the faculty of the University of Minnesota.

**Charles Schulz:** The man behind "Peanuts" is a St. Paul native.

**Robert Vaughn:** The Man from U.N.C.L.E. was originally a man from Minneapolis.

**Roy Wilkins:** The former director of the NAACP was raised in St. Paul.

**Dave Winfield:** The 3,000-hit man of baseball also has St. Paul roots.

of St. Paul who have never seen Chaska. Get to know these people, if you can, and share with them the parts of this book that will encourage them to enjoy the Twin Cities in its entirety.

## The Cost of Living

It's hard to categorize the Twin Cities as either expensive or inexpensive. After all, so many factors conspire to set prices — geography, supply, demand, climate, trendiness and the area's general financial health, to name a few.

Take housing costs, for instance. Like other metropolitan centers in the Midwest, the Twin Cities enjoys a housing market that is less expensive than the national average. In many parts of the area, within the cities or in the suburbs, you can find good houses in respectable areas for well under $100,000. But once you move in, what's it going to cost to heat that place? There's a winter here, in case you haven't heard, and you'll be amazed at how quickly your new home will absorb gas, electricity or heating oil. As a result, the cost of home ownership is hard to meaningfully categorize.

Rents are in the intermediate range, lower than New York City

Headlines from the 1930s "gangster" era in St. Paul.

and higher than Fargo. A continuing surplus of rental properties has kept rent increases moderate in recent years. This writer can state with authority that you can rent a spacious two-bedroom apartment in a good building in a fine neighborhood for $525 a month, including utilities and parking. For details on the renting and home-buying market, see our Real Estate chapter.

What about another necessity — food? Again, the verdict is split. If you're a glutton for meat, milk, cheese and butter, you'll get off easy here, thanks to the proximity of meat and dairy producing operations. (You'll also likely have to take advantage of the region's oft-praised medical facilities; see the chapter on Health Care.) If instead you graze upon fruits and vegetables, watch out for high prices in the produce department, especially during the winter when locally grown goods are not available in farmers markets.

Because of lower than average crime rates, car and property insurance come as a relief to people used to the going prices on the coasts. But watch out for property taxes. Even more, watch out for income taxes! (That money for government-supplied services has to come from somewhere. During the 1970s and '80s, taxation critics were fond of calling the state "The People's Republic of Minnesota.")

It costs $6.50 to see a first-run movie, $1.23 to buy a gallon of gas, a quarter to make a phone call and $400 to get a recreation membership at the YMCA. And if you lose track of your expenses, a bounced check could run you $22.

### Minnesota Nice

If your memory stretches back more than a few years, you'll recall that the term "politically correct" was once a phrase of praise used to indicate tact, courtesy or social diplomacy. Nowadays, of course, it's a slur, a label indicating a lock-step

## Twin Cities Statistics: A Random Selection

**Population (1992 figures)**
Seven-county metropolitan area: 2,352,121 (16th largest in the United States)
Minneapolis: 368,559
St. Paul: 272,692
Metro area growth rate, 1980 to 1990: 15.2 percent
Twin Cities' percentage of Minnesota population: 52.3 (1990)

**Twin Cities racial diversity (1992)**
White 91.6 percent
African American 3.9 percent
Asian/Pacific Islander 2.8 percent
American Indian/Eskimo/Aleut 1.0 percent
Other 0.6 percent
(The U.S. Census Bureau believes that people of Hispanic origin can be of any race.)

**Weather**
Coldest month: January, 11.8 degree average
Warmest month: July, 73.6 degree average
Annual mean temperature: 44.9 degrees
Snowiest month: March, 9.6 inches average
Rainiest month: June, 3.9 inches average
Driest month: October, 1.8 inches of precipitation average
Sunniest month: July
Cloudiest month: December

conformity of thought and an unwillingness to risk offending anyone. The term "Minnesota nice" has undergone a similar metamorphosis.

Through the 1980s, Twin Citians liked hearing that their culture was imbued with "Minnesota nice." It meant that store clerks were sincerely helpful, strangers smiled at each other on the street, and such commercial establishments as movie theaters and fast-food restaurants took checks. It indicated that you would rarely encounter someone who was habitually rude, boastful, vulgar or boorish. It characterized the efforts of good Samaritans who would appear from nowhere to assist snow-stuck drivers, direct lost tourists (the lost ones always seem to be from Iowa), and guard ducklings attempting to cross busy streets.

All those nice things still happen in the Twin Cities, much more often than they do in other metropolitan areas of comparable size. (Syndicated newspaper columnist Molly Ivins recently described Minnesotans as the nicest people in the United States.) But don't try to praise a Twin Citian by referring to "Minnesota nice" any more. Over time, the term has come to mean something not so nice.

These days, "Minnesota nice" evokes different images: people who offer a false smile instead of telling you what they really think, folks who avoid talking about unpleasant things, those who avert their eyes from troubling sights, and cooks who prepare bland, inoffensive food. These flaws are by no means unique to Minnesotans. But be forewarned — the term "nice" is becoming bad. Try another term if you want to extend praise: "kind," "generous," "thoughtful," whatever. And, remember: If you avoid the problem entirely by ceasing to offer praise altogether, you're exemplifying "Minnesota nice" yourself.

# Inside
# Getting Around

Not all that long ago, the Twin Cities boasted one of the nation's finest streetcar systems, a network of tracks that could carry you from neighborhoods far east of St. Paul to the shores of Lake Minnetonka, 20 miles west of Minneapolis. Destroyed in the 1950s by corrupt public officials and the machinations of various bus manufacturers, the streetcar system is now reduced to a single line, a thread of rails that connects Lake Harriet and Lake Calhoun in Minneapolis. Volunteer conductors operate it out of love, riders board the cars out of nostalgia, and people stop to watch it as it chimes its bell and clatters by. As charming as the old streetcar is, it's more an attraction than a means of transport.

Even if the streetcars had remained, however, it is doubtful that the system could have kept up with the Twin Cities' urban and suburban growth during the past 40 years. (Yes, some light-rail plans are currently creeping forward, particularly corridors to link Minneapolis and St. Paul and to serve Minneapolis' southern suburbs, but it will be years before they materialize.) Unfettered by the mountains, basins and large bodies of water that confine some other metropolitan areas, Minneapolis-St. Paul has sprawled in all directions. Only the snaking of the Mississippi and Minnesota rivers has lent a natural hindrance to the growth, and even that hasn't done much to slow it.

In the old days, when the streetcars whisked you out to Snelling Avenue in St. Paul or to Lake Street in Minneapolis, they were carrying you to the edge of town. Now those streets run through the inner cities. In the 1990s, the Twin Cities covers a geographic region that technically spans seven counties, and it can take some ingenuity to get from one place to another in the most efficient and fun manner. Never despair — there's always a way.

## Doing It By Car

Minnesota is not the world's easiest place to operate a car. Winter not only causes the awesome automotive demands that car battery commercials are so fond of showing, but it also coats the roads with ice, narrows the roads with piles of snow, breaks apart asphalt to form vertigo-inducing potholes, and forces fuel suppliers to oxygenate gasoline to levels that not all cars enjoy.

But winter's only half the year, right? The other half, according to Minnesota highway veterans, is road

*A view of downtown St. Paul showing I-94 and I-35E.*

construction season. It does seem as if all major roads are under construction when you need them most, but all that work has resulted in a metropolitan highway system that functions well when the orange construction cones go away.

Like many major urban centers, the Twin Cities is served by a "ring" system of interstate highways. Interstate 35 — with a 35W fork that runs through Minneapolis and a 35E fork that runs through St. Paul — is the main north-south artery. Interstate 94 (a coast-to-coast highway that connects Minneapolis and St. Paul) and Interstate 394 (from Minneapolis going west) carry much of the east-west traffic. Forming a ring around most of the metro area is Interstate 494/694 (494 is the designation for the southern half of the ring; 694 is the northern segment). These interstates connect with many state and county highways that fill the gaps. In general, north-south routes bear odd numbers, while east-west highways have even numbers.

Rush-hour traffic has picked up noticeably during the past decade, with the most consistent trouble spots being I-394 approaching downtown Minneapolis; the I-35W/Minn. Highway 62 interchange south of Minneapolis, known as the "Crosstown Commons"; and "Spaghetti Junction" in downtown St. Paul, where I-35E and I-94 cross paths. Gawkers anywhere, however, can turn a minor accident into a major slowdown. Although many radio stations offer traffic updates, the best source of highway information is KBEM 88.5 FM, which taps the resources of the Minnesota Department of Transportation.

The Department of Transportation also maintains a set of phone numbers for traffic information.

Call 296-3076 to hear about Minnesota highway road conditions, 297-4103 to keep up on highway lane closings, and 296-3000 (TDD 296-9930) for general transportation information.

While on the highways, you'll notice a full complement of Minnesota driving styles. The Speed Limit Enforcer, for example, drives at a steady 55, even in the left lane, and refuses to move over for speedier traffic. (Some would argue that this civilian enforcement is necessary, because the Minnesota State Patrol is more lax in enforcing speed limits than its counterparts in other states.) When two Speed Limit Enforcers cruise alongside each other they form the famous Minnesota Wedge, which can slow traffic for miles.

You also may find yourself behind the Surprise Decelerator, a nervous driver who slows down on highway entrances rather than accelerating to merge with traffic. Or maybe you'll encounter the Disintegrator, who pilots a car so eroded by rust and salt that at least one part falls off every trip.

All drivers should be on guard for "black ice," the exhaust of autos that freezes and camouflages itself on the roadway, as well as potholes and the raccoons and deer that stray onto the roads in suburban areas. Do not underestimate the ability of snow and ice to make you slip and slide — slow down! Despite these hazards, Minnesota has one of the lowest rates of highway fatalities of all the states, and Twin Cities drivers are safe and often surprisingly courteous.

Natives of Minneapolis and St. Paul both claim to get lost in each other's cities. In the downtown area, where some streets follow the trail of old footpaths and the barrier of the Mississippi River dictates some peculiarities, navigating in St. Paul can be somewhat confusing. Street addresses often do not follow the course that logically minded visitors would prefer, with numbers in the 800s, say, sometimes jumping an intervening cross-street to appear on the next block. Still, the uninitiated will get around just fine with a map or by asking for directions.

On the surface, the street layout of Minneapolis seems better ordered. In general, avenues run east-west and streets run north-south. In addition, many thoroughfares are numbered, and some areas have alphabetical sequences of streets, based on the names of former residents, presidents, and even chemical elements. But some drivers become confused by the existence of pairs of numbered avenues with the same name (Second Avenue N. lies northwest of Nicollet Avenue, while Second Avenue S. lies southeast of that dividing line) and by identical addresses on numbered streets north or south of Nicollet. Also perplexing to some are the numbered streets east of the Mississippi River that run diagonally compared with the rest of the street grid (they bear the designation "northeast" or "southeast"). You'll get used to it.

Traffic laws and customs in the Twin Cities are pretty normal. You can turn right on red, except at the frustratingly high number of Minneapolis intersections where signs prohibit it. Motorcyclists don't have to wear a helmet (but they should anyway). If you're using your windshield wipers at any time of the day, turn on your headlights. Don't even think about driving close to the Aquatennial Parade in Minneapolis and the Winter Carnival Parade in St. Paul. Watch out for one-way streets in downtown Minneapolis and St. Paul. And if you try to drive on the Nicollet Mall in Minneapolis (reserved for pedestrians, buses, bicyclists and taxis) someone will call out and ask what part of Iowa you're from. If you're in the front seat of your car, you must wear your seat belt. Don't drive drunk.

## Parking

Suburbanites tremble at the idea of parking in downtown Minneapolis and St. Paul, but the parking situation isn't too bad in either place because of an ample supply of lots and ramps. It's just expensive — daily rates can top $10 for a stall in a primo heated ramp. Downtown street parking is regulated by meters whose hours and allotted time vary considerably. Meters in Minneapolis take only quarters, and down by the Metrodome the meter cops remain vigilant until 10 PM, even on Sundays.

Other troublesome parking areas are the neighborhood near St. Thomas University and the Grand Avenue area in St. Paul, anywhere near the University of Minnesota (although new ramps have eased the problem), and the Uptown area of Minneapolis.

The parking situation becomes greatly complicated when a heavy snowfall occurs. If city officials declare a genuine snow emergency — which you'll hear about in all the news media — special parking rules go into effect. St. Paul's snow emergency parking system is the simplest: Plows first attack snow emergency routes and the labeled side of streets bearing special signs, where parking is prohibited until the work is completed. Drivers then move their cars to the cleared portions of the streets as the plows dig into the other side of the street.

Minneapolis' snow emergency system is a devilish scheme in which citizens need to move their cars from odd to even sides of the street, or vise versa, in a manner that changes in alternate years. Call 348-SNOW for details on the current year's system.

In suburban areas where off-street parking is more plentiful, some municipalities simply prohibit street parking until the plows clear the roads of snow.

If you leave your car where it

shouldn't be, there's a good chance it will be towed. In Minneapolis, your car will likely end up in the municipal impound lot at 51 Colfax Avenue N.; call 673-5777 to find out if your car is really there. St. Paul's impound lot is at 830 Bard's Channel Road, just east of Minn. Highway 3; call 292-3642.

## Share A Ride

Commuting to work solo in a car can be expensive, environmentally unsound, tiresome and lonely, so many drivers take advantage of Minnesota Rideshare (call 348-RIDE or TDD 349-7746), a government-funded service that helps people set up or join carpools and vanpools. About 16,000 people are currently on the Rideshare database. Poolers enjoy many benefits: shared expenses, the use of designated highway express lanes, special highway access ramps, free or reduced-cost parking in downtown Minneapolis and St. Paul, and preferential parking granted by many employers.

## Hail a Cab

Except at the Minneapolis-St. Paul International Airport, trying to hail a taxi in the Twin Cities can be a time-consuming, if not impossible, effort. Phone the taxi services instead, well in advance. Check the Yellow Pages for the latest listing or ask a hotel desk clerk for recommendations. Some cab companies provide smoke-free taxis. Rates vary somewhat by municipality, as do special fares for seniors.

## Take the Bus

The Twin Cities boasts some 145 bus routes that run 903 peak-hour and 277 midday buses on any given weekday. Since many of the riders are commuters who want to go to downtown Minneapolis or downtown St. Paul, service into the central corridors is strongest. Metropolitan Council Transit Operations is by far the biggest provider of public bus service, but a number of other bus companies meet the needs of riders in suburban areas.

### METROPOLITAN COUNCIL TRANSIT OPERATIONS

During 1993, fully one-third of all Twin Cities residents took an MCTO bus for one reason or another, and its buses carry 66 million passengers a year. Local service most often radiates from downtown Minneapolis or downtown St. Paul, while express service carries commuters on highways (often traveling in special lanes designated for buses). There is also special service to such locations as the Minnesota State Fairgrounds and the Mall of America.

By calling 373-3333, you can have access to bus schedules, help in planning a route to your destination, customer relations and other services. The fare is currently $1; it goes up to $1.25 during the peak hours of 6 to 9 AM and 3:30 to 6:30 PM. Express bus rides cost $1.50 and $1.75 (peak hours). Seniors aged 65 and older, people with disabilities, and kids 6 to 17 pay only 25 cents during non-peak hours. Up to three kids 5 and young-

*Downtown St. Paul skyway.*

er can ride free with a paid fare at any time. Rides within special downtown zones in Minneapolis and St. Paul cost only 25 cents (50 cents during peak hours). Transfers are free. Monthly passes and discounted ride tickets are available, and recently installed fare boxes accept dollar bills, automatically count the money you drop into them (sometimes inaccurately; they don't easily recognize Canadian coins), and do not make change. In general, bus service ceases between 1 and 4:30 AM.

The drivers are a varied bunch, ranging from friendly folks who call out the names of streets and tell jokes ("Attention ladies and gentlemen: The letters MCTO stand for Metropolitan Council Transit Operations, not My Cafeteria Travels On — please don't eat or drink on the bus") to behind-the-wheel drudges who consider it a strain to grunt hello. Most, though, are real people who can rise to such heroic heights as navigating snow-clogged streets, gently guiding a bus down an icy hill, and waiting out a light to let a patron cross the street and board.

The MCTO employs 187 police officers, and on-board crime is uncommon on most routes. Some of the express routes, in fact, are known for commuter camaraderie, and riders have enjoyed bus-bound celebrations of anniversaries and birthdays. Some of the most interesting routes are the 16, connecting downtown Minneapolis and downtown St. Paul via the University of Minnesota and the State Capitol; the 21, linking Minneapolis' chic Uptown neighborhood, several St. Paul residential neighborhoods and downtown St. Paul; St. Paul's route 12, heading far out into the countryside east of the city; and Minneapolis' route 7, running through north Minneapolis and the city's warehouse district on the way, at some times of the day, to the Minneapolis-St. Paul International Airport. Compared with the buses in other large cities, the MCTO's fleet is very clean.

Six transit hubs in the Twin Cities — located at Rosedale Center, Mall of America, downtown St. Paul, Plymouth Road, Louisiana Avenue, and downtown Minneapolis — let riders make transfers and await their buses in climate-controlled comfort. Many streetside bus stops also have shelters that will keep the snow, sleet and rain off your head. You can recognize bus stops by the red sign with a "T" enclosed in a circle.

For commuters in outlying areas, the Park & Ride lots can be convenient. Sprinkled throughout the metro area, the 148 lots hold more than 7,000 cars and allow their occupants to easily hop aboard at a nearby bus stop.

### OTHER PUBLIC BUS SERVICES

The MCTO claims the lion's share of bus passengers, but other smaller companies provide local transit, dial-a-ride trips and otherwise unavailable services.

| | |
|---|---|
| Anoka County Transit | 422-7088 |
| Medicine Lake Bus Co. | 545-9417 |
| Carver Area Rural Transit | 361-1631 |
| Columbia Heights Shared Ride | 782-2800 |
| Dakota Area Referral and Transportation Service | 455-1560 |
| Dakota County Volunteer Transportation Services | 450-2874 |
| Hopkins Hop-A-Ride | 935-8474 |
| Human Services Inc. "Transporter" (Washington County) | 777-5222 |

| | |
|---|---|
| Maple Grove Transit System | 420-4000 |
| Minnesota Valley Transit Authority | 431-4311 |
| Mound Westonka Rides | 472-0349 |
| North Suburban Lines | 784-7196 |
| Northeast Suburban Transit | 777-1872 |
| Plymouth Metro Link | 550-5072 |
| Roseville Area Circulator | 645-1959 |
| St. Louis Park Emergency Program | 925-4899 |
| Scott County Transportation Program | 496-8277 |
| Senior Community Services (Minnetonka) | 541-1019 |
| Senior Community Services (Westonka) | 472-0340 |
| Senior Transportation Program (Champlin) | 323-9017 |
| Shakopee Area Transit | 445-3650 |
| Southwest Metro Transit Commission | 949-8544 |
| University of Minnesota Transit Service (Route 52) | 625-9000 |
| Lake (White Bear) Area Transit | 770-1872 |

### METRO MOBILITY

As the Twin Cities' public transit service for people with disabilities who are unable to use regular route bus service, Metro Mobility operates a fleet of 150 vans specially designed to be comfortable and safe for disabled passengers and equipped with wheelchair lifts and tie-downs. The program provides door-to-door service, helping passengers through the first set of doors at both the pickup point and at the destination. About 100,000 riders make use of the service each month.

Riders can schedule their trips up to 14 days in advance by calling 221-1928. Fares and hours are similar to those for regular bus service.

### INTERCITY BUS SERVICE

### GREYHOUND BUS STATIONS

| | |
|---|---|
| 29 N. 9th Street, Minneapolis | 371-3323 |
| 25 W. 7th St., St. Paul | 222-0509 |

*Northwest Airlines at Minneapolis-St. Paul International Airport.*

Photo: Neal Lambert, Pioneer Press

Greyhound (which began in Minnesota in the early decades of the century) and Jefferson Lines, a bus carrier that serves many towns throughout the Upper Midwest, share passenger stations in the Twin Cities. Neither one is the kind of place you'd want to visit all day, but they're clean and quiet as far as bus stations go. There are also suburban Greyhound pickup points in Anoka, Bloomington and Shakop-ee, as well as at the Minneapolis-St. Paul International Airport.

## Train Service

### AMTRAK TWIN CITIES PASSENGER STATION

*730 Transfer Rd., St. Paul        644-1127*

The Twin Cities are at mile 418 on the 2,209-mile route of the "Empire Builder," running from Chica-

---

### If It's Tuesday, It Must Be ...

When some Twin Citians think about getting around, that activity extends *outside* the area, especially to warmer climes during those long winter months. That's where charter vacations come in. Most such excursions from the Twin Cities are packaged by two companies. The most easily accessible is **Trans Global Tours**, 8200 Normandale Boulevard in Bloomington, 831-1980 or 948-8333 for the 24-hour recorded hotline. The other is **MLT Vacations**, which is not open directly to the public. Check the ads in Sunday newspaper travel sections for details of current tours offered by both these companies, then call your travel agent for booking.

go's Union Station to Seattle. Other Minnesota cities with stops along the route are Winona, Red Wing, St. Cloud, Staples, and Detroit Lakes. Overall, though, Amtrak keeps a low profile in the Twin Cities, and few people use the train to get around.

## *Air Travel*

### MINNEAPOLIS/ST. PAUL INTERNATIONAL AIRPORT - WOLD CHAMBERLAIN FIELD

*Near Bloomington at the junction of I-494 and Highway 5*          *726-8100*

Even beyond the transatlantic heroics of Charles Lindbergh (who grew up in Little Falls, Minnesota, about an hour's drive north of the Twin Cities), aviation has a distinguished history in the region. In 1926, the Twin Cities-based Northwest Airways (now Northwest Airlines) won the government's air mail contract and began using the only hangar within an abandoned car race track that had been converted to an air field three years before, south of Minneapolis-St. Paul. Northwest inaugurated passenger service in 1929, and the airport's rapid growth was on. Soon the U.S. Weather Bureau opened a station there, a control tower rose over the field, and paved runways replaced the grass strips. The airport took its present ungain-

ly name in 1948. (Ernest Wold and Cyrus Chamberlain were early Minnesota aviators killed in France during World War I.)

To this day, the airport is dominated by the presence of Northwest, which uses it as a major hub. During a recent year, the airline accounted for 77 percent of all the passenger boardings. Nineteen other major and regional airlines serve the airport, however, along with an additional 35 charter and cargo carriers. Each year, the airport serves 21 million passengers bound for 100 domestic and 13 international nonstop destinations. The Hubert H. Humphrey Terminal, a separate facility on 34th Avenue S. that handles charter and international flights, is linked with the main terminal (called the Lindbergh Terminal) by a shuttle bus that runs frequently.

Outside of rush-hour times, it takes about 20 minutes to drive to the airport from either downtown Minneapolis or downtown St. Paul. Bus service is available on five MCTO lines (call 373-3333 for schedule information), but none has luggage racks. The taxi stand is located across the street from the baggage pickup area; a cab fare into town could run as high as $30, although the average fare is around $20. Airport Express, 726-6400,

Consider carpooling, riding the bus or a bike to the University of Minnesota campus, because the parking is difficult at best.

*Lake Harriet Band Shell in Minneapolis.*

Photo: Buzz Magnuson, Pioneer Press

provides van transportation to downtown Minneapolis, downtown St. Paul and many suburbs, and other companies connect the airport with towns outside the Twin Cities.

Recent improvements have made parking more pleasant. An enclosed skyway joins the parking ramp with the main terminal. Options include short-term, general, valet and long-term parking (the latter available in the EconoLot located just north of the Humphrey Terminal). All areas have handicapped parking, and people with disabilities can use the valet parking at general parking rates.

### St. Paul Downtown Airport
*644 Bayfield St., St. Paul      224-4306*

This airport, located just minutes from downtown St. Paul and also known as Holman Field, is becoming increasingly popular among business and corporate travelers. It has a new 6,700-foot runway, along with restaurant and catering facilities. The airport also offers fuel service, no tie-down fees in front of the main terminal, and transportation into town via taxis and rental cars.

### Other Airports

Several other airports handle the Twin Cities' business and general

Insiders' Tips

Hennepin County alone spends about $2 million annually to clear snow from roads and apply salt to streets.

aviation needs. These include Flying Cloud Airport in Eden Prairie, 941-3545; Crystal Airport in Minneapolis' northern suburbs, 537-2058; Anoka County/Blaine Airport, 786-9490; Lake Elmo Airport, 777-6300; and AirLake Airport near Lakeville, 469-4040.

## Pedals and Spokes

Minnesotans bicycle at nearly twice the national average, and our 4.3 bikes per capita leads the country. Many of the hearty pedalers use their bikes to commute to work and just generally get around. Even in the dead of winter, it's not unusual to see a helmeted and bundled cyclist atop a pair of spinning wheels, wrapped head to toe in protective garb, peering out from a narrow scarf opening. Aside from their penchant for riding on sidewalks along busy streets, they're a welcome sight. The city of Minneapolis recently gave bicycle commuting a huge boost by creating 93 blocks of on-street bike lanes downtown, including a specially graded set of lanes that barrels right down the middle of main drag Hennepin Avenue. For information on using a bike to commute, contact the Minnesota Extension Service Bicycle Program at 625-5737.

In 1994 Metropolitan Council Transit Operations began a new program to rent bicycle lockers to people who want to commute with their bikes in conjunction with bus trips. The lockers are located throughout the Twin Cities at Park & Ride lots and other areas where there is heavy bus traffic. Each location has four to six lockers available for rent seasonally or annually. Rental rates are $5 monthly plus a refundable deposit. For more information, call Minnesota Rideshare at 349-RIDE.

For decades, Minnesota has been a leader in the development of off-the-road bike trails. An extensive bike path system is a renowned feature of the Minneapolis parks system; its 38 miles of linked bike paths provide views of city lakes, downtown, Minnehaha Creek and Minnehaha Falls, and the Mississippi River. St. Paul offers 5 miles of paved trails at Hidden Falls-Crosby Farm Regional Park and the 17-mile Gateway Trail starting at Arlington Avenue and I-35E north of downtown. In addition, many of the Hennepin Park reserves — including Baker Park Reserve, Carver Park Reserve, Clearly Lake Regional Park, Elm Creek Park Reserve and Hyland Park Reserve — each contain 3 to 9 miles of bike paths, and the 7-mile North Hennepin Trail Corridor connects Elm Creek Park Reserve with Coon Rapids Dam Regional Park.

Finally, one of Minnesota's fabulous state bike trails, developed by the Department of Natural Resources, lies within the Twin Cities area. The Luce Line Trail, built along a 30-mile-long former railbed, connects Plymouth with the town of Winsted. Following a route used long ago by Dakota Indians, it skirts tree groves, pastures, lake beaches and farmland. You can find its Plymouth trailhead on Vicksburg Lane between County Roads 6 and 15.

Color maps outlining bicycle routes throughout the Twin Cities and the entire state are available from the map sale office of the Minnesota Department of Transportation, 395 John Ireland Boulevard, St. Paul, 296-2216.

## On Foot Via the Skyways

Visitors to Minneapolis and St. Paul stare up at them in amazement, searching for the right word to describe them. Some newcomers try to call them "bridges," "connectors" or "walkways." One or two even try to call them "tunnels," which is emphatically wrong. They are, in fact, skyways — enclosed, second-story sidewalks that link most of the major buildings in the two downtowns.

In the more than 30 years they've stretched above our heads — the first Twin Cities skyway was one built in 1962 across Marquette Avenue to connect the Northstar Center and the old Northwestern National Bank Building in Minneapolis — skyways have forever altered the dynamics and atmosphere of Minneapolis and St. Paul. Many of the healthiest retail establishments in the downtowns are now on the skyway-served second floors, and buildings have to deal with the benefits and problems of essentially having two main floors. In both cities, landlords often charge higher rents for skyway-level space than for first-floor space. During the cold season, when people most heavily use the climate-controlled skyways, the street-level foot traffic can dwindle to practically nothing.

As a result, many of the sights and sounds of street life have moved upstairs. The skyways have their own beat police officers, musical buskers strumming their hearts out for quarters, flower stands, Salvation Army bell-ringers and even parades.

St. Paul eventually began its own skyways, and they now cover about 4 miles, making it the world's largest publicly owned system. It connects department stores, office buildings, apartment and condo residences, and parking ramps.

In Minneapolis, the system is actually larger, but each skyway is separately owned and maintained by building owners. Via skyway you can avoid the frigid winds, that hurtle through the downtown canyons, and travel all the way from the municipal parking ramps on the north end of downtown to the Minneapolis Convention Center — a distance of 12 blocks. Along the way, you'll pass through (or have the opportunity to pass through) virtually every building of importance in the downtown core. Min-

24•

neapolis' busiest skyway, the one spanning Marquette Avenue from the IDS Center to the Baker Building, carries something like 20,000 people each day.

In both cities, the skyway hours vary somewhat, depending on the hours of the buildings they connect. But most open early in the morning and remain navigable into the evening.

Additions to the systems are built every few months, as a new building rises or a structure undergoes renovation. You can find the most up-to-date skyway maps in the Minneapolis and St. Paul editions of the *Skyway News*, a weekly publication (available free in downtown racks) that serves as the community newspapers of the downtowns.

# *Inside*
# Accommodations

*"To sleep, perchance to dream."*

A good hotel room is a traveler's necessity that, too often, is simply taken for granted. But that's as it should be.

A hotel, after all, isn't the "be all and end all" of one's journey. Rather, it provides a pleasing backdrop, a canvas on which to paint your vivid travel adventures.

The best hotels are those that are hospitable yet non-intrusive, quiet and serviceable — like a good pair of shoes.

But, just as a persistent squeak or pinched toes can ruin one's day, so too can thin walls, a lumpy bed or sourpuss desk clerk spoil even the most well-planned vacation or business trip.

Travelers to the Twin Cities needn't despair of finding good-quality lodging in a range of price brackets. Downtown Minneapolis alone has around 4,500 hotel rooms, boosting its position as a magnet for national conventions.

While hotels are less numerous in downtown St. Paul, those that are there are as fine as can be found in any major U.S. city — most notably the peerless St. Paul Hotel and the St. Paul Radisson.

The southern suburb of Bloomington, home to the Mall of America and close neighbor to the Twin Cities International Airport, is teeming with convenient and comfortable hotels and motels, all within a stone's throw of a major freeway and, therefore, minutes from any Twin Cities attraction.

Many business travelers opt for suburban hotels, because many corporate headquarters have moved to the suburbs and suburban lodgings offer free parking — a rarity in the cities.

Here's a listing of the major hotels, motels, inns and bed and breakfasts in the Twin Cities, broken down into geographical areas. The rates quoted here do not include hotel tax, which is 12 percent in Minneapolis and Bloomington, 13 percent in St. Paul.

Room rates (double occupancy) are indicated as follows:

| | |
|---|---|
| *Less than $75* | **$** |
| *$75 to $95* | **$$** |
| *$95 to $115* | **$$$** |
| *More than $115* | **$$$$** |

## *Minneapolis*

### CROWN PLAZA NORTHSTAR
*618 Second Ave. S.*           *338-2288*
**$$**

The Crown Plaza Northstar, located above a six-story parking

ramp, may be hard to locate, but it's worth the search. This high-quality, 17-story hotel with 224 rooms underwent a $40 million renovation last year. The result is a lush, rich look of deep greens, burgundies, dark woods and Victorian accents. Several nonsmoking floors were created as part of the overhaul. This is the home of an award-winning restaurant. While there is no on-site pool, guests have access to the pool in the nearby Minneapolis Club via an underground tunnel. The hotel offers several package deals.

### CROWN STERLING SUITES
*425 S. Seventh St.*     *333-3111*
**$$$$**

For those who feel cramped in the conventional hotel room, this facility offers expansive suites comprising a living room, bedroom and small kitchen area complete with refrigerator, microwave and wet bar. There are also two TVs and two telephones in each suite. Guests may enjoy a complimentary cooked-to-order breakfast in the hotel's atrium area. Recreational facilities include an indoor pool, sauna, steam room and weight-lifting area, plus guest privileges at the nearby Arena Athletic Club for an extra nominal charge. There are 218 suites in this six-story hotel. For fine dining at a reasonable price, check out Cornell's Restaurant on the premises.

### MINNEAPOLIS HILTON HOTEL AND TOWERS
*1001 Marquette Ave.*     *376-1000*
*Minneapolis*
**$$-$$$$**

From it crytsal chandeliers and fine wallpaper to the handsome bronze statue that graces its lobby, the Minneapolis Hilton has brought a touch of luxury and elegance to the Minneapolis hospitality scene. Built in 1992, this huge facility has 814 guest room, including 51 suites, an in-house health club with swimming pool, two acclaimed restaurants, and 43,000 feet of retail and

Photo: Richard Marshall, Pioneer Press

*Whitney Hotel, a converted flour mill, in the Minneapolis riverfront area.*

specialty shops. Primarily a conventioneer's hotel, the Hilton has several large meeting rooms and a 2,500 square foot ballroom. Special attention is paid to guest who stay on the concierge level, where there's a fax machine in every room. Skyways connect the hotel to the nearby Minneapolis Convention Center and Nicollet Mall stores.

### HOLIDAY INN-METRODOME
*1500 Washington Ave. S.*      333-4646
**$$$**

This local branch of the national chain is located in Minneapolis' "Seven Corners" area and within walking distance of several theaters, such as the Hey City Stage, Theater in the Round and Mixed Blood, not to mention nightlife from blues bars to folk houses. There are five good restaurants within a block of this hotel, plus the Holiday Inn's own Grill Room. Hotel amenities here include a small indoor pool, whirlpool, sauna and exercise room. The famous Hubert H. Humphrey Metrodome is six blocks away, and the Nicollet Mall is eight more beyond that. (Hint: Ask for a "great rate" special.) Parking is $7 extra per day. There are 265 rooms on 14 stories.

### HYATT REGENCY MINNEAPOLIS
*1300 Nicollet Mall*           370-1234
**$$$$**                (800) 233-1234

This luxury hotel in the heart of downtown has 532 comfortable rooms and 21 suites with city views, complimentary HBO and cable news. Some rooms are grouped on nonsmoking floors. A nice extra here is the Regency Athletic Club, a private athletic facility with enclosed tennis and racquetball courts, running track, weight room, sauna and Jacuzzi, which hotel guests may use for a nominal daily fee. All guests have access to a large on-premises swimming pool.

The Hyatt is also home to three good restaurants: Manny's Steakhouse, Pronto (Italian fare) and Taxxi (American bistro), plus Spike's sports bar. The Hyatt is strategically located close to the Minneapolis Convention Center, Nicollet Mall shops, Orchestra Hall and the Music Box Theater, specializing in cabaret entertainment.

On weekends, the room rate drops. There's also a luxury-level rate, which includes a private lounge, honor bar, complimentary continental breakfast and refreshments. The Hyatt offers discounts for AAA members, senior citizens and convention groups and runs frequent specials. Parking is available in nearby city-run ramps for $9 daily.

### HOTEL LUXEFORD SUITES
*1101 LaSalle Ave.*           332-6800
**$$$**

Oriental vases, classical columns and elegant furniture fill the small lobby of this cozy, all-suites hotel. Each of the 230 suites contains a sitting room (with a queen-size sleeper-sofa), bedroom, kitchenette, phone and TV. The hotel offers discounts to AAA members and runs frequent specials. Guests also have access to an in-house fitness center with whirlpool and sauna. Cafe Luxeford, on the main floor, specializes in live jazz by local and nationally known musicians.

### THE MARQUETTE

*Seventh St. and Marquette Ave.*     *332-2351*
**$$$$**

President Clinton slept here during a whistle-stop visit in 1994. There are 277 rooms, including 13 suites, in this 19-story, luxury hotel, part of the Hilton International chain. The Marquette is located in the IDS building, Minneapolis' tallest skyscraper, and because of the building's design, all rooms are corner rooms, with about 20 percent more space that the average hotel room. Amenities include steam baths in some rooms and basic cable TV in all rooms. There's also a workout facility — sans pool — on the fifth floor. The hotel restaurant is the moderately priced Basil's, specializing in traditional fare — from Angus beef to specialty pizzas — prepared with fresh herbs. There's also a bar, the Mark 7. Discount room rate packages are available.

### MARRIOTT CITY CENTER

*30 S. Seventh St.*     *349-4000*
**$$$$**

This deluxe hotel, located above the bustling City Center indoor shopping complex, has 584 rooms, including suites, in 31 stories. There's also an on-premises health club with hot tub, sauna and weight rooms but no swimming pool. For those who simply can't be separated from Ma Bell, there are some rooms with bathroom phones. Hotel restaurants are Gustino's, featuring singing waiters and Northern Italian fare, and Papaya's, for family dining. An advantage to staying here — apart from the sheer indulgence — is the proximity to downtown shopping via the skyway system. The Cinnebar Lounge is a pleasant hotel bar. The Marriott offers a special weekend package.

### NICOLLET ISLAND INN

*95 Merriam St., Nicollet Island*     *331-1800*
**$$$**

This classy, cozy 24-room inn on an island in the Mississippi River is only a block away from downtown — yet in atmosphere, it's worlds removed. Built in an old sash and door factory, this inviting hostelry boasts an award-winning gourmet restaurant, awesome river views, individually decorated rooms (some with four-poster beds), a roaring fireplace in the lobby and charm aplenty. You'll never want to go home! Several "getaway packages" are available.

### PARK INN INTERNATIONAL

*1313 Nicollet Ave.*     *332-0371*
**$$$$**

A midsize, 14-story hotel near the Minneapolis Convention Center, the Park Inn has an indoor pool, Jacuzzi, sauna and 325 rooms, including suites. Group discounts and packages are available. George's in the Park restaurant and bar is on the premises. Several restaurants and cultural and shopping venues are within a few blocks.

### RADISSON PLAZA

*35 S. Seventh St.*     *339-4900*
**$$$$**

A Minneapolis landmark, this flagship hotel of the locally owned Radisson chain was virtually rebuilt in the 1980s, and the result is an elegant, grand hotel with amenities

Photo: Craig Borck, Pioneer Press

*Nicollet Island Inn is located on an island in the Mississippi River in Minneapolis.*

for the 20th-century traveler. The Radisson is in a prime shopping locale, next-door to Dayton's and within easy walking distance to the Conservatory, City Center and Gaviidae Common. A stunning focal point in the lobby is a huge marble ball suspended on a fountain. Tucked away on the third floor is Festival, a small formal restaurant with an adjoining intimate, hushed bar, seemingly worlds away from the madding crowd. Rooms are designed for business executives, with generous desks and bedside and bathroom phones. There's an on-site fitness center with classes and aerobic and weight-training equipment. Special packages are available. Higher rates apply to the hotel's upper three floors which comprise the Plaza Club. Here, guests stay in more luxurious rooms and receive complimentary drinks and continental breakfast.

### WHITNEY HOTEL

| | |
|---|---|
| *150 Portland Ave.* | *339-9300* |
| *$$$$* | *(800) 248-1879* |

This elegant hotel on the banks of the Mississippi offers a stately lobby with spiral staircase and grand piano, and great dining at the intimate Whitney Grill or the outdoor Garden Plaza. There are 94 richly decorated rooms and 40 suites in this eight-story hotel. Some of the suites are bi-level, with spiral staircases and breathtaking views of the Mississippi. If you're looking for a really special experience, rent the three-bedroom penthouse suite with two living rooms, a grand piano, fireplaces, whirlpools and a deck overlooking the river — it goes for a mere $1,500 a night. Five private meeting rooms provide an elegant setting for meetings or dinners of up to 200 people. The hotel also offers several weekend package deals.

### BEST WESTERN REGENCY PLAZA
*41 N. 10th St.* 339-9311
$

This no-nonsense downtown motel has more than 200 rooms, an indoor pool, whirlpool, Harrigan's restaurant and coffee shop and, best of all, free parking. This motel isn't as centrally located as the other luxury hotels, but, for the price, it's a good deal. And there's free shuttle service to a variety of downtown destinations.

### BEST WESTERN NORMANDY INN
*405 S. Eighth St.* 370-1400
$

This smaller (160-room) motor hotel looks like a Swiss chalet from the outside, yet, on the inside, offers all the modern amenities, including swimming pool, whirlpool and sauna. Pets are allowed in rooms. Your room rate includes free parking. Some package deals are available. A dining room, coffee shop and bar/lounge are on-site.

### SHERATON METRODOME
*1330 Industrial Blvd.* 331-1900
$$$

Don't let the name fool you. This hotel is 15 minutes — by car — from the Metrodome. If you don't mind the drive, you'll find this a pleasant hostelry with 254 rooms, an indoor pool, whirlpool and sauna. The hotel's Anchorage Restaurant is a very popular dining destination among locals. Weekend packages are available.

## St. Paul and Suburbs

The hotel rates quoted below do not include the 13 percent hotel tax that is levied in St. Paul.

## Downtown St. Paul Hotels

### ST. PAUL HOTEL
*350 Market St.* 292-9292
$$$$

The St. Paul, a highly acclaimed grand old hotel overlooking Rice Park, the historic Landmark Center and the Ordway Music Theatre, is THE place to stay for that special occasion. A Mobil Guide four-star rated hotel, the 254-room St. Paul offers the traveling business executive modern amenities in a setting of Old World charm. The deluxe rooms and suites are all elegantly appointed with tasteful artwork and upholstered chairs and settees, and some contain big old armoires (just like Grandma's) and queen-size four-poster beds.

Why not pull out all the stops and conduct your next sales meeting in the Park Suite, furnished with a comfortable sitting area and a stunning walnut dining/meeting table for eight. Imagine what a power lunch you could have here. The suite contains a separate room for sleeping and terry bathrobes to make you feel right at home.

Though there is no health club on premises, exercise equipment can be brought to your room. Just check with the concierge. The St. Paul also contains seven large-function rooms that accommodate up to 260 people for meetings and 380 for banquets. The hotel's St. Paul Grill, with its clubby atmosphere, walls filled with historic photos, gourmet cuisine and park views, is one of the best restaurants in the Twin Cities. The Cafe, on the lower level, is an upbeat eatery with a fun touch — a huge chalkboard wall detailing all the week's doings in the Saintly City. The hotel is linked, via above-ground skyways, to an extensive array of downtown restaurants, shops and museums. Weekend packages are available. Parking is $10 a day.

### THE RADISSON HOTEL ST. PAUL
*11 E. Kellogg Blvd.*      *292-1900*
**$$**

Overlooking the Mississippi, the 22-story Radisson encompasses 475 elegantly appointed rooms, including luxurious suites and cabana rooms adjacent to the indoor garden court and Olympic-size pool. The popular top-floor Le Carousel Restaurant slowly revolves, affording an unforgettable panoramic view of the city and the Mighty Mississippi. Those booking a two-room executive suite enjoy complimentary breakfast, newspaper and evening cocktails. A popular convention hotel, the Radisson offers flexible spaces for any type of business meeting or social gathering, including a simply grand ballroom with glittering chandeliers. The hotel is linked, via skyway, to the shops and cultural venues of downtown St. Paul.

### BEST WESTERN KELLY INN
*161 St. Anthony Blvd.*      *227-8711*
**$$$**

Politicians wheel and deal here in the dark and intimate Capitol Lounge or bustling Benjamin's restaurant. If only the walls could talk! This is a popular hostelry for government employees and lobbyists mainly because of its location — almost in the front yard of the State Capitol. The 125-room Kelly Inn boasts a large, pleasant indoor pool, whirlpool, sauna and children's pool. And it's easy to reach — just off the Marion Street exit of I-94.

### CROWN STERLING SUITES
*175 E. 10th St.*      *224-5400*
**$$$$**

A Mediterranean villa transplanted to the snow country — that's the atmosphere at the Crown Sterling Suites of St. Paul. The interior is dominated by a huge atrium traversed by a flagstone walkway that winds around palms, street lamps and rock-hewn waterfalls and leads to a jewel box gazebo and dining area. Eight floors of suites—adorned with tons of wrought iron and hanging plants — surround this tropical garden. You may feel like you're at a theme ride in Disney World. Actually, it all comes together to create a sunny, pleasant getaway.

The two-room suites (210 in all) are contemporary in style, tastefully decorated in light woods and modern fabrics. Each contains two TVs, two phones, separate sleeping and living quarters and a small kitchenette with microwave, coffee maker and refrigerator. A made-to-order complimentary breakfast is included with the room. Work off breakfast with a dip in the indoor pool or nearby whirlpool and sauna. Fine dining is offered at Woolley's Restaurant and Lounge. Each floor has an executive conference suite for business meetings, and there's a large ballroom for meetings and seminars.

### Days Inn Civic Center

*175 W. Seventh St.* 292-8929
$

A stone's throw from the St. Paul Civic Center and the Ordway Music Theatre, this serviceable, clean 205-room facility offers a double-occupancy room rate that's very affordable. The lobby was being renovated at press time and the progress was looking promising. Dining is available in Jazzmin's lounge and cafe. Pets are accepted in rooms.

## Other St. Paul Area Hotels

### Best Western Maplewood Inn

*1780 E. County Rd. D*
*Maplewood* 770-2811
$

Shopaholics, take note! Maplewood Mall, a large suburban shopping center, is located right across the street from this motel, which caters mostly to tourists and families. Kids will love splashing in the indoor pool. There's also a sauna, whirlpool, game room, Nickelby's restaurant and Nick's lounge. Nick's hosts the Totally Bonkers Comedy Club Thursdays through Saturdays, to which guests receive free tickets.

### Country Inn by Carlson

*6003 Hudson Rd.* 739-7300
$

True to its name, this new 158-room motel serves up country charm, from hardwood floors to quilted comforters. There's also a full-service restaurant and the Jug-

gernaut Lounge, indoor pool, saunas, game room, free parking and free HBO.

### Holiday Inn-East

*2201 Burns Ave.* 731-2220
$$

This 192-room version of the national chain has all the usual amenities, including indoor pool, sauna, whirlpool, exercise area, game room, restaurant, bar, gift shop and laundromat. This motor lodge is very close to 3M headquarters, which supplies most of its business, and 10 minutes from downtown St. Paul. For a few bucks more, you can qualify for the executive level, which comes with a private lounge, refreshments, complimentary breakfast and newspaper, and speedy checkout.

### Holiday Inn Express

*1010 Bandana Blvd. W.* 647-1637
$$

Built in an old railroad repair shop, this colorful 109-room motel has tracks running through the lobby and is connected via skyway to the Bandana Square shopping center. There's an indoor pool, wading pool, whirlpool and sauna. Complimentary continental breakfast is served.

### Sheraton Midway

*400 Hamline Ave. N.* 642-1234
$$$

Conveniently located near I-94 and within minutes from both Twin Cities' downtowns, this 197-room motor hotel has an indoor pool, whirlpool, sauna and exercise area, TV, complimentary coffee, Bigelow's restaurant and a bar. Ask

*Thorwood Inn Bed & Breakfast, Hastings.*

about the "best-value" rate, based on availability.

### St. Paul Ramada Hotel
*1870 Old Hudson Rd.*      *735-2330*
$

Just 10 minutes east of downtown St. Paul, off I-94, the St. Paul Ramada has an attractive sunlit indoor pool area and a casual ambiance. This is a refreshingly non-pretentious, 200-room strip motel with meeting rooms for business conferences and social gatherings. A pleasant surprise is Summerfield's Restaurant and Lounge, where you sip a drink next to a roaring open-hearth fireplace.

---

## South Suburbs

---

### Best Western Seville Plaza Hotel
*8151 Bridge Rd., Bloomington*      *830-1300*
$

Situated on the intersection of Highway 100 and I-494, the Spanish-themed Seville has an indoor pool, whirlpool and sauna, restaurant and lounge.

### Best Western Thunderbird Hotel
*2201 78th St. E., Bloomington*      *854-3411*
$$$

There are 263 rooms and suites in this hotel filled with an extensive collection of Native American handiwork and artifacts. Guests enjoy indoor and outdoor pools, exercise facilities and a game room and restaurant. Catch some live music in the Totem Pole restaurant and lounge. The Mall of America is located almost in the backyard.

### Bloomington Super 8 Motel
*7800 S. Second Ave., Bloomington*    *888-8800*
$

This basic motel offers whirlpool and sauna, cable TV and complimentary coffee. There is no restaurant on premises, though several good ones are nearby.

### BRADBURY SUITES BEST WESTERN
*7770 Johnson Ave., Bloomington 893-9999*
$

Located on the corner of I-494 and France Avenue, this hotel offers 126 "corporate suites," large rooms with a divider between the sleeping and sitting areas. They also are equipped with refrigerators. Microwave ovens are available for guest use on the first and sixth floors. There is no swimming pool.

### COMFORT INN-AIRPORT
*1321 E. 78th St., Bloomington 854-3400*
$$

Minutes from the airport and Mall of America, the Comfort Inn is an attractive, moderately priced hotel offering free mall shuttle service, an indoor pool, exercise area, free HBO and a restaurant and lounge. In the special king-size rooms, you'll find a touch of home — a comfy recliner!

### CROWN STERLING SUITES-AIRPORT
*7901 34th Ave. S., Bloomington 854-1000*
$$$$

The lobby of this all-suites hotel opens onto a skylit indoor courtyard accented with brick pillars, lush greenery and fountains. There are also an indoor pool, sauna, whirlpool, restaurant and bar. The two-room suites contain refrigerator, microwave, coffee maker, two TVs and two phones. Guests enjoy a cooked-to-order complimentary breakfast.

### DAYS INN AIRPORT
*1901 Killebrew Dr., Bloomington 854-8400*
$$-$$$$

This motor lodge has an indoor pool and free shuttle to the airport and Mall of America, which is right across the street.

### EMBASSY SUITES BLOOMINGTON
*2800 W. 80th St., Bloomington 884-4811*
$$$$

Like others in the chain, this all-suites hotel offers a lovely open

atrium, two-room suites with two phones, two TVs and a kitchenette with coffee maker. Guests receive a free full breakfast and complimentary cocktails.

### EXEL INN
2701 E. 78th St., Bloomington    854-7200
$                                (800) 356-8013

Located so close to the Mall of America you can almost smell the bargains, this basic motel offers reasonable rates plus a free continental breakfast. Combination microwave-refrigerators are available for a nominal charge.

### FANTASUITE HOTEL
250 N. River Ridge Center
Burnsville        890-9550, (800) 666-7829
$-$$$$

Live out your wildest fantasies in theme rooms ranging from Arabian Nights, Sherwood Forest and Le Cave to Jungle Safari and Space Odyssey, among others. Conventional rooms and whirlpool suites are also available. The hotel has an indoor/outdoor pool complex and whirlpool. The rates range from $45.95 for a standard room to $199 for a fantasy suite on Saturday.

### HAMPTON INN-BLOOMINGTON
4201 W. 80th St., Bloomington    835-6643
$

This inn offers a double-room

rate of $67, free deluxe continental breakfast, sports bar/grill and an adjacent Denny's restaurant. If you're here on business, meeting rooms are available. Some rooms have private balconies. It's 3.5 miles from the Mall of America.

### HAWTHORN SUITES HOTEL
*3400 Edinborough Way, Edina   893-9300*
*$$$*

This hotel contains 142 one-bedroom suites with separate living rooms and complete kitchens. Guests enjoy a free hot buffet breakfast and have access to lovely indoor Edinborough Park and free use of its pool, track and ice rink. The Mall of America bus stops here.

### HOLIDAY INN EXPRESS MPLS.-AIRPORT
*814 E. 79th St. Bloomington   854-5558*
*$*

Both standard rooms and suites with fridges are found at the Holiday Inn Express. This newly remodeled, limited-service hotel offers a free continental breakfast buffet and free shuttle service to Mall of America and the airport. There is no pool.

### HOLIDAY INN INTERNATIONAL AIRPORT
*3 Appletree Sq., Bloomington   843-9000*
*$$$*

This deluxe 431-room, 13-story hotel boasts an Olympic-size pool, a well-stocked health club, two restaurants, a lounge, gift shop and free shuttle service to the airport and Mall of America. There are extensive convention facilities. Come January, you'll appreciate the hotel's covered parking!

### HOTEL SOFITEL
*5601 78th St. W., Bloomington   835-1900*
*$$$$*

Vive le France! This elegant six-story French hotel is one of the classiest in Bloomington. There are 287 lovely rooms and suites surrounding an atrium lobby filled with fresh flowers and chairs and couches arranged in conversational groupings. Guests enjoy a pool and health spa, turndown service with truffle and rose and a baguette as a parting gift.

This is home to three acclaimed French restaurants: Chez Colette for hearty provincial fare; Le Cafe Royal for haute cuisine; and La Terrasse for casual dining (with some summertime outdoor seating). Not to be missed is the hotel's gift shop for all that's French, fun and fanciful! The hotel's Executive Meeting Center offers spacious conference rooms with adjacent private dining rooms. The Grand Ballroom accommodates up to 500. Weekend packages are available.

### MALL OF AMERICA GRAND HOTEL
*7901 24th Ave. S., Bloomington   854-2244*
*$$$-$$$$                  (800)222-8733*

After a long day of shopping, relax and put your feet up in a luxury room at the 15-story Mall of America Grand Hotel, formerly known as The Registry Hotel. Located across the highway from Mall of America, this deluxe hotel offers free mall and airport shuttle service. Its 322 rooms (including six suites) come equipped with alarm clocks and color TVs with Showtime, ESPN and in-room movies.

There's an indoor heated pool, whirlpool, sauna and full-service exercise room. Ravels nightclub offers dancing to live music, and at the new Nine-Mile Grill, guests can enjoy a casual but classy dining experience. If you really want to pamper yourself, spring for a room on the Concierge Floors (14 and 15), where you can relax in a private lounge that affords one of the best views of the Twin Cities' skyline and enjoy complimentary cocktails, hors d'oeuvres and a continental breakfast. The hotel also has a 5,568-square-foot ballroom, a 2,800-square-foot Grand Salon and seven small conference rooms for business meetings and conventions.

### MINNEAPOLIS AIRPORT MARRIOTT
*2020 E. 79th St., Bloomington    854-7441*
$$$

This deluxe, full-service, 478-room hotel has an indoor pool, health club, whirlpool, two popular restaurants, a lounge and gift shop.

If you really want to live it up, stay in one of the suites or rooms on the luxurious concierge level, where you'll enjoy a private lounge, complimentary breakfast and newspaper and evening cocktails. Every guest enjoys complimentary shuttle service to the Mall of America and the airport.

### MINNEAPOLIS/ST. PAUL AIRPORT HILTON
*3800 80th St., East Minneapolis    854-2100*
$$$

A business-oriented hotel offering state-of-the-art audio/visual support for meetings, the Airport Hilton also features an indoor pool and health club, casual and fine-dining restaurants and Flamingos nightclub.

### RADISSON HOTEL SOUTH AND PLAZA TOWER
*7800 Normandale Blvd.*
*Bloomington                835-7800*
$$$

Boasting 575 rooms, numerous

conference suites and meeting rooms (including a 2,500-square-foot ballroom), this suburban hotel is a popular convention facility. Guest amenities include a full-size iron and ironing board in every room and coffee makers in the oversized rooms of the hotel's Plaza Tower. For a special experience, stay on the Plaza Club level and receive complimentary breakfast, evening cocktails and hors d'oeuvres in your own private lounge. Poolside cabana rooms have private patios or balconies. There's a large indoor pool, whirlpool, sauna, a bar-lounge and the Shipside restaurant, where fresh seafood is flown in daily. For less-formal dining, try the Scandinavian-themed Cafe Stuga.

### SELECT INN
*7851 Normandale Blvd.*
*Bloomington      835-7400, (800) 641-1000*
**$**

This 140-room economy motel offers free continental breakfast, indoor pool, satellite TV and an airport shuttle. While there is no on-premises restaurant, several good eateries are nearby.

### SHERATON AIRPORT INN
*2500 E. 79th St., Bloomington      854-1771*
**$$**

A highly rated hostelry, the 235-room Sheraton has a snazzy health club with an indoor pool and extensive exercise equipment. After you've sweated off all those calories, add a few back at the Timbers restaurant and lounge. Large meeting facilities here can accommodate up to 400 people. The Mall of America is a stone's throw away. Special weekend packages are available.

## Western Suburbs

### BEST WESTERN AMERICAN INN
*3924 Excelsior Blvd., St. Louis Park      927-7731*
**$**                              *(800) 528-1234*

Newly remodeled and just minutes away from Minneapolis' Chain of Lakes, this 36-room motel offers complimentary continental breakfast, free parking and a very inviting room rate. There is no pool. But who needs a pool when you can walk the lovely lakes?

### BEST WESTERN KELLY INN
*2705 Annapolis Lane N., Plymouth      553-1600*
**$**

You can't help but have a good time here — if you take advantage of the very popular in-house Plymouth Playhouse Theater and Green Mill restaurant. The theater is know for its boisterously fun musical-revue offerings, including *Pump Boys and Dinettes*, and the Green Mill, part of a well-regarded local chain, consistently wins raves for its pizza and extensive beer selection. The hotel also has an indoor pool, sauna and Jacuzzi, plus an exercise area with weights and Stairmasters. There are 141 recently remodeled rooms, plus several meeting rooms, the largest of which accommodates a group of 200.

### DAYS INN-PLYMOUTH
*2955 Empire Lane, Plymouth      559-2400*
**$**

Surrounded by several office parks and corporations, this motel caters primarily to business travelers. Although there's no pool, the motel offers complimentary continental breakfast, satellite TV and free phone calls. The 113 rooms include some corporate suites with microwaves and refrigerators. There is no on-site restaurant, but you can follow your nose to the Perkins located right next door.

### HAMPTON INN MINNETONKA
*I-394 and Hwy. 169, Minnetonka 541-1094*
$

Business executives like this limited-service hotel for its quiet atmosphere, reasonable rates and convenient location, just 10 minutes from downtown Minneapolis and near several west metro corporations. There is no swimming pool or food service, except for the complimentary continental breakfast. The 127 guest rooms are equipped with free cable TV. Some suites are available. For business meetings, the Hampton Inn offers three conference rooms, the largest with a seating capacity of 75.

### HOLIDAY INN WEST
*9940 Wayzata Blvd.*
*St. Louis Park           593-1918*
$$

You'll find an indoor pool, fitness center and spa here, plus cozy fireside dining in Martha's Vineyard restaurant. For business meetings and conventions, there are two large ballrooms that break down into several meeting rooms. The 196 guest rooms include a number of suites.

### RADISSON HOTEL AND CONFERENCE CENTER
*3131 Campus Dr., Plymouth           559-6600*
$$

Serious fitness buffs are attracted to this hotel's full-service fitness center, which features an extensive array of free weights and strength-training machines, as well as Stairmasters and other aerobic equipment, two racquetball courts and an indoor basketball court. The hotel's conference center includes 10 expansive meeting rooms and 21 smaller hospitality rooms for groups of six to eight. The 243 sleeping rooms were recently redecorated in dark green and burgundy hues. Enjoy views of the surrounding woods from the Creekside Cafe restaurant and adjoining bar-lounge.

### RAMADA HOTEL PLAZA MINNEAPOLIS WEST
*12201 Ridgedale Dr., Minnetonka 593-0000*
$$

Watch Canada geese soar overhead or catch a glimpse of deer running through the nearby woods from the windows of this four-story deluxe suburban hotel. Though it's located across the street from bustling Ridgedale shopping center, the Ramada backs up to a scenic woodland and wetlands lush with migrating waterfowl. Guests enjoy such amenities as an indoor pool, whirlpool, exercise area, Christy's restaurant, and Winners sports bar, an intimate setting for cocktail talk. Refreshments are also served in the large pleasant atrium lobby. A popular spot for traveling executives during the week, the hotel is also a favorite venue for weekend wedding receptions. There are three ballrooms and several smaller meeting rooms. Guests may also use the nearby YMCA for a nominal fee.

### SHERATON PARK PLACE HOTEL
*5555 Wayzata Blvd.*
*St. Louis Park* 542-8600
$$

There are 268 rooms and 30 poolside suites in this distinctive newer hotel located just 5 minutes west of downtown Minneapolis. Guests here enjoy a stunning skylit indoor pool. Live music and gourmet fare are served up at the hotel's Dover Restaurant. There are 18 banquet rooms for business meetings and conventions. The hotel offers lots of package deals, and youths 18 and younger stay free in their parents' room.

## North Suburbs

### BEST WESTERN KELLY INN
*5201 Central Ave. N.E., Fridley* 571-9440
$

This attractive motel is newly remodeled with a pleasant tropical courtyard featuring an indoor pool, whirlpool and game room. There are 96 rooms and an on-premises restaurant.

### BROOKDALE INN
*6500 River Rd. W.*
*Brooklyn Center* 561-5650
$

If peace and quiet is what you seek, check out this small 25-unit motel with very reasonable rates. Via freeway, it's conveniently located near both Twin Cities.

### BUDGETEL INN
*6415 James Circle N.*
*Brooklyn Center* 561-8400
$ (800) 4-BUDGET

Stretch out in one of Budgetel's 99 "roomy" rooms furnished with easy chairs and extra-long double beds. You'll enjoy a complimentary continental breakfast and free phone calls.

### BUDGET HOST FRIDLEY
*6881 Hwy. 65 N.E., Fridley* 571-0420
$

Picturesque Rice Creek borders this 14-unit motel. The rooms are equipped with microwaves, TVs and refrigerators. There also are biking and hiking trails.

### DAYS INN ROSEVILLE
*2550 Cleveland Ave. N., Roseville* 636-6730
$

The Days Inn offers clean and comfortable basic lodging with free continental breakfast.

### HOLIDAY INN MINNEAPOLIS NORTH
*2200 Freeway Blvd.*
*Brooklyn Center* 566-8000
$$

You can jog off your stress on the nature trails next to this attractive hotel or take a dip in the indoor pool and whirlpool. There's free parking and free in-room movies, plus an on-premises nightclub and restaurant.

### HOLIDAY INN ROSEVILLE
*2540 Cleveland Ave., Roseville* 636-4567
$

This Holiday Inn offers an indoor pool and a restaurant.

### Northland Inn
### and Conference Center

*7101 Northland Center*
*Brooklyn Park*          536-8300
*$$$*

This five-year-old luxury hotel and conference center offers 231 two-room suites, each furnished with double-wide whirlpool tubs, with the exception of 10 rooms with handicapped-accessible showers. A bustling conference center houses two ballrooms and 20 other meeting rooms. The hotel is handsomely furnished in warm woods, Minnesota granite and hues of burgundy and forest green. There are two restaurants, Wadsworth's and America's Harvest.

### Super 8 Minneapolis North

*6445 James Circle*
*Brooklyn Center*          566-9810
*$*

The 103-room Super 8 offers hard-to-beat rates, free continental breakfast and satellite TV. Restaurants and shopping are within easy access.

## Bed and Breakfasts

These homey accommodations often lend a very special ambiance to one's travels. Here are a few of the bed and breakfasts found in the Twin Cities area. The list is by no means complete — consult friends or travel agents for their personal recommendations. And remember, in most cases, breakfast is included in the prices listed below. Most bed and breakfasts are smoke-free.

### St. Paul

### Chatsworth Bed & Breakfast

*984 Ashland Ave.*          227-4288
*$-$$*

Located in the heart of St. Paul, near the Governor's Mansion, this bed and breakfast is a spacious Victorian home with five guest rooms, two with private whirlpool baths. Colorful Grand Avenue is within walking distance. Breakfast is served in a richly paneled dining room.

### COMO VILLA BED & BREAKFAST

*1371 W. Nebraska Ave.*   647-0471
$-$$

This antiques-filled 1872 Victorian home is located two blocks from lovely Como Park. The rooms are exquisitely decorated with period furniture. Lower rates apply during the week. Weekend breakfast guests are serenaded by music from the grand piano.

### PRIOR'S ON DESOTO

*1522 Desoto St.*   774-2695
$-$$

Unlike many bed and breakfasts, Dick and Mary Prior's establishment is a relatively new (1991), handsome, modern structure boasting all the comforts of home — and then some. Relax by the fire in a dramatic living room with vaulted ceiling and spectacular windows. You have your choice of two sleeping areas. The Victorian room offers landscape views through lace-curtained windows, a queen-size four-poster bed, and an adjoining loft complete with desk and phone. Overlooking the patio, the Paisley Room is equipped with twin beds (convertible to one king-size bed) furnished in blue and rose paisley fabric, and it too opens to a loft area. Each room has a private bath. An inviting communal sun deck and front porch are just right for bird-watching and quiet conversation. It's conveniently located near I-35 and Larpenteur Avenue, just 5 min-

utes from downtown St. Paul. Bring your checkbook because the Priors don't accept credit cards.

## Minneapolis

### COE CARRIAGE HOUSE

*1700 Third Ave. S.*   871-4249
$$$$

Relax in this converted 1883 carriage house, located one block from the Minneapolis Convention Center. A pleasant alternative to chain hotels, the Coe Carriage House is a recently renovated National Historic Register home. Inside this handsome brick and wood-paneled structure, you'll find a modern, gourmet kitchen and tastefully decorated large living room with overstuffed chairs and elegant artwork. A spiral staircase leads to the three bedrooms accented with period furniture. There is a marble bathroom with a Jacuzzi, tub and spa and another half-bath. The living room and bedrooms have cable TV. Unlike most bed and breakfasts, the entire home is rented as a unit, with nightly rates based on the number of guests. From here, it's a healthy six-block walk to Orchestra Hall and Nicollet Mall.

### ELMWOOD HOUSE

*1 Elmwood Place*   822-4558
$

Pluck out a tune on the baby grand in the parlor or just chew the fat 'round the living room fireplace. Whatever your mood, you're bound to feel at home in this gracious 1887 Norman chateau-style historic home. This South Minneapolis inn, just 15 minutes from downtown, offers three sleeping rooms and one suite with private bath. An added attraction are nearby nature trails.

### EVELO'S BED AND BREAKFAST
2301 Bryant Ave. S.          374-9656
$

This 1897 Victorian home is conveniently located near Uptown and downtown attractions. In original condition, it is graced with heavy, dark oak millwork and period furnishings. It offers three nicely appointed upstairs rooms with a shared bath.

### LEBLANC HOUSE
302 University Ave. N.E.          379-2570
$$

An 1896 restored and elegantly furnished home, the LeBlanc House is just minutes away from Riverplace and downtown. It offers three rooms, one with a private bath. Zofi's Room is a floral fantasy with a walnut bed and marble-top dresser and private bath. Amelia's room looks out on the city skyline and is furnished in elegant white with a walnut bed, table and chairs. In Marissa's Room, you'll enjoy oak furnishings and an antique brass bed topped with handmade quilts. Save room for the generous breakfast of rum-raisin French toast, filled crepes and pistachio quiche.

## Minneapolis Suburbs

### BLUFF CREEK INN
1161 Bluff Creek Dr., Chaska     445-2735
$$

Dating to 1864, this Minnesota River Valley inn encompasses five tastefully decorated, antique-filled rooms, each with a private bath. Some rooms also have balconies and whirlpools. Enjoy a gourmet three-course breakfast and evening hors d'oeuvres. With 20 miles of cross-country ski trails nearby, this is a perfect wintertime destination.

### INN ON THE FARM
6150 Summit Dr. N.
Brooklyn Center          569-6330
$$-$$$$          (800) 428-8382

Housed in a cluster of farm buildings on what was once a sprawling country estate, this large inn offers 11 exquisitely decorated period rooms, each with a double whirlpool, private bath and queen-size bed. Before turning in for the evening, enjoy a spot o' tea next to the cozy stone fireplace in the antiques-filled parlor. This is a very popular destination for honeymooners. Breakfast is served in the inn's dining room, and there's also Earle's restaurant for fine dining on Friday and Saturday nights. Also on the grounds is the Earle Brown Heritage Center exhibition hall which frequently hosts antique fairs and arts and crafts shows. Credit cards and checks are accepted.

### THE NICHOLAS HOUSE
### BED & BREAKFAST
134 4th Ave. E., Shakopee     496-2537
$$

Guests at this 1895 Queen Anne home can sip lemonade on a huge wraparound porch shaded by 100-year-old-trees or relax in the formal parlor or living room, both filled with antiques, Oriental carpets and period wallpapers. There

The Rivertown Inn in Stillwater.

are three sleeping rooms, all located on the second floor. One has its own bath.

## Stillwater and Vicinity

### AFTON HOUSE INN
*3291 S. St. Croix Trail, Afton     436-8883*
*$-$$$$*

Built in 1867, this historic inn is listed on the National Register of Historic Places. Here you'll find country-style hotel rooms with fireplaces and such modern amenities as Jacuzzis. The inn's restaurant is a popular destination for the aprés-ski crowd from nearby Afton Alps. This may feel like a bed and breakfast, but it's actually not — sorry, no free eats in the morning. Still, it's a fine choice for cozy accommodations.

### ANN BEAN HOUSE
*319 W. Pine St., Stillwater     430-0355*
*$$$-$$$$*

A grand old (c. 1878) mansion built by a prosperous lumberman, the Ann Bean House boasts 11-foot ceilings and a 55-foot tower, original oak woodwork and antiques galore. There are five large sleeping rooms, some with double whirlpools and wood-burning fireplaces. All have private baths.

*Downtown Minneapolis*

### ASA PARKER HOUSE

*17500 St. Croix Tr. N.*
*Marine on St. Croix*        *433-5248*
*$$-$$$$*

Nestled in this picturesque little burg overlooking the St. Croix River, the Asa Parker House, dating to 1856, features five antique-filled guest rooms with English wallcoverings and decor. One suite contains a whirlpool. The breakfast here is legendary. Communal areas include a double parlor, wicker-filled porch, yard gazebo and tennis court. Canoes are available for river exploring.

### THE BRUNSWICK INN

*114 E. Chestnut St., Stillwater        430-2653*
*$$$-$$$$*

One of the oldest structures in Stillwater, this 1848 Greek Revival inn nonetheless has such modern amenities as oversized double whirlpools in each of its three sleeping rooms, not to mention wood-burning fireplaces. For a real treat, call ahead and make reservations for the Victorian multi-course dinners Friday and Saturday evenings.

### THE ELEPHANT WALK

*801 Pine St., Stillwater        430-0359*
*$$$$*

This Victorian home sends guests on "round-the-world" tours via uniquely themed bedrooms. Among them are the Rangoon Room, containing a whirlpool and four-poster bed draped in mosquito netting; the Raffles Room with a bamboo bed and fireplace; and the Spanish-style Cadiz Room with its own private sunroom. Long-term and mid-week discounted rates are available.

### JAMES A. MULVEY RESIDENCE INN

*622 W. Churchill St., Stillwater        430-8008*
*$$-$$$*

This Italianate Victorian home built by a lumber baron is filled with art, antiques and loads of charm. There are five sleeping rooms, some containing fireplaces and whirlpools. All have private baths. During the summer, the four-course breakfast is served on the sun porch.

### THE RIVERTOWN INN

*306 W. Olive St., Stillwater        430-2955*
*$-$$$$*

A sprawling three-story lumberman's mansion, this 1882 inn offers nine rooms elegantly decorated in period furnishings, some with whirlpools and fireplaces. Its hillside location offers breathtaking views of historic Stillwater and the St. Croix River Valley. Dinner packages are available.

### WILLIAM SAUNTRY MANSION

*626 N. Fourth St., Stillwater        430-2653*
*$$-$$$$*

Listed on the National Register, this Queen Anne-style 1890s home is decorated with historically correct wallpapers and room settings. Fantastic views are afforded through stained-glass windows. There are five guest rooms with fireplaces, private baths and whirlpools. Victorian dinners are offered on weekends.

---

## Hastings

### HEARTHWOOD BED & BREAKFAST

*17650 200th St.        437-1133*
*$-$$*

A multilevel Cape Cod log

home built in 1986 is the setting for this bed and breakfast with five guest rooms. Four of the five rooms have private whirlpools and fireplaces. Hearthwood's great room features a massive stone fireplace set amid an eclectic decor of traditional and antique furnishings. Guests greet the day with a candlelit full breakfast. The Hearthwood is located on 10 acres of land 5 miles south of Hastings and within easy reach of attractions along the Mississippi River and historic Red Wing.

### THORWOOD INN
### ROSEWOOD INN
*Hastings*           *437-3297*
*$$-$$$$*

These two inns — the Thorwood (at 315 Pine Street) and the Rosewood Inn (at 620 Ramsey Street) — are both listed on the National Register of Historic Sites. Filled with reading nooks, fireplaces and antiques, they provide a cozy retreat from the 20th century. Some suites have double whirlpools and fireplaces. All have private baths. There are 15 rooms in all. Intimate in-house dinners are available upon request.

## Convention and Visitors Bureaus

For other lodging information, as well as general information about Twin Cities destinations, the area convention and visitors bureaus can provide help.

### MINNEAPOLIS CONVENTION
### AND VISITORS BUREAU
*4000 Multifoods Tower*
*Minneapolis*          *661-4700*

### ST. PAUL CONVENTION
### AND VISITORS BUREAU
*55 E. Fifth St., St. Paul*     *297-6985*

### BLOOMINGTON CONVENTION
### AND VISITORS BUREAU
*1550 E. 79th St., Bloomington*   *858-8500*

### BURNSVILLE CHAMBER OF
### COMMERCE AND CONVENTION BUREAU
*14577 Grand Ave., Burnsville*    *435-6000*

### EAGAN CONVENTION
### AND VISITORS BUREAU
*1380 Corporate Center Curve*
*Eagan*     *452-9872, (800) 324-2620*

# Inside
# Restaurants

Here's the fattest chapter in the book — one that, consulted too often, may cause you to assume larger proportions. But, seriously, the size of this chapter testifies to the variety and quality of eating establishments in the Twin Cities. Old-timers can wax nostalgic about some of the region's now-vanished restaurants of repute, such as Charlie's Cafe Exceptionale in Minneapolis, but nobody with his or her palate on straight will deny that the eating is much better in these parts than it has ever been before.

Why? There are many answers, but recent immigrants are most responsible for the rising quality of Twin Cities dining. Twenty years ago, you would have been hard-pressed to locate many authentic African, Middle Eastern, Vietnamese, Thai or even Italian restaurants in the area. Since then, newcomers have arrived in Minneapolis and St. Paul from all over the globe, and you can see it in the menus. Asian food, in particular, is especially good and plentiful here, contributing to the Twin Cities' status as one of the Midwest's ethnic-eating capitals.

There's a venerable saying among restaurant hoppers: Those who have poor noses have unsatisfied appetites. In other words, if you want to be a fulfilled restaurant goer, you'll have to keep your nostrils always open to sniff out your own favorite haunts. Think of the restaurants listed here as just the starting steps on your path to eating nirvana. Hundreds of other fine, interesting and challenging restaurants in the Twin Cities are not included here, and they are for you to discover.

The dollar sign code with each restaurant entry indicates the likely cost of dinner for one, excluding beverages, tips and taxes. Lunch at most restaurants costs less. Here's how the code works:

| | |
|---|---|
| *Less than $10* | **$** |
| *$10 to $20* | **$$** |
| *$20 to $30* | **$$$** |
| *More than $30* | **$$$$** |

Unless we note that an establishment does not accept credit cards, you can be fairly confident that the restaurant will take one of the cards you carry. Certainly ask *before* your meal if you want to make sure.

Grab your fork and let the eating begin!

## African and Middle-Eastern Cuisine

### THE BARBARY FIG
720 Grand Ave., St. Paul          290-2085
$$

The Barbary Fig is the Twin Cities' only couscous restaurant, with a small, enticing menu of gently spicy North African dishes and a smattering of foods from Provence. Recommended are the vegetarian couscous, fish and eggplant specials, and garlicky olives served with crusty bread. Hours are 11:30 AM to 2 PM and 5 to 9 PM Monday and Wednesday through Saturday; 5 to 9 PM Sunday. Wine and beer are served.

### CARAVAN SERAI
2175 Ford Pkwy., St. Paul          690-1935
$$

You can sit in a chair if you want, but it's much more fun to dine while reclining at this sumptuously appointed Middle Eastern restaurant. The soups, naan, tandoori chicken and sheer chai, a cardamom-scented tea with cream, are all recommended. Lunch is served 11 AM to 2 PM Tuesday through Friday. Dinner is 5 to 9:30 PM Sunday through Thursday; 5 to 10:30 PM Friday and Saturday. Reservations are recommended.

### CASPIAN BISTRO
2418 University Ave. S.E.
Minneapolis                      623-1113
$                        No credit cards

Here you'll find Middle Eastern food bargains for cautious and adventurous diners alike. Recommended choices are the lemony chicken kebabs, shawirma and snowy buttered rice. Hours are 10:30 AM to 9 PM Tuesday through Thursday; 10:30 AM to 10 PM Friday; 11:30 AM to 10 PM Saturday; noon to 9 PM Sunday. Reservations are recommended.

### DUPSY'S AFRICAN CUISINE
474 W. University Ave., St. Paul   225-1525
$

The first of its kind in the area, this friendly West African cafe serves authentic dishes that range from comforting to challenging. Rice, beans, beef and fried plantains are easy to like; soups and fufu are satisfying, especially when eaten with fingers. Hours are 11 AM to 9 PM Tuesday through Saturday. Reservations are recommended.

### EMILY'S LEBANESE DELI
641 University Ave. N.E.
Minneapolis                      379-4069
$                        No credit cards

Come here for the smooth, addictive hummos, the tabbouleh for parsley lovers and the big flat spinach pies that taste great even as leftovers. It's a good choice for takeout, but the crowded, ultra-casual dining room has a certain charm, too. Hours are 9 AM to 9 PM Sunday, Monday, Wednesday and Thursday; 9 AM to 10 PM Friday and Saturday.

### JACOB'S
101 N.E. Broadway, Minneapolis 379-2508
$$

Experience the surprise of excellent Middle Eastern food in a northeast Minneapolis bar and restaurant. If you find it hard to decide

Photo: Mark Morson, Pioneer Press

The Lexington, St. Paul

what to order from the long, tempting menu, consider the appetizer sampler plate as a nice, light meal for two. Reservations are suggested. Hours are 7 AM to 10 PM Monday through Thursday; 7 AM to 11 PM Friday; 7 AM to 2 PM and 5 to 11 PM Saturday; 7 AM to 2 PM Sunday.

### JERUSALEM'S
*1518 Nicollet Ave. S., Minneapolis    871-8883*
**$$**

Among the city's best Middle Eastern restaurants, this cozy den serves hearty food prepared with care. You'll discover smooth, garlicky hummos, a crunchy Jericho salad, lamb curry, combination plates and much more. On Friday and Saturday nights, dancers do their best to distract diners. Hours are 11 AM to 10 PM Monday through Thursday; 11 AM to 11 PM Friday; noon to 11 PM Saturday; noon to 10 PM Sunday.

### ODAA
*408 Cedar Ave., Minneapolis    338-4459*
**$$**

If you've never eaten with your fingers as an adult, this is the place to start. Odaa features a variety of West African dishes in a comfortable, West Bank setting, marred only by sometimes lackadaisical service. Try lukuu waaddi gubaa (curried chicken with jalapenos) and a gingery beef stew called itto sa'a. Hours are 11 AM to 10 PM Monday through Thursday; 11 AM to 11 PM Friday and Saturday; 3 to 9 PM Sunday. Reservations are recommended.

### OLD CITY CAFE
*1571 Grand Ave., St. Paul    699-5347*
**$**                          *No credit cards*

Old City offers strictly kosher food prepared with care. The choices range from Middle Eastern specialties — hummos and eggplant — to a swell New York-style pizza.

• 53

Yemenite rice and falafel parmesan are also recommended. Take it out or eat in. Hours are 11 AM to 8:30 PM Monday through Thursday; 11 AM to 2 PM Friday; 10 AM to 8:30 PM Sunday; closed Saturday.

### PORT OF BEIRUT
*1385 S. Robert St., West St. Paul 457-4886*
**$$**

Hearty seasonings are a trademark of this reliable West St. Paul cafe (garlic-lovers, dip into the creamy, pungent sauce accompanying many dishes). The Port Sampler for two offers a little of almost everything. Dancers undulate every Friday and Saturday night, beginning at 8 PM. Hours are 11 AM to 9 PM Monday through Thursday; 11 AM to 10 PM Friday and Saturday. Reservations are recommended.

## American Cuisine

### APPLEBEE'S
### NEIGHBORHOOD GRILL AND BAR
*1600 W. University Ave., St. Paul 642-9757*
**$$**

This consistent and competent chain offers a wide variety of appetizers, sandwiches, salads and entrees, with regular updates to follow seasons and trends. You'll find a visually busy atmosphere and a staff that's accommodating to children. Hours are 11 AM to midnight Monday through Saturday; 11 AM to 11 PM Sunday. There are 13 other locations, including Town Center in Eagan; and Ridgedale in Minnetonka.

### BEAN COUNTER
*World Trade Center, 30 E. Seventh St.*
*St. Paul                    227-8283*
**$**

The Bean Counter's warm, regular-folks service, good coffee and food make it a valuable find. In addition to the basics, the cafe offers its own hard-core creation, "The Quad," four shots of espresso and steamed milk — perfect for groggy executives. The lunch chow is good to take out or eat in: there's a satisfying cold club sandwich and food supplied by the Old City Cafe. Hours are 6:30 AM to 7 PM Monday through Friday; 10 AM to 6 PM Saturday; noon to 5 PM Sunday.

### THE BLUE POINT
*739 E. Lake St., Wayzata          475-3636*
**$$$**

There's more seafood here than you can shake a pole at, with a daily special sheet telling you the precise origin of your fish. Hours are 4 to 9 PM Sunday; 4 to 10 Monday through Thursday; 4 to 11 PM Friday and Saturday. (Call for special

# Exceptional Dining.

Our breathtaking vista creates the perfect atmosphere for dining on truly exceptional food while our fireplace creates a cozy atmosphere.

## Toby's
### On The Lake

I-94 & Century Ave. (MN 120) • 739-1600

winter hours.) Reservations are recommended.

### CALIFORNIA CAFE

*Mall of America, Bloomington* 854-2233
$$$

This is a tasteful San Francisco-based eatery serving satisfying, upscale California cuisine. Recommended menu items are the bruschetta trio, oak-fired pizza, farmers market salad, trout with red onion sauce and beets, creme brulee and lemon-berry shortcake. The menu changes regularly. Lunch is served 11 AM to 4 PM daily. Dinner is 5 to 10 PM Monday through Thursday; 5 to 10:30 PM Friday and Saturday; 4:30 to 8:30 PM Sunday. It's best to call for reservations.

### THE CAFE

*St. Paul Hotel, 350 Market St.*
*St. Paul* 292-9292
$$

The Cafe offers a sedate country atmosphere and a varied menu. Best bets are the cream of chicken

soup with brie and artichokes and the spinach-strawberry salad. Hours are 6:30 AM to 2:30 PM Monday; 6:30 AM to 9 PM Tuesday through Thursday; 6:30 AM to 10 PM Friday; 6:30 AM to 1 PM and 4:30 to 10 PM Saturday; 6:30 AM to 1 PM Sunday. Reservations are recommended.

### CAFE MINNESOTA

*Minnesota History Center*
*345 W. Kellogg Blvd., St. Paul* 297-4097
$ *No credit cards*

This better-than-basic cafeteria offers imaginative salads, great vegetarian chili, top-notch burgers and a full range of entrees. There's also a continental breakfast (juice, coffee, muffins, etc.) on weekday mornings. Hours are 8 AM to 3 PM Monday through Friday; 11:30 AM to 3 PM Saturday and Sunday.

### CARIBOU COFFEE

*2138 Ford Parkway, St. Paul* 690-9934
$

This is a slick, upscale nook next

• 55

to Bruegger's Bagel Bakery. It employs a legion of perky, well-trained workers who serve coffee, espresso drinks and a hefty selection of top-notch baked goods supplied by Goodfellow's. Hours are 6:30 AM to 10 PM Sunday through Thursday, 6:30 AM to 11 PM Friday and Saturday. (There's another Caribou at 1055 Grand Avenue, St. Paul.)

### CAROUSEL

*Radisson Hotel, 11 E. Kellogg Blvd.*
*St. Paul* 292-1900
**$$**

This revolving restaurant with a view boasts a full bar and a whole new look and menu, with lower prices and lighter fare. Specialties include coconut fried shrimp, sirloin steak and mushroom escargots. Hours are 6:30 AM to 10:30 PM Monday through Thursday; 6:30 AM to 11:30 PM Friday; 7 AM to 11:30 PM Saturday; 7 AM to 10:30 PM Sunday.

### CHEROKEE SIRLOIN ROOM

*886 S. Smith Ave., West St. Paul* 457-2729
**$$**

This bustling steakhouse offers plenty for the chicken-eaters in the family, too. While you're there, take a look at the mirrors, chandeliers and a mural that pays homage to the High Bridge. The Cherokee is a place where deals are sealed, both personal and professional. Lunch is served 11 AM to 2:30 PM Monday through Friday; 11 AM to 3 PM Saturday. Dinner is 5 to 11 PM Monday through Thursday; 5 PM to midnight Friday and Saturday; 3 to 10 PM Sunday. Sunday brunch is 10 AM 'til 2 PM. A second Cherokee

Sirloin Room is at 4625 Nichols Road in Eagan.

### COGNAC MCCARTHY'S

*162 N. Dale St., St. Paul* 224-4617
**$** *No credit cards*

Here's a friendly neighborhood bar with a staggering selection of spirits. It also offers bar food and beyond: little tortilla "pizzas," great burgers, meat loaf sandwiches, fried potatoes and Cuban chicken. The cozy booths are perfect for true confessions. Food is served 7 AM to 11 PM Monday through Saturday; 9 AM to 9 PM Sunday.

### DARI-ETTE

*1440 E. Minnehaha Ave., St. Paul* 776-3470
**$** *No credit cards*

In addition to burgers, malts and cherry cokes, this drive-in (complete with carhops) serves pasta, meatball sandwiches and a nifty Italian soup. Make sure to allow time to do your drive-in duty: Tilt back the car seat and contemplate nothing in particular. Hours are 11 AM to 10 PM Sunday through Thursday; 11 AM to 11 PM Friday and Saturday.

### DAY BY DAY CAFE

*477 W. Seventh St., St. Paul* 227-0654
**$** *No credit cards*

Looking for an atmosphere where you can get your life, not to mention your morning, together? Try the delish Red Earth breakfast, which mixes eggs with hashbrowns and tops it with cheese and salsa. Here you'll find nicely mismatched chairs and silverware, along with live entertainment on Friday nights. Hours are 6 AM to 8 PM Monday

*Photo: Buzz Magnuson, Pioneer Press*

*Bad Habit Cafe in St. Paul*

through Thursday; 6 AM to 10 PM Friday;

### FABULOUS FERN'S BAR AND GRILL
*400 Selby Ave., St. Paul      225-9414*
*$$*

The atmosphere may be a little predictable, but the food at this friendly and casual place is steps above the typical fern bar. Appetizers include spicy black bean dip with chips and fried salmon patties; recommended entrees are fettuccine with chicken and the Southwestern flank steak. For dessert, sink into the super-rich Jack Daniels chocolate and walnut pie. Hours are 11 AM to 10 PM Monday through Thursday; 11 AM to 11 PM Friday; 10 AM to 1 PM Saturday; 10 AM to 9 PM Sunday (brunch 10 AM to 2 PM). Reservations are recommended.

### FIGLIO
*Calhoun Square, 3001 Hennepin Ave.*
*Minneapolis      822-1688*
*$$*

Cosmopolitan charm, luscious pasta and a sunny, upbeat waitstaff create a most pleasant dining ambiance at Figlio. This bustling eatery specializes in California-Italian fare at moderate prices. The people-watching is primo, especially in the big dining room overlooking Hennepin Avenue and Lake Street. Outdoor sidewalk dining is available in the summer. Hours are 11:30 AM to 1 AM Sunday through Thursday; 11:30 AM to 2 AM Friday and Saturday.

### FOUR INNS
*American National Bank Building Skyway*
*St. Paul      291-7939*
*$      No credit cards*

This is an efficient, bustling skyway lunch spot offering traditional dinners and sandwiches. The pies are great — order early to avoid missing your favorite. Hours are 6:30 AM to 3:30 PM Monday through Friday.

### GALLIVAN'S
*354 N. Wabasha St., St. Paul      227-6688*
*$$*

This is a woody, relaxing bar and restaurant, the ideal place to sink in and discuss the meaning of it all. For dinner, stick to basics like the steak sandwich. There are generous and free happy hour hors d'oeuvres. Hours are 11 AM to 10 PM Monday through Thursday; 11 AM to 11:30 PM Friday and Saturday; 4 to 8 PM Sunday. Reservations are recommended.

### GOOD EARTH
*Calhoun Square, 3001 Hennepin Ave.*
*Minneapolis      824-8533*
*$-$$*

Wholesome food prepared with fresh, natural ingredients is the specialty of this pleasant, completely smoke-free restaurant chain. The baked goods here are exceptional. There's no bar, but wine and beer are served. Hours are from 11:30 AM to 10 PM Monday through Thursday; 11:30 AM to 11 PM Friday and Saturday; 9 AM to 11 PM Sunday. Other Good Earths are found in the Galleria shopping center in Edina and at 1901 W. Highway 36 in Roseville.

### GOPHER BAR
*241 E. Seventh St., St. Paul      291-9638*
*$          No credit cards*

Here you'll find four-star Coneys with a buttery grilled bun; don't order fewer than two, or you'll just have to ask for seconds. There are burgers, gyros and tostadas, too. Hours are 9 AM to midnight Monday through Friday; 9 AM to 9:30 PM Saturday; 7 AM to 3 PM Sunday.

### GRANDVIEW GRILL
*1818 Grand Ave., St. Paul      698-2346*
*$          No credit cards*

Great big burgers, nice fries and a neighborhoody feeling make this diner a good choice for lunch. Hours are 6 AM to 3 PM Monday through Saturday; 8 AM to 3 PM Sunday.

### GREEN MILL INN
*57 S. Hamline Ave., St. Paul      698-0353*
*$$*

Pizza's the point at these bustling cafes featuring delightful deep dish specimens bursting with tomatoes alongside crisp, saucy flat ones. There's a full menu of entrees, burgers, salads and kids' items. Other Green Mill locations include those at 2626 Hennepin Avenue, Minneapolis; 8266 Commonwealth Drive, Eden Prairie; 2705 Annapolis Lane, Plymouth; 6003 Hudson Road, Woodbury; 1595 W. Highway 36, Roseville. Call for hours. Reservations are recommended.

### HIGHLAND GRILL
*771 Cleveland Ave. S., St. Paul      690-1173*
*$          No credit cards*

A onetime ice-cream shop finally found its true identity in this friendly grill. The fare is fresh and surprisingly eclectic; in addition to burgers and pancakes, there's veggie hash, ratatouille, curried beef and black bean cakes. Breakfast is served all day. Hours are 7 AM to 3 PM and 5:30 to 9 PM Monday through Friday; 8 AM to 3 PM and 5:30 to 9 PM Saturday; 8 AM to 3 PM Sunday.

### IVORIES

*Hwys. 55 and 169, Plymouth      591-6188*
*$$*

Classic American fare of fresh seafood, steaks and chops, salads and appetizers is served in this elegant, modern restaurant. Cap off your dinner with a visit to the piano lounge. With its wall of windows and cozy candle-lit tables, it's one of the most romantic spots in the Twin Cities, where talented co-owner Jimmy Martin tickles the ivories and sings his heart out. Lunch hours are 11 AM to 2 PM Monday thourgh Friday; brunch is from 11 AM to 2 PM Sunday. Dinner is served from 5 to 9 PM Monday; 5 to 10 PM Tuesday through Thursday; and 5 to 11 PM Friday and Saturday.

### JAX CAFE

*1928 University Ave. N.E.*
*Minneapolis      789-7297*
*$$*

Jax is an enduring favorite among locals, especially for its fresh lobster, rainbow trout (catch it yourself from Jax's brook) and steaks. A pianists performs Thursday through Sunday. Hours are from 11 AM to 10:30 PM Monday through Thursday; 11 AM to 11 PM Friday and Saturday; and 3:30 to 9 PM Sunday. Brunch is served from 10 AM to 3 PM Sunday.

### J.D. HOYT'S

*301 Washington Ave. N.*
*Minneapolis      338-1560*
*$$$*

There are steaks, chops and Ca-jun specialties in this hopping warehouse-district bar. Try the stick-to-your-ribs breakfasts, too. Hours are 7 AM to 3 PM and 5 to 11 PM Monday through Friday; 7 AM to 2:30 PM and 5 to 11:30 PM Saturday; 10 AM to 2 PM and 5 to 10 PM Sunday. Reservations are recommended.

### KEYS

*767 Raymond Ave., St. Paul      646-5756*
*$*

Keys specializes in big, buttery food in a well-worn atmosphere that lures you back. And they do come back — the regulars are legendary. Popular menu items are the weighty, spicy Italian hash, the thick homemade toast, and the huge caramel rolls. Hours are 6 AM to 3 PM Monday to Friday; 7 AM to noon Saturday; 8:30 AM to noon Sunday. Other Keys restaurants are at 500 North Robert Street, St. Paul; 1682 North Lexington Parkway, Roseville; and 1192 Fifth Avenue N.W., New Brighton.

### LAKE ELMO INN

*3442 Lake Elmo Ave. N.*
*Lake Elmo      777-8495*
*$$$*

Want fancy dining with a grandmotherly Minnesota touch? Here you'll discover a varied continental menu and the best salt and pepper shaker collection around. It's an appropriate dining choice for special occasions. Hours are 11 AM to 2 PM and 5 to 10 PM Monday through Saturday; 10 AM to 2 PM and 4:30 to 8:30 PM Sunday. Reservations are recommended.

## LAKE STREET GARAGE

*3508 E. Lake St., Minneapolis*     *729-8820*
*$*     *No credit cards*

This is a wholesome hangout in a former garage, adorned with signs for Quaker State and Prest-O-Lite. The menu includes superior burgers, malts and fries, a nice Italian salad and a sundae called the Wrecker. Enjoy free popcorn with your beer. Hours are 11 AM to 10 PM Monday through Thursday; 11 AM to 11 PM Friday; 11:30 AM to 11 PM Saturday.

## THE LEXINGTON

*1096 Grand Ave., St. Paul*     *222-5878*
*$$*

This venerable restaurant has an updated menu, but the comfortable, clubby atmosphere remains unchanged. Steaks are a reliable choice; among the newer offerings, try Shaw's crab cakes, the chicken fettuccine rosa, and The Beans, a spicy Oriental appetizer. Hours are 11 AM to 10 PM Monday through Thursday; 11 AM to midnight Friday and Saturday; 10 AM to 3 PM and 4 to 9 PM Sunday. Reservations are recommended.

## LINDEY'S PRIME STEAK HOUSE

*3610 N. Snelling Ave., Arden Hills 633-9813*
*$*     *No credit cards*

The choosing's easy — sirloin, sirloin or chopped sirloin. The tender meat arrives juicy and sizzling, along with plenty of potatoes and garlic bread. Here the ambiance is dark and northwoodsy. Hours are 5 to 10:30 PM Monday through Thursday; 5 to 11:30 PM Friday and Saturday.

## LOON CAFE

*500 First Ave. N., Minneapolis*     *332-8342*
*$$*

Chili reigns supreme at this bustling, sportsy bar and cafe, located a block from Target Center. For a real kick in the pants, try the hot version of Pecos River Red. Food is served 11 AM to 11:30 PM Monday through Saturday; 11:30 AM to 10:30 PM Sunday. Bar hours are until 1 AM.

## LORD FLETCHER'S ON LAKE MINNETONKA

*3746 Sunset Dr., Spring Park*     *471-8513*
*$$*

Diners come by boat and by car to this popular lakeside restaurant reminiscent of an old English tavern. Fare includes fresh fish and other seafood, prime rib and chicken. While the main restaurant is formal (or dressy casual), a lower-level cafe is strictly for the jeans and shorts crowd. Whether you're upstairs or down, the lake views are stunning. Outdoor dining is available in the summer. Lunch is served from 11 AM to 2 PM; dinner from 5 to 10 PM Monday through Saturday and from 4:30 to 9:30 Sunday. Brunch is served from 11 AM to 2 PM Sunday.

## MAGNOLIA'S

*1081 Payne Ave., St. Paul*     *774-3333*
*$*     *No credit cards*

Magnolia's offers hearty Mom food served with friendly efficiency. Notable are the low prices, tender chicken, enormous dumplings, and breakfast served all day. Hours are 5:30 AM to 10:30 PM Monday through Saturday; 6:30 AM to 9:30 PM Sunday.

### THE MALT SHOP
*1554 Concordia Ave., St. Paul     645-4643*
*$*

The old malt shop just ain't what it used to be: now ratatouille and spanakopita share menu space with burgers and fries. The food and service are uneven, but kids feel right at home, plied with crayons and live piano music. (Other locations are at 50th Street and Bryant Avenue S., Minneapolis; and highways 7 and 10 in Minnetonka.) Hours are 7 AM to 10:30 PM Monday through Thursday; 7 AM to 11 PM Friday; 8 AM to 11 PM Saturday; 8 AM to 10:30 PM Sunday.

### MANCINI'S CHAR HOUSE
*531 W. Seventh St., St. Paul     224-7345*
*$$*

This is a lively center of the St. Paul steak-and-potatoes universe. It's also a great place to unwind after a long week — but be prepared to wait during peak hours, for hordes are hooked on Mancini's no-nonsense charms. A bonus is the glitzy lounge with frequent live music. Hours are 5 to 11 PM Sunday through Thursday; 5 PM to midnight Friday and Saturday.

### MARKET BAR-B-QUE
*1414 Nicollet Ave. S., Minneapolis     872-1111*
*$$*

Choose from spare ribs, beef ribs, chicken and even barbecued sirloin, with a choice of sauces on every checkered tablecloth. Although relocated from its original downtown location, the Market still has the charm of the old place, with all the celebrity photos on the wall. Hours are 11:30 AM to 2:30 AM Monday through Saturday; noon to midnight Sunday. Youll find another Market at 15320 Wayzata Boulevard in Minnetonka.

### MAYSLACK'S
*1428 N.E. Fourth St., Minneapolis     789-9862*
*$$     No credit cards*

Do you like garlic? Love beef? Then this old-time Nordeast bar is for you. The roast beef sandwiches are bigger than a wrestler's bicep, loaded with sliced onions and juice. Hours are 11 AM to 11 PM daily.

### MINNESOTA STEAKHOUSE
*1655 W. County Rd. B2, Roseville 628-0350*
*$$*

This is a family-friendly restaurant boasting big portions and reasonable prices. Don't miss the deep-fried Paul Bunyan onion. Hours are 4 PM to 10 PM Sunday through Thursday; 4 PM to midnight Friday and Saturday. Other Minnesota Steakhouse restaurants are at 13050 Aldrich Avenue S., Burnsville; and at 16396 Wagner Way, Eden Prairie.

### MONTE CARLO
*219 Third Ave. N., Minneapolis     333-5900*
*$$*

Come for reliable, predictable sandwiches, burgers and wings in a cozy, bustling atmosphere. Take note of the gorgeous ceiling and huge selection of liquors; hang out for Sunday brunch and enjoy the hefty helpings. Hours are 11 AM to 11:45 PM Monday through Saturday; 10 AM to 10:45 PM Sunday.

There's a full bar. Reservations are recommended.

### NAPA VALLEY GRILLE

*Mall of America, Bloomington* 858-9934
**$$$**

Another winner from the proprietors of California Cafe, this elegant cafe offers a serious wine list, imaginative seasonal salads, fish and pasta, grilled steaks and chops. Even if you hate shopping, it's worth a trip to the mall to eat here. Lunch is served 11 AM to 4 PM daily. Dinner is 5 to 10 PM Monday through Thursday; 5 to 10:30 PM Friday and Saturday; 5 to 8:30 PM Sunday. Sunday brunch is served 11 AM to 3:30 PM.

### NO WAKE CAFE

*100 Yacht Club Rd., St. Paul* 292-1411
**$$** *No credit cards*

At least once a summer, you've got to visit St. Paul's wonderful floating restaurant, located at a Harriet Island dock. This cozy diner serves homey fare — Wednesday is fish night. Hours are 8 AM to 2 PM Tuesday; 8 AM to 2 PM and 5 to 9 PM Wednesday; 8 AM to 2 PM Thursday; 8 AM to 2 PM and 5 to 10 PM Friday; 8 to 11 AM and noon to 10 PM Saturday; 8 AM to noon Sunday.

### ON THE WAY CAFE

*340 N. Wabasha St., St. Paul* 222-5208
**$** *No credit cards*

Here's an oasis of well-brewed coffees, spirited espresso drinks and real lunch food, including spicy chicken chili and salads. You'll also find plenty of sweet pastries for breakfast. Proprietor Bookie Read

hosts writers support groups 7 to 9 PM Tuesdays and Thursdays. Hours are 6:30 AM to 7 PM Monday through Friday; 8 AM to 5 PM Saturday; closed Sunday.

### ORIGINAL CONEY ISLAND

*444 St. Peter St., St. Paul* 293-9999
**$** *No credit cards*

Come here for small Coneys with a cautious soul, unchanged since 1923. In the bar, find friendly conversation, but in the cafe, just watch the slow cracks on the old brown walls, wonder what year Eddie Cantor recorded "If You Knew Susie" and realize that no news really is good news. Call for hours.

### PALOMINO

*825 Hennepin Ave., Minneapolis* 339-3800
**$$**

Minneapolis movers and shakers eat, drink and make merry at this sleek and sophisticated "Eurometro" bistro specializing in Mediterranean cuisine, including spit-roasted garlic chicken, Roma-style pizza, prime rib and seasonal game. Lunch is served from 11:15 AM to 2:30 PM Monday through Saturday; dinner is from 5 to 10 PM Monday through Thursday, 5 to 11 PM Friday, and 4 to 9 PM Sunday.

### PRACNA ON MAIN

*117 S.E. Main St., Minneapolis* 379-3200
**$$**

Billing itself as the "oldest restaurant-bar in Minneapolis," Pracna on Main is located in the historic and charming St. Anthony Main buildings along the east bank of the Mississippi River, just across from downtown. The view is terrific, especially from the outdoor tables on

Photo: Sully Doroshow, Pioneer Press

*The Dakota, a jazz club and restaurant in St. Paul.*

a golden fall afternoon. Pranca serves a menu of American fare — from pasta and pork chops to spinach salad and burgers. Hours are from 11:30 AM to 1 AM Monday through Saturday and 11:30 AM to midnight on Sunday.

### RAINFOREST CAFE

*Mall of America, Bloomington      854-7500*
**$$**

The food is almost an afterthought at this exotic eatery filled with tropical birds, splashing fish and lush foliage. A range of dishes from pasta to burgers is offered in this unusual setting. Hours are from 11 AM to 10 PM every day of the week.

### ROSEN'S

*430 First Ave. N., Minneapolis      338-1926*
**$$**

Things are always hopping at this popular sports bar/cafe in the Warehouse District. Chomp on pasta, burgers or stir fries while catching the latest Vikings game on one of Rosen's 10 giant TVs. Hours are 11 AM to 1 AM Monday through Saturday; 10 AM to midnight Sunday.

### RUDOLPH'S BAR-B-QUE

*1933 Lyndale Ave. S., Minneapolis 871-8969*
**$$**

Rudolph's is a local landmark for delicious, sloppy, lip-smacking ribs and barbecued chicken. A full menu also includes steaks, chops and sandwiches. With walls smothered in autographed Hollywood photos and movie posters, Rudolph's is a popular after-movie or - theater meeting spot. Namesake Rudolph Valentino would be proud. Hours are 11 AM to 1 AM Monday through Saturday; 11 AM to midnight Sunday. There are three other Rudolph's restaurants in the Twin Cities: at Galtier Plaza in St. Paul;

Highway 7 at Williston Road in Minnetonka; and 815 Hennepin Avenue E. in Minneapolis.

### RUTH'S CHRIS STEAK HOUSE

*Minneapolis Centre, 920 Second Ave. S.*
*Minneapolis*            672-9000
**$$$$**

This national franchise is the latest addition to Minneapolis' upscale meat scene. Prime steaks and seafood abound, including Minnesota walleye and live Maine lobster. There are also eight kinds of potatoes and wonderful bourbon bread pudding. Eye the elegant decor and extensive wine list. Dinner is served 5 to 10:30 PM daily. Reservations are recommended.

### SEBASTIAN JOE'S

*1007 Franklin Ave. W.*
*Minneapolis*            870-0065
**$**            *No credit cards*

Here's the home of arguably the best ice cream in town, in dozens of mind-bending flavors: raspberry chocolate chip, chocolate with cinnamon and cayenne. They serve espresso drinks and muffins, too. Another Sebastian Joe's is at 4321 Upton Avenue S., Minneapolis. There's outdoor seating at both locales. Hours are 7 AM to 11 PM Sunday through Thursday; 7 AM to midnight Friday and Saturday.

### SHANNON KELLY'S PUB

*395 Wabasha St., St. Paul*        292-0905
**$**

Here's a woody watering hole with burgers, chili, hot roast beef with mashed potatoes and plenty of bar snacks. You'll be impressed by the huge cheesy helpings of potato skins. The kitchen is open 11 AM to

9 PM Monday and Tuesday; 11 AM to 10 PM Wednesday to Saturday; noon to 8 PM Sunday.

### SHELLY'S WOODROAST

*Hwy. 394 and Louisiana Ave.*
*St. Louis Park*            593-5050
**$$**

This is the best-smelling restaurant in town, due to wood-burning ovens that cook fish, fowl and tender beef brisket. Check out the tart apple pie and bread pudding, too, as well as a daily special of "basic American fare," such as meat loaf sandwiches and corned-on-the-premises beef and cabbage. Hours are 11 AM to 10 PM Monday through Thursday; 11 AM to 11 PM Friday and Saturday; 10 AM to 10 PM Sunday. There's a full bar. Reservations are recommended; smoking is allowed in the bar only.

### STONE'S FINE BAR-B-Q

*1532 University Ave., St. Paul*        646-3861
**$$**            *No credit cards*

This cheery, bustling cafe serves smoky, saucy and generously portioned food — the sort that makes you forget your manners and concentrate on how quick you're going to get the meat off that bone. The pork and beef ribs are tops. Hours are 11 AM to 9 PM Monday through Thursday; 11 AM to 10 PM Friday and Saturday; noon to 8 PM Sunday.

### SUNSETS

*700 E. Lake St., Wayzata*        473-LAKE
**$$**

Overlooking picturesque Lake Minnetonka, this casual but classy restaurant serves up a feast for the eyes as well as the palate. The decor is one of clean lines, uncluttered spaces and generous windows. The menu offers a range of palate-pleasing entrees — from fresh seafood, ribs and pastas to sandwiches and soups. There's also a full bar that bustles on weekend nights, especially in the summer. Outside dining is available during balmy weather. Hours are 6:30 AM to 1 AM Monday through Saturday; 9:30 AM to midnight Sunday.

### SWEENEY'S
*96 N. Dale St., St. Paul          221-9157*
*$*

This energetic bar makes you feel like you're on vacation. Burgers, sandwiches, salads and fries are just the thing with a glass of locally brewed Summit ale on tap. There's also $2.95 pasta on Sunday and Monday nights. Hours are 11 AM to 11 PM Monday through Wednesday; 11 AM to midnight Thursday and Friday; 9 AM to midnight Saturday; 9 AM to 11 PM Sunday.

### TOBIE'S TAVERN
*23 N. Sixth St., Minneapolis          376-9614*
*$$*

Although this friendly establishment sits within shouting range of the Target Center, don't assume it serves sports-bar grub. In recent months, Chef Tobie Nidetz has won raves for his acclaimed chicken stir-fry as well as for a hearty offering of soups, salads, steaks and sandwiches. The atmosphere evokes a pub or tavern, which makes it a popular stop among downtown office workers. Hours are 11 AM to 1 AM Monday through Saturday and 10 AM to midnight Sunday.

### TOBY'S ON THE LAKE
*249 N. Geneva Ave., Oakdale          739-1600*
*$$*

The lake in question is Tanner's Lake, and Toby's deck overlooking the water offers a lovely spot for summertime dining. Prime rib, barbecued ribs and fresh seafood are the specialties here, all served amidst a quaint and woody English atmosphere. There are also banquet facilities and a full bar. Hours are 11 AM to 2:30 PM and 5 to 10 PM Monday through Thursday; 11 AM to 2:30 PM and 5 to 11 PM Friday; 11 AM to 11 PM Saturday; and 11 AM to 9 PM Sunday. A sit-down Sunday brunch is served 11 AM to 2 PM.

### TROTTER'S COUNTRY BAKERY
*232 N. Cleveland Ave., St. Paul          645-8950*
*$                    No credit cards*

Visit for tasty muffins without the sugar rush, along with a bevy of other fine baked goods. The strong coffee is from Dunn Brothers; there are sandwiches, soups and salads, too. It's a low-key, friendly spot to escape from the busy routine, good for take-out, as well. Hours are 7 AM to 7 PM Tuesday through Friday; 7 AM to 4 PM Saturday.

### TROUT HAUS
*14536 W. Freeway Dr.*
*Columbus Township          464-2964*
*$$*

You can just order off the menu, but it's more fun to work for your supper at the Trout Air fish farm, where the odds are always with you. Toss your line into a stocked pond (indoors during cold weather) and have the very fish you catch cooked up in the rustic, corny Trout Haus restaurant. This is a great place to take kids and out-of-town visitors who think they've seen it all. Reservations are recommended. Hours are 11:30 AM to 9 PM Sunday through Thursday; 11:30 AM to 10 PM Friday and Saturday.

## Asian Cuisine

### AUGUST MOON
5340 Wayzata Blvd.
Golden Valley                    544-7017
$$

Eat by the light of a lava lamp at this fun, casual cafe. Brother and sister owners Martin and Vivika Olander serve Vietnamese staples, as well as wild Asian hybrids. Try the spicy water buffalo chicken wings, stuffed Peking pancakes, stir fries, or goat-cheese stuffed tandoori chicken breast on curried potatoes. The coconut ice cream is wonderful, but the ginger and pepper frozen yogurt packs the greatest punch. Hours are 11 AM to 9 PM Monday through Thursday; 11 AM to 10 PM Friday; 4 to 10 PM Saturday; 4 to 9 PM Sunday. Wine and beer only are served.

### CARAVELLE
799 W. University Ave., St. Paul    292-9324
$$

More than 100 Chinese and Vietnamese dishes fill the menu here. Recommended are the poached fish and the crisp spring rolls. Dine in the bamboo-and-beaded booths for optimum effect. (Other Caravelle locations are at 783 Radio Drive, Woodbury; 1 E. Little Canada Road, Little Canada; 2529 Nicollet Ave-

nue S., Minneapolis; and 2233 Energy Park Drive, St. Paul.) Hours are 11 AM to 9 PM Monday through Thursday; 11 AM to 10 PM Friday and Saturday. Reservations are recommended.

### CHINATOWN
1533 W. Larpenteur Ave.
Falcon Heights                    644-9194
$$                        No credit cards

Every region of China is represented at this tasteful contemporary restaurant. Chinatown is noted for its soups and Peking duck. Hours are 11 AM to 9 PM Monday through Thursday; 11 AM to 10 PM Friday; noon to 10 PM Saturday; 5 to 9 PM Sunday. Reservations are recommended.

### DELITES OF INDIA
1123 W. Lake St., Minneapolis    823-2866
$$

This cozy establishment is owned and operated by a Hindu couple who are strict about what they serve: no meat, seafood or dairy products. The variety is still astounding. Careful curries range from hot to explosive — watch out for "vindaloo." Don't miss the homemade pickles — mango, lemon, mixed vegetable. Lunch is served 11:30 AM to 2 PM Tuesday through Sunday. Dinner is 5 to 9 PM Tuesday through Saturday; 5 to 8:30 PM Sunday.

### HOA BIEN
1129 W. University Ave., St. Paul 647-1011
$                        No credit cards

You won't find a fancy restaurant setting here, just reliable, authentic Vietnamese food, including a mean ban xeo (crisp rice flour pancake). Hours are 9 AM to 9 PM Sunday through Thursday; 9 AM to 10 PM Friday and Saturday.

### KHAN'S MONGOLIAN BARBECUE
*2720 N. Snelling Ave., Roseville    631-3398*
*$$*

At this novelty restaurant, diners select raw meats, vegetables and noodles from a buffet, then watch as they are cooked by a chef at an enormous griddle. Try some curry, but go easy on the dragon sauce, or you'll be breathing fire. (Another Khan's restaurant is at 418 13th Avenue S.E., Minneapolis.) Hours are 11 AM to 9:30 PM Monday through Thursday; 11 AM to 10 PM Friday; noon to 10 PM Saturday; noon to 9 PM Sunday (5 to 9 PM Sunday in Minneapolis). Reservations are recommended.

### KHYBER PASS CAFE
*1399 St. Clair Ave., St. Paul    698-5403*
*$$*                    *No credit cards*

This is the place to go for delicious, carefully prepared Afghani specialties. Try the aushak (leek dumplings), lean lamb dishes, korma-e murgh (chicken stew) and excellent dal. Finish off with firni, a silken pudding flavored with cardamom and rosewater. Lunch is served 11 AM to 2 PM Tuesday through Saturday. Dinner is 5 to 9 PM Tuesday through Saturday.

### LEEANN CHIN
*Union Depot Place, 214 E. Fourth St.*
*St. Paul                    224-8814*
*$$*

The Depot location of this mega-chain offers an attractive setting with a reliable buffet of stir-fried entrees, salads, dumplings and more. The efficient take-out outlets around the Twin Cities offer an even greater selection. Lunch is served 11 AM to 2:30 PM daily. Dinner is 5 to 9 PM Sunday through Thursday; 5 to 10 PM Friday and Saturday. Reservations are recommended. (Other Leeann Chin restaurants are at Har Mar Mall, Roseville; Highland Village Mall, St. Paul; Milton Mall, St. Paul; Norwest Skyway, St. Paul; Bonaventure Shopping Center, Minnetonka; Ninth Street and Second Avenue S., Minneapolis; and many other locations.)

### MIRROR OF KOREA
*761 N. Snelling Ave., St. Paul    647-9004*
*$$*

When this family restaurant changed locations, Minneapolis' loss was St. Paul's gain. The rich flavored, often peppery, dishes all come with delightful ban chan — small bowls of kimchee, sliced radishes and other tempting condiments. Recommended are the bulgogi (tender Korean barbecue), the

Minnesotans lead the nation in the per-capita consumption of popcorn.

Insiders' Tips

dahk bokgeum (chicken stir-fry), and bibim bahp (rice with toppings to toss with pepper sauce). Hours are 11 AM to 10 PM Monday and Wednesday through Friday; noon to 10 PM Saturday; noon to 9 PM Sunday.

### MY LE HOA

*2900 Rice St., Little Canada      484-5353*
*$$*

Chinese food came to Little Canada by way of Vancouver, where owner Alex Ha learned his trade. The food at this pretty mall restaurant is a wide-ranging culinary adventure. Recommended are the two-course Peking duck, singing chicken hot pot, and the pork and salted cabbage soup. Lunch is a buffet, and dim sum is served every day. Hours are 11:30 AM to 9 PM Monday through Friday; 10:30 AM to 10 PM Saturday and Sunday. Reservations are recommended.

### ORIGAMI

*30 N. First St., Minneapolis      333-8430*
*$$$*

Japanese cuisine's special affinity for the sea is shown to good advantage at this pleasant warehouse-district cafe and sushi bar. Recommended are the hamachi shioyaki, a simply grilled yellowtail, the miso soup, and sashimi. Lunch is served 11 AM to 2 PM Monday through Friday. Dinner is 5 to 9:30 PM Monday through Thursday; 5 to 11 PM Friday and Saturday.

### ROYAL ORCHID

*1835 Nicollet Ave., Minneapolis  872-1938*
*$$*

Looking for the Twin Cities' best Thai menu? Don't miss the mieng kham, a wrap-your-own appetizer in which coconut, ginger, dried shrimp, lime bits and other ingredients are rolled up in lettuce leaves. The Orchid's lavender decor won't win any awards, but the gai tom kha, a fragrant chicken and coconut soup, should. Hours are 11 AM to 2:30 PM and 5 to 10 PM Tuesday through Thursday; 11 AM to 2:30 PM and 5 to 11 PM Friday; noon to 11 PM Saturday; noon to 10 PM Sunday.

### RUAM MIT THAI

*544 St. Peter St., St. Paul      290-0067*
*$$                    No credit cards*

This cozy cafe is a perfect place to begin a culinary love affair with sensually pleasing Thai food. Roll your own mieng kham appetizer, and try the lemony toam yum soup, roast duck curry and sticky rice with fresh mango. Hours are 11 AM to 10 PM Monday through Thursday; 11 AM to 11 PM Friday and Saturday; 3 to 9 PM Sunday. Reservations are recommended.

### SAJI-YA

*695 Grand Ave., St. Paul        292-0444*
*$$*

Perhaps the best way to dine at Saji-Ya is to order appetizers and sushi — the restaurant does swell things with fish (both cooked and raw), tofu and vegetables. Flashy tableside teppanyaki cooking is available, too, but only certain nights. Don't be alarmed if shouting ensues when you first walk over the restaurant's wooden bridge — the host calls out the number in your party; when the rest of the staff responds, they are simply saying "Welcome." Lunch is served 11 AM to 2 PM Monday through Friday. Dinner is 5 to 10 PM Monday through Thursday; 5 to 11 PM Friday and Saturday; 5 to 9 PM Sunday. Reservations are recommended.

## SAKURA
*Galtier Plaza, 175 E. Fifth St.*
*St. Paul* 224-0185
*$$*

A warm, friendly owner and carefully prepared food make this a fine spot to explore Japanese cuisine. The serious sushi, filling bento box combination lunch, tasty teriyaki and tempura are all recommended, as is the ika shoga yaki (broiled cuttlefish) and goma ae (spinach and sesame) appetizers. Hours are 11 AM to 2:30 PM and 5 to 9:30 PM Monday through Thursday; 11 AM to 2:30 PM and 4:30 to 10 PM Friday and Saturday; 4 to 9:30 PM Sunday. Reservations are recommended.

## SAPPHIRE DRAGON
*Maplewood Square, 3035 White Bear Ave.*
*Maplewood* 779-8623
*$$*

This is a friendly, family-operated restaurant offering a variety of fresh, expertly-prepared Vietnamese foods with some concessions to Midwestern tastes. The egg rolls are tops, as are the shrimp stir-fry chow mein and curried mock duck. Hours are 11 AM to 2:30 and 4 to 8:30 PM Monday through Thursday; 11 AM to 2:30 PM and 4 to 9 PM Friday; noon to 9 PM Saturday. Reservations are recommended.

## SAWATDEE
*118 N. Fourth St., Minneapolis* 373-0840
*$$*

The restaurant-bar's raw brick, red ceiling and cobalt blue walls make an attractive setting for Supenn Harrison's spicy Thai food. Recommended are the fresh spring rolls, shrimp salad with lemongrass, chicken with cashews and, for a delightful dessert, sticky rice with fresh mango. Hours are 11:30 AM to 1 AM Monday through Saturday (kitchen closes at midnight); 5 PM to midnight Sunday (kitchen closes at 11 PM). Other Sawatdee locations are at 607 Washington Avenue S., Minneapolis; 8501 Lyndale Avenue S., Bloomington; and 289 E. Fifth Street, St. Paul.

## SHILLA
*694 N. Snelling Ave., St. Paul* 645-0006
*$$* *No credit cards*

The hot dishes here are tongue-tingling; the mild offerings are equally adventuresome. Shilla features delicious barbecued meats, noodle dishes and soups. Hours are 11 AM to 9:30 PM Tuesday through Sunday.

## SUN SUN
*854 W. University Ave., St. Paul* 291-0212
*$$* *No credit cards*

This pleasant, humble Chinese restaurant is good news for seafood lovers. Recommended are the lobster with five-spicy salt, the fresh walleye, duck with preserved vegetables, and the beef and mustard-greens soup for two. Hours are 11:30 AM to 9 PM Monday through Friday; 5 to 9 PM Saturday; 5 to 8

PM Sunday. Reservations are recommended.

### TANG'S GINGER CAFE
*1310 Hennepin Ave., Minneapolis 339-9220*
$$

The menu at this groovy-looking cafe soars all over Asia and beyond. Among the taste sensations are walleye-scallop potstickers and "blazing don don noodles," along with lemongrass chicken soup with peanuts, steamed shrimp with red curry and grilled beef tenderloin with black bean horseradish sambal. Lunch is served 11:30 AM to 2 PM Tuesday through Friday. Dinner is 5 to 10 PM Tuesday through Saturday. Tang's is closed Sunday and Monday. There's free parking in the Wilson Tower ramp, on Laurel Avenue, behind the restaurant.

### TASTE OF INDIA
*1745 Cope Ave. E., Maplewood    773-5477*
$$

Don't let the suburban strip architecture fool you — there are spicy surprises in store inside. Try the scallop masala (melt-in-your-mouth shellfish, tomatoes, peppers and onions in a cumin sauce) or chicken vindaloo (potato-based sauce with a tamarind tang), dal, kheer and mango ice cream. The lunch buffet is a delicious bargain

at $5.95. Wine and beer are served. Here are the hours: lunch 11:30 AM to 2:30 PM Monday through Friday, 11:30 AM to 3 PM Saturday and Sunday; dinner 5 to 10 PM Monday through Sunday.

### TO CHAU
*823 W. University Ave., St. Paul   291-2661*
$$                    *No credit cards*

The adventuresome Vietnamese menu offers everything from quail to eel, with plenty of noodle and stir-fry dishes, too. To Chau boasts a pleasant setting and big portions. Hours are 10 AM to 8 PM Sunday through Thursday; 10 AM to 9 PM Friday and Saturday. Beer is served. Reservations are recommended.

### VILLAGE WOK
*610 Washington Ave. S.E.*
*Minneapolis                    331-9041*
$$

Skip the Americanized standbys and order off the wall — signs explain the seafood specials. Walleye is wonderful at this homey cafe, which is especially lively on weekend nights. Hours are 11 AM to 2 AM daily. Reservations are recommended.

### VINA
*756 S. Cleveland Ave., St. Paul    698-8408*
$$                    *No credit cards*

Vina features Vietnamese spe-

*Lord Fletcher's on The Lake, Lake Minnetonka.*

Photo: Buzz Magnuson, Pioneer Press

cialties, with a few Chinese standbys thrown in. For a fun change of pace try the crisp, filling rice pancake, bites of which may be picked up with bits of lettuce and dipped in a sweet fish sauce. Around dinner time, the peach-colored restaurant is as sunny as the servers' dispositions. Hours are 11 AM to 9 PM Monday through Thursday; 11 AM to 10 PM Friday and Saturday; noon to 9 PM Sunday. Reservations are recommended.

### WHITE LILY
*758 Grand Ave., St. Paul          293-9124*
*$$*

Here you'll find reliable, non-threatening Vietnamese food in an airy, flowery setting. Hours are 11 AM to 9 PM Monday through Thursday; 11 AM to 10 PM Friday and Saturday; 4:30 to 9 PM Sunday. Reservations are recommended.

### YIN YANG
*2645 White Bear Ave.*
*Maplewood                    777-1893*
*$$*

Enjoy hot and mild Chinese food in a sleek, clean atmosphere. Cooks in white caps are visible behind a glass window, turning out some of the best fried dumplings in town. Hours are 11 AM to 9 PM Tuesday to Thursday; 11 AM to 10 PM Friday; noon to 9 PM Saturday and Sunday.

## Eclectic Cuisine

### ALEXANDER'S
*714 Second Ave. S., Minneapolis   339-2893*
*$*

Here's a pleasant, casual two-level eatery serving all the necessary burgers, sandwiches and salads with tasty ethnic daily specials such as Mediterranean chicken kebabs. The breakfasts are hearty, too. Breakfast is served 7 to 10:45 AM Monday through Friday. Lunch is served 11:15 AM to 3 PM Monday through Friday.

### BAD HABIT CAFE

*418 St. Peter St., St. Paul*     224-8545
$            *No credit cards*

Not all of downtown St. Paul throws in the towel after dark. This cozy hangout serves coffee, sweets and light meals into the weekend wee hours. Spoken word performances are at 8:30 PM on Mondays; live music cranks at 8:30 PM most Wednesdays and Thursdays, 10 PM Fridays and Saturdays. A relaxed ambiance and outdoor tables (in warm weather) help make mid-afternoon coffee breaks habit forming. Hours are 7 AM to 11 PM Monday through Thursday; 7 AM to 2 AM Friday; noon to 2 AM Saturday; noon to 6 PM Sunday.

### BREAD AND CHOCOLATE

*867 Grand Ave., St. Paul*     228-1017
$            *No credit cards*

Here you'll find special muffins flavored with espresso and pecans one day, cardamom and lemon the next. The rich caramel rolls display a delicate balance between crunch and tenderness. There are also nice made-to-order sandwiches.

### BRUEGGER'S BAGEL BAKERY

*1 W. Seventh Pl., St. Paul*     225-4363
$            *No credit cards*

Bruegger's fresh, chewy bagels will challenge your choppers; they're sold singly, by the dozen or as sandwiches. The garlic bagels, so fragrant they need their own bag, are especially good with Bruegger's olive-pimento cream cheese spread or hummos and cucumber. Hours are 6:30 AM to 6 PM Monday through Friday; 6:30 AM to 8 PM Saturday; 6:30 AM to 5 PM Sunday. Other Bruegger's restaurants are at 796 Grand Avenue, St. Paul; 2233 Energy Park Drive, St. Paul; 2136 Ford Parkway, St. Paul; 1100 Nicollet Mall, Minneapolis; 4953 Penn Avenue S., Minneapolis; 1808 S. Plymouth Road, Minnetonka; and many other locations.

### BRYANT-LAKE BOWL

*810 W. Lake St., Minneapolis*     825-3737
$$

At this combination cafe, coffeehouse, bowling alley and experimental theater, the nifty menu offers plenty of vegetarian fare, including a swell burrito, potato salad and vegetarian chili. Also good is the Bryant-Lake Bowl plate and bete noir. The atmosphere is wholesome, in a funky sort of way. Hours are 7 AM to 1 AM Monday through Saturday; 7 AM to midnight Sunday.

### CAFE BRENDA

*300 First Ave. N., Minneapolis*     342-9230
$$

Vegetarians will go for the macrobiotic plate, open-faced blackbean enchiladas and soba noodles in ginger-tahini dressing. There are plenty of temptations for seafoodlovers, too, in this calm and airy restaurant. No dishes contain red meat or processed sugar. Lunch is served 11:30 AM to 2 PM Monday through Friday. Dinner is 5:30 to 9:30 PM Monday through Thursday; 5:30 to 10 PM Friday and Saturday. Reservations are recommended; smoking is not allowed.

## CAFE CON AMORE

*917 Grand Ave., St. Paul* 222-6770
$ *No credit cards*

Here's an artsy nook featuring dandy coffee drinks and food that's above coffeehouse average — try the Michelangelo (a hot panino sandwich of turkey, provolone, sun-dried tomatoes and herbs) and the excellent heart-shaped scones. As a bonus there is a private meeting room available for reservations. Hours are 6:30 AM to 10 PM Monday through Thursday; 6:30 AM to 11 PM Friday; 7 AM to 11 PM Saturday; 7 AM to 8 PM Sunday.

## CAFE LATTE

*850 Grand Ave., St. Paul* 224-5687
$

This busy cafeteria is equally appropriate for a light healthy meal or a chocolate binge, offering a changing array of killer desserts and inventive salads and soups. There's a full selection of espresso drinks and heavenly scones (try the English currant variety). Hours are 10 AM to 11 PM Monday through Thursday; 10 AM to midnight Friday; 9 AM to midnight Saturday; 9 AM to 10 PM Sunday.

## CAFE SFA

*Saks Fifth Avenue, 655 Nicollet Mall*
*Minneapolis* 333-7200
$

Models in expensive duds wander through this small cafe, while shoppers and downtown workers nibble on chicken Caesar salad and a sinful almond fudge pot (you can just bet those models don't indulge in *this* dessert very often). Hours are 11 AM to 4:30 PM Monday through Saturday.

## CARVERS

*Minneapolis Hilton and Towers, 1001*
*Marquette Ave., Minneapolis* 376-1000
$$$

This formal, continental-American hybrid is perfectly situated for pre- or post-Orchestra Hall meals. Recommended are the crab cakes, steak salad and chestnut Charlotte. Lunch is served 11:30 AM to 2 PM Monday through Friday. Dinner is 5:30 to 10 PM Monday through Thursday; 5:30 PM to 11 PM Friday and Saturday. Reservations are recommended. Use the valet parking or hotel garage.

## CECIL'S

*651 S. Cleveland Ave., St. Paul* 698-0334
$$C

This homey family-owned and -operated deli has been serving comforting knishes and chicken soup for more than 20 years. Try the terrific chopped liver; take a dozen buttery hamantaschen home. Hours are 9 AM to 8 PM daily; the deli is open until 9 PM.

## COSSETTA'S

*211 W. Seventh St., St. Paul* 222-3476
$ *No credit cards*

Here you'll find unsurpassed New York-style pizza with a thin, foldable crust. There's a cafeteria line for pastas, salads and sandwiches, too. Hours are 8:30 AM to 10 PM Monday through Saturday; 10 AM to 8 PM Sunday.

## GALLERY 8
*Walker Art Center, 725 Vineland Pl.*
*Minneapolis* 374-3701
$ *No credit cards*

Rest your eyes and exercise your palate at this tasteful top-of-the-museum restaurant. If only all cafeterias were this good: there are daily special entrees, straight-ahead sandwiches and salads, and artful desserts. Hours are 11:30 AM to 8 PM Tuesday through Saturday; 11:30 AM to 5 PM Sunday. (Call to verify dinner hours; special events may close the restaurant some nights.)

## KAPOOCHI'S
*815 Nicollet Mall, Minneapolis* 339-1011
$$

This is a quirky yet elegant cafe and bar offering a seductive merging of Italian and Asian cuisines. Recommended are the sesame Caesar salad, Peking duck with parsley risotto, pan-roasted chicken with mashed potatoes and sesame sauce, panko-crusted sea scallops in green apple-lemongrass broth, and macaroon nut tart. Breakfast is served 7 to 10 AM Monday through Friday. Brunch is 11 AM to 3 PM Saturday and Sunday. Lunch is 11 AM to 2 PM Monday through Friday. Dinner is 5:30 to 10 PM Sunday through Thursday; 5:30 to 11 PM Friday and Saturday. Validated parking is available in the Eighth Street Ramp adjacent to the restaurant. Live jazz begins at 6:45 PM nightly.

## LORING CAFE AND BAR
*1624 Harmon Pl., Minneapolis* 332-1617
$$$

This hipper-than-hip cafe boasts a menu that's sensitive to the season. The appetizers shine: bucheron and sun-dried tomato pizza, and pretty composed salads. The sprawling bar, which offers a limited menu and nightly entertainment, is big on theatrical ambiance and attitude. The Bar has outdoor seating with a view of Loring Park; the cafe has a cozy courtyard. Lunch is served 11:30 AM to 2:30 PM Monday through Friday. Dinner is 5:30 to 10 PM Monday through Wednesday; 5:30 to 11 PM Thursday; 5:30 PM to midnight Friday and Saturday; 5 to 10 PM Sunday. (Food is served in the bar 11:30 AM to 3:30 PM Monday through Saturday and 4:30 PM to midnight daily; also Sunday brunch is served 11:30 AM to 3 PM.) Reservations are recommended.

## LUCIA'S
*1432 W. 31st St., Minneapolis* 825-1572
$$$

Lucia's offers quiet, eclectic food, served in a room that hovers between casual and romantic. Though the selections are slim at the wine bar next door, it's a nice spot for a sip and a nibble of, say, bread with goat cheese, pesto and seasoned lentils. Lunch is served 11:30 AM to 2:30 PM Tuesday through Friday. Brunch is served 10 AM to 2 PM Saturday and Sunday. Dinner is from 5:30 to 9:30 PM Tuesday through Thursday; 5:30 to 10 PM Friday and Saturday; 5:30 to 9 PM Sunday. Reservations are recommended. (Wine bar hours are 11:30 AM to midnight Tuesday to Thursday; 11:30 AM to 1 AM Friday; 2

PM to 1 AM Saturday; 2 PM to midnight Sunday.)

### MANHATTAN BAGELS

*1672 Grand Ave., St. Paul       690-5138*
**$**                          *No credit cards*

This bagel shop offers not only fresh-baked bagels with cream cheese or delish homemade chicken salad, but also a genuine New York accent, courtesy of the brothers from the Big Apple who run it. Hours are 7 AM to 6 PM Monday through Saturday; 7:30 AM to 6 PM Sunday.

### MUD PIE

*2549 Lyndale Ave. S., Minneapolis 872-9435*
**$$**

A long, international list of vegetarian specialties is on the menu of this earthier-than-thou cafe, which is famous for its veggie burgers (also available in your grocer's freezer). Tamale pie, rotti, and peanut butter dandies are recommended, too. Hours are 11 AM to 10 PM Monday through Thursday; 11 AM to 11 PM Friday; 8 AM to 11 PM Saturday; 8 AM to 10 PM Sunday. No smoking is allowed.

### THE NM CAFE

*Neiman Marcus, 651 Nicollet Mall*
*Minneapolis               339-2600*
**$$**

This cafe offers a high-quality lunch and snack menu of sandwiches, salads and skinny pizzas. The afternoon tea, served 2 to 5 PM Thursday through Saturday, is a classy pick-me-up, with tea sandwiches, scones, sweets and Ashby's tea. Hours are 11 AM to 5 PM Monday through Saturday. Free parking is available in the Gaviidae Commons ramp; bring in your parking ticket for validation.

### NEW RIVERSIDE CAFE

*329 Cedar Ave., Minneapolis      333-4814*
**$**                          *No credit cards*

Food and politics mix in a gentle way at this worker-owned West Bank institution. There is reliable, inexpensive, healthful food, including Mexican dishes, rice and beans, salads, omelettes and some awe-inspiring tofu specialties. The cafe hosts live music almost nightly, and there's always terrific people-watching. Hours are 7 AM to 11 PM Monday through Thursday; 7 AM to midnight Friday; 8 AM to midnight Saturday; 10 AM to 3 PM Sunday.

### PLANET HOLLYWOOD

*Mall of America, Bloomington      854-7827*
**$$**

Owned in part by Demi Moore, Arnold Schwarzenegger, Sylvester Stallone and Bruce Willis, this movie museum/hype machine/restaurant is crammed with old and new memorabilia (check out the life-size cyborg from *Terminator 2*, Freddie Krueger's claw glove, and outfits worn by Judy Garland and Prince). The menu — casual and eclectic — isn't really the point. But you might enjoy the Chicken Crunch appetizer, fajitas, turkey burger, and ebony and ivory brownie. Hours are 11 AM to 1 AM daily.

### RISIMINI'S

*1670 Grand Ave., St. Paul        699-0013*
**$**                          *No credit cards*

This counter-service eatery, popular among Macalester College students and staff, offers many choices of pizzas, pastas, salads and sandwiches. The calzone is impressive inside and out. Hours are 11 AM to 10 PM Monday through Thursday; 11 AM to 11 PM Friday; 11 AM to 10 PM Saturday; 4 to 8 PM Sunday. No alcoholic beverages are available.

## THE RIVER ROOM
*Dayton's, Sixth and Cedar Sts.*
*St. Paul*      292-5174
$$

This is a pink, relaxing place for ladies (and well-mannered men) who lunch, with a menu of trend-conscious staples and terrific popovers. Try the Moroccan salad. Hours are 11 AM to 7 PM Monday through Friday; 11 AM to 3 PM Saturday; noon to 3 PM Sunday. Reservations are recommended for lunch.

## ROCK BOTTOM BREWERY
*825 Hennepin Ave., Minneapolis*   332-2739
$$

The made-on-the-premises ales are the main reason to visit this popular bar and restaurant; the food tends toward the heavy. Best bets are the salads and appetizers such as Asiago cheese dip, smoked Rocky Mountain trout and the glutton-sized plate of maroon and gold nachos. Food is served 11 AM to 11 PM Sunday through Thursday; 11 AM to midnight Friday and Satur-

day. Bar hours are until 1 AM nightly, with live jazz 10 PM to midnight Wednesday through Saturday.

## SCULLY'S BROILER AND BAR
*1321 E. 78th St., Bloomington*   854-0107
$$

Outstanding fresh fish and many creative pasta combinations head the eclectic menu at this pleasant airport area bar and grill. Hours are 6 AM to 11 PM Monday through Friday; 7 AM to midnight Saturday and Sunday.

## SIDNEY'S PIZZA CAFE
*2120 Hennepin Ave., Minneapolis* 870-7000
$$

Here's a great place for unique pastas and pizzas, beautiful salads and more, with an emphasis on fresh and delish. Try the Asian spicy chicken pizza, the Greek salad, fiesta chicken linguini and fettuccine with chicken and sun-dried tomatoes. The wine menu offers a fine variety by the glass and the half-glass "taste." There's a bustling atmosphere, with a view of the rotisserie and wood-burning oven. Breakfast is served 7 to 11 AM Monday through Friday. Brunch is Saturday and Sunday 10 AM to 2 PM. Lunch/dinner is 11 AM to 11 PM Sunday through Thursday; 11 AM to midnight Friday and Saturday. No smoking is allowed. (There are also Sidney's restaurants at

15600 Highway 7, Minnetonka; and at the Galleria in Edina.)

### TABLE OF CONTENTS

*1648 Grand Ave., St. Paul*     *699-6595*
$$

This consistently good restaurant, attached to a bookstore, offers a sophisticated array of fresh, creative food. Recommended are the fish specials, wafer-crust pizzas, the chicken salad and the sinful sauteed pound cake. Lunch is served 11:30 AM to 2 PM Monday through Saturday. Sunday brunch is 10 AM to 2 PM. Dinner is 5:30 to 9:30 PM Monday through Thursday; 5:30 to 10:30 PM Friday and Saturday; 5 to 9 PM Sunday. Reservations are recommended; smoking isn't allowed.

### THE TOUR CAFE

*4924 France Ave. S., Edina*     *929-1010*
$$$

Scott Kee's clever cookery thrives at his new cafe, which has recently lowered prices but not standards. Here you'll find heady, sophisticated flavors with many an international accent. Don't miss the polenta with prosciutto and spicy melon, smoked mozzarella risotto cakes, fettuccine with mushrooms, gorgonzola and cream, jerk chicken breast, and rhubarb crisp. Hours are 5 to 10 PM daily. Reservations are recommended.

## European Cuisine

### AZUR

*Gaviidae Common, 651 Nicollet Mall*
*Minneapolis*     *342-2500*
$$$

The menu and wine list zero in on the Mediterranean, while the decor is reminiscent of an Italian space colony. The menu is full of temptations, both standard à la carte offerings and a nightly "platter menu," which offers multiple courses to share, for $21 to $24 per person. Azur is a good choice for sophisticated fun. Lunch is served 11:30 AM to 2 PM Monday through Friday. Dinner is 5:30 to 9 PM Monday through Thursday; 5:30 to 10 PM Friday and Saturday. Reservations are recommended.

### BLACK FOREST INN

*1 E. 26th St., Minneapolis*     *872-0812*
$$

Here's all the German food you could want in a well-worn, utterly comfortable setting. Take note of the espresso drinks and a hearty selection of beers. Don't miss the weighty ham and sauerkraut balls. The outdoor seating goes fast in good weather. Hours are 11 AM to 1 AM Monday through Saturday; noon to 1 AM Sunday.

### BRASSERIE

*1400 Nicollet Ave., Minneapolis*   *874-7285*
$$

The French fare plied by Brittany-born Paul Laubignat can be the model of uncomplicated clarity — it's cooking that showcases the quality of the food rather than the ego of the chef. Try the assiette de charcuterie, roast rack of pork, chicken and sun-dried tomato pasta, profiteroles, and chocolate ganache. There's a romantic ambiance and superior service. Hours are 11 AM to 11 PM Monday through Thursday; 11 AM to midnight Friday and

Saturday; 11 AM to 9 PM Sunday (Sunday brunch 11 AM to 3 PM). A limited menu is offered 2 to 5 PM Monday through Saturday. Reservations are recommended.

### BRITS' PUB

*1110 Nicollet Mall, Minneapolis   332-3908*
**$$**

Steak and kidney pie, cock-a-leekie soup and other comforting aspects of British food are here aplenty, served in an attractive setting. Take some time to sit by the fire, below a portrait of the Queen Mum. Food is served 11 AM to midnight Monday through Friday; 8 AM to midnight Saturday; 8 AM to 11 PM Sunday.

### BUCA

*1204 Harmon Place, Minneapolis 638-2225*
**$$**

Ideal for hungry groups, Buca offers southern Italian food, served family-style in great quantity, in an ambiance of bustling bonhomie. Recommended dishes are the bruschetta, mixed green salad with gorgonzola and prosciutto, spaghetti marinara, chicken Marsala, green beans with lemon, and tiramisu. Hours are 4:30 to 10 PM Sunday; 5 to 10 PM Monday through Thursday; 5 to 11 PM Friday; 4:30 to 11 PM Saturday. Buca also has a St. Paul restaurant at 2728 Gannon Road.

### CAFE UN DEUX TROIS

*114 S. Ninth St., Minneapolis     673-0686*
**$$**

This is Minneapolis' own version of the New York brasserie, serving French basics in a setting that looks fashionably crumbling due to trompe l'oeil paintings. Try the fish specials, the grilled steak, escargots, salads and the creme brulee for dessert. Lunch is served 11:30 AM to 5 PM Monday through Friday. Dinner is 5 to 10 PM Monday through Thursday; 5 PM to midnight Friday and Saturday. Reservations are recommended; there is free valet parking in the evening.

### CAFFE SOLO

*123 N. Third St., Minneapolis      332-7108*
**$$**

Goat cheese and sun-dried tomatoes are still in style at this contemporary Italian cafe. The menu contains a long list of gourmet pizzas, pastas and well-executed fish specials (look for sauteed snapper with leeks and scallions). Also good are the grilled eggplant appetizer, shrimp and scallop lasagne, galette and spumoni. The atmosphere is spacious and often noisy. Hours are 7 AM to 11 PM Monday through Thursday; 7 AM to 3 AM Friday; 8 AM to 3 AM Saturday; 8 AM to 11 PM Sunday. Reservations are recommended.

### CARMELO'S RISTORANTE

*238 S. Snelling Ave., St. Paul      699-2448*
**$$**

This family-owned and -operated cafe offers simple Italian fare, including a tasty chicken parmigiana, bracioletti (steak rolled around cheese and herbs), and salad with balsamic vinaigrette. All pasta is made on the premises; focaccia pizzas are a good choice for lunch. Hours are 11 AM to 9 PM Monday through Thursday; 11 AM to 10 PM Friday;

4:30 to 10 PM Saturday. Sundays are reserved for private parties. Carmelo's serves wine and beer. Reservations are recommended.

### CHRISTOS
*2632 Nicollet Ave. S.*
*Minneapolis*       871-2111
*$$*
Come here for a hearty helping of Greek cuisine; the long menu is good for experimenting. The appetizers are especially recommended: hearty hummos, light calamari, creamy taramosalata — and they even know how to do octopus right. Hours are 11 AM to 9:30 PM Monday through Thursday; 11 AM to 10:30 PM Friday; 4 to 10:30 PM Saturday; 4 to 9 PM Sunday. Reservations are recommended.

### COCOLEZZONE
*5410 Wayzata Blvd.*
*Golden Valley*       544-4014
*$$$*
This is a bustling trattoria serving course after course of fine Italian food. There are great pastas and pizzas — even the vegetables are memorable. Driving down 394, look for the sign to the north that reads "Coco's." Lunch is served 11:30 AM to 2 PM Tuesday through Thursday; dinner is 5:30 to 9 PM Monday through Saturday. Reservations are recommended.

### D'AMICO CUCINA
*100 N. Sixth St., Minneapolis*    338-2401
*$$$$*
The food looks as good as it tastes at this elegant Italian restaurant. You'll find no heaps of pasta here, but delicate dishes that de-

mand to be slowly savored — artful arrays of wild mushroom preparations, gnocchi that melts in your mouth, sumptuous roast birds and irresistible desserts. The waitstaff is always top-notch. Hours are 5:30 to 10 PM Monday through Thursday; 5:30 to 11 PM Friday and Saturday; 5 to 9 PM Sunday. Call for reservations.

### FRANCESCA'S BAKERY AND CAFE
*W. Seventh Pl. and St. Peter St.*
*St. Paul*       227-5775
*$*       *No credit cards*
Francesca's wholesome Italian-influenced fare is a delicious gift to hungry downtown workers. Recommended choices are the black bean soup, chicken and turkey salad sandwiches, wild rice salad, savory tarts and better-than-Mom-makes cookies. Francesca's serves wine and beer and also handles private parties and catering. Hours are 6:30 AM to 6:30 PM Monday through Thursday; 6:30 AM to 9 PM Friday; 7 AM to 9 PM Saturday.

### GIORGIO'S
*2451 Hennepin Ave., Minneapolis 374-5131*
*$$*       *No credit cards*
Tasty Italian pastas, salads, meats and small courses, informal charm and the reasonable prices all recommend this small cafe. Lunch is served 11:30 AM to 2:30 PM Tuesday through Friday. Dinner is 5 PM to midnight Sunday through Thursday; 5 PM to 1 AM Friday and Saturday. Brunch is served 10:30 AM to 2 PM Saturday and Sunday.

## It's Greek to Me

*626 W. Lake St., Minneapolis    825-9922*
**$$**

This is a casual, bustling, inexpensive eatery with some of the cities' best baklava. The spanakopita and lamb kebabs are also recommended. Hours are 11 AM to 11 PM daily.

## Italian Pie Shoppe and Winery

*777 Grand Ave., St. Paul    221-0093*
**$**

For a richly sauced thin-crust pizza, and a deep dish that's memorably crisp, stop here. The casual atmosphere drips with nostalgia. Hours are 11 AM to 10 PM Monday through Thursday; 11 AM to midnight Friday and Saturday; 1 to 10 PM Sunday. There's a second location at 1438 Yankee Doodle Road in Eagan.

## Kramarczuk Sausage Company

*215 E. Hennepin Ave.*
*Minneapolis    379-3018*
**$    No credit cards**

Belly up to the cafeteria line to order deep-fried piroshki, nalesnyky (meat-stuffed crepes covered with cheese), varenyky (soft folded dumplings stuffed with meat, potatoes or sauerkraut), cabbage rolls and sandwiches made with krakowska and other sausages. There are low prices and a sunny, spacious lunchroom. Hours are 8 AM to 4 PM Monday through Saturday.

## Linguini and Bob

*Butler Square Building, 100 N. Sixth St., Minneapolis    332-1600*
**$$**

This restaurant, popular before events at Target Center, features classy Italian food in a high-energy setting. Recommended are the spicy shrimp with angel hair cake, calamari, pizza with caramelized hot peppers and onions, linguini in parchment, and chicken breast with lemon mashed potatoes. Hours are 11:30 AM to 3 PM and 4 to 10:30 PM Monday through Thursday; 11:30 AM to 3 and 4 PM to midnight Friday; noon to 3 and 4 PM to midnight Saturday; 4 to 10 PM Sunday.

## Lowry's

*1934 Hennepin Ave. S.*
*Minneapolis    871-0806*
**$$**

Lowry's offers a fun menu concentrating on Italian preparations — pastas, polentas, risottos — often with a hearty twist. Try the polenta with mozzarella and black bean sauce. The kitchen also prepares many types of salads and some fish dishes. Check out the good wine and beer selection. Reservations are recommended. Hours are 7 AM to 10 PM Monday through Thursday; 7 AM to 11 PM Friday; 10 AM to 11 PM Saturday; 10 AM to 9 PM Sunday.

## Muffuletta Cafe

*2260 Como Ave., St. Paul    644-9116*
**$$**

Muffuletta's long menu with both French and Italian influences is strongest on pizzas, pastas and appetizers. The tortellini baronessa is especially good; so's the steak au poivre. During spring and summer, take advantage of outdoor dining on the deck. Lunch is served 11:30 AM to 2:30 PM Monday through Saturday. Dinner is 5 to 9 PM Monday through Thursday; 5 to 10 PM Friday and Saturday; 5 to 8 PM Sunday. The sumptuous brunch is 10 AM to 2 PM Sunday. Reservations are recommended.

### NYE'S POLONAISE ROOM
*112 Hennepin Ave. E.*
*Minneapolis*            379-2021
$$

One of the few old-time restaurants with the sense to leave a good thing alone, Nye's features great 1960s decor and hearty Polish food. Recommended are the pierogi, kielbasa, and sauerkraut — and plenty of time to let the weighty food and pleasant ambiance sink in. Cap off your evening with a visit to Nye's legendary piano bar. Hours are 11 AM to 11 PM Monday through Thursday; 11 AM to midnight Friday and Saturday. Reservations are recommended.

### OLD SPAGHETTI FACTORY
*233 Park Ave., Minneapolis*      341-0949
$

Italian gusto graces this recently opened family eatery. So does a life-size trolley car in the center of the dining room! Naturally, the specialty is pasta, smothered in a variety of sauces. Lunch is served from 11:30 AM to 2 PM Monday through Friday; dinner is from 5 to 10 PM Monday through Thursday; from 5 to 11 PM Friday and Saturday; and from 4 to 10 PM Sunday.

### PANINO'S
*244¹ Rice St., Roseville*      481-7009
$$

The best bets here are the unusual rolled sandwiches called paninos, which make an enormous meal. There are pizzas and pastas, too. (Another Panino's is at 857 Village Center Drive, North Oaks.) Hours are 11 AM to 10 PM Monday through Thursday; 11 AM to 11 PM Friday and Saturday; 11 AM to 9 PM Sunday.

### PIZZAIOLA ROMA
*704 S. Cleveland Ave., St. Paul*      699-8321
$                    *No credit cards*

This clean, pleasant cafe serves top-notch gourmet pizzas, including a delicious Thai chicken version. There are also nice salads and hearty calzone. Order at the counter, then relax while you're served. Hours are 11 AM to 9 PM Sunday through Wednesday; 11 AM to 10 PM Thursday through Saturday.

### RISTORANTE LUCI
*470 S. Cleveland Ave., St. Paul*      699-8258
$$

Olive oil, mushrooms and cheeses make beautiful music together at this cozy, family-owned and -operated cafe. The menu includes regional Italian pastas and entrees; there are lovely fruit tarts and moderate prices. Hours are 5 to 9:30 PM Monday through Thursday; 5 to 10:30 PM Friday and Saturday; 4:30 to 9 PM Sunday. Reservations are highly recommended.

### RUSSIAN TEA HOUSE
*1758 W. University Ave., St. Paul* 646-4144
$                    *No credit cards*

This no-frills cafe serves great piroshki — mild ground beef and rice baked inside a chewy, leavened roll. Russian potato salad, cabbage rolls and borscht are also available. It's good for take-out. Go on a nice day, for the best seating is out front on a picnic table under a pine tree. Hours are 11 AM to 6 PM Tuesday through Friday.

### STEPHANO'S

*11849 Millpond Ave., Burnsville   895-1639*
**$$**                         *No credit cards*

This is the place for honest, home-cooked Italian food, served in a family-friendly atmosphere overflowing with knickknacks. Recommended are the ravioli, spaghettini alla Napolitana, pollo con carciofini (chicken with artichoke hearts), bistecci alla Italiana, pizza, and the house salad. Lunch is served 11 AM to 2 PM Monday through Friday; dinner is 4:30 to 9:30 daily.

### TULIPS

*452 Selby Ave., St. Paul   221-1061*
**$$**

This cozy, reasonably priced Cathedral Hill cafe serves meats, poultry and seafood, personalized with French sauces. It's a popular spot for romancing. Lunch is served 11:30 AM to 3 PM Monday to Friday. Dinner is 5 to 10 PM Sunday through Thursday; 5 to 11 PM Friday and Saturday. Reservations are recommended.

### YVETTE

*65 S.E. Main St., Minneapolis   379-1111*
**$$$**

Romance is almost required in this elegant Riverplace spot. You'll find white tablecloths, evocative murals and French-influenced foods as well as steaks; there's music

and dancing in the open bar most nights. Hours are 11 AM to 3 PM and 5 to 11 PM Monday through Thursday; 11 AM to midnight Friday and Saturday. Reservations are recommended.

---

## Four-star Cuisine

### DAKOTA BAR AND GRILL

*Bandana Square, 1021 E. Bandana Blvd.*
*St. Paul   642-1442*
**$$**

The town's classiest jazz club is also one of its best restaurants. A changing menu emphasizes seasonal ingredients and creative combinations. The fish is uniformly fine; garlic fans will worship the Dakota's Caesar, others will swoon over the brie and apple soup. Who says Midwestern cuisine is unsophisticated? Hours are 5:30 to 10:30 PM Monday through Thursday; 5:30 PM to midnight Friday and Saturday; 5:30 to 9:30 PM Sunday. The bar offers a food menu 4 PM to 1 AM daily. Sunday brunch is 10 AM to 2 PM. Reservations are recommended.

### THE 510 RESTAURANT

*510 Groveland Ave., Minneapolis 874-6440*
**$$$**

The 510 has lowered prices and cut down on the formality, but still has charms, including its grand old room, a $19 three-course meal and bargain featured wine list, with prices just a buck over average retail. Recommended are the luncheon salads, scallop-risotto cakes, wild mushroom fettucine and grilled flank steak. Lunch is served 11:30 AM to 2 PM Monday through Friday. Dinner is 5:30 to 10 PM Monday through Saturday. Reservations are recommended.

### FOREPAUGH'S
*276 S. Exchange St., St. Paul*   224-5606
*$$$*

Forepaugh's serves traditional continental favorites in the pretty, intimate rooms of a historic Victorian house. There's no question — this is a very popular special-occasion choice. Hours are 11:30 AM to 2 PM and 5:30 to 9:30 PM Monday through Friday; 5:30 to 9:30 PM Saturday; 10:30 AM to 1:30 PM and 5 to 8:30 PM Sunday. Reservations are recommended.

### GOODFELLOW'S
*The Conservatory, 800 Nicollet Mall*
*Minneapolis*   332-4800
*$$$$*

Allow yourself a big budget and a lot of time to enjoy this wonderful restaurant's creative food and classy, soothing ambiance. Goodfellow's also features a top-notch wine list and great artwork. Lunch is served 11:30 AM to 2 PM Monday through Friday. Dinner is 5:30 to 9 PM Monday through Thursday; 5:30 to 10 PM Friday and Saturday. Reservations are recommended.

### KINCAID'S
*8400 Normandale Lake Blvd.*
*Bloomington*   921-2255
*$$$*

This is one of the Twin Cities' best-liked restaurants, a home for those who love Nebraska corn-fed beef as well as pasta, fresh fish and oysters. It's a popular dining stop for executives with food as well as business on their minds, plus couples and others wanting to create a good impression. Try the mesquite-grilled meats and homemade bread. Lunch hours are 11 AM to 2:30 PM Monday through Saturday. Dinner hours are 4 to 9:30 PM Monday through Thursday; 4 to 10:30 PM Friday and Saturday; and 4 to 8:30 PM Sunday. There's also a Sunday brunch from 10 AM to 2 PM.

### MANNY'S
*Hyatt Regency Hotel, 1300 Nicollet Mall*
*Minneapolis*   339-9900
*$$$$*

Waiters at this classy steak house wheel around a cart of raw dry-aged beef, pork and live lobsters, just in case you need help deciding. A winning menu boasts a fine Caesar salad and a whole section of potatoes and onions (try the hash browns). The food is excellent, and all of it is offered à la carte. Hours are 5:30 to 10 PM Monday through Thursday; 5:30 to 11 PM Friday and Saturday; 5:30 to 9 PM Sunday. Reservations are recommended.

### MORTON'S OF CHICAGO
*555 Nicollet Mall, Minneapolis*   673-9700
*$$$$*

The meals are enormous, and so are the prices. But if you have the dough to blow, Morton's is worth it for the simple, well-prepared food and pleasant, professional service. The steaks are superb, as is the grilled swordfish. There are also great baked and Lyonnaise potatoes and beefsteak tomato salads. Don't forget your doggie bag. Lunch is served 11:30 AM to 2:30 PM Monday through Friday. Dinner is

5:30 to 11 PM Monday through Saturday; 5 to 10 PM Sunday. Reservations are recommended. Valet parking is offered at the Sixth Street entrance, just east of Nicollet.

## MURRAY'S
*26 S. Sixth St., Minneapolis      339-0909*
$$$$

The sign on the outside proclaims that Murray's is "home of the silver butter-knife steak" — a characterization left by a traveling gourmand of the 1950s who found perfect steaks in precious few establishments throughout the United States. Forty years later, this restaurant is still preparing mouth-watering beef, as well as very good fish entrees (try the salmon and walleye). If for no other reason, come here to see the professional, veteran waitstaff at work and to enjoy the violin and piano sounds Thursday through Saturday evenings. Hours are 11 AM to 10:30 PM Monday through Thursday; 11 AM to 11 PM Friday; 4 to 11 PM Saturday; and 4 to 10 PM Sunday. There's also a weekday afternoon tea from 2 to 3:30 PM.

## NEW FRENCH CAFE
*128 N. Fourth St., Minneapolis     338-3790*
$$$

Fresh interpretations of all manner of French food are the game at this gallery-district cafe. The place is hopping most all of the day, serving breakfast croissants and omelettes, lunchtime sandwiches and entrees, all-out dinners, sumptuous weekend brunches and late-night suppers. The New French is the home of arguably the best French bread in town. Hours are 7 to 11 AM, 11:30 AM to 1:30 PM and 5:30 to 9:30 PM Monday through Thursday; 7 to 11 AM, 11:30 AM to 1:30 PM and 5:30 PM to midnight Friday; 8 AM to 2 PM and 5:30 PM to midnight Saturday; 8 AM to 2 PM and 5:30 to 9 PM Sunday.

## NICOLLET ISLAND INN
*95 Merriam St., Nicollet Island*
*Minneapolis                331-1800*
$$$

This is a charming country inn serving sophisticated comfort food. The four-course Minnesota-made menu includes pan-fried chicken that is out of this world. Also recommended are the lamb chops, goat cheese with red-pepper compote, and walleye and scallop cakes. Breakfast is served 7 to 10 AM Monday through Friday; 8 to 11 AM Saturday. Brunch is 9:30 AM to 2:30 PM Sunday. Lunch is 11:30 AM to 2 PM Monday through Friday; 11:30 AM to 2:30 PM Saturday. Dinner is 5:30 to 9 PM Sunday; 5:30 to 9:30 PM Monday through Thursday; 5:30 to 10 PM Friday and Saturday. Reservations are recommended.

## ST. PAUL GRILL
*St. Paul Hotel, 350 Market St.*
*St. Paul                   224-7455*
$$$

The woody, understated dining room looks as though it has been listening to business dealings and lovers' secrets for years. Here you'll find solid, uncomplicated American food, including steaks, tasty grilled chicken breast and fish. The smoked salmon appetizer is recommended. Lunch is served 11:30 AM to 2 PM Monday through Saturday. Dinner is 5:30 to 10 PM Monday; 5:30 to 11 PM Tuesday through Saturday; 5 to 10 PM Sunday. Brunch is 11 AM to 2 PM Sunday. A bar menu is available 2 PM to midnight daily. Reservations are recommended.

### WHITNEY GRILLE
*Whitney Hotel, 150 Portland Ave.*
*Minneapolis* 339-9300
*$$$*

For fine dining, few places can compare with this elegant, hushed setting in the lower level of the Whitney Hotel. A feeling of intimacy is enhanced by the use of dark woods, plants and waist-high dividers that promote privacy without compromising the people-watching quotient. The Whitney serves contemporary American cuisine prepared with fresh, seasonal ingredients. Live entertainment is featured Wednesday through Saturday nights. Breakfast hours are 6:30 to 11 AM Monday through Friday; 7 to 11 AM Saturday. Lunch is served from 11 AM to 2:30 PM Monday through Saturday. Dinner is from 5:30 to 10:30 PM all week. Brunch is offered from 9:30 to 2:30 PM Sunday.

## Hispanic and Caribbean Cuisine

### EL AMANECER
*194 Concord St., St. Paul* 291-0758
*$* *No credit cards*

Come here for a variety of filling Mexican basics, including tasty, chewy tacos al pastor. For $4.50 weekdays at lunchtime, you can choose from several hefty meat stews, served with rice, beans and tortillas; there are menudo and caldo specials Friday through Sunday. Breakfast is served every day, hence the name "the dawn." Hours are 8 AM to 10 PM Sunday through Thursday; 8 AM to 3 AM Friday and Saturday.

### BOCA CHICA
*11 Concord St., St. Paul* 222-8499
*$$*

This 26-year-old institution has added a snappy new bar for sipping those killer margaritas and nibbling on nachos or chips with hot, hot sauce. Mexican-American basics are served, as well as lesser-known regional specialties, such as pork with nopales and enchiladas in a tangy green sauce. Hours are 11 AM to 10 PM Sunday and Monday; 11 AM to 10:30 PM Tuesday through Thursday; 11 AM to midnight Friday and Saturday. Reservations are recommended on weekends.

### EL BURRITO
*200 Concord St., St. Paul* 227-2192
*$* *No credit cards*

This neighborhood Mexican grocery includes a swell deli for take-out food. Try the chile chipotle or burrito filled with chili verde. Hours are 8 AM to 8 PM Monday through Saturday; 8 AM to 6 PM Sunday.

### LA CAZUELA
*197 Concord St., St. Paul* 291-0498
*$* *No credit cards*

This humble tortilla factory and cafeteria serves fresh corn torts smothered with spicy stews: chile verde, chipotle, nopales and much more. The borracho beans will set a happy little fire in your mouth. Hours are 8 AM to 9 PM daily.

### CHEZ BANANAS
*129 N. Fourth St., Minneapolis    340-0032*
**$$**

This restaurant offers spicy, creative Caribbean specialties in a goofy atmosphere — rubber bats mingle with plastic Godzillas. Where else can you eat expertly prepared fish, perfect cornbread and black beans while gazing at a picture of Pee Wee Herman or an inflatable version of Edvard Munch's "The Scream"? Hours are 5 to 10 PM Monday; 11:30 AM to 10 PM Tuesday to Thursday; 11:30 AM to 11 PM Friday; 5 to 11 PM Saturday; 5 to 9 PM Sunday.

### LA CORVINA
*1570 Selby Ave., St. Paul    645-5288*
**$$**    *No credit cards*

This friendly family-operated cafe serves comforting, yet not always predictable, Mexican-Latin food. Recommended are the fajitas, burritos, garlic chicken and sopa de albondigas. Outdoor seating is available. Hours are 11 AM to 10 PM Monday through Friday; noon to 10 PM Saturday and Sunday.

### LA CUCARACHA
*36 S. Dale St., St. Paul    221-9682*
**$**

The food's zippy and so's the service. Order the nachos Azteca, the puerco guisado verde, and the pollo loco. There's also a new Minneapolis location at 315 First Ave-

nue N. Hours are 11 AM to 11 PM Sunday through Thursday; 11 AM to midnight Friday and Saturday.

### JUANITA'S
*201 Concord St., St. Paul    290-2511*
**$**    *No credit cards*

Juanita's offers a variety of inexpensive, authentic Mexican food — burritos, enchiladas and soft tacos with onions, fresh cilantro and sauces on the side. Hours are 11 AM to 8 PM Tuesday through Thursday; 11 AM to 10 PM Friday; 9 AM to 2 AM Saturday; 9 AM to 5 PM Sunday. There are no alcoholic beverages served.

### EL MESON
*3450 Lyndale Ave. S.*
*Minneapolis    822-8062*
**$$**

Here's a rare taste of Spanish and other Latin-influenced eats, which are marked by plenty of garlic, sweet peppers and, often, saffron. Call ahead for paella in this cozy, friendly nook. Hours are 5 to 10 PM Monday; 11 AM to 10 PM Tuesday through Friday; noon to 10 PM Saturday; noon to 9 PM Sunday. Reservations are recommended. Alcoholic beverages are limited to low-alcohol beer.

### PASQUAL'S
*2528 Hennepin Ave.*
*Minneapolis    374-1415*
**$**

This solid Southwestern deli offers a full menu of enchiladas, tacos, burritos and the like; there are also fresh salsa, guacamole and foods to cook at home. (Another location is at 5057 France Avenue S., Minneapolis.) Hours are 10 AM to 10 PM daily. Eat in or take out.

## Outside the Twin Cities, But Worth the Drive

### THE CREAMERY

*County Rd. C, East of Hwy. 25*
*Downsville, Wis.* (715) 664-8354
*$$* *No credit cards*

A little over an hour's drive from St. Paul, this country getaway offers a relaxing atmosphere and simple, sometimes sophisticated, food. There are good prices and friendly service, too. Lunch is served 11:30 AM to 2 PM Tuesday through Saturday. Brunch is 10 AM to 2 PM Sunday. A light menu is served in the lounge from 2 to 9 PM Tuesday through Thursday; 2 to 10 PM Friday; 2 to 4:30 PM Saturday; 2 to 8 PM Sunday. Dinner is served 5 to 9 PM Tuesday through Thursday; 5 to 10 PM Friday and Saturday; 4:30 to 8 PM Sunday.

### DICK'S BAR

*III Walnut St.*
*Hudson, Wis.* (715) 386-5222
*$$*

When you order a Chicken in a Hubcap here, you really get a car part with your meal. Dick's cozy ambiance, cheerful staff and good fries make it a neat stop off. The best bets are chicken, burgers and fresh pasta dishes. Specials are offered every night, along with cheap appetizers. Hours are 8 AM to 10 PM daily.

### DOCK CAFE

*425 E. Nelson St., Stillwater* 430-3770
*$$*

Grilled fish, meat and fowl, an eclectic appetizer list and plenty of salads appropriate to the season — they're all there in a tasteful, airy building that peers out onto the St. Croix River. There's an attractive, expansive deck on the riverfront. Hours are 11 AM to 9 PM Monday through Thursday; 11 AM to 10 PM Friday and Saturday; 10 AM to 8 PM Sunday. Reservations are recommended.

### HARBOR VIEW CAFE

*First and Main Sts.*
*Pepin, Wis.* (715) 442-3893
*$$* *No credit cards*

Lunch or dinner at this casual riverfront restaurant is worth the drive — and the usually long wait for a table. The blackboard menu boasts a changing array of fresh fish, meats and much more. Try the magnificent coq au vin, the plump garlic prawns on pasta, or the satisfying Caesar salad. Prices are moderate to boot. Do go early; the fall color season creates a breathtaking dinner rush. Hours are 11 AM to 2:30 PM and 5 to 9 PM Thursday and Friday; 11 AM to 2:30 PM and 4:45 to 9 PM Saturday; noon to 7:30 PM Sunday; 11 AM to 2:30 PM and 5 to 8 PM Monday.

# *Inside*
# **Nightlife**

No matter your feelings on the benefits or detriments of drinking, you can learn a great deal about an area from its bars.

Set yourself down on a stool, lean your elbows on the oak and order up a beer, wine or drink (hard or soft). Then listen in on neighboring conversations or engage a friend or new acquaintance in some friendly banter. Soon, you'll find yourself swept up into the homey warmth of pub culture, making connections often eschewed by our increasingly isolationist society.

Like any vibrant metropolitan area, the Twin Cities has a lively bar scene, with intimate, old-fashioned neighborhood joints complemented by large commercial operations and nightclubs of varying sizes and styles.

When it comes to the latter, live music is where it's at in the twin towns. The area is internationally famous for its music scene — especially in the rock genre — and the cities' lively club scene has become an incubator for nationally acclaimed talent. (The area has been nicknamed "The land of 10,000 bands.")

But, like any dynamic urban area, you can have a good time on the town, even without the music. What we've assembled here are a number of "pub crawls" that will take you through Twin Cities neighborhoods and let you glimpse some of the local flavor.

Within each walk, you'll find an interesting mix of styles, from small watering holes to expansive music clubs.

In the case of the more lengthy crawls (for example, the bar-heavy Minneapolis Warehouse District), you're advised to pick and choose. Please don't try to hit 'em all, unless you're feeling restless and plan on ordering only iced tea or soda.

The crawls are, for the most part, intended as walks. No driving should be necessary if you're drinking.

A warning on that account: Unlike such bustling burgs as Chicago or New York, you're rarely able to step from the door of a Twin Cities restaurant, bar or theater and hail a taxi. It seems that legendary Midwestern sense of independence extends to owning and driving your own car. Hence, demand for taxis here is as meager as the supply.

It may be a good idea start the evening by looking up a cab company in the Yellow Pages and scrawling down the number. Then, when you feel you've had your fill of crawling, give them a call and they'll come get you. For those on a budget, MCTO buses are a reliable source of transportation to any area within the Twin Cities.

Although local liquor laws are a constant source of debate in the city halls of Minneapolis, St. Paul and surrounding suburbs, the standard closing time is 1 AM. Some pubs listed here will serve food, but no alcohol, after that time.

So, let's get started. We'll begin with what could be called Bar Central in the Twin Cities: Minneapolis' Warehouse District, located on the northwest edge of downtown.

## Pubs and Bars

### Minneapolis

#### WAREHOUSE DISTRICT PUB CRAWL

The grand old brick buildings of the Warehouse District—once used promarily for storage — are now home to the Twin Cities' highest concentration of art galleries and feature some of Minneapolis' best restaurants within its loosely defined boundaries.

Like any center for artists (yes, many of them live and work in the neighborhood's renovated lofts), the attire and attitude are primarily Bohemian. It's especially fun to take a crawl when the galleries are hosting opening receptions for new exhibits (on a Saturday night, roughly every six weeks) and the crowded sidewalks take on the ambiance of a street festival.

We'll start off in the real Warehouse District, close to the mighty Mississippi, where most of the structures actually are warehouses. Here, off by itself, away from the bustle at downtown's heart, sits the **Acme Comedy Co.**, 338-6393, 708 N. First Street. It's located in the Itasca Building, amidst a stretch of storefronts that also includes the rehearsal spaces for the Minnesota Opera and the Guthrie Theater's Laboratory offshoot. The Acme is regarded by many as the Twin Cities' best comedy club, thanks to its booking of national acts (four or five nights a week) and its unforced jovial atmosphere.

If you walk a few blocks east, you'll come upon **Nikki's**, 340-9098, 107 Third Avenue N., a friendly midsized pub with a thrown-together, but inviting, feel. Nikki's hosts music every night, with pianist Cornbread Harris (father of pop and R&B giant Jimmy "Jam" Harris) tickling the ivories a few times a week. If you're in town during the summer months, the neighboring garden area is the nicest outdoor bar in the Warehouse District.

The dividing line between the old and new Warehouse Districts is Washington Avenue, Downtown Minneapolis' principal north-south thoroughfare. It has a far more commercial climate than any of the dimly lighted side streets, and many of its bars have a far more raucous atmosphere than the aforementioned old area places.

Exhibit A, on that account, is **Bunker's**, 338-8188, 761 Washington Avenue N., a boisterous, noisy live music bar that specializes in blues and R&B of the old school (loads of horns, lengthy guitar solos and throaty vocals). The sightlines are limited, but the tunes are generally satisfying. Every Monday and Tuesday since the early '80s, Dr. Mambo's Combo has held forth with soulful funk, aided by guests from some of the area's most prominent bands (Prince's players, among them). Another regular is the blues-based big band, Mick Sterling and the Stud Brothers.

Head a few blocks south on Washington and you'll find **Mollie Malone's**, 333-1675, 119 Washington Avenue N. To call Mollie's Minneapolis' best Irish pub would be faint praise: Unlike the more ethnic St. Paul, the Mill City is not known for its high concentration of Irish Americans. But Mollie's is a charming little place to put away a pint or two and, on weekends, hear some folk music from the Emerald Isle.

Continue south to **Runyon's**, 332-7158, 107 Washington Avenue N. Once the hottest pub in the neighborhood, Runyon's has settled into its niche as a dark, chatty, checkered bar bursting with noise and energy. Now turn west on First Avenue and you'll be headed into the Warehouse District's more bustling environs, closer to the heart of downtown.

If you're in the mood for music, there are few better places to hear it than the **Fine Line Music Cafe**, 338-8100, 318 First Avenue N. The acoustics and sightlines are outstanding at this tiered den of pop, folk and rock, where you'll find a blend of emerging local bands and concerts by national acts with commensurate cover charges. Alas, the drink prices are steep, the kitchen's inconsistent and the waitstaff is notorious for its disappearing act. But if all you care about is listening to the music, it's a nice club.

Cut north on Fourth Street and you'll encounter a couple of stops worth consideration. Duck in through the doorway of the **New French Cafe** (a first-rate restaurant) and follow the serpentine hallway to the **New French Bar**, 338-3790, 128 N. Fourth Street. Here, you'll find a selection of outstanding wines of various vintages, best when imbibed at one of the bar's sidewalk tables in summer. But the inside is intimate and oak-laden, with a relaxing atmosphere that offers a sharp contrast to the neighboring **Urban Wildlife**, 339-4665, 331 Second Avenue N., a once-out-of-the-way watering hole that today has become a social hotbed for those in their 20s who clearly miss the frat-house parties.

No visit to the neighborhood would be complete without at least looking in the door and finding that you can't get a table at the **Loon Cafe**, 332-8342, 500 First Avenue N. There may be times when this institution isn't almost bursting out its big windows with people, but never in the evening. The chief attractions are the good chili, people-watching and pedestrian traffic patterns that are conducive to uninterrupted conversation.

Now, a word about Prince (now known as a male/female symbol rather than by his name): Although some say the Minneapolis native's music has never climbed back to the level of popularity it achieved c. 1984 (thanks to his film and album, *Purple Rain*), he is still regarded as one of the Twin Cities' most prominent personalities. After years of surprise gigs at such nearby clubs as First Avenue and the Fine Line, he decided to set up a home base for these impromptu concerts and opened **Glam Slam**, 338-3383, 110 N. Fifth Street. As contemporary discos go, it could be the Twin Cities' best, with each night given over to a different theme ('70s disco, '60s psychedelia), and it also plays host to some of the most popular acts on the urban contemporary charts.

On Sixth Street is an old favorite for many locals: **Gluek's**, 338-6621, 16 N. Sixth Street. The spacious woody interior is reminiscent of a German *rathskeller*, with towering ceilings and long tables down the center of the room, ideal for large parties. If relaxing is what you have in mind, the afternoon or early evening are your best times to stop. In the evening, a college-party spirit overwhelms the place, with all of the requisite rowdiness. But it's one of the only places you can still get Gluek's beer, an old Minneapolis label.

Depending upon your age and energy level, you may now be ready for the Twin Cities' premier music club, **First Avenue**, 338-8388, 701 First Avenue N. Don't expect anything clean or fancy, such as the Fine Line or Glam Slam: First Avenue is a concert club that delights in its grubbiness and laissez-faire ambiance. Music is what it's all about here, and the management is fiercely proud to have introduced local audiences to many acts that have since achieved international fame (the outside wall is emblazoned with a roster of them). Stain-resistant black is the color scheme here, and the music (either recorded or live) runs nonstop from your arrival to your departure. Check the Friday entertainment sections in the local papers or one of the weeklies for the schedule, for most nights are given over to touring acts, offering anything from grunge rock and reggae to R&B and African. If a table is a top priority, arrive early and don't expect wait service. The balcony is best for viewing, but the bustling dance floor is always a memorable experience.

First Avenue also has a smaller auxiliary room called the **Seventh Street Entry**, accessible through an unmarked entrance on, you guessed it, Seventh Street, as well as through First Avenue's main room. It's an intimate, grubby little club that makes its big brother next door look like the Waldorf Astoria by comparison. But, if alternative rock is your brew of choice, this is the best place to hear up-and-coming local bands or catch an emerging national act on its way through town. Just be prepared to stand or dance and don't lean on anything if you value your clothing.

## DOWNTOWN
## MINNEAPOLIS PUB CRAWL

There are bars and restaurants throughout downtown Minneapolis, so many that you can choose any downtown street, start walking and duck into a number of interesting pubs. For our purposes here, we'll concentrate on downtown's two main north-south commercial streets: Hennepin Avenue and the Nicollet Mall. The former is the Main Street of downtown, home to theaters, restaurants, bars, crowds and, unfortunately, some accompanying crime. Nicollet Mall, on the other hand, is a retail district made for walking, with only city buses, taxis and bicycles allowed along its narrow center.

You can start your journey at Hennepin Avenue's hottest club, **Rogue**, 371-0706, 10 S. Fifth Street, which stylishly combines dancing and dining in an environment that's bright but rarely blaring and always alive with music and the hum of conversation. Although "hipness" is a label that comes and goes with the changing winds, Rogue has managed to hold on to that elusive quality over the past couple of years.

The granddaddy of Twin Cities gay bars, **The Gay 90s**, 333-7755, 408 Hennepin Avenue, is located nearby. The popularity of this multiroom nightclub never seems to flag, with crowds pouring in and out of its doors on most nights but

especially on weekends. Among the rooms are a dance annex, specializing in disco of the old school, a cabaret featuring flamboyant drag shows, a piano bar where standards and ballads are the tunes of choice and a quiet bar near the entrance if you need a break from all of the activity.

Located in the City Center shopping mall, the **Nankin**, 333-3303, 2 S. Seventh Street, is best-known as one of the city's oldest Chinese restaurants. Its bar area offers hideaway booths where you can munch on fried wontons and sip one of the town's legendary concoctions, the Wanderer's Punch. We'd suggest you limit your intake to one: They're much stronger than they taste.

Back down on street level, you'll find a few interesting watering holes near the Historic State and Orpheum theaters. **The Rock Bottom Brewery**, 332-2739, 825 Hennepin Avenue, is a fairly new entry in the brew pub movement that's mushrooming nationally. They brew their own on the premises, but you can find tastier ales and lagers elsewhere, for example, at **Mackenzie**, 333-7268, 918 Hennepin Avenue, a bar that boasts of its Scottish heritage and backs it up with a nice selection of ales and scotches.

On Hennepin off of Ninth Street is an unmarked bar known as the **Y'All Come Back Saloon**, 332-0835, 830 Hennepin Avenue. While The Gay 90s may be the patriarch of local gay bars, The Saloon (as regulars call it) is considered the hipper hangout, with a more subdued, less theatrical clientele but an equally hopping dance floor.

If you continue on Hennepin a few blocks, you'll come upon one of downtown's nicest little bars, **Eli's**, 332-9997, 1225 Hennepin Avenue. Here, you can hold a quiet conversation unattainable at most of the noisy downtown hangouts while enjoying the wide variety of spirits and beers.

A couple of blocks farther, the hippest of the hip gather at the **Loring Bar**, 332-1616, 1624 Harmon Place. This self-described Bohemian pub, filled with mismatched overstuffed couches and chairs, exudes an attitude that may make some uncomfortable. But the waitstaff isn't nearly as rude as it used to be, and it's a nice place to hear music, which is delivered from one of the smallest stages in the city. It's especially pleasant on summer nights, when the large front windows are open and patrons can look out upon Loring Park. If you're lucky, you'll be there on a night when the rooftop sax player is in session.

Heading back into the center of downtown, you'll happen upon a few intriguing places near the end of Nicollet Mall that deserve mention. Each is located within a block of Orchestra Hall and makes for a pleasant post-concert destination. **The Times**, 333-2762, 1036 Nicollet Mall, is a narrow little old-fashioned bar with good pub grub and a full schedule of local musicians who hold forth each evening at the reasonable price of no cover charge. The music is a mix of jazz and standards, with the emphasis on

singers, but Thursday nights are given over to local blues legends Dave Ray and Tony Glover.

Speaking of music, you can find some of the area's best jazz musicians at **Cafe Luxeford**, 332-6800, 1101 LaSalle Avenue, in the lobby of the Luxeford Suites hotel down the block. Expect a mixture of traditional and straight-ahead, performed by trios and quartets.

Right across from Orchestra Hall is a friendly joint, **Brit's Pub**, 332-3908, 1110 Nicollet Mall, which does its best to recreate the ambiance of a bar in merry old England, complete with the cuisine (such as it is) and an assortment of ales and single-malt scotches. And you can imbibe while sitting in a puffy chair beneath a portrait of the Queen Mum.

Not located along the Nicollet Mall, but just around the corner, are a couple of friendly dramshops. The **Court Bar**, 332-5589, 212 S. Seventh Street, used to be a quiet little neighborhood pub that attracted mostly newspaper and radio people, but now it's a popular stop for the college crowd, as well. And why not? It's an inoffensive old place with big tables that accommodate lively conversations among big groups.

**Lyon's Pub**, 333-6612, 16 S. Sixth Street, is similar in atmosphere and clientele and is at its most energetic and interesting right after work.

### BEFORE OR AFTER
### A GAME AT THE METRODOME

If you plan on attending a Twins baseball game, Vikings or Gophers

*Gatlin Brothers Music City Restaurant at the Mall of America.*

Photo: Buzz Magnuson, Pioneer Press

football game or other event at the Hubert H. Humphrey Metrodome (located on the southeast end of downtown), there are a few nice bars nearby for meeting friends beforehand or catching a nightcap afterward. At one time, there were more, but, in one of those classic urban tradeoffs, socializing was sacrificed to the automobile: Many bars were wiped out in an effort to provide more Metrodome parking.

The happiest beneficiary of that change is **Hubert's**, 332-6062, 601 Chicago Avenue, now the only watering hole within four blocks of the Dome. Its location is prime: right across the street from the principal entrance for Twins games, hence, it's always packed around game time. As food and drink go, it's pretty standard fare (burgers and Budweiser), but it's nice to gaze

upon the walls of local sports memorabilia while you're waiting for your game date.

One of the more pleasant places to meet before a game is **Maxwell's**, 338-1980, 1201 Washington Avenue S., a small, narrow, wood-laden bar with elevated chairs and tables. The atmosphere is always friendly (even after a loss) and the burgers and the appetizers are pretty good. A few doors down is **Maxwell's Roadhouse**, 340-9738, 1111 Washington Avenue S., a slightly larger offshoot that features the same menu and a few billiards tables.

If you prefer something a little more classy and expensive (and feel yourself suitably dressed), try the upscale bar at the **Whitney Hotel**, 339-9300, 150 Portland Avenue. Here, you can be serenaded by a singing pianist while sipping top-shelf liquor or wine from the amply stocked cellar. In summer, the fountainside patio is a soothing place to sit and sip before taking a quiet walk along the nearby Mississippi.

If that sounds a little too rich for your blood, but you still like the idea of outdoor imbibing, you'll probably enjoy **Knickerbockers**, 375-1766, 1501 S. Sixth Street. Located on the other end of a walkway that connects the Metrodome with the Cedar-Riverside area, Knickerbockers is a friendly, multilevel brick building with an intimate bar, a back dining room (again, burger and sandwich fare) and an upstairs pool room that features a round table in a window-lined round tower. But the bar's best feature is a rooftop patio that's simply perfect for Twins fans who have just spent the better part of a beautiful summer evening trapped beneath the Metrodome's inflated roof. Lean back and stare at the stars — or at one of the best views of the Minneapolis skyline you'll find anywhere — and let that claustrophobic feeling float away.

## WEST BANK PUB CRAWL

If you're in the mood for music, but you don't necessarily know what kind of music you're in the mood for, then, friend, welcome to the West Bank.

Here, you'll find bars, cafes, coffeehouses and concert halls of many stripes, all located (roughly) along a 10-block stretch of Cedar Avenue from Seven Corners (Cedar and Washington Avenue) to the railroad yards down around Franklin Avenue.

We'll begin at the north end of the area, at the bustling Seven Corners. Actually, construction has limited the intersection to a more manageable four corners, and that's where a few of the bars are located. If you want to make the transition from University culture to Cedar-Riverside counterculture, these bars will ease the shift.

**Bullwinkle's**, 338-8520, 1429 Washington Avenue S., has all the ambiance of a typical East Bank college bar, but it's considerably cozier, especially in the loft section that overlooks the intersection. Across the street is **Winners**, 375-0166, 1501 Washington Avenue S., ostensibly a sports bar, but a fairly quiet place for a sandwich and a beer before you move on.

**Sgt. Preston's**, 338-6146, 221 Cedar Avenue S., is a narrow, intimate, mahogany-hued pub with a cafeteria line for sandwiches in the back, while **Grandma's**, 340-0516, 1810 Washington Avenue S., is the neighborhood "meat market," designed for making fresh acquaintances and sustaining a more refined version of the University house party.

A few doors down, you'll find an interesting little place called **Nostalgia**, 330-0926, 247 Cedar Avenue S., which has few tables and a small bar but periodically hosts local jazz singers and the occasional cabaret-style show.

Once you've crossed the bridge over Third Street, you've entered the music center of Minneapolis. On your right you'll come upon the **Red Sea**, 333-1644, 316 Cedar Avenue S., the Twin Cities' foremost world-music bar, presenting the sounds of the Caribbean, South America and Africa on weekends but leaning upon the area's populous alternative-rock milieu on weeknights.

Now you've reached the legendary intersection of Cedar and Riverside, the hub of Twin Cities radicalism, where aging hippies and mellowing anarchists mingle with holistic healers and environmentalists. This is also the most warmly multicultural neighborhood in the Twin Cities, a place where immigrants and exchange students from around the world are made to feel welcome.

This warmth is nowhere more palpable than at the **New Riverside Cafe**, 333-4814, 329 Cedar Avenue S., one of the Twin Cities' best vegetarian restaurants. Here, you can grab a cup of herbal tea — served cafeteria style — and listen to the tunes of local folk artists five nights a week, with early shows Tuesdays through Thursdays. Across the street is a musical landmark, the **400 Bar**, 332-2903, 400 Cedar Avenue S., where local bands hold forth nightly, mostly playing the kind of alternative rock descended from the late-'70s punk movement and early-'80s new wave.

A couple of doors down is the **Cedar Cultural Centre**, 338-2674, 416 Cedar Avenue S., the Twin Cities' premier folk music venue, which hosts two or three concerts a week by nationally and internationally known acts. Passing through the Cedar once or twice a year are such performers as wry singer-songwriter Loudon Wainwright III, Iowa troubadour Greg Brown and some of the top traditional music acts from Africa, South America, China, India, Ireland and elsewhere. Basically, the inside of the Cedar looks like a movie theater, which it was at one time, but the sightlines are good and the acoustics fine for a night of folk. See The Arts chapter for more information on the Cedar.

Now you're getting into blues territory. The Cedar-Riverside area is home to some of the Twin Cities' top blues musicians, with such local legends as Koerner, Ray and Glover and Willie Murphy regularly playing in the area, along with bands led by any of the local "big" men: Big Walter Smith, Big John Dickerson and Big George Jackson. On Riverside, just off Cedar, you'll find the **Viking Bar**, 332-4259, 1829 Riverside Avenue, a corner pub that is given over to the blues a few nights a week, including regular gigs by Willie Murphy and Joel Johnson.

But the place to find blues, reggae or jams in the Grateful Dead vein seven nights a week is the **Five Corners Saloon**, 338-6425, 501 Cedar Avenue S. It's an intimate, casual place where dancing is encouraged, with a fairly regular clientele that gladly accepts new faces. And there's rarely a cover charge. If you want to rest your ringing ears from all of this music, **Palmer's**, 333-7625, 500 Cedar Avenue S., is another friendly neighborhood pub where you can have a quiet conversation. Similar in style is **Blondie's on the Avenue**, 333-0105, 629 Cedar Avenue S., drawing heavily on students from nearby Augsburg College.

Pass under I-94 and keep on straight ahead and you'll hit a couple more reliable music bars. **Whiskey Junction**, 338-9550, 901 Cedar Avenue S., has music seven nights a week at no cover, with an almost permanent roster of local blues jams and favorites of the local bikers. Next door is one of the Twin Cities' main music venues: **The Cabooze**, 338-6425, 917 Cedar Avenue S. Its odd shape makes for difficult viewing sometimes, as it's constructed like a big, wide train car, with the band in one corner. However, the Cabooze books national acts every week or two (ranging from surf guitar idol Dick Dale to funk icon George Clinton) and is respected as one of the granddaddies of area clubs. But a hint: If there's a band you really want to catch here, arrive early and get one of the only seats available opposite the stage on the tiered balcony.

### UPTOWN PUB CRAWL

Even though it has been discovered by suburbanites, the Uptown area of South Minneapolis hasn't shaken its Bohemian roots.

Today, teenage punks share the sidewalks with gray-bearded professional types, artists and the ultra-hip.

Naturally, this mix lends itself to a fantastic bar/cafe scene.

The Uptown area, roughly speaking, could be described as consisting of the thoroughfares that form The Wedge, a densely populated community shaped like an isosceles triangle. These streets are Lyndale Avenue on the east, West Lake Street on the south end and the curving South Hennepin Avenue on the western border.

Warning: This crawl is not a short one if you're on foot, so you might want to think about alternative transportation between some of the stops.

We'll start at **Lyle's**, 870-8183, 2021 Hennepin Avenue S. (or Liquor Lyle's, as it's known to many a local, thanks to the frenetic chaser lights that spell "liquor" above the front door). That should give you an idea of the ambiance: Drinking is unabashedly the first order of business here, as the plaster walls are lined with those uniquely American hand-printed signs advertising nightly drink and beer specials. The decor, service and menu are no great shakes, and the place is crowded, noisy and smoky, but still everybody comes here! Perhaps it's because it's the only old-fashioned neighborhood bar on South Hennepin for miles, refreshingly unencumbered by a modern marketing strategy.

Now you're approaching Hennepin and Lake, the hub of the Uptown area (sometimes called Yuptown for its high concentration of young urban professionals). The most popular bar near the intersection is also the area's oldest, **William's Pub**, 823-6271, 2911 Hennepin Avenue S. There's a restaurant on street level, but the most pleasant part of the pub is its basement, which houses the peanut bar. Here, you'll find groups of various sizes engaged in earnest conversation while leaning on checkered tablecloths and mulling over their choices from one of the Twin Cities' legendary beer lists. A fun activity for a large group is making your way around the world with beers, forming a human chain across the continents, country by country. As we said, it's best for large groups.

The trendy **Figlio**, 822-1688, 3001 Hennepin Avenue S., always attracts a large post-work contingent and is great for people-watching. While Italian cuisine is Figlio's specialty, drinking is the chief objective at its upstairs neighbor, the **Smiling Moose**, 822-5988, 3001 Hennepin Avenue S. This Colorado-based chain specializes in a variety of potent concoctions and one of the area's most impressive tap-beer selections (yes, the neighborhood is a brew fan's dream). Say what you will about the bland shopping-mall decor; you can ignore it and enjoy the people-watching out the big windows.

If you're intrigued by alternative rock performed by up-and-coming Twin Cities ensembles — spiced with the occasional national act — then the **Uptown Bar**, 823-4719, 3018 Hennepin Avenue S., is a must. Yes, the decor is reminiscent of a VFW hall that's fallen into disrepair, but the music's often worthwhile and, if the volume gets to be too much, there's a much quieter bar section to which you can retreat.

**Lucia's Wine Bar**, 825-1572, 1432 W. 31st Street, could be described as the Uptown Bar's antithesis. Here, patrons sip chardonnays and pinot noirs in a subdued atmosphere with low lighting, perhaps partaking of the appetizers from the restaurant section, which specializes in the culinary arts of northern Italy.

Follow Lake Street eastward and you'll see one of the most interesting places to emerge in recent years on the local pub scene: **Bryant-Lake Bowl**, 825-3737, 810 W. Lake Street. Now, granted, the bowling alley has existed for years, but it's only recently become a gathering place for the Twin Cities' copious number of progressive and experimental theater artists. It's a friendly place, where stereotypes are broken by creatively coiffed social rebels who like to toss a ball or two. There's also a theater on the premises with cabaret tables, where small troupes perform along with alternative rockers and modern dancers. There's also an occasional film.

A few blocks down Lyndale is a bar that could be described as the eastern Wedge's version of Lyle's: the **C.C. Club**, 874-7226, 2600 Lyndale Avenue S. It's an unassuming neighborhood bar, best for darts and pitchers of beer. It has a lived-in atmosphere that not even Lyle's can match, and you always get the feeling that the majority of your fellow patrons are from the neighborhood. In the early to mid-'80s, the C.C. became best-known as the favored watering hole of the Replacements, one of the most critically acclaimed bands to ever come out of the Twin Cities. Sitting at the bar and watching the locals come and go, you can see where the band's chief songsmith, Paul Westerberg, found the inspiration for "Here Comes a Regular."

If the Bryant-Lake Bowl is the main haunt of the Twin Cities' many theater people, then it has stolen the title from **Oliver's**, 871-5591, 2007 Lyndale Avenue S., for this is where actors and techies have gathered for years after the show, flamboyantly recounting the peaks and valleys of the evening's performance while relaxing in a woody, tiered bar. True, Bryant-Lake may get the more adventurous performance artists, but Oliver's is still where the casts from such nearby theaters as the Guthrie, Children's Theater, the Minneapolis Theatre Garage and the innumerable small companies gather for a post-show drink.

### SOUTH MINNEAPOLIS

South Minneapolis' primary east-west artery is Lake Street and, because of distances, it's best navigated by wheels rather than feet. Apart from the usual shot-and-a-beer joints, the thoroughfare is home to a decent sports bar (**Champions**, 827-4765, 105 W. Lake Street) and a grungy little rock bar that offers new local bands their first gig (**Fernando's**, 721-2107, 1501 E. Lake Street). Speaking of music, **Dulono's Pizza**, 827-1726, 607 W. Lake Street, is the unlikely venue for live bluegrass performed by local and national acts every Friday and Saturday night. The staff

sometimes asks the band to tone it down when the phone rings so they can take delivery orders.

The bars in the area of 26th Avenue and 26th Street are patronized by a mix of area factory workers and the left-wing Bohemians from around Franklin Avenue and the Cedar-Riverside area. Their haunts include one of the Twin Cities' most popular old-fashioned bowling alleys, **Stardust Lanes**, 721-6211, 2520 26th Avenue S., as well as a friendly shot-and-beer joint, the **Hexagon Bar**, 722-3454, 2600 27th Avenue S.

One of the Twin Cities' more unusual music venues is around the corner: **Mirage**, 729-2387, 2609 26th Avenue S. This large nightclub seems to have everything going for it: a large stage, high-tech lighting and sound systems and plenty of seating. Unfortunately, Mirage limits its bookings to heavy-metal and hard-rock bands, and — unless hosting a concert by a well-known national act — it just doesn't draw the crowds.

Also in the area, you'll find a local favorite, **Matt's**, 722-7072, 3500 Cedar Avenue S., where they serve the legendary Juicy Lucy, a popular cheese-filled hamburger that bursts at first bite.

As mentioned, there are dozens of little grogshops throughout

Nobody grooves like Dr. Mambo's Combo
Tuesday nights at Bunkers.

Insiders' Tips

• **99**

South Minneapolis that offer the minimum necessities and few frills. But most of them will probably remind you of Nick's, the place in *It's a Wonderful Life*, where, as bartender Sheldon Leonard rasped, "Men come to drink and get drunk. And we don't need any characters around to lend the place atmosphere, know what I mean?"

### NORTH MINNEAPOLIS

The pubs of the North side are similar in style to those of the South side: mostly working-class places with little flair, some of them located in neighborhoods that you might want to avoid after dark unless you have a specific destination. Yes, the Twin Cities area has one of the lowest per capita crime rates of any American metropolis, but a city's a city, and the working-class neighborhoods are usually the first to feel the sting of crime. Hence, the North and South sides both have rough pockets (as do some sections of St. Paul, but we'll get to that).

The hub of activity for pub crawlers is an area on the east end of the North side: the intersection of Washington and Broadway (or I-94). Here, you'll find such bustling gin mills as **Standup Frank's**, no phone, N. Second Street and 21st Avenue N. — so named for its lack of seating—where the drinks are powerful and cheap. It's a point of pilgrimage for University of Minnesota students of legal age, and the atmosphere is predictably rowdy.

A much more subdued stop is the **Broadway Bar**, 529-7666, 2025 N. West River Road, an unassuming caboose-shaped saloon specializing in beer and pizza. Nearby is the **Riverview Supper Club**, 521-7676, 2319 N. West River Road, one of the only upscale cocktail lounges in the neighborhood, which offers jazz and rhythm-and-blues, sometimes by internationally known artists like Bobby "Blue" Bland and Evelyn "Champagne" King. But the east end of the North side isn't the only place you can find a friendly dramshop: **DeLisi's**, 529-9265, 2119 W. Broadway, is located toward the west end of the neighborhood and serves up good pizza and Italian food, along with the occasional rock band or theatrical venture in the upstairs hall.

### NORTHEAST MINNEAPOLIS PUB CRAWL

This fiercely ethnic area (often called "Nordeast" by locals) is home to a high concentration of families who have lived in the area for generations, and they all seem to be proud of their cultural heritage, whether it be Polish, Slavic, Italian, Norwegian, Swedish, German or Lebanese. Just about every bar in the area has an ethnic affiliation of some sort, and most of them are very colorful places, rich in the kind of character you'll find missing in the newer, pre-fab places on the other side of town.

For Northeasters, a pub acts as a community gathering place where generations — and perhaps social classes — come together.

For this pub crawl, we'll give you some interesting taprooms that not only act as a social hub for their neighborhoods but also embrace visitors and offer a glimpse into the rich history of the area. Of all the pub crawls in this chapter, you may find this the cheapest, as prices for both drinks and food in Northeast are refreshingly low.

If you're feeling like a little exercise, this crawl is possible on foot. We'll start at a typically intimate rathskeller, **Dusty's**, 378-9831, 1319 N.E. Marshall Street. Although its Italian influences don't show through as much as they used to, Dusty's still serves a variety of cheap sandwiches and a couple of tap beers while locals sit and smoke in a jovial atmosphere. It lies in the shadow of the old Grain Belt Brewery (since closed), which kept it bustling for decades.

Although Grain Belt was the largest brewery in Northeast, it certainly wasn't the only one. A few blocks down Marshall, you'll find Gluek Park, site of the now-defunct Gluek Brewery. That's right, the same Gluek mentioned earlier as lending its name (and limited supply of beer) to a Warehouse District bar. You can't get Gluek's at the **Polish Palace**, 789-6626, 2124 N.E. Marshall Street, but it used to be the after-work stop for the brewery crew. And the tiny tavern still hops almost every night, serving Polish beers and specialty sandwiches to a youngish crowd.

**Tony Jaros' River Garden** (referred to as "Jaros's" by most locals), 789-9728, 2500 N.E. Marshall Street, bears the name of a player for the old Minneapolis Lakers, a team that took five NBA titles in the '40s and '50s (before flying off to Los Angeles). Jaros' is best known for the Greenie, a vodka-based concoction both sweet and

potent. It could be that a lot of the young crowd at the Polish Palace is merely overflow from Jaros', as some nights it's difficult to even get in the door, much less find a seat.

Go east on Lowry and you'll discover another popular community haunt. **Stasiu's**, 788-2529, 2500 University Avenue N.E., serves cheap sandwiches to a crowd often dominated by softball players and billiard aces. The tables seem to always be covered with pitchers of beer here. A block down the road is the **Chance Bar**, no phone, Lowry Avenue N.E. and N.E. Fourth Street, similar in atmosphere to Stasiu's. The reason is simple: As you approach from the west, its sign reads "Last Chance Bar"; if you're coming from the east, it says "First Chance Bar." And they're right — it's the only bar for miles if you're traveling eastward on Lowry Avenue. So, if you live east of the Chance, it's your corner bar.

Now head back south toward downtown and you'll come upon the **Sun**, 781-4405, 1528 University Avenue N.E. Don't be intimidated by the motorcycles out front: It's an amiable enough place, not rough at all. It's just that many bikers like the blues, and that's what the Sun often features on weekends.

A block or so away is a Northeast institution (although just about any of these bars could claim that title): **Mayslack's Polka Lounge**, 789-9862, 1428 N.E. Fourth Street. Although ex-professional wrestler Stan Mayslack has sold the place, it still specializes in the kind of heaping garlic-laced roast beef sandwiches that Stan himself used to build while manning a buffet line. And the kitchen stays open late.

We'll conclude this crawl at another Northeast landmark, **Nye's Polonaise Room**, 379-2021, 112 Hennepin Avenue E. Although visitors flock from all over to this multiroom "temple to the traditional," it's still a personal favorite of Northeasters. The attraction here is the piano bar, which draws singers (and those who attempt it) for the warm encouragement they get from the pianists. It's the Twin Cities' best stop if you're interested in a full-bar sing-along. And one of the neighboring rooms often hosts a polka band for your dancing pleasure.

## St. Paul

### DOWNTOWN ST. PAUL PUB CRAWL

If you're looking for a vibrant hotbed of activity, where crowds mingle in the streets after dark, traversing from one rowdy bar to the next, each bursting with noise and music, then downtown St. Paul is definitely not the place to go.

But bustle isn't everything. If what you want is a nice quiet place to walk around and visit interesting bars and restaurants, downtown St. Paul is a perfectly pleasant place to hang out.

Locals in the know will tell you that downtown St. Paul is actually more like two downtowns, each centered around a tree-filled urban park. On the west end of downtown, near Rice Park, is an area of beautiful restored buildings and new ones with old-fashioned elegance. On the east end is Lower-

town, an area dominated by residential buildings and artists' lofts. The center of this neighborhood is Mears Park.

We'll start off by hitting a few pubs near Rice Park, considered the crown jewel of downtown St. Paul. Each of the four sides of Rice Park is graced with a lovely piece of architecture. The major attraction here is the newest, the lovely Ordway Music Theatre, which hosts concerts by the Saint Paul Chamber Orchestra and esteemed soloists who offer Schubert Club recitals. It's also the chief venue for the Minnesota Opera and presents an eclectic mix of ballet, modern dance, jazz and world music.

Before or after the concert or show, you'll find crowds gathering at the **St. Paul Grill**, 224-7455, 350 Market Street. Located in the St. Paul Hotel, the Grill not only offers one of the best dinners downtown, but also features its most endearing bar. The rich history of the capital is displayed all over the walls, but in a classy, clubby manner that makes you feel as if F. Scott Fitzgerald and Charles Lindbergh were just faces in the colorful crowd here. This dimly lighted dark-oak bar mixes first-class drinks with a healthy wine list and an ample collection of single-malt scotches and small-batch bourbons. There's also an economical and excellent bar menu. It's one of the only places in downtown St. Paul where you really feel like you've walked into history.

After stopping to step into Rice Park and admire the beauty of Landmark Center and the St. Paul Public Library, you're ready to move on.

Photo: Mark Morson, Pioneer Press

*St. Paul Grill in the St. Paul Hotel.*

The **Bad Habit Cafe**, 224-8545, 418 St. Peter Street, is a nearby coffeehouse with an amiable atmosphere and music of the folk and jazz idioms a few nights a week. One of downtown St. Paul's oldest bars is **Gallivan's**, 227-6688, 354 N. Wabasha Street. Although, like the St. Paul Grill, it's dominated by a restaurant that specializes in traditional fare such as steaks and seafood, Gallivan's differs from its art deco compatriot by exuding the ambiance of an elegant old library. It's the principal post-work hangout for those employed in the judicial or bureaucratic professions, a place where deals are struck and differences set aside. But, on St. Patrick's Day, all of this grace and dignity takes a holiday, as Gallivan's becomes the raucous postparade hangout for St. Paul's large Irish-American population. Then, it's more like a beer hall with a bacchanalian electricity in the air.

An apt transition between the old establishments and the modern joints might be **Shannon Kelly's**, 292-0905, 395 N. Wabasha Street, a woody dramshop with an intimate air. It looks and feels incongruous amidst the rows of concrete and brushed-steel shops on Wabasha Street, presenting a relaxed retreat from its commercial surroundings.

Speaking of commercial, much of this section of Wabasha is dominated by two monumental paeans to shopping, Dayton's department store and the World Trade Center. The latter houses a couple of prefab watering holes, the most popular being the **Heartthrob Cafe**, 224-2783, 30 E. Eighth Street. The theme is an early-'60s malt shop, with tunes of the times pouring from the stereo speakers. But it's probably downtown's most popular bar and is sometimes the only place you can find a good-sized crowd on weeknights.

Now, let's head to Lowertown. As mentioned earlier, this neighborhood is more residential than commercial, but it's also a smaller variation on Minneapolis' Warehouse District, filled with lofts, galleries, artists' housing and, of course, actual warehouses. The area's primary bow to the retail sector is Galtier Plaza, a combination highrise/shopping mall that features a few decent restaurants and some pleasant pubs, as well. Among them is **Rudolph's Tapas Bar**, 222-2226, 366 Jackson Street, which sits at street level beneath Rudolph's Barbeque, the Twin Cities' most popular rib chain. The bar here is one of the only parts of Galtier that feels older than the '80s building that houses it. And for good reason: It's part of the old McColl Building, the only structure on the block that didn't meet the wrecking ball in preparation for the construction of Galtier Plaza.

Over on the eastern side of the building, you'll find three levels of pubs overlooking Mears Park. On street level is **O.J.'s**, 225-8105, 175 E. Fifth Street, a friendly sports bar with dark windows, a late-night menu and a balcony that looks out upon the park. Upstairs is **Amelia's**, 291-1590, which really bustles on weekends, especially when the music is provided by some of the top-notch Latin jazz bands from points west. Otherwise, it's still downtown's best place for dancing to live music and mingling with a diverse clientele. On the third floor is **Plaza Billiards**, 291-1779, which might answer a commonly asked question from first-time visitors to downtown St. Paul: "Where is everybody?" Well, they're chalking up their cues at the Plaza tables.

Sharing the third floor is **Scott Hansen's Comedy Gallery St. Paul**, 331-5653, which offers standup comedy by national and local acts.

As you move northward toward the State Capitol area, the nightlife becomes fairly sparse, but there are a couple of haunts here. **The Gopher Bar**, 291-9638, 241 E. Seventh Street, has thrown off its ancient image as a bowery dive and become a favorite stop for Lowertown residents and after-work downtowners. The specialty of the house is the Coney Island, arguably the Twin Cities' best.

Toward the confluence of freeways known to locals as Spaghetti Junction, you'll find a couple of places. **Rumours**, 224-0703, 490 N. Robert Street, is one of St. Paul's most popular gay bars, although it doesn't pack them in as it once did. **Woolley's**, 224-5111, 175 E. 10th Street, is a chain bar, albeit a pleasant one, in the Crown Sterling Suites hotel.

### SUMMIT HILL-GRAND AVENUE PUB CRAWL

Lest you think St. Paul is a lifeless backwater burg where they roll up the sidewalks after dark, be advised there are some parts of town where nightlife is the chief attraction.

Perhaps one of the reasons that downtown doesn't seem to catch on as a social center is the proximity of Summit Hill and Grand Avenue, where the bars are always hopping on weekends and often on other nights, as well.

Here's a pub crawl that can be done in one night or two. It will take you in an uncomplicated "Z" pattern down the main streets of the two neighborhoods, Summit Hill and Grand Avenue. We'll start off on the eastern end, near the lovely, green-domed Cathedral of St. Paul. This neighborhood is often referred to as Cathedral Hill, and our first stop is at its most popular restaurant and bar, **W.A. Frost**, 224-5715, 374 Selby Avenue. This historic brick building houses not only an elegant restaurant but the nicest bar in the neighborhood. Like the St. Paul Grill, this is old St. Paul, with a subdued, high-class feel that seems to cry out for cognac in large snifters. But the chief attraction at Frost is the large, tiered outdoor patio, where Chinese lanterns burn into the night and tree boughs loom above you. This is the Summit Hill that inspired F. Scott Fitzgerald, a neighborhood of great mansions and a little smart-set stuffiness.

Speaking of literary figures, a few doors down is **Fabulous Fern's**, 225-9414, 400 Selby Avenue, which, under previous management, used to be a daily stop for playwright August Wilson, winner of the Pulitzer Prize for his gripping dramas, *Fences* and *The Piano Lesson*. Wilson used to live upstairs in the Blair Arcade building, but he was well-known for doing much of his writing in St. Paul bars, sometimes catalyzed by the conversations at neighboring tables. Wilson has since left the Twin Cities, but his spirit lives on in this friendly establishment.

A few blocks up is another pleasant pub in a historic old building: **Chang O'Hara's**, 290-2338, 498

Selby Avenue. What was once an old fire station is now a bar with three distinctly different sections: a window-lined bar with elevated booths, a white-linen restaurant that sometimes hosts jazz bands, and a multilevel outdoor deck that offers a cozier variation on the garden at W.A. Frost.

Travel west on Selby Avenue, then turn left at Dale and you'll come upon the neighborhood's most pleasant pub, **Cognac McCarthy's**, 224-4617, 162 N. Dale Street. It's a homey little place with scratched-up wood booths and a small dining room where they serve consistently fine home-style meals such as pot roast and turkey with all the trimmings. It's easily the friendliest bar in the neighborhood, and its regulars come from near and far.

A couple of blocks farther down Dale is **Sweeney's**, 221-9157, 96 N. Dale Street, which shares some of the same ownership as Chang O'Hara's and Cognac McCarthy's but is clearly the flagship of the fleet. It seems that Sweeney's has been bustling every night since it opened in the late '70s, constantly awash in conversation and taped music. The library area is especially conducive to group discussions, and, of course, there's a patio.

You can stop now and say that you've conquered Summit Hill, but if you still crave some social interaction, you can continue on to Grand Avenue. Sometime in the '70s, Grand changed from a conventional commercial strip to a hip hangout, both for living and for socializing. It's now lined with trendy boutiques that dispense such commodities as spices and socks. Some might call it "yuppified," but it's still an amiable place to stroll on a summer night.

Take a right when you reach Grand and, on the first block, you'll see **Tavern on Grand**, 228-9030, 656 Grand Avenue. Some locals call this "the last real bar left on Grand," inferring that others lack the neighborhood watering-hole ambiance that rules at the Tavern. The decor is reminiscent of a northern Minnesota fishing lodge, and that's the kitchen's metier: the fish indigenous to Minnesota lakes, most notably the walleye pike. All of the bars on this crawl have celebrity stories, but the Tavern tops them all: Mikhail Gorbachev once dropped in for some walleye while visiting St. Paul. He reportedly pronounced it delicious.

Up the block is **Dixie's**, 222-7345, 695 Grand Avenue, which serves up a mildly seasoned menu of Southern dishes. It's an expansive place by Grand Avenue's intimate standards, but that's fine, for it's also one of the street's most popular bars. Model trains chug by above your head as you sample from the lengthy beer list or sip one of their Southern variations on the martini or Bloody Mary.

One block west stands **Lyons' Pub**, 224-1787, 788 Grand Avenue, which caters to the college crowd with pitchers of beer and tables designed for large groups. If you're over a certain age, this is the one bar on the crawl that can really make you feel it: Virtually half of the pub is given over to video games,

and the constant cacophony of crashes may be the idea of Hell's soundtrack, for some.

Downright tasteful and restrained by comparison is **Billy's**, 292-9140, 857 Grand Avenue, a meandering, multiple-room bar and restaurant that offers a few different options, depending upon your mood: The summer patio is a pleasant meeting place for a summer night; you can hedge your bets on the weather and retreat to the window-lined area just off the garden; or you can catch the constant activity in the bustling bar section.

Once you make it through the crowd, you'll be right next to **Music City Cafe**, 292-1316, 857 Grand Avenue, one of the Twin Cities' nicest little places to sit and listen to acoustic folk, blues or jazz. It's a candlelighted L-shaped tavern that might remind you of a Greenwich Village coffeehouse. The conversation is always quiet and the music is almost invariably as laid back as the atmosphere. It provides a wonderful wind-down after a lengthy crawl.

### WEST SEVENTH STREET

Every major city in America (with the possible exception of Salt Lake City) has a main drag or two lined with working-class bars that specialize in mainstream tap beers and an occasional shot of the hard stuff. As a city with large parcels of land devoted exclusively to industry, St. Paul is, of course, no exception. And the city's longest street is the one that provides a bumper crop of these alehouses: West Seventh Street (also known as Fort Road).

For the sake of convenience and

stamina, we won't view this as a pub crawl (the street is several miles long). Instead, we'll just tell you about some of the typical watering holes on the avenue and let you choose one that fits your style. Starting at the St. Paul Civic Center, which acts as the gateway to (or exit from) downtown St. Paul, you can head down a block and come upon **Patrick McGovern's**, 224-5821, 225 W. Seventh Street. This is one of the nicest pubs on West Seventh, with a relaxed atmosphere inspired by old wood booths and a long bar with an old-fashioned brass rail. It's a popular after-work stop for those with offices toward the west end of downtown, and it serves as the corner bar for those who live in the Irvine Park area, one of St. Paul's oldest neighborhoods.

An interesting stop on this stretch is the **Babylon Cafe**, 225-9885, 267 W. Seventh Street, a combination wine bar and art gallery that features music (mostly folk and jazz) almost every night. It's a favored hangout for some of the artists who live and work in downtown lofts.

Perhaps the most popular establishment on all of West Seventh is **Mancini's**, 224-7345, 531 W. Seventh Street, one of the Twin Cities' favorite steak houses and a hotbed of local color. The current mayor was wise to headquarter all of his campaign parties here, for it has the kind of "all things to all people" reputation that politicians desire. The bar area plays host to a crowd of many ages and social classes, and they all get up to polka when the band strikes up. But beware of bad Elvis impersonators.

**Flanagan's**, 224-2452, 1026 W. Seventh Street, is a former Knights of Columbus hall that's been converted to an expansive multiroom bar and restaurant. It periodically plays host to prominent Irish acts such as the Wolfe Tones and Tommy Makem, and it's a perfectly fine concert hall, though not very rich in character or decor.

Farther down West Seventh, you'll find **Champps**, 698-5050, 2431 W. Seventh Street, the original sports bar that inspired the popular Twin Cities chain. It's a wide-open place, with TVs galore and some of the best burgers in the Twin Cities. Nearby is a popular supper club, the **Manor**, 690-1771, 2550 W. Seventh Street, with both a piano bar and a lounge that hosts an old-fashioned show band every weekend.

## HIGHLAND PARK AND MACALESTER-GROVELAND

Looking to take a pub crawl through these two nicely appointed St. Paul residential neighborhoods? Good luck. Believe it or not, ancient city liquor laws have made it darn near impossible to open an alehouse in these large and densely populated neighborhoods. The word we've heard (and we're not making this up) is that the dramshop laws are based upon the police department's complaint that their horses couldn't make it all the way from downtown to Highland Park in order to deal with disturbances in bars. That's right, it's a holdover from the 19th century.

Hence, one of St. Paul's largest geographical areas, Highland Park, only has three (count 'em, three) bars. **The Tiffany Bar**, 690-4747, 2051 Ford Parkway, is a slightly cleaner version of the corner shot-and-beer joint, with tiffany lamps above the tables and plenty of pool tables. It's long been a popular hangout with students from the College of St. Catherine and the University of St. Thomas, but business has become more scarce from such quarters since the drinking age was raised to 21.

The other two Highland Park bars are located virtually next door to one another. **Plums**, 699-2227, 480 S. Snelling Avenue, used to fancy itself a yuppie fern bar with a lively singles scene until it was decided that it was better for business to be all-embracing than exclusive. So, it's now more like an even-nicer version of the neighborhood beer joint. A few doors down is **Goby's Grille & Pub**, 690-5731, 472 S. Snelling Avenue, a dimly lighted but airy bar that's built for talk, not a party atmosphere.

The Macalester-Groveland area is indeed St. Paul's most densely populated neighborhood, but it has the distinction of having virtually no bars in the area. If locals feel like having a drink, the stop of choice is generally **O'Gara's Bar & Grill**, 644-3333, 164 N. Snelling Avenue, an old family-owned establishment that's been around for many a generation. Over the past 15 years, O'Gara's has grown from a small corner pub with wholesome home-style cooking into a popular hangout that has expanded into almost all of the stores next door. There are five distinct sections to O'Gara's:

the humble old restaurant; the intimate old bar; a newer central bar area; the Shamrock Room, which features jazz and a piano bar on most nights; and the Garage, a large room where local rock bands hold forth on weekends.

### UNIVERSITY AVENUE, MIDWAY AND FROGTOWN

The closest thing you can find in the Twin Cities to a main street that runs all the way through the metropolitan area is University Avenue. It begins at the northwest end of Northeast Minneapolis and ends just east of the State Capitol in St. Paul. The nature of the street takes on different styles as you continue down it. It's residential in Nordeast, lined with houses and corner pubs before hitting one of its many industrial sections, then giving way to the University of Minnesota campus and the towering trees of Prospect Park. But, in St. Paul, it's almost unrelentingly industrial and commercial, dominated by small businesses in the service and retail sectors.

The bars of University Avenue are primarily working-class joints frequented by blue-collar workers after a hard day at the plant. But there are exceptions. Traveling eastward from the St. Paul-Minneapolis border, we'll try to fill you in on some of the highlights. The first bar you'll hit is the **Cromwell**, 646-1243, 2511 W. University Avenue, a shot-and-beer joint disguised as a supper club serving steaks and seafood. The atmosphere is usually rowdy on a weekend, exacerbated by the occasional country band. The

Cromwell is located in one of St. Paul's most intensely industrial areas, near the intersection of University Avenue and Highway 280, but much of its clientele seems to come from elsewhere.

The city of St. Paul has done an admirable job of converting many of the empty warehouses in the area into studio and office space for artists. Writers, painters, sculptors, dancers, filmmakers — the intersection of University and Raymond Avenue is teeming with them. Where do they go to wind down after a creative endeavor? None other than **Johnny's Bar**, 645-4116, 2251 W. University Avenue. And they aren't the only ones. Johnny's is a favorite of beer-lovers from throughout the Twin Cities area. The bland interior is nothing to look at, but the ever-changing tap-beer menu on the wall certainly is. There are always a few obscure ales or pilsners from Europe on draught, but the specialty of the house is whatever the neighboring microbrewery, Summit, is currently trying out.

One of St. Paul's classic shot-and-beer joints is just down the street: the **Ace Box Bar**, 646-5551, 2162 W. University Avenue. Named for its cube-shaped building and intimate feeling, the Ace is a friendly place favored by workers at the neighboring Waldorf paper mill and other nearby businesses.

The intersection of University and Prior has a couple of bars, each located at the edge of a motel. **The Irish Well**, 645-7162, 1975 W. University Avenue, is the more popular of the two, and it is, indeed, a pleasant place to visit, especially if

you enjoy traditional Irish music and pints of Guinness Stout and black-and-tans. The sound and sightlines are good, and the jiggers are often up for the fast numbers.

Across the street, **Tracks**, 645-8681, 1964 W. University Avenue, is an intimate sports bar that bustles on game nights.

University and Snelling is the Twin Cities' busiest intersection, and most of the bars here are of the no-frills, working-class variety. **The Turf Club**, 647-0486, 1601 W. University Avenue, has the most character of the bunch, as it specializes in country music and lively two-stepping. Nearby is a pleasant, albeit rather bland, chain bar, **Applebee's**, 642-9757, Spruce Tree Centre, West University and North Snelling avenues.

One of the Twin Cities' oldest gay bars, the **Town House**, 646-7087, 1415 W. University Avenue, is along this stretch, but, in the tradition of old gay bars, it's unmarked. Just look for a gray freestanding building west of Hamline Avenue on the north side of the street. The clientele is a mix of younger folks and others who have been regulars for decades. A couple of blocks away is **Arnellia's**, 642-5975, 1183 W. University Avenue, a nightclub that offers a live mix of jazz and old-fashioned R&B under swirling lights.

Before we leave the Midway area, we'd be remiss not to mention some of the other appealing nightspots of the area. **Ginkgo**, 645-2647, 721 N. Snelling Avenue, is a coffeehouse that offers concerts once a week by local and national folk acts.

In a neglected shopping center called Bandana Square stands the Twin Cities' top stop for jazz, the **Dakota Bar & Grill**, 642-1442, 1021 E. Bandana Boulevard. Not only is this clean, classy club a first-rate restaurant (one of the Twin Cities' best, in the opinion of many), but it also hosts jazz combos of various sizes and styles every night. Most often it's a local group (and there are many very good ones), but it's also the prime place for concerts by such legendary luminaries as Elvin Jones and Max Roach, as well as "young lions" such as Marcus Roberts and Terrence Blanchard. It's sometimes traditional, sometimes contemporary, but always worth a listen.

A couple of blocks east is **Gabe's by the Park**, 646-3066, 991 N. Lexington Parkway, which would be a fairly typical sports bar were it not for its position as official pre- and post-game hangout for fans of the St. Paul Saints, an independent minor league baseball team that packs them in for every game. Although the outdoor deck sits beside busy Lexington Parkway, it's a pleasant place to spend a summer evening.

Continue east and you'll come upon the **Half Time Rec**, 488-8245, 1013 Front Avenue, the Twin Cities' most popular pub for listening (and perhaps dancing) to traditional Irish music. Most of the bands are local (although usually born and bred across the pond), and it's a marvelous place to acquaint yourself with St. Paul's rich Irish music scene. Half of the Half Time seems like a concert hall in miniature, while the other half is more like a typical shot-and-beer joint. But not many bars can boast of having bocce ball in the basement.

About a mile southeast, you'll find yourself in the middle of Frogtown, a working-class St. Paul neighborhood that's run into some problems with crime in recent years, but nonetheless has some worthwhile places to visit. The most famous is the **Blues Saloon**, 228-9959, 601 N. Western Avenue, the Twin Cities' premier venue for the blues. Music is offered every Thursday through Monday, usually with a nominal cover charge. More often than not, Friday and Saturday nights are given over to respected blues artists from around the country, and the club seems to have a pipeline for players from the rich Chicago scene that never seems to run dry.

Frogtown is the unlikely home of St. Paul's most popular gay and lesbian bar, **Club Metro**, 489-0002, 733 Pierce Butler Route. Actually, it sits off by itself on an expressway alongside the Burlington Northern railyards. Club Metro is packed on many nights and is known for being a lively, sprawling place that offers a warm reception to new faces. The club is also host to Unicorn Theater Company, which specializes in plays about gay issues.

### THE EAST SIDE OF ST. PAUL

St. Paul's East Side is, geographically, the city's largest neighborhood (although longtime residents might argue that it comprises several neighborhoods). Roots run deep in this working-class community. Many families have lived here for generations — since their European-immigrant ancestors first settled these streets. Italian names stand out most prominently on local business signs. But many new faces have moved into the area within the past decade, as well.

The bars of the East Side reflect the area's blue-collar population. The majority of the bars along the area's main drags — Payne Avenue, East Seventh Street, Arcade Street and White Bear Avenue — are the kind of shot-and-a-beer joints we've detailed above: pressed wood paneling, lots of beer lights and billiard tables. The ones we list here have exceptional characteristics that make them among the most popular haunts of Eastsiders, many of whom also enjoy the nightlife in the neighboring suburb of Maplewood. Due to the enormity of the East Side, this pub crawl is only possible by car.

**Peppercorns**, 776-2314, 1178 Arcade Street, is a hard-rock bar that provides young and 30ish Eastsiders with their music of choice.

It's a clean, neon-infused pub with decor reminiscent of a '50s malt shop, but it has everything an Eastside bar needs (pool tables, dart boards, all of the usual suspects on tap).

Off Highway 36, you'll find a paean to kitsch that's remained popular for decades. **Bali Hai**, 777-5500, 2305 White Bear Avenue, Maplewood, is a Polynesian restaurant that presents not only the cuisine of the South Pacific islands but the traditional music, dancing and drama, as well. Depending upon your tastes, it's either wildly entertaining or just plain too much. But the umbrella-adorned tropical drinks are potent and tasty, and the dimly lighted bar has an infectious party atmosphere.

Maplewood Mall is the area's temple to shopping, and it's surrounded by many national-chain bars that look as if they've been manufactured elsewhere for assembly on the suburban plains. But there are a couple of interesting bars nearby that have been serving Eastsiders and suburbanites for a number of years. **T-Bird's**, 779-2265, Maplewood Square, White Bear and Woodlynn avenues, Maplewood, has the open, tiered look of a sports bar, but it's really an old-fashioned watering hole that offers dancing most nights.

Nearby is the **Red Rooster**, 770-7822, 2029 Woodlynn Avenue, Maplewood. From the outside, it looks like a little motel bar, but the interior is reminiscent of a country roadhouse, with rustic walls and an arched, beamed ceiling. You can always tell a place that draws regulars from the bartender's familiar manner with the customers and signs that list the birthdays of patrons. There's karaoke, darts and a genuine small-town feel in the place.

Our final stop is a bit distant from the rest. Off Century Avenue near I-94 stands **Blackie's**, 738-3333, 271 N. Geneva Avenue, Oakdale, a barbecue restaurant with a popular bar area. Another place with Old World decor, Blackie's is a brick-lined hangout for those in their 20s who like to dance to pop and funk heavy on the backbeat (the place positively throbs sometimes). But those uninterested in the music can retire to the deck overlooking Tanner's Lake and sip one in relative quiet.

## The Suburbs

### BLOOMINGTON PUB CRAWL

Bloomington is a prototypical American suburb. You know, the kind that started out as a provincial little extension of its neighboring metropolitan area and eventually turned into one of the largest communities in the state. Population-wise, Bloomington is now the third-largest city in Minnesota behind Minneapolis and St. Paul.

But, as far as nightlife goes, Bloomington has undergone some major changes in recent years. When Metropolitan Stadium was home to the Twins and Vikings, and the neighboring Met Center hosted North Stars hockey games and most of the national concert tours that came to town, Bloomington had an energetic after-dark atmosphere.

But then the Twins and Vikings set up shop at the Metrodome in downtown Minneapolis in 1982, the North Stars left town in 1993, and the face of Bloomington changed: It ceased to be a fashionable place to party.

Along came the Mall of America, the temple to American consumerism that has put Bloomington back on the national map. Transcending all that came before it in the way of retail clusters, the "megamall" not only houses department stores and boutiques by the hundreds, but bars and restaurants as well. And you'll find these pubs hopping almost any night of the week.

However, the Mall's effect upon the legendary I-494 strip has evidently not been particularly favorable. Popular old haunts have closed, and most of the clubs left standing are part of national chains. Unfortunately, these places aren't usually rich in character. Like your average fast-food restaurant, they seem to have come out of the same factory, ready for assembly in any American suburb. **Bennigan's**, 881-0013, 1800 W. 80th Street, is a classic example of this style, although it's still one of the more popular pubs among what's left of the Bloomington singles scene.

A local minichain that packs them in most nights is **Joe Sens-er's**, 835-1191, 4217 W. 80th Street. Bearing the name of a former Vikings tight end and broadcaster, the bars are of the classic sports-bar variety, expansive and multileveled, with TVs galore. On the same stretch, there's a more intriguing stop, the Australian-themed **Billabong**, 844-0655, 5001 W. 80th Street. Yes, it's just a gimmick, and neither the food nor drink is particularly Aussie, unless you count Foster's on tap. But the tropical decor is pleasant, as is the waitstaff, and the food is consistently good, for pub grub.

As nightlife goes, much of the fun is found at **Steak and Ale**, 884-0124, 2801 Southtown Drive. Granted, the restaurant section is standard franchise, but the nightclub area hops on weekends to the sounds of tight, professional R&B bands.

Well, now it's off to the Mall of America, and we'll warn you in advance: You're either going to love it or hate it.

If you think suburban shopping malls are either a lot of fun or, at worst, unobjectionable, then you'll have no problem with the mother of all malls. In fact, you'll be in shopping nirvana. But, if there's something about excessive commercialism and large, enclosed courtyards that make you feel a little queasy, do yourself a favor and stay away.

That said, there are some bars in the Mall that are among the Twin Cities' best for their type. For example, **Gatlin Brothers Music City Grille**, 858-8000, is the Twin Cities' No. 1 club for booking national country acts that aren't quite big enough to fill an arena — people such as Carlene Carter and John Michael Montgomery before his explosion of popularity. Most nights, it's a pretty hopping club for the country set, with all of the requisite hats, boots and line dancing.

If comedy is your favorite form of entertainment, **Knuckleheads**, 854-5233, is one of the nicer laugh emporiums in the Twin Cities area. Unlike some places that stack the audience a tad too tightly, Knuckleheads is comfortable and intimate. Its headliners are always national acts, usually visiting from New York, Chicago or Los Angeles.

The Mall's version of a college bar, **Gator's**, 858-8888, attempts to recreate the atmosphere of a frat party — that is, if you attended keggers beside a tropical swamp.

A few doors down, you'll find a cluster of bars. The biggest is **America's Original Sports Bar**, 854-5483. Remember what we said about the layout of your average sports bar? Multiply its acreage by 10 and you'll have this stadium-sized shrine to all things athletic. Despite its roominess, the place is inevitably crowded and, unfortunately at times, its inebriated clientele lacks "Minnesota nice" social manners.

To escape this unruly mob scene, slip through the door of **Lil' Ditty's**, 854-5483, a quiet piano bar with dueling ivory-ticklers and jovial sing-alongs. Another laid-back oasis is **Players**, 858-5505, the Mall's fairly good imitation of a friendly corner bar. It certainly offers a more pleasant atmosphere than **Hooters**, 854-3110, a national chain that's fine if you don't mind mediocre food and a sexist atmosphere. Minnesota nice, it ain't.

### LAKE MINNETONKA PUB CRAWL

Most of the suburbs that surround Minneapolis and St. Paul have more similarities than differences. Some are more commercial; others more distinctly rural; some downright small-townish. But the many small suburbs that surround Lake Minnetonka, west of Minneapolis, have a culture quite different from anything else in the Twin Cities area.

Perhaps the best environment to use for comparison would be the blue-blooded leisure ports of Newport, Rhode Island, or Cape Cod. But, while those bastions of boating and old-money families are set against the majestic Atlantic, these communities are wrapped around the labyrinthine bays and satellite lakes of the Minnetonka chain. These small suburban areas (Navarre, Greenwood, Tonka Bay) are set away on islands, peninsulas and isthmuses, sheltered by forests and often easier to reach by boat than car.

Two things that you should know before undertaking a Minnetonka pub crawl. One, there's a maritime feel to just about everything. Boating is a central activity for people of all ages, and many of the bars and restaurants are accessible by boat, with slips available out back. And two, it shares with the aforementioned Newport a clear stratification of economic classes. This makes for a not-necessarily-friendly atmosphere at some places (at least by Minnesota standards), but there's still plenty of character to be found at the local watering holes.

If you're traveling westward on Highway 7 toward the Lake Minnetonka area, keep your eyes open for a joint called the **Will Hop Inn**, 938-9892, 14824 Highway 7, Minnetonka. Typical of old Minnetonka before the post-war suburban sprawl struck, the Will Hop Inn is like a big, friendly fishing shack.

One of the more popular places in Minnetonka is **T. Wright's**, 475-2215, 3310 S. Highway 101, Wayzata, which looks like an airplane hangar from the outside but is more like a suburban supper club on the inside, filled with curved-back wooden captain's chairs (naturally) and red leather booths. On weekends, it has the reputation of being a meat market for those interested in mingling with strangers.

One of the most monied of Twin Cities suburbs is Wayzata, and it features a main drag that runs alongside the shore of a large open section of Lake Minnetonka. Along this stretch, you'll find **Sunsets**, 473-5253, 700 E. Lake Street, Wayzata, a window-lined pub that seems to be crowded every night. It has a touch of class that some of the other bars on this crawl lack, but it's also more casual than many (Docksiders and polo shirts allowed).

**The Minnetonka Mist**, 471-8471, 4050 Shoreline Drive, Spring Park, is an artificially weather-beaten building constructed in the style of a New England Colonial home. The Mist is permeated with the maritime motif that dominates the bars of the area, and the upstairs deck overlooks a public boat landing where there is a fairly constant stream of activity.

Although **Al and Alma's**, 472-

3098, 5201 Piper Road, Mound, is best-known as a popular family restaurant and bar, the old establishment also owns a fleet of yachts with well-stocked bars. Some of their onboard bacchanals are the stuff of legend.

The centerpiece of the Lake Minnetonka social circle is **Lord Fletcher's on the Lake**, 471-8513, 3746 Sunset Drive, Spring Park, a virtual Disneyland of a bar/restaurant complex, set on what was once the edge of a swamp. But the founders discovered paydirt by dredging up a canal, installing some slips for passing boats and building a sprawling wooden deck referred to as "the wharf." Inside are three other bars and a couple of restaurants. Lord Fletcher's offers a somewhat incongruous combination of decor, blending nautical New England with the mutton-and-ale ambiance of Old England. And, outside, the volleyball sandpits stretch on for acres and are crowded throughout the summer.

If all of the suburbs leave you longing for something a bit more urban than urbane, the closest thing you'll find is the town of Excelsior. There once was a popular amusement park in Excelsior, and you may be happy to see some architecture here that's actually pre-World War II. The most popular bar in town is **Haskell's Port of Excelsior**, 474-0935, 1 Water Street, Excelsior, a small pub that's almost bursting out its few windows with youngish drinkers every night. The socializing is loud and raucous, but don't expect mingling if you're not from the area.

The overflow crowd heads to **Park Tavern Excelsior**, 474-1113, 685 Excelsior Boulevard, Excelsior, part of a small local chain, where things are considerably quieter. The tavern's bay windows and sprawling deck look out upon, appropriately enough, a bay. There's a dock with abundant slips for the boating crowd, and Park Tavern tries to grab some of the Lord Fletcher's overflow as well by offering volleyball on the beach.

A little restaurant and bar with a German flavor, **The Copper Stein**, 474-5805, 5635 Manitou Road, Excelsior, sits just outside of town, and it's a nice place to stop for a brew. On the wall inside the door is a large portrait of Excelsior Jimmy, a legendary local eccentric. Just a little celebrity story here: In the early years of their career, the Rolling Stones performed at the Excelsior Amusement Park. During their stay, Mick Jagger had a prescription filled at a town pharmacy, where he was said to have fallen into conversation with the town's chief character, Excelsior Jimmy. There are those who claim that this exchange provided the inspiration for a story in the Stones song, "You Can't Always Get What You Want," and that the name was changed from "Excelsior" to "Chelsea" for rhythmic purposes.

A little farther from the lake area (but still within the Minnetonka border) is **Sherlock's Home**, 931-0203, 11000 Red Circle Drive, Minnetonka, which was the Twin Cities area's first brew pub, meaning that most of its beer is created on premises from original recipes. It's a homey place that's designed to look considerably older than its years, with the decor feigning that of an Old English pub. Across the way is **Toros of Aspen**, 938-9100, 6001 Shady Oak Road, Minnetonka, a restaurant-bar known for its singles scene. It feels more like one of the pre-fab chain bars on the 494 Strip than it does like a Minnetonka bar (read: no maritime motif).

### STILLWATER PUB CRAWL

Out on the eastern edge of the Twin Cities area is the quaint little town of Stillwater, which refers to itself as The Birthplace of Minnesota. The devoted preservation of its historic feel is one of the charms of this little St. Croix River Valley village.

Stillwater is close enough to St. Paul that workers in the capital city often commute. There are few more pleasant places east of the Mississippi River that can still be considered part of the Twin Cities metropolitan area, and few better for a pub crawl.

All of the bars near the Main Street area of Stillwater have some historic ties. We'll begin our journey at **Cat Ballou's**, 439-4567, 112 N. Main Street, which affects the decor of a 19th-century bordello, complete with gawdy, bawdy life-size paintings and ornate etchings on the windows. But it's just a brightly lighted fern bar without the ferns. However, there's music on weekends (mostly blues and alternative rock), and there's a separate entrance for the upstairs pool hall. A block down, you'll find a much more appealing (and lively) watering hole, **The Mad Capper**, 430-3710, 224 S.

Main Street. Beer is the specialty of the house here, with a list of 20-odd imports and a tap-beer selection that includes the wares of obscure micro-breweries and such delights as the Czech beer Pilsner Urquell. The interior is adorned in a hodgepodge of stuffed armadillos, antique clocks, beer signs and Grandma Moses-style sports paintings, if you can imagine that.

**Brine's**, 439-7556, 219 S. Main Street, is a trilevel bar and restaurant with three distinctly different atmospheres. The main floor is given over to the brick-lined bar, which offers a copious selection of tap beers and the same etched-mirrors decor that you'll find in most Stillwater bars. The second floor is the restaurant section, bathed in old-fashioned malt shop ornamentation, while the third floor has the best view of any pool hall in the Twin Cities area, looking out upon the lovely St. Croix River. A few doors down is **Trumps**, 439-0024, 317 S. Main Street, occupying the top floor of a small mall loaded with boutiques and the kind of specialty stores that line the streets of Stillwater. The view of the river out the back windows is the main attraction here, although there's something to be said for the clean, woody, well-lighted interior and the erratic but intriguing music schedule (blues and reggae seem to be the genres of choice). About a half-block off Main Street, you'll see a music store called Water Music. When you get there, look down and you'll find a subterranean haunt called the **Blue Guitar**, 430-1211, 116 E. Chestnut Street. It's a cozy little coffeehouse reminiscent of a Greenwich Village cafe (sans the smoke), and Friday and Saturday nights are given over to performances by local and national folk acts (with the occasional rocker tossed in for good measure).

Now let's go down to the riverfront. Stillwater's social centerpiece is the **Freighthouse**, 439-5718, 305 S. Water Street, an 1883 railroad warehouse that's listed on the National Register of Historic Places (although much of the town could qualify for the honor). There are restaurant and bar sections both inside and out at the Freighthouse (depending on what time of year you visit). The gazebo bar is pleasant on a summer evening, but the area that really hops is the nightclub, a big split-level room with a large dance floor. Continue north along the river's edge and you'll find **P.D. Pappy's**, 430-1147, 422 E. Mulberry Street. Upon arrival, it shouldn't take you long to figure out that this was once the social center of the Stillwater Yacht Club. It's an open, airy place with a sparse maritime decor and a big deck outside that overlooks the crowded slips of local boaters. It's clearly the favored dramshop of those who cruise the river, but it also draws urbanites who like the full and varied music schedule. And, if all of this hanging out by the river makes you feel too much like a landlubber, give the folks at **Andiamo Showboat** a call at 430-1236. They operate a nightclub on wheels — paddlewheels, that is — on Saturdays from spring to fall, hosting parties that cruise up and down the St. Croix with local bands on deck.

## OTHER SUBURBS

Every local suburb has its own little subculture, and the bars in each run the gamut from friendly corner pubs to glitzy national chains.

The fastest-growing section of the Twin Cities metropolitan area is Dakota County, but (although housing starts have skyrocketed in recent years) the development of nightlife hasn't kept pace. Most of the bars in Dakota County are either roadhouse holdovers from its days as a farm district (some pretty colorful) or franchise places in search of a mall. Among the more interesting places in the area are the **Chart House**, 435-7156, 11287 Klamath Trail, Lakeville; **Russ' Pub**, 890-5710, 3080 W. Highway 13, Burnsville; and **J. Doolittle's**, 452-6627, 2140 Cliff Road, Eagan.

There's also a St. Paul export, the **Cherokee Sirloin Room**, 454-6744, 4625 Nicols Road, Eagan, which, in addition to great steaks, offers music and dancing on weekends. A little closer to St. Paul, within the usually sleepy old town of Mendota, you'll find the **Ragin' Cajun**, 452-9191, 1351 Sibley Memorial Highway, Mendota, offering blues and boogie a few nights a week. Across the road is the **Mendota Saloon**, 452-9582, 1352 Sibley Memorial Highway, serving up country and old-fashioned rock 'n' roll in a roadhouse atmosphere.

Speaking of roadhouses, you'll find a number of cavernous honky-tonks along Highway 61 south of St. Paul as it runs parallel to the Mississippi River. Highway 61 is good for that kind of thing, no matter what part of the Twin Cities area you're in. There are some nice bars in the town of White Bear Lake, located along 61 north of St. Paul, and a string of working-class places — with cold beer and dancing — stretching down south to the river town of Hastings.

A center of nightlife in the near-north suburb of Arden Hills is **McGuire's Manhattan Grille**, 636-412, Ramada Hotel and Conference Center, 1201 W. County Road E. It features music a few nights a week (pop and R&B, mostly) and has several rooms full of activity.

One of the prime gathering places in Blaine is the **Blainbrook Entertainment Center**, 755-8686, 12000 Central Avenue N.E., offering music on weekends in a room as sprawling as the suburb that houses it.

The Mounds View area has a few interesting places. **The Mermaid**, 784-7350, 2200 E. Highway 10, has been through several incarnations but has always seemed to find its greatest success with hard-rock fans who like the smoky, rough-hewn atmosphere.

But most of the nightlife in the northern suburbs can be found at such chains as the **Bombay Bicycle Club**, 786-0380, 199 Northtown Drive N.E., Blaine, and **Tequilaberry's**, 780-1850, 133 N.W. Coon Rapids Boulevard, Coon Rapids. They pack 'em in even though the ambiance is a bit contrived and sterile.

So, let's finish up with the western suburbs. Yes, you can find the same kind of chain bars mentioned above (add **T.G.I. Friday's** and **Chili's**, as well as the **Champps** local sports bar chain), but there are also some friendly places with good music by local bands.

**Dover**, 542-1060, 5555 Wayzata Boulevard, St. Louis Park, located inside the Sheraton Park Place Hotel, is a classy bar. Out in Crystal is the **Iron Horse**, 533-2503, Hennepin County 81 and Bass Lake Road, one of the Twin Cities' old standbys for heavy metal and hard rock by local and national acts.

**Ivories**, 591-6188, 605 Highway 169, Plymouth, is one of the classiest piano bars in the Twin Cities, featuring talented Jimmy Martin tickling the keys. It's located on the northwest corner of the intersection of highways 55 and 169. If you're traveling farther west on Highway 55, there are a couple of stops worth making. **J.P. Mulligan's**, 559-1595, 3005 N. Harbor Lane, Plymouth, is a friendly bar and restaurant that occasionally offers music. **The Country House**, 546-4655, 10715 South Shore Drive, Medicine Lake, is tucked away alongside Medicine Lake and prides itself on being an old-fashioned roadhouse with a country clientele in the midst of the ever-developing western suburbs.

Speaking of country, the Twin Cities' foremost venue for national country acts (as well as the best of the local lot) has long been the **Medina Entertainment Center**, 478-6661, 500 Highway 55, Medina, a honkytonk of the first order. Whether the music is provided by Waylon Jennings or such hot down-home locals as the Killer Hayseeds, you'll find a friendly atmosphere and a large dance floor designed for two-stepping.

# Movies

From arty foreign-film houses to suburban multiscreen complexes, there's a movie theater to fit every taste and budget in the Twin Cities. Here's a look at the variety of it all. (For complete listings, check either daily newspaper, the *St. Paul Pioneer Press* or the *Star Tribune*. For capsule reviews, call the *Pioneer Press* audiotext service, The Line, at 222-1000.)

## Foreign and Art Film Houses

The **Uptown Theatre**, 825-4644, 2906 Hennepin Avenue, Minneapolis, specializes in first-run foreign and art films, plus revivals of great vintage flicks such as *Casablanca* and *Lawrence of Arabia*. Serious film buffs also flock to the **U Film Society**, 627-4430, housed in the Bell Auditorium at 17th and University avenues, Minneapolis, on the University of Minnesota campus. The society also sponsors a terrific annual film festival of new works from around the world.

The **Walker Art Center**, 375-7622, Vineland Place, Minneapolis, frequently shows new and old controversial works, sometimes pairing them with live music performances. In the summer, the Walker sponsors a popular Movies and Music in the Park series, presenting free flicks on an outdoor screen in Loring Park, preceded by live music.

**The Parkway**, 822-3030, 4814 Chicago Avenue, Minneapolis, is a second-run theater where you'll find foreign and off-beat fare at reduced prices.

## Bigger than Life

The **Omnitheater** at the Science Museum, 221-9444, Wabasha and Exchange streets, St. Paul, shows nature films on a gigantic "you are there" Omni screen. (A word of caution: Arrive early and purchase your tickets hours in advance, because this is a very popular attraction, especially during the summer months.) Also, during the summer, you'll find a similar Omni theater at **Valleyfair** amusement park, 445-6500, in Shakopee.

## Some Great Mainstream Houses

### SOUTHTOWN THEATRE
*Hwy. 494 and Penn Ave.*
*S. Bloomington*                884-2111
The Southtown is a big old movie house that has admirably withstood the trend toward multiplexes and shrunken screens. Built in the '60s, the Southtown boasts two large screens in cavernous, high-ceilinged rooms, each filled with 500-plus comfortable bucket seats.

### CENTENNIAL LAKES CINEMA
*8731 I France Ave. S.*
*Edina*                920-3334
This modern multiplex offers state-of-the-art projection and booming stereo acoustics in eight screening rooms. And not content to just serve the old popcorn and Milk Duds menu, Centennial Lakes also sells tacos at its refreshment stand!

Photo: Sully Doroshow, Pioneer Press

*Guthrie Theatre in Minneapolis.*

## MALL OF AMERICA

*14 Mall of America, I-494 and 24th Ave.*
*Bloomington                546-5700*
This is the perfect spot for indecisive types. With 14 screens of new releases to choose from, there's something for everyone and every mood at this huge General Cinema multiplex. It's on the fourth floor of the Mall's south side.

## Bargain Venues

The following are second-run houses, showing features just months after their first run at bargain prices (around $1.50). Considering some of Hollywood's dubious "hits," it's definitely worth the wait.

### RIVERVIEW THEATRE

*3800 42nd Ave. S.*
*Minneapolis                729-7369*
This old second-run moviehouse is loaded with kitsch and character. Its decor is a happy blend of '40s and '50s — comfy lobby couches, coffee tables and gold cylinder lamps, plus lots of turquoise. It's an enjoyable trip down memory lane.

### ROSEVILLE 4 THEATRES

*1211 Larpenteur Ave.*
*Roseville                488-4242*
Looking for comfort? This bargain house is reputed to have the cushiest seats in town: plush, neck-supporting rockers.

## Second-run Houses

Here's a quick list of other second-run houses:
- **Ridge Square**, 546-1404, Highway 394 and Plymouth Road, Minnetonka
- **Excelsior Dock**, 474-6725, 26 Water Street, Excelsior
- **Spring Brook**, 780-3706, 4 Theatre 141 N. 85th Avenue, Coon Rapids
- **Plaza Maplewood Theater**, 770-7969, 1847 Larpenteur Avenue E., Maplewood

## For Something a Little Different

### CINEMA 'N' DRAFTHOUSE

*2749 Winnetka Ave. N.*
*New Hope                546-6305*
Order a pizza, glass of wine or mug of beer and munch away to your heart's content while you watch a second-run movie on one of six screens in this comfortable blend of restaurant and movie house. All seats are $2.50.

**50TH & FRANCE**

Stroll the charming walkways where you'll find distinctive shops and services catering to your every need.

...At 50th Street & France Avenue, where Minneapolis and Edina meet.

# Inside
# Shopping

Once upon a time, sophisticated Twin Citians eschewed our stodgy Midwestern retail emporiums and flew to Chicago or New York to shop for the latest designer fashions or furnishings.

Well, baby, times have changed.

Today, local trendsetters can find their hearts' desires in fashions, furnishings and bric-a-brac right here in their own back yard — thanks, in large part, to the Twin Cities' new temple to consumerism, the Mall of America — not to mention numerous other unique retail complexes and shopping centers that have sprouted here in the past decade.

Minneapolis and St. Paul have developed into a shopping mecca for the Upper Midwest. Now, Chicagoans — heck, even the French, Japanese and Swedes — are coming here to shop 'til they drop.

In reality, the twin towns have a long tradition of innovative retailing. After all, the country's first enclosed shopping mall, Southdale, was built here in suburban Edina in the late '50s. The concept proved so successful that other "Dales" soon sprouted in other suburbs. Not to be outdone, the downtowns fought back with attractive, upscale stores linked by enclosed skyways to draw shoppers year round, even in blustery January.

In the '60s, Minneapolis turned its retail center, Nicollet Avenue, into a pedestrian (plus buses) boulevard, named it Nicollet Mall, and adorned it with benches, shade trees and unique sculptures and water fountains. The '80s saw such upscale shopping centers as The Conservatory and Gaviidae Common join the more middle-class, bustling City Center complex on this retail avenue.

St. Paul has created attractive shopping centers in the stunning new World Trade Center and Town Square, the latter encompassing an indoor park with waterfalls and greenery. The Saintly City also is home to Galtier Plaza, a complex of shops, restaurants and movie theaters in historic Lowertown, located on the eastern edge of downtown. For those who prefer to shop on a more intimate scale, there are numerous old-fashioned neighborhood retail clusters — typically hardware stores, bakeries and quaint gift shops — sprinkled throughout both cities and the suburbs, not to mention an abundance of less-attractive strip malls.

A new wrinkle on the local shopping scene is the large discount outlet centers offering prestigious, famous-label fashions and furnishings at discount prices.

The following "shopping tour" will highlight major retail centers as well as one-of-a-kind shops in the Twin Cities. Be forewarned: In the topsy-turvy world of retail, favorite old stores can close with little notice, while new shops seem to sprout up overnight. We've tried to be up-to-date, but inevitably, changes might have occurred since press time.

Let's begin with the obvious.

### MALL OF AMERICA
*24th Avenue S. and I-494*
*Bloomington*          *883-8800*

This shopper's paradise is the largest, enclosed retail/entertainment complex in the United States.

In addition to its four anchor stores — **Bloomingdale's, Macy's, Nordstrom** and **Sears** — the mega-mall houses nearly 400 specialty stores, tons of freestanding kiosks and carts, a seven-acre indoor **Camp Snoopy** amusement park with 23 rides, a dinner theater, a 14-screen movie theater, a huge Lego play center, a miniature golf course and more than 30 restaurants (including Planet Hollywood), in addition to 30 fast-food outlets, plus nightclubs, sports bars, comedy clubs and entertainment spots such as **Starbase Omega**, a cool place where you dress up in sci-fi gear and play shoot-em-up (no, it's not just *kids* you find here).

The 4.2-million-square-foot center is laid out along four "avenues" surrounding Camp Snoopy. These avenues are three or four levels high with an anchor store at each corner.

In addition to the nationally known large anchor stores, MOA retailers include the upper-crusty **Brooks Brothers, Banana Republic, Filene's Basement, Abercrombie & Fitch, The Gap, Scala Milano** and **Guess?, Chico's** women's apparel, plus specialty stores such as **Linens-N-Things, Lechter's Home Store, Warner Brothers Studio Store, Williams-Sonoma** and oodles more. Not to be missed is the innovative **Oshman's Super-Sports** store, complete with basketball courts and batting cages.

One can literally spend days in MOA, visiting a mind-boggling array of shops. Here are a few of the more unusual ones: **BareBones**, offering skeleton-themed games, gifts and science kits; **Butterflies by Nancy**, where butterflies aren't free; **Lotta Hotta**, a hot-sauce emporium; **Bead It!**, offering beads from around the world; **Love From Minnesota**, selling North Star State mementoes; **Enchanted Tales**, where kids (and, be honest, even adults) love the specialty stuffed animals; **Peanuts**, where you can find Charles Schulz's favorite pup on everything from ties to bookmarks; and **The Lost Forest**, an enchanting collection of stuffed species in a tropical-forest setting.

The Mall can literally fill your every need — even those needs you didn't think you needed!

At the Mall, it's possible to:

• Buy a home security system (**Security Store**)

• Dress up in a Victorian gown and have your photo taken (**Old Time Photography** or the **Victorian Photographer**)

• Buy intriguing 3D holographic items (**Hologram Fantastic**)

• Dress up in satin and sequins and have your photo taken (**Glamour Shots**)

• Book a cruise (**Cruise Holidays**)

• Get your teeth cleaned (**Group Health Dental Clinic**)

• Build a LEGO dinosaur with your kids (**LEGO Imagination Center**)

• Go to the same movie theater every day of the week and never see the same film twice (**General Cinema 14**)

• Attend a dinner theater (**Ford Playhouse**)

• Buy a snazzy-looking bird feeder (**Natural Wonders**)

• Get a foot massage (via machine, in Nordstrom women's lounge)

• Find a job (**Hennepin Employment Brokerage**)

• Buy a dreamcatcher (**Painted Tipi** or **Pueblo Spirit**)

• Complete your cow collection (**Cowabuddies**)

• Find lip-smackin' boysenberry jam (**Knott's Berry Market**)

• Find products especially suited for left-handers (**The Leftorium**)

• Get that just-right Minnesota-type gift or card (**Minnesot-ah**)

• Delight a duffer (**Mac Birdie Golf Gifts**)

• Delight your spouse (**Victoria's Secret**)

• Visit rock star Prince's **New Power Generation** boutique

• Find automobile paraphernalia (**Runkel Bros. American Garage**)

• Add to your music box collection (**San Francisco Music Box Co.**)

• Delight in the fanciful, painted animals created by local artist Christopher Tully (**Animalia**)

Book-lovers need not go home empty-handed. There are three bookstores to feed your hunger for the written word. **B. Dalton's**, of course, is part of popular national chain. You'll also find **P.B. Pages**, an intimate shop with an extensive collection, and**Readwell's**, a friendly, service-oriented bookstore.

A great place to take kids — without denting the pocketbook — is the **Everything's a $1.00** store, with two locations in MOA, or the **Buck Boutique**, which follows the same $1 pricing theme. Give the kids $5 each and let them loose!

Restaurants include **Wolfgang Puck's Pizzeria** and the **California Grill** in Macy's, the wildly popular **Planet Hollywood**, **Tony Roma's**, **Tucci Benucch** and many more. Perhaps the most imaginative is the expansive, exotic **Rain Forest Cafe**, complete with jungle decor, sounds of the wild and even primordial mists. In addition, there are two large food courts offering an array of fast food.

One of the more pleasant surprises about the Mall of America is its incredibly convenient, free parking. Even though there are more than 12,700 spaces on two parking decks and four ground-level parking lots, no parking space is more than 300 feet from a mall entrance. And there's little chance of experiencing the shopper's nightmare — forgetting where you've parked the car. Each parking section is labeled with the name of a state. We find it easier to park at the Mall of America than at any suburban mall in the Twin Cities.

But if you'd rather leave the car at home, the Twin Cities' Metropolitan Council Transit Operations offers daily express bus service to the Mall from both downtown Minneapolis and St. Paul every half-hour. There's also an airport shuttle from the Minneapolis/St. Paul Airport to the Mall every half-hour.

Visiting this gigantic complex can be a daunting experience. But it needn't be that way — if you keep things in perspective. Here are a few guidelines on how to make your Mall of America experience one you will remember:

1) Get there early and, if you can, go on a weekday when the crowds are slimmer.

2) Wear comfortable shoes and clothes! This is a must, as you will be walking, walking, walking.

3) Don't try to see it all in one visit. Take your time, breathe deeply, and keep your sense of perspective.

4) When things get a bit overwhelming, head for Nordstrom or Macy's, where they have terrific restroom-lounges.

5) If you're planning to eat in one of the fast-food courts, go during a non-peak time to avoid the crowds and noise. These expansive courtyards can be stressful and clangy. The food courts in the Camp Snoopy area seem to be less crowded. Another option is to choose one of the Mall's many nice, sit-down restaurants. It may be worth it to pay a bit more for the peace of mind and relaxation.

6) If you're planning to ride Paul Bunyan's Log Chute in Camp Snoopy, make it the last stop before going home, because you'll get drenched!

One final note: There are eight Guest Service Centers located at all Mall main entrances. Here, friendly staff members are available to provide directions, answer questions and offer such services as foreign language interpretation, messaging, strollers, wheelchairs, lockers, electronic convenience vehicles, lost and found, automatic teller machines, telephones (including devices for the deaf), directories and shopping bags. Also, restrooms are located near these centers.

Tours of the Mall are offered Monday through Saturday at 11 AM, 2:30 PM and 6 PM and on Sunday at 11 AM and 2:30 PM. Tours depart from level one, South Avenue. The fee is $2.

The Mall of America is open from 10 AM to 9:30 PM Monday through Friday, 9:30 AM to 9:30 PM Saturday and 11 AM to 7 PM Sunday. Camp Snoopy and the Upper East Side entertainment venues are open beyond Mall hours — call for information.

To get to the Mall from the airport, take I-494 west toward 24th Avenue. Watch for the MOA signs and turn south. From the west, take I-494 until you approach Cedar Avenue. Watch for the signs. Technically, the Mall is located at the intersection of I-494 and Highway 77. You can't miss it!

Photo: Mark Morson, Pioneer Press

*Gaviidae Common along Nicollet Mall in downtown Minneapolis.*

## *Minneapolis*

### Downtown Minneapolis

Despite the numerous malls that dot the suburbs, many Twin Citians still prefer to shop downtown Minneapolis and St. Paul, where they can enjoy a variety of traditional department stores and specialty shops, terrific restaurants and nightlife in a cosmopolitan ambiance you just can't find in suburbia.

In downtown Minneapolis, most shopping centers on the Nicollet Mall. In addition to the many indoor shopping areas detailed below, there are lots of boutiques, gift shops and specialty stores located at the south end of the mall and on streets to the east and west of the mall.

Here's an overview of downtown Minneapolis shopping.

**City Center**, 33 S. Sixth Street, is a multilevel indoor shopping center with 77 stores, including **Montgomery Ward, Filene's Basement** and **B. Dalton Bookseller**. There are also restaurants (including the legendary **Nankin** and **Chi-Chi's**), plus a fast-food court.

**The Conservatory on Nicollet**, 800 Nicollet Mall, offers 20 attractive, high-calibre shops such as **Mark Shale** (menswear), **Ann Taylor** (women's clothing), **Williams-Sonoma** (gourmet cooking), **Banana Republic** (men's and women's clothing), **The Nature Company** and **Sharper Image** (yuppie gadgets), among others. The award-winning **Goodfellow's** restaurant is also located in The Conservatory.

• *127*

**Gaviidae Common**, located on Nicollet Mall between Fifth and Seventh streets, is named for the Minnesota state bird, the common loon (Gavia in Latin), which is memorialized here in a handsome bronzed sculpture. But there's nothing loony about this classy shopping emporium. In addition to **Saks Fifth Avenue** and **Neiman Marcus**, Gaviidae is home to more than 60 specialty shops and restaurants. Among them is **Juster's Clothiers**, a local favorite for elegant menswear and women's casual clothing, and **Room & Board**, a locally based home furnishings store that specializes in high-quality contemporary and classical (i.e. Shaker, Mission) styles of furniture, upholstery and kitchenware.

Other well-known stores include: **Anne Klein, Burberrys, Eddie Bauer, Jessica McClintock, Laurel** (Escada), **Lillie Rubin, Pendleton, Rodier Paris, Cole-Haan, Lenox China, Joan Vass** and **Talbots**.

Hints for bargain-hunters: **Neiman Marcus' Last Call on 4** (on the fourth floor, obviously) is an entire department of greatly reduced merchandise. Saks also has a similar department, called the **Clearinghouse**, also located in its fourth floor. Great buys for serious shoppers!

Located on Gaviidae's fifth level is the stunning **Azur** restaurant, specializing in Mediterranean fare, and on the concourse level is **Morton's of Chicago Steakhouse**, purveyors of huge steaks and fresh lobster.

Parking, available in ramps off Fifth and Sixth streets, is free for up to 3 hours with a minimum $20 same-day purchase at Gaviidae.

A block south of Gaviidae is **Dayton's**, 700 Nicollet Mall, the flagship store of the locally based department-store chain, offering quality merchandise and great customer service. There are eight floors of men's, women's and children's apparel, appliances, home furnishings, gourmet food and much, much more. Dayton's lower level Marketplace area is especially fun with its gourmet foods, trendy furnishings and kitchenware. In fact, Dayton's has a popular wedding registry service. This shopping emporium is a local favorite of Twin Citians, who come here to shop, socialize or meet for lunch at the **Oak Grill** or **Sky Room**.

In addition to its retail offerings, Dayton's also sponsors many annual special events in its eighth-floor auditorium. These include the annual wintertime displays with animated figures (it has become a family tradition to go see them during the holiday season) and spring flower show extravaganzas. Watch for these Dayton's sales: Anniversary Sale in March, Daisy Sale in June and Jubilee Sale in October. Also legendary are the sales in Dayton's ritzy Oval Room.

Adjacent to Dayton's is **J.B. Hudson Jewelers**, a must-see for fine jewelry, crystal and collectibles such as Limoges pill boxes, Lladro and Beatrix Potter figurines. This place is a real feast for the eyes.

The **Polo/Ralph Lauren** store at Ninth Street and Nicollet Mall is remarkable not only for its internationally famous fashions for men, women and children, not to mention home furnishings, but also for

# NEW ART.    NEW LOOK.    NEW LOCATION.

 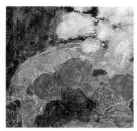 

Part of the pleasure of owning beautiful things is feeling

at home with them. ❧ Find that feeling at White Oak

Gallery where art is as comfortable as your favorite blue

jeans. ❧ From simple treasures to modern masterpieces;

original work by more than one hundred artists. ❧ Come

in and experience our new gallery at 3916 West 50th Street

in Downtown Edina, 612-922-3575. ❧

Artists, clockwise from top left:
B.R. Gates, Roy Fairchild, David Schneuer, Malcom Liepke ©Eleanor Ettinger Inc., B.D. Hultmann, M.R. Smith

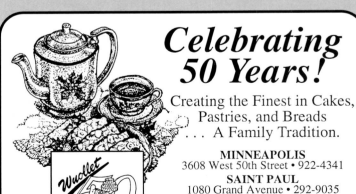

# 50TH & FRANCE
*So Much, So Close, So Easy!*
## Apparel & Accessories
### Children
| | |
|---|---|
| Simply Splendid | 922-6830 |
| Spirit | 920-8191 |

### Men
| | |
|---|---|
| Belleson's | 927-4694 |
| Burwick 'n Tweed | 926-9551 |
| Al Johnson Clothier | 920-5450 |

### Women
| | |
|---|---|
| Chico's | 925-5474 |
| Dana's | 927-5052 |
| Doncaster Studio 53 | 928-9988 |
| Grethen House N Etc. | 926-8725 |
| Spirit | 920-8191 |
| Talbots | 925-6155 |
| Tonya's | 929-2928 |
| Vestiges, Ltd. | 926-2804 |

## Gifts, Galleries, Furnishings & Accessories
| | |
|---|---|
| The Accessory Collection | 922-0111 |
| Cottages to Castles | 920-8090 |
| The Cottage Sampler | 925-9672 |
| The Garden Sampler | 925-4859 |
| Images Under Glass • Picture Framing | 927-6041 |
| J-Michael Galleries | 920-6070 |
| Patio Village Casual Furniture | 926-2771 |
| Periwinkles | 925-4221 |
| RSVP | 922-7777 |
| White Oak Gallery | 922-3575 |

## Jewelry
| | |
|---|---|
| Diamonds Direct | 929-0054 |
| R.F. Moeller Jeweler | 926-6166 |
| Van Guilder's Goldsmith | 920-6907 |

## Personal Services
| | |
|---|---|
| Edina Five-O Florist | 920-5665 |
| Edina Shoe Repair | 922-4356 |
| 50th & France Chiropratic | 920-4528 |
| Kids' Hair | 929-3614 |
| Spalon Montage | 929-4411 |

## Restaurants, Bakeries & Beverage
| | |
|---|---|
| Cuppa Java | 928-9004 |
| Pearson's Edina Restaurant | 927-4464 |
| Starbuck's Coffee | 927-7055 |
| Tejas | 926-0800 |
| The Tour Cafe | 929-1010 |
| Wuollet Bakery | 922-4341 |

*More than 175 businesses to serve you!*

the elegant, old Young-Quinlan building it inhabits. This is, in fact, the third-largest Polo shop in the world. Step inside and enjoy the history.

Also on this block is **Crate & Barrel**, 915 Nicollet Mall, packed with contemporary home furnishings and kitchenware. This store also has a popular bridal registry service.

The **IDS Crystal Court**, 80 S. Eighth Street, was made famous in the opening scenes of "The Mary Tyler Moore Show." The shot pictured Mary riding one of the Crystal Court escalators and eating lunch here. The expansive courtyard has

also played host to President Clinton who gave speeches here in the summer of 1994. This is a smaller retail center offering several boutiques, plus local branches of **The Gap** and **Banana Republic**. Oh, by the way, it's housed in the tallest building in Minneapolis.

The **Dublin Walk**, 1200 Nicollet Mall, offers a little bit o' the old sod — Irish sweaters and Claddagh jewelry, plus Waterford crystal and Belleek china. Even though it has changed its downtown address a few times over the years, this tasteful shop is an enduring favorite of Twin Citians. Also on the mall, you'll find lots of bridal shops, art galler-

*St. Paul's Mears Park*

ies and import gift shops, including **Mhiripiri Gallery** (African art) and **Esperanto**, for home furnishings. And don't forget about the second floor shopping arcade of the **Hyatt Regency Hotel**, 1300 Nicollet Mall.

Don't make the mistake of limiting your shopping only to the Nicollet Mall. There are other surprises just blocks away.

**Baxter's Books**, 608 Second Avenue S., is an inviting emporium of volumes on every subject, specializing in business, travel and children's books. The large wooden bookcases create intimate nooks for browsing and reading on a world of subjects. This independent book shop specializes in personalized service and special events and clubs for readers and writers.

For the latest in traditional and contemporary furnishings, **Design Studio 1200**, 1200 Second Avenue

S., offers personalized design services.

Also worth a visit is **Hubert W. White**, 611 Marquette Avenue, a classy shop for the latest in men's fashions.

**Haskell's**, 81 S. Ninth Street, is the flagship store of a local chain of liquor stores specializing in an extensive wine selection and friendly, helpful staff. Psst — they give samples.

For the new and unusual in gifts, books and wearable art, check out the gift shops at **Walker Art Center** and the **Guthrie Theater**, Vineland Place. Both have great one-of-a-kind baubles, books, sarcastic T-shirts and mementoes you just won't find in a department store or mall. Both are located just southwest of downtown, across Loring Park.

## Minneapolis' Warehouse District

The Warehouse District, located west of Hennepin Avenue between Ninth Street and Washington Avenue, is home to several antique shops, art galleries, nightclubs and restaurants in historic buildings. The Wyman Building, at Sixth Street and First Avenue, contains many first-rate art galleries such as **MC Gallery** and **Carolyn Ruff Gallery**.

**Architectural Antiques**, 801 Washington Avenue N., is a unique source of marble table tops, stained-glass windows, plaster columns and other architectural remnants salvaged from old buildings, homes and churches.

Just for the fun of it, check out **Sister Fun**, 121 N. Fourth Street, where you can buy an Elvis lamp, squeeze toys, zany T-shirts and assorted whimsies for the person who has everything.

**Nate's Clothing Co.**, 27 N. Fourth Street, is a local institution, offering a wide selection of discounted men's clothing.

Off on the western side of the Warehouse District is **International Market Square**, at 275 Market Street, a first-class showplace of home furnishings housed in, of all places, a converted underwear factory. The public is invited to come in and browse, but purchases must be made through a trade professional.

## Northeast Minneapolis

Check out **Surdyks** liquor store, East Hennepin and University Avenue N.E., for its wide selection of beer, wine and cheese. (They have *great* sales.)

**International Gallery and Gifts**, 207 E. Hennepin Avenue, sells Ukrainian Easter eggs and other decorated eggs from Poland and other Eastern European countries.

Also in this ethnic enclave, stop in at **Kramarczuk Sausage Co.**,

215 Hennepin Avenue E., for tasty Polish sausages and old-fashioned franks, and **Emily's Lebanese Deli**, 641 University Avenue N.E., for to-die-for takeout tabbouleh.

Nearby are **Riverplace** and **St. Anthony Main**, lovely riverfront shopping/entertainment/office complexes in historic buildings housing a few interesting gift shops; the fascinating **Museum of Questionable Medical Devices**; and restaurants such as **Pracna on Main** (American bistro fare with summertime outdoor seating), **Yvette** (French fare in an elegant setting), **Kikugawa** (Japanese food) and **Tuggs Saloon** (pub fare).

## Uptown Minneapolis

The Uptown area, roughly located south of downtown along Hennepin Avenue between Franklin Avenue and 32nd Street, offers many unusual shops — from antiques shops to bookstores to counterculture grunge venues.

**Calhoun Square**, an indoor shopping center at Hennepin and Lake, houses 80 stores, with an emphasis on contemporary/global apparel and gifts. Shops include **Kitchen Window, Main Street Outfitters, Borders Bookstore, Urban Traveler, Uptown Art, Games People Play** and **Comic Book College** for lovers of comics. (There's also another Comic Book College store just down the street at 3151 Hennepin Avenue S.). When you're tired of browsing, grab an outdoor table at **Figlio** and enjoy the people-watching. Just across Hennepin from Calhoun Square are a large new branch of **The Gap**, 3000 Hennepin Avenue, and **Urban Outfitters**, 3006 Hennepin Avenue S., specializing in the funky grunge look.

Across Lake Street from Calhoun Square is the **New Power Generation** boutique, 1408 W. Lake Street, owned by rock star Prince, and, to the east, several antiques shops. Up and down Hennepin, you'll find mountaineering stores, futon outlets, espresso shops and interesting little nooks and crannies.

Of special note, at 3505 Hennepin Avenue S., is **Play It Again Sports**, a secondhand sports equipment store that's a favorite among parents of Little Leaguers and budding sports stars. The store buys used equipment for cash or as a trade-in on other equipment. There are 14 Play It Again Sports outlets in the Twin Cities metro area.

Farther up Hennepin, where it intersects with Lake Street, **Fleetham Furnishings and Design** has been offering top names in home furnishings for decades.

**Lunds Food Store**, 1450 W. Lake Street, is part of a local grocery chain that puts a high emphasis on attractive ambiance, a wide variety of specialty and import foods, quality produce and meats and customer service. This food store also is a nonthreatening place for Uptown's many young and beautiful singles to meet. ("Our eyes locked over the cantaloupe display.") There are nine Lunds stores in the Twin Cities and, best of all, they're open 24 hours a day.

**Calhoun Cycle**, 1622 W. Lake Street, is a bicycle shop that also

Come

For

A

Visit.

You'll

Never

Want

To

Leave.

Shop over 400 stores, including Bloomingdale's, Macy's, Nordstrom, and Sears. Thrill to Knott's® Camp Snoopy® indoor amusement park. Unwind in restaurants and nightclubs. "One Call For The Mall," (612) 883-8800, answers any question.

**MALL OF AMERICA**®
Bloomington, MN

carries homemade boomerangs call Z-rangs.

---

### South Minneapolis

Check out **Ingrebretsen's Scandinavian Gifts**, 1601 E. Lake Street, for specialty foods, cookware, albums and other Scandinavian imports. Another source of Scandinavian goods is the gift shop at the **American Swedish Institute**, 2600 Park Avenue.

For those hooked on whodunits, **Uncle Edgar's Mystery Bookstore**, 2864 Chicago Avenue, in south Minneapolis, is just the place. Then, leave the mysteries and head next door for the outer limits at **Uncle Hugo's Science Fiction Bookstore**.

Hungry? **Broder's Cucina Italiana**, 50th Street and Penn Avenue S., serves up all types of Italian specialties and groceries.

**Wild Rumpus Bookstore**, 2720 W. 43rd Street, is an enchanting children's bookstore filled with fun surprises and an array of animals (see the Kidstuff chapter for details).

The area at 43rd Street and Upton Avenue is a wonderful antidote for "megamallitis." It's a fun little collection of yarn shops, gift shops and the great **Sebastian Joe's** ice cream parlor, all located just a stone's throw from Lake Harriet.

# St. Paul

## Downtown St. Paul

Over the past decade, St. Paul's retail offerings have expanded, thanks to the relatively new World Trade Center and Galtier Plaza centers. Here's an overview of shopping in the Saintly City's downtown core.

**Town Square**, 445 Minnesota Street, offers 40 stores, including **Braun's**, **Casual Corner**, **Regency Gourmet Coffee Shop**, **The Limited**, **Accent Minnesota** (for Minnesota-themed gifts) and many others in a picturesque setting that includes an indoor park, complete with **Cafesjian's Carousel**. And, if all the great shopping has left you with a growling stomach, check out the lower level fast-food court, where you'll dine amid the sound of gurgling water fountains.

Just across the street (or skyway), the **World Trade Center**, 30 E. Seventh Street, is home to **Eddie Bauer**, **Juster's**, **Lane Bryant**, **Caren Charles**, **The Gap**, **Victoria's Secret** and 45 other specialty stores, plus a food court — all in an attractive multilevel setting, the centerpiece of which is a 52-foot fountain. A popular destination for tourists is **The Map Store**, especially for its helpful local maps and guides. Restaurants here include **Favore**, a popular, contemporary Italian eatery on the third floor, **Pig's Eye Grill and Brew Annex**, offering the popular local brew and pub fare, and the **Heartthrob Cafe** on the first floor, where your burger and fries are delivered by waiters on roller skates. If you're in a hurry, check out **Au Bon Pain** for great sandwiches and soups that you can eat in or take out.

Next door to the World Trade Center and across the street from Town Square is **Dayton's Department Store**, 411 Cedar Street, offering the same amenities as the Minneapolis version in a setting that's a bit more friendly and a lot less crowded. Dayton's has two popular restaurants: the intimate Iron Horse on the lower level and the larger, elegant River Room on the main floor.

Located in Lowertown, **Galtier Plaza**, 175 E. Fifth Street, has 30 specialty shops, including **Inside Africa**, a shop featuring African arts and crafts, including stone carvings and batiks, a four-screen movie theater, the **Comedy Gallery** comedy club, a fine Japanese restaurant, **Sakura**, plus a main-floor food courtyard that overlooks attractive Mears Park.

There also are several individual downtown St. Paul stores worth noting. **Frank Murphy**, St. Peter and Fifth streets, is a landmark offering women's designer fashions. Since 1906, **Nakashian-O'Neil**, 23 W. Sixth Street, has been selling incomparable antiques, including French, Chinese and English porcelain, and fine, one-of-a-kind gifts.

The **Science Museum of Minnesota**, 30 E. 10th Street, and the **Minnesota History Center**, 345 W. Kellogg Boulevard, have great gift shops brimming with books and rare finds.

Along West Seventh Street in St.

Paul you'll find interesting shops and antiques stores, not to mention one of the best hardware stores in St. Paul, **Seven Corners Ace Hardware**, 216 W. Seventh Street. Across the street is a great Italian restaurant/deli, **Cossetta's Market and Pizzeria**, 211 W. Seventh Street.

## Grand Avenue

St. Paul's eclectic, homespun Grand Avenue offers a refreshing change of pace from the modern, hermetically sealed suburban malls.

This bustling thoroughfare is lined with specialty and gift shops selling everything from world crafts to kitchenware, books, clothing and home furnishings. Be sure to make a stop at the **Jubilee Shop**, 1051 Grand Avenue, a nonprofit store that sells handmade crafts from around the world. Profits are returned to the village artisans.

Also worth a visit are **The Bibelot Shop**, 1082 Grand Avenue, selling one-of-a-kind gifts and clothes; **Irish on Grand**, 790 Grand Avenue, catering to children of the Old Sod with Belleek china, Celtic jewelry and apparel; **Trade Winds International**, 857 Grand Avenue, featuring world crafts; and **The Gathering**, 850 Grand Avenue, offering contemporary gifts and jewelry. **Chico's**, 1068 Grand Avenue, sells cotton casual apparel with ethnic touches.

Last but not least, Grand Avenue is home to some wonderful independent bookstores, including the **Hungry Mind Bookstore**, 1648 Grand Avenue, which publishes its own literary review and houses an extensive collection in a rambling old building; **Odegard Books**, a book-lover's bookstore conveniently located in Victoria Crossing, 857 Grand Avenue; and the **Red Balloon Bookshop**, 891 Grand Avenue, a fun children's bookstore. Also located at and nearby the Victoria Crossing locale are **Books for Travel** and **Odegard Encore Books**, of-fering a selection of remaindered books and publishers' overstocks.

You should know that parking can be a challenge along Grand Avenue. Check the Victoria Crossing lot for space.

## Bandana Square

Bandana Square, 1021 E. Bandana Boulevard, is a shopping/entertainment complex housed in a former railroad-car repair warehouse. While it's not as popular as other venues, it nonetheless has fine specialty shops including **Europa European Imports**, and **Miniature Merchants**, featuring dollhouse furnishings and military miniatures. There's also a huge model railroad display and the **Dakota Bar & Grill**, one of the best jazz clubs in the Twin Cities.

## St. Anthony Park

This colorful neighborhood shopping area, located at the intersection of Como and Carter avenues in St. Paul, is home to such interesting little shops as **Micawber's** bookstore, the **Bibelot Shop** and **Country Peddler Quilt Shop**, plus a great little restaurant, **Muffuletta**.

Insiders' Tips

Antique-hunters flock to St. Paul's Payne Avenue (north of East Seventh Street) and West Seventh Street (west of Kellogg Boulevard).

## Suburban Specialties

### West Metro Suburbs

**Excelsior**, a quaint little town on the shores of Lake Minnetonka, is sprinkled with boutiques, gift shops, a knitting shop, antiques stores, plus the **Frog Island** bookstore and a genuine old-fashioned drugstore (**Bacon Drug** at 205 Water Street) with a working soda fountain. After shopping, stop for lunch at **Park Tavern** on the lake.

On the way to Excelsior, you'll pass the **General Store**, located a quarter-mile west of I-494 on Highway 7 (14401 Highway 7, Minnetonka). Set in a rustic old building, the General Store is crammed with homemade crafts, Victoriana, folk-art primitives and Minnesota mementoes, plus a great selection of kids' toys.

**Wayzata** is another picturesque Lake Minnetonka community whose main street is lined with fun — but pricey — boutiques, galleries and restaurants. Especially worth visiting are **Wuollet Bakery; Chico's** (women's clothing); the **Bookcase**, a great little bookstore; **Overland Gallery**, specializing in Russian Impressionist art; and, last but not least, **The Foursome**, a family-run clothing store with an extensive, high-quality collection for men, women and children.

The up-and-coming southwestern suburb of **Eden Prairie** is home to **Eden Prairie Center**, located at Prairie Center Drive near I-494. This modern shopping mall has many clothing and gift stores, including **The Limited, Braun's, Gigi Fashions, Gantos** and **Lane Bryant**, all women's clothing stores; **The Gap**, men's/women's clothing; and **J. Riggins** men's clothiers.

In Minnetonka, you'll find **Ridgedale Shopping Center** at 12301 Wayzata Boulevard (or I-394). This attractive enclosed mall has nearly 100 stores, including anchors **Sears, Dayton's, JCPenney** and **Carson Pirie Scott**. Other stores include **Ann Taylor, Braun's, Victoria's Secret, Eddie Bauer, The Gap, The Limited, The Museum Store, Natural Wonders, Lechter's** kitchenware, and **Waldenbooks**, plus **Applebees** and **Uno Pizzaria** restaurants.

West of Ridgedale — across the parking lot, actually — is **Bonaventure** shopping mall, housing **Borders Book Shop and Espresso Bar**, a huge, inviting book emporium that also sponsors readings and lectures. Also in Bonaventure are **Filene's Basement, Joanne Fabrics, Champps** sports bar and **Leeann Chin** Chinese restaurant.

Across Plymouth Road from Ridgedale and Bonaventure is another small complex housing an ever-popular **Target** discount store and **Byerly's**, part of a prestigious, upscale grocery-store chain, whose flagship store in St. Louis Park, that emphasizes a luxurious shopping atmosphere (i.e. carpeting and chandeliers), fine imported foods, freshness and customer service while also offering an on-site liquor store and a nice all-night restaurant. A huge **Barnes and Noble** bookstore here caters to your lust for literature.

Suburban **St. Louis Park** is home to two smaller, older shopping centers, **Knollwood** and **Miracle Mile**. Knollwood, at 8332 Highway 7, houses many clothing and specialty shops, including **Montgomery Ward, Everyday Hero**, a new **Kohl's** department store, **Braun's** women's store and many other shops.

Miracle Mile, 5009 Excelsior Boulevard, is noteworthy as the home of **Half-Price Books**, offering used and new books, records and CDs at a 50 percent discount (there are also stores in St. Paul and Maplewood); **Once Upon a Child**, featuring high-quality used children's clothing; **Mike Lynne's Tennis Shop**; **Cafe Sorella**, dishing up scrumptious brownies and strong java; **B. Dalton Bookseller**; and many other small and interesting shops. (There are other Once Upon a Child stores in several other suburbs.)

Just a few miles west of Miracle Mile on Excelsior Boulevard, you'll come to the little town of **Hopkins**. It has a quaint, old-fashioned main street that is nice for strolling and leisurely shopping. Here you'll find antique and clothing stores, home furnishings shops and cafes. Two stores of note are **Little Blind Spot**, 811 Main Street, and **Shutters 'N' Shades**, also at 811 Main, featuring custom shades and wood shutters.

## South Suburbs

The intersection of 50th Street and France Avenue S. in the tony suburb of **Edina** is just teeming with trendy shops and boutiques such as **White Oak Gallery** and **Doncaster** women's fashions, plus **Lunds** grocery store, **Clancy's** drugstore, **Pearson's** family restaurant, **Edina Five-O Florist**, **Kids' Hair** (with another location in Eden Prairie), **Wuollet Bakery**, and **Edina Shoe Repair**. Other standouts include **Chico's** women's clothing, **Durr Ltd.** for fine traditional home furnishings, **R. F. Moeller, Jeweler**, with other stores on W. 50th Street in Edina and in Highland Village in St. Paul, and **Stay Tooned**, a very animated gallery. And, if you find yourself in need of a little adjustment after all the shopping, you can conveniently visit the **50th and France Chiropractic Clinic**. Free parking for the area is available in the ramp behind the Edina Theater.

**Southdale**, at 66th Street and France Avenue S. in Edina, was the country's first enclosed shopping mall, built in 1958. Its original 800,000 square feet has grown into 1.6 million square feet, thanks to recent remodeling. There are more than 150 retail stores, including **Dayton's, Carson Pirie Scott** and **JCPenney**, at this attractive mall. Other popular shops include **Ann Taylor, Banana Republic, Casual Corner** and **The Limited Express**. Go ahead and indulge! Stock up on fine soaps at **Crabtree & Evelyn,** a skimpy teddy at **Fredericks** or a lovely piece of wildlife art at the **Wooden Bird**.

Just south of Southdale, at 69th and France, is **The Galleria**, an upscale collection of boutiques and shops, anchored by a large **Gab-**

*At Oshman's Superstore in the Mall of America customers can test sporting goods before buying them.*

berts furniture store. The Galleria houses more than 25 designer fashion stores plus gift shops offering one-of-a-kind wares. The **Good Earth** health-food restaurant here is popular among locals. Stash the kids at the **Fun Station** indoor play/ day-care center and steal away for a few great hours of shopping at such venues as **Bellini** (kids' furniture), **Timbuktu, Epitome** or **I.B. Diffusion** clothing shops, and the German boutique **Mondi.**

Nearby, at 76th Street and France Avenue, is the smaller **Centennial Lakes Plaza,** home to the huge**Computer City SuperCenter,** plus **Austad's** golf store, other shops and a popular movie theater.

**Southtown** is an older shopping center, located at I-494 and Penn Avenue S. in **Bloomington.** Here you'll find **B. Dalton Bookseller, Braun's** women's clothing, a big and tall shop and several other stores, along with a great movie theater.

**Burnsville Center,** located in the suburb of the same name, is a large, modern shopping mall housing **Dayton's, Carson Pirie Scott** and 160 other retailers.

## Northern Suburbs

**Brookdale,** Highway 100 and Brooklyn Boulevard in Brooklyn Center, features four anchor stores, **Dayton's, Carson Pirie Scott, Sears** and **JCPenney,** in addition to 50-plus specialty and clothing stores, including **Lane Bryant, The Limited, Braun's** and **Casual Corner** for women's apparel, and **Northern Getaway** for North Woods kids' clothes. For the gourmet, there's the pungent and inviting **Gloria Jean's Coffee Bean** shop selling great grinds and a delightful assortment of teapots and mugs. Strollers and wheelchairs are available at the mall's Customer Service Counter.

Farther north in **Blaine** is **Northtown,** University Avenue and Highway 10, a large complex catering to the down-to-earth, practical shopper with such moderately priced stores as **Kohls, Walgreens, Montgomery Ward, Best Buys** and **Carsons.** The place is usually packed with young families and teens. There's also an attractive food court.

**Rosedale,** Highway 36 and Fairview Avenue in Roseville, is a step up from Northtown. On our recent visit, we were serenaded by a harpist in **JCPenney's** fine jewelry and a tuxedo-clad pianist in **Dayton's** cosmetics. All that was missing were the ballroom dancers!

There's flowers, foliage and benches galore in this clean, attractive, modern complex. In addition to the usual fare — **Montgomery Ward, Dayton's, Carson Pirie Scott, JCPenney, Eddie Bauer, The Gap** — Rosedale is home to **American Eagle Outfitters** (men's and women's casual), **Northern Reflections** (casual women's with a North Woods theme), **The Museum Company** and **Natural Wonders** (both offering tasteful, high-quality gifts and collectibles), **The Bombay Company** (traditional home furnishings in dark woods and brass), **Franklin Quest** (specializing in calendars and daily planners), **Computer City,** and **Air Traffic** (windsocks and kites). Restaurants include the **Green Mill,** a very popular local chain that touts the best pizza in town.

Farther east, at the busy intersection of White Bear Avenue and I-694, lies another shopping mecca,

**Maplewood Mall,** with approximately 60 stores. In addition to **Carson Pirie Scott, Sears,** and **Kohl's,** this pleasant suburban complex boasts such familiar names as the **Body Shop, Goodman's Jewelers** and **Footlocker,** as well as one-of-a-kind shops such as **Evening Moon,** a gallery of original art and home furnishings. Maplewood Mall is as much an entertainment complex as it is a retail center. Within its walls, you'll find **Circus,** a children's pizza emporium and playland, popular restaurants and a multi-screen movie theater.

If you venture north a bit — and you really should — you'll find yourself in **White Bear Lake.** Veer off the busy highways (96 and 61) into the old downtown near the intersection of Washington and Fourth streets and you'll discover a charming commercial area of tree-shaded streets, old-fashioned storefronts and no-nonsense barbershops (**Benny's** and **Dale's**). Each store is distinctive. Here's a sampling: **Heritage II** (Scandinavian and British Isles wares), **White Bear Lake Pottery, Sassafras Whole Foods Market, White Bear Lake Children's Shop,** the **Country Goose** (handmade gifts), **Conrad's** women's boutique, plus the **Cupping Room** for a sip of espresso. During the summer, there's street entertainment on certain nights and a farmers market every Friday.

## Eastern Suburbs

East of St. Paul in the picturesque, booming suburb of Woodbury, you'll find great shopping at **Woodbury Village**, located east of I-494 on Valley Creek Plaza Road. In addition to a spacious, new **Barnes & Noble Bookstore** this strip mall contains **Creative Kidstuff**, part of a chain of terrific stores that sells imaginative arts and crafts kits, tapes, books and other quality toys for children. Other offerings at Woodbury Village include **Casual Corner** (women's apparel), **Kohl's** department store, **Target**, **Rainbow** grocery store and popular restaurants such as **Ciatti's** and **Applebees**.

Just 20 minutes northeast of St. Paul, lovely, old Stillwater offers tons of antiques shops, a phenomenal number of bookstores (antiquarian and contemporary), gift shops and art galleries in a picturesque setting along the St. Croix River.

## Outlet and Bargain Shopping

**Manufacturers Marketplace Outlet Center**, located off I-94 and County Road 19 (Exit 251), in the St. Paul suburb of Woodbury, offers more than 40 outlet stores, from Eddie Bauer, Van Heusen and Geoffrey Beene to Leslie Fay, Corning/Revere cookware and Spiegel. For more information, call 735-9060 or (800) 866-5900.

**Tanger Factory Outlet** in North Branch, 40 miles north of the Twin Cities, features brand names such as Liz Claiborne, Woolrich, Nine West, Van Heusen, Capezio, Kitchen Collection and Carter's Childrenswear. To reach Tanger, take Exit 147 off I-35 and follow the signs. For more information, call (612) 674-5885 or (800) 727-6885.

About 50 miles south of the Twin Cities, but well worth the trip, is the **Medford Outlet Center** in Medford. This center offers 30 shops, from Bass Shoe, Liz Claiborne, The North Face (sportswear and outdoor equipment) and Adolfo II to Jordache, Guess?, Nike and Mikasa china. To reach the Medford Outlet Center, take I-35 south to Exit 48 and follow the signs.

On a smaller scale, you can find high-quality department-store merchandise at discounted prices at such Twin Cities stores as **TJ Maxx**, **Marshall's** and **Filene's Basement**, each with several locations in the Twin Cities.

Last but not least, there's a store for people who spurn copycat fashion. It's **Ragstock**, a funky shop selling secondhand — or shall we say "vintage" — clothing. There are Ragstock stores in Uptown, Dinkytown (near the University of Minnesota East Bank campus) and in St. Paul at 1515 University Avenue W.

# *Inside*
# **Kidstuff**

The Twin Cities abound in delightful adventures for the young and the young at heart. In true Midwestern spirit, Minnesotans genuinely adore children and the pleasures of family life. Indeed, much of that ballyhooed Minnesota "quality of life" centers on the easy availability of wholesome recreational and cultural offerings for all ages.

First and foremost, Minneapolis and St. Paul's many lakes and parks serve as Mother Nature's own playground for the younger set. In Minneapolis, Thomas Beach on the south shore of Lake Calhoun and the beaches at Lake Harriet, Cedar Lake and Lake Nokomis are ideal spots to laze away a summer day. Cap off your summer evening with a free concert at the Lake Harriet Pavilion, where dancing in the aisles is encouraged — and sometimes even applauded!

When the weather turns frosty, families lace up the skates and cut figure 8s on those same crystalline waterways. Minneapolis' Minnehaha Park, with its roaring Minnehaha Falls and rolling lawns, is another fun-filled year-round destination for families. In St. Paul, Lake Phalen sports a sandy beach and jogging/walking paths aplenty. Another popular destination, Lake Como, boasts paddleboats, picnic areas, a restored concert pavilion, not to mention a Japanese garden, conservatory, zoo and amusement park — all just 3 miles north of downtown St. Paul.

In St. Paul itself, Rice and Mears parks are quiet, green refuges from bustling urban life. In winter, Rice Park becomes a frozen fairyland with a jewel box skating rink, bordered by thousands of twinkling lights and ice sculptures.

The Twin Cities suburbs also offer countless parks, fanciful outdoor playgrounds and beaches. For further details, consult the chapters on Rivers, Lakes and Creeks, and Parks and Recreation.

Minneapolis and St. Paul also boast many man-made attractions for children — from unstuffy museums to tummy-churning amusement parks, not to mention a nationally acclaimed Children's Theatre Company and other cultural offerings. (For information on the performing arts, see The Arts chapter.) The following are capsules of the best and brightest childhood delights.

By the way, while you're driving to these fun spots, entertain the kids by turning your radio dial to

Photo: Ginger Pinson, Pioneer Press

*Children add finishing touches to a "memory mural" at St. Paul's Children's Museum.*

Radio Aahs (1280 AM), the Twin Cities' own children's radio station (now nationally syndicated). Its lively tunes and soothing stories are sure to transform the most restless critters into happy campers. (The radio station, housed at 5501 Excelsior Boulevard, St. Louis Park, also offers tours every Tuesday, Thursday and Saturday. Call ahead for a reservation at 926-1280.)

## Major Kids' Attractions

### MINNESOTA CHILDREN'S MUSEUM
*1217 Bandana Blvd., St. Paul        644-3818*

In this hands-on, free-wheeling funhouse, children can play "make-believe" in the grown-up worlds of medicine, construction, television,

mass communications and other pursuits. They can take over the controls of a construction crane and try their hands at hoisting foam-rubber "concrete" blocks; or play TV news reporter in a genuine TV studio; or, traveling back in time, sit behind a telegraph machine and tap out cryptic messages or take over the controls of a real railroad engine.

There's also an adventure maze of tunnels and secret passages that no kid can resist. Even infants and tots have their own tunnel-like play space called Habitot.

The facility, ranked among the Top 10 children's museums in the country, also hosts ever-changing exhibitions on various scientific and cultural subjects throughout the year.

The Children's Museum has proven so successful, it has outgrown its current space and is slated to move into new, expansive quarters at Wabasha and Seventh streets in downtown St. Paul by mid-1995.

Hours are 9 AM to 5 PM Tuesday, 9 AM to 8 PM Wednesday through Saturday; noon to 5 PM Sunday. Admission is $3.50 for ages 3 to 60 and $2 for toddlers and seniors, except after 5 PM Wednesday through Saturday when it's $2 for everyone.

### SCIENCE MUSEUM OF MINNESOTA AND THE WILLIAM L. MCKNIGHT-3M OMNITHEATER
*30 E. 10th St., St. Paul          221-9488*

Iggy, a whimsical 40-foot metal iguana sculpture, greets visitors at the entrance to this science showcase. The "kid-tested" scaly critter symbolizes the museum's fun-filled, "please-touch" approach to the sciences.

The museum features permanent exhibits in biology, paleontology, technology and geography. In the East Building, visitors learn about the geology and natural history of the North Star State in a colorful "Our Minnesota" permanent exhibit. There's also a Hall of Paleontology featuring huge re-creations of dinosaurs and a lab where fossils are cleaned and categorized.

The West Building boasts three floors of "neat stuff," all connected by a musical stairway — as they say, getting there is half the fun! The first floor features traveling exhibits and an auditorium for experiments and lectures. On the second floor is the Hall of Anthropology, where the most popular exhibit is a mummy in a rather alarming state of undress. Also showcased here are intricate Native American and Southeast Asian weavings (plus a loom where kids try their hand at weaving), Egyptian hieroglyphics, a model of a Southeast Asian farm home and much more.

Undoubtedly, the most popular exhibits for children are found on the third floor, which houses the Experiment Gallery, a collection of participatory, hands-on experiments in weather, electronics, robotics, energy, chemistry and physics. Kids can pedal a stationary bicycle to power various electronic devices — a light bulb, radio and fan. They can try their hands at lifting a compressed auto using air pressure, or witness the formation of a tornado in a wind tunnel. Adults find themselves elbowing out the youngsters for a turn at these fun and fascinating science lessons.

Nature in all its glory comes alive on the "aahh-some" 76-foot-diameter dome screen of the Omnitheater, located in the Science Museum. Omni films — on topics ranging from mountain gorillas to sharks to the rain forest — feature spectacular "you are there" footage, accompanied by stereo sound. The Omni is so popular that reservations are strongly recommended. Showtimes are Monday through Friday, 1, 3, 7 and 8 PM (also 9 PM Friday only); Saturday and Sunday, 11 AM, noon, 1, 2, 3, 4, 7 and

Valleyfair amusement park in Shakopee.

*Photo: Pioneer Press*

8 PM (plus 10 AM and 9 PM Saturday only). The Science Museum is open Monday through Friday from 9:30 AM to 9 PM; Saturday 9 AM to 9 PM; and Sunday 10 AM to 9 PM. Admission is $4.50 for exhibits; $5.50 for Omnitheater; $6.50 for both exhibits and Omni. For children 12 and younger, admission is $1 less in all categories. Gift shops and food concessions are located on premises.

### CAFESJIAN'S CAROUSEL AND TOWN SQUARE PARK

*Sixth and Cedar Sts., St. Paul     290-2774*

Built in 1914 by the Philadelphia Toboggan Co., this beautiful carousel was a favorite permanent attraction at the Minnesota State Fair until 1989, when it was disassembled to be sold in pieces at auction. A community-wide fundraising effort — including a $600,000 gift from St. Paul resident Gerard L. Cafesjian — saved the carousel.

Today, youngsters and young-at-heart adults still delight in taking a spin on the merry-go-round in its new home on the top level of indoor Town Square Park in downtown St. Paul. The finely crafted restored carousel features 68 carved wooden horses and two chariots.

Rides are offered on the quarter hour from noon to 7 PM Thursday and Friday, from 10 AM to 5 PM Saturday and noon to 5 PM Sunday. It is closed Monday through Wednesday. Cost per ride is $1.

After your carousel ride, spend a few minutes enjoying Town Square Park, one of the world's largest indoor public parks, complete with skylights, lush greenery, waterfalls and dining alcoves. Noontime live entertainment is offered weekdays on the upper-level entertainment area of this four-story complex. Offices, shops and a lower-level fast-food area make this a one-stop shopping/recreation center.

### JAMES FORD BELL MUSEUM OF NATURAL HISTORY

*17th Ave. and University Ave. S.E.*
*(On the University of Minnesota*
*East Bank campus)*
*Minneapolis                        624-7083*

While this museum houses an impressive collection of more than 100 works of wildlife art, visiting kids make a beeline to the Touch and See Room, where everything is displayed at child height and the motto is "please DO touch." There are animal skins, skeletons and bones and even live snakes. In addition to this fun exhibit, children will enjoy the museum's lifelike displays of animals in their natural habitat.

Hours are 9 AM to 5 PM Tuesday through Friday, 10 AM to 5 PM Saturday, and noon to 5 PM Sunday. The Touch and See room closes at 2 PM Tuesday through Friday. Admission is $3 for adults, $2 for youths (3 to 16) and seniors, and free for children younger than 3. There is no charge on Thursdays.

### MINNEAPOLIS PLANETARIUM

*300 Nicollet Mall , Minneapolis   372-6644*

Built within the Minneapolis Public Library in 1961, the Minneapolis Planetarium offers dazzling simulated tours of the night sky under a domed 40-foot ceiling. The astronomy shows are multimedia presentations with laser lights, soundtracks and stunning visual effects. Shows change frequently to highlight seasonal sky changes and various astronomical themes. For showtimes, call the Planetarium at 372-6644. Admission is $3.50 for adults and $2 for children 12 and younger.

### MINNEAPOLIS SCULPTURE GARDEN

*Vineland Place, Minneapolis      375-7622*

This 11-acre urban garden, located across the street from the renowned Walker Art Center, is dappled with more than 40 sculptures — ranging from "Spoonbridge and Cherry," a gigantic spoon and cherry creation by Claes Oldenburg and Coosje van Bruggen, to a fanciful leaping acrylic fish by Frank Gehry.

Kids love skipping over the expansive rolling greenery while their parents ponder the weighty meaning of these provocative pieces. The Cowles Conservatory, which houses the Gehry fish and indoor tropical plants, is a special treat. Hours are 6 AM to midnight daily; Conservatory hours are 10 AM to 8 PM Tuesday through Saturday; 10 AM to 5 PM Sunday; closed Monday. Admission is free. See The Arts chapter for complete information. While you're here, check out the internationally acclaimed Walker Art Center and Guthrie Theater, both of which are described in detail in The Arts chapter. (Hungry? The Walker's Gallery 8 Restaurant offers cafeteria-style lunch Tuesday through Sunday.)

## *And If You Have The Time — Small Treasures*

Sometimes the best gifts come

*"Alice in Wonderland" performed by The Children's
Theatre Company in Minneapolis.*

in the smallest packages. The
following are a few less-publicized, off-the-beaten track destinations that are nonetheless
worth a visit.

### FIREFIGHTERS MEMORIAL MUSEUM
*Broadway and Central Ave. N.E.*
*Minneapolis               623-3817*

This is the place for every kid
who's ever dreamed of climbing
aboard a gleaming red fire truck
and blowing the sirens! Children
are encouraged to live out the fantasy in this engaging museum that
also spotlights many other historic
and modern pieces of firefighting
equipment. Hours are 9 AM to 3
PM Saturday and 6 to 9 PM Thursday. Admission is $4 for adults and
$2 for children.

### TRAINS AT BANDANA SQUARE
*Bandana Square in Energy Park*
*1021 Bandana Blvd. E. , St. Paul     647-9628*

Even in the jet age, trains continue to fascinate children. This
small railroad "museum," with its
extensive operating model railroad
(one of the largest in the country),
brings alive the romance and adventure of riding the rails.

Great care was taken in creating these exact reproductions of
locomotives, passenger and freight
cars — even down to the replica
mini-spikes in the railroad ties. The
model trains are on the O-gauge
scale of ¼-inch-to-the-foot. Several pieces of artwork depicting the
mighty ironhorses also line the
walls. Appropriately, the exhibit,
run by the Twin City Model Railroad Club, is located at Bandana
Square, a renovated complex of

turn-of-the-century Northern Pacific railway "shop" buildings, where passenger cars were once constructed. Today, the cavernous buildings house shops, restaurants, nightclubs and offices, so plan in a little time for browsing. There's plenty to see. Hours are Monday through Friday, 10 AM to 8 PM; Saturday, 10 AM to 6 PM; Sunday, noon to 5 PM. Admission to the train exhibit is on a donation-only basis. Free parking is plentiful in the shopping center lot.

### THE ORIGINAL BASEBALL HALL OF FAME OF MINNESOTA

*910 Third St. , Minneapolis       375-9707*

Former Minnesota Twins equipment manager Ray Crump has compiled a baseball-lover's dream-come-true collection of memorabilia in a hole-in-the-wall setting. In a couple of the meandering rooms in a tattered old building, there are 10,000 autographed baseballs and World Series bats, plus informative exhibits on how bats, baseballs and gloves are made. This little gem is located in the shadow of the Hubert H. Humphrey Metrodome, home of the Minnesota Twins. Hours are 9 AM to 5 PM Monday through Friday, 11 AM to 3 PM Saturday, and before and after all Metrodome events. Admission is free.

### COMO-HARRIET STREETCAR LINE

*Linden Hills Depot (at Lake Harriet)*
*Queen Ave. S. at W. 42nd St.*
*Minneapolis       291-7588*

Treat the children to a ride on a genuine antique streetcar, that colorful, clangy and very efficient

*Knott's Camp Snoopy inside the Mall of America.*

precursor to the Twin Cities' current mass-transit bus system. As recently as the 1950s, the bright yellow streetcars crisscrossed the entire Twin Cities. At one time, there were more than 1,000 streetcars running on 523 miles of track stretching from Stillwater to Excelsior. Today, the streetcar only traverses the rolling parkland between lakes Harriet and Calhoun in a two-mile round-trip jog. Passengers may board at Linden Hills Depot on the northwest shore of Lake Harriet or at the Lake Calhoun Platform, located on East Lake Calhoun Parkway, south of W. 36th Street. Short but sweet, the ride is a refreshing change of pace.

From Memorial Day weekend through Labor Day, the streetcar runs from 6:30 PM to dusk Monday through Friday; from 1 PM 'til dusk Saturday, and from 12:30 PM to dusk Sundays. In September (after Labor Day), it operates only on weekends during the hours listed above. Hours are shortened in October to 1 to 5 PM Saturday and 12:30 to 5 PM Sunday. It closes after October. Fare is 75 cents; ages 4 and younger are free.

### WILD RUMPUS
### CHILDREN'S BOOKSTORE
*2720 W. 43rd St. , Minneapolis    920-5005*
In most cases, children and shopping DON'T mix. But Wild Rumpus is a delightful exception to the rule. This magical store is a child's pet-filled playhouse. Kids can peer through a plexiglass floorboard to view the shop's pet rat, enjoy the pleasant coo of the resident mourning dove and pet two very spoiled house cats. Oh, yes, and there's the books . . . all enchanting and within easy reach of little fingers. Store hours are 10 AM to 8 PM Monday through Friday; 10 AM to 5 PM Saturday; noon to 5 PM Sunday.

## Zoos

### MINNESOTA ZOO
*13000 Zoo Blvd. , Apple Valley    432-9000*
This 500-acre zoological garden, located in the southern suburb of Apple Valley, is home to more than 2,700 mammals, birds, fish, reptiles and amphibians living in natural-habitat settings. A series of winding trails brings visitors nose-to-snout with the Earth's creatures.

The Ocean Trail offers dolphin performances and underwater views of sea creatures from around the world. The Tropics Trail takes visitors through an indoor oasis of lush greenery, exotic birds and gibbons. A new coral reef exhibit showcases sharks and brilliantly colored tropical fish.

The Minnesota Trail spotlights regional wildlife such as puma, beavers and otters in indoor and outdoor habitats. The Northern Trail offers glimpses of timber wolves, moose, Asian wild horses and camels. And, finally, the Discovery Trail features a Children's Zoo and a "please touch" Zoolab tank of interesting critters.

If the trails prove too daunting, hop aboard the Skytrail monorail ($2) for a treetop look at the animals. A new amphitheater features the World of Birds show, plus evening concerts by well-known musical groups. In the winter, Nordic skiing trails crisscross the zoo grounds.

The zoo offers extensive educational outreach programs for people of all ages. Summer zoo hours are 9 AM to 6 PM Monday through Saturday and 9 AM to 8 PM Sunday. Winter hours are 9 AM to 4 PM daily. Admission is $8 for adults; $4 for children 12 and younger; $5 for seniors 65 and older; and free for ages 2 and younger. The Skytrail fee is $2 (ages 2 and younger, free).

### COMO PARK ZOO, CONSERVATORY
### AND AMUSEMENT PARK
*Midway Pkwy. and Kaufman Dr.*
*St. Paul                     488-5571*
Como Zoo is an enduring old favorite for Twin Cities children and their parents, many of whom spent their own childhood days at

Como — feeding the seals, grunting at the gorillas and soaring on amusement park rides.

The zoo's collection is impressive, ranging from snow leopards and Siberian tigers to Alaskan timber wolves; from gorillas to sea lions; from polar bears to flamingos. Children especially enjoy the seal shows, presented at 11 AM, 2 and 4 PM daily May 15 through August (except Mondays), with an extra 5 PM show on weekends. Shows are at 2 and 4 PM weekends only in September.

The Como Park Conservatory, located on zoo grounds, features seasonal blooming plants and tropical and semitropical vegetation year round. And a formal Japanese tea garden is open on a limited basis from May through August. The zoo has an adjoining amusement park and picnic area.

Como Zoo is, by no means, as expansive or modern as the Minnesota Zoo located in suburban Apple Valley, but even so, it has definite advantages — it's more centrally located than the Minnesota Zoo and, best of all, it's free. There are fees for the amusement park rides, however, and donations are happily accepted at the Conservatory.

Also on the expansive Como Park grounds are an 18-hole golf course, swimming pool, and lakeside walking and biking trails. Zoo hours, from April through September, are 8 AM to 8 PM (buildings are open from 10 AM to 6 PM). In winter, the zoo is open from 8 AM to 5 PM (buildings from 10 AM to 4 PM). Parking is free.

## Amusement Parks

### VALLEYFAIR FAMILY AMUSEMENT PARK

*1 Valleyfair Dr., Shakopee*        445-6500

Located in the southwest suburb of Shakopee, Valleyfair is Minnesota's answer to Disneyland with more than 40 thrilling rides, a terrific water park, concert stages and an Imax giant-screen theater — all laid out on immaculately maintained, landscaped grounds. A single admission fee covers the cost of all rides.

The park is staffed, for the most part, by perky, wholesome teenagers, and the rides themselves range from the pleasant Tilt-O-Whirl to the stomach-flipping Corkscrew and gravity-defying Excalibur rollercoaster. Not for the fainthearted!

A new attraction at Valleyfair is Berenstain Bear Country, based on the popular children's book series. Children can tour the bears' family treehouse, visit Dr. Grizzley's office, dig for fossils in the dinosaur pit and view the Bears' daily show. Also included are an Actual Factual Museum and a variety of hands-on activities.

Admission to Valleyfair includes entry into the adjacent Whitewater Country Waterpark. Fun-lovers can choose among many slippery attractions, including the Raging Rapids inner-tube slide and — for the daring — the Speed Slide, a very vertical 50-foot fall. Valleyfair hours are early May (weekends) and, after about the middle of May, open daily through Labor Day from

10 AM to late evening (closing hours vary). Admission is $19.95 for adults; children age 4 and up to 48 inches tall pay $4.95; children 3 and younger are free; and seniors 62 and older $11.95. A two-day pass is $25.95. Starlight admission after 5 PM is $11.95. Season passes are $56 per person.

In addition to the amusement and water park, Valleyfair also operates Challenge Park, a go-cart track and miniature-golf course. There is no entry charge for Challenge Park, but a fee (generally in the $3 to $5 range) is charged for each ride or round of golf.

### MALL OF AMERICA AND CAMP SNOOPY
*(Located just south of the intersection of I-494 and Hwy. 77)*
*Bloomington*                883-8600

America's largest enclosed shopping mall is described in detail in the Shopping chapter, but it's worth noting here that the huge facility offers activities beyond marathon shopping at more than 400 specialty stores. No. 1, of course, is Knott's Camp Snoopy, a seven-acre landscaped indoor amusement park with 23 rides, 14 eating places and four entertainment stages. Attractions include the overhead Ripsaw roller coaster and a wet and wild ride called Paul Bunyan's Log Chute, which splashes down a 40-foot waterfall. There's also a "fly by the seat of your pants" 3-D movie theater that places viewers in the middle of the action. Hours are 9:30 AM to 9:30 PM Saturday; 10 AM to 7:30 PM Sunday; 10 AM to 9:30 PM Monday through Friday. There's no admission fee to the

park, but each attraction has a point value. Visitors purchase point passes in varying amounts. To enter each ride, a visitor merely runs the point pass under a scanner, which reads a bar code — à la the modern grocery store.

Also of interest for kids is the free Lego Imagination Center, a shrine to those little interlocking plastic blocks. It houses more than 30 giant Lego creations as well as a Lego play area for kids.

Aspiring duffers can try out Golf Mountain, an 18-hole miniature golf challenge overlooking Camp Snoopy. For movie buffs, the Mall's General Cinema sports 14 screens showcasing the latest from Hollywood. For more details, see the chapters on Shopping and Restaurants.

## *Water Parks — Indoor and Outdoor*

### WHITEWATER COUNTRY WATERPARK AT VALLEYFAIR
(See complete details above under Amusement Parks.)

### EKO BACKEN
*22570 Manning Tr., Scandia*        433-2422

This outdoor park, situated in the midst of rolling farmland in the northern suburb of Scandia, has two huge (350-foot) slides for water-sliding in the summer and plentiful hills with tows for snow-tubing in the winter. There's also a brand-new miniature golf course, picnic area, volleyball courts and concession stand. Hours are 10 AM to 7 PM daily in summer (June 1 through Labor Day). Winter hours are 11 AM to 10:30 PM weekends and holidays and 6:30 to 10 PM Monday through Friday evenings. Admission fee is $7.50 ($6.50 for 12 and younger). Directions: from St. Paul, take I-35E north to Highway 97. Go east on 97 to Manning Trail (County Road 15). Go north on Manning Trail 1.5 miles to Eko Backen.

### BEAVER MOUNTAIN WATER SLIDE
*15100 Buckhill Rd., Burnsville      435-1700*

This south suburban water park has six slides, ranging from "kiddie" to "black hole." It's open during daylight hours, all summer. Admission is $12 for all day; $9 for 20 slides; $7 for 10 slides.

### BUNKER HILLS WAVE POOL
*701 County Parkway Rd. A*
*Coon Rapids                      755-3672*

This is as close to California surf as you get in landlocked Minnesota. Patrons rent inner tubes and "surf" over machine-generated waves in this popular outdoor pool located in the northwestern suburb of Coon Rapids. Admission is $4 for all day; $3 for kids younger than 18. Tube rental is $1 per hour.

### WILD MOUNTAIN
*Country Rd. 16*
*(7 miles north of Taylors Falls)  1-465-6315*

This wintertime downhill ski area northeast of the Twin Cities transforms itself into a water park during the summer months, offering water slides, alpine slides, a go-kart track and canoe rentals. The park also operates riverboat cruises on the scenic St. Croix riv-

er. Summer hours are 10 AM to 8 PM seven days a week, beginning Memorial Day weekend. Fees: Superday pass (unlimited water and dry rides), $18.80 plus tax for ages 6 and older; unlimited water rides and three dry-ride tickets, $14.95 plus tax; unlimited water rides, $10.95 plus tax. For ages 3 to 5, the fee for unlimited water rides is $5.95 plus tax. The park also offers several riverboat cruises at varying fee levels.

### SHOREVIEW COMMUNITY CENTER
*4600 N. Victoria St. Shoreview    490-4700*

This modern city-owned recreation center in the northern suburb of Shoreview is a wet 'n' wild place for the whole family with a huge water slide and swimming pools equipped with rope swings and fountains, hot tub, two basketball courts, a weight room and running track. Hours are noon to 7:45 PM on weekends and noon to 9:45 PM on weekdays. Admission is $4.75 for adults and $3.75 for children (add $1 for the waterslide). Shoreview residents receive discounts.

### CHASKA COMMUNITY CENTER
*1661 Parkridge Dr.*
*(two blocks east of the intersection of Hwy. 41 and Anchor Blvd.), Chaska      448-5633*

This facility was modeled after the Shoreview Community Center and offers basically the same attractions in a clean, modern indoor setting located in the southwest suburb of Chaska. Hours are 1 to 5 PM and 7 to 8:30 PM Monday through Thursday, and 1 to 5 PM and 6 to 9 PM Friday through Sunday. Admission is $3.75 for

Photo: Buzz Magnuson, Pioneer Press

*The community center in Shoreview, a St. Paul suburb.*

adults (17 and older) and $3.25 for children. Discounts are offered for residents of Chaska.

## Indoor Play Centers

### LEAPS & BOUNDS
*Burnhill Shoppers Corner*
*14103 Irving Ave. S., Burnsville    898-2299*
### LEAPS & BOUNDS
*8601 Springbrook Dr. N.E., Blaine    785-8910*

These family-centered play centers are filled with secret tunnels, bridges, cargo nets, slides and ball pools — all the "gym dandy" paraphernalia that active children love. There's also a quiet room for ages 3 and younger. Hours are 9 AM to 8 PM Monday through Thursday; 9 AM to 10 PM Friday and Saturday; 9 AM to 7 PM Sunday. Admission is $5.95 for unlimited play; adults are admitted free with a child. The center is designed for ages 1 through 12.

### DISCOVERY ZONE
*In the Minneapolis suburbs:*
*Springbrook Mall, 139 85th Ave. N.W.*
*Coon Rapids                    783-9707*
*Yorktown Mall, 3441 Hazelton Rd.*
*Edina                          893-9950*
*In the St. Paul suburbs:*
*Rosedale Square, 1619 W. County Rd. C*
*Roseville                      628-9009*
*Woodbury Village, 1505 Queens Dr.*
*Woodbury                       735-4386*

Like Leaps & Bounds, these playlands offer tunnels, ball pools, rope climbing and lots of physical fun. Hours are 10 AM to 8 PM Sunday through Thursday; 10 AM to 10 PM Friday and Saturday. Admission is $5.99 for ages 2 through 12 and $2.99 for ages 24 months and younger.

### EDINBOROUGH PARK
*7700 York Ave. S. , Edina    893-9890*

This lushly landscaped indoor park features a skating rink, playgrounds, picnic area, swimming pool and an amphitheater with free entertainment — all enclosed in an attractive high-rise setting. Admission is free except for a pool charge of $3 per person. Call for the pool hours.

### KIDSPORTS
*Maplewood Commons Shopping Center*
*1900 E. County Rd. D*
*Maplewood*      773-9530

This center, for ages 1 through 12, offers an ambitious 10,000 square feet of tunnels, obstacle courses and equipment, plus a hide-and-seek maze, carpeted gym and snack bar. Hours are 9 AM to 9 PM Monday through Friday; 9 AM to 10 PM Friday and Saturday; 10 AM to 8 PM Sunday. Admission is $4.95 Monday through Friday; $5.95 Saturday and Sunday.

### FUN STATION
*Galleria Shopping Center*
*3460 W. 70th St., Edina*      922-1773

Fun Station is another marvelous mix of tube slides, ball crawls and other physical fun for the younger set. This center also offers short-term child care (two hours max) for ages 3 and older while Mom and Dad browse the interesting shops of the Galleria. Hours are 10 AM to 8 PM Monday through Thursday; 10 AM to 10 PM Friday and Saturday; 11 AM to 6 PM Sunday. Fees are $4.95 per child when accompanied by a parent; no charge for parents. (For drop-off child care, it's $4.95 for the first hour and $3 for the second hour.)

### NEW HORIZON KIDS QUEST
*2228 Eden Prairie Center*
*Eden Prairie*      941-1007

This is a top-of-the-line play center that offers such extras as free, nonviolent video games and an obstacle course with rope swings, karaoke room, computer art and a Barbie corner. This facility offers drop-off day care only, with no time restrictions. Hours are 9 AM to 10 PM Monday through Thursday; 9 AM to midnight Friday and Saturday; 11 AM to 8 PM Sunday. The fee is $5 per hour.

## Outdoor Playgrounds

The Twin Cities boast many state-of-the-art outdoor playgrounds where children can run and jump in the fresh air and sunshine. Note that in all Hennepin County system parks, you are charged a $4 daily parking fee. The following are a few outstanding examples:

### BAKER PARK RESERVE
*3800 County Rd. 24, Maple Plain 476-4666*

This park, part of the Hennepin County park system, has a wonderful playground filled with wooden climbing structures, slides and tire swings. It's adjacent to rolling picnic grounds on the shores of Lake Independence. The park is located in the western suburb of Maple Plain, on County Road 24, between highways 12 and 55.

### FRENCH REGIONAL PARK
*12605 County Rd. 9, Plymouth    559-8891*

Also part of the Hennepin County system, this park's exceptional wooden playground is a kid's dream come true with tire swings, extensive jungle-gym ropes and cargo nets, plus winding slides and great hide 'n' seek areas.

### CHUTES AND LADDERS
*Hyland Lake Park Reserve*
*8737 E. Bush Lake Rd., Bloomington 941-4362*
The "chutes" are several 40- to 50-foot enclosed slides that offer thrills aplenty. Also available at this Hennepin County park is the usual complement of traditional playground equipment for all ages.

### ELM CREEK PARK RESERVE
*13080 Territorial Rd., Maple Grove 424-5511*
Located in yet another Hennepin County park, this playground offers popular pulley rides, extensive tunnels, slides and swings.

### LAKE REBECCA PARK RESERVE
*8600 Rebecca Park Tr., Rockford 972-3407*
This lovely park sports a fanciful playground with a climbing tower, swings and curving slides.

### LONG LAKE REGIONAL PARK
*New Brighton 777-1707*
This Ramsey County park has a new playground with climbing areas, swings and slides. The park is located off Country Road 77 near the intersection of interstate highways 35W and 694.

**Other playgrounds worth visiting:**

### LINDEN HILLS PARK
*34th St. and Xerxes Ave. S., Minneapolis*

### POWDERHORN PARK
*33rd St. and 10th Ave. S., Minneapolis*

### HARRIET BISHOP PLAYGROUND
*Harriet Island, St. Paul*

### CENTRAL PARK
*Victoria Ave. between county roads B and C, Roseville*

### SKYLAND PARK
*Cliff Road (.35-mile east of I-35W), Burnsville*

*Snowboarding at Wild Mountain, a ski area north of the Twin Cities.*

# *Inside*
# Recreation and Parks

The real joys of Twin Cities living are found in the area's many outdoor pleasures.

The greater metro region offers a dizzying array of outdoor pursuits. You can swim, canoe or drop a fishing line in a sparkling urban lake; hike the St. Croix riverbanks; listen to the call of a trumpeter swan in a peaceful park reserve; camp out under the stars; or sprint the Mississippi River roads on a blazing autumn day.

Tree-shaded parks and shimmering lakes are the crowning glories of the Twin Cities, home of one of the most extensive park systems in the country.

Within the seven-county metropolitan area there are four state parks, 19 wildlife management/refuge areas, 43 regional parks and approximately 1,000 municipally owned parks. This is truly the land of lakes: 31 large lakes in the Twin Cities proper and about 1,000 in the greater metro area. Let's not forget Old Man River, the Mighty Mississippi; its brother, the Minnesota River; the nearby scenic St. Croix River; or lovely Minnehaha Creek, a ribbon of water that meanders willy-nilly through South Minneapolis to a crashing finale at the legendary Minnehaha Falls.

(See our In, On and Around the Water chapter for a comprehensive look at recreational opportunities on our lakes and rivers.)

In this chapter, we provide an overview of the parks and recreation scene in the Twin Cities and suburbs, including city, state and county parks, golf courses, swimming pools, health and fitness clubs and much more. (See the Winter's Wonderland chapter for information on wintertime recreation.)

Let's begin with a look at city parks.

## *City Parks*

### Minneapolis

Minneapolis has approximately 170 city parks and 18 lakes, not to mention 38 miles of designated walking trails and 36 miles of biking trails. For detailed information on specific parks, call the Minneapolis Park and Recreation Board at 348-2142.

Here are a few of our local favorites.

#### MINNEHAHA PARK
*Minnehaha Ave. and 50th St.*

Steeped in history, legend and natural beauty, Minnehaha Park consists of 142 acres of rolling lawns and thick woods, crowned by the lovely Minnehaha Falls, a breathtaking 40-foot waterfall that cascades through a wooded glen. The cataract has inspired artists, poets, composers and photographers, not to mention sweethearts, their passions presumably stirred by the roaring waters.

Henry Wadsworth Longfellow was so taken by a picture of the falls that he used it as the setting for his narrative poem "Song of Hiawatha," even though he never actually visited the falls. The epic's lovers, Hiawatha and Minnehaha, are memorialized here in a statue by Jacob Fjelde that was purchased in 1893 with pennies collected by Minnesota schoolchildren.

Another historical note: While visiting the falls, an inspired Antonin Dvorak scribbled down the musical notes that eventually became his Opus 100, the "Indian Maiden."

The falls are created by Minnehaha Creek, a stream that begins in Lake Minnetonka, winds through South Minneapolis and bisects the park before joining the Mississippi to the east. During dry spells, the creek water is augmented by water piped in from wells.

Many a Twin Citian recalls childhood jaunts to Minnehaha Park: climbing down the long stone stairway to the lower lookout bridge, leaping from boulder to boulder across the creekbed (more often than not, getting soaked in the process) and playing hide 'n' seek on the park's many wooded paths.

Minnehaha Park is located in South Minneapolis. It's also the site of the historic Stevens House, the first framed dwelling on the Mississippi's western banks in Minneapolis. Originally located near St. Anthony Falls, the house was moved to its present locale around the turn of the century. For tour information, call 722-2220.

### LAKE HARRIET AND LYNDALE PARK GARDENS
*Lake Harriet Pkwy.*

From the falls, take a drive down gorgeous Minnehaha Parkway and enjoy the parade of bikers and walkers whizzing past elegant old homes. Turn north on Lyndale Avenue, go a few blocks, then jog west again to hook up with Lake Harriet Parkway, which circles Minneapolis' most picturesque urban lake.

At the north end of the lake are a swimming beach and an attractive bandshell and pavilion where free concerts are offered regularly in the summer. There are also rental canoes and the *Queen of the Lakes* sternwheeler.

Across the parkway to the north you'll see a beckoning expanse of greenery and lush color: the Lyndale Park Rose and Rock Garden, the second-oldest public rose garden in the United States, and the Thomas Sadler Roberts Bird Sanctuary, home to numerous bird species.

The rose gardens in their full summer glory are a gorgeous attraction. Many new hybrids are planted here in the test garden for the All American rose selections. There's also an adjoining garden

*Photo: Pioneer Press*

*Itasca State Park, headwaters of the Mississippi River, north of the Twin Cities.*

of annuals and perennials. The rock garden is graced by a Japanese-style bridge containing peace stones found near the site of the atomic bomb explosion at Hiroshima and Nagasaki.

Continuing north on William Berry Drive, you'll converge with Lake Calhoun Boulevard for a scenic drive around Lake Calhoun. If you choose, you may continue northward and circle picturesque Lake of the Isles. For more information on both lakes, see the In, On and Around the Water chapter.

### LORING PARK
*Harmon Place and Willow St.*

Just northeast of Lake of the Isles and in the shadow of downtown, this jewel of a park is Minneapolis' version of New York's Washington Square, attracting a mix of urban professionals and office-workers, young arty types, ne'er-

do-wells, hipsters and hoops-playing kids.

In addition to the basketball courts, there are shuffleboard courts, horseshoe pits, tennis courts and a children's playground — all surrounding the tiny, picturesque Loring Lake.

One of the Twin Cities' loveliest water fountains, the Berger Fountain, is found here at 14th and Willow streets. Rising like a large dandelion puff, the fountain spews water from 250 copper tubes in a spherelike configuration. It's a glistening sight on a sunny summer day.

Loring Park is hip and happening. On the northwest side of the park, at 1624 Harmon Place, is the Loring Cafe, a trendy *salon* filled with artistes, sneering waiters and black-clad sax players. To the east is an interesting neighborhood of theaters, bars and ethnic restaurants adjoining downtown. And to the west is . . .

### MINNEAPOLIS SCULPTURE GARDEN
*Hennepin Ave.*

A whimsical pedestrian bridge designed by Siah Armajani takes you across bustling Hennepin Avenue to the Minneapolis Sculpture Garden, an 11-acre park filled with 40-plus works by renowned sculptors. The park is a collaborative project of the Minneapolis Park and Recreation Board and Walker Art Center, located just south of the park.

The landmark piece is the huge, soaring "Spoonbridge and Cherry" fountain sculpture by Claes Oldenburg and Coosje van Bruggen. One can't help but smile at the sight of this monstrous spoon — measuring 52 feet — topped by a 9½-foot cherry.

Other artists whose works are found in the garden include Henry Moore, George Segal and Jackie Ferrara. The grounds also feature the glassed-in Cowles Conservatory, housing the vibrant "Standing Glass Fish" sculpture designed by Frank Gehry, as well as seasonal floral displays.

This striking garden is an attraction for all ages. Open year round, it makes a pleasant stop in conjunction with a visit to the nearby Guthrie Theater or Walker Art Center. Hours of operation for the park are 6 AM to midnight. The conservatory is open 10 AM to 8 PM Tuesday through Saturday and 10 AM to 5 PM Sunday; it is closed Monday.

### POWDERHORN PARK
*14th Ave. S. and 35th St.*

Smack-dab in the middle of a lively, culturally diverse urban neighborhood is this 65-acre patch of green known as Powderhorn Park, a historic magnet for family gatherings and the site of a colorful Mayday parade and summertime arts fair. At the park's center is Powderhorn Lake, deriving its name from its unique shape.

The park also boasts four fanciful children's playgrounds — one for each season — and, in the winter, the only speed-skating ice oval in Minneapolis.

### THEODORE WIRTH PARK
*Wirth Pkwy.*                       *521-9731*

This sprawling 957-acre wooded park, the largest in the Minneapolis parks system, offers something for everyone.

For gardeners and nature lovers, there's the spectacular 13-acre Eloise Butler Wildflower Garden and Bird Sanctuary, featuring plant species and wildlife native to woodland, bog and prairie habitats. A world away from the urban madness, the Butler garden is open from 7:30 AM to dusk daily April 1 to October 31. Naturalists are at hand to offer tours and programs.

Also of interest to green-thumbers are the lovely J.D. Rivers' 4-H Children's Garden and a daylily-perennial garden.

Theodore Wirth Park also contains extensive evergreen groves, a five-acre tamarack bog and several natural springs.

Wirth Lake attracts swimmers with its sandy beach and adjacent

Photo: Joe Rossi, Pioneer Press

*The Twin Cities Marathon is an annual event.*

picnicking and play areas. The lake is also a popular fishing spot.

This is a year-round park. An 18-hole golf course attracts summer duffers and, in the winter, is transformed into a Nordic sports complex, offering downhill and cross-country skiing, snowshoeing, skating, snow-tubing and sledding — not to mention hot cocoa in the Swiss chalet clubhouse. Call ahead for complete program information.

To get to Wirth Park, take I-394 west from downtown Minneapolis to Wirth Parkway. From there, go north to the park.

## St. Paul

St. Paul's parks are as varied and charming as the city itself: expansive Como Park with its gently rolling lawns; the sedate and Victorian Irvine Park; the urban and urbane Rice Park; and scenic Mounds Park with its mysterious Indian burial mounds and magnificent river views. There are more than 50 recreational sites covering 2,000 acres in the St. Paul park system, not to mention several lakes and 29 miles of Mississippi River shoreline. For more information on St. Paul parks, call 266-6400.

Here is a listing of St. Paul's most popular parks.

### COMO PARK AND LAKE
*1431 N. Lexington Pkwy.*

| | |
|---|---|
| Conservatory | 489-1740 |
| Zoo | 488-5571 |
| Golf course | 488-9673 |

The 450-acre Como Park is a delightful family destination that features a free public zoo and adjacent amusement park, a nature conservatory bursting with flowers and fountains, Japanese gardens, swimming pools, picnic areas, athletic fields, a lake for fishing and paddleboating, biking and jogging trails and an 18-hole golf course. The park's recently restored, picturesque Lakeside Pavilion offers food and free evening concerts during the summer months. (See the Kidstuff chapter for more information on the zoo.)

It's easy to see why this handsome park is an enduring favorite of Twin Citians young and old.

Como Park is about 2.5 miles north of I-94.

### PHALEN PARK AND LAKE
*Wheelock Pkwy. and Arcade St.*

A popular St. Paul destination, this park is centered on Lake Phalen, with its sandy swimming beach, volleyball courts and 3 miles of shoreline jogging and biking paths. At the park activity center, you can rent paddleboats, canoes, rowboats, sailboards and sailboats.

You'll also find an 18-hole golf course (used as a downhill and cross-country ski area in the winter), tennis courts, an indoor recreation center, picnic pavilion and an amphitheater offering free summer concerts.

### MOUNDS PARK
*Mounds Blvd. and Burns Ave.*

Mounds Park, laid out on the scenic Mississippi River bluffs east of downtown St. Paul, is the site of 2,000-year-old burial sites of the Hopewell Indians, ancestors of the Dakota tribe.

This 77-acre park offers a not-to-be-missed panoramic view of downtown St. Paul, its bustling river barges, Holman airfield and surrounding areas.

Cherokee Park, in St. Paul's West Side along the river bluffs of Cherokee Heights Boulevard, also affords great views, playgrounds, picnic areas and tennis courts.

### IRVINE PARK
*Walnut St. and Ryan Ave.*

Escaping to Irvine Park is like stepping back in time to the Victorian era of elegance and grace. In an age of artificial noise and mayhem, Irvine gives us water dancing in a graceful old fountain, acorns crunching underfoot, mothers and babes quietly chatting on park benches. Created in the mid-1800s in one of St. Paul's first neighborhoods, the park and surrounding area experienced years of neglect before being lovingly restored in the 1970s. Today, this urban jewel just southwest of downtown St. Paul is surrounded by many well-tended Victorian homes, including one that houses Forepaugh's, a popular restaurant. A block away is the Alexander Ramsey House, the stately mansion of the first governor of Minnesota. (See the Architecture and Historic Sites chapter for more on the Ramsey House.)

### RICE PARK
*Washington and Fourth Sts.*

New York may have Rockefeller Plaza, but St. Paul has charming little Rice Park, a peaceful urban escape complete with gurgling fountains, hotdog vendors, flower gardens and plenty of stone benches for people-watching. This is where downtown workers go to loosen their collars, kick off their shoes and shake off their cares.

During the annual Winter Carnival, Rice Park is illuminated by thousands of sparkling lights, enchanting ice sculptures and a small ice rink.

Rice Park is surrounded by four St. Paul landmarks: the elegant St. Paul Hotel, the Ordway Music Theatre, Landmark Center and the historic St. Paul Public Library.

### MEARS PARK
*Wacouta and Sixth Sts.*

Another spot of urban greenery is found at Mears Park in St. Paul's Lowertown district. Located across Sibley Street from Galtier Plaza, this recently renovated city park boasts a trickling stream, Norway pines, Japanese birch, maples and lindens, plus a perennial garden and abundant benches and paths. There's also a bandstand for concerts.

### HIGHLAND PARK
*Montreal Ave. and Edgcumbe Rd.*

So ya think you got us Minnesotans pegged, huh? You think we're just a bunch of cribbage-playing Lutherans? Well, head on over to Highland Park for a dose of reality. That's where we indulge our secret passion for Frisbee golf — on a regulation 12-hole course, no less. Top it off with a dip in one of St. Paul's best swimming pools, followed by a heaping bowl of booya, if you're lucky enough to happen upon a Belgian picnic!

*Ice-skating is an activity enjoyed by young and old alike.*

Photo: Richard Marshall, Pioneer Press

## The Suburbs

Here are a few green treasures tucked away in the suburbs.

### CAPONI PARK
*1215 Diffley Rd., Eagan      454-4338*

Art and nature come together in the 60-acre Caponi Park, where sculptures are conceived and built on site as an outgrowth of their natural surroundings. Tours are by appointment.

### NORMANDALE JAPANESE GARDEN
*9400 France Ave. S.*
*Bloomington      881-8137*

This two-acre Japanese garden on the grounds of Normandale Community College is a tranquil retreat in the bustling suburb of Bloomington. The traditional Japanese garden features footpaths and carved bridges that span pools and provide vantage points for viewing this contemplative setting. There is no admission charge.

### WESTWOOD HILLS
### ENVIRONMENTAL EDUCATION CENTER
*8300 Franklin Ave. W.*
*St. Louis Park      924-2544*

Tucked between the hilly neighborhoods of northern St. Louis Park and I-394 is this natural retreat filled with thick woods and a wetlands rich with waterfowl. Owned by the city of St. Louis Park, Westwood Hills sponsors many educational programs for children and families. There are numerous paths through the woods and a boardwalk circling the wetlands. There is no admission charge.

### Wood Lake Nature Center
*735 Lake Shore Dr., Richfield      861-9365*
This Richfield nature area totals 150 acres, 70 acres of which is the Wood Lake wetlands, filled with myriad wildlife. The park features 3 miles of walking paths and a floating boardwalk. The nature center offers many educational programs throughout the year. There are no entry fees.

### Springbrook Nature Center
*100 85th Ave. N.E., Fridley      784-3854*
This 127-acre refuge of woods and wetlands also boasts a visitors center filled with natural-history displays. The center sponsors many educational programs and is open to the public free of charge.

### Staring Lake Outdoor Center
*13765 Staring Lake Pkwy.*
*Eden Prairie                949-8479*
This nature park encompasses 159 acres dotted with lakes, ponds and woods, plus a genuine log cabin. There is no admission fee to this refuge.

### Thomas Irvine Dodge Nature Center
*1795 Charlton St. W., St. Paul    455-4531*
This private natural refuge consists of 300 acres of marshes, ponds, meadows, woodlands and restored prairie. There are also such educational facilities as a model farm, apiary, live animal displays, maple-syruping room, boardwalk,

greenhouse and classrooms. Weekdays, the refuge is reserved for school groups and educational programs. Its trails are open to the general public for hiking from 10 AM to 4 PM Saturdays.

# County Parks

## Hennepin County

Encompassing Minneapolis and many of its western suburbs, Hennepin County offers more than 24,000 acres of park reserves and regional parks in a variety of woodland settings.

These well-maintained natural areas offer something for the whole family — from state-of-the-art playgrounds and cross-country ski trails to environmental programs led by park naturalists.

Hennepin parks charge a daily parking fee of $4. Frequent users may be interested in the annual $20 pass, permitting unlimited use from the date of purchase. This annual pass is reciprocal with Carver, Washington and Anoka counties, allowing free admission to their county parks.

In this section, we describe several of the most popular Hennepin Parks and their offerings. Other Hennepin parks worth visiting are: Bryant Lake Regional Park in Eden Prairie, Carver Park Reserve in Victoria, Cleary Lake Regional Park and Murphy-Hanrehan Park in Prior Lake, Coon Rapids Dam Park, Crow-Hassan Park Reserve in Hassan Township, Elm Creek Park Reserve in Osseo, Fish Lake

*Dog sledding.*

Regional Park in Maple Grove and Lake Rebecca Park Reserve near Rockford.

For complete information on all Hennepin parks, call 559-9000.

### BAKER PARK RESERVE
*County Rd. 19, Medina*

This park, located just 20 minutes west of the metropolitan area on Lake Independence, offers a diversity of recreational activities in addition to its popular campground.

Attractions include an imaginative children's play area, well-groomed swimming beaches, a golf course, 6 miles of paved biking/hiking trails with bike rentals, 8 miles of cross-country ski trails and 9 miles of snowmobile trails.

To get to Baker Park, take I-394 (Highway 12) west about 20 miles to Maple Plain. Then take county roads 26 and 19 north to the park.

### FRENCH REGIONAL PARK
*Rockford Rd., Plymouth*

Within view of the Minneapolis skyline, this park on Medicine Lake in the western suburbs offers many lake-oriented activities, from swim-

Photo: Joe Rossi, Pioneer Press

ming in the summer to skating in the winter. There's also a great multilevel maze of cargo climbing nets and slides for the younger set. Cross-country skiers enjoy the 9 miles of trails, some of which are lighted for night skiing.

French Park is located off Highway 9 (Rockford Road) between highways 169 and 494.

### HYLAND LAKE PARK RESERVE
*County Rd. 28, Bloomington*

Located in the bustling suburb of Bloomington, Hyland Lake Park is a quiet, green refuge for deer, pheasants and wild songbirds. There's a nature center offering year-round programs, and you'll enjoy the lake for fishing and canoeing (no swimming), 8 miles of hiking trails, 5 miles of biking trails, 7 miles of cross-country ski trails and a downhill skiing area with a chalet and 14 runs.

The park's Chutes 'n' Ladders play area, including a 60-foot enclosed slide, is popular with kids.

To reach Hyland, take Highway 169 South. Continue south of I-494 where 169 turns into County Road 18. Take a left at County Road 1 and another left at County Road 28. Continue to the park entrance.

### NOERENBERG MEMORIAL PARK GARDENS
*2840 North Shore Dr., Wayzata*

These pristine formal flower gardens on the shores of Lake Minnetonka attract many people for tours, informal viewing and weddings. No food or recreation is allowed, however. The gardens' Oriental boathouse provides an expansive view of the famous lake.

## Dakota County

We have provided information about some of the larger parks in Dakota County. Two others that you may want to visit are Spring Lake Park Reserve on the Mississippi River, just northwest of Hastings, and Thompson County Park in South St. Paul. For more information on Dakota parks, call 437-6608.

### LEBANON HILLS REGIONAL PARK
*Cliff Rd., Eagan*

This pine- and birch-filled park is dotted with a dozen woodland lakes and ponds and includes two major picnic areas, 7 miles of hiking trails, 10 miles of horseback trails and 2 miles of canoe trails and portages. Horses are available at nearby stables. Schultz Lake boasts a nice swimming beach.

Lebanon Hills Park is located off Cliff Road, between Pilot Knob Road and Highway 3.

### LAKE BYLLESBY REGIONAL PARK
*County Rd. 88, east of Randolph*

This Dakota County park is situated on a deep fishing lake formed by a dam on the Cannon River. It has a swimming beach, picnic area, camping facilities and a boat launch. This 1,490-acre reservoir is the largest body of water in the metropolitan area south of the Mississippi and Minnesota rivers.

To get there, take Highway 52 south from the St. Paul area to County Road 86. Take a right, then

Photo: Pioneer Press

Mears Park in Lowertown in downtown St. Paul.

exit on Harry Avenue and continue south to the park.

## Ramsey County

Ramsey County, encompassing St. Paul and east metro suburbs, has set aside 25 percent of its land for use as public parks. Here's a listing of a few Ramsey parks. Others are located at Long Lake, Snail Lake, Beaver Lake, Island Lake, Lake Johanna, Lake Josephine, Silver Lake, McCarron's Lake, Lake Owasso, Turtle Lake and White Bear Lake in St. Paul and suburbs. For information on Ramsey County Parks, call 777-1707.

### BALD EAGLE-OTTER LAKESREGIONAL PARK
*Near County Rds. 149 and 60*
*White Bear Township*
### TAMARACK NATURE CENTER
*5287 Otter Lake Rd.* 429-7787

This 862-acre park encompasses the northeast side of Bald Eagle Lake as well as land between Bald Eagle and Otter lakes in White Bear Township. The entrance is off Hugo Road. Amenities include picnic facilities, a swimming beach, shoreline fishing and a playground. The nearby Tamarack Nature Center offers cross-country skiing, hiking and year-round educational programs.

### BATTLE CREEK REGIONAL PARK
*Upper Afton Rd. in Maplewood and St. Paul*

This 805-acre park affords sweeping views of the Mississippi while offering 5 miles of cross-country ski trails, 4 miles of hiking trails, great sledding hills, picnic areas and playgrounds. The park, located in both St. Paul and Maplewood, is one block east of McKnight Road.

### KELLER REGIONAL PARK
*Phalen and Maplewood Drs.*

This 103-acre park offers access to Keller, Gervais, Kohlman, Phalen and Round lakes in St. Paul and Maplewood, with picnic areas, hiking trails and other amenities.

## Washington County

Washington County, east of St. Paul, has five county parks. We've described the largest, Lake Elmo Park Reserve; others are Point Douglas, Square Lake, Pine Point and Cottage Grove Ravine parks. For additional information, call 731-3851.

### LAKE ELMO PARK RESERVE
*Between Inwood and Lake Elmo Aves. N.*
*Lake Elmo*

Encompassing 2,165 acres of rolling hills, wetlands, lakes, prairies and forests, the park offers 80 camping sites, 20 miles of hiking trails, 12 miles of cross-country ski trails and 5 miles of biking trails, swimming beach and playground. The entrance is north of I-94 on Country Road 19.

## State Parks

Want a quick getaway from the city's hustle and bustle? Pack the cooler, throw the tent in the trunk and head out to one of the three Minnesota state parks within the

Twin Cities greater metropolitan area.

Entrance fees may be paid on a daily basis or with an annual pass. Parks are open to the public year round from 8 AM to 10 PM. For more information, call 296-6157 or (800) 766-6000. The TDD number for the hearing impaired is (800) 657-3929. To reserve a campsite or cabin, call (800) 765-CAMP. Campsites can be reserved from three to 120 days in advance for a nonrefundable fee.

### AFTON STATE PARK

*County Rd. 20, Afton*          *436-5391*

This is a great hiking park filled with rugged hills and St. Croix River overlooks. There are 18 miles of trails for hiking and cross-country skiing, plus 24 hike-in backpack camping sites. The park also features 5 miles of horse trails and 4 miles of biking trails.

From St. Paul, go 8 miles east on I-94, 7 miles south on County Road 15, then 3 miles east on County Road 20.

### MINNESOTA VALLEY STATE PARK

*U.S. Hwy. 169, Jordan*          *492-6400*

Just west of Jordan lies one of Minnesota's best-kept secrets. This attractive wooded park offers outstanding recreational opportunities only minutes from the Twin Cities: Minnesota River trails, historic farmsteads, lakes and abundant wildlife.

Minnesota Valley has 25 drive-in camping sites, plus eight hike-in backpack camping sites. The park also offers 34 miles of snowmobile trails and 4 miles of cross-country ski trails.

### WILLIAM O'BRIEN STATE PARK

*Minn. Hwy. 95*
*Marine on St. Croix*          *433-0500*

This very popular park on the St. Croix River features rolling wooded hills and flood-plain forests. Recreational activities include camping, canoeing, hiking, swimming, interpretive programs, picnicking and cross-country skiing. There are 125 drive-in campsites.

To reach William O'Brien, take State Highway 95 2 miles north of Marine on St. Croix.

### FORT SNELLING STATE PARK

*Post Rd.*          *725-2390*

This park, located below and separate from Historic Fort Snelling, offers 18 miles of hiking trails and 5 miles of biking trails in a stunning setting at the confluence of the Mississippi and Minnesota rivers. The park also has canoe and paddleboat rentals, as well as a popular beach on Snelling Lake.

To get to Fort Snelling State Park, take State Highway 5 to Post Road and look for the entrance.

## Not to Be Missed

### MINNESOTA LANDSCAPE ARBORETUM

*3675 Arboretum Dr.*
*Chanhassen*          *443-2460*

This 905-acre showcase harbors woods, gently rolling hills, native prairies and formal display gardens ranging from serene Japanese rock gardens to colorful English formal gardens. There are thousands of varieties of flowers, trees and shrubs, all visible from 6 miles of hiking trails, paved paths and a 3-mile drive. Tram rides are offered through the grounds several times daily. Open year round is the arboretum's Tearoom restaurant and Linden Tree Gift Shop, as well as the Andersen Horticulture Library. From May through October, free walking tours are offered at 10 AM Tuesday and Wednesday and the first Saturday of the month. Admission is $4 for adults (16 years and older) and $1 for children younger than 16 (free with parent). The arboretum grounds are open 8 AM to sunset daily. The buildings are open from 8 AM to 4:30 PM Monday through Friday and from 11 AM to 4:30 PM Saturday and Sunday.

## Golf

Minnesotans love the links!

Although the seasonal sport can be played here only six months a year (if it's a good year), golf has an enthusiastic following in the North Star State.

In fact, Minnesota has hosted several important golf tournaments — the 1991 U.S. Open at Hazeltine National Golf Club in Chaska is one — precisely because of the sport's popularity here.

There are more than 100 golf courses, public and private, in the greater Twin Cities area. That's more than in any other urban area in the country. Among the private courses are the upper-bracket, nationally known Hazeltine and Interlachen clubs with their equally upper-bracket membership fees.

There are also two new high-profile golf courses in the area: the Wilds in Prior Lake (a public course

and residential development) and Bearpath in Eden Prairie, a private facility. For us common folk, we'll start with a look at some of the most challenging and popular public courses in the Twin Cities.

By the way, a storehouse of information on local golf events and tournaments is the Minnesota Golf Association at 927-4643.

## Public Courses

### BAKER NATIONAL GOLF COURSE
*2935 Parkview Dr.*
*Medina*                    473-0800

Hennepin Parks operates this 18-hole regulation course, nine-hole executive course, driving range and new clubhouse. Greens fees are $20 for 18 holes, $12 for nine and $7 for the executive course. Carts are available for $20 for 18 holes and $11 for nine. Reservations may be made up to three days in advance.

### BRAEMAR GOLF COURSE
*6364 Dewey Hill Rd., Edina    941-2072*

This tree-filled, rolling course is owned and operated by the city of Edina. Edina residents may reserve tee times; the general public may golf on a walk-on, space-available basis. Greens fees are $18 for 18 holes and $10.50 for nine.

### BUNKER HILLS GOLF COURSE
*Hwy. 242 and Foley Blvd.*
*Coon Rapids*                755-4141

Bunker Hills, with its abundant woods and bunkers, is reputed to be the toughest public course in the metropolitan Twin Cities. Greens fees for 18 holes are $24 weekends and $22 weekdays; for nine holes, $12. Reservations are accepted.

### COLUMBIA GOLF COURSE
*St. Anthony Pkwy. and Central Ave.*
*Minneapolis*                789-2627
The focus at this municipal golf course (one of five operated by the city) is a state-of-the-art learning center. Fees are $16.50 for 18 holes and $11.50 for nine. Reservations may be made for weekends and holidays only.

### COMO PARK GOLF COURSE
*1431 N. Lexington Pkwy.*
*St. Paul*                488-9673
Reopened in 1988, this picturesque course is riddled with traps, trees and several ponds. It is owned and operated by the city of St. Paul. Greens fees are $17 for 18 holes and $12 for nine. Reservations are accepted.

### EDINBURGH USA GOLF COURSE
*8700 Edinbrook Crossing*
*Brooklyn Park*                424-7060
Robert Trent Jones designed this new golf course, which is handsome — yet hazardous to your golf score. Watch out for the treacherous third and 17th holes; those water hazards will get you every time! Greens fees are $29 for 18 holes and $14 for nine (after 6 PM only). Reservations are accepted four days in advance. This course, owned by the city of Brooklyn Park, also features a stately clubhouse and an elegant restaurant.

### GOODRICH GOLF COURSE
*1820 N. Van Dyke Rd., St. Paul*  777-7355
Owned by Ramsey County, this

course charges $17 for 18 holes and $12 for nine. Reservations are accepted four days in advance.

### FRANCIS GROSS GOLF COURSE
*St. Anthony Pkwy. and 27th Ave. N.E.*
*Minneapolis*                789-2542
Serious golfers like the distinctive topography at this municipal course. Greens fees are $16.50 for 18 holes and $11.50 for nine. Reservations are accepted. Holes three and 12 can be especially challenging.

### HIAWATHA GOLF COURSE
*4553 Longfellow Ave. S.*
*Minneapolis*                724-7715
Another municipal course, this one skirts lakes Hiawatha and Nokomis in South Minneapolis and is a longtime favorite for its easy accessibility and challenging layout. Minnehaha Creek winds through the links. Greens fees are $16.50 for 18 holes and $11.50 for nine. Reservations are accepted for weekend use only.

### HIGHLAND PARK GOLF COURSE
*1403 Montreal Ave., St. Paul*  699-0193
A par 72, city-owned course, Highland Park is well-trapped and challenging and offers scenic views of gently rolling hills and a meandering creek. Greens fees are $17 for 18 holes and $12 for nine. Reservations are accepted.

### HOLLYDALE GOLF CLUB
*4710 Holly Lane N., Plymouth*  559-9847
This suburban course offers challenges for every skill level. Greens fees weekdays are $16 for 18 holes and $11 for nine; week-

ends, $18 for 18 holes, $12 for nine. Reservations are accepted.

### KELLER GOLF COURSE
*2166 Maplewood Dr., St. Paul  484-3011*

Challenges aplenty await duffers at this handsome public course, the site of LPGA and PGA tournaments. Greens fees are $17 for 18 holes, $12 for nine.

### THE LINKS AT NORTHFORK
*9333 153rd Ave. N.W.*
*Ramsey                    241-0506*

The only Scottish links-style course in Minnesota, Northfork is characterized by large areas of roughs and nearly constant winds. Greens fees (18 holes only) are $25 for weekdays and $28 for weekends. After 4 PM, fees are $17 weekdays and $20 weekends.

### MAJESTIC OAKS GOLF COURSE
*Hwy. 65 N. and Bunker Lake Rd.*
*Ham Lake                   755-2142*

Play here is characterized by deep, unforgiving bunkers on a handsome course that is the site of many corporate and local tourneys. There are two 18-hole courses — Platinum and Gold. Hole seven on the Platinum Course is particularly challenging. The greens fees: Platinum, $22 weekends and $18 weekdays; Gold, $19 weekends and $16 weekdays. There's also an executive nine-hole course for $7.50.

### MANITOU RIDGE
*3200 N. McKnight Rd.*
*White Bear Lake            777-2987*

This Ramsey County course sports a newly constructed club-

house with pro shop, bar and grill. Watch out for Hole 10 with its devilish water hazard. Greens fees are $17 for 18 holes, $12 for nine.

### MEADOWBROOK GOLF COURSE
*300 Meadowbrook Rd.*
*Hopkins                    929-2077*

The fifth hole here can give you gray hair! A well-maintained course, it's easy to get to — just off Excelsior Boulevard in suburban Hopkins. Greens fees are $16.50 for 18 holes and $11.50 for nine. Reservations are accepted.

### PHALEN PARK GOLF COURSE
*1615 Phalen Dr., St. Paul   778-0413*

An 18-hole, city-owned course, this one stretches along the west shore of Phalen Lake, presenting enough doglegs, water hazards and sand bunkers to test all ability levels. Greens fees are $17 for 18 holes; $12 for nine.

### SUNDANCE GOLF AND BOWL
*15240 113th Ave.*
*Maple Grove                420-4700*

The rolling landscape here is deceptively challenging. Greens fees are $18 for 18 holes and $11.50 for nine. Reservations are accepted.

### THEODORE WIRTH GOLF COURSE
*Wirth Pkwy. and Plymouth Ave.*
*Minneapolis                522-4584*

Just minutes from downtown Minneapolis, Wirth offers a beautiful wooded setting for golf enthusiasts. Greens fees are $16.50 for 18 holes, $11.50 for nine. Reservations are accepted.

*Snow sliding at the Highland Golf Course in St. Paul.*

Photo: Chris Polydoroff, Pioneer Press

### UNIVERSITY OF MINNESOTA GOLF CLUB
*2275 Larpenteur Ave. W.*
*St. Paul*                              627-4000
This is an 18-hole course filled with delightfully difficult holes. Greens fees are $17 weekdays and $20 weekends. For University of Minnesota students, fees are $8 weekdays, $12 weekends.

---

### Indoor Driving Ranges

For those duffers who just can't let go of the game when the mercury dips, here are two places to swing your clubs without hitting a snowdrift.

•**Fore Seasons Golf Inc.**, 473-4813, 2465 W. Industrial Boulevard, Long Lake

•**Tony's Clubhouse**, 647-0233, 1526 Larpenteur Avenue W., Falcon Heights

---

### Outdoor Miniature Golf

A round of miniature golf and a hot summer's day are a perfect match for all ages. Here are a few fun minigolf courses in the Twin Cities.

### NORA'S
*3118 W. Lake St., Minneapolis    927-5781*

Work off one of Nora's home-cooked meals at the restaurant's very own 18-hole miniature golf course. It's a quaint course with a popular target hole and windmill obstruction.

### GASOLINE ALLEY
*10300 Central Ave. N.E.*
*Blaine                    784-7223*

A super-dooper course, it features fast fairways and challenges aplenty. It's part of a popular entertainment complex that also has a go-kart track and video game center.

### CHALLENGE PARK AT VALLEYFAIR
*1 Valleyfair Dr., Shakopee    445-7600*

This park is adjacent to Valleyfair and offers miniature golf, bumper boats and go-karts, all with separate fees.

### SPRING LAKE AMUSEMENT PARK
*1066 N.E. Hwy. 10*
*Spring Lake Park            786-4994*

Choose from two 18-hole miniature golf courses and two water slides. The park also has battery-powered cars for tots and a water-balloon tossing area.

### FORE SEASONS GOLF
*2465 W. Industrial Blvd.*
*Long Lake                  473-4813*

This large complex has an outdoor mini-golf course in addition to an indoor driving range.

## Indoor Miniature Golf

### GOLF MOUNTAIN
*Mall of America, Bloomington    883-8899*

Overlooking Camp Snooty, this 18-hole course is great for people-watching.

### GRAND SLAM SPORTS & ENTERTAINMENT CENTER
*3984 Sibley Memorial Hwy.*
*Eagan                      452-6569*

Miniature golf is just one part of this state-of-the-art sports center. There are also batting cages, a video arcade, basketball courts and much more.

## Swimming Pools

Even in the land of lakes, some prefer swimming in pools. Here's information on popular public pools in the Twin Cities area.

## Minneapolis

In Minneapolis, there are three public, outdoor 50-meter swimming pools. Daily fees are $1.50 per person. Season passes for families and individuals are also available at prices ranging from $27.50 for resident families to $14.50 for resident individuals. For nonresidents, season passes range from $41.25 for families to $21.50 for individuals. Please note: The prices quoted are for 1994 and are subject to change.

Minneapolis outdoor public pools are:
•**Rosacker Pool**, 348-8840, 1520 N.E. Johnson Street

•**North Commons Pool**, 348-2266, 1701 Golden Valley Road
•**Webber Pool**, 348-6412, 4400 Dupont Avenue N.

There also is public indoor swimming at:

•**Franklin Junior High**, 348-2226, 1501 Aldrich Avenue N.
•**Phillips Community Center**, 348-2373, 2323 11th Avenue S.

## St. Paul

St. Paul has two outdoor public pools. Admission is $2.50 for adults and $1.50 for kids 17 and younger.

•**Como Pool**, 489-2811, Horton and Lexington avenues
•**Highland Pool**, 699-7968, 1840 Edgcumbe Road. The city also operates an indoor pool, open daily except Sunday.
•**Oxford Pool**, 647-9925, 1079 Iglehart Avenue

## The Suburbs

There are a number of public outdoor pools in the outlying communities that cater to the public.

### WESTERN SUBURBS
•**St. Louis Park Recreation Center**, 924-2545, 5005 W. 36th Street, St. Louis Park

### NORTHWESTERN SUBURBS
•**Crystal Public Swimming Pool**, 531-0950, 4800 N. Douglas Drive, Crystal
•**Honsey Outdoor Pool**, 531-5177, 4301 Xylon Avenue N., New Hope

### SOUTHWESTERN SUBURBS
•**Eden Prairie Community Center**, 937-8727
•**Edina Aquatic Center**, 927-9829, Valley View Road and W. 66th Street, Edina

### SOUTH SUBURBS
•**Richfield Municipal Outdoor Pool**, 861-9355, 630 E. 66th Street, Richfield
•**Redwood Community Building and Outdoor Pool**, 431-8850, 311 County Road 42, Apple Valley
•**Valley View Pool**, 881-4937, 201 E. 90th Street, Bloomington

### NORTHERN SUBURBS
•**Edgewood Pool**, 784-0618, 5100 Edgewood Drive, Mounds View

### EASTERN SUBURBS
(These are indoor pools.)
• **Woodbury Junior High School**, 458-4300, 425 School Drive, Woodbury
• **Woodbury Senior High School**, 458-4320, 2665 Woodlane Drive, Woodbury

### SOUTHEASTERN SUBURBS AND COMMUNITIES
•**Cottage Grove Pool**, 458-2834, 6541 85th Street, Cottage Grove
•**Hastings Outdoor Pool**, 437-6111, Highway 55 and Maple Street, Hastings
•**Northview Pool**, 450-8744, 19th Avenue N. and Thompson Avenue, South St. Paul
•**McClain Pool**, 450-8744, Third Avenue and Seventh Street N., South St. Paul

• **West St. Paul Pool**, 552-4150, 92 W. Orme Street, West St. Paul

## Water Parks

### SHOREVIEW RECREATION CENTER
*4600 Victoria St., Shoreview    490-4700*
### CHASKA COMMUNITY CENTER
*1661 Parkridge Dr., Chaska    448-5633*
These two facilities are state-of-the-art indoor water parks. See the Kidstuff chapter for complete details on both parks.

### EDINBOROUGH PARK
*7700 York Ave. S., Edina    893-9890*
This indoor park has a pool, ice rink and health club on premises.

### MAPLEWOOD RECREATION CENTER
*2100 White Bear Ave.*
*Maplewood    770-4570*
This new city-owned facility, just completed in fall 1994, features pools, water slides, banquet facilities and an athletic club equipped with strength and cardiovascular machines.

## Bowling

This traditionally blue-collar sport is an enduring favorite in the Twin Cities, perhaps because it provides an easy and affordable recreational outlet during our long winters. Many families are taking up the sport, and alleys are encouraging this new trend by offering other attractions for children and smoke-free bowling times.

The Twin Cities boast many modern, attractive family-oriented bowling centers, as well as a smattering of old-time, smoke-filled "al-

leys." There isn't space to list them all. Here we've selected a few that stand out from the rest.

### BRYANT-LAKE BOWL
*810 W. Lake St., Minneapolis    825-3737*
This is '90s-style bowling! The oh-so-trendy Bryant-Lake serves up espresso, designer beer and brie to black-ball enthusiasts, who, after hurling a few strikes, can catch the latest live performance at the in-house cabaret theater.

### BRUNSWICK EDEN PRAIRIE LANES AND FAMILY FUN WORLD
*12200 Singletree Ln.*
*Eden Prairie    941-0445*
There are 40 lanes and 45,000 square feet of space in this new, high-tech bowling alley/entertainment center. Also on the grounds are a pro shop, a fun pizza parlor, a three-level children's indoor playground/day-care center and bar. Scoring is done by computer.

### NICOLLET BOWLING LANES
*3813 Nicollet Ave.*
*Minneapolis    822-4112*
This old neighborhood alley has a humble eight lanes, but that's part of its appeal. We're talking cozy and quaint here. Built in the '40s, Nicollet Lanes' alleys feature the old-fashioned above-the-floor ball returns. The beer bar has great burgers at rock-bottom prices. There's also pingpong and pool tables and steel and electric darts.

### STARDUST LANES
*2520 26th Ave. S., Minneapolis    721-6211*
This 20-year-old alley with 30 bowling lanes, video games and a

bar is an enduring favorite of Twin Citians. It's open 24 hours.

### MAPLEWOOD BOWL & FUN MALL
*1955 English St., Maplewood    774-8787*

This bowling entertainment center features 40 lanes and also has billiards, darts, foosball and a sports bar with live entertainment and karaoke. Wouldn't Norton and the guys be impressed!

## Martial Arts

People study the martial arts for a variety of reasons: to develop muscular strength and self control, for self defense, to meet new people or just for the fun of it.

There are many schools in the Twin Cities teaching a variety of martial-arts forms — everything from tae kwon do and Okinawa shirite karate to judo. For information on specific studios or schools, consult the Yellow Pages under "Karate." A word to the wise: Many so-called associations or organizations are simply fronts for specific schools or studios and are unreliable sources of objective information.

The best introduction to the martial arts may be through a low-cost community education class offered through local school districts. Many martial arts centers also offer a free introductory lesson.

## Running

Every October, 6,000 runners come from all over the world to race in the Twin Cities Marathon. Acclaimed as "the most beautiful urban marathon in America," this 26-mile course encompasses stately tree-shaded neighborhoods, Mississippi River boulevards and even the State Capitol lawns in St. Paul.

It is one of the major marathons in the country, attracting world-class runners who vie for the top prize of $12,000.

For information on running in or working as a volunteer for the Twin Cities Marathon, call its headquarters at (612) 673-0778.

Minneapolis and St. Paul are swarming with running and jogging enthusiasts who pursue the sport year round. That's right, year round! In the dead of winter, you'll see these daring (some might say foolhardy) runners, clad in sweats and earmuffs, leap over snowbanks and stride through slush to log their daily 5-miler. Racing events are held virtually every weekend of the year, including a half-marathon during the St. Paul Winter Carnival in late January and early February.

Favorite running spots in the Twin Cities: any of the major lakes, most notably Lake of the Isles, Lake Calhoun and Lake Harriet in Minneapolis and lakes Phalen and Como in St. Paul; Minneapolis' Minnehaha and Theodore Wirth parkways; St. Paul's mansion-lined Summit Avenue; and Hyland Lake Park Reserve in Bloomington.

Along the Mississippi River, popular runs include the loop between Franklin and Washington avenues; S. River Boulevard south of the Lake Street Bridge in St. Paul; Minneapolis' Minnehaha Park and Crosby Lake Park and Hidden Falls Park in St. Paul.

There are several running clubs in the Twin Cities. One of the largest is the **Minnesota Distance Running Association**, 927-0983, which meets at the Edina Community Center, 5701 Normandale Road. (This organization also maintains a race-information line, 925-4749, offering updates on Twin Cities running events.) Another is the **American Lung Association Running Club**, 227-8014. One caveat: This club is only for runners who have completed a marathon.

Several health and fitness clubs also have running clubs, such as the 500-member **Northwest Club Run**, 673-1282, sponsored by Northwest Racquet, Swim and Health Clubs. The club meets for runs every Monday and Wednesday evening, offers guidance from professional trainers and sponsors several racing and social events. The catch here is you have to join the Northwest clubs to be a member of the running group.

## Rock Climbing

The bluffs at Taylors Falls along the St. Croix River and the craggy cliffs along the North Shore of Lake Superior attract many rock-climbing enthusiasts.

Two indoor climbing facilities in the Twin Cities offer rock climbers a place to hone their skills by literally scaling the walls!

• **Peak Adventure**, 884-7996, 9208 James Avenue S., Bloomington

• **Vertical Endeavors**, 776-1430, 844 Arcade Street, St. Paul

Another organization, **Footprints**, 788-1414, teaches rock climbing at various sites in Minnesota and Wisconsin.

## Walking, Hiking

To discourage wintertime sloth and dissipation among the citizenry of these cold climes, several enclosed shopping malls in the Twin Cities suburbs have started walking clubs. Members meet early in the morning, before the stores open, to walk from the halls and byways of these modern indoor shopping centers.

The Mall of America's walking club is called the **Mall Stars**, 885-8500.

For information on walking clubs in other malls, such as Southdale, Ridgedale or Rosedale, call each mall's management office.

While there are great hiking areas all over the Twin Cities — the Chain of Lakes, river roads and the Minnesota Landscape Arboretum come to mind — two trails in particular are worth noting.

• **Luce Line Trail** — Beginning at Vicksburg Lane in Plymouth, this DNR-maintained trail continues west for 30 miles to Winsted. There's a rest area and picnic table at mile 6.

• **Gateway Trail** — This trail begins on Arlington Avenue, just west of Westminster Street in St. Paul, and continues through 17 miles of woods and wetlands to Stillwater.

Here are other resources for walking and hiking enthusiasts.

• **Minneapolis Municipal Hiking Club**, 661-4875

• **City of St. Paul Seniors Hiking Club**, 266-6370 or 266-6377

• **Meandering Minnesotans**

**Volksmarch**, 890-7560 or 894-3213

**Twin Cities Volksmarch Club**, 699-9026 or 348-7896

• **Minnesota State Parks Hiking Club**, 296-6157

• **Hennepin Parks Hiking Program**, 559-9000

• **Summit Avenue Walking Tours**, 297-2555

• **St. Anthony Falls Walking Tours**, 627-5433

## In-line Skating

Every park in the cities is filled with these crazies on wheels. After all, this is the home of Rollerblade Inc. The lakes of Minneapolis — especially Calhoun and Lake of the Isles — are favorite spots for 'bladers, and there are many in-line skate rental outlets nearby along Lake Street. Many of the county parks also sponsor in-line skating clinics and rent all the necessary equipment, including helmets, knee and elbow pads — vital necessities for this free-wheeling sport.

Both Minneapolis and St. Paul discourage in-line skating and skateboarding on downtown sidewalks. In-line skaters are welcome to use the bike paths around the lakes.

## League Events

### Kids

A myriad of leagues offer youth baseball, basketball, soccer, gymnastics, tennis, swimming and other sports. Your best source of in-formation on a specific youth league is the local parks and recreation department. Minneapolis and St. Paul and virtually all suburbs have such departments. Local schools are also important resources for youth sports.

### Adults

Don't let the kids have all the fun! Local parks and recreation departments offer plenty of team sports for adults as well — everything from women's hockey leagues to coed volleyball to softball to tennis ladders. Call local city or suburban offices for complete information.

## Tennis, Health and Fitness Clubs

The Twin Cities area is a competitive market for health clubs, and, for that reason, many facilities frequently offer membership specials and discounts. Keep your eyes open — it could save you some bucks! By all means, visit and try out any club before you commit yourself to a membership plan. Here's a quick survey of some of the Twin Cities' most popular facilities.

**BALLY'S U.S. SWIM AND FITNESS**
*1166 University Ave., St. Paul*     644-2444

This national fitness chain offers a full range of options in a bright, modern setting. Amenities include strength and cardiovascular machines, aerobics classes, pool, gym, jogging track, plus racquet-

Photo: Buzz Magnuson, Pioneer Press

*Shoreview Community Center.*

ball courts in some locations. There are other Bally's clubs in Bloomington, Little Canada, Eagan, St. Louis Park, Richfield, New Hope and Fridley.

### CALHOUN BEACH CLUB
*2925 Dean Pkwy., Minneapolis    927-9951*

On the northern shore of Lake Calhoun, this recently renovated, attractive club offers courts for tennis, racquetball and squash; swimming pools; strength and cardiovascular machines; a members' dining room; and full range of social activities. The Calhoun Beach Club, Regency Athletic Club and University Club of St. Paul have reciprocal membership agreements.

### CATHEDRAL HILL YWCA
*198 Western Ave. N., St. Paul    225-YWCA*

This is a small but appealing coed facility where you can take advantage of strength-training and cardiovascular machines, aerobics classes, an Olympic-sized pool and other amenities. Child care is available.

### EAGAN ATHLETIC CLUB
*3330 Pilot Knob Rd., Eagan    454-8790*

Smaller than the chains, this club has a cozy, neighborhood feel. Amenities include strength and cardiovascular machines, four indoor tennis courts, racquetball, volleyball, indoor and outdoor swimming pools, aerobics classes and children's programming.

### FLAGSHIP ATHLETIC CLUB
*755 Prairie Center Dr.*
*Eden Prairie    941-2000*

The first thing you see when you walk through this club's front door is a grand piano and an elegant restaurant, indications this is as much a social scene as it is a health club.

Flagship offers a full range of fitness services, including 11 outdoor and seven indoor tennis courts, four racquetball courts, cardiovascular and strength machines, indoor jogging track, indoor and outdoor pools, hair salon, plus the aforementioned formal restaurant with bar.

### LIFETIME FITNESS CLUB
*7970 Brooklyn Blvd.*
*Brooklyn Park    493-9393*
*1565 Thomas Center Dr.*
*Eagan    688-3000*

The 3-year-old Brooklyn Park club and the brand-new (fall '94) Eagan branch of LifeTime are modern, attractive facilities loaded with cutting-edge cardio and weight machines, pools, aerobics studios and health-food cafes. The new Eagan facility also has a climbing wall and a children's play center/day care.

### LILYDALE CLUB
*Hwy. 13 and I-35E, Lilydale    457-4954*

This is a well-maintained older facility with a serious tennis program. There are nine indoor tennis courts, four racquetball courts, an aerobics studio, an outdoor swimming pool and indoor jogging track, plus a limited number of strength and cardiovascular machines.

### NORTHWEST RACQUET, SWIM & HEALTH CLUBS
*5525 Cedar Lake Rd.*
*St. Louis Park    546-5474*

This is the premier local chain

of athletic clubs, with heavy emphasis on tennis. With 13 locations in Minneapolis and the western suburbs, Northwest clubs are well-run, top-notch facilities. While some of the branches are strictly tennis clubs, others, including the flagship St. Louis Park club, offer a full range of services, including strength and cardiovascular machines, swimming pools, jogging tracks, racquetball and classes in aerobics, self defense and dance. Squash courts are available at some locales.

Northwest's Arena Club, located in the Target Center in downtown Minneapolis, is especially popular for young, single professionals. The suburban clubs are more family-oriented.

For tennis buffs, Northwest is the place to be for year-round play. The Northwest system offers more than 100 indoor courts and 46 outdoor courts in addition to a staff of nearly 50 tennis pros who coach group lessons, women's daytime leagues, club leagues and youth lessons and drills. All staff are U.S. Professional Tennis Association members.

### REGENCY ATHLETIC CLUB
*Hyatt Regency Hotel, 1300 Nicollet Mall*
*Minneapolis* 343-3131
This deluxe club, housed in the posh Hyatt Regency, offers strength and cardiovascular machines, aerobics classes, indoor pool, six racquetball courts, two squash courts and four indoor tennis courts, basketball gym, plus restaurant, spa and hair salon. Hotel guests may use the club for a nominal daily fee.

### SWEATSHOP
*171 Snelling Ave. N., St. Paul* 646-8418
This is a small but friendly workout spot specializing in aerobics classes. The Sweatshop also offers strength-training machines and free weights, cardiovascular machines, child care, personal trainers and counseling.

### TERI MAYERS FITNESS
*St. Anthony Main Complex*
*200 Second St. S.E.*
*Minneapolis* 371-9541
Popular aerobics/dance guru Teri Mayers teaches aerobics weekdays after work and Saturday mornings. Package deals are also available.

### UNIVERSITY CLUB
*420 Summit Ave., St. Paul* 222-1751
This stately old club has the usual complement of machines, aerobics classes, an outdoor pool and tennis courts, plus lovely Summit Avenue for jogging.

### UPTOWN YWCA
*2808 Hennepin Ave. S.*
*Minneapolis* 874-3171
This relatively new YWCA branch offers weight-training and cardiovascular machines, a gym, swimming pool and aerobics classes in a modern, attractive setting. Membership is transferable to other Ys in the area that feature tennis and racquetball courts.

### WHITE BEAR LAKE RACQUET & SWIM
*4800 White Bear Pkwy.*
*White Bear Lake* 426-1308
This handsome, modern facility exudes a private-club atmo-

sphere. Amenities include strength and cardiovascular machines, a children's wading pool, indoor and outdoor pools, 10 tennis and four racquetball courts, squash courts, a basketball gym and an aerobics studio with a cushioned wood floor. There's also an extensive tennis program of leagues and classes. This club doubles as a social center with a restaurant and bar on premises and a full calendar of social events.

## YMCA

*1130 Nicollet Mall*
*Minneapolis*                   *332-0501*

This clean and spacious facility includes a weight-training center, basketball and racquetball courts, a swimming pool, plus educational programs on a variety of subjects.

### YMCA OF GREATER ST. PAUL

*194 Sixth St. E., St. Paul      292-4130*

The Y offers full-service clubs with strength training and cardiovascular machines, swimming pools, jogging tracks, racquetball courts and a range of fitness classes for all ages. In addition to the downtown St. Paul club, the Y has five other facilities sprinkled throughout St. Paul and its suburbs. The Northeast Y, in White Bear Lake, has a popular water slide.

### OTHERS WORTH CHECKING OUT

• **Chaska Community Center**, 448-5633, 1661 Parkridge Drive, Chaska

• **Commodore Squash & Fitness Club**, 228-0501, 79 N. Western Avenue, St. Paul

• **Cottage Grove Racquet & Fitness**, 458-0722, 8401 W. Point Douglas Road, Cottage Grove

• **Decathlon Athletic Club**, 854-7777, 1700 E. 79th Street, Bloomington

• **Edinborough Park**, 893-9890, 7700 York Avenue S., Edina

**Jewish Community Center**, 698-0751, 1375 St. Paul Avenue, St. Paul

• **Jewish Community Center of Greater Minneapolis**, 377-8330, 4330 S. Cedar Lake Road, St. Louis Park

• **Lonna Mosow's Hot Workouts**, 941-9448, 7500 Flying Cloud Drive, Eden Prairie

• **Maplewood Recreation Center**, 770-4570, 2100 White Bear Avenue, Maplewood

• **Northland Fitness Centers**, 425-5880, 7624 Boone Avenue N., Brooklyn Center

• **Roseville King's Court Racquet Club**, 633-0744, 2560 N. Fry Street, Roseville

• **Shoreview Community Center**, 490-4700, 4600 N. Victoria Street, Shoreview

• **Williston-Sagedahl Sports & Fitness**, 935-8638, 14509 Minnetonka Drive, Minnetonka

## *Where the Champs Compete*

### NATIONAL SPORTS CENTER AND BLAINE SOCCER COMPLEX

*1700 105 Ave. N.E., Blaine      785-5600*

No discussion of Twin Cities amateur sports and recreation is complete without mention of the National Sports Center in Blaine. This state-of-the-art sports complex is one of the nation's finest sports training and competition centers, having hosted the likes of Carl Lewis, Jackie Joyner-Kersee, Greg LeMond, the U.S. National Men's and Women's Soccer Teams, the National Weightlifting Championships, the 1991 International Special Olympics and the 1992 U.S. Olympic Cycling Trials — just to mention a few!

The NSC's velodrome, seating up to 2,500 spectators, is the only all-wood, all-weather cycling track in the United States.

Outdoor arenas and fields include 32 soccer fields and a 400-meter performance track. The indoor arena offers basketball courts, indoor soccer fields, tennis courts and track and field space.

Many local and national amateur sporting events take place at the Blaine facility, located just 20 minutes north of the Twin Cities. It's definitely worth the trip just to see the facility!

## Finally . . . If You Have Any Energy Left

The possibilities for a variety of recreational activities continue with these popular pasttimes.

### Biking

Biking is becoming increasingly popular in the Twin Cities, so much so that Minneapolis, for example, has greatly expanded its number of streets with designated bike lanes (see the Getting Around chapter for more information).

- **Metro Mountain Biking Resource Group**, 452-9736
- **Twin Cities Bicycling Club**, activity hotline, 924-2443
- **Minnesota Cycling Federation**, 729-0702
- **Road Explorers Bike Club**, 559-6700

### Bird-watching

Bird-watchers have much to gaze upon in Twin Cities skies. For that, you can thank our strategic location on the great Mississippi flyway migration route. Because we're so centrally located, we also are visited by migrating eastern and western birds. The Minneapolis Audubon Society sponsors bird walks in the Thomas Sadler Roberts Bird Sanctuary every Tuesday at 9 AM in April and May.

- **Minneapolis Audubon Society**, 926-6338
- **St. Paul Audubon Society**, 291-2596

### Bocce Ball

Bocce ball is a cross between bowling and curling — without the kilts and ice! This is an especially popular sport on the east side of St. Paul, home to a large Italian enclave. The Bocce association counts about 600 members.

- **Minnesota Bocce Ball Association**, 772-2357

### Frisbee

The University of Minnesota lawns and Highland Park in St. Paul

Photo: Chris Polydoroff, Pioneer Press

A ski lift at Welch Village near the Twin Cities.

are a few favorite Frisbee-tossing areas. The Minnesota Frisbee Association, with a membership of around 200, sponsors tournaments in disc golf and other Frisbee activities.

•**Minnesota Frisbee Association**, (toll call) 612-255-0966

## Horseback Riding

There's a lively horse community in the Twin Cities metro area. The Minnesota Horse Council is an advocacy organization for the promotion of horseback riding and trails. Here are a few popular stables.

### BRASS RING STABLES
*9105 Norris Lake Rd., Elk River    441-7987*
This facility offers guided trail rides and riding lessons.

### BUNKER HILLS STABLES
*Hwy. 242 and Foley Blvd.*
*Coon Rapids*                757-7010
This stable leads rides through scenic Bunker Hills Park.

### EAGLE CREEK STABLES
*7301 Eagle Creek Blvd.*
*Shakopee*                   445-7222
Eagle Creek offers horse rentals, riding instruction and hay and sleigh rides.

### HANSON'S RANCH
*1401 County Rd. 18, Shakopee    445-9970*
You can rent horses or go on a sleigh or hay ride here through 650 wooded acres.

### DIAMOND T RIDING STABLES
*4889 Pilot Knob Rd., Eagan      454-1464*
In this pretty wooded spread,

you can rent a horse or lean back on a hay wagon and just enjoy the view.

•**Minnesota Horse Council**, 755-7729

## Outdoor Adventure Club

Founded at the University of Minnesota decades ago, the Rovers in now community-based and offers countless outdoors activities and social events for active individuals of all ages. Recent excursions have included Boundary Waters canoeing, apple-picking and St. Croix River hiking trips. From September through May, the club meets every Tuesday at various locations on the University of Minnesota campus.

•**Minnesota Rovers Outing Club**, 522-2461

## Outdoor Adventures for Women Only

The following organization leads rather challenging excursions into nature — everything from dog sledding to canoe trips.

•**Woodswomen Inc.**, 822-3809

## Skydiving

For instruction in this daredevil sport, contact:

•**Minnesota Skydivers Club**, 469-2730

# *Inside*
# Winter's Wonderland

Minnesota is a meteorologist's dream.

From winter's Arctic blasts to summer's sultry haze, the weather here is never boring.

Due to our location — near the geographic center of North America and far away from the tempering oceans — we are blessed with a hardy climate of extremes. On occasion, temperatures have been known to range from 30 degrees below zero to 100 above within the same calendar year. Typically, the average high in January is 19 degrees, while in July, readings of 83 are common.

Making life even more interesting are the blizzards, impulsive tornadoes and nasty wind and hail storms that regularly visit our state.

While each season has its unique charms, it is winter that stirs our deepest emotions. And it's easy to see why. Total seasonal snowfall is more than 40 inches. Days are grayer and shorter, with darkness setting in around 5 PM during bleakest January. And, worst of all, it's so darned unrelentingly cold.

In all this misery, there is only one consolation. We could be in North Dakota. That frigid piece of real estate has the distinction of being the coldest of the lower 48 states.

But you can't win 'em all. Many Minnesotans give up the good fight and head south every winter. By the thousands, they migrate to Florida, Las Vegas or Texas for a couple of weeks or, if they can swing it, the entire season. To those wimps, we say, "Good riddance!" Their loss is our gain. Real Minnesotans love winter. We can't get enough of it! Maybe our brains are permanently frostbitten or maybe we're just plain loopy, but our hearts tremble with excitement at the mere mention of "black ice," "wind-chill factor" and "goose down."

For us, there aren't words to describe the peace and contentment that come when the first giant flakes fall from the heavens, blanketing the world in white . . . the sensual pleasure of coming in from the cold to dinner in a warm, fragrant kitchen . . . the joy of strapping on a pair of cross-country skis and gliding silently through a pristine frozen forest . . . the grace of steel blades on glassy ice . . . the fun of pushing a kid's sled down a billowy slope.

And guess what? Some of us — admittedly, the more perverse ones — even get a kick out of winter's minor highway mishaps. There's a special "misery loves company" camaraderie in going shoulder-to-shoulder with total strangers to free cars from snowbanks and sharing a few jokes while hunched over crackling jumper cables. These are bonafide social events in January.

Some consider winter their favorite season even though they rarely step outdoors. For them, it's a wonderful excuse for cocooning and recharging emotional batteries: reading a good book by a roaring fire or watching videos 'til the eyes glaze over. It's no small coincidence that the Twin Cities are filled with voracious readers, countless book clubs and busy libraries, not to mention a thriving community of writers. You can, in part, thank the long winter months for that.

But perhaps the best thing about winter is the fact that it makes us truly appreciate spring. When the first warm breezes of April roll in, we're out the door, strolling, biking, jogging — one mass of humanity pouring onto lake shores and walking paths. You can almost hear a collective sigh of relief.

In this chapter, we offer a winter survival guide filled with practical pointers on adapting to the elements, plus fun things to do.

## The Basics

### Clothing

The layered look is chic during Minnesota winters. Dress in layers that can be easily discarded as the temperatures warm during the day, and top it all off with a sturdy wool or down-filled jacket. Gloves, scarves, hats and waterproof boots are all winter necessities. You might even want to throw in a set of silk long underwear if you're planning to spend a lot of time outdoors.

Don't forego comfort for the sake of fashion. During wintry cold spells, you'll see Guthrie or symphony audiences dotted with sweaters, wool shirts and down vests. Nobody thinks twice about it.

### Your Home

Here are a few tips for maintaining your home in winter:

• Make sure the exterior of your home is well caulked, especially around vents and windows.

• Install a CO (carbon monoxide) monitor, and check it routinely.

• Have your gas furnace professionally examined once a year, as well as cleaned regularly.

• Change your furnace filters regularly.

### Vehicles

Be kind to your car, and it will serve you well all winter. In fall, take time for that winter tune-up, oil change and battery check. It's well worth it. And don't forget windshield washer fluid! It's also a good idea to keep your gas tank at least half full during cold weather.

Slow down during snowy conditions and allow extra space between your car and the vehicle in front of you. Remember, under Minnesota law, you must drive with your lights on during any form of precipitation — and that includes snow flurries!

Photo: Chris Polydoroff, Pioneer Press

## *Motorists Should Carry This Winter Survival Kit*

Here's an idea from the Minnesota Safety Council for an inexpensive but useful winter survival kit to be carried in your car during Minnesota winters. This is especially important for motorists traveling in less-populated out-state Minnesota, where a minor car problem can leave one stranded for hours in the freezing cold.

### AUTO SURVIVAL KIT

Inside one large empty coffee can, place the following items:

1. A quarter for a phone call, taped to the inside of the plastic lid
2. A small candle and matches (or disposable lighter)
3. A bandana or piece of bright red or orange fabric (approximately 18 inches square) to serve as a face mask, signal banner or makeshift bandage for first aid
4. A couple of safety pins
5. A few adhesive bandages
6. A small pack of facial tissues (or a few paper towels)
7. A large plastic garbage bag, which serves as a wind- or water-repellent poncho if you cut holes for arms and head
8. A stick of chewing gum, which could serve as adhesive
9. A small box of raisins (or bag of peanuts)
10. Wrapped hard candies (or chocolate bar)
11. Packets of dehydrated tea, cocoa, coffee and/or soup
12. Plastic spoons to stir and eat with

13. A piece of wire, which could be used to suspend a can from the rearview mirror. The can could then be used to heat food or melt snow. (Punch a few holes around the top edge of the can.)

14. An extra scarf and mittens

Place this emergency kit in a safe place in the interior passenger compartment of your vehicle.

Other useful items for winter trips include: booster cables, a small shovel, a tow chain and sand or traction mat, road flares, a flashlight with spare batteries, a compass, a windshield scraper, a snow brush, a fire extinguisher, a plastic whistle, canned heat, plastic cups, a can opener, a knife, work gloves, a snowmobile suit and sleeping bag or blankets and 30 feet of cord or heavy string, which becomes a homing line for anyone who must check outside the vehicle during blizzard conditions.

For other wintertime safety information, call the Minnesota Safety Council at 291-9150 or (800) 444-9150.

## Weather Reports

It's important to heed storm warnings and road reports, because driving can be difficult during wintry weather. While many radio and TV stations provide adequate service, WCCO Radio (830 AM) has developed weather reporting to a fine art. It is nationally known for its up-to-the-minute weather coverage, even to the point of being excessive about it. WCCO is also the station to turn to for information about weather-related school or business closings. Speaking of weather reporting, you'll undoubtedly hear the phrase "wind-chill factor." This is a number that expresses the combined effect of low temperatures and high winds on exposed skin. Ouch!

If you're planning an outstate trip and wondering about road and weather conditions throughout Minnesota, call the state Department of Transportation hotline at 296-3076 for detailed information.

## What Every Minnesotan Needs to Know...

**Black Ice**: This is a very slick road surface created when car exhaust meets frigid temperatures. It commonly happens during rush hour when there's more idling (and exhaust) than real movement. Because you can't see black ice, it's a good idea to drive cautiously during heavy-traffic conditions.

**Skids**: If you don't heed the above advice, you WILL need to know how to maneuver through a skid. The best rule of thumb is to ease up on the brakes, steer in the direction of the skid and hope against all hope that no one's in your way. Gradually, gently accelerate and try to regain control of your steering. A skid can be a terrifying experience — no matter how many times you've experienced it. This is one time when landing in a snowbank is a definite blessing, considering the alternatives. Cars are especially skid-prone on icy bridges and highway ramps.

**Lock Freeze-up**: Now, you know it's cold when you can't even get a key in your car door because the locks are frozen. What to do? Do NOT pour hot, boiling water into your locks. They'll only freeze up again. Do NOT kneel down and breathe into the keyhole. One misstep and you'll find yourself frozen in a liplock with your Buick. No. 1: It's not a pretty sight to cement your face to car metal. No. 2: It's very difficult to explain to onlookers. No. 3: It's painful!

Here's what may work. If you have time, just wait a few hours and let the sunlight thaw the locks. If you're in a hurry, use one of those aerosol-spray de-icers. Short of that, try the good, old-fashioned hair dryer, either a battery-operated type or a plug-in with a long extension cord. If nothing else, try your other car doors — you may be able to jimmy open the back door and maneuver yourself into the front seat.

## HELPFUL TELEPHONE NUMBERS

### DEPARTMENT OF TRANSPORTATI
*Road condition hotline*        *296-3076*

### AMERICAN AUTOMOBILE ASSOCIATION (AAA) ROAD SERVICE
*In Minneapolis and western suburbs        927-2727*
*In St. Paul Ramsey County and other metro areas        891-8000*
*For membership information        927-2567*

## *Winter Recreation*

### Cross-country Skiing

Cross-country skiing (also known as Nordic skiing) gained widespread appeal in Minnesota during the 1970s, and it remains a very popular sport. There are hundreds of miles of cross-country ski trails in the Twin Cities and environs, in city, county and state parks. Most facilities require skiers to purchase and wear a Great Minnesota Ski Pass, which helps pay for trail upkeep. The season pass costs $5 for individuals and $7.50 for husband and wife. The pass also may be purchased on a daily basis for $1. County and state parks also charge daily or seasonal vehicle parking fees. Several parks also offer rental equipment and lessons.

Here's a listing — by no means complete — of parks offering cross-country skiing.

### CITY PARKS — ST. PAUL

**Como Park Golf Course** (Kaufman Drive and Lexington Avenue), 4.5 miles of trails

**Phelan Golf Course** (1615 Phalen Drive), 6 miles of trails

### CITY PARKS — MINNEAPOLIS

**Theodore Wirth Park** (1301 Wirth Parkway), 8.5 miles of trails

**Columbia Golf Course** (St. Anthony Parkway and Central Avenue), 3 miles of trails

**Hiawatha Golf Course** (46th Street and Longfellow Avenue), 3 miles of trails

**Francis Gross Golf Course** (St. Anthony Parkway and Fillmore Street N.E.), 3 miles of trails

### RAMSEY COUNTY PARKS

The following Ramsey County parks have cross-country ski trails and no parking fees but do require a Great Minnesota Ski Pass:

**Battle Creek Regional Park** (Winthrop Street and Lower Afton Road, St. Paul), 6.5 miles of trails

**Tamarack Nature Center** (5287 Otter Lake Road, White Bear Township), 4.5 miles of trails

**Keller Golf Course** (2166 Maplewood Drive, Maplewood), 4.75 miles of trails

**Snail Lake Regional Park** (580 Snail Lake Boulevard, Shoreview), 1.5 miles of trails

**Long Lake Regional Park** (1500 Old Highway 8, New Brighton), 1.5-mile beginner trail

**Manitou Ridge Golf Course** (3200 N. McKnight Road, White Bear Lake), 3-mile intermediate/advanced trail

### HENNEPIN COUNTY PARKS

These parks require a daily parking fee of $4, plus the Great Minnesota Ski Pass.

**Carver Park Reserve** (7025 Victoria Drive, Victoria), 12.7 miles of trails

**Lake Rebecca Park Reserve** (County Road 50, Rockford), 6.2 miles of trails

**Crow-Hassan Park Reserve** (11629 Crow-Hassan Park Road, Rogers), 10.9 miles of trails

**French Lake Regional Park** (Medicine Lake, Plymouth), 5.4 miles of trails

**Elm Creek Park Reserve** (Highway 152, Osseo), 9.8 miles of trails

**Coon Rapids Dam Regional Park** (Highway 242, Coon Rapids), 3.7 miles of trails

**Hyland Lake Park Reserve** (10145 E. Bush Lake Road, Bloomington), 6.7 miles of trails

**Baker Park Reserve** (County Road 19, Medina), 8 miles of trails

**Cleary Lake Regional Park** (18106 Texas Avenue, S. Prior Lake), 9.7 miles of trails

**Murphy-Hanrehan Park Reserve** (County Road 74 and 164th Street, Prior Lake), 17 miles of trails

### STATE PARKS

**Afton State Park** (6959 Peller Avenue, S. Hastings), 18 miles of trails

**Fort Snelling State Park** (Post Road and State Highway 5, St. Paul), 17 miles of trails

**Minnesota Valley State Park** (19825 Park Boulevard, Jordan), 4 miles of trails

**William O'Brien State Park** (16821 O'Brien Trail N., Marine on St. Croix), 15.5 miles of trails

### FOR SOMETHING A LITTLE DIFFERENT

Ski past elk, buffalo and a Siberian tiger or two on the Minnesota Zoo's unusual trails. Admission is $8 for adults, $4 for children. The zoo is located at 13000 Zoo Boulevard, Apple Valley.

## Downhill Skiing

Several downhill skiing slopes have sprouted in the Minnesota prairie. Here are a few of the most popular in the Twin Cities and nearby communities. Most also have areas for snowboarding, a cold-weather marriage between skateboarding and surfing. Call the **Minnesota Ski Council** at 673-0828 for information on local ski clubs, equipment swaps, tours and clinics.

### AFTON ALPS
*6600 Peller Ave. S., Hastings    436-5245*

This picturesque ski area boasts a 350-foot vertical drop, night skiing, 36 runs plus a snowboard half-pipe, 18 chairlifts, one T-bar and two rope tows.

### BUCK HILL
*15400 Buck Hill Rd., Burnsville    435-8178*

Buck Hill has a 306-foot vertical drop, 10 runs, four chairlifts, one T-bar and three rope tows.

### COMO PARK
*1431 N. Lexington Pkwy.*
*St. Paul                    488-9673*

This small course has two runs, two tow ropes and night skiing.

### HYLAND HILLS
*8800 Chalet Rd., Bloomington    835-3604*

Hyland Hills offers a 175-foot vertical drop, night skiing, 14 runs, plus a snowboard half-pipe, three chairlifts and three rope tows.

### MOUNT FRONTENAC
*Red Wing*
*Toll call              612-338-5826*

Mount Frontenac offers a 420-foot vertical drop, two chairlifts, one T-bar and two rope tows.

### POWDER RIDGE SKI AREA
*St. Cloud    398-7200, (800) 348-7734*

Located 16 miles south of St. Cloud on State Highway 15, Powder Ridge offers three chairlifts, a J-bar and two rope tows. There's also an on-site cafeteria and bar.

During a Minnesota cold snap, you have to run backwards in order to spit.

Insiders' Tips

## THEODORE WIRTH REGIONAL PARK
*1301 Wirth Pkwy.*
*Golden Valley*          *661-4867*
   This small city ski area has two runs, a tow rope, snow tubing and night skiing.

## WILD MOUNTAIN SKI AREA
*County Rd. 16, Taylors Falls*     *462-7550*
   Wild Mountain has a 300-foot vertical drop, 21 ski runs, night skiing, four chair lifts and one rope tow.

## WELCH VILLAGE
*County Rd. 7, Welch*          *222-7079*
   Welch Village offers a 350-foot vertical drop, 36 runs, eight chairlifts and one T-bar.

---

## Snowmobiling

   Snowmobiles — mobile, fast and loud — are the Harley Davidsons of the Great North.

   The recreational machines were invented in northern Minnesota in 1953. The Polaris snowmobile company was founded in the northern Minnesota town of Roseau. And nearby Thief River Falls is the original home of Arctic Cat, now called Artco. Today, one in 20 Minnesotans owns a snowmobile.

   There are more than 2,000 miles of state-groomed trails, plus another 10,200 miles of locally maintained trails.

   In the Twin Cities area, snowmobile trails are located in several Hennepin County parks, such as Baker Park Reserve (9 miles), Carver Park Reserve (5 miles), Cleary Lake Regional Park (1 mile), Crow-Hassan Park Reserve (5 miles),

Lake Rebecca (5.5 miles) and Elm Creek Park Reserve (11 miles), plus the North Hennepin Trail Corridor (7 miles) linking Coon Rapids Dam Regional Park to Elm Creek Park Reserve.

   In Dakota County, Lebanon Hills Regional Park affords 5 miles of trails. In Ramsey County, snowmobiling is permitted on many lake surfaces and prohibited on all other park land except for designated trails along Keller Creek (connecting Keller Lake and Phalen Lake) and between Otter Lake and Bald Eagle Lake.

   As for local state parks, Minnesota Valley State Park has 34 miles of snowmobile trails and William O'Brien State Park has a 1-mile trail.

   The Luce Line State Trail, west of Stubbs Bay Road in Orono to Thompson Lake near Cosmos, offers a 50-mile trail with connections to other state trails.

   The Rice Creek Trail, based at the Rice Creek Chain of Lakes in Lino Lakes, affords 70 miles of snowmobile trails.

   Outstate Minnesota is riddled with snowmobile trails. For information on trails, check with local snowmobile dealers. The state also is home to many snowmobiling races, including the I-500, a grueling three-day competition from White Bear Lake to Thunder Bay, Ontario.

   Call the Minnesota United Snowmobile Association at 427-5024 for more information on trails and regulations.

*Ice sculpture at the St. Paul Winter Carnival.*

## Ice-Skating and Hockey

In the state of 10,000 frozen lake surfaces, ice skating and hockey are understandably popular sports.

In fact, hockey enthusiasm reaches manic proportions every March when the entire state is mesmerized by the State High School Hockey Tournament in St. Paul.

That's the culmination of a dream for every Minnesota kid who has donned 50 pounds of padding and chased a wily puck through the ranks of mini-mites to pee-wee to bantam leagues and then on to the big time in high school teams and state competition. In fact, many successful players in the National Hockey League had their beginnings on Minnesota rinks. Minnesotan Herb Brooks coached the

1980 Miracle on Ice Olympic team that won the gold medal. Twelve members of that team were from Minnesota.

Incidentally, hockey isn't just for the guys anymore. Girls' hockey is now officially sanctioned in the state and at least 20 high schools now have girls' hockey teams.

Those who prefer the more genteel sport of figure skating or the thrill of speed skating will find ample opportunity to do both on Twin Cities frozen lakes, such as Lake of the Isles in Minneapolis and Como Lake in St. Paul, and other local rinks. In downtown St. Paul, during the Winter Carnival, there's usually a small but picturesque ice rink in the middle of Rice Park ringed with ice sculptures.

## St. Paul Area Rinks

St. Paul boasts around 30 outdoor rinks for pleasure skating and another 30 outdoor rinks specifically for hockey. Some of the more popular pleasure-skating rinks are on Como Lake and at Langford Park, Edgecumbe, Battle Creek, Hazel Park, Phelan, North Dale and Palace recreation centers. Here's a listing of public indoor ice arenas in the St. Paul area. Because many of these facilities reserve ice time for hockey practice and figure-skating lessons, it's important to call ahead for open-skating hours and admission fees.

**Aldrich Arena**, 777-2233, 1850 N. White Bear Avenue, White Bear Lake

**Biff Adams Arena**, 488-1336, 743 N. Western Avenue, St. Paul

**Gustafson-Phalen Arena**, 776-2554, 1320 Walsh Street, St. Paul

**Harding Arena**, 774-2127, 1496 E. Sixth Street, St. Paul

**Highland Arena**, 699-7156, 800 S. Snelling Avenue, St. Paul

**Ken Yackel-West Side Arena**, 228-1145, 44 E. Isabel Street, St. Paul

**Oscar Johnson Arena**, 645-7203, 1039 DeCourcy Circle, St. Paul

**Pleasant Arena**, 228-1143, 848 Pleasant Avenue, St. Paul

**Roseville Ice Arena and John Rose Minnesota Oval**, 484-0268, 1200 Woodhill Drive, Roseville

**Shoreview Arena**, 484-2400, 844 W. Highway 96, Shoreview

**Wakota Arena**, 451-1727, 141 E. Sixth Street S., St. Paul

**White Bear Lake Sports & Ice Center**, 429-8571, 1328 Highway 96, White Bear Lake

**White Bear Arena**, 777-8255, 2160 Orchard Lane, White Bear Lake

## Minneapolis Area Rinks

The city of Minneapolis boasts about 50 outdoor public skating rinks in parks and on lake surfaces. The most popular of these are at Lake of the Isles and Lake Harriet, Folwell Park in North Minneapolis, Theodore Wirth Park on the western edge of the city, Logan and Van Cleve parks in Northeast Minneapolis and Lynnhurst Park, Keewaydin Park, Lake Nokomis and Powderhorn Park in South Minneapolis, which has the city's only outdoor speed-skating oval.

For a unique skating experience à la New York's Rockefeller Center, strap on your skates and go for a spin on the ice at **Peavey Plaza**, smack dab downtown near Orchestra Hall!

Minneapolis also has a large public indoor skating arena, **Parade Ice Garden**, 348-5724, 800 Kenwood Parkway, on the western edge near the Guthrie Theater. Open skating hours are 11:30 AM to 1 PM Monday through Friday; 6:30 to 8:15 PM Monday; and 4 to 5:45 PM Tuesday, Thursday, Saturday and Sunday. It's adults only from 7:45 to 9:30 PM Friday. Admission is $2.50 for adults and $2.25 for juniors and seniors.

Here's a partial listing of indoor skating arenas in Minneapolis and surrounding suburbs.

**Braemar Arena**, 941-1322, 7501 Highway 169, Edina

**Brooklyn Park Community Activity Center**, 493-8333, 5600 85th Avenue, Brooklyn Park

**Edinborough Park**, 893-9890, 7700 York Avenue S., Edina

**Fogerty Ice House**, 780-3323, 9250 Central Avenue N.E., Blaine

**Hopkins Pavilion**, 939-1410, 1515 County Road 3, Hopkins

**Minnetonka Ice Arena**, 939-8310, 3401 Williston Road, Minnetonka

**Victory Memorial Ice Arena**, 627-2952, 1900 42nd Avenue N., Minneapolis

**St. Louis Park Recreation Center**, 924-2545, 5005 W. 36th Street, St. Louis Park

Among Hennepin County parks, Carver Park Reserve, Fish Lake Regional Park and French Regional Park offer ice-skating rinks.

Also, because of the popularity of hockey, many area high schools have their own indoor or outdoor rinks that are available for public open skating at specific times. Check with individual school districts for more information.

## Curling

This quirky ice sport involving "stones" and brooms originated in Scotland and has an enthusiastic following in the Twin Cities. In fact,

the St. Paul Curling Club, with 650 members, is the largest curling club in the United States.

The game is played in this way: One player slides a big, rounded 42-pound curling stone down a lane of ice toward a target; other teammates then rush ahead of the stone and "sweep" the ice to alter the stone's speed and direction. The goal is to land your team's stones closer to the center of the "house," or target, than the opposing team's stones.

In the 1880s, curlers played the game on the Mississippi River at St. Paul. The St. Paul Curling Club was established on Christmas Day 1885, and in 1912 it built its present clubhouse at 470 Selby Avenue, St. Paul.

Curling is a game long on tradition and camaraderie. For more information on the sport, call the St. Paul Curling Club at 224-7408. The club welcomes new members and, every winter, hosts a newcomers bonspiel (tournament) as an introduction to the sport.

## Ice Fishing

No discussion of Minnesota winter recreation is complete without mentioning the infamous sport of ice fishing, wherein otherwise sane individuals drive their vehi-

Locals know to leave that infamous Scandinavian delicacy, lutefisk, well enough alone.

Insiders' Tips

Photo: Chris Polydoroff, Pioneer Press

*This woman is using a phone booth in St. Paul in November 1991, a month that shattered records for snowfall in Minnesota.*

cles out onto frozen lake surfaces in 30-below weather, saw holes in the ice, drop in a fishing line, pop open a brewski and wait eternally in the wind and cold for the BIG ONE to bite.

Serious ice-fishing enthusiasts haul little fishing houses — complete with heaters — onto the ice and keep them there the entire winter. In fact, many of the larger lakes have fish-house communities. One fish-house "town" even elects a mayor!

The 1993 filmed-in-Minnesota movie *Grumpy Old Men*, starring Walter Matthau, Jack Lemmon and Ann-Margret, depicted this loony sport in all its glory.

## Winter Festivals

Several winter celebrations and events are testimony to our Nordic fortitude. Here's a glimpse at a few.

### ST. PAUL WINTER CARNIVAL
*297-6953*

This annual celebration melts winter's gloom with a dazzling array of events and attractions. One of the oldest winter celebrations in the United States, the Winter Carnival was founded in 1886 in reaction to a New York reporter's comment that St. Paul was so cold it was worse than Siberia. A group of St. Paul businessmen decided to hold a celebration to prove how much fun winter can be.

And fun it is! The carnival boasts a parade, parties, ice sculpting in Rice Park, winter-sports competitions, ice slides, a King Boreas Me-

dallion Hunt and the coronation of mythical figures. Ruling the carnival are King Boreas and the Queen of the Snows. And to provide mischief and drama, the carnival also selects a Vulcanus Rex and Krewe, evil forces that try to drive out winter and spoil the festival. They wreak all kinds of mischief on city streets — including smudging the faces of innocent folks with black ash marks.

In some years, an ice palace is constructed using frozen blocks from Minnesota lakes. Its size varies, depending on the carnival's budget. In 1992, a grand ice palace — measuring 150 feet high and costing nearly $1 million — captured international attention. The Super Bowl was held in Minneapolis that year, increasing the exposure of the palace.

The Winter Carnival is traditionally held in late January and early February.

### HOLIDAZZLE PARADES
*Minneapolis*

To light up the wintry skies — and attract holiday shoppers away from suburban malls — downtown Minneapolis offers enchanting lighted parades down Nicollet Mall virtually every night during the holiday shopping season — from late November to New Year's Day.

### HOLIDAY IN LIGHTS
*13000 Zoo Blvd., Apple Valley    432-9000*

The Minnesota Zoo also offers a dazzling display of holiday lights during the same time period.

*Blizzards can seriously affect modes of transportation in Minnesota.*

Photo: Joe Oden, Pioneer Press

### CHILLY OPEN

*Wayzata*

Those crazy folks in Wayzata shake off their winter woes at the annual Chilly Open, a golf tournament on the frozen surface of Lake Minnetonka. It's usually slated for early February.

### FESTIVAL OF TREES

*Minnesota Landscape Arboretum*
*Chanhassen                     443-2460*

The Minnesota Landscape Arboretum dresses up its greenery and displays creatively decorated Christmas trees in this lovely festival usually held throughout the month of December.

### OTHER CELEBRATIONS

Other can't-miss events during the winter months include the annual staging of Dickens' *A Christmas Carol* at the Guthrie Theater, plus several other holiday productions by local troupes; an exhibit, "Christmas in the Period Rooms," at the Minneapolis Institute of Arts; a holiday bazaar at the Landmark Center in St. Paul; the American Swedish Institute's St. Lucia Day celebration; and the Minnesota Zoo's annual Tropical Beach Party in February, not to mention several local observances of Black History Month (February).

---

## Inside Escapes

---

It's mid-January. Outside, the snowbanks are dirty, the sky is gray and your discarded Christmas tree sits forlornly on the curbside waiting for the garbage truck.

Inside your home sweet home, you're surrounded by cranky, sniffling loved ones, a droning TV set and petrified fruitcake. You're so restless you could climb the walls. It's a classic case of the wintertime blues.

Even the hardiest Minnesotan eventually catches this malady sometime during our long, long winter. Short of a charter to Cancun, what's a Minnesotan to do?

Here are a few great Twin Cities "escape" destinations to help cool that cabin fever.

• **The Minneapolis and St. Paul skyway systems.** You can escape the elements and stroll forever in these glass-enclosed, above-street walkways without retracing your steps. Go to lunch, take in a movie, browse in the shops or just indulge in some fantastic people-watching. In Minneapolis, stop by the Crystal Court and check out Mary Tyler Moore's famous lunch spot and do some power-shopping at the Conservatory or Gaviidae Common. In St. Paul, head for Town Square Park, take in a noontime concert and go for a spin on Cafesjian's Carousel on the upper level. (See the Getting Around chapter for more information on skyway routes.)

• **The Mall of America.** Go for shopping, lunch and a visit to Camp Snoopy, the fantastic indoor amusement park. There are also 14 movie theaters and a miniature golf course, not to mention one-of-a-kind shops.

• **Museums.** Now's the time to absorb some of the great culture in the Twin Cities. Visit the always provocative Walker Art Center, check out the sun-splashed landscapes of Van Gogh and Gauguin at the Minneapolis Institute of Arts or drop by the stunning new Weisman Art Museum. In St. Paul, let the kids run out their ya-yas at the Children's Museum or the Science Museum. Nearby are the new Minnesota History Center and the Minnesota Museum of American Art.

• **Indoor parks.** Edinborough Park in Edina is a lush indoor refuge with vegetation, playgrounds, picnic area, swimming pool and indoor skating rink. Or take a plunge at these great indoor water parks: the Chaska Community Center and Shoreview Community Center.

• **Tropical restaurants.** Take a gastronomic vacation to the southern climes. Try the Pickled Parrot and Chez Bananas for some Southern and/or tropical fare or any of a number of Indian, Ethiopian or Southeast Asian eateries.

• **Casinos.** It may be cold outside, but the action's hot inside these Las Vegas-style gaming emporiums featuring blackjack, slots, bingo, food and entertainment. Within a few hours' drive of the Twin Cities are Mystic Lake Casino in Prior Lake, Treasure Island Casino near Red Wing and Grand Casino at Hinckley.

• **Minnesota Zoo.** Head for the zoo's Tropics Trail, an indoor oasis of lush greenery, vibrant birds, gibbons and other tropical animals. Don't miss the coral reef exhibit of sharks and brilliantly colored tropical fish.

• **Como Park Conservatory.** Escape the frozen north in this lovely showcase of tropical plants and flowers.

Photo: Pioneer Press

*A giant ice slide at the St. Paul Winter Carnival.*

• **Hotel getaways.** Many Minnesota families take weekend minivacations in local resort hotels, where they soak in the pool or hot tub to recharge their batteries.

If all else fails, take heart. Coming just around the corner in late winter are the annual boat and vacation, camping and RV shows at the Minneapolis Convention Center. Featuring the latest models of recreational equipment, they bring a splash of summer into the darkest winter.

Photo: Joe Oden, Pioneer Press

*Fishing in Chisago Lake.*

# *Inside*
# In, On and Around the Water

Ever wonder why people in the Twin Cities love their water so much? The answer is simple: If you can see water flowing, lapping, dripping, falling or simply accumulating in a pool, that means it's warm enough NOT to be winter. And for most folks, that's real good news.

It is lucky, then, that we're blessed with so many lakes, rivers, creeks and ponds — not to mention the abundant opportunities for fishing, boating and swimming that go with them. All told, Minnesota has 6,564 rivers and streams (totalling 92,000 miles in length) and 11,842 lakes with more than 10 acres each of surface area (adding up to 4,967,510 acres of lake water). There is also one boat for every six residents — more than for any other state — and 2.3 million people who like to go fishing. Obviously, counting all the lures, oars, life jackets and flippers would be an impossible task.

A newcomer might assume that all this water activity must take place in northern and central Minnesota, where most of the lakes lie. Not so! Dozens of large lakes dot the Twin Cities metropolitan area, and we have creeks, marinas and the mighty Mississippi and Minnesota rivers,

as well. Not too far to the east, straddling the Wisconsin border, flows the St. Croix River, one of the Mississippi's major tributaries.

Visitors often express surprise at all the lakes in Minneapolis, whose name, after all, is an Indian-Greek hybrid meaning "city of water." Minneapolis even has its own annual festival devoted to water — Aquatennial. (For more details about Aquatennial, consult the Annual Events chapter.) Amazingly, nearly 7 percent — 2,324 acres — of Minneapolis' total area is water. St. Paul has its lakes as well, and together with Minneapolis it forms the northernmost major metropolis on the Mississippi River.

So there's no excuse for remaining a landlubber. Dip your toe into the water activities of the Twin Cities, and you'll soak up plenty of fun and exercise, along with an enhanced appreciation for the element that, more than any other, makes this urban area physically distinctive.

## *Boating*

It must be human nature: Where there's water, there's someone who wants to travel on it. Minnesota, it sometimes seems, has almost as many boats as people. A Twin Cit-

*Jet skiing on the Mississippi River.*

ies boat census would include sailboats, canoes, kayaks, motorboats of all sizes, dinghies, inflatable rafts, houseboats, floating restaurants, tugs, barges and sternwheelers. You can buy them, rent them, borrow them or build them. Most boats are not exactly status symbols, but they do identify their owners as members of the water/fishing/outdoorsy urban culture.

Canoeists can have a great time in the Twin Cities. In addition to all kinds of opportunities on area lakes, they can take advantage of 57 miles of scenic canoeing on the Mississippi River, between Anoka and Hastings. From the canoe's unique vantage point in the river, you can see dramatic wooded bluffs, wildlife, water traffic and a side of the Twin Cities normally not viewed. You do, though, need to deal with river locks in Minneapolis and farther south, but usually

even novice canoeists can handle them. Other popular canoeing rivers are the Crow River west of the Twin Cities, the St. Croix River to the east, and the Cannon River to the south.

All canoes need to be licensed. In the Twin Cities, you can rent canoes from **Ketter Canoeing**, 560-3840; **Midwest Mountaineering**, 339-3433; or at several area lakes. For general information on canoeing in Minnesota, contact the Minnesota Department of Natural Resources, 296-6157.

Users of sailboats and windsurfers abound. The area is lucky to have several lakes that provide public landings for sailboats. Lake Calhoun in Minneapolis appears to be the center of windsurfing activity in the Twin Cities.

Boat enthusiasts who want someone else to do the piloting should check out some of the many boat excursion businesses whose crafts ply the Twin Cities' waters. Most of the firms are in operation Memorial Day through Labor Day. Here are a few of them.

### ANSON NORTHROP RIVERBOATS
*Boom Island Park, Minneapolis*   227-1100
This company offers Mississippi River cruises in Minneapolis aboard the *Anson Northrop* or the *Betsy Northrop*. Cruise highlights include views of the Falls of St. Anthony, the Stone Arch Bridge and downtown; a trip through the river's upper lock; and, in some cases, meals.

### CREATIVE RIVER TOURS
*Shakopee*   445-7491
This firm's excursion boat, the *Emma Lee*, gives history and wildlife tours of the Minnesota River.

### EXCELSIOR PARK CHARTERS
*701 Minnetonka Blvd.*
*Excelsior*   474-4772
Lake Minnetonka is the cruising territory of the *Excelsior Park*, which offers Sunday and holiday brunch trips as well as scenic and historic excursions to such spots as Big Island.

### PADELFORD PACKET BOAT COMPANY
*Harriet Island, St. Paul*   227-1100
Two of the Twin Cities' best-known cruisers, the *Jonathan Padelford* and the *Josiah Snelling*, churn water on the section of the Mississippi between St. Paul and Fort Snelling. During the past 25 years, more than 3 million people have cruised the river on these boats — about 150,000 a year.

### QUEEN OF EXCELSIOR
*10 Water St., Excelsior*   474-2502
From May through September, the *Queen of Excelsior* offers brunch, dinner and cocktail cruises that explore Lake Minnetonka's coves, islands and bays.

## Fishing
From the shore, in a boat, on a bridge or off a dock, fishing in the Twin Cities is good. The fish are generally plentiful, can sometimes tip the scales (record-big crappies, sunfish, bass and catfish have been pulled out of Twin Cities lakes and rivers) and include such prized gamefish as northern pike, walleye and trout. And for city fish, these are reasonably clean critters. Women who are or plan to become pregnant, nursing mothers and children, however, should be especially careful not to eat fish that are high in contaminants. Call the Minnesota Department of Health at 627-5146 for a booklet of advisories and updates about eating fish.

Step number one in going fishing in the Twin Cities, if you're 16 or older, is to get a Minnesota fishing license, available at bait shops, sporting goods stores and county license offices all over town. There are special licenses for nonresident fishers, seniors and trout anglers. The next step is to know the seasons for different fish species and the limits on your catch, both set by the Minnesota Department of Natural Resources, 772-7950. In addition to these restrictions, municipalities and individual lakes may have their own rules on what fish you can catch, how you catch them and what kind of boat you can use. Regulations are usually posted at public landings or near public docks. If you're fishing from a boat (rental boats are available at most of the larger lakes), you must wear a life jacket.

Fishing, of course, is a great kids' activity, and the Department of Natural Resources annually stocks 24 Twin Cities area ponds with crappies, bluegills and other species ideal for younger anglers. For a tape-recorded update on this kids' fishing program, call 296-9131. Children younger than 16 do not need a license to fish.

Several books give the ins and outs of fishing in the Twin Cities, some complete with lake charts giving depths and favorite biting grounds for different species. One of the most popular and readable is Ron Schara's *Twin Cities Fishing Guide*, available at many area bookstores.

## Lakes

More than just places to swim, boat or fish, the Twin Cities lakes, in many cases, are recreational focal points, offering opportunities to skate or bike around their shorelines on dedicated bikeways, stroll on pedestrian pathways or simply hang out and get an eyeful of the passing fauna. (In addition to humans, you can admire the dogs, part-wolves, cats, ferrets, potbellied pigs, gerbils and lizards they take on their walks for company.) Some of our urban lakes are for dedicated anglers, some attract yuppies and their families, some lure bathers and others bring out the boats. There's a lake in the Twin Cities for every personality, activity and persuasion.

### BROWNIE LAKE
*Cedar Lake Pkwy., Minneapolis*

Located at the head of Minneapolis' chain of lakes, Brownie is a little piece of water, just 18 acres, situated at Cedar Lake Parkway south of Highway 394. The anglers who visit it find crappies and bluegills aplenty.

### CEDAR LAKE
*Minneapolis*

Less visible from main roads than many of Minneapolis' other lakes, Cedar Lake, located south of U.S. Highway 394 along Cedar Lake Parkway, is snuggled on the west end of the city, near the border with St. Louis Park. On its 168 acres of weedy and lily-padded water you can canoe (and also take in Lake of the Isles via a canal; call 348-5364 for rental information);

Photo: Bill Alkofer, Pioneer Press

*Boating on the St. Croix River*

swim at lifeguard-staffed beaches at Southeast Point and Cedar Point; and take a dip at an unguarded area on the northeast shore that has long served as an unofficial (and technically illegal) nude beach. The area surrounding the lake also contains numerous trails. Cedar Lake is the only Minneapolis lake with private access to some of its 2.9 miles of shoreline, so don't trespass.

On the lake's north shore are rare remnants of the prairie that once covered much of the Twin Cities. The red cedar evergreens for which the lake is named can still be seen on the west side.

For anglers, Cedar offers bass, muskies and northern pike, along with the smaller bluegills and crappies that live in most of the city's other lakes. Like lakes Harriet, Calhoun and Nokomis, it has a public fishing dock.

## COMO LAKE

*St. Paul*

Located in St. Paul's delightful Como Park, this lake holds a peculiar distinction in Minnesota's angling history. In 1882 it became one of the first lakes in the state in which carp *(Cyprinus carpio)* swam. With the mistaken idea that people would line up to catch and eat the imported Asian fish, the Minnesota Fish Commission stocked Como Lake with the big fat minnows and waited to see what would happen. What has happened, of course, is that carp have joined suckers, dogfish, buffalofish and other unsavory, nongame species in the "rough fish" category, and have spread throughout much of the state.

In addition to carp, there are crappies and bluegills in Como's waters, and many fishers take advantage of the public fishing dock to catch them.

Another popular activity at the

The annual
Minnesota Carp Festival
on the Mississippi River.

lake is renting a foot-operated paddleboat for a spin in the sun.

### DIAMOND LAKE

*Minneapolis*

This small wetland lake in a
south Minneapolis residential
neighborhood near the southern
border of Minneapolis attracts waterfowl and other wildlife. On the
lake's east shore is a walking path
that, if you're lucky, can allow you
a view of the wild birds.

### LAKE CALHOUN

*Minneapolis*

Calhoun, at 518 acres the largest of Minneapolis' lakes, is one of
the city's best places to go for sailing, windsurfing, fishing, swimming and strolling. In its waters
idle bass, northern pike, and crappies, and at its shore idles a fairly
young crowd of sun-worshipers,
wind surfers, walkers and swimmers. Its location near the busy
Uptown district and in a heavily
residential area attracts plenty of
people and keeps them there. Its
waters are by no means ignored
during the winter — you'll undoubtedly spot ice fishing houses
during the chilly season.

Named after U.S. Vice President John Calhoun, who was instrumental in the establishment of
Fort Snelling, the lake long served
as home ground for Dakota Indians and was then surrounded by
deer-filled woods. In 1834, the city's
first dwelling built by whites was a
cabin that the Pond brothers raised
on its shores.

Nowadays, a walk around the
lake is 3.4 miles. Your stroll will

take you past a food concession stand (the buttered popcorn is recommended), a canoe rental area and the canal leading to Lake of the Isles, all on the north end. At times of peak use, driving around the lake can be an arduous process. Parking lots are located on the north and south ends.

## LAKE HARRIET
*Minneapolis*

Who was Harriet, anyway? Her full name was Harriet Lovejoy Leavenworth, and she was the wife of a U.S. Army colonel at the time the region was surveyed.

Lake Harriet lies near the chain formed by Cedar Lake, Lake of the Isles and Lake Calhoun in southwest Minneapolis, but it is not connected to the other lakes. Covering 337 acres and reaching a depth of up to 70 feet, it bears muskie, crappie and the occasional largemouth bass. Even better, it is a rare urban source of walleye, the Minnesota state fish and a highly sought-after main course. The public-access boat landing is located at the lake's northwestern corner, just off William Berry Drive and W. Lake Harriet Parkway.

Perhaps the visual highlight of the shoreline is the Lake Harriet Bandshell, near W. 42nd Street, a splendid venue for outdoor concerts that take place throughout the summer. It's the fifth bandshell that has stood on that site since 1888. Nearby are restrooms, a refreshment stand and the dock used by the sternwheeler *Queen of the Lakes*, which plies the Lake Harriet waters for paying passengers.

Another stone's throw away, along Queen Avenue S., is the boarding area of the Harriet-Como Streetcar (see Attractions) and a hand-operated water pump providing liquid refreshment that many people swear by.

Lake Harriet is undeniably pretty, the haunt of families with kids and older walkers. It carries a tamed beauty, however, and the only whiff of wilderness here is at the magical grounds of the Thomas Sadler Roberts Bird Sanctuary, just to the north. Here, with a sharp eye, you can see wild birds and forget that you're right in the middle of a city. Adjacent to the bird sanctuary you'll find the Lyndale Park Rose and Rock Gardens. For more on this parkland, see the Recreation and Parks chapter.

## LAKE MINNETONKA
*Minnetonka, Wayzata, Orono, Deephaven, Excelsior, Shorewood and Mound*

If you claim to know Lake Minnetonka like the back of your hand, you're either a liar, a real old-timer or a fishing fanatic. It is huge, easily the largest lake in the metropolitan area, with more than 100 miles of shoreline and covering 14,528 acres. Much of the water laps in chains of cozy bays.

Like most of the bodies of water in the Twin Cities, Lake Minnetonka has many identities. To anglers, it offers a compendium, of sorts, of virtually every kind of fish available in the area — walleyes, northern pike, largemouth bass and different varieties of panfish. Boaters appreciate it as a lake where you can sail or motor in a straight line for a goodly distance (provided nobody else is in your way — Lake Minnetonka's waters can get quite congested at peak times). Others like to view the water from the vantage point of a cafe window or, even better, their own picture window.

Back when Lake Minnetonka was still well beyond the boundaries of the metropolitan area, it had yet another identity: summer resort. For most of the 19th century, the lake was the playground of the wealthy, many of them visitors from the southern states, who stayed in lavish shoreline hotels. One of the most famous of the ritzy hostelries was the Hotel Lafayette, constructed by railroad magnate James J. Hill in 1882 on a hill between Crystal and Holmes bays. The 300-room hotel rose in only 100 days, gobbling up 3 million feet of lumber, three carloads of nails and nearly a mile of shingles. Its visitors included U.S. presidents Ulysses Grant and Chester Arthur. The Lafayette burned to the ground in 1897 despite the efforts of the Minneapolis Fire Department, which made a then-record 50-minute run to Lake Minnetonka to battle the blaze.

After the turn of the century, year-round lake living became more common, and folks of more modest means began to frequent the lake. Streetcars carried in people from Minneapolis and St. Paul, sternwheelers plied the waters with more than 1,000 passengers each, and several amusement parks offered roller coasters and other thrills. Popular songs such as "By

the Waters of Minnetonka" and "Land of the Sky Blue Water" praised the lake.

Today, boating remains one of Lake Minnetonka's biggest attractions. There are nine public boat landings scattered among the bays, and boats for rent are available from several area businesses.

### LAKE NOKOMIS
*Minneapolis*

Removed from the other lakes in Minneapolis, Nokomis has its own nontrendy, slower-paced atmosphere. Its shores are a popular picnic choice, and its 2.7 miles of paths for biking, skating or walking do get their share of users. Its waters are a reliable source of panfish, and there's a public concessions stand if you'd prefer to let someone else catch your food.

Lake Nokomis, along with lakes Harriet and Calhoun in Minneapolis, offers sailing opportunities that are almost unheard of in other large cities. There are public-use sailboat buoys and launches, along with frequent sailboat races. Restrooms are available, and parking is usually no problem.

### LAKE OF THE ISLES
*Minneapolis*

Located in the heart of Kenwood, Lake of the Isles is far busier at its edges than on the water. On summer days and weekends, it boasts one of the area's most trodden strips of asphalt along the shoreline, and an outer path whizzes with bikers and in-line skaters. Eavesdroppers can hear deep discussions about relationships, the birthing of business deals, astute restaurant reviews and even an occasional marriage proposal. One circumnavigation is about 3 miles.

Due to the lake's shallows (Isles was originally a marsh; the city transformed it into a lake by dredging it at the turn of the century, and the deepest point is only 31 feet), canoers rarely stray beyond the southern end, and there is no access for larger boats. During the winter, one of the northern arms becomes a popular skating rink. There are two islands, both designated as wildlife refuges and unwelcome to people.

There's definitely no shortage of wildlife. Sharp eyes can spot black-crowned night herons and great egrets. Canada geese and ducks are notoriously numerous spring through fall, and their presence sometimes transforms the walking path into a guano-streaked obstacle course. The lake also harbors bass and northern pike. Several years ago, high water filled off-shore depressions with carp of legendary proportions.

Canals connect Lake of the Isles with Lake Calhoun and Cedar Lake. Its total area is 109 acres.

### LAKE PHALEN
*St. Paul*

Covering 198 acres in St. Paul's

northeast corner, Lake Phalen is one of the Twin Cities' most dependable sources of walleyes, bass and northern pike. There are also walking and biking paths, canoes for rent (call 774-9759) and ample sites for picnics and play.

### LORING LAKE
*Minneapolis*

The geese, ducks and carp have the run of this little man-made pond, which covers only seven acres and surrounds a very small island. The fishing is poor, and the shallows preclude any boating. It's a prominent feature of downtown Minneapolis' Loring Park, however.

### MEDICINE LAKE
*Plymouth*

Medicine Lake is a medium-sized body of water (885 acres) planted smack dab in the middle of Hennepin County, north of Highway 55 and east of County Road 61. The angling there is considered very good, even during the winter, and the most common catches are largemouth bass, northern pike and various kinds of panfish. There's a public fishing dock and a public boat landing on the north end, which is also the site of French Regional Park (for more on the park, see the Recreation and Parks chapter).

The official state fish is the walleye, which gained that status by a legislative vote of 128-1 in 1965.

*Sailing on Lake Minnetonka near Minneapolis.*

### POWDERHORN LAKE
*Minneapolis*

Powderhorn Lake is the jewel of Powderhorn Park in south Minneapolis. It's really not much more than a wedge-shaped pond, but people (mostly kids) do fish there and catch the bluegills and crappies with which it is stocked.

### WHITE BEAR LAKE
*Dellwood, Mahtomedi and city of White Bear Lake*

A Native American legend tells of a magnificent white bear that was slain by an Indian brave just as it was about to attack a family near the lake. From that point on, the story relates, the spirit of the bear has haunted the place. Nowadays, the lake is haunted by anglers, recreational walkers and thrill-seeking in-line skaters.

This is one of the larger lakes in the Twin Cities, with 2,416 acres of unusually clear water. A Ramsey County beach offers a good spot for swimming, and paths for walkers, bikers and skaters line the west end. Boaters use two public-access landings on the northwest side. Boat rental is available from **Nelson Marine**, 429-4388.

Anglers like White Bear Lake for its walleyes, smallmouth and largemouth bass, muskies, northern pike and panfish.

Manitou Island, which is quite large, was known as Spirit Island in the old days and provided an annual bounty of maple syrup to Native Americans.

## *Rivers and Creeks*

### Minnehaha Creek

Passing through many Hennepin County communities, Minnehaha Creek runs 22 miles from Lake Minnetonka to the Mississippi River. It never gets very wide, allowing kids to wade in it and ride its surface in inner tubes for much of its length.

Not long before it reaches the Mississippi, it makes a dramatic 40-foot drop at Minnehaha Falls, which has always drawn all kinds of visitors. The 19th century Bohemian composer Antonin Dvorak paid a visit there, and Henry Wadsworth Longfellow's famous poem "Song of Hiawatha" pays tribute to the falls, although he never set foot there.

Visitors to Minnehaha Falls can get drastically different views, depending on the season and state of drought. But regardless of whether the water is dropping at a trickle or in a torrent, the falls is one of the most charming spots in the Twin Cities.

## Mississippi River

It all begins more than 200 miles north of the Twin Cities at Lake Itasca, where the trickling source of one of the world's great rivers eluded European searchers for more than a century. Now, at the Mississippi headwaters in Itasca State Park, you can pick your way across the water on stones rubbed smooth by the soles of countless other visitors who wanted to walk across Old Man River.

By the time the Mississippi rolls into the Twin Cities area as part of its 2,552-mile journey to the Gulf of Mexico, it's already a great big highway of water. In years past, people in this region tapped that force to move forests of logs, power mills that for many years made Minneapolis the world's largest flour producer and turn the turbine of the Western Hemisphere's first hydroelectric power generator. The Mississippi River is the main reason why both Minneapolis and St. Paul exist at all, and it is a bit puzzling that both cities in the past turned their backs on the river.

Nowadays, however, the river is a focus of attention in the Twin Cities. In downtown Minneapolis, where the Mississippi River Regional Park stretches for 150 acres, a project to create bikeways and walking paths along the river, connected to the trails of other city parks, has reached completion. For a few years now, one of the most wondrous spots in the city has been the area along the west bank of the river just north of the Hennepin Avenue bridge, a place heavy with past significance and contemporary beauty. It was here that the first bridge ever built across the Mississippi was erected (it has since had two successors). It's here that you can see runners, bikers and walkers passing at a steady clip on the trails — as President Bill Clinton did on a recent jog. And it's here that you can look across the river at Nicollet Island, downriver at the Falls of St. Anthony and, with some neck craning, farther downriver at the historic Stone Arch Bridge. No one knows what things will look like when the Federal Reserve Bank, which forced its way onto this historic real estate at the old bridgehead and leveled several important old buildings in the process, raises its new building, a facility in which checks will be processed.

In Minneapolis, the Mississippi River is just as important for what has floated down it as for what is permanently fixed in its course. Nicollet Island, a residential and commercial hybrid community that falls under the shadow of the Hennepin Avenue Bridge, is one of those oft-fantasized areas right in the middle of things that seems way out of things. First settled in the mid-1800s, the northern half still boasts 19th-century rowhouses, duplexes and single-family dwellings that are among Minneapolis' oldest and most architecturally interesting. The homes are arranged along narrow streets that suggest a small town, and an old one at that. Up until a few years ago, a donkey grazed this piece of land within view of the downtown skyscrapers. In the center of Nicollet Island are a few businesses and De La Salle High School. At the south end of the island is an amphitheater that hosts frequent summer concerts and plays, a deck that allows a splendid view of downtown, and the William Brothers Boiler Works building, now a public pavilion.

Downriver from Nicollet Island is the site of the Falls of St. Anthony, the only falls anywhere on the Mississippi. What we see now — a concrete apron that supports a modest rush of water — is just a shadow of what this waterfall used to be. For 200 years it was the region's best-known physical feature: a natural marvel that early European explorers compared favorably against Niagara Falls and that inspired countless paintings, drawings and poems. At the end of the 19th century, though, the development of log and flour mills along the river, along with poorly planned efforts to divert Mississippi water to power them, had reached a feverish pitch, eventually causing a nearly catastrophic fracture of the river's channel that threatened to flood everything. The river obviously had to be tamed, and the falls were mastered in the process.

Also subdued was Spirit Island, a small, rocky outpost below the falls and practically in its froth. A Dakota legend held that a woman paddled over the falls with her children when her husband introduced a second wife into the household and that her spirit haunted the island. Starting at the end of the 1800s, Spirit Island shrank with each mining of gravel from its shores, and an effort to make the river more navigable in the early 1960s finally did it in.

From downtown Minneapolis, the Mississippi flows past the sites of the old flour mills on both banks and between the halves of the University of Minnesota's Minneapolis campus, spanned by the Washington Avenue Bridge that poet John Berryman jumped from to take his own life. One more bridge crosses it at Franklin Avenue and another at Lake Street. Near this stretch is the Great River Road, a system of walking trails, bike paths and scenic overlooks. The river is already gliding along residential St. Paul here.

On the way to downtown St. Paul, it passes Fort Snelling at a confluence with the Minnesota River. A sojourner through much of the southern part of the state, the Minnesota is the main waterway of that region. Most Twin Citians see little of this river except at crossings, which is too bad. Running for 34 miles along its banks from Fort Snelling to Jordan is the Minnesota Valley National Wildlife Refuge, an 8,000-acre oasis for wildlife in the heart of the metropolitan area. Several trails in the refuge offer great bird-watching and the chance to escape from the pressures of the city; one of the trails is accessible to people with disabilities. There are also wildlife programs and exhibits. Call 854-5900 for details.

When it nears downtown St. Paul, the Mississippi bends, actually running northeast for a while and causing some directional confusion. West St. Paul is actually south of St. Paul, but it is so named because it lies on the former west side of the river. Here the channel is wider and deeper, allowing the passage of barges that glide low in the water, seemingly without end. Swede Hollow, a St. Paul riverfront neighborhood that housed waves of Scandinavian, Italian, Jewish, Hispanic and other immigrants for nearly 100 years, was regularly flooded by the Mississippi until its residents vacated for good in the 1960s.

Many people fish the Mississippi (as well as the Minnesota River) in all manners possible, and they catch catfish, muskies, walleyes — you name it. Carp aficionados should head straight to part of the river near Coon Rapids Dam (upriver of Minneapolis); this area has such a good reputation for carp angling that the dam is the site of an annual carp festival each June.

River fish should not be eaten without first consulting the fish advisories of the Minnesota Department of Natural Resources. The Mississippi, after all, has always been the Twin Cities' main liquid dump. It's lovely in spots, historic and dignified, but nobody would call Old Muddy Waters pristine.

# Inside
# Spectator Sports

When it comes to spectator sports, the Twin Cities has been a big-league town far longer than most people realize. In 1884, St. Paul fielded a team in the Union Association, one of that era's major baseball leagues, although a financially unstable one. The local nine went on to lose six of eight games before ignobly disbanding. That brief existence still stands as the record for the shortest life of any American major-league baseball team.

Though it wasn't a success, the St. Paul baseball team at least got out the gate and paved the way for a long procession of professional teams that would follow. Right now, the Twin Cities is the home of major-league teams in baseball, basketball and football, with some local minor-league activity in other sports, along with a wealth of intercollegiate and high school competition. To contain all the flying balls and whizzing pucks, the area boasts a good assortment of stadiums and arenas, most of them recently built.

You can judge sports teams not only by their win-loss records, but also by the amount of entertainment and civic pride they generate. We've had World Series cham-

pionships, Super Bowl appearances (no victories yet), All Star games on the home fields and great players who have become important members of the community — Kirby Puckett immediately comes to mind. And don't forget the recently concluded drama of who would own the Minnesota Timberwolves and where that team was going to play in the future. That was rich entertainment in itself, and nobody knew how it would play out until the final seconds.

The phone numbers listed for all sports teams will connect you with ticket sales and information.

## Professional Sports

### Baseball

#### MINNESOTA TWINS
*338-9467*

Until recently, the players of the Minnesota Twins used to have little TCs on their caps — now supplanted by an M that is undoubtedly easier for the opposing team's fans to figure out. The Twins arrived here in 1961 from out East, where they were once known as the Washington Senators. They started out playing in Metropolitan Stadium in Bloomington, a classic

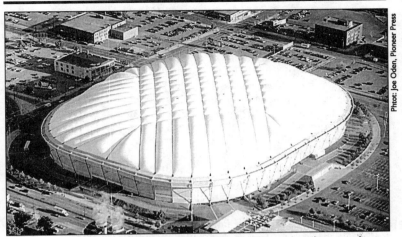

*Hubert H. Humphrey Metrodome in downtown Minneapolis is home to the
Minnesota Twins and the Minnesota Vikings.*

Photo: Joe Oden, Pioneer Press

open-air field that had been built
five years earlier precisely to attract a big-league team. The Twins
had many good seasons at Met Stadium, winning an American League
championship in 1965 and division championships in 1969 and
1970. Some of their best players
during these years were Harmon
Killebrew, Tony Oliva, Rod Carew,
Jim Kaat, Jim Perry, Dean Chance,
Zoilo Versailles and Earl Battey.

In 1982, the Hubert H. Humphrey Metrodome opened at the
edge of downtown Minneapolis.
The Twins moved to this new home
field and old Met Stadium — along
with its 4,300 tons of steel, 2.1 million bricks, 9 miles of pipe rails, 71
turnstiles, 460 doors, 5,200 light
fixtures and more than 40,000 seats
— fell to the bulldozers. The site is
now occupied by the Mall of America, and there is a marker showing
the old location of home plate on

the floor of the shopping and entertainment complex.

Some losing years followed for
the Twins, and it took the team
several seasons to adjust to these
new surroundings. In 1987, however, the team won the World Series, an effort duplicated in 1991.
Since the move to the Metrodome,
some of the team's most outstanding players have been Kirby Puckett, Kent Hrbek, Frank Viola, Gary
Gaetti, Greg Gagne, Jack Morris,
Brian Harper, Jeff Reardon, Chuck
Knoblauch and Rick Aguilera.

Unless you're undyingly attached
to sunlight, the Metrodome is a
good place to watch a baseball game.
Most of the lower-deck seats surrounding the infield go to season-
ticket holders, however. For occasional attendees, that means some
of the best seats are on the lower
deck, running from first and third
bases to the outfield. For the thrill

of sitting next to the more expensive season-ticket sections, order early to get Sections 118 or 132. If you're more economically minded and like the view from left field, try the lower left-field bleachers. Upper-deck seats behind home plate (Sections 222 through 226) are a good deal and offer an excellent view of the action. The upper-deck outfield seats are cheap at $4, but they place you far away (sometimes pitched and batted balls are invisible), and at the Dome you don't have the benefit of catching rays. A stadium-wide bonus for some fans and a drawback for others is one hard and fast rule, expressed with gusto at the start of each game by the Metrodome's announcer: "There is noooooooooooo smoking in the Metrodome! No smoking!"

Of the food at the Metrodome, the less said, the better. (If it does to the inside of you what it does to the bottom of your shoe, that's genuine cause for alarm.) But, hey, they've started serving espresso and gourmet coffees, so who needs to eat anyway?

Many independently operated parking lots scattered throughout the area serve Dome fans. Street parking is also available, but most of the nearby meters are in force until 10 PM. If you're willing to make a 10-minute walk, you might be able to find free on-street parking in downtown Minneapolis.

Purchase tickets by phone, mail or in person at the Metrodome, which is located at the downtown Minneapolis intersection of Chicago Avenue S. and South Fifth Street. (Just look for the white hump.)

## St. Paul Saints
*644-6659*

In 1993, outdoor professional baseball made a big comeback in the Twin Cities with the arrival of the St. Paul Saints, competitors in the independent Northern League. (Other teams in the league represent Sioux Falls, Thunder Bay, Sioux City, Winnipeg and Duluth-Superior.) With a roster made up of major-league wannabes, couldbes and never-willbes, the Saints from the start displayed plenty of marketing savvy and the kind of on-the-field irreverence that made fans happy. For instance, a young pig, the team's mascot, delivers balls to the umpire, and a nun is sometimes on hand in the stands to give massages during the game. There's also a barber providing haircuts. The Saints have also sponsored a post-game Arnold Schwarzenegger film festival, a hot tub night, and Call In Sick Day. The team's home field, the 6,305-seat Municipal Stadium in St. Paul, located at 1771 Energy Park Drive, just off N. Snelling Avenue, is unabashedly nostalgic. Part of the zaniness of this team's on-the-field antics could be because movie star Bill Murray is one of the owners (another is Mike Veeck, son of the former White Sox owner Bill Veeck).

## Football

### Minnesota Vikings
*333-8828*

The same year the Twins started up in business in the Twin Cities, the Minnesota Vikings also

# Out of the Race

Besides the big three of the Twins, Vikings and Timberwolves, the Twin Cities has been hometown to a handful of other professional clubs. They've since folded or moved, but do you remember them?

Minneapolis Bruins (ice hockey)
Minneapolis Lakers (basketball)
Minneapolis Millerettes (women's baseball)
Minnesota Fighting Saints (ice hockey)
Minnesota Fillies (women's basketball)
Minnesota Kicks (soccer)
Minnesota Muskies (basketball)
Minnesota North Stars (ice hockey)
Minnesota Pipers (basketball)
Minnesota Strikers (soccer)

came to town. Wearing their distinctive purple, white and gold uniforms, along with those horned helmets, the Vikings quickly won a dedicated following. During their time at Metropolitan Stadium in Bloomington, they posted several remarkable seasons — particularly the "golden years" of 1969 through '77 — going four times to the Super Bowl. For some Twin Citians, that quartet of appearances on Super Sunday, all losses, evokes deep humiliation and frustration, but the fans of few other cities received as many football thrills during those years as did Vikings followers.

The Vikes moved out of the Met in favor of the Metrodome in 1982, with mixed results in the new stadium. The 1984 season under the coaching of Les Steckel was a notable low point (3-13), but in recent years the team has reached the playoffs with some consistency. Many great players have filled the Vikings roster over the years, including Alan Page (now a Minnesota Supreme Court Justice), Carl Eller, Fran Tarkenton, Chris Doleman, Keith Millard, Ahmad Rashad, Anthony Carter, Matt Blair, Chuck Foreman and Sammy White.

As configured for football, the Metrodome's seating is dominated by season-ticket holders. Often, they take up virtually the entire 30,000-seat lower deck. Although many people think the best seats for football are those closest to the 50-yard line, the seats near the end zones and the corners of the field will spare you much cranking of the head. In fact, the seats that are physically closest to the field are behind the end zones in the first rows of lower-deck Sections 100, 101, 117, 118 and 141. On the other hand, plenty of fans prefer the panoramic view afforded by upper-deck seats.

## Basketball

### MINNESOTA TIMBERWOLVES
*337-3865*

Although the Minnesota Timberwolves have made plenty of headlines during the past year, this attention had nothing to do with the team's rather dismal efforts on the court. Instead, everyone was clamoring about the attempts of former team owners Marvin Wolfenson and Harvey Ratner (universally referred to as "MarvandHarv") to sell the franchise. During the spring of 1994, they had entered into an agreement to sell the Wolves to a group who wanted to move the team to New Orleans, but the NBA blocked the deal. Eventually, Glen Taylor, a former state senator from Mankato, Minnesota, and a wealthy printing mogul, agreed to plunk down $90 million for the team *and* keep it in the Twin Cities. For the foreseeable future, NBA action is here to stay.

The Timberwolves, which began as an expansion team in the 1989-90 season, had big shoes to fill. From the late 1940s through the mid-'50s, the Minneapolis Lakers were the dominant team in the NBA. Led by superstar center George Mikan, the Lakers won a string of championships that end-ed only with the big man's retirement. After several more seasons in small-capacity arenas, the Lakers moved to Los Angeles (thus creating the curiosity of a Lakers team in semi-desert Southern California).

The Wolves, kept going in past seasons by such players as Doug West, Tony Campbell, Pooh Richardson, Randy Breuer, Christian Laettner, Felton Spencer and Thurl Bailey, are still looking for their first winning year. Nobody can fault lack of support from the fans, who crowd the Target Center arena for each home game. In this facility, built for the Wolves and located at 600 First Avenue N., downtown Minneapolis, seats on the lower level near midcourt are virtually sold-out to season-ticket holders, but that still leaves good seats in the corners — Sections 109, 113, 129 and 133 — where you can watch without swiveling your head. Seats behind the baskets also can provide exciting views. Up on the second level, however, the behind-the-basket seats are significantly farther from the action than those on the sides, and the side seats opposite the team benches allow you to watch the coaches scream and whine. If you're in a particularly expansive mood, reserve one of the 12-seat suites, running more than

$2,000 a game, that come with leather sofas, a private bathroom, a TV, some fleeting prestige and, for a little more money, a well-stocked refrigerator and bar.

## Ice Hockey

### MINNESOTA MOOSE
*26-MOOSE (266-6673)*

After the Minnesota North Stars of the National Hockey League abandoned the Twin Cities in favor of Dallas in 1993, Minneapolis-St. Paul was, quite amazingly, without a professional hockey team. But that situation changed in the fall of 1994 when the Minnesota Moose, a new franchise in the 50-year-old International Hockey League, came to town. Playing its home games at the St. Paul Civic Center at 143 W. Fourth Street — the first time this facility has regularly hosted pro hockey since the old Minnesota Fighting Saints folded midway through the 1977 World Hockey Association season — the Moose have an 81-game season that lasts from late September through mid-April. Their competitors in the IHL's Midwest Division are teams representing Atlanta, Houston, Kansas City and Milwaukee. All told, the IHL has 17 teams for the 1994-95 season.

The Moose are by no means the first Minnesota team to skate into IHL action. Two Twin Cities franchises, the St. Paul Saints and the Minneapolis Millers (adopting the names of the area's minor-league baseball teams), joined the IHL in 1959, and the Saints went on to win the league championship in 1960 and 1961 before both teams went out of business in 1962.

At this point, it's hard to predict how well the local fans will take to these new kids on the ice, but it's good to see pucks flying in professional competition once again.

## Rollerblade Hockey

### MINNESOTA ARCTIC BLAST
*3800 First Bank Pl., Minneapolis 376-PUCK*

If the arrival of summer leaves you still longing for hockey action, check out the Arctic Blast, a team that plays on Rollerblades. During the 1994 season (which ran from June through August), the Arctic Blast racked up a 18-3-1 regular season record. It competed in a 24-team league of American and Canadian clubs, some of whom probably won't make it to the '95 season. Games take place at Target Center in Minneapolis and tickets are available through Ticketmaster, 989-5151, or in person at Target Center's Box Office.

## Soccer

### MINNESOTA THUNDER
*P.O. Box 19378*
*Minneapolis 55419          893-1442*

Minnesota's earlier pro soccer clubs, the Kicks and the Strikers, were able to gain a certain measure of popularity, but neither ever put together the astounding win-loss record that the Thunder, a member of the United States Interregional Soccer League, has amassed. Since

*The Minnesota Twins won both the 1987 and 1991 World Series.*

the team began in 1990, its record has been 64-7-9, finishing with a perfect 20-0 record in 1994. Other teams in the league represent such places as Milwaukee, Long Island, Los Angeles, Charleston (South Carolina) and Greensboro (North Carolina). Most home matches are played at the National Sports Center in Blaine (see the Recreation and Parks chapter for more information on this center).

## Intercollegiate Sports

Just about every college and university in town fields a varsity team of some kind, and many have very full intercollegiate schedules for men and women. The most closely followed teams, however, are those of the University of Minnesota, whose Golden Gophers compete in the Big Ten conference. The teams' archrivals, of course, are the Wisconsin Badgers and Iowa Buckeyes. To order tickets for men's or women's Gopher events, call the Gopher Ticket Hotline at 624-8080. Here's a round up of U of M sports.

### Men's Athletics

#### BASEBALL

The Gophers baseball team plays at Siebert Field on the East Bank Minneapolis campus, at Ninth Street S.E. and 15th Avenue S.E., a fine no-beer stadium. The squad has a great winning tradition, with 80 winning seasons over the past 111 years. During 1994, the team came in second in the Big Ten and played well in the NCAA Atlantic I Regionals in Miami.

The team has a lot of young talent and should do well in the coming seasons.

## BASKETBALL

The basketball team, playing its home games at the recently renovated Williams Arena at Fourth Street S.E. and 18th Avenue S.E. in Minneapolis, last year advanced to the second round of the NCAA Division III Tournament. It was the fifth time in the past six years that the dribblers qualified for post-season play. Coach Clem Haskins has been popular and successful.

## FOOTBALL

It's been a loooooong time since the Gophers won the Big Ten and went on to the Rose Bowl (more than 30 years). The last three seasons, in fact, have been losing ones. Part of the problem, some fans would argue, is the team's move several years ago to play its home games at the Metrodome, whose downtown location and scattered parking has effectively ended the tradition of pre-game tailgating.

## ICE HOCKEY

Two-year-old Mariucci Arena, located on the East Bank of the Minneapolis campus at Fourth Street S.E. and 19th Avenue S.E., is the home for the men on ice, who in 1994 became one of the NCAA Final Four for the fifth time in the past nine years. It wasn't an easy trip to the finals, however, because the Gophers went through their first six games of the season without a win. For 1994-95, the Gophers are losing four key seniors, but the returning team looks strong.

## TENNIS

The Gopher Men's tennis team is one of the biggest success stories in U of M athletics. Playing on the courts next to Mariucci Arena, the team recently won its third consecutive Big Ten title and has put together a record of 39 consecutive victories against conference opponents.

## OTHER MEN'S SPORTS

The Gophers also field teams in swimming and diving, track and field/cross country, wrestling, golf and gymnastics. Call the Gopher Ticket Hotline, 624-8080, for more information on these teams.

## Women's Athletics

### BASKETBALL

Last year the Gopher women's basketball team, which plays in the spiffed up Sports Pavilion (old Mariucci Arena) on the East Bank, made its first trip ever to the NCAA tournament, lasting into the second round of competition. Overall their record was 18-11, with one

Three players — Harmon Killebrew, Tony Oliva and Rod Carew — have had their numbers retired by the Minnesota Twins.

Insiders' Tips

senior, Carol Ann Shudlick, finishing her career with 2,097 points, the most in the team's history and third all-time among Big Ten players. In 1995 the team hosts the NCAA Basketball Final Four at Target Center.

### SOCCER

In its first year of intercollegiate soccer play during 1993, the Gopher women ran up a 13-6 overall record, playing home games at Bierman Field on the East Bank Minneapolis campus. 1994 marked the first year in which the Big Ten recognized women's soccer as a conference sport, so watch for a lot more visibility for the women kickers.

### OTHER WOMEN'S SPORTS

The Gopher women also have teams in cross country, softball, gymnastics, swimming and diving, tennis, track and field, and golf. Call the Gopher Ticket Hotline, 624-8080, for more information.

# *Inside*
# Attractions

There are so many things to do and see in Minneapolis and St. Paul that it's a wonder Twin Citians ever manage to spend a night at home. From history museums to honky-tonks, from art galleries to amusement parks, from sculpture gardens to skywatches, Minneapolis and St. Paul have something for everyone.

In this chapter, we describe major attractions that aren't already found in other chapters. For example, the Twin Cities' vibrant cultural offerings, such as art museums, theaters and concert series, are outlined in The Arts chapter; most historic locales are enumerated in the Historic Sites chapter; sporting events are in the Spectator Sports chapter. Whatever's left is included here. It's an admittedly eclectic mix. We've also included offbeat — but fascinating — specialty attractions. Enjoy! A note of caution: Although our information on these attractions, their hours of operation and fees was current at press time, things can change at a moment's notice. It's best to call a specific attraction before visiting to confirm details or, better yet, check in at the following tourist information outlets for any last-minute changes.

### MINNESOTA OFFICE OF TOURISM
*100 Metro Square , 121 Seventh Place E.*
*St. Paul, Minn. 55101*     296-5029
*(800) 657-3700*

The friendly folks at this tourism office offer reams of information on everything from art galleries to zoos. Call their travel counselors even before you step on Minnesota soil. They'll happily help customize a trip that fits both your interests and pocketbook, providing lists on hotels, campgrounds and cultural offerings. The tourism office also publishes the *Minnesota Explorer*, a seasonal tabloid highlighting various attractions throughout the state.

### ST. PAUL CONVENTION AND VISITORS BUREAU
*101 Norwest Center 55 E. Fifth St.*
*St. Paul, Minn. 55101*     297-6985
*(800) 627-6101*

This bureau offers visitor assistance and tourism brochures. Its main office is staffed from 8 AM to 5 PM Monday through Friday. The bureau also operates information centers throughout downtown St. Paul: at Town Square, 444 Cedar Street; the World Trade Center, Wabasha and Seventh Place; the Landmark Center, 75 W. Fifth Street; City Hall and Courthouse, 15 W. Kellogg Boulevard; the Sci-

Photo: Eric Miller, Pioneer Press

*The riverboat Josiah Snelling on the Mississippi River.*

ence Museum, Wabasha and Exchange Street; and the Minnesota State Capitol, Aurora and Constitution avenues.

### GREATER MINNEAPOLIS CONVENTION AND VISITORS ASSOCIATION
*4000 Multifoods Tower, 33 S. Sixth St.*
*Minneapolis, Minn. 55402       661-4700*

This tourism association, a source of valuable information on hotels, restaurants and attractions, may be reached at the above address or at its offices on the skyway level of the City Center, located on Nicollet Mall between Sixth and Seventh streets. Hours at the City Center office are 10 AM to 8 PM Monday through Friday, 10 AM to 6 PM Saturday and noon to 5 PM Sunday.

## Guided Tour Services

A bus tour can provide the first-time visitor with a basic orientation to Minneapolis and Saint Paul, their landmarks, lakes and lore. The following are reliable tour companies.

### MEDICINE LAKE LINES/ GRAY LINE TOURS
*835 Decatur Ave. N.*
*Golden Valley            469-5020*

This company conducts sightseeing bus tours plus specialty tours to sporting events, shopping areas and the airport during the summer months only. Bilingual guides are available. Fees for a 4-hour guided tour of the Twin Cities are $15 for adults, $13 for seniors and $7 for children ages 7 through 14. Also available is a 6½-hour tour of the cities that includes a boat ride on the Mississippi aboard the paddlewheeler *Anson Northrup*. Fees for the latter are $25 for adults, $23 for seniors, and $13 for children ages 7 through 14.

### METRO CONNECTIONS
*1219 Marquette Ave., Ste. 110*
*Minneapolis*                    *333-8687*

These tours feature commentary by experienced guides while you relax in a deluxe motorcoach. During summer, two daily tours are offered seven days a week — a four-hour morning tour and a three-hour afternoon tour. In September, tours are offered Wednesday through Sunday. In October, tours run Friday, Saturday and Sunday. Tours depart from several locales. Ask about their Sunday morning tour of '30s gangster hideouts. Fees: $16 for adults, $14 for seniors and $9 for children. Bilingual guides are available.

### AIRPORT EXPRESS
*3920 Nicollet Ave. S.*
*Minneapolis*                    *827-7777*

Tours of major attractions depart from downtown Minneapolis and St. Paul hotels. Reservations are required.

---

### And For Something a Little Different . . .

#### PADELFORD PACKET BOAT COMPANY
*Harriet Island, St. Paul and*
*Boom Island Park, Minneapolis*
*(For both locales)*            *227-1100*

See the cities from the vantage point of the grand old Mississippi River on these sternwheel riverboats. The Padelford company operates four riverboats — two sailing from St. Paul's Harriet Island to Fort Snelling; the other two leaving Minneapolis' Boom Island and navigating through the locks near downtown. Hours are: Memorial Day through Labor Day, daily at noon and 2 PM. During the month of May, tours are limited to 2 PM Saturday and Sunday. Cost is $8 for adults, $7 for seniors, $5.50 children younger than 12. Dinner and Sunday brunch cruises are also available.

### HERE COME THE TROLLEYS!

Beginning in 1995, St. Paul visitors will be able to ride colorful trolleys throughout the downtown area. The route will include such attractions as the State Capitol, the Minnesota History Center, Rice Park, the Raddisson Hotel, Lowertown, Town Square, Dayton's, the World Trade Center and the Science Museum of Minnesota. Rides cost a quarter.

## General Attractions

### MINNESOTA HISTORY CENTER
*345 W. Kellogg Blvd.*
*St. Paul*                      *296-6126*

This spanking-new museum and research center on state history boasts hands-on exhibits, lively demonstrations and costumed interpreters. Grammar-school history was never like this — visitors can view Prince's *Purple Rain* costume and a birch-bark voyageur's canoe, sit on a milking stool next to a full-sized plaster Holstein cow, run their fingers over a beaver trap, peek inside a model of a sod house, listen to Minnesota's own Andrews Sisters' recording of "Boogie Woogie Bugle Boy" . . . and much more! The History Center can be enjoyed on many levels by people of all ages.

While many of the exhibits seem targeted to adults, children will delight in climbing around and in two special exhibits: a real 24-ton boxcar, representative of Minnesota's railroad heritage, and the Grain Elevator, an interactive play area that allows children to travel the same path that grain takes as it goes through processing. The museum also boasts a restaurant, Cafe Minnesota, and two museum stores featuring Minnesota and Native-American books, games, toys, jewelry and more.

Every Sunday afternoon from 1 to 4 PM, the museum offers "History Hijinks," free programs in which visitors participate in activities such as bread-baking, beading and storytelling. Museum hours are 10 AM to 5 PM Tuesday, Wednesday, Friday and Saturday; 10 AM to 9 PM Thursday; noon to 5 PM Sunday (closed Mondays). Admission is free, except for parking.

## HISTORIC SUMMIT AVENUE

Lofty Summit Avenue is home to an impressive span of stately Victorian mansions, including the fortress-like home of railroad magnate James J. Hill (No. 240), the Governor's Mansion (No. 1006) and the rowhouse once inhabited by F. Scott Fitzgerald (No. 599). From downtown St. Paul, Summit begins at the Cathedral of St. Paul and continues west for nearly five miles to the Mississippi. It's a grand drive.

## JAMES FORD BELL MUSEUM OF NATURAL HISTORY
*17th Ave. and University Ave. S.E.*
*(On the U. of Minnesota East Bank campus)*
*Minneapolis*          624-7083

This museum houses more than 100 works of wildlife art, tracing the development of the art form from the early artist-naturalist through the sporting era to the modern emphasis on ecological awareness. Recently, the museum's collection was merged with that of the American Museum of Wildlife Art, and the result is an impressive, comprehensive display. In the children's Touch and See Room, everything is displayed at child height — the motto is "please DO touch." People of all ages will enjoy the museum's lifelike displays of animals in their natural habitat. Admission is $3 for adults, $2 for youths (3 to 16) and seniors and free for children younger than 3. There is no charge on Thursdays. Hours are: 9 AM to 5 PM Tuesday through Friday, 10 AM to 5 PM Saturday and noon to 5 PM Sunday. The Touch and See room closes at 2 PM Tuesday through Friday.

## FOSHAY TOWER
*821 Marquette Ave. S.*
*Minneapolis*          341-2522

When baby boomers were wee tots, the 32-floor Foshay Tower was the tallest "skyscraper" in Minneapolis, and a visit to its observation

deck for a panoramic view of the city was a grand outing. Completed in 1929 by utilities magnate Wilbur B. Foshay, and restored in 1992, the Foshay was the first skyscraper built west of the Mississippi and remained Minneapolis' tallest building until 1971. A splendid art deco showcase with ornate terrazzo floors and marbled walls, the Foshay was modeled after the Washington Monument. Upon its completion on August 30, 1929, John Phillip Sousa himself performed a march dedicated to the edifice.

While nowadays the view is somewhat obstructed by the "big shoulders" of the 57-floor IDS Tower and its lofty cohorts, the top of the Foshay still affords a great panorama. The observation deck and Foshay Tower Museum detailing the history behind the colorful edifice are accessed through the 30th floor. Hours are noon to 4 PM Monday through Friday and 11 AM to 3 PM Saturday. Admission is $2 for adults and $1 for seniors and children.

### THE AMERICAN SWEDISH INSTITUTE
*2600 Park Ave.*
*Minneapolis*                    *871-4907*

Founded in 1929 in the sprawling, ornate mansion of Swedish newspaper publisher and self-made millionaire Swan J. Turnblad, the

American Swedish Institute is a tribute to more than 150 years of the Swedish experience in America, housing everything from immigrants' trunks to more than 600 examples of exquisite Swedish art glass. The 33-room mansion, with its two-story grand entrance hall, ornate mahogany woodwork, sweeping staircases and 11 rare porcelain fireplaces, is worth the trip alone. Two gift shops offer an extensive collection of Swedish-language books, music and handicrafts. For a more complete description, see the Ethnic Diversity chapter. Hours are: noon to 4 PM Tuesday, Thursday, Friday and Saturday; noon to 8 PM Wednesday; and 1 to 5 PM Sunday. Admission is $3 for adults; $2 for senior citizens and students.

### UPPER ST. ANTHONY
### FALLS LOCK AND DAM
*332-3660*

The legendary St. Anthony Falls and the Mississippi River have been tamed by a series of 29 locks that enable boat traffic to navigate the river over varying elevations from Minnesota to the Gulf of Mexico. The Upper Lock lifts towboats, barges and other river crafts 50 feet and above the falls, utilizing about 11 million gallons of water for every lockage. This is the highest lift of any lock on the Mississippi. The nearby Lower Lock lifts and lowers the water level about 25 feet.

There are many ways to view the locks, which are owned and operated by the Army Corps of Engineers. Visitors may observe the process from the Upper Lock Public Observation Deck, located on the west bank of the river, just off Portland Avenue (immediately north of the Whitney Hotel at 150 Portland Avenue). There's no admission fee, and the view is great. The observation deck is open 8 AM to 10 PM April 1 to December 1. Another interesting way to view the lock system up close and personal is to ride through the Upper Lock on the *Anson Northrup* paddleboat. You can board the boat at Boom Island (Eighth Avenue N.E. and the river). More information on the boat rides is available at the front of this chapter.

After visiting the observation deck, take an unforgettable stroll across the Mississippi on the historic Stone Arch Bridge. This 112-year-old limestone structure, originally a railroad bridge, was recently reopened for pedestrian and bicycle traffic and trolley rides. The picturesque span, built by railroad magnate James J. Hill, is the second-oldest bridge remaining on the Mississippi River. On the river's east bank, the bridge leads to Father Hennepin Park, believed to be where Father Louis Hennepin first sighted St. Anthony Falls in 1680. Guided tours of the historic St. Anthony Falls district are offered by the Minnesota Historical Society on Saturdays, Sundays and Thursdays. Call 627-5433 for more information.

Down river — take Minneapolis' West River Road south about 3 miles to just below Ford Parkway — is Lock and Dam No. 1, providing another breathtaking view of

**Best Entertainment Value in Town**

- Nation's largest dinner theatre
- Lavish productions
- Choice of entree served tableside

• • • • •

**Chanhassen**
Dinner Theatres
**612-934-1525**
**or 800-362-3515**

Ole Miss from a modern visitors center and promenade. The center here is open from April through October (8 AM to 10 PM) and offers a 45-minute tour. Visitors are offered a bird's-eye view of the lock, the 674-foot-long dam and the Ford Power Plant, one of only a handful of hydroelectric plants on the river.

### NICOLLET MALL
*Downtown Minneapolis*

Built in 1967 to revitalize the city's retail center in the face of mushrooming suburban malls, this 12-block pedestrian walkway meanders through downtown Minneapolis' shopping district from Washington Avenue south to 13th Street. Significantly remodeled in 1991, the mall on any given summer day is home to street musicians, farmers market booths, outdoor cafes and great browsing. Dayton's department store at the 700 block is a historic anchor and a favorite of locals. Nearby are the newer shopping complexes of Gaviidae Common (housing Neiman Marcus and Saks Fifth Avenue), The Conservatory (with Mark Shale and other quality shops), City Center and the IDS Crystal Court. See the Shopping chapter for a complete description of these stores.

A visit to the Farmers Market is a great way to spend a Saturday morning.

Insiders' Tips

## FARMERS MARKETS

*In St. Paul: 290 E. Fifth St.*     *227-6856*
*In Minneapolis: 312 Lyndale Ave. N.*
*(Take the Hwy. 55 Exit off I-94)*   *333-1718*

No Minnesota experience is complete without a bite into a juicy, red homegrown Big Boy tomato. Few culinary experiences compare with that sloppy, sensuous, flavorful indulgence. There are Big Boys aplenty at the Farmers Market, plus much more — exotic "designer" vegetables, organic breads, fish and meats, locally harvested honey and flowers galore. You'll also undoubtedly find members of the local Hmong community selling their colorful embroidery at very reasonable prices.

The Farmers Market — bursting with vibrant color and pungent odors — is a Minnesotan's reward for suffering through nine months of frozen winter. Both markets are open from April through October. The Minneapolis Farmers Market is open seven days a week from 6 AM to 1 PM. On Thursdays, it moves to the Nicollet Mall and runs from 6 AM to 6 PM. In St. Paul, the Farmers Market is open Saturday and Sunday mornings. On Thursdays, it is conveniently located at Seventh Place in downtown St. Paul.

## Specialty Attractions

### THE BAKKEN: A LIBRARY AND MUSEUM OF ELECTRICITY AND LIFE

*3537 Zenith Ave. S.*
*Minneapolis*     *927-6508*

Housed in a historic mansion overlooking Lake Calhoun, this collection is positively electrifying, featuring scientific instruments and rare books on electricity and medicine. The handsome grounds also offer a medicinal herb garden. Hours: 9:30 AM to 4:30 PM Saturday and by appointment from 9 AM to 5 PM Monday through Friday. Admission: $3 for adults; $2 for children and seniors.

### CHAUTAUQUA ON THE RIVER

*Downtown St. Paul*

A charming relic of yesteryear will come alive again in the summer of 1995 in downtown St. Paul when the Chautauqua on the River raises its tent near the Mississippi. Based on the educational and recreational outdoor summer seminars made popular in New York in the mid-19th century, St. Paul's Chautauqua will highlight Mississippi River folklore and traditions through musical and theatrical presentations that appeal to all ages. They will be presented over a five-week period. A modest admission fee will be charged.

### HENNEPIN HISTORY CENTER

*2303 Third Ave. S.*
*Minneapolis*     *870-1329*

Housed in an old mansion kitty-corner from the world-class Minneapolis Institute of Arts, this museum has an impressive collection of historical data about the county, plus North American Indian artifacts such as beadwork and a genuine birch-bark canoe. Hours: 10 AM to 5 PM Tuesday through Saturday; noon to 5 PM Sunday. Admission: $1.50 (50 cents for children younger than 12).

Photo: Chris Polydoroff, Pioneer Press

*Farmers Market in downtown St. Paul*

### HUMPHREY FORUM
### UNIVERSITY OF MINNESOTA
*301 19th Ave. S.*
*Minneapolis* 624-5799

The life of Hubert Horatio Humphrey, one of Minnesota's most colorful and influential public servants, is showcased in this exhibit, which includes life-size photo murals, a replica of Humphrey's 1964 Senate office, videos of his speeches and other political memorabilia. Hours are 9 AM to 8 PM Monday; 9 AM to 5 PM Tuesday through Friday; and 10 AM to 1 PM Saturday. Closed Sundays. Admission is free.

### THE KERLAN AND HESS
### COLLECTION, RESEARCH CENTER
### FOR CHILDREN'S BOOK
*Walter Library, U. of Minnesota*
*East Bank campus* 625-5000

A book-lover's affinity for children's books was the source of this now-extensive literary collection. Included are original manuscripts, artwork and galleys for more than 5,000 children's books. The late Dr. Irvin Kerlan devoted decades to children's literature, collecting quality books, corresponding with authors and gathering original manuscripts and art work. The collection is now housed at the University of Minnesota and may be viewed by the public upon request.

### MINNESOTA AIR GUARD MUSEUM
*Air National Guard Base*
*Mpls.-St. Paul International Airport* 725-5609

Aviation buffs will delight in this out-of-the-way museum's collection of 15 vintage planes. An indoor gallery chronicles the history of the Minnesota Air Guard. Admission is free. Hours are 11 AM to 4 PM Saturday and Sunday from mid-April through mid-September; the second and third Saturdays of the month, October through March.

### MINNESOTA VIETNAM MEMORIAL
*State Capitol Grounds*
*St Paul*                                    536-1792

This solemn landmark honors those Minnesotans who served in the Vietnam War. Its granite wall is carved with the names of more than 1,000 Minnesotans who were killed or are listed as missing in action.

### MUSEUM OF QUESTIONABLE MEDICAL DEVICES
*219 S.E. Main St.*
*Minneapolis*                                379-4046

More than 250 outrageous examples of medical quackery throughout history are showcased in this collection. Among the items are a piece of Martian-like headgear that judges your character, countless devices to change one's breast size, the infamous foot x-ray machines commonly found in shoe stores during the early '50s, plus fascinating literature on the tragic results of such "cures" as radium suppositories (alleged to boost one's sexual prowess). Museum curator Bob McCoy is a cheery extrovert brimming with stories about these supposed cure-alls. This museum is a real find. Hours are 5 to 9 PM Monday through Thursday, 5 to 10 PM Saturday. Admission is free.

While you're here, take a few minutes to enjoy the view. Cobblestoned Main Street meanders past historic grain mills and old warehouses that are now home to Riverplace and St. Anthony Main, two complexes comprising restaurants, shops and offices. Across Main Street, down a rolling embankment, are the wide, churlish waters of the mighty Mississippi. This is one of the loveliest views of the Minneapolis skyline. Historic St. Anthony Falls, the rapids that attracted the original settlers, have given way to an elaborate system of locks and dams, but the river is still a mesmerizing sight.

### PAVEK MUSEUM OF WONDERFUL WIRELESS
*3515 Raleigh Ave.*
*St. Louis Park*                             926-8198

Founded by the late Joseph Pavek, an amateur radio authority and historian, this museum takes viewers back to the days when the wireless was king. Included are extensive displays of radio sets, primitive crystal sets and ham radio equipment. Admission is $2 ($1 for children younger than 13 and senior citizens). Hours are 10 AM to 6 PM Tuesday through Friday; 9 AM to 5 PM Saturday. Closed Sundays, Mondays and holidays.

### PLANES OF FAME AIR MUSEUM
*Flying Cloud Field, 14771 Pioneer Tr.*
*Eden Prairie*                               941-2633

Dedicated to preserving American aviation history, the Planes of Fame Air Museum harbors such famous flying machines as the P38 Lightning, British Spitfire, a B-25 Bomber and many, many more. Also displayed are combat films and aviation artifacts. For a real thrill, go for a spin in the open-cockpit *Stearman* trainer. Hours are 1 to 5 PM Tuesday through Friday; 11 AM to 5 PM Saturday, Sunday and holidays. Admission is $5 for adults, $2 for ages 7 to 17, younger than 7, free.

## RAPTOR CENTER

*1920 Fitch Ave., St. Paul        624-4745*

The Gabbert Raptor Center, known informally as the Raptor Center, is a rehabilitation hospital and research center for eagles, hawks, owls, falcons and other raptors. Located on the University of Minnesota-St. Paul campus, the center offers tours, by reservation, for groups of eight or more. (Individuals and smaller groups can usually be added to tour groups on Saturdays.) There also are exhibits of live, "unreleasable" eagles, hawks and other birds and educational displays. Tours include a slide show and video on the history of the center and the rehabilitation process. Hours are 9 AM to 4 PM Monday through Friday and 11 AM to 4 PM Saturday. Admission is $3 for adults, $1.50 for children and $2 for seniors.

## SCHUBERT CLUB
## MUSICAL INSTRUMENT MUSEUM

*Landmark Center, 75 Fifth St. W.*
*St. Paul        292-3268*

This small museum showcases an amazing collection of historic musical instruments and phonographs. Included are a 1542 harpsichord, a rare art deco piano made by Wurlitzer in 1935 and many, many more fine and rare creations. If only those keys could talk! Admission is free. Hours are 11 AM to 3 PM Monday through Friday.

# *Inside*
# Annual Events
# and Festivals

Here's a true story: There was once a Twin Cities vegetarian who had an unusual ritual. For 364 days of the year he'd refuse to place meat in his mouth because of his health and humanitarian convictions. But once a year, during the waning days of August, with great deliberation and ceremony he'd make a trip to the Minnesota State Fair to eat a foot-long hot dog. He just couldn't make it through the year without that one juicy lapse.

Twin Citians of all convictions have their own reasons for attending any of the region's many annually recurring events, and many of them are undoubtedly stranger than the vegetarian's. Nevertheless, we go again and again to these yearly happenings, getting our needed fixes of music, community spirit, holiday cheer, noise, crowds, people-watching or hot dogs.

And there's no shortage of opportunities. You'd need a very large personal calendar, not to mention several lifetimes of weekends, to log in all the festivals, carnivals, parades, holiday celebrations and music extravaganzas that the Twin Cities offers. You couldn't possibly attend even most of them. But there's no harm in trying.

Consult the daily newspaper for specific dates, times and admission costs (if any) of these events. The Minnesota Department of Tourism also lists statewide festivals and events in its free, seasonal *Minnesota Explorer* publication. Call them at 296-5029 or (800) 428-4322.

---

## January

### St. Paul Winter Carnival
*Downtown St. Paul and*
*other locations*                    297-6953

Launched in 1886 to rebut assertions in the eastern press that Minnesota was just another Siberia, the country's oldest and best-known winter festival annually runs from late January through early February. The Winter Carnival is a 12-day celebration of everything that non-Minnesotans and other people ignorant about the winter dread most about the frigid season: snow, ice, and windchill. If you've got it, you might as well make the most of it, right?

A distinctive, and some say peculiar, mythology has mushroomed alongside the carnival. According to the folklore, King Boreas, the ruler of snow and ice, and Vulcanus, the deity of fire, are rivals and enemies. When Boreas decides to make Minnesota his paradise and establish a celebration of the winter with his Queen of the Snows, Vulcanus mischievously makes repeated attempts to disrupt the proceedings and melt them to a puddle. That's all an explanation why, during the St. Paul Winter Carnival, there are King Boreas and Queen of the Snows coronations as well as frequent appearances by otherwise honorable citizens dressed as Vulcanus and his stooges who interrupt events, scream through town on fire engines, and try to smear soot on people's faces.

Among the most popular Winter Carnival events are the two parades. The first, the daytime King Boreas Grand Day Parade, features marching bands, richly decorated floats, a "bouncing girl" (who is tossed aloft from a blanket), and a presiding grand marshal — usually a nationally known celebrity. The Vulcan's Victory Torchlight Parade, held at night, concludes with a fireworks show.

All told, about 1.5 million folks turn out for the 80 or so Winter Carnival events. Many of the activities take place out on the snow or ice: skating, tubing, team sports, ice-carving competitions, snow sculpting, kite flying, golf, even motorcycle racing. The closely followed hunt for the Winter Carnival Medallion, hidden somewhere

in the city, gets people bundling up and digging holes in the darndest spots after they interpret clues printed daily in the *St. Paul Pioneer Press*. Often (though not every year), the carnival sponsors the construction of a spectacular ice castle that raises its chilly and colorfully lit walls high into the sky. Some of these castles have been among the largest such structures ever built.

But don't worry — not all the activities are held outdoors. Carnival-goers wishing a respite from the cold weather can attend such things as the Indoor Fun Fair, complete with a county fair-like "midway," and indoor concerts.

If you dislike the winter, the Winter Carnival can be a good incentive to change your attitude. If you already enjoy the cold season in the Twin Cities, the carnival can be one of the biggest reasons why.

## March

### ST. PATRICK'S DAY PARADES
*Downtown St. Paul and Minneapolis*

For several years now, the twin towns have both sponsored St. Patrick's Day parades. They're both impressive efforts, especially considering the risk of blizzard or ice storm each faces in mid-March. St. Paul's is the bigger, older and more

At the first St. Paul Winter Carnival in 1886, 200 workers erected a 140-foot-tall ice palace that weighed 100 tons and cost $5,210.

Insiders' Tips

Photo: Valica Boudry, Pioneer Press

*Grand Old Day Festival is an annual summer gathering and
parade held on Grand Avenue in St. Paul.*

established event, one that can count on the support of a sizable resident Irish-American community and many Irish-style pubs. In Minneapolis, the sudden splash of green still seems a bit out of place, but the parade is usually well-attended. They're both welcome breaks for downtown workers.

May event that your eyes will be seeing patterns for days afterward. There are also bagpipers, highland dancing, a parade, sheepherding demonstrations, living history demonstrations, an art fair, kids' activities and food. Most notable are the athletic events — can those guys in kilts really throw telephone poles?

## April

### FESTIVAL OF NATIONS
*St. Paul Civic Center, 143 W. Fourth St.*
*St. Paul* 647-0191
The state's largest multi-ethnic event, held annually in April, features great ethnic bands, continual folk dance performances, food from around the world, folk art demonstrations, arts and crafts exhibitions and an international bazaar.

## May

### HEART OF THE BEAST MAY DAY PARADE
*Bloomington Ave. S. near E. Lake St.*
*Minneapolis* 721-2535
It's an unforgettable sight: enormous, 15-foot puppets marching down the street into Powderhorn Park, where a pageant performance takes place. More than 25,000 people come to watch this parade by the jumbo figures of the In the Heart of the Beast puppet troupe, traditionally held on the Sunday nearest May 1.

### SCOTTISH COUNTRY FAIR
*Macalester College, 1600 Grand Ave.*
*St. Paul* 696-6239
There's so much tartan at this

## June

### EDINA ART FAIR
*50th St. and France Ave. S., Edina 922-4413*
This arts and crafts fair, held annually in June, began back in the mid-1960s and now attracts more than 250 exhibitors and crowds of buyers. There's also live music and food.

### GRAND OLD DAY
*Grand Ave., St. Paul* 224-3324
This is the biggest one-day street festival in the Midwest, and the Grand Day Parade is just one of its many highlights. Held annually on a Sunday in June, it features bands, street entertainers and plenty to eat and drink. There's also a special kiddie parade, a family area, and lots of fun.

### LYN-LAKE STREET FAIR
*Lake St. at Lyndale Ave. S.*
*Minneapolis* 822-4002
Only two years old, this south Minneapolis street festival has really taken root, drawing together artisans and craftspeople, kids, street entertainers, popular bands and big crowds. It's held in June and includes a parade and food and refreshments.

## MIDSOMMAR CELEBRATION
*American Swedish Institute, 2600 Park Ave.*
*Minneapolis* 871-4908

This is a cheery and traditional Scandinavian-style summer celebration, complete with arts and crafts exhibitors, Swedish folk dancers, a real Maypole, and lots of food and music.

## MINNESOTA CRAFTS FESTIVAL
*College of St. Catherine, St. Paul* 333-7789

Traditionally held on the last weekend in June and sponsored by the Minnesota Crafts Council, this is regarded by many as the state's highest quality, though certainly not the largest, arts and crafts festival. Representing artistry in ceramics, glass, wood, fiber and metal, 110 craftspeople from throughout the country come to display and sell their work to a quite discriminating crowd. Also on hand are food vendors and live entertainment.

## SUMMERFOLK
*Hyland Hills Park, Bloomington* 338-8388

Red House Records, a St. Paul-based producer of folk and urban-folk music recordings, every year transforms a weekend in June into a tuneful showcase of its best talent. Past artists in this free festival have included Greg Brown, Shawn Colvin, Claudia Schmidt, Trova, Peter Ostroushko and many others.

## TWIN CITIES JUNETEENTH CELEBRATION
*Theodore Wirth Park, Minneapolis* 377-7000

This annual June event dating to 1986 — which includes a 5K run, live music, a parade, kids' activities and an African American Marketplace that features hundreds of food and crafts vendors — celebrates the day, June 19, 1865, when African-American slaves in Texas finally learned they had been freed from bondage.

---

# July

## ALL-STAR FESTIVAL OF THE BLUES
*Municipal Stadium, 1771 Energy Park Dr.*
*St. Paul* 922-9000

Since 1990, this event, sponsored by the Upper Mississippi Blues Society, has brought some of the bluest performers in the country to the Twin Cities. Past stars have included Lowell Fulson, Anson Funderburgh and Big Jay McNeely. Presented annually on a Saturday in July, the event also features food and arts and crafts.

## GAY AND LESBIAN PRIDE FESTIVAL
*Loring Park, Minneapolis* 377-8141

The Twin Cities' most free-spirited and raucous parade, marching down Franklin and Lyndale avenues to Loring Park, is the signature of this two-day July festival. Vendors, artists and craftspeople, street entertainers and a huge crowd fill up Loring Park in celebration of gay and lesbian pride.

## LOLLAPALOOZA
*Harriet Island, St. Paul* 989-5151

Launched in 1991 as a cutting-edge pop music festival, Lollapalooza now includes an occasional oldies act as well as such trailblazers as Smashing Pumpkins, The Breeders, Beastie Boys and Arrested Development. St. Paul is an annual July stop of this outdoor, one-

*Photo: Marcj. Kawanishi, Pioneer Press*

*Minneapolis Aquatennial milk carton boat race.*

day touring event, which also includes spoken-word artists, interactive computer activities and food.

### MINNEAPOLIS AQUATENNIAL

*Downtown Minneapolis and
other locations*                      *331-8371*

For more than 50 Julys, the Aquatennial has celebrated all the water Minneapolis has within its borders — with milk-carton boat races, two big parades, fireworks, a downtown block party, an arts and crafts fair, kids' events, a sand sculpture competition, music and 11 days of mirth. Communities from all around the state nominate young women who vie for the Queen of the Lakes crown. The 10-day event is one of Minneapolis' strongest traditions, and lately it has taken pains to make the event more culturally inclusive by adding youth arts events and a music festival.

It all started in 1939, when a group of Minneapolis business leaders witnessed a crowd of a million people who turned out to view the British royalty in Winnipeg, Manitoba. Convinced that their city could do just as good a job in attracting throngs to see homegrown royalty, the business people launched the Aquatennial to improve Minneapolis' public image. It was a success from the start, taking on an early emphasis in promoting the fight in World War II.

For many years, the festival's most popular attraction was the Aqua Follies, which until 1964 featured swimming, diving and water ballet. Over time the Aquatennial has also featured such celebrities as Jayne Mansfield, Jimmy Stewart, Aretha Franklin, and Hubert Humphrey. An annually changing theme gives the festival focus and direction.

Taking place throughout the city, Aquatennial includes skydiving shows, sports tournaments, art exhibitions, a gelatin slide, senior walks and dances, a sailing regatta, a kite flying contest, fishing clinics and a fishing derby, concerts, a 5K run and a fireworks finale. The two parades, the Grande Day Parade and the concluding Torchlight Parade, are the best-attended events. If you're alive and breathing, some part of Aquatennial will be of interest to you.

### MINNESOTA HERITAGE FESTIVAL
*Nicollet Island and vicinity*
*Minneapolis* 338-3807

If you're interested in an entertainment- and food-filled couple of days all about the state's cultural diversity and heritage, this end-of-July festival in downtown Minneapolis is for you. Set on Nicollet Island and old Main Street in the oldest part of Minneapolis, the three-day event includes live music, exhibitions, dancing, historic tours and demonstrations, sports tournaments, and a fireworks show. An international bazaar featuring crafts from around the world is a special highlight.

### MOVIES AND MUSIC IN THE PARK
*Loring Park, Minneapolis* 375-7622

Walker Art Center sponsors this annual Monday-evening series, spanning July and August, that allows you to watch a movie outdoors in the company of hundreds of other people, with band music still ringing in your ears. The bands are on first, and they range from funk groups to folk-rockers. The film that follows is usually a cult favorite or crowd pleaser. It's all free.

### RICE STREET FESTIVAL
*Rice St., St. Paul* 488-1039

Featuring one of the Twin Cities' longest parades, this festival, held in July, also includes a coronation of royalty, arts and crafts displays, food booths, kids' activities, sports tournaments and live music.

### RONDO DAYS
*Hallie Q. Brown/Martin Luther King Ctr.*
*270 N. Kent St., St. Paul* 488-1039

When the eight lanes of I-94 rolled across the Twin Cities in the 1950s and '60s, they split St. Paul's largest black neighborhood and obliterated its main street, Rondo Avenue. It took years for the community to recover from this disruption. Each year, the Rondo Days festival, held in July, seeks to recall the sights and sounds of the old neighborhood by bringing people together for a parade, arts and crafts displays, kids' activities and food.

### A TASTE OF MINNESOTA
*State Capitol Mall, St. Paul* 228-0018

The most spectacular fireworks show in town is only one of the attractions of this annual Independence Day weekend extravaganza in the shadow of the State Capitol building. The name of the 12-year-old event tells most of the story: This gathering is about edibles. Each year some 35 Twin Cities restaurants band together to offer an incredible array of food from their booths. You can partake of cabbage rolls, ribs, chicken wings, and many other types of traditional American and ethnic foods. At the same time, you can enjoy nationally known bands on the main stage, an arts and crafts fair, puppet shows and other kids' events, and, of course, the nightly fireworks. Proceeds benefit the St. Paul Downtown Council.

### TWIN CITIES RIBFEST

*Downtown Minneapolis*     *338-3807*

Do you know the difference between pork back ribs, spareribs, country-style ribs and boneless ribs? The poor porkers themselves may not find delectable ribs a cause for celebration, but rib connoisseurs (and downtown workers on their lunch hour) smack their lips at this food event, held annually at the end of July. Chefs from around the country vie for the national barbecue rib championship. Also part of the festivities are a hog-calling contest and pig races (they have good reason to run).

### VIENNESE SOMMERFEST

*Orchestra Hall, 1111 Nicollet Mall*
*Minneapolis*     *371-5656*

If you're interested in Brahms, Beethoven and bratwurst (and not necessarily in that order), read on. Viennese Sommerfest began in 1980 when the Minnesota Orchestra decided to create its own summer festival inspired by the music, food and spirit of Vienna. Now running four weeks in July and August, the event has grown into one of America's most engaging classical music festivals, one that attracts top-flight artists, local restaurateurs who prepare ethnic cuisine, and folks who love music and like to hang out in the Marktplatz, the

modest re-creation of a European common that takes shape on Peavey Plaza outside Orchestra Hall.

More than just music, the festival also includes dance, kids' events, tongue-in-cheek programming (last year there was "Late Night with David Zinman," hosted by the conductor and Sommerfest artistic chair) and movies. It's not stuffy at all — there's usually a "candlelight recital" and "piano extravaganza" — and even those who don't normally partake of classical music fall under its spell.

## August

### MINNESOTA RENAISSANCE FESTIVAL

*Renaissance Festival Grounds, Hwy. 169*
*Shakopee*     *445-7361*

Want to see jousting? Eager to hear olde-style musicians? Care to try your hand at dunking a foul-mouthed, insulting blackguard? Interested in gnawing a turkey leg? You can do all this, as well as enjoy arts and theater, crafts, and other 16th-century diversions at the Minnesota Renaissance Festival. Long one of the state's biggest attractions, the festival runs successive weekends from mid-August through the end of September. You'll learn that Renaissance folks — while they had to deal with things like 100-year wars and the plague — certainly had fun.

### MINNESOTA STATE FAIR

*Minnesota State Fairgrounds*
*Falcon Heights*     *642-2200*

In the brief two weeks leading up to (and including) Labor Day,

*Photo: Pioneer Press*

*This ice palace was constructed during the 1992 St. Paul
Winter Carnival held on Harriet Island.*

this marvelous, inter-species gathering — which simultaneously delights and torments the eye, ear, nose and stomach — manages to sum up the entire experience of living in Minnesota. Within the space of a day, you can experience a pig barn, a trout pond, an art gallery, a church diner, a salesman's spiel, a game operator's leer, a race car's whine, a tractor's rumble, mini-donuts, pronto pups, butter sculpture, sand sculpture, musicians on parade, talent show winners, vintage autos, monster-sized squash, seed art, free carrots, bees in the hive, Ferris wheels in the air, cheese on a stick, pickle on a stick, gefilte fish on a stick, and just about any other foodstuff that can be impaled with wood. There are he-men, hucksters, dazed tourists, proud sheep breeders, people selling silos, people carrying yardsticks, dairy princesses, TV news anchors, politicians who are all hands, barkers who are all voice, farm folks in overalls, teens in hardly anything, equestrians, cremation advocates, insemination specialists, weight guessers and weirdos — and everywhere kids . . . kids in strollers, crying kids, chewing kids, sticky kids, laughing kids.

Where else in the world can you: 1) drink all the milk you can for 50 cents; 2) see the state's fattest hog; 3) lose your lunch on the Gravitron, and still have fun; 4) eat guilt-free battered and fried cheese curds; 5) hear jazz in one ear and polka music in the other; 6) watch a dog being spayed; 7) see how slovenly those rock station DJs really are; 8) wait in line for a plastic bag imprinted with the name of a seed company; 9) see a sizable percentage of all the llama in Minnesota; 10) pet a water buffalo; 11) step in melted taffy (it could be worse); 12) meet a genuine chainsaw artist or; 13) learn the latest turkey recipes?

The fairgrounds, located in the tiny St. Paul suburb of Falcon Heights along North Snelling Avenue, are enormous, so come prepared to walk because you can't exactly drive through the place. (Special trams for those who can't or don't want to walk do inch through the crowds; the Alpine Lift ride, which connects two ends of the fairgrounds via cable-suspended cars, is a quick way to get from one place to another.) Official parking lots surround the grounds, and you can park for free if there are four or more in your car. (Others pay $3 to park.) If you don't want to deal with that particular sea of cars, just park on the property of the many nearby homeowners who don't mind subjecting their lawns to hot tire treads . . . you'll pay handsomely for the privilege. Extensive MCTO bus service lets savvy riders bypass the traffic jam.

In 1994, tickets to the fair ran $5 for adults and $4 for kids 5 to 12 and seniors. Imps younger than 5 were free. Discounted tickets are available in advance at the fairgrounds ticket office or at any Holiday gas station in Minnesota or western Wisconsin.

### POWDERHORN FESTIVAL OF THE ARTS
*Powderhorn Park, Minneapolis      823-0597*
Powderhorn Park, a green oasis in a richly urban neighborhood of Minneapolis, hosts 170 artists from a four-state area, ethnic-food makers, multinational musicians, kids' activities and, in a recent year, a live Holstein cow in this early-August, two-day salute to the diversity of the city's arts.

### UPTOWN ART FAIR
*Vicinity of Lake St. at Hennepin Ave. S.*
*Minneapolis                827-8757*
Minneapolis' trendiest neighborhood fills with 525 national artists, 400 volunteers and 350,000 visitors in this mammoth arts and crafts show, which is the largest in the Upper Midwest. Since the early-August fair's founding in the early 1960s, local residents have tended to feel overwhelmed by this three-day crush of people, but art lovers from around the region flock to it for its encyclopedic selection of handmade goods that range from schlock to masterworks. In addition to the artists, the fair features food, street performers, live music and children's activities. Each year it raises a quarter of a million dollars that funds neighborhood projects.

### October

### EUROPEAN OKTOBERFEST
*E. Hennepin Ave., Minneapolis      379-3018*
East Hennepin Avenue in the Old St. Anthony district of Minneapolis, across the river from downtown, becomes a veritable Common Market of European cultures during the annual European Oktoberfest, held in September or October. The neighborhood's ethnic restaurants — representing German, Polish, Ukrainian, Rumanian, Italian and Russian cuisines, among others — offer old-world food to tempt visitors. Also on hand

are ethnic bands, horse-drawn carriages and folk dancers. You can take a historic tour of the neighborhood, chomp on a perogie, or visit the children's Gingerbread Village.

## December

### FOLKWAYS OF CHRISTMAS
*Murphy's Landing, Shakopee*      445-6901

Running on weekends from Thanksgiving through the end of the year at a living history museum, Folkways of Christmas gives visitors a chance to see the decorations and customs of a variety of 19th-century Minnesota ethnic groups. Some examples from past years: The Polish and Czech houses featured straw on the floor to honor Jesus' humble origins, as well as decorations paying tribute to the legend of St. Nicholas, and the German house had a Christmas tree and advent wreath. You can also hear a variety of ethnic holiday music and learn about the Scandinavian legends of Christmas elves that guard the house and the brightly lit menorah for the Jewish holiday of Hanukkah.

### HOLIDAZZLE PARADES
*Nicollet Mall, downtown*
*Minneapolis*      338-3807

Between Thanksgiving and Christmas, downtown Minneapolis businesses mark the arrival of the holiday season with a quite spectacular series of lighted evening parades down Nicollet Mall. From your vantage point on the sidewalk or in one of the overhead skyways, you can hear electrically wired musicians, see spectacular floats and, of course, Santa. Kids love 'em.

### INTERNATIONAL FESTIVAL OF TREES
*Minnesota Landscape Arboretum*
*Chanhassen*      443-2460

First celebrated in 1981, this annual holiday treefest runs from December through the first of the year at the Minnesota Landscape Arboretum. The festival features live evergreens that bear handmade holiday decorations from many cultures and centuries, including trees with Colonial American, Tahitian, Norwegian, English, Irish and Japanese themes. There are also horse-drawn sleigh rides, kids' activities and family entertainment.

# Inside
# The Arts

The Twin Cities, it seems, has always bustled with the arts. As far back as 1856 — when St. Paul was still a dusty river town subject to cholera epidemics and Minneapolis was a frontier outpost less than a year old — the great Norwegian violinist Ole Bull, one of the most famous classical artists of the 19th century, came to the area accompanied by a 13-year-old Spanish girl named Adelina Patti, already on her way to becoming the best-known soprano of her generation. The duo gave a pair of recitals, but the performing conditions were not ideal. Before performing in Minneapolis, Bull had to insist that the floor of the concert hall, located above Arthur McGhee's grocery store, be reinforced to prevent collapse. And because the owner of the only grand piano in town demanded the exorbitant fee of $50 to move the instrument to the hall, the touring musicians had to engage a smaller, much inferior, piano offered by another early settler.

Aside from the fact that big names like Bull and Patti still come to town, much has since changed in the artistic life of the Twin Cities. We've built outstanding facilities for enjoying the output of artists — places that include concert halls such as the Ordway Music Theatre and Orchestra Hall, theaters such as the Guthrie and Theatre de la Jeune Lune's stage, art museums such as the Weisman and Walker Art Center and other performing venues as diverse as Northrop Auditorium, the main stage at the Loft and the Chanhassen Dinner Theatres. We've grown into a metropolitan area that strongly supports the arts through patronage and philanthropy. Most important, we've long ago ceased being simply a stop in the touring schedules of out-of-state artists and have developed a homegrown and vital community of musicians, visual artists, dancers, film and video professionals and writers who attract national attention and influence the work of others.

Of course, there are some Twin Citians who wouldn't be caught dead in a playhouse and yawn at the idea of waiting in line to see a groundbreaking art exhibit. They are viewed curiously by all the others in town who can't imagine not dipping into the artistic wealth that distinguishes the Twin Cities from so many other Midwestern communities.

The role of Old Man Winter in making this region an artistic mec-

Photo: Joe Rossi, Pioneer Press

*Saint Paul Chamber Orchestra in Landmark Center.*

ca by freezing the outdoors five months a year is probably exaggerated; those arts organizations that maintain schedules during the glorious spring and summer, such as the Minnesota Orchestra and its spectacularly successful Viennese Sommerfest, report no problems getting crowds to attend such performances. Perhaps the annual freeze does give Twin Cities artists fewer distractions in which to work, but more noteworthy is the encouragement and support — private, corporate and otherwise — that creative people find here. There's a reason why Minnesota outpaces 46 other states in the amount of federal support it receives for the arts: The money can sniff out the talent.

An excellent and free guide to the arts in the Twin Cities is *Art Town*, a directory published by the Metropolitan Regional Arts Council. Call 292-8010 for a copy. And if you're a fan of automated telephone information lines, try calling ArtsPhone, a free and easy-to-use service that provides information on Twin Cities arts and performance events and can even connect you with the presenting organizations. ArtsPhone is updated every Friday afternoon; the number is 377-0241.

## Dance

### BALLET ARTS MINNESOTA
*528 Hennepin Ave., Ste. 201*
*Minneapolis*          340-1071
Ballet Arts Minnesota is a school and performance organization that uses such locations as Northrop Auditorium in Minneapolis and O'Shaughnessy Auditorium in St. Paul to give traditional and contemporary ballet performances.

### ETHNIC DANCE THEATRE
*1940 Hennepin Ave.*
*Minneapolis*          872-0024
Featuring skilled dancers, great costumes and unusual musicians, Ethnic Dance Theatre is dedicated to presenting the traditional dance and music of many world cultures. The group gives performances throughout the year at such locations as Orchestra Hall and O'Shaughnessy Auditorium, and it also offers workshops and school residencies.

### MINNESOTA DANCE ALLIANCE
*528 Hennepin Ave., Ste. 600*
*Minneapolis*          340-1156
The Alliance is the state's largest organization that supports dance arts. It sponsors several dance performance series that are presented on stage at Hennepin Center for the Arts, Walker Art Center and other locations. It also offers a newsletter and other services for dancers.

### MINNESOTA DANCE THEATRE AND SCHOOL
*528 Hennepin Ave., Ste. 5B*
*Minneapolis*          338-0627
This ballet school for students of all ages is best known to Twin Cities eventsgoers for its annual holiday presentation of Loyce Houlton's *Nutcracker Fantasy* at the Historic Orpheum Theatre in downtown Minneapolis. This pro-

duction — which, during 27 years, has paired members of the Minnesota Orchestra and the Minnesota Dance Theatre in a magical combination of beautiful dancing and Tchaikovsky's beloved ballet music before audiences totaling more than 1 million people — is now the longest-running and most widely attended arts event in Minnesota history.

### NANCY HAUSER
### DANCE COMPANY AND SCHOOL
*1940 Hennepin Ave.*
*Minneapolis* 871-9077
Although the company's founder died several years ago, this organization remains a strong dance force in the Twin Cities, offering classes and presenting modern dance programs.

### TAPESTRY FOLKDANCE CENTER
*310 E. 38th St., Minneapolis* 825-3668
If you're anxious to learn how to dance a sher, cut a czarda or rock into a rhumba, check out this folkdance center providing instruction and the chance to take part in all kinds of ethnic and national dancing with like-minded people. Its programs take place in Sabathani Center in Minneapolis.

---

## Literary arts

### THE LOFT
*66 Malcolm Ave. S.E.*
*Minneapolis* 379-8999
Housed in a former school building in Minneapolis' Prospect Park neighborhood, the Loft brings some of the world's finest writers to the Twin Cities for readings and other programs. Gary Soto, Andre Codrescu, Claribel Alegria and many others have mounted the Loft's stage to present their work, as have such area writers as Judith Guest, Kate Green, Carol Bly and Alexs Pate. Viewed as a whole, the organization's hefty schedule of writing classes is the finest in the region, and its grant programs, writing support groups and other services do much to strengthen the Twin Cities' active writing community. Special mentorship programs serve African American, Hispanic, Native American, Asian American and gay and lesbian writers.

### MINNESOTA CENTER FOR BOOK ARTS
*24 N. Third St., Minneapolis* 338-3634
Located in the Minneapolis Warehouse District, the Center for Book Arts promotes the practice of book arts and book design. It involves writers and book designers in innovative collaborations and offers classes and workshops on the art of the physical book. Its exhibitions explore the ways in which artists are changing the presentation of printed ideas.

### THE PLAYWRIGHTS' CENTER
*2301 E. Franklin Ave.*
*Minneapolis* 332-7481
Itching to see some new plays — some *really* new plays? Several times each season, this nationally renowned organization holds informally staged or unstaged readings of playwrights' works in progress, providing a rare glimpse of the dramatic muse at work (or asleep at the wheel). The Playwrights' Center also offers grant

support, workshops, classes and other performance opportunities for writers of plays.

### SCREENWRITERS' WORKSHOP
P.O. Box 580800
Minneapolis 55458                 331-3880

Participants in Screenwriters' Workshop programs are people who are interested in screenplays (and teleplays) or want to improve their skills in writing them. This organization offers public readings of new works, classes, lectures, a newsletter and a competitive production program that brings members' scripts to the screen.

## Moving Images

### MINNESOTA MOTION PICTURE AND TELEVISION BOARD
401 N. Third St., Ste. 460
Minneapolis                 332-6493

Funded by the state and from private donations, the film board works to attract movie and video projects to Minnesota and to assist film makers in a variety of ways once production begins. As a result of its efforts, 30 feature-length film projects have been undertaken in the state since 1990, creating thousands of jobs and bringing in millions of dollars. The film board also sponsors a couple of movie premieres each year, screening films that were made in Minnesota. The 24-hour tape-recorded film board hotline (333-0436) lists upcoming opportunities for crew, talent and extras.

### UNIVERSITY FILM SOCIETY
425 Ontario St. S.E.
Minneapolis                 627-4431

Created and still directed by movie czar Al Milgrom, the U Film Society is the area's most ambitious and risk-taking presenter of international cinema. Films that never appear anywhere else between the coasts frequently land on this organization's screen in the Bell Auditorium on the University of Minnesota campus, including gems, soon-to-be classics and a few dogs. The society also hosts the Rivertown Film Festival, an annual orgy of independently made and foreign films.

## Multidisciplinary Arts

### INTERMEDIA ARTS MINNESOTA
425 Ontario St. S.E.
Minneapolis                 627-4444

Multimedia installations, performance art, video programs, sound sculptures and electronic music are all part of the territory of Intermedia Arts Minnesota, which sponsors exhibits, schedules classes and administers grants for artists working in a variety of new media and technologies. Among the Twin Cities "mainstream" arts organizations it has been one of the most active in presenting the work of artists of color.

## Music

### BACH SOCIETY OF MINNESOTA
P.O. Box 39292
Minneapolis 55439          649-4692

Embracing three separate performing groups — the Bach Society Chorus, the Sebastian Singers and the Motet Choir — this choral music organization gives several performances a year in different locations.

### CEDAR CULTURAL CENTER
416 Cedar Ave. S.
Minneapolis          338-2674

This is one of the area's main folk, blues, international music and folk dance hangouts, with appearances by such artists as Greg Brown, Blind Boys of Alabama, Pierre Bensusan, Peter Ostroushko and Rory Block. A former movie theater, it has rather uncomfortable seating of the folding-chair variety, but everyone in the audience is up close to the stage, and the acoustics are fine. Every month there are several contradance and other footstomping events, and instruction is always provided.

### THE FREDERICK CHOPIN SOCIETY
P.O. Box 8131
Minneapolis 55408          870-0604

If you like the music of Chopin — or Beethoven, Brahms, Bartók or anybody else who wrote for the piano — take advantage of the annual recital series that this keyboard-loving organization sponsors. Its recent concerts have spotlighted such well-known artists as Stephen Hough and Cynthia Raim, and rising stars in the classical-music scene also make frequent appearances. Most concerts take place at the Janet Wallace Fine Arts Center, Macalester College, St. Paul.

### CORN PALACE PRODUCTIONS
1420 Washington Ave. S.
Minneapolis          340-1725

Each year, this feisty organization presents the Corn Palace Festival of Theatrical Music, a month-long set of musical theater shows that feature new tunes and collaborations between some of the area's most accomplished composers and librettists. It all takes place in the Southern Theater, a venerable old place built in 1909 and conveniently located in the Seven Corners area of Minneapolis, that has seen everything from Swedish theater productions to avant-garde operas.

### THE DALE WARLAND SINGERS
120 N. Fourth St., Minneapolis    339-9707

These vocalists, who together make up one of the region's best choral groups, often embark upon international concert tours and sponsor their own concert series in the Twin Cities. They've frequently appeared on radio, have recorded extensively and often commission new works. Their director, Dale Warland, is an internationally known vocal-music master.

*Minneapolis Sculpture Garden across from the Walker Art Center and the Guthrie.*

Photo: Pioneer Press

### Ex Machina
*230 Crestway Ln., W. St. Paul   455-8086*

Guided by the inventive mind of artistic director James Middleton, Ex Machina is a baroque opera company whose productions are always interesting and often eye-poppingly costumed and designed. See just one Ex Machina production, and you'll forever forget the notion that old music is sedate. The group's orchestra, performing on period instruments, is uniformly excellent, as are the singers who take on the sometimes bizarre roles that the featured baroque composers wrote.

### Minnesota Bluegrass and Old-Time Music Association
*P.O. Box 11419*
*St. Paul 55111          870-7432*

The two biggest programs of this organization are a midwinter bluegrass fest held at a Twin Cities location and a much larger summer festival held outside the metropolitan area usually in August, in Zimmerman. MBOTMA also publishes a monthly newsletter for members.

### Minnesota Chorale
*528 Hennepin Ave., Ste. 211*
*Minneapolis                333-4866*

Another of the Twin Cities' excellent professional-level choruses, the 150-voice Minnesota Chorale frequently performs with the Minnesota Orchestra and St. Paul Chamber Orchestra. It focuses on the great works of symphonic choral literature.

### Minnesota Composers Forum
*26 Exchange St., Ste. 200*
*St. Paul                228-1407*

This is the nation's largest organization dedicated to the creation and appreciation of new music through the promotion of composers. Despite its name, MCF has members nationwide. It sponsors concerts of new music (often in collaboration with Walker Art Center), provides grants and performance opportunities to composers and connects composers with others who are seeking new works.

### MINNESOTA GUITAR SOCIETY

P.O. Box 14986
Minneapolis 55414                374-4681

Fans of the guitar pay homage to this organization for bringing to town some of the country's finest players in the classical, jazz and blues styles. Its annual Classical Guitarathon, a spring fund-raising event, is a big audience favorite, as is the annual Jazz Guitarathon in the fall. Members receive a newsletter and other benefits.

### MINNESOTA OPERA

620 N. First St., Minneapolis    224-4222

Once known nationwide for its productions of new opera, the Minnesota Opera now focuses on the classics, sometimes presented with a contemporary twist. Its shows always look good and often boast impressive musical talent. Many of its productions use surtitles, English translations projected above the stage. It mounts its productions at Ordway Music Theatre and the Fitzgerald Theater, both in St. Paul. Ordway patrons can take advantage of Opera Insights, half-hour pre-show sessions that explore the opera's story, characters, staging and music. The Minnesota Opera also offers several types of opera classes.

### MINNESOTA ORCHESTRA

1111 Nicollet Mall               371-5656
Minneapolis              (800) 292-4141

Founded in 1903 as the Minneapolis Symphony Orchestra, this world-renowned orchestra has worked under such music directors as Eugene Ormandy (1931 to 1936), Dimitri Mitropoulos (1937 to 1949), Antal Dorati (1949 to 1960; the orchestra made some of its best-known recordings under his baton), Stanislaw Skrowaczewski (1960 to 1979) and Sir Neville Marriner (1979 to 1986). Edo de Waart, the music director since 1986, has shaped the orchestra into a powerful ensemble that performs music of the 19th and 20th centuries most convincingly. During recent years, such composers as Strauss, Mahler and Berlioz have received the most sympathetic readings of their works from the Minnesota Orchestra. (Lovers of music by Bach and Haydn should look across the river to the Saint Paul Chamber Orchestra for unforgettable performances.) If not one of the nation's "big five" orchestras, the Minnesota Orchestra certainly ranks among the top dozen.

Starting with the 1995-96 season, de Waart will be succeeded by Eiji Oue, the young and enthusiastic music director of the Erie (Pennsylvania) Philharmonic. His selection to fill the post came as a surprise, because Oue was not very well-known to Twin Cities audiences. The orchestra loved him, however. We'll see if Oue can sustain the continual improvement that de Waart demanded or if he can attract the top-ranked musicians that were drawn to his predecessor.

In addition to its regular subscription-series concerts that run from the fall through the spring, the Minnesota Orchestra also performs Weekender Pops and summer Cabaret Pops concerts (former "Tonight Show" bandleader Doc Severinsen serves as principal pops conductor); offers informal Casual Classics concerts and plays at multicultural Kaleidoscope events; and sends each summer spinning with its annual, four-week-long Viennese Sommerfest. Led by artistic director David Zinman, Sommerfest is a high-energy and often irreverent music festival that features dozens of guest artists and more than its share of surprise events.

The Minnesota Orchestra uses Orchestra Hall in Minneapolis as its home field. Built in 1975, it is an acoustically amazing place that holds 2,300 people. Huge acoustical cubes on the ceiling and behind the stage scatter the sound in all directions, sometimes startlingly so. Some of the best sound is on the top tier, but many of the seats there suffer from obscured viewing. The view is best from Tier One. An adjoining parking ramp is connected to Orchestra Hall via a skyway.

Minnesota Public Radio offers live broadcasts of many orchestra concerts, and Public Radio International (formerly American Public Radio) carries them to stations around the country.

### PLYMOUTH MUSIC SERIES
*1900 Nicollet Ave.*
*Minneapolis*                                690-6700

For the past 26 years, the Plymouth Music Series has been exploring the world of music for voices and instruments. Directed by Philip Brunelle, a nationally prominent and Grammy Award-winning conductor, the series tackles fresh new compositions (including frequent world premieres); audience favorites and works that involve the talents of such guest artists as Garrison Keillor, James Earl Jones and Jubilant Sykes. Performances take place in several Twin Cities venues, including Orchestra Hall, Ted Mann Concert Hall on the University of Minnesota campus, the Ordway Music Theatre and Plymouth Congregational Church.

### SAINT PAUL CHAMBER ORCHESTRA
*75 W. Fifth St., St. Paul*          224-4222

People often wonder why the Twin Cities has two major orchestras. Compare the sound of the Saint Paul Chamber Orchestra with that of the crosstown ensemble, the

When the Beatles appeared at Met Stadium in Bloomington in 1965, it was the only concert in their American tour that did not sell out.

Photo: Joe Rossi, Pioneer Press

*Ghanaian drummer Sowah Mensah performing with the Minnesota Orchestra.*

Minnesota Orchestra, and you'll realize that the presence of both is due to more than plain sibling rivalry. Smaller and in possession of its own jewel-like sound, the 36-year-old SPCO is the nation's only full-time chamber orchestra and is renowned around the world for the caliber of its live performances and many recordings. In recent decades, its music directors have included Dennis Russell Davies, violinist Pinchas Zukerman and now Hugh Wolff, an increasingly prominent American conductor whose brightest years are still in the future. The ensemble has mastered an incredible range of material, from 16th-century works to brand-new pieces (winning several ASCAP awards for the performance of new music in the process). The orchestra shines the most in the new music and in its frequent performances of pieces by such 17th- and 18th-century composers as Vivaldi, Bach, Corelli, Haydn and Mozart.

Because the 34-member SPCO is smaller than a symphony orchestra and often plays in more intimate settings than the traditional cavernous concert hall, it sometimes seems more like a family than an orchestra. The players obviously like each other, work well together and have fun at what they're doing. Many members of the audience recognize the musicians on the street and stop to talk with them.

The SPCO, which appears to have shaken off the worst of the financial troubles that have dogged it for the past couple of years, has a 40-week, 150-concert season. (Its players take a summer break.) In addition to performing at the Ordway Music Theatre and Orchestra Hall, the orchestra presents series at United Church of Christ and O'Shaughnessy Auditorium in St. Paul, Temple Israel and Ted Mann Concert Hall in Minneapolis and Wooddale Church in Eden Prairie. Most concerts are broadcast locally by Minnesota Public Radio and nationally by Public Radio International.

## THE SCHUBERT CLUB
*75 W. Fifth St., Ste. 302*
*St. Paul*                    292-3267

During the last decades of the 19th century, it was common for groups of music-minded citizens to band together to present enjoyable evenings of music, sometimes bringing in a renowned artist from outside the community. The Schubert Club is a miraculous holdover from that period that has expanded and adapted to the 20th century. For more than 100 years, it has invited the world's greatest classical musicians to the Twin Cities for recitals; the 1994-95 International Artist Series schedule, for instance, includes pianist Alicia de Larrocha, soprano Kathleen Battle and the Borodin String Quartet. In addition, the Schubert Club sponsors 40 other recitals each year, competitions and scholarships for young musicians and educational programs.

## THURSDAY MUSICAL
*1410 W. Skillman Ave.*
*St. Paul*                    333-0313

Like the Schubert Club, Thursday Musical originated during the

19th century as an organization founded by music lovers. It's evolved in its own distinctive way, however, emphasizing the showcasing of local musicians and ensembles and providing scholarships to young artists. Its concerts are performed at many venues around the Twin Cities.

### TWIN CITIES GAY MEN'S CHORUS
*528 Hennepin Ave., Ste. 701*
*Minneapolis                891-9130*
Founded in 1981, this ensemble gives four major concerts a year in various Twin Cities locations. It also commissions many new works and performs a great deal of contemporary music.

### TWIN CITIES JAZZ SOCIETY
*P.O. Box 4487*
*St. Paul 55104            633-0329*
Jazz aficionados find this organization a good source of information on upcoming concerts. The society also sponsors its own jazz series and offers other programs. Its newsletter is an essential part of any jazz lover's monthly reading.

## Theater

### BRAVE NEW PRODUCTION COMPANY
*2605 Hennepin Ave.*
*Minneapolis                332-6620*
Founded decades ago by Dudley Riggs, this is one of the oldest comedy-and-satire companies in the country. Its productions, which invariably sport such playful titles as *Cinderella and the Glass Ceiling* or *What's So Funny About Being Female?*, routinely skewer conservative greed, liberal guilt and "Minneso-

ta nice" in shows that mix high hilarity and music. The group's Hennepin Avenue storefront theater is a worn and cramped cave perfectly suited for in-your-face entertainment.

### BRYANT LAKE BOWL THEATER
*810 W. Lake St., Minneapolis    825-8949*
Here you can hear the crash of strikes and the agonized screams of those who throw gutter balls as you enjoy theater in an decidedly unorthodox setting. Satire and dark comedy are the normal fare in this surprisingly large theater that adjoins a popular bowling hangout. The tableside seats at the front of the theater are definitely better (and less prone to aural interruption from bowlers) than the rear row seating.

### CHANHASSEN DINNER THEATRES
*501 W. 78th St., Chanhassen    934-1525*
About a half-hour drive southwest of Minneapolis is a large complex of theaters where cooks are employed as well as actors, waiters as well as lighting techs and bus help as well as box office staff. Since 1968, theatergoers have been coming to the Chanhassen Dinner Theatres to have their appetites for good food and stylishly produced plays satisfied simultaneously. Its high quality productions run the full gamut of popular theater — *Phantom*, *Brighton Beach Memoirs* and *Fiddler on the Roof* are some recent examples — and the setting, a semirustic building with fireplaces and snug alcoves, is memorable. Many TV and film stars such as Loni Anderson and Linda Kelsey

Photo: Joe Oden, Pioneer Press

*Prince's Paisley Park recording studio in Chanhassen.*

started their climb to the big time here.

### THE CHILDREN'S THEATRE COMPANY
*2400 Third Ave. S.*
*Minneapolis* 874-0400

One of America's largest and most highly respected producers of kids' theater, CTC stages new adaptations of classics like *The Adventures of Tom Sawyer* and *The 500 Hats of Bartholomew Cubbins,* as well as theater versions of such contemporary works of childrens' literature as *Amazing Grace* and *East of the Sun and West of the Moon.* High quality productions are the norm, often with original music and outstanding child and adult actors. The company's modern theater, located in an arts complex that the CTC shares with the Minneapolis Institute of Arts, is designed with little viewers in mind (although adults typically constitute more

than half of the audience) and features great sightlines, wide aisles and very comfortable seats.

### CHILD'S PLAY THEATRE COMPANY
*5701 Normandale Rd., Ste. 343*
*Edina* 925-5250

The Twin Cities is lucky to have a second company dedicated to the production of childrens' theater. Usually presenting its programs at Eisenhower Community Center in Hopkins, Child's Play focuses on giving kids stage experience through performances and classes.

### CRICKET THEATRE
*821 Marquette Ave., Ste. 229*
*Minneapolis* 337-0747

It's hard to believe that this groundbreaking theater company, which specializes in works by such living playwrights as Sam Shepard and Alan Ball, is already 25 years old. With many near-bankruptcies in its past, the Cricket has always hung on to deliver high quality shows in locations all over Minneapolis. Currently most shows are being mounted at the Hennepin Center for the Arts.

### GREAT AMERICAN HISTORY THEATRE
*30 E. 10th St., St. Paul*          *292-4323*

Charles Lindbergh, St. Paul's lost African-American Rondo neighborhood, Zelda and F. Scott Fitzgerald and other Minnesota figures and stories have been brought to the stage by this company specializing in musicals, dramas and comedies that detail the lives of people in this region. Many of its shows are world premieres. It gives its performances in the theater of the St. Paul Arts and Science Center. Finding a parking place can be tough, even with a few ramps in the area.

### GUTHRIE THEATER
*725 Vineland Pl.*          *377-2224*
*Minneapolis*
*(800) 848-4912, Ext. 2712*

Although other Twin Cities theaters — most notably the Old Log and Theatre in the Round — antedate it, the Guthrie is the Big Bopper of the frisky local theater world, the institution that receives the most attention from the local press, the national media, funders and area theatergoers. It opened in 1963, the brainchild of British impresario Sir Tyrone Guthrie, who wanted to plant a high-quality repertory theater in the fertile ground of America's heartland. Nearly 200 productions later, Guthrie's dream has taken root with a vengeance: Some of

the world's best directors, stage designers, costumers and actors work there, and its shows are invariably top-quality and thought-provoking. Recent seasons have included productions of such classics as *Othello, As You Like It, A Woman of No Importance* and *The Bacchae*, as well as such contemporary masterworks as *The Screens, Home* and *Naga Mandala*. The Guthrie's annual holiday production of Charles Dickens' *A Christmas Carol* is a decades-old tradition in the Twin Cities.

The Guthrie Theater occupies the west half of a cool and solid arts complex it shares with Walker Art Center at the southwest edge of downtown Minneapolis. A recent exterior renovation of the theater displeased some patrons, but there can be few who would complain about the sightlines of the 1,500-seat interior. The best seats are on the main floor, because even some professionally trained voices can get lost up in the balconies. Areas 2, 3 and 4 of the theater allow seating for users of wheelchairs and their guests. Rush seats, available for most performances at $8, provide some great ticket bargains. The theater is also an excellent and frequently used concert venue.

Don't arrive at the last minute for Guthrie performances — traffic can get congested and parking can be hard to find in the largely residential neighborhood. There are pay lots next to the Minneapolis Sculpture Garden and on Groveland Avenue. The Guthrie is also accessible via bus lines 1, 4, 6, 12 and 28.

## HEY CITY STAGE
*1430 S. Washington Ave.*
*Minneapolis*                    333-1300

Since 1991 this combination restaurant and cabaret has played host to a very lively production of *Forever Plaid*, an irreverent homage to the guy vocal groups of the 1950s and '60s. It will undoubtedly keep running as long as the crowds keep pouring in.

## ILLUSION THEATER
*528 Hennepin Ave., Ste. 704*
*Minneapolis*                    338-8371

Presenting most of its shows in the Hennepin Center for the Arts, Illusion Theater is unusually focused on sparking personal and social change. It produces the work of many emerging and well-established contemporary playwrights and is perhaps best known for its annual Fresh Ink Series, a weeks-long parade of new and in-progress plays by American writers of all kinds. Starting out in 1974 as a mime troupe, Illusion Theater has grown into one of the Twin Cities' most intriguing and rewarding companies.

## IN THE HEART OF THE BEAST PUPPET AND MASK THEATRE
*1500 E. Lake St., Minneapolis*    721-2535

If you've attended many parades or festivals in the Twin Cities, you've undoubtedly encountered an army of the Heart of the Beast's trademark jumbo puppet figures. It's an awesome sight. With permanent quarters in a former porn theater, the company employs puppets of many types to create surprisingly poignant shows for adults and families, often touching upon serious social issues. The group also offers many productions in various community settings.

## JUNGLE THEATER
*709 W. Lake St., Minneapolis*    822-7063

One of the area's hottest and most successful new theaters, the Jungle has, in just a few years, drawn much attention and exerted its own special influence. It productions — ranging from classics like *The Diary of Anne Frank* and *Who's Afraid of Virginia Woolf?* to such relatively unfamiliar works as local playwright Kevin Kling's *The Ice Fishing Play* — are routinely outstanding. Situated in a storefront facility, the Jungle offers cramped (and very limited) seating that somehow increases the intensity and effectiveness of its shows. A forthcoming expansion into a neighboring building should ease the crowding without, we hope, diminishing the high quality. The Jungle's productions are for audiences who love expert directing, splendid acting and unforgettable theater.

## LORING PLAYHOUSE
*1633 Hennepin Ave. S.*
*Minneapolis*                    332-1617

Ensconced in a formerly elegant car dealership building (now also the quarters of the chic Loring Bar and Cafe), this avant-garde company presents irreverent and intriguing shows that resist simple categorization as comedies, dramas, etc. They're all complex and playful, often arguments for different concepts of beauty or normalcy than mainstream theater usually presents.

## MINNESOTA CENTENNIAL SHOWBOAT
*East River Rd., Minneapolis      625-4001*

An old paddlewheeler moored on the banks of Old Man River may seem an unusual place to attend a play, but decades worth of comedies, melodramas and musicals have strained the boards of this floating playhouse operated by the University of Minnesota's theater department. Open only during the summer, the Showboat features energetic and usually young casts, along with a gentle rise and fall that is certainly not part of your imagination.

## MIXED BLOOD THEATER
*1501 S. Fourth St., Minneapolis   338-0937*

At one time the nation's largest employer of Equity actors of color, Mixed Blood is a company that has never shied away from controversial and thought-provoking productions. Its managing director, Jack Reuler, has long espoused a color-blind casting policy that only gradually have some other theaters imitated. Whether its shows are probing the causes and effects of the Crown Heights riots or examining the soul of Cyrano de Bergerac, they're always memorable.

## MUSIC BOX THEATRE
*1407 Nicollet Ave*
*Minneapolis                   871-1414*

After having served for years as the Cricket Theatre's home, this former cinema at the edge of downtown Minneapolis has been again refurbished to provide a congenial home for musicals and musical revues. One recent production, *The All Night Strut*, seamlessly paraded 27 favorite songs from the 1930s and '40s. Audiences of a surprisingly wide range of ages have proven susceptible to this type of musical fare.

## NEW CLASSIC THEATRE
*1832 Carroll Ave., St. Paul      645-7547*

Area premieres of new plays are the specialty of this company that puts together only one or two shows a year, usually presenting them at the Minneapolis Theater Garage or Mixed Blood Theater. Founded by artistic director Peter Moore, a well-known local actor, the company delivers strongly acted performances and challenging plays.

## NORTHERN SIGN THEATRE
*528 Hennepin Ave., Ste. 308*
*Minneapolis       338-7876, TTY 338-7549*

The mission of this company is to spark dialogue between deaf and hearing people through the theater. Audiences can take in everything it produces — stage shows, touring productions, workshops and videos — in both American Sign Language and English.

### OLD LOG THEATER
*5175 Meadville St., Excelsior      474-5951*

In business since 1941, this is the oldest professional theater concern in the Twin Cities. Beautifully set near the shore of Lake Minnetonka, the current Old Log replaced the original theater decades ago and has more than 600 seats. (The old structure now serves as a scene shop.) British bedroom farces such as Ray Cooney's popular *Run for Your Wife!* constitute the bulk of the stage offerings at this renowned and much-loved dinner theater, whose alumni include movie star Nick Nolte.

### PARK SQUARE THEATRE
*253 E. Fourth St., St. Paul      291-7005*

For years, Park Square staged its shows exclusively at the auditorium of the Minnesota Museum of American Art building in St. Paul, but now the company has begun using Seventh Place Theatre, 20 W. Seventh Place, St. Paul, as the home stage for its performances of classic plays from the European and American repertory. Its season runs winter through summer.

### PENUMBRA THEATRE COMPANY
*270 N. Kent St., St. Paul      224-3180*

Penumbra, the Twin Cities' only professional company presenting works from an African-American perspective, performs at St. Paul's Martin Luther King Center. Long associated with Pulitzer Prize-winning playwright August Wilson (a former St. Paul resident), Penumbra has recently come into the public eye even more with solid stagings of plays by other writers. Each holiday season, Penumbra fills the Fitzgerald Theater with many performances of Langston Hughes' *Black Nativity*, an uplifting and music-filled retelling of the nativity story.

### PLYMOUTH PLAYHOUSE
*Hwys. 55 and 494, Plymouth      333-3302*

With offerings such as *Pump Boys and Dinettes* and *The Lovely Liebowitz Sisters in a Krakatoa Homecoming*, this is a place to go for light musicals, nostalgia and cute comedy. The theater is a part of a Best Western Kelly Inn.

### RED EYE COLLABORATION
*15 W. 14th St., Minneapolis      870-0309*

New multimedia theater works are Red Eye's bread and butter, and the group is well-known for its presentations of experimental, nontraditional and provocative shows. It also sponsors occasional music series and media exhibitions.

### THE REFRESHMENT COMMITTEE
*801 Dayton Ave., St. Paul      227-0775*

The Refreshment Committee, a professional company that performs at Seventh Place Theatre in St. Paul, presents shows for adults and kids that illustrate biblical values and promote racial equality and social responsibility.

### TEATRO LATINO DE MINNESOTA
*3501 Chicago Ave. S.*
*Minneapolis      432-2314*

This is a multicultural theater

company that often presents issues-packed or exploratory Hispanic plays — many of them performed bilingually.

### THEATER MU
*1201 Yale Pl., #911*
*Minneapolis*      *332-5763*

This two-year-old theater company, specializing in plays that explore Asian-American issues, has made a fast entry into the Twin Cities' admittedly crowded stage scene. It's garnered great reviews, however, for such productions as *Yellow Fever* by Rick Shiomi, a parody of the hard-boiled detective genre that delved into anti-Asian racism in Canada during World War II. Its most recent productions have been staged at the Southern Theater and the Ordway.

### THEATRE DE LA JEUNE LUNE
*105 N. First St., Minneapolis*      *333-6200*

If the Guthrie Theater gets the lion's share of media and public attention among the Twin Cities' theaters, Theatre de la Jeune Lune challenges other venues for second place. An ensemble theater created by American and French actors, it stages richly imaginative and grandly conceived shows that are usually jointly created by many members of the company. For many seasons now, its productions, such as *Germinal* and *Conversations After a Burial*, have drawn international raves. Jeune Lune performs in a stylish old downtown Minneapolis building — a former storage warehouse — that was partly designed by Cass Gilbert (architect of the U.S. Supreme Court building

in Washington and New York's Woolworth Building). It gives the company the room it needs to mount productions that typically bulge with cast members and ideas. The company's name means "Theater of the New Moon," an oblique homage to the innovative Parisian Theatre du Soleil — "Theater of the Sun."

### THEATRE IN THE ROUND PLAYERS
*245 Cedar Ave., Minneapolis*      *333-3010*

Now creeping up on its 45th birthday, Theatre in the Round is the region's oldest community theater, and its stage certainly ranks among the busiest. Each year about 10 productions are mounted in the company's Seven Corners building; they range from classics to contemporary works and Broadway hits. Theatre in the Round also offers classes and training in theater crafts.

### VENETIAN PLAYHOUSE
*2814 Rice St., St. Paul*      *484-1108*

This theater features extended-run productions of cabaret- and vaudeville-style shows, often staged by such companies as Troupe America. Dinner service is available before most shows. The playhouse is inside the Venetian Inn Restaurant.

## The Visual Arts

### BLOOMINGTON ART CENTER
*10206 Penn Ave. S.*
*Bloomington*      *887-9667*

This center supplies one of the best arguments that the suburbs are not arts-free deserts. It frequently exhibits the work of Bloomington-area artists and also offers art classes and workshops for kids and adults.

### FREDERICK R. WEISMAN ART MUSEUM
*333 E. River Rd. (East Bank of U. of Minn.)*
*Minneapolis* 625-9494

Crossing the Washington Avenue Bridge or taking in the view across the Mississippi River, you can't miss this wonderful pile of improbably angled sheets of metal, designed by Los Angeles architect Frank Gehry, that sits atop the east bank and sends blinding reflections of sunlight in all directions. Named after its major donor, it's spectacular on the outside and very functional and friendly on the inside (although smaller than it appears from the exterior). This museum, run by the University of Minnesota, just opened a couple of years ago and has had a lot of visitors singing its praises. It houses the University's extensive art collection and also hosts visiting exhibitions from around the country. The permanent collection is especially strong in 20th-century American art. Recent showings have included "Light from the Yellow Star," a collection of gouaches by Holocaust survivor and U of M professor Robert Fisch, and "The Crucible," a site-specific installation by Minnesota artist Stuart Nielsen. Parking is available in a ramp located beneath the museum. Admission to the museum is free.

### MINNEAPOLIS INSTITUTE OF ARTS
*2400 Third Ave. S.*
*Minneapolis* 870-3266

Back in 1911, a group of prominent Minneapolis citizens pooled their money to establish an ambitiously conceived art museum and classroom facility for the city. The original beaux-arts building, designed by the famed architectural firm McKim, Mead and White and completed in 1915, still stands, raising its columns to Fair Oaks Park across the street and the more distant skyscrapers of downtown. In recent decades, however, various additions have expanded the facility, creating one of America's great comprehensive art museums and luring art lovers from throughout the region.

The 80,000-item collection of the Art Institute is strong in many areas — particularly in decorative art, textiles and the art of ancient times, Asia, the United States before 1950 and Europe of the 14th through 19th centuries. Wandering its high-ceilinged galleries, you'll encounter works by Titian, Georgia O'Keeffe, Monet, Van Gogh, Grant Wood, Picasso, Miró and Magritte. You'll also see a 2,000-year-old mummy, a world-famous Oriental jade collection (that includes a magnificent mountain carved from a single block of the mineral), the throne of a Chinese king, rooms representing many periods from American and European history, a fine collection of African masks, a remarkable hoard of prints and drawings, a photo gallery and a wondrous sand mural created on-site by a group of visiting Tibetan monks.

Don't miss Rembrandt's "Lucretia," the gathering of French impressionist paintings in Gallery 330,

Photo: Bill Alkofer, Pioneer Press

*Frederick R. Weisman Art Museum overlooks the Mississippi River from the University of Minnesota's Minneapolis campus.*

the American gallery on the first floor and the displays of the Minnesota Artists Exhibition Program that feature the recent works of regional artists. The Art Institute also boasts a gift shop, educational exhibits, a coffee shop, video and film programs and art classes for kids and adults.

A half-million people visit this museum every year. Like most art museums, the Institute is closed Mondays. Admission is free, except for some special or touring exhibitions usually displayed on the second floor.

### MINNESOTA CRAFTS COUNCIL
*528 Hennepin Ave., Ste. 308*
*Minneapolis*                    *333-7789*

This organization's most visible activity is a high-quality annual crafts fair, held in June or July at the College of St. Catherine in St.

Paul. The Council, focused on promoting excellence in craft media and handmade objects, also sponsors other exhibitions and connects crafts artists with one another.

### MINNESOTA MUSEUM OF AMERICAN ART
*75 W. Fifth St., Second Fl.*
*St. Paul*                       *292-4380*

Probably because it maintains two separate locations — in St. Paul's Landmark Center and a couple of blocks away in a wonderful art deco building at 305 St. Peter Street — this museum has always operated in the shadows of its Minneapolis counterparts. It is less financially secure than the other art museums in town, as well, which has recently prevented it from showing off the luster of its collection. Strong in American paintings (especially from the decades around the turn of the century) and the art of Asia, Africa and Oceania, the Minnesota Museum of American Art reserves the Landmark Center gallery space for temporary exhibitions, many of which focus on the work of contemporary artists. Recent exhibitions have spotlighted African-American quilts and photo portraits of jazz artists.

### NORTHERN CLAY CENTER
*2375 University Ave. W.*
*St. Paul*        642-1735

Get your wheels spinning and your fingers dirty at this ceramic arts center that sponsors classes and exhibitions of the work of regional and national artists.

### WALKER ART CENTER
*725 Vineland Pl., Minneapolis*    375-7636

Sharing a building with the Guthrie Theater is one of the nation's greatest centers of contemporary art. Walker Art Center began, however, as the private collection of T.B. Walker, a Minneapolis lumber baron who collected Old Master paintings, Oriental pottery and jade carvings, musical instruments, ancient Greek vases and many other kinds of art objects. After Walker's death, the art foundation he had established decided to make 20th-century art the focus of its galleries at the foot of Lowry Hill in Minneapolis.

The thousands of pieces in the Walker's permanent collection now span the full range of American and European art movements in the 20th century: everything from Pop Art and Minimalism to Abstract Expressionism and Neo-Ex-

pressionism. Some of the nation's best touring contemporary art exhibitions also make a mandatory stop at the Walker.

The Walker, though, is much more than just an art museum. Through its renowned performing arts program, it sponsors or co-sponsors an amazing variety of events: film and video screenings, dance performances, concerts, appearances by performance artists, lectures, music and theater events, and children's programs. Many of these events take place at the Walker, but others take the stage at venues around the area.

Across the street from the Walker and jointly operated by it and the Minneapolis Park Board is the seven-acre Minneapolis Sculpture Garden, an outdoor area that opened in 1988 and has rapidly become one of the Twin Cities' most popular hangouts for tourists, families and arts lovers. The beautifully landscaped Sculpture Garden contains exemplary works by such sculptors as Henry Moore and Frank Gehry, sprouts a great flower garden at its north end and includes a 52-foot-long sculpture and fountain that has become a symbol of Minneapolis' status as an arts-conscious city: Claes Oldenburg's and Coosje van Bruggen's "Spoonbridge and Cherry." The Irene Hixon Whitney Bridge, a long and delicate connection between the Sculpture Garden and Loring Park, designed by Siah Armajani, is also a part of the collection.

## Other Venues

### HENNEPIN CENTER FOR THE ARTS
*528 Hennepin Ave.*
*Minneapolis*                    332-4478

This rugged sentinel at the corner of Fifth Street and Hennepin Avenue in downtown Minneapolis, built in 1890 as a Masonic Temple, houses many small arts organizations and contains two public performing spaces. The larger one, the 300-seat Bower Hawthorne Theatre on the top floor, is used by such companies as Illusion Theatre, Cricket Theatre, Lyric Theatre and Troupe America, as well as some music and dance groups. It suffers from the high elevation of the stage, which forces performers to look down at much of the audience. The second-floor Little Theater, a 140-seat space, is encumbered by poor lighting. In the works is a $2 million refurbishing of the building that would dramatically reconfigure the seating of the Bower Hawthorne Theatre and improve the technical equipment in the Little Theater. If the money is raised, it all could happen as early as 1996.

### TED MANN MUSIC HALL
*West Bank, University of Minnesota*
*Minneapolis*                    624-2224

Only a couple of years old, this concert hall has quickly become a major performing space for all kinds of musical organizations in addition to the many university ensembles that play there. Its acoustics are fine-tuned enough for a solo guitar recital and solid enough for a concert band. Sightlines are fine, especially from the side balconies.

### MINNEAPOLIS THEATER GARAGE
*711 W. Franklin Ave.*            870-0723

This theater in the Wedge neighborhood, a former repair facility that now hosts occasional productions by the Jungle Theater and other companies, is excellent from the audience's perspective. All seats are close to the stage, and sightlines are great. It's pretty small, perhaps accommodating a crowd of 100. Only street parking is available.

### NORTHROP AUDITORIUM
*University of Minnesota*
*Minneapolis*                    624-2345

This formidable auditorium, built in 1929 and capable of seating a crowd of 5,000, spent its early years mainly as a home of university events and as a classical-music concert hall where audiences cheered the likes of Vladimir Horowitz and Sergei Rachmaninoff. (The Minnesota Orchestra cut some of its most famous early recordings there, as well.) Nowadays Northrop does much of its own programming, putting on its stage some of the world's best ballet and dance ensembles and bringing in a variety of prominent pop and jazz musicians.

Two areas of the auditorium are best for dance performances: the first rows of the balcony and the side sections of the main floor, where you can follow the footwork without turning your head back and forth like a tennis fan. On the main floor, Row 25 has an advantage because its elevation over the preceding row is abnormally high. Northrop's balcony spotlights spill more light than their counterparts in other halls, so light-sensitive people may want to stick to the main floor. Acoustically, there are few advantageous seats; the stage's acoustical shell has improved the sound in the first 10 rows.

### ORDWAY MUSIC THEATRE
*345 Washington St., St. Paul*    224-4222

The Ordway serves as the primary home of the Saint Paul Chamber Orchestra, the Minnesota Opera and the Schubert Club, but it also offers interesting and ambitious programming of its own. Along with the Historic Orpheum Theatre in Minneapolis, it is the only place in town that can accommodate such gigantic and stage-busting Broadway shows as *Angels in America, Phantom of the Opera* and *Les Miserables*. It also programs highly regarded (and well-attended) dance and music series, both of which have a strong international and multicultural component. There are special programs for kids, as well.

Built in 1984 and reputedly inspired by the great concert halls of Europe, the Ordway has an 1,800-seat music hall that has never been as acoustically stunning as Minneapolis' Orchestra Hall but offers its own charms: a beautiful, old-world feel; comfortable seats with good sightlines; and a magical (especially during the winter) location at the edge of Rice Park — near the St. Paul Hotel, Landmark Center and the St. Paul Public Library. Seats to avoid are the first eight rows of the orchestra level, where the minimal slope makes viewing difficult. The side boxes of the balcony level offer only a partial view of the stage, but these seats are cheap, acoustically good and may allow you to see all the action if you're attending a chamber music concert or a piano recital.

The Ordway's McKnight Theater, with 300 seats, is equally handsome.

Several parking lots and ramps in the area serve Ordway patrons, but it almost always seems possible to find street parking (free at night and on Sundays) within a 10-minute walk.

### O'SHAUGHNESSY AUDITORIUM
*2004 Randolph Ave., St. Paul*    690-6700

Until the arrival of the Ordway, O'Shaughnessy — located on the campus of the College of St. Catherine — was St. Paul's biggest and best concert hall. It's seen everything in its 25 years: concerts by the Minnesota Orchestra and the Saint Paul Chamber Orchestra; dance; and pop, folk and bluegrass music. If you're attending a dance performance, the front of the balcony is the place to head, and these seats also put you right on top of the musicians during concerts. The back rows of the balcony, 125 feet from the stage, are too far away for nonbinocular vision. If the hall is notorious for anything, it's for the absence of any center aisle on the main floor or balcony levels. There can be as many as 63 seats unbroken by an aisle. So if you're expecting to leave in midperformance, pick an aisle seat to avoid climbing over 31 others.

## Services for Artists and Audiences

### ARTS MIDWEST
*528 Hennepin Ave., Ste. 310*
*Minneapolis*               *341-0755*
Arts Midwest is one of the area's major funders and information providers for artists and arts presenters involved in everything from jazz to the visual arts. It administers, for example, the Midwest's Meet the Composers grants, which give money to arts organizations that have arranged visits from composers around the country. It's also active in helping develop organizations that serve artists of color.

### ARTSPACE PROJECTS
*400 First Ave. N., Ste. 518*
*Minneapolis*               *339-4372*
This unusual and useful organization helps locate and construct living, working and exhibition space for artists in the Twin Cities area. Several of its cooperatives for low-income artists have been very successful.

### ASIAN AMERICAN RENAISSANCE
*1564 LaFond, St. Paul*          *641-4040*
Presenting conferences, exhibitions, performances and lectures at several locations in the Twin Cities, this organization helps support Asian-American artists who are active in many disciplines.

### BLACK MUSIC EDUCATORS OF THE TWIN CITIES
*764 Dayton Ave., #2, St. Paul*   *No Phone*
Created to advance the music of African-American composers and increase the number of performance opportunities for black musicians, this group sponsors scholarships, concerts and other programs.

### CABLE ACCESS ST. PAUL
*213 E. Fourth St., St. Paul*     *224-5153*
St. Paul residents who want to try their hand at cable-TV video production should take advantage of the training, facilities and equipment offered by this organization.

### CENTER FOR ARTS CRITICISM
*2402 University Ave. W.*
*St. Paul*                  *644-5501*
Aspiring critics and people already accomplished in the world of arts criticism make use of the services of this organization, which provides grants, sponsors conferences and workshops and helps make criticism more accessible to artists and the public.

Photo: Joe Rossi, Pioneer Press

*Ordway Music Theatre in downtown St. Paul.*

### COMMUNITY CABLE CHANNEL 33
*10816 Normandale Blvd.*
*Bloomington*                    *888-6702*

This is a public-access cable channel in Bloomington that offers residents the chance to produce and watch homegrown TV programs.

### COMPAS
*75 W. Fifth St., Ste. 304*
*St. Paul*                    *292-3249*

Artists can participate in this organization's school and community residencies, apply for its grants and take advantage of its other special programs. COMPAS, like several other St. Paul arts organizations, is located downtown in Landmark Center, a former federal courts building renovated to house the arts.

### FORECAST PUBLIC ARTWORKS
*2324 University Ave. W.*
*St. Paul*                    *641-1128*

Public art projects and the public discussion of the arts is the business of FORECAST, which provides assistance to artists who are working for their communities. It also publishes a respected public-art publication.

### INDEPENDENT FEATURE PROJECT/NORTH
*119 N. 4th St., Ste. 202*
*Minneapolis*                    *338-0871*

Serving independent filmmakers throughout the region, IFP/North offers classes and workshops as well as screenings of locally produced film and video work.

### METROPOLITAN REGIONAL ARTS COUNCIL
*345 St. Peter St., Ste. 700*
*St. Paul*                    *292-8010*

Unlike most other states, Minnesota has established a group of regional arts councils to administer a chunk of state funds earmarked for the arts. The Metropolitan Regional Arts Council handles this administration for the seven-county Twin Cities area. It gives grants to arts organizations, encourages diversity in the arts, helps community groups generate arts activities and works to increase people's accessibility to the arts.

### MIDWEST CENTER FOR ARTS, ENTERTAINMENT AND THE LAW
*749 Simpson St., St. Paul*     *644-1891*

This organization (nicknamed MiCAEL) helps connect artists with resources on the law and censorship.

### MINNESOTA ASSOCIATION OF COMMUNITY THEATRES
*521-5692*

MACT's telephone hotline, a recorded message updated on Sundays, gives valuable information on community theater auditions and other theater activities in the seven-county metropolitan area.

### MINNESOTA CITIZENS FOR THE ARTS
*708 N. First St., Ste. 235D*
*Minneapolis*     *338-2970*

This is a lobbying and advocacy group that strives to increase government funding for the arts and works within the government to improve the financial health of artists and arts organizations.

### MINNESOTA CULTURAL MEDIA
*4937 Aldrich Ave. N.*
*Minneapolis*     *529-1435*

Minnesota Cultural Media concentrates on helping minority audiences gain access to the arts and assisting artists of color by sponsoring festivals and other arts programs in various communities and schools.

### MINNESOTA STATE ARTS BOARD
*432 Summit Ave., St. Paul*     *297-2603*

This state-funded agency, whose arts-assistance budget has amazingly increased in recent years, gives a big boost to Minnesota artists and arts organizations by providing expertise, information and financial assistance. Individual artists benefit from fellowships, career opportunity grants, cultural pluralism programs, support for folk artists and a variety of useful publications. The arts board also supports the work of artists who obtain residencies in schools.

### NATIONAL WRITERS UNION, TWIN CITIES LOCAL
*P.O. Box 50507*
*Minneapolis 55403*     *879-4114*

This labor union helps writers of journalism, textbooks, fiction and poetry strengthen themselves economically by promoting model contracts, offering grievance assistance and providing contacts with other writers.

### NATIVE ARTS CIRCLE
*1433 Franklin Ave. E.*
*Minneapolis*          870-7173
Promoting the artistic expression of people in the Native American community is the focus of this organization that sponsors exhibitions, writing workshops, film festivals and other programs.

### RESOURCES AND COUNSELING FOR THE ARTS
*75 W. Fifth St., Ste. 429*
*St. Paul*          292-4381
Know a dancer who needs sharper bookkeeping skills? How about a sculptor in need of marketing tips or a musician seeking tax assistance? RCA helps by providing business and management assistance to artists of all kinds and to arts organizations. It offers workshops, individual counseling, job listings, publications and an artist loan program.

### ST. LOUIS PARK COMMUNITY TELEVISION
*5005 Minnetonka Blvd.*
*St. Louis Park*          924-2660
This is another public-access TV station that serves a suburban community by helping residents produce their own programs and by ultimately airing them.

### VERY SPECIAL ARTS MINNESOTA
*528 Hennepin Ave., Ste. 305*
*Minneapolis*          332-3888
          TTY 332-3888
Very Special Arts strives to serve the needs of artists and arts patrons with disabilities by providing information on the physical accessibility of arts events, training and programs that raise awareness of the disabled.

Photo: Scott Takushi, Pioneer Press

World Trade Center in St. Paul with the Assumption Church in the foreground.

# *Inside*
# Architecture and Historic Sites

Perhaps a little more than most places, the Twin Cities has tended to undervalue the richness of its architecture and history. It's a reticence inspired not by modesty but by a mistaken interpretation of historical fact. After all, many Minnesotans reason, we've produced no U.S. presidents, have no nearby major battlefields, did not spawn any important architectural movements and have no landmarks that rank among the most visited (unless you count the Mall of America). Fortunately, however, politics, wars and postcard images do not define history any more than home-grown architectural movements necessarily produce memorable buildings.

Instead, what makes history interesting and buildings beautiful are people and structures that are full of life and can move us. These the Twin Cities has as much as any place. History is simply someone's story, and architecture is the translation of a personal story — or an emotion or philosophy — to the physical form of a structure. If people have dwelled here, there is good history and architecture here.

The best place to start any historical exploration of the Twin Cities, indeed, of the entire state, is the Minnesota History Center in St. Paul. This visionary and ambitiously conceived history museum — easily one of the best in the country — tells history largely in terms of people's personal stories. The experiences of the rich and prominent are given no more weight than the stories of the poor and common, to the extent that surviving historical materials allow the museum's staff to do so. The historical paths of African Americans, Native American and other Minnesotans of color are also receiving increasing attention there. For more information on the Minnesota History Center, see Attractions.

To state the obvious, architecture is best viewed by getting outside and looking. Look on foot, not by car. Get up close. Resist nostalgia. The Twin Cities has lost more than its share of great old buildings, most notably the Metropolitan Building in Minneapolis, but many worthless old dumps fell to the wrecking ball as well. By the same token, many newer structures speak well and with feeling. (The Minnesota History Center is a good example.)

Walk the streets of the Twin Cities and listen to its stories. You'll encounter plenty of great architecture and lots of wonderful history.

## ARMSTRONG HOUSE
*233-235 W. Fifth St., St. Paul*

This startling and formerly elegant double-residence, built in 1886, is boarded up, so you'll have to be content with viewing it from the outside and imagining its grandeur. One of the last surviving houses anywhere in downtown St. Paul, it is currently owned by the State of Minnesota and has an uncertain future. Edward P. Bassford, an early Twin Cities architect whose other buildings are mostly demolished, designed it for the family of George Washington Armstrong, combining Romanesque features with elements of the Queen Anne style. The house will almost surely be razed in the coming years; moving it is not a possibility because its weight of 600 tons makes any travel an expensive and risky proposition.

## FIRST NATIONAL BANK BUILDING
*Minnesota and Fifth Sts., St. Paul*

Long the most recognizable building on St. Paul's skyline (and still the classiest), this skyscraper was built in 1931 and renovated 40 years later. Indiana limestone, arranged in bands on the exterior, emphasizes its height. Don't miss the "1st" sign at the summit and the high-spirited sculpture by George Sugarman presiding over the main entrance.

## F. SCOTT FITZGERALD HOUSE
*599 Summit Ave., St. Paul*

On the third floor of this rowhouse, during the summer of 1919 at the age of 22, F. Scott Fitzgerald completed his first novel, *This Side of Paradise*. He and his family had previously lived at several other St. Paul addresses, but this home, located tantalizingly close to the residences of the city's ultra-rich, apparently provided ample fodder for the young author's literary preoccupation with class, social climbing and money. (In one of his works of fiction, Fitzgerald describes a Crest Avenue, obviously based on Summit Avenue, which he characterized as "a museum of American architectural failures.") Although a plaque details Fitzgerald's connection and the residence is registered as a National Historic Landmark, the interior of the rowhouse is not open to public view.

## FITZGERALD THEATER
*10 E. Exchange St., St. Paul*     290-1200

The Fitzgerald, which opened as the Schubert Theater in 1910, was never a really fancy place, but it gained national fame during the 1980s as the home base of Garrison Keillor's "A Prairie Home Companion" public radio show. A renovation during that period uncovered a long-lost upper balcony,

---

*Insiders' Tips*

Fort Snelling was nearly bulldozed in 1958 to make way for a highway, until the Minnesota Historical Society stepped forward to lead efforts to save the historic site.

moved the main entrance from Wabasha Street to Exchange, spiffed the place up and stopped the ceiling plaster from falling on people's heads. Long known as the World Theater, it was renamed in September 1994 in honor of native son F. Scott Fitzgerald. Nowadays the theater hosts concerts and shows, as well as Keillor's revived "A Prairie Home Companion" program.

### FORT SNELLING
*Fort Rd. at Hwys. 5 and 55*
*St. Paul*                    725-2413

Fort Snelling, a federal garrison established in 1820 to keep an eye on the northern portion of the land acquired years earlier with the Louisiana Purchase, was never attacked, which is one reason why the fort is around today for us to enjoy. Another reason, however, is the efforts of the Minnesota Historical Society, which shouldered the archaeological and preservational task of preventing the fort from crumbling into the Mississippi and Minnesota rivers, at the junction of which the military complex rises. Thanks to that work, we can now enjoy a site loaded with nationally significant history: Countless exploratory teams began there in missions to map and explore the frontier; Dred Scott, the slave whom the Supreme Court ultimately ruled a nonperson, lived there; Civil War volunteers, bound for the Battle of Gettysburg, trained there; and Dakota Indians camped outside its walls during conflicts with the U.S. Government in the 1860s. Now a National Historic Landmark, the site uses a living-history approach in presenting itself to the public, with authentically costumed guides working in the re-created barracks, kitchens, laundry rooms, hospital, blacksmith shop and officers' quarters. Most of Fort Snelling is open to visitors during the spring and summer months, although a recently constructed on-site history center remains open year round.

### ARD GODFREY HOUSE
*University and Central Aves. S.E.*
*Minneapolis*                870-8001

Open for summer public tours, this residence dates to 1848, when Maine native Ard Godfrey was active developing the dams and sawmills that tapped the immense energy of the St. Anthony Falls on the Mississippi River.

### GOVERNOR'S RESIDENCE
*1006 Summit Ave., St. Paul*    297-8177

Designed by William Channing Whitney in the English Tudor Revival style and built for St. Paul attorney Horace Hills Irvine in 1910, this residence has only housed the families of the state's governors since the 1960s. Before that, governors lived in their own homes and the state booked space in hotels or the capitol building for official receptions. The 20-room house has undergone several renovations and redesigns over the decades to accommodate the particular needs of the first families. Public tours are available during the spring and summer months.

## HENNEPIN COUNTY GOVERNMENT CENTER

*Fifth St. between Third and Fourth Aves. S.*
*Minneapolis* 348-3848

So distinctive are the twin 24-story towers of this structure spanning Sixth Street and rising 24 stories into the air that they have been incorporated into the graphic logo that Hennepin County uses to identify itself. Designed to surrender more than half of the block to a welcome urban plaza and fountain, the complex also contains a striking 350-foot-high glass atrium. A tunnel connects it with the Minneapolis City Hall and Courthouse across Fifth Street. Inside are licensing bureaus, courtrooms and offices of the county commissioners and many other county agencies. Daily tours are offered.

## JAMES J. HILL HOUSE

*240 Summit Ave., St. Paul* 297-2555

A visit to this dark, imposing and magnificent mansion — the most awesome of all the Victorian residences on St. Paul's Summit Avenue — will convince any doubters out there that the railroad business truly was a rewarding enterprise in the 19th century. James J. Hill, who purchased the sickly St. Paul and Pacific Railroad and transformed it into the immensely successful Great Northern Railroad, invested nearly $1 million in his red-sandstone-faced house in 1891 and built it with size in mind. Designed by the Boston firm of Peabody, Stearns and Furber, it originally included 22 fireplaces and 13 bathrooms to accommodate the Hills and their eight children, as well as a massive reception room, full servants' quarters and a dining room (able to seat 40) whose furnishings must have been responsible for the clearing of several tracts of forest. After Hill's death in 1916 and that of his wife Mary five years later, the mansion fell into the hands of the archdiocese of St. Paul, becoming a National Historic Landmark in 1961. Now owned by the Minnesota Historical Society, the house hosts concerts and art exhibitions in the skylighted, pipe-organ-equipped gallery that Hill built for his own art collection. Guides give illuminating tours of the mansion and also lead occasional tours of the Summit Avenue neighborhood.

## HISTORIC ORPHEUM THEATRE

*910 Hennepin Ave.*
*Minneapolis* 339-7007

With nearly 3,000 seats at the time of its opening in 1921, the Minneapolis Orpheum (actually the second Orpheum Theatre to open its doors in the city) was the second-largest vaudeville house in the country, after New York's Lowe's State Theater. The Marx Brothers headlined the first bill of entertainers. The Orpheum has a fascinating past and a promising future, thanks to a city-sponsored renovation that returned the building to its former glory. Bestowing a new backstage area and improved dressing rooms and restrooms, the restoration also gave the Orpheum a cleaned-up exterior and a wonderful vertical neon sign that pulses in purple. Once even owned by Bob Dylan, the theater now hosts a

Photo: John Doman, Pioneer Press

*Downtown St. Paul's Rice Park with Landmark Center in the background.*

variety of Broadway, pop, jazz and rock events.

### HISTORIC STATE THEATRE
*805 Hennepin Ave.*
*Minneapolis*                    339-7007

Across the street and a block away from the Orpheum is the Italian Renaissance-style State Theatre, an eye-popping palace of entertainment that has survived nearly 80 years as a movie theater and vaudeville house, church and vacant hulk. Fully restored in 1991, it now has 2,200 seats, period murals on the walls, glittering chandeliers, a golden proscenium arch above the stage and admirable sightlines from almost everywhere in the house. Concerts, dance events and Broadway shows fill its schedule.

### IDS CENTER
*777 Nicollet Mall, Minneapolis*

Often hailed as one of the world's finest skyscrapers and perhaps architect Philip Johnson's best design, the IDS Center single-handedly transformed the Minneapolis skyline when it was completed in 1973. Now that the skyline has filled in and the IDS Center no longer appears to be a lonely digit stretching toward the heavens, the building nonetheless retains its supremacy. (In physical terms, that supremacy can be measured in inches, as other buildings have approached, but not surpassed, IDS' height.) Anyone who remembers "The Mary Tyler Moore Show" (and apparently 98.9 percent of Twin Citians do) can still picture the opening credits in which Mary

rapturously descends the building's escalator before tossing her hat into the air outside on the Nicollet Mall. But the 51-story building and its revolutionary Crystal Court — home to American Express Financial Advisors Inc. (formerly known as IDS Financial Services), The Marquette Hotel and many shops and restaurants — have seen far more important events: presidential appearances, concerts of full symphony orchestras and thundering sports rallies. It has provided the setting for countless romantic trysts, as well — don't forget, this is the heart of a great city!

### LANDMARK CENTER
*75 W. Fifth St., St. Paul*        292-3272

Nowadays, Landmark Center houses galleries of the Minnesota Museum of American Art and the offices of several other arts and community organizations, but in days past an intriguing assortment of gangsters, judges and postal officials walked through its doors. Back then, in fact until 1967, the granite building with the notable clock tower gathered together under one roof federal courts, the city's main post office and customs offices. When the federal offices vacated the building, it was threatened with demolition. Fortunately, community preservationists rallied together to preserve the Neo-Romanesque castle, designed by Willowby J. Edbrooke and constructed in 1906. They mounted a 10-year, $12.5 million restoration, and now Landmark Center presides over Rice Park and the Ordway Music Theatre in one of downtown St. Paul's most visually attractive districts. It was the first building in the state to be nominated for the National Register of Historic Places.

### LOWERTOWN HISTORIC DISTRICT
*Vicinity of E. Sixth St. near Sibley St., St. Paul*

Originally a bustling St. Paul neighborhood that sprouted off a Mississippi River landing and later a district of warehouses and merchandise distribution centers, Lowertown is now a unique mix of artists' lofts, residences, converted warehouses and commercial spaces. A 17-block area listed on the National Register of Historic Places, it includes Depot Place (1917 to '23, formerly Union Depot, 214 E. Fourth Street), which handled millions of tons of rail freight and millions of passengers before closing down in 1971 to become a space for restaurants and retailers; First Trust Center (1914 to '16, formerly the Railroad and Bank Building, 176 E. Fifth Street), a Classical Revival structure that was for decades the largest office building in the Twin Cities, recently restored for banking purposes; the Pioneer Building (1889, 340 N. Robert Street), boasting the only surviving open light court in the Twin Cities and a fascinating period elevator; and the First Baptist Church (1875,

499 Wacouta Street), the original 190-foot-high spire of which, too heavy for the swampy ground, had to be removed in 1945. At the heart of the district is Mears Park, a plot of ground on which landscaping and history mix engagingly. An excellent brochure detailing a walking tour of the district is available from the St. Paul Heritage Preservation Commission, 266-6580.

### LUMBER EXCHANGE BUILDING
*425 Hennepin Ave., Minneapolis*

In the halls that lumber barons once stalked now wafts the scent of aroma therapy, thanks to a 1980s restoration that infused the Lumber Exchange with new life and made it the home of such businesses as a Horst hair salon. A hunkering Richardsonian Romanesque structure designed by the renowned Twin Cities firm of Long and Kees and crafted in 1885 out of rough cut granite and Lake Superior brownstone, it is one of the few remaining signs that the lumber business, now much reduced in importance, once built the state.

### MILWAUKEE ROAD DEPOT
*Washington Ave. S., Minneapolis*

Yes, it's dirty and boarded up, and the clock in the tower hasn't worked for years, but this train depot and its accompanying shed are

In 1888, Minneapolis architect LeRoy Buffington received the first U.S. patent for a method of skyscraper construction.

a historical treasure. Urban renewal projects of the 1950s and '60s, along with a couple of foolish razings right here in the 1990s, have erased most other traces of the working-class, down-and-out culture that formerly thrived in the Gateway district (not to romanticize it; the neighborhood was gritty, dangerous and the last stop for many of its residents). Virtually all the flophouses, saloons and bums' meeting places are long gone, leaving only this empty depot, the landing place of many unskilled workers who flocked to Minneapolis during the first half of the century. Designed by Charles Frost and built in 1898, the depot originally had a smashing rotunda, patterned marble floors and carved-wood ceilings. The 625-foot-long train shed is one of the very few such structures still standing in America. In its peak years, 29 scheduled trains departed daily. The depot closed to the public after a 1971 conversion to railroad office space and locked its doors for good about eight years later. Since then, the site has been considered for everything from a shopping mall to a gambling casino, but nothing ever seems to work out. The site remains in limbo.

### MINNEAPOLIS ARMORY
*500 S. Sixth St., Minneapolis*

Currently empty and destined for an undetermined use, the Minneapolis Armory is at least not now threatened with demolition, a possibility that loomed large when Hennepin County coveted the site for a new jail. It would have taken

quite a bit of force to bring this streamlined WPA-era building to its knees. Inside is a hangar-sized drill area with an 85-foot-high ceiling, seating for 4,500 and cavernous facilities that could swallow army trucks, other motorized vehicles and thousands of national defenders. Though sparsely ornamented and given rounded corners to make it resemble a military machine, the armory does have its cultured side, as well. Two large interior murals, created by artists Elsa Jemne and Lucia Wiley, illustrate Minnesota's origins and show scenes of peace and battle.

### MINNEAPOLIS CITY HALL AND COURTHOUSE
*400 S. Fourth St., Minneapolis    673-3000*

If you're looking at the Minneapolis skyline and you see an old building with a steeply pitched green roof and a big clock tower (the clock face is bigger than Big Ben's), you've caught sight of the Minneapolis City Hall and Courthouse. Get closer, because this magnificent and well-worn Romanesque building, faced with limestone and granite and filled with marble, pulses with the drama and frustration of everyday life. When completed in 1906, it signalled that Minneapolis was a metropolis of importance. The local architecture firm of Long and Kees designed it with a courtyard and a dignified entrance facing the Mississippi River, the direction in which most of the city then lay, but the subsequent demand for city services filled the courtyard with offices, removed the skylights and even flipped the main entrance to the opposite side. But no matter, there's still history here — hangings, police investigations, payoffs to corrupt mayors. The building is best known for the 345-foot-high clock tower and its 15-bell carillon, along with the main lobby's "Father of Waters" statue, carved by Larkin Goldsmith Mead from the biggest block of Italian marble ever hauled out of the famous Carrara quarries.

### MINNESOTA STATE CAPITOL
*Cedar and Aurora Sts., St. Paul*    296-2881

Architect Cass Gilbert, who later designed the U.S. Supreme Court building and New York's famed Woolworth Building, concentrated his formidable talents on Minnesota's third capitol structure (the first burned down, the second became too small after only a few years), even contributing to the design of the furniture. Just as it did when first built in 1905, the capitol building awes visitors with its monumental dome (modeled after St. Peter's in Rome), huge columns, stenciled ceilings, symbolic murals and vivid hues in the restored Senate and House chambers. On a bright day, there are few Minnesota sights as grand as the sunlight glinting off the gold-leaf horses. They're part of a statue themed "The Progress of the State," that sits atop the main entrance. The Minnesota Historical Society offers free guided tours year round, and all galleries and legislative meetings are open to the public.

### MINNESOTA WORLD TRADE CENTER
*Wabasha and Eighth Sts., St. Paul*

Easily the flashiest skyscraper in St. Paul, this 40-story office tower casts a warm glow over the city — thanks to its yellowish granite and bronze glass. Raised in 1987, it was the first international trade center built in the Midwest.

### MISSISSIPPI RIVER STONE ARCH BRIDGE
*Mississippi River, near Main St., Minneapolis*

Dating from 1883, this limestone and granite bridge was the brainchild of railroad magnate James J. Hill, who needed an improved rail link across the Mississippi River. His builders crafted it to last — its 23 arches and sound structure needed no major repairs for the next eight decades. Reminiscent of a Roman viaduct, the bridge remains the only stone-arch span ever built across the river. It closed as a railroad bridge in the early 1980s, but a recently completed restoration has given it new life as a pedestrian and bicycle crossing.

### MURPHY'S LANDING
*2187 E. Hwy. 101, Shakopee*    445-6900

The Minnesota River, the region's other important waterway, cut a long valley in the southern part of Minnesota. Beginning in the middle years of the 19th century, settlers moved there, farmed there and built towns there. The Twin Cities' metropolitan spread has started to transform some of the valley towns into suburban communities, but Murphy's Landing re-creates what life was like before this change took place. Focusing on the years 1840 to 1890, this living-history museum brings back the rhythm of daily life in a typical Minnesota River Valley settlement, with historically dressed interpreters going about their tasks in a fur trader's cabin, farm and other village settings. In addition to offering period dinners, river boat excursions, trolley rides and an in-depth look at 19th-century activities, Murphy's Landing sponsors seasonal events on the Fourth of July, Halloween and Christmas, as well as theme days that pay tribute to such icons of Americana as the Civil War, Tom Sawyer and Laura Ingalls Wilder. The site has a gift shop and restaurant.

## NICOLLET MALL
*Running from Washington Ave. S. to W. Grant St., Minneapolis*

During the 1960s, Minneapolis built the Nicollet Mall, a gently winding thoroughfare for pedestrians and buses that erased a congested business street, foisted the auto traffic upon neighboring avenues, drew international praise and reigned as the longest urban mall in the country. The millions it cost to build (and later to extend and redesign) have been well spent, if only for the attention it has received and the controversy it has generated. Was the mall better as a winding route, as in the past, or relatively straight, as now? Who cares? Nowhere else in the Twin Cities can you regularly encounter street musicians (some of the regulars play cello, trumpet, sax, drums and bagpipes), street-corner evan-

gelists, pushcart food vendors, illuminated holiday parades and wandering conventioneers.

## NORWEST CENTER
*Sixth St. and Marquette Ave., Minneapolis*

Cesar Pelli, designer of this rosy and graceful 57-story office tower that appeared on the Minneapolis skyline in 1988, drew his inspiration from both the past and the present. For a half-century, Norwest Bank (formerly Northwestern National Bank) had occupied a venerable and well-loved structure on this same site, but a catastrophic fire on Thanksgiving Day 1982 reduced it to rubble. Pelli salvaged many artifacts from the old building — chandeliers, bronze medallions, cast railings — and built a modern setting in which they would look comfortable. Especially when dramatically lighted at night, Norwest Center plugs a gap in the skyline as it discreetly fails to overshadow the nearby IDS Tower. Don't miss the set of 16 vitrines in the main lobby that showcase Norwest's splendid collection of modernist decorative art, including pieces representing the arts-and-crafts, art nouveau, de Stijl, Bauhaus and art deco movements.

## PILLSBURY "A" MILL
*Third Ave. and Main St. S.E., Minneapolis*

LeRoy Buffington, a prolific Minneapolis architect who worked on university buildings, hotels and office structures throughout the Upper Midwest, produced this limestone building that long symbolized the supremacy of flour milling in Minneapolis' economic life.

Photo: Scott Takushi, Pioneer Press

*Historic State Theatre in downtown Minneapolis*

Erected in 1881 and for years the largest and most productive mill on earth, it now houses limited storage and packing facilities. Even so, a sign still towers above the roof proclaiming "Pillsbury's Best Flour."

### ALEXANDER RAMSEY HOUSE
*265 S. Exchange St., St. Paul     296-0100*

When Alexander Ramsey raised his home in 1872 at the St. Paul intersection of Walnut and Exchange streets, he already had an impressive political career behind him: He had served as the first territorial governor of Minnesota and the second governor after statehood, mayor of St. Paul, a U.S. senator and the U.S. Secretary of War. Even so, Ramsey lived another 31 years in the house, leading an active social life and running his real estate affairs. The house, located in the Irvine Park neighborhood, remained in the family

until 1964, when the Minnesota Historical Society acquired and restored it. Today the Ramsey House still retains the carved walnut woodwork, marble fireplaces, and crystal chandeliers that make it one of the best preserved Victorian homes in the country. In addition, visitors can take in sparkling accumulations of silver and crystal and the Ramsey girls' remarkable doll house. Ramsey House is open April through December, and the Society's guides offer tours and operate a gift shop.

### ST. ANTHONY FALLS HISTORIC DISTRICT
*Nicollet Island and both sides of the Mississippi River, downtown Minneapolis     627-5433*

A 165-acre area encompassing old flour mills, riverside warehouses, historic Main Street, one of Minnesota's earliest African-American neighborhoods and an entire island, the St. Anthony Falls Historic District provides a glimpse into the lives of some of the state's earliest urban dwellers. With many structures eligible for National Register listing and two National Historic Landmarks, the district is almost too much to take in and is best surveyed via walking tours organized by the Minnesota Historical Society. (The Society maintains an office in the district at 125 S.E. Main Street.) One tour covers the East Bank of the river, including old Main Street and other commercial areas; another traverses the West Bank and its rich milling history; and a third focuses on the industrial, residential and architectural history of Nicollet Island.

### ST. PAUL CITY HALL AND COURTHOUSE

*15 W. Kellogg Blvd., St. Paul    266-8500*

Except perhaps for Mickey's Diner, few places in downtown St. Paul can so immediately transport you to another era as St. Paul's city hall and courthouse. The 41-foot-high Fourth Street lobby, which achieves striking effects with walls of blue Belgian marble (it appears nearly black), is one of the most enchanting art deco spots on the globe. Designed by Holabird and Root and Ellerbe Architects and completed in 1931, the building features the statue "God of Peace" by Carl Milles, that was carved from an enormous, 55-ton chunk of Mexican white onyx. The elevators are worth a view, too, because their doors are paneled with scenes from the city's history, painted by Albert Stewart.

### JOHN H. STEVENS HOUSE

*4901 Minnehaha Ave.*
*Minneapolis    722-2201*

This house, the Twin Cities' first white-owned dwelling on the west side of the Mississippi River, dates from 1849. Originally occupying a site farther north, it is the building in which the name "Minneapolis" was first proposed and Hennepin County organized. Very simple in design, it is built in the New England Colonial style.

### UNITED STATES POST OFFICE

*100 S. First St., Minneapolis*

They could film a 1930s movie in this place, because the interior public spaces of this Moderne-style behemoth, erected in 1933, seem to have changed little from the day it witnessed the selling of its first stamp. Handsome and clean-looking, the post office is a survivor of a massive urban renewal effort that cleared the Gateway district of many of its older buildings.

### WAREHOUSE HISTORIC DISTRICT

*Vicinity of First Ave. N. between Second and Seventh Sts., Minneapolis*

Functionality can inspire beauty — that much is evident from the stone and brick structures that brush shoulders in Minneapolis' 14-block Warehouse District. Now housing restaurants, nightclubs, office buildings, artists' quarters and even theaters and galleries, many of the old edifices have been scrubbed, gutted and restored to produce a city district that remains as lively and prosperous as it was a century ago. The district, officially designated "historic" by the National Register of

Historic Places, includes more than 150 buildings, cobblestone streets and a pair of steel bridges. Some of the most interesting structures are Butler Square (1906, 100 N. Sixth Street), the trailblazing renovation project that changed an enormous dry goods warehouse of questionable utility into a warm home for restaurants and offices; the Wyman Building (1896, 400 First Avenue N.), another design by the distinguished Minneapolis architecture firm of Long and Kees, a former warehouse that now counts galleries, designers and other small businesses among its tenants; and the former Minneapolis Van and Warehouse Company Building (First Street and First Avenue N., now the home stage of the Theatre de la Jeune Lune), a magnificent structure with an exterior that was altered early this century by the young Cass Gilbert. Many other buildings in the district deserve examination, however, and the Minneapolis Heritage Preservation Commission, 673-2422, offers highly recommended walking tours.

*The Ojibwa dance at a Cinco De Mayo parade.*

# Inside
# Ethnic Diversity

It's a cliche, but it's worth repeating — people of the Twin Cities come in all shapes, sizes, colors and places of national origin. They speak a hundred languages or more, wax nostalgic over an equal number of Old Countries, speak in many accents and eat a rainbow of ethnic foods.

The U.S. Census, speaking in statistics, reports that German Americans are the largest single ethnic group in Minnesota. After them, in descending numbers, come the Norwegians, Swedes, Irish, "unclassified," "other groups," "race or Hispanic," Finns, English, Poles, "U.S./American," Italians, Czechs, the Dutch and Danes. Many other groups — Ukrainians, Ethiopians, Palestinians, Russians, Croatians — contribute to the Twin Cities as well, and this chapter can't possibly cover them all.

Even so, you can get to know many of them. Eat in their restaurants, attend their festivals, browse their shops, see their exhibits, visit their places of worship. At the same time, don't neglect to investigate your own ethnic background. How can you explain yourself to others if you don't know where you came from?

## The African Americans

The number of African Americans living in the Twin Cities — 89,459, representing 3.9 percent of the population, according to 1990 census figures — has nearly doubled since 1980. Although that percentage is still small compared with that of other American urban regions, African Americans have always had an important presence in the area.

As early as the late 18th century, African Americans were involved in the region's fur trade, and other black people arrived in succeeding decades as slaves owned by soldiers assigned to Fort Snelling. One of the latter group, Dred Scott, used his two years in residence at the fort (which was technically in free territory) as the basis of a legal suit to win his freedom. In the now-infamous 1857 case of Dred Scott vs. Sanford, the U.S. Supreme Court ruled that Scott was a noncitizen, an article of property who could not even file a legal suit.

The first Minnesota territorial census in 1849 determined that 40 free people of African ancestry lived in the region, most of them in St. Paul. That number gradually grew with the arrival of fugitive slaves. In 1868, two years before the 15th

Amendment to the U.S. Constitution made it mandatory, Minnesota became one of a handful of states to voluntarily extend the vote to African-American men. The following year, the state legislature outlawed the racial segregation of public schools.

Up until about 1910, St. Paul remained the center of the Twin Cities' black community. An early group of free African Americans had settled near the Falls of St. Anthony, however, giving Minneapolis its own community. In both cities, they increased in numbers as they established churches, ran businesses and formed social organizations. By 1930, the Rondo neighborhood of St. Paul and the near-north side and Seven Corners area of Minneapolis emerged as the hearts of the community.

Though not as overt as in Southern cities, discrimination existed in the Twin Cities, preventing African Americans from eating in many restaurants, renting halls in major hotels or earning wages comparable to those of whites. The black community was hit hard by the Great Depression, and 60 percent unemployment rates did not drop until the industrial mobilization of World War II. From 1950 to 1970, the African-American population of Minneapolis and St. Paul quadru-

pled, and a migration of black people from other northern industrial states has continued into the 1990s.

Nowadays, about half of the Twin Cities' African Americans live in Minneapolis, with the remainder split between St. Paul and the suburbs. *Black Enterprise* magazine recently lauded Minneapolis as a hot spot for upwardly mobile African-American businesspeople, noting that the city has the highest number of black professionals per capita in the nation.

A few notable members of the Twin Cities' African-American community, past and present, are: Sharon Sayles Belton, mayor of Minneapolis; Alan Page, associate justice on the Minnesota Supreme Court and former Minnesota Vikings football star; William Finney, St. Paul chief of police; Roy Wilkins, a longtime leader of the national organization of the NAACP; and Curman Gaines, superintendent of the St. Paul Public Schools.

## Organizations

**COUNCIL ON BLACK MINNESOTANS**
*2233 University Ave., Ste. 426*
*St. Paul*                    642-0811
The council serves as a liaison between African-American Minnesotans and the state government, calling black issues to the attention

Photo: Scott Takushi, Pioneer Press

*Festival of Nations, a multicultural event featuring folk dances, ethnic food and an international bazaar.*

of the governor and legislature and working to open access to state services and programs to all African Americans.

### SABATHANI COMMUNITY CENTER
*310 E. 38th St., Minneapolis    827-5981*
A full range of counseling, education, senior, kids' and referral programs are offered by the several different agencies housed here.

### SURVIVAL SKILLS INSTITUTE INC.
*1501 Xerxes Ave. N.*
*Minneapolis    522-6654*
This organization helps families and children of color by providing community-based family development programs.

### PHYLLIS WHEATLEY COMMUNITY CENTER
*919 Fremont Ave. N.*
*Minneapolis    374-4342*
Providing a broad range of ser-

vices — including education, counseling and assistance — to the primarily African-American residents of the near north side of Minneapolis is the primary focus of this community center.

## The Asians and Asian Americans

Like the Latinos who live in the Twin Cities, the Asians and Asian Americans in the region have greatly varied backgrounds and ethnicity. The 65,000 people of Asian descent in the metropolitan area (representing almost 3 percent of the population) trace their origins to Laos, Korea, Vietnam, China, India, the Philippines, Cambodia and Japan, among other countries. They are the Twin Cities' fastest-growing ethnic community.

The greatest in size are the Hmong (which means "free men"),

Photo: Scott Takushi, Pioneer Press

*St. Paul teenagers celebrate the Hmong New Year's Day*
*with the traditional ball-toss.*

a group that long lived in the mountains of Laos. During the 1960s and '70s, many Hmong aided the U.S. government in its fight against Laotian communists, and when the communists gained power, Hmong came to the United States in large numbers. The influx of Hmong into Minnesota has been steady since 1975, and the state has become the home of more Hmong than any other except California. There is a sizable Hmong community in St. Paul. Among the Twin Cities' many notable Asian Americans is St. Paul school board member Choua Lee, the first Hmong elected to public office in the United States.

Other Southeast Asian people — from Laos, Cambodia and Vietnam — settled in the Twin Cities around the same time the Hmong did. Some were involved in the fighting of the Vietnam War, while others left to escape "re-education camps," government oppression,

social abuse or poor economic opportunities.

About 10,000 of the state's Asian Americans are Koreans who were adopted by American families after the Korean War ended in 1953. Again following California, Minnesota ranks second nationally in the number of Korean children who have come for adoption. Many of the adoptees are now adults, and the South Korean government has drastically reduced the number of Korean children available for overseas adoption.

The Asian Indian, Chinese and Japanese communities in the Twin Cities have older roots. Chinese people arrived in Minnesota as early as the 1870s to establish businesses. In this century, more Chinese (from both China and Taiwan), as well as Asian Indians, arrived in Minnesota for university study and remained here. A group of Japanese workers came to the state around the turn of the century to work on the railroads, and the Japanese Americans increased their numbers during World War II when they settled in the Twin Cities after serving in the Military Intelligence Service Language School at Fort Snelling.

## Organizations

### ASSOCIATION FOR THE ADVANCEMENT OF HMONG WOMEN IN MINNESOTA
*3137 Chicago Ave. S.*
*Minneapolis*                823-4238
Providing a connection between refugee women and Minnesota culture, this group helps Hmong women develop skills in self-sufficiency, leadership and self-respect.

### CENTRE FOR ASIANS AND PACIFIC ISLANDERS
*1304 E. Lake St., Minneapolis*   721-1229
This agency helps Asians and Southeast Asians as they adjust to life in Minnesota. It offers legal aid, youth programs, a food shelf and health projects.

### CHINESE AMERICAN ASSOCIATION OF MINNESOTA
*P.O. Box 382584*
*Minneapolis 55458*          *No phone*
This organization promotes the activities of Chinese Americans, offers programs that increase awareness of Chinese culture and keeps the Chinese-American community abreast of significant news.

### FIL-MINNESOTA ASSOCIATION
*7415 Fifth Ave. S.*
*Richfield*                  861-2397
The purpose of this group is to provide support and cultural offerings to the large community of Filipino Americans and educate others about the Philippines.

### HMONG AMERICAN PARTNERSHIP
*450 N. Syndicate, Ste. 35*
*St. Paul*                   642-9601
The main focus of this organization is helping Minnesota's Hmong become fully participating members of the community.

### HMONG YOUTH ASSOCIATION OF MINNESOTA
*379 University Ave. W., Ste. 214*
*St. Paul*                   225-9421
Hmong youth can receive educational assistance, job counseling and cultural support from this community organization.

### INDIA CLUB OF MINNESOTA
*P.O. Box 130158*
*St. Paul 55113*             894-1273
The India Club sponsors events of Indian interest, works to serve the Indian community and acts to increase the public's understanding of Indians in Minnesota.

### JAPANESE AMERICAN CITIZENS LEAGUE
*P.O. Box 582864*
*Minneapolis 55458*          822-3659
This long-established organization works to protect the rights of Japanese Americans, preserve their culture and promote events of interest to members.

### KOREAN INSTITUTE OF MINNESOTA
*P.O. Box 8094*
*St. Paul 55208*             644-3251
Classes in language, dance, culture, martial arts, cooking and art

are offered by this Korean cultural organization.

### LAO FAMILY
### COMMUNITY OF MINNESOTA INC.
*976 W. Minnehaha Ave.*
*St. Paul*                    *487-3466*
Created by Hmong people to assist other Southeast Asian refugees, this organization operates a variety of programs — focusing on literacy, youth, health, employment, legal aid and other areas — to foster self-sufficiency.

### MINNESOTA ADOPTED KOREANS
*3511 Edward St. N.E.*
*Minneapolis*               *788-5859*
This organization for adopted Koreans sponsors support groups and holds educational programs about Korean culture.

### MINNESOTA CHINESE
### STUDENT ASSOCIATION
*P.O. Box 14157*
*Minneapolis 55414*        *No phone*
Through a variety of programs and special events, this group serves Chinese people in the area and promotes understanding between Americans and Chinese.

### STATE COUNCIL
### ON ASIAN-PACIFIC MINNESOTANS
*205 Aurora Ave., Ste. 100*
*St. Paul*                    *296-0538*
This council, created by the Minnesota Legislature, focuses on involving Asian-Pacific people in governmental decisions, giving them greater access to government services and providing them with increased opportunities.

### VIETNAMESE CULTURAL
### ASSOCIATION OF MINNESOTA
*2985 Northview St., Roseville*    *296-1879*
Housed in a new building, this organization helps preserve Vietnamese culture in Minnesota as it assists Vietnamese adjust to life in the United States.

### UNITED CAMBODIAN
### ASSOCIATION OF MINNESOTA INC.
*1821 University Ave., Ste. 360S*
*St. Paul*                    *645-7841*
*60 N. Kent St., St. Paul*     *225-9571*
UCAM helps Cambodians in Minnesota by sponsoring youth programs, providing educational opportunities and employment services and preserving the Cambodian ethnic heritage.

## The Chicanos and Latinos

Chicanos and Latinos in the Twin Cities account for the largest concentration of that group in the state, although there are also sizable numbers in counties scattered throughout Minnesota. The biggest group of the 36,000 Twin Cities Chicanos and Latinos live in the suburbs, with 11,000 in St. Paul and 8,000 in Minneapolis. Their numbers, bolstered by a large number of recent arrivals from such places as Puerto Rico, Colombia, Cuba, Panama and El Salvador, have increased by two-thirds in the past decade alone.

The Twin Cities' first Spanish-speaking people came from Mexico and the U.S. Southwest. As late as 1910, there were only 52 people of Mexican origin in the entire state, but the availability of agricultural field work (mainly working with the sugar-beet crop) soon drew others, who arrived as migrant workers and later became permanent residents. These people primarily settled in St. Paul, occupying housing on the lower West Side. Their population increased tenfold during the 1920s, reaching more than 3,600. Hampered by high unemployment during the Depression, they still managed to launch places of worship — such as Our Lady of Guadalupe Church — and found social and service groups. Meanwhile, a much smaller community of Mexicans and Mexican Americans was kindled in Minneapolis.

Gradually these communities switched from seasonal to year-round work, their workers joining the staffs of such businesses as meatpacking plants and textile factories. An important change in St. Paul's Chicano community took place in the early 1960s, when most remaining families in the flood-plagued lower West Side moved to higher ground elsewhere on the West Side. During the next two decades, in both St. Paul and Minneapolis, the use of Spanish in the communities became more widespread.

Starting in the late 1970s, the community in the Twin Cities began to become more diversified

with the arrival of people from Central and South America seeking better economic opportunities or fleeing political oppression. Even now, however, people of Mexican origin account for two-thirds of all Hispanics in Minnesota.

## Organizations

### CATHOLIC CHARITIES — HISPANIC OUTREACH

*2201 Nicollet Ave. S*
*Minneapolis*                    874-1412
*401 Concord St., St. Paul*      224-0799
Catholic Charities offers referral services, financial assistance and other human services for the Hispanic and Latino community.

### CENTRO CULTURAL CHICANO INC.

*2201 Nicollet Ave. S.*
*Minneapolis*                    874-1412
This is a community cultural organization that provides employment assistance, educational programs, health counseling, activities for seniors and arts programs.

### CENTRO LEGAL INC.

*2929 Fourth Ave. S., Ste. L*
*Minneapolis*                    825-5503
*179 E. Robie St., St. Paul*     291-0110
This organization is a source of legal assistance in the areas of immigration, family law and consumer law.

---

Many Finnish Americans in Minnesota celebrate St. Urho's Day, which commemorates the man who drove all the grasshoppers out of Finland.

Insiders' Tips

### HISPANOS EN MINNESOTA
*155 S. Wabasha, Ste. 128*
*St. Paul*                    227-0831
Health, chemical dependency and HIV education services are the emphasis of this community agency.

### MINNESOTA HISPANIC FEDERATION INC.
*162 College Ave. W., St. Paul*    224-4855
This is an advocacy and lobbying organization that seeks to educate the public and government officials on Hispanic cultures and their needs.

## The Germans

More Minnesotans trace their ancestry to Germany than to any other country in the world. In the Twin Cities there are some very sizable Germanic pockets — Cottage Grove, 55 percent; Chaska, 58 percent; and Shakopee, 64 percent — but they've got nothing on Hamburg, Minnesota, where the German-American population stands at 92 percent. The metropolitan area's overall German share is 43 percent.

Unlike Irish immigrants, who primarily settled along the Atlantic seaboard, the majority of the 5 million immigrant Germans of the 19th century came to the Midwest, making such cities as Milwaukee and Cincinnati veritable burgs. They also came in large numbers to southern and central Minnesota. In the Twin Cities, the German population swelled from 27 to more than 2,000 between 1850 and 1860, climbing further to about one-third of the population with the passage of another 10 years. St. Paul, in particular, acquired a strong German character, giving birth to more than 20 German-language newspapers in the 19th century.

Bringing more skills from their home country than many other immigrant groups, the Germans took up work in banking, brewing, shopkeeping and other nonmanual trades. They differed from other foreign-born groups in another important respect: They boasted a remarkable religious diversity, representing the Catholic, Lutheran, Methodist and Jewish faiths, among others.

Early on, German Americans established institutions of higher learning in the Twin Cities. They founded St. Paul's Luther Seminary, which later moved to Iowa. Concordia College in St. Paul, founded in 1892 by Missouri Synod Lutherans, long had a strong German atmosphere. Also carrying to Minnesota their deep musical traditions, they started most of the Twin Cities' major classical-music organizations. Emil Oberhoffer, the first music director of the Minnesota Orchestra (then called the Minneapolis Symphony Orchestra), was a native of Bavaria.

When World War I erupted, many German immigrants in the Twin Cities found themselves harassed by the Minnesota Commission of Public Safety, a hyper-patriotic organization created by the state legislature to aid the war effort. At the same time, the Minneapolis Board of Education restricted the teaching of German in public schools. Anti-German sentiment

*Performers at the Cinco De Mayo Festival*

in Minnesota was much reduced during World War II.

Now, among many of the descendants of the German immigrants, nostalgia for the old country has faded. Even so, there is still quite a bit of enthusiasm for the preservation of German culture.

## Organizations

### VOLKSFEST ASSOCIATION OF MINNESOTA INC.

*301 Summit Ave., St. Paul*   222-7027

Germanic culture remains alive in the activities of this organization that sponsors language classes, music and dance groups, activities for seniors and social events.

## *The Irish*

Although people of Irish origin make up a smaller percentage of the Twin Cities population than they do in many other U.S. metropolitan areas, they have always exerted a great influence in St. Paul, which became known as an Irish city even while Germans reigned as the capital city's largest ethnic group. When the Irish-born man of letters Oscar Wilde toured the country in 1882, St. Paul gave him one of the warmest welcomes he received anywhere in the United States. St. Paul has Irish pubs, Irish politicians, a huge St. Patrick's Day parade and reportedly has contributed more than its share to the coffers of the Irish Republican Army. Irish music and dance are popular throughout the Twin Cities, and Irish performers frequently make tour stops in these parts.

Minnesota, then a largely agricultural state, received only a small share of the great wave of Irish immigration in the 19th century. Some came as lumberjacks or soldiers in the U.S. Army, while others were railroad workers, craftspeople or domestics. Many settled in St. Paul because it was the headquarters of a Catholic archdiocese (one of the earliest arrivals was John Ireland, a native of County Kilkenny, who would eventually become the archbishop), and volunteer Irish laborers help erect the city's first Catholic school in 1851. That same year, the city reeled through its first St. Patrick's Day celebration. As the decades passed, the Irish spread more or less evenly throughout the city. In Minneapolis, the Irish lived primarily in the northeast portion of the city and downtown.

Many of the Irish went on to build careers in the civil service, law enforcement, politics and law. One of the state's most popular turn-of-the-century Irish politicians, Ignatius Donnelly, was a chronic party-switcher, lieutenant governor, member of the legislature, humorist, proponent of the existence of the lost continent of Atlantis and author of an internationally famous book about hidden cryptograms in the works of William Shakespeare. Nine out of the 10 mayors of St. Paul between 1932 and 1972 had Irish surnames.

Today, the Irish population of certain Twin Cities areas remains strong. Mendota Heights and Deephaven both have Irish concentrations of more than 20 percent, while Lilydale tops the charts at 25 percent. Overall, about 15 percent of Twin Citians claim some Irish blood.

## Organizations

**IRISH AMERICAN CULTURAL INSTITUTE**
*University of St. Thomas, No. 5026*
*2115 Summit Ave., St. Paul* 647-5678
The nation's largest organization devoted to Irish culture is located right here in St. Paul, offering educational programs, lectures, trips to Ireland for high school students, research stipends and arts grants.

**O'SHAUGHNESSEY-FREY LIBRARY**
*Department of Special Collections*
*University of St. Thomas, No. 5004*
*2115 Summit Ave., St. Paul* 647-5726
This library contains a Celtic collection that includes more than 10,000 volumes on Irish folklore, history, literature, language and religion — as well as materials about the culture of Scotland and Wales.

## The Native Americans

Many of the Twin Cities' Native Americans can trace their ancestry to people who have lived for centuries in the land now known as Minnesota. Through the mid-19th century, several different native peoples had lived in the region, including the Dakota, Ojibwa, Assiniboin and Cheyenne. But when white soldiers, traders and settlers began arriving in significant numbers in 1819, the Dakota and Ojibwa had settled virtually all the land. The Dakota, spread out along much of the Midwest, were represented in southern Minneso-

Photo: Scott Takushi, Pioneer Press

*Dancers at an American Indian Pow Wow.*

ta by four tribes — the Mdewakanton, Wahpekute, Wahpeton and Sisseton — and had been in the area for several hundred years. The Ojibwa, who entered Minnesota from the east around 1700, occupied the more heavily forested northern regions. All told, approximately 15,000 American Indians dwelt here when the first whites arrived.

Starting in 1837, through a series of treaties and land successions, they lost most of their territory. The area that now includes much of the Twin Cities was among the earliest chunks of Minnesota land lost to the Native Americans. In return for the land, the U.S. government paid the Ojibwa and Dakota bargain-basement prices and promised them reservations and other benefits. Often, however, the government was slow to pay, or Congress wouldn't establish the reservations. When the Dakota tired of these breaches of contract, they sometimes tried to resettle the lands they had given away. Disastrous conflicts of culture resulted, sparking the bloody U.S.-Dakota War of 1862 in which hundreds of people died and 38 Dakota Indians were hanged in Mankato, the largest mass execution in American history. Many Dakota fled Minnesota. In just a few years, the Dakota population in the state fell to only 176.

Meanwhile, the government concentrated on consolidating the various bands of the Ojibwa people on reservations. Seven reservations were created in the northern half of the state. Government bu-

reaucrats, as well as some influential Indians, hoped that Native Americans would eventually assimilate into the dominant culture. Many reservation parcels, doled out to individuals, eventually fell into white hands.

In the late 19th and early 20th centuries, the Dakota began a return to Minnesota. They established small communities in the southern part of the state. By the time the post-World War II period arrived, Minnesota's Native Americans were ripe for a major migration to the Twin Cities, which the federal government officially encouraged. By 1960 one-fifth of Minnesota's Indians lived in the Twin Cities, a proportion that grew to more than one-third in the decades that followed.

Now there are about 23,000 Native American people in the Twin Cities, representing 1 percent of the population. Most live in metro Minneapolis, where those of Ojibwa ancestry are the majority. More than 7,000 live in the suburbs. St. Paul's smaller Native American community includes many Winnebago people originally from Wisconsin, as well as Ojibwa and Dakota. Minneapolis, in particular, emerged as a center of American Indian activism, serving as headquarters of the American Indian Movement (AIM) and the Upper Midwest Indian Center. In recent years, Twin Cities Native Americans have also spearheaded a nationwide effort to convince school and professional sports teams to do away with their Indian names and mascots. (In 1993, the

Minneapolis-based *Star Tribune* become only the second daily newspaper in the country to refuse to print the Indian names of such teams as the Cleveland and Atlanta baseball clubs and the Washington and Kansas City football clubs.)

Of the 11 reservations in Minnesota, only one — the Shakopee-Mdewakanton Reservation in Carver County, a Dakota community — lies within the Twin Cities metropolitan area. It owns the very successful Mystic Lake Casino complex (for more on casinos, see the Weekend and Daytrips chapter).

---

## Organizations

### MINNEAPOLIS AMERICAN INDIAN CENTER
*1530 E. Franklin Ave.*
*Minneapolis*          871-4555
This is a large cultural resource and community center that has programs focused on everything from social services to the arts.

### MINNESOTA INDIAN AFFAIRS COUNCIL
*500 Rice St., St. Paul*          296-3611
Serving as the official liaison between Minnesota's Native American communities and the state government, the Indian Affairs Council involves itself in such issues as education, housing, the environment, tribal rights and health.

### RED SCHOOL HOUSE
*643 Virginia St., St. Paul*          488-6626
Offering an Ojibwa and Dakota culture-based curriculum for students in prekindergarten through the 12th grade, this alternative school has long served native families in the Twin Cities.

### ST. PAUL AMERICAN INDIAN CENTER
*811½ University Ave., St. Paul*     487-3241
This community center offers a variety of services: child care, youth programs, music groups and other organized activities and a food shelf.

### UPPER MIDWEST AMERICAN INDIAN CENTER
*1113 W. Broadway*
*Minneapolis*          522-4436
Child welfare services, mental health programs, adult education, a learning center for high school students and an intergenerational program are a few of this center's offerings.

## The Scandinavians

Lumped together (which you must never do, because the Norwegians, Swedes, Danes and Icelanders protest it vociferously), the Scandinavians dominate much of the ethnic scene in the Twin Cities. What Garrison Keillor says on the radio is true — there are a lot of Scandinavians here. It's actually common here to hear Norwegian/Swede jokes, have the opportunity to sample acquired-taste delicacies like lutefisk that have long vanished in the Old Country and major in Nordic languages at the University of Minnesota. And if you're looking for someone named, say, Donald Peterson, in the Minneapolis phone book — forget it, there are just too many of them. In the Twin Cities, 30 percent of the people claim some Nordic blood, with some areas — like Richfield, Fridley and Ham Lake — exceeding 40 percent.

The Norwegians in Minnesota outnumber the Swedes by a slight margin, with the Danes far behind. All three groups, however, originally came here because of economic troubles at home, an affinity for working the land and an oft-declared visual similarity between the new land and the old.

More Norwegians came to Minnesota than to any other state. When they settled in, starting in the 1850s, they sent "America letters" back home that made their relatives and former townspeople feverish to join them.

By the 1880s, many were heading for Minneapolis, which was destined to become the second-biggest Norwegian city in the world. At the start of World War I, Norwegians ran many of the city's banks, newspapers and churches. With the Swedes, they established a residential enclave along Cedar Avenue that was nicknamed Snooze Boulevard, after the reputedly heavy use of snuff by the residents. Later they moved to south Minneapolis and other sections of the city.

The Swedish immigrants, too, favored Minnesota more than any other state. They began their arrival just when the state was opening up for settlement, and they kept coming in substantial numbers for another 80 years. Much of this tide washed over the Twin Cities. At first Swedes tended to settle in the Phalen Creek area in St. Paul (which became known as Swede Hollow), St. Paul's East Side, the Snooze Boulevard neighborhood of Minneapolis and the shanties of Bohemian Flats along the Mississippi River. Later they migrated to northeast and south Minneapolis. By 1905, fully 7.5 percent of the Minneapolis population were natives of Sweden, and the city became a center of Swedish-American culture and life. Wherever they went, they formed businesses, music groups and social clubs.

The Danes did not come to the region in nearly as large numbers, and their migration ended sooner than the Norwegians or Swedes. The Danish were also more spread out, moving to Iowa and Wisconsin in large numbers. They began populating the Twin Cities in the 1880s, most of them living in Minneapolis. Dania Hall, in Minneapolis' Cedar-Riverside neighborhood, became a center of their community activities.

Although all three groups are now largely assimilated in the Twin Cities, they maintain strong cultural ties through organizations and celebrations.

## Organizations

### AMERICAN SWEDISH INSTITUTE
*2600 Park Ave. S., Minneapolis    871-4907*
Founded by Swedish American newspaperman Swan Turnblad and housed in the fortress-like 1904 mansion he built as his home, the American Swedish Institute fosters an interest in Swedish settlers, the immigrant experience and the mingling of American and Swedish affairs. Its remarkable collection of

Photo: Chris Polydoroff, Pioneer Press

*The Rondo Days Parade is named after Rondo Avenue, the center of the city's black community in the 1960s. The street was demolished to construct a freeway.*

more than 6,000 artifacts includes Swedish provincial costumes, a painting from 1712 by Gustaf Hesselius (the first Swedish-American artist), exquisite glassware, looms from the old country and Swedish books. Traveling exhibitions are also frequently on display. The building itself is a marvel, featuring a wall-sized enameled glass copy of a Swedish historical painting by Carl Gustav Hellqvist, 11 decorative and rare porcelain tile stoves and one of America's largest installations of carved African mahogany.

### DANISH AMERICAN FELLOWSHIP
*4200 Cedar Ave. S.*
*Minneapolis* 729-3800
This organization preserves Danish culture through special events, cultural activities and educational programs.

### SONS OF NORWAY INTERNATIONAL
*1455 W. Lake St., Minneapolis* 827-3611
This is the international headquarters of an organization that promotes Norwegian heritage and culture. Through its 50 district offices throughout the state, it sponsors educational programs, social activities and special events.

### SWEDISH CULTURAL SOCIETY IN AMERICA
*P.O. Box 8042*
*St. Paul 55108* 645-8578
A promoter of Swedish culture and language in the United States, the society sponsors programs about the life and literature of Sweden.

# *Inside*
# Weekend and Daytrips

While the Twin Cities offer many weekend pleasures, sometimes the most diverting Saturdays and Sundays are spent miles away from the cities' borders, exploring Minnesota's small towns, lake resorts, dairy and wheat farms, river valleys or magnificent Lake Superior shoreline.

### CABIN FEVER

For some, getting away simply means going "up north" to the family's second home, a summer cabin on one of Minnesota's 10,000 lakes. A large number of Minnesotans own second homes — usually humble one-bedroom cottages — on lakes in the state's northern and northwestern resort areas. In many cases, owning these cabins is a matter of disposable income — many residents are sufficiently well-off to afford a second mortgage.

But, we suspect this phenomenon is more a matter of tradition and culture than economics. Many of these summer cabins have been in the same family for years and years. The lakeshore lot was purchased cheap decades ago, a makeshift cottage was built, and the deed was passed from generation to generation, in some cases, shared piecemeal by siblings or an assortment of relatives.

Owning a cabin keeps your feet on the ground and your priorities straight. What otherwise would be spent on a wild resort weekend or evening out instead is invested in that little shack in the woods.

Beyond the mortgage and property taxes, however, the cost of maintaining a cabin is minimal. Heaven knows, no one puts much money into furnishing these little abodes. In fact, Minnesotans compete to see how incredibly tackily they can decorate their cabins. If they replace anything in their primary homes, that castoff chair, rusty appliance or lumpy mattress finds a new home in the cabin.

It may be the '90s in the Twin Cities, but "up north" at the cabin, it's eternally the '50s and '60s — a world of gold shag carpeting, mismatched Melmac dishes, vinyl dinette sets and avocado green stoves.

More often than not, the beds are covered with old sleeping bags (no Ralph Lauren comforters here) and the floors blanketed with wet bathing suits and sand. There are leeches (for bait) and beer in the fridge and a hot card game in progress at the table.

Truth be told, you wouldn't want it any other way. After all, the whole idea of going to the cabin is to shake off "the city" — all the burdensome cares, criteria, agendas, schedules, labels and expectations of civilization — and just hang out, preferably at the end of the dock with your toes in the water and a fishing pole in your hands.

Going "up north" to the summer cabin isn't so much a destination as it is a frame of mind.

Newcomers, if you happen to get yourself invited to somebody's cabin for a weekend or a day, accept without hesitation. (And if you don't get invited, invite yourself — "We'll be up in Alexandria this weekend. Maybe we'll stop over and see you at the lake." This is acceptable cabin etiquette. If your hosts really don't want to see you, they'll just go fishing.) Then pack your swimsuit, grab some potato salad at the neighborhood deli — better yet, make a hot dish — and head on up. It's a Minnesota experience that's not to be missed.

### HIGHWAY DISCOVERIES

On those rare weekends when Minnesotans aren't at the cabin, they're undoubtedly at a summer festival. Blame our long, cold winters, but when summer comes around, we find any reason to celebrate. Minnesota abounds in summer festivals. There's the **Woodtick Music Jubilee** in Akeley, the **Spam** (yes, Spam) **Jamboree** in Austin, **River City Days** in Red Wing, the **Waterfront Festival** in Duluth and the **Polka Fest** in Bird Island, not to mention **Sauerkraut Days** in Henderson.

The best reason to visit these festivals is to rediscover the soul of Minnesota — its small communities bursting with ethnic pride, its rambling river towns, romantic bed and breakfasts, the glory of Superior, the aching beauty of the St. Croix.

Fortunately, many of these destinations are just outside our back door — close enough to the Twin Cities for a day or weekend trip.

In this chapter, we're listing a few suggestions for short trips from Minneapolis and St. Paul. This is just a sampling. There are many other fascinating locales within reach, and, if you make the effort, you'll find your own favorite spot.

It's fun to plan your trip around a community festival. Check with the **Minnesota Department of Tourism**, 296-5029 or (800) 657-3700, for a schedule of year-round celebrations.

A word to the wise: If you have your heart set on staying in a specific bed and breakfast or eating at a popular historic inn, it's a good idea to make reservations ahead of time. Also, keep in mind that fall, with its blazing color displays, is as much a tourist season as summer in certain areas of the state, including Duluth and the North Shore Drive and the St. Croix, Mississippi and Minnesota river valleys.

(A final note: Unless another area code is specifically mentioned, the destination listed here is within the 612 area code.)

## Rivertown Ramble

The **St. Croix River**, often called the "Rhine of the Midwest," is a delightful destination just minutes from the Twin Cities. From its origins in northern Wisconsin, the waterway forms part of the Minnesota-Wisconsin border before joining the Mississippi River near the city of Hastings. Many interesting cities and towns sprouted on the banks of both rivers. Travelers may choose to ramble along the river banks and visit them all. The alternative is to throw out an anchor in any one of them for a day or two and soak up the ambiance. In an effort toward practicality, we will journey from north to south, from Taylors Falls to Red Wing.

### TAYLORS FALLS/ST. CROIX FALLS

Taylors Falls (population 694) offers historic charm, small-town friendliness and the natural beauty of the Dalles of the St. Croix, an impressive gorge cut by the river. Like other St. Croix River burgs, Taylors Falls was a bustling lumbering community in the late 19th century, and its many existing Victorian homes are reflective of that boom period.

Tourism is nothing new to Taylors Falls. In the late 1880s, the town was the site of a log jam of monumental proportions: 30 feet high and more than 2 miles long. It took months to clear the mess, and, in the meantime, visitors came from far and wide to see the unbelievable phenomenon. It remains a source of local bragging rights. There's even a **Log Jam Restau-**rant, where the historic event is depicted on placemats and historic photos.

Attractions here include the lovely old **Folsom House**, 465-3125, in the Angel Hill Historic District. This artifact-filled home of lumber baron William Folsom overlooking the St. Croix is open from late May through mid-October.

But perhaps Taylors Falls' greatest attribute is its natural setting amid the fascinating Dalles and the breathtaking beauty of the St. Croix. The Dalles are a geologic wonder — strange formations of limestone and shale that tower dramatically over the rushing St. Croix. Closer inspection will reveal many fossils in the rock. A fascinating stop is **Interstate Park**, located just a mile south of Taylors Falls and straddling both banks of the river. Go for a hike on the park's infamous "Pothole Trail," containing unusual holes drilled in rock by glacial waters. The park's **Ice Age Interpretive Center** tells you everything you wanted to know about glaciers.

Many visitors choose to view the river up-close and personal by renting canoes at the **Taylors Falls Canoe Rentals** facility in the park, 462-6315. Other canoeing information is available across the river in St. Croix Falls, Wisconsin, at the **Riverway Headquarters Visitors Center**, Massachusetts and Hamilton streets, (715) 483-3284.

Water activity is also found at **Wild Mountain** outdoor amusement area, 465-6315, located 7 miles north of Taylors Falls on

*Stillwater, 20 miles northeast of St. Paul, is the birthplace of Minnesota.*

County Road 16. This downhill ski park turns into a water park during the summer months, offering both water slides and "dry slides" down the slopes, plus a go-kart track, canoe rental and paddleboat tours of the river. See the Kidstuff chapter for complete details. Like any small town, Taylors Falls offers a rather limited range of restaurants; nonetheless, a few stand out. For instance, you can cruise back to the '50s at **The Drive-In**, on the north end of Main Street. Here you'll find carhops in poodle skirts delivering hamburgers and homemade root beer to your car window à la *American Graffiti*.

Other dining options include the new **Romayne's** restaurant/bar, serving everything from sandwiches to grilled salmon, and less-formal eateries, such as the **Log Jam Restaurant** and **Chisago House**.

Many an innocent tourist has spent the night in jail in Taylors Falls. No, this isn't a case of late-night revelry or an overzealous police department. One of the city's most unique guest houses is the two-story **Old Jail Co. Bed & Breakfast**, 465-3112, 100 Government Road. While the exterior has been authentically restored, the interior has been transformed into a comfortable living area, complete with modern kitchen and loft bedroom. Suites also are available next door in the historic Schottmuller Building.

If you're looking for something a bit more luxurious than the jail, the **St. Croix River Inn** in nearby Osceola, Wisconsin, is the ultimate. This 80-year-old Dutch colonial home, on a bluff overlooking the St. Croix, boasts seven bed and breakfast rooms filled with antique-looking furniture, Jacuzzis and oodles of charm. Of course, charm comes with a price tag. Room rates range from $100 to $200 nightly.

Call (715) 294-4248 for reservations and information.

### STILLWATER

Just 30 minutes east of the Twin Cities, Stillwater, a town steeped in history, sits picturesquely on the bluffs of the St. Croix. Founded in 1843, Stillwater lays claim to being Minnesota's oldest town. The state's territorial charter was drawn up here in 1848 and passed in Congress a year later, making the city the birthplace of the Minnesota Territory.

Stillwater was a thriving logging town until the industry dwindled in the early 1900s. Yet, through a rigorous preservation program, many of its historic buildings and homes have been painstakingly restored. And today, tourists, rather than logs, spill into this town of 14,000 to shop for antiques and oddities, dine overlooking the river or just enjoy its small-town yesteryear pace.

Stillwater was once a contender to be the state capital but settled instead for the state penitentiary. The three-story Territorial Prison housed notorious criminals of its day, including Cole Younger, a member of the Jesse James gang. The sprawling old edifice still stands, but its prison days are over. Today, convicts are held in a much larger facility in neighboring Bayport.

Stillwater is filled with Victorian homes (many transformed into bed and breakfasts), a picturesque Main Street lined with antique shops, galleries and bookstores, not to mention several good riverfront restaurants.

For antique buffs, there are innumerable shops for browsing, including many dealers in the historic 1869 **Isaac Staples Sawmill Complex**, located on North Main Street.

Book-lovers will want to check out the new **Stillwater Book Center**, at 229 S. Main Street, just across the street from another find, the **St. Croix Antiquarian Booksellers**. Housing 27 used-book sellers, the center also offers rare maps and prints, as well as hard-to-find books printed by university and small presses.

Dining ranges from casual to formal Victorian. For the former, try **The Dock**, 430-3770, 425 E. Nelson, where a riverfront deck attracts boaters and tourists, as well as locals, or **Savories**, 430-0702, 108 N. Main, a European bistro serving interesting sandwiches and soups.

The **Freight House Restaurant**, 439-5718, 305 S. Water Street, is steeped in railroad memorabilia and offers river views, plus an expansive outdoor deck. After your meal, go next door for a spin on the **Rivertown Trolley**, which offers 40-minute narrated tours of the town.

Hedonists head for the **Lowell Inn**, 439-1100, 102 N. Second Street, which serves a generous fare in three elegant dining rooms of a graceful estate known as the "Mount Vernon of the West." The inn also has 21 rooms for overnight guests ($119 to $189). And you may need a room after that sumptuous repast!

Hike up the hill behind the Low-

ell Inn to **Pioneer Park**, offering a sweeping view of Stillwater and the St. Croix River valley.

Another interesting stop is the **Joseph Wolf Brewery Caves**, open Memorial Day through Labor Day, 439-3588, 402 S. Main Street. These hand-dug caves were originally used by fur trappers and later for beer storage by the Wolf Brewery. They are now the site of picturesque **Vittorio's Restaurant**. Call for tour information.

Other historic sites include the **Warden's Home Museum**, 439-5956, 602 N. Main Street, an 1853 building that housed wardens of the first Territorial Prison, and the **Washington County Historical**

**Courthouse**, 430-6233, 101 W. Pine Street, circa 1870, one of the oldest courthouses in the state.

Just 15 miles north of Stillwater is **William O'Brien State Park**, a year-round recreation area on the St. Croix River that's great for camping, picnicking, canoeing and swimming. And just 8 miles northeast of Stillwater is Somerset, Wisconsin, notorious for the Apple River, a great "tubing" river for kids of all ages.

### HUDSON

Located just 12 miles east of St. Paul on I-94, this Wisconsin town on the St. Croix River was named for its physical resemblance to the Hudson River Valley in New York.

Founded in the 1840s by fur traders, Hudson was a thriving lumbering center in the 1850s and '60s. And today many grand Victorian homes built by lumber barons and wealthy merchants of the period still grace Hudson neighborhoods, especially along Third Street. Check in at the **Hudson Chamber of Commerce**, (715) 386-8411, 421 Second Street, for information on a self-guided tour of Hudson's old homes.

Or begin your sightseeing at the **Octagon House**, (715) 386-2654, 1004 Third Street. Listed on the National Register of Historic Places, the Octagon House — yes, it is truly eight-sided — contains a wealth of memorabilia, including a grand piano notable because it was dumped in the river twice on its way up the Mississippi to Hudson.

Across the street, at 1005 Third Street, is the historic 1884 **Phipps Inn**, a sprawling Queen Anne home divided into six comfortable bed and breakfast suites. Rates range from $119 to $159. Call the inn at (715) 386-0800 for more information and reservations.

Picturesque Hudson is also home to the very modern, expansive **Phipps Center for the Arts**, (715) 386-2305, First and Locust streets, offering art exhibits, plays and popular and classical music concerts. Recently expanded, the Phipps boasts an awesome view of the St. Croix from the upper-floor gallery.

To get a real feel for the hometown appeal of this pretty city, just wander through Hudson's downtown, which centers on Second Street.

Pop into **Dick's Bar and Grill**, (715) 386-5222, Walnut and Second streets, an unpretentious eatery with concrete floors and wall murals, for some notoriously good down-home cooking, including "chicken-in-a-hubcap." This is baked or fried chicken served, just as it says, in a real hubcap. It's Dick's specialty! Other good bets are **Sunsets**, (715) 386-4001, 500 First Street, for lunch or dinner (if the weather's good, grab an outdoor table on the deck) and the **North Shore Coffee Company**, (715) 386-4122, upstairs from Valley Bookseller at 112½ Walnut Street, for a steaming jolt of espresso and proprietress Maureen's freshly baked goodies.

Then walk off the calories at nearby **Lakefront Park**, which boasts a swimming beach, bandshell, walkways and a new amphitheater.

**St. Croix Meadows Greyhound Park**, just south of I-94, offers both matinee and evening races at a new, state-of-the-art track. Dining is available in the clubhouse. Call the racetrack at (715) 386-6800 for a racing schedule or dinner reservations.

Just northeast of Hudson, County Highway A leads to **Willow River State Park**, featuring a nature center, prairie land, a great trout stream, three dams, three lakes and a pleasant sandy beach.

North Hudson (population 3,100-plus) is a longstanding Italian enclave. Check out its Italian restaurants, or plan ahead and visit during the community's annual **Pepper Festival**, usually held in mid-August.

### RED WING

Pottery and work shoes have made the name Red Wing world-renowned, but you couldn't tell it from the looks of this pretty Mississippi River town. With its gorgeous 19th-century mansions, historic St. James Hotel and restored Main Street, Red Wing seems frozen in an earlier time of quiet elegance.

Located just 50 miles southeast of the Twin Cities, Red Wing (population 13,134) is nestled amid the craggy bluffs surrounding the Mississippi. A 1.5-mile climb up one of the most popular, Barn Bluff, affords a commanding view up and down the Mississippi.

The recently restored **T.B. Sheldon Auditorium Theatre**, 388-2806, Third Street at East Avenue, is not to be missed. This jewel box theater opened in 1904 and today hosts a variety of performances from films to plays to classical music concerts.

History buffs will want to visit the **Goodhue County Historical Society and Museum**, 388-6024, at 1166 Oak Street.

Be sure to take time for a stop at the **Red Wing Pottery Salesroom**, 388-3562, 1995 W. Main Street, where original pieces of the old Red Wing Pottery are still sold, along with other gifts and collectibles.

**Pottery Place Outlet Center**, 388-1428, 2000 W. Main Street, is a complex of factory outlets, shops and restaurants in a converted old stoneware factory.

Have lunch or dinner — or spend the night — in the elegant antique-filled **St. James Hotel**, 388-2846, 406 Main Street, c. 1875, which also boasts an adjacent shopping mall.

Nearby **Frontenac State Park** (15 miles south on U.S. Highway 61) has been called the bird-watching capital of southern Minnesota. And during the winter months, downhill skiers flock to **Mount Frontenac** and **Welch Village** ski resorts.

**Treasure Island Casino**, just outside of Red Wing off highways 61 and 316, blasts the traveler back to the 20th century with its video slots, bingo and blackjack tables. See the Casinos section of this chapter for more details.

## Southern Stops

### ROCHESTER

There's always a doctor in the house in this bustling city whose claim to fame is the world-renowned Mayo Clinic.

Located about 80 miles south of the Twin Cities (via U.S. Highway 52) or about 46 miles south of Red Wing, Rochester is a city of roughly 70,000, with a thriving cultural and educational scene, thanks, in part, to its large concentration of doctors and other well-educated folk.

One of the jewels of Rochester is the sprawling **Mayowood** estate, former home of the famed Mayo family. Built in 1911, this gorgeous 57-room mansion overlooking the Zumbro River served as a social center for such visiting dignitaries as Franklin Roosevelt, Helen Keller and Adlai Stevenson. Reservations are required for tours; call (507) 282-9447. The **Mayo Clinic**, at 200 First Street S.W., also offers tours and there's plenty to see — distinctive architecture, a well-adorned chapel, a carillon tower, not to mention those hallowed clinic halls visited by more than a quarter-million people every year. The tours are free and no reservations are required. Tours are given at 10 AM and 2 PM Monday through Friday. For more information, call (507) 284-2511.

Other attractions include **Quarry Hill Nature Center**, featuring a fossil-filled limestone quarry; **Whitewater State Park** with its climbing bluffs and trout fishing; **Olmstead County History Center and Museum**; and, to the west, the old town of **Mantorville**, containing many buildings listed in the National Register of Historic Places.

Mantorville's **Hubbell House** draws diners from near and far. Housed in an 1854 inn, the restaurant serves traditional fare in a historic setting as comfortable as an old armchair. Call (507) 635-2331 for reservations.

### New Ulm

Ninety miles southwest of the Twin Cities on the banks of the Minnesota River sits New Ulm, a little piece of Germany in the Midwest.

Traces of New Ulm's Teutonic heritage are everywhere — from the 45-foot Glockenspiel downtown to its neatly planned streets to the August Schell Brewery to the annual Oktoberfest revelry. Dominating this city of 13,000 is a statue of Hermann the Cheruscan, the 9th-century warrior who united Germany.

Highlights include the **Schell Brewery**, a family-owned brewery dating back to 1861, and surrounding gardens and deer park; the home of children's author/artist **Wanda Gag**; the **Harkin Store**, an 1870 general store; **Brown County Historical Museum**; and **Veigel's Kaiserhoff**, a restaurant renowned for its barbecued ribs.

To experience the town's "gemutlichkeit" in full bloom, visit during **Oktoberfest** (usually the second week in October) when the polka music and the beer spill forth unceasingly for a rollicking good time.

### St. Peter

In 1857, St. Peter was a contender to be the state capital, but a scheming legislator hid the crucial bill authorizing the capital's move from St. Paul. The deadline passed and so did St. Peter's chance for lasting glory — all because Legislator Joseph Roulette hated the idea of having to travel to St. Peter from his home in northern Minnesota.

This city on the Minnesota River 70 miles south of the Twin Cities is an interesting stop on the way to New Ulm or a good destination in its own right.

Dating to 1854, St. Peter (population 9,421) contains several well-

# BED & BREAKFAST
# AND
# HISTORIC INNS

preserved historic buildings, including the home of St. Peter's first mayor, E. St. Julien Cox. This 1871 home is a magnificent example of Gothic Revival architecture.

Other interesting attractions include **Gustavus Adolphus College**, the **Nicollet County Historical Museum** and the **St. Peter Arts and Heritage Center**.

Stop for lunch or dinner at **Mitterhauser's Grill & Restaurant**, (507) 931-3833), 429 S. Minnesota Avenue, owned and operated by award-winning Austrian chef, Claus Mitterhauser.

Too tired for the drive home? Turn in at the **Park Row Bed & Breakfast**, (507) 931-2495, 525 W. Park Row, a cozy Victorian retreat.

### New Prague

On your way back to the Cities, swing eastward and stop in the Czech town of New Prague (highways 13 and 19), which is noteworthy for its colorful wall murals, the copper-domed **St. Wenceslaus Church** and a delightful old inn, **Schumacher's New Prague Hotel**, 758-2133, 212 W. Main Street. The latter is an elegant Greek Revival brick building designed by famed architect Cass Gilbert in the late 1890s. Inside, the European-styled hotel features 11 lodging rooms, each individually decorated. Three cozy Old World-themed dining rooms serve homemade Czech and German specialties, accompanied by imported beers.

### Northfield

Located 40 miles south of the Twin Cities at the junction of state highways 3 and 9, the town of Northfield (population 14,684) lays claim to two prestigious private colleges, **Carleton College** and **St. Olaf College**, and one colorful historic event: a foiled robbery attempt by the notorious Jesse James and his gang.

On September 7, 1876, James and his gang attempted to rob the First National Bank, but the cashier, Joseph Lee Heywood, refused to open the safe. He was shot to death, but the citizenry retaliated, killing two gang members and chasing the rest out of town. One other innocent bystander was killed in the melee. Three gang members were apprehended in Madelia, Minnesota, and sent to Stillwater State Prison. Six years later, Jesse James was murdered in Missouri. The foiled bank robbery is a source of community pride and is re-enacted every September during "Defeat of Jesse James Days." The bank has been restored and is now a museum housing exhibits about the famous event.

In fact, Northfield contains many restored buildings and storefronts in its historic downtown, which is well worth a stroll. Also noteworthy is the **Archer House**, (507) 645-5661, 212 Division Street, a charming 1877 38-room inn along the banks of the Cannon River.

Thanks to its two colleges, Northfield has a vibrant cultural scene, including several interesting art galleries. Both colleges are worth touring. The Arboretum at Carleton College offers hiking and jogging trails along the Cannon River and tours by reservation, 663-4309.

Just west of Northfield, on Highway 19, is **Fireside Orchard**, a great "pie and cider stop" before you hit I-35 back to the cities.

## Northern Exposures

### ST. CLOUD

Located 65 miles northwest of the Twin Cities, St. Cloud, with its population of about 80,000 (including suburbs), is large enough to be interesting, yet small enough to be friendly.

In this prosperous city are found world-famous granite quarries; **St. Cloud State University** with its planetarium, anthropology and art museums; the **Stearns County Heritage Center**, 253-8424, 235 S. 33rd Avenue; distinctive gardens, such as the colorful **Munsinger Gardens** (Riverside Drive and Michigan Avenue); and several theater groups and art galleries.

Nearby **Collegeville** is home to **St. John's University**, the breathtaking **St. John's Benedictine Abbey** and the **Hill Monastic Manuscript Library**, 363-3514, possessing one of the largest collections of early manuscripts. Well worth a side trip is the **Charles A. Lindbergh State Park**, 632-9050, located about 26 miles north of St. Cloud at Little Falls. This secluded park in the woods skirting the Mississippi River contains the boyhood home of famous aviator and environmentalist Charles Lindbergh. Filled with his boyhood toys and period household furnishings, the comfortable old homestead with its big screened-in sleeping porch offers a fascinating look at the forces that shaped the man. The garage houses a Volkswagen Bug that Lindbergh drove on adventure trips throughout Africa.

Nearby, the park's visitors center offers films and exhibits on Lindbergh and his famous flight, as well as an interesting bookstore.

### BRAINERD

Brainerd, 125 miles north of the Twin Cities, is the hub of a region filled with 450 lakes and more than 135 resorts, hotels and campgrounds. As such, it's a popular weekend destination for many Twin Citians. Most people come just to relax and recharge their batteries by lolling about on the beach, fishing, water-skiing or boating.

Apart from the dazzling lakes and serene woods, points of interest include the **Crow Wing County Museum**, (218) 829-3268, 320 Laurel Street; **Brainerd International Raceway**, (218) 829-9836, Highway 371, where Paul Newman has raced; **Paul Bunyan Fun Center** amusement park, (218) 829-6342, highways 210 and 371; **Lumbertown U.S.A.**, a re-creation of an 1870 logging camp, (218) 829-8872, at Madden's Resort on Gull Lake, 8001 Pine Beach Peninsula; and the **Paul Bunyan Arboretum**, (218) 829-8770, N.W. Seventh Street; not to mention various water-slide parks, mini-golf courses and shopping galore.

### DULUTH

Lake Superior winds buffeting seagulls off Canal Park, the boom of foghorns in the mist, old neighborhoods clinging to hillsides, others squatting on sandbars, the elegant Glensheen Mansion, falcons circling over Hawk Ridge.

These are but a few of the great reasons for visiting Duluth (population 85,493), bustling Lake Superior port city and gateway to the picturesque North Shore Drive. Duluth is the final stop on the St. Lawrence Seaway, which connects the Atlantic Ocean to the Great Lakes.

The heart of the city is the harbor and the aerial-lift bridge, through which thousands of domestic and foreign vessels arrive each year, lending an exciting international ambiance to the surroundings.

To get a real feel for Duluth, take a boat cruise of the harbor or tour the *William A. Irvin*, a retired ore carrier that's been transformed into a 610-foot floating museum.

The **Canal Park Marine Museum**, (218) 727-2497, operated by the U.S. Army Corps of Engineers, offers fascinating exhibits on maritime history and the Great Lakes, including dioramas of shipwrecks and models of famous shipping vessels, plus enough marine equipment to incite sailing fever in the most ardent landlubber.

Of course, no trip to the harbor and Canal Park is complete without a lunch or dinner stop at **Grandma's Saloon & Deli**, (218) 727-4192, with its convivial atmosphere, old-time decor and hearty sandwiches. Top off lunch with a brisk walk on Duluth's **Lake Walk**, a colorful walkway that skirts Lake Superior from Canal Park to just past Fitger's Brewery.

Children of all ages will enjoy **The Depot**, (218) 727-8025, 506 W. Michigan Street, a renovated 1892 railroad depot that now serves as an art center, housing several museums and performing arts spaces. The lower level contains a train museum, complete with real, operating locomotives and historic storefront displays. This is great kidstuff. They love climbing all over the trains.

Drive north of town to **Glensheen Mansion**, (218) 724-8864, 3300 London Road, for a glimpse at how the other half lived in turn-of-the-century prosperity. Built on 22 acres in 1908 by attorney and legislator Chester Adgate Congdon, Glensheen is reminiscent of an English country estate with its elegant 39-room manor house and formal gardens overlooking Lake Superior. Call ahead for tour times and admission fees.

Other attractions include **Fitger's Brewery**, (218) 722-8826, 600 E. Superior Street, a complex of shops, restaurants and lodging, and for gamblers, **Fond-du-luth Gaming Casino**, (218) 722-0208, 129 E. Superior Street. See the Casino section at the end of this chapter for more information.

To take in the lovely sweep of city and water, drive along **Skyline Parkway**, a dramatic hilltop route in the western part of Deluth. In the fall, bird-watchers converge here at Hawk Ridge to watch migrating hawks and eagles soar over the city.

As you can see, Duluth, located

Photo: John Doman, Pioneer Press

*The St. Croix River.*

150 miles north of the Twin Cities, is a destination in itself, or it can serve as a stop on your way up **North Shore Drive**, a breathtaking roadway that skirts crashing waves, verdant forests and crystalline streams for 150 miles to the Canadian border.

Plan your trip for a long weekend in order to do justice to the many attractions of Duluth and/or the North Shore. And make reservations. This area is a favorite destination for Twin Citians, especially in the summer and fall. You don't want to be stranded without a bed for the night. Several wonderful accommodations are the **Spinnaker Inn**, 5427 North Shore Drive, (218) 525-2838; and **Fitger's Inn**, 600 E. Superior Street, (218) 722-8826. Another good option is the **Radisson Duluth**, 505 W. Superior Street, (218) 727-8981.

## Casinos

It's enough to make those Scandinavian pioneers roll over in their graves — Minnesotans are becoming gambling fools!

They're flocking in droves to the glitzy, new American Indian-owned casinos to wager at the blackjack tables, pour quarters into video slots or dab bingo cards, then celebrate their winnings or mourn their losses at the casino-operated restaurants and lounges.

It's a 1990s phenomenon with no end in sight. With more casinos than Atlantic City, Minnesota is the largest American Indian gaming market in the United States. There are 17 Indian-operated casinos in the state, and in 1993, it was estimated they produced a combined gross revenue of more than $3 billion.

We're not talking about cozy little gambling halls reminiscent of those found in Las Vegas' historic downtown. Many Minnesota facilities are big-time casino complexes — some of the largest in the Midwest.

For example, Mystic Lake Casino in the Twin Cities suburb of Prior Lake measures 340,000 square feet — the biggest casino between Atlantic City and Las Vegas. Several other casinos are larger than 100,000 square feet. And it's not uncommon for every square foot to be absolutely packed — even on Saturday mornings!

All this action began in the late 1980s and today — moral issues aside — it's become a major industry.

In this section, we're listing various casinos in the Twin Cities area and those that are close enough for a day trip or weekend outing.

But first, here are some general characteristics of gambling — Minnesota style.

### ALCOHOL

Unlike the scene in Vegas or Atlantic City, the booze doesn't pour from the bar like coins from the slots. Many of Minnesota's casinos are dry — including the big Mystic Lake complex in suburban Twin Cities. In other casinos, it may be carefully controlled. At Grand Casino Hinckley, for example, there's a two-drink limit in the entertainment lounge. Other casinos sell alcoholic drinks, but not in the gaming areas.

### LIGHTING UP

The "no smoking" movement is very big in Minnesota and it has extended to casinos, where several have set aside large no-smoking areas. Be aware of where you light up or you could face a large fine.

### FOOD, GLORIOUS FOOD

Many casinos have initiated large buffets to lure gamblers. At bargain prices, these feasts may be worth the trip alone.

### BLACKJACK, À LA MINNESOTA

This is currently the only table game allowed in Minnesota. It's played in the traditional Las Vegas fashion. Except for aces, double downs are permitted after splits, and dealers are required to stand on all 17s, at most casinos. There are no bet limits imposed by the state, but don't expect to go any higher than $1,000 or even a couple hundred at some facilities.

All "slots" in Minnesota are actually video gaming devices, not the traditional spinning reels. This is because the former are considered more tamper-proof than machines that employ the actual spinning reels.

In Minnesota, as a general rule, video slots must return no less than 80 percent for non-skill games and no less than 83 percent for games with more player input, such as video poker. This state also has limits on how much the machines can pay out — no more than 95 percent for non-skill games and no more than 98 percent for games such as video poker.

Whatever the payout, remember the goal is to have fun, whether you win or lose. Bring your smile, loose change and your sense of perspective and you'll undoubtedly have a great time!

The casinos are listed alphabetically. We're concentrating on those that are close enough to be comfortable weekend destinations from the Twin Cities. For detailed information on other Minnesota casinos, contact the Minnesota Office of Tourism at 296-5029 or (800) 657-3700.

### BLACK BEAR CASINO
*Carlton*                    (218) 878-2327

Located about 25 miles south of Duluth in the city of Carlton, Black Bear Casino is a new 87,000-square-foot facility operated by the Fond du Lac band of Chippewa Indians.

Inside the faux-limestone facility is a two-story main rotunda filled with 24 blackjack tables ($2 to $200 betting range), surrounded by 1,000 video slots and games. An upstairs 500-seat bingo parlor doubles as the casino's lunch and dinner buffet area.

Liquor is served in the gaming area, and the Blackbear Lounge offers a popular walleye fish dinner (entrees are in the $10 to $12 price range). There's also a sports bar and the Lady Slipper Lounge, with live music on weekends. The casino is open around the clock every day.

Location: Go north on I-35 from the Twin Cities. After about 100 miles, as you near the Duluth area, take the Highway 210 Exit. You'll see the casino from the interstate.

### FIREFLY CREEK CASINO
*Granite Falls*                    564-2121

Set in a pleasant valley along the Minnesota River in southwestern Minnesota, this smaller casino has a friendly, down-home atmosphere, in addition to 350 slot and video games and 10 blackjack tables ($2 to $200). There's a country-style cafe and a lounge.

The Firefly is open 24 hours on Fridays and Saturdays, 8 AM to 1 AM all other days.

When you tire of the action at the Firefly, you can hop in your car and head for Jackpot Junction Casino in Morton, just 40 miles away.

Location: From the Twin Cities, take Highway 212 west to Granite Falls. From Granite Falls, take Highway 67 south for 5 miles to the casino. It's about 120 miles west of the Twin Cities.

### FOND-DU-LUTH CASINO
*129 E. Superior St., Duluth*   (218) 722-0280
                                      (800) 873-0280

Run by the Fond du Lac band of Chippewa, this casino offers 400 slot and video keno machines, plus an upstairs 525-seat bingo parlor. Due to a legal squabble between the Indians and the city of Duluth, no blackjack is currently offered.

There's a snack bar serving grilled food and an adjacent parking ramp (free parking with validation).

The Fond-du-Luth is open 24 hours Fridays through Sundays and from 10 AM to 2 AM Mondays through Thursdays.

Conveniently located on one of Duluth's major streets, the casino is east of the intersection of County Highway 23 and I-35.

### GRAND CASINO HINCKLEY
*Hinckley* (800) 472-6321

A 75-minute drive from the Twin Cities brings you to the door of this deluxe gaming emporium. Inside are more than 1,500 slot and video games, 48 blackjack tables ($3 to $1,000), plus video craps and video blackjack tables and a computerized horse-racing game.

The casino is owned by the Mille Lacs band of Chippewa, which also owns the nearby Grand Casino Mille Lacs.

This prosperous facility is growing like crazy. By the end of 1995, this Hinckley complex is expected to include three hotels, an amphitheater and an 18-hole golf course, in addition to the 240-site RV park and 50-unit "chalet" (mini-mobile home) development that are already operating.

Connected to the casino via an enclosed corridor is the Grand Grill Americana bar and restaurant. Inside the casino itself are the Silver 7s Lounge and the Grand Grill, however. The Grand Buffet has received rave reviews. There's free entertainment nightly in the casino lounge.

The casino also has a state-of-the-art Kid's Quest child-care center, for children between the ages of 6 weeks and 12 years. Grand Casino Hinckley is open 24 hours every day.

Location: Go north on I-35 from the Twin Cities. Take the Hinckley Exit and go a mile east on Highway 48.

### GRAND CASINO MILLE LACS
*Onamia* (800) 626-5825

Located on the southwest shore of huge Lake Mille Lacs, a year-round magnet for serious anglers, Grand Casino Mille Lacs is a smaller version of the Hinckley gaming complex and offers 1,200 slot and video games, 35 blackjack tables ($3 to $1,000), a 400-seat bingo parlor and a computerized horse-racing game.

Like its Hinckley sibling, Grand Casino Mille Lacs has on-site lodging (an attached 180-room hotel with pool), child-care facilities, a video arcade, plus one of the best buffets of any casino in the state. However, no liquor is served in the casino, which is open 24 hours a day.

Location: From the Twin Cities, take Highway 169 north for about 100 miles. The casino is located between Onamia and Garrison on the southwest shore of Mille Lacs.

### JACKPOT JUNCTION
*Morton (507) 644-3000 or (800) 538-8379*

Ironically, Jackpot Junction, one of the first successful Indian-run casinos in the state, sits near the site of the tragic Dakota Conflict, a six-week war between Indians and whites more than 100 years ago that resulted in the forced exodus of the Sioux, or Dakota, tribes.

Today it seems the Dakota are exacting sweet justice at the gaming tables and slot machines.

Jackpot Junction offers 1,200 slot and video games, 63 blackjack tables ($2 to $1,000), using 2- and

4-deck shoes, plus a 385-seat bingo hall.

Because of its out-of-the-way location, 100 miles southwest of Minneapolis and St. Paul, Jackpot Junction offers regular low-cost busing from the Twin Cities and is generous with its coupon offers.

This large, sprawling facility has a full-service restaurant, Impressions, that is considered one of the better eateries in the area. There's also a buffet, three full-service bars and a concert area with nightly entertainment, including national celebrities.

The casino operates a 90-site campground and RV park.

Jackpot Junction is open 24 hours daily.

Location: From Minneapolis, take Highway 212 to Olivia, turn south on Highway 71 and follow the signs to the casino near Morton. Or, from I-90, take Highway 71 north to Redwood Falls, then take Highway 19 east to the casino.

### MYSTIC LAKE
### ENTERTAINMENT COMPLEX
*Prior Lake*      *445-6000 or (800) 262-7799*

Mystic Lake is the biggest casino complex in the Midwest. Technically, the complex comprises the Little Six Casino, the down-home Dakota Country Casino and the upscale Mystic Lake Casino. The latter two are huge domed gambling palaces connected by an enclosed mall. The Little Six, Mystic Lake's humble forerunner, is a half-mile away.

Mystic Lake Casino screams "Las Vegas" with its glitzy aura and giant chandeliers. At Mystic's high-stakes blackjack area, minimum bets are in the $100 range.

The adjacent Dakota Country Casino is designed to attract smaller-stakes gamblers, with tons of nickel slots, video poker machines and $3 blackjack tables.

Overall, there are 2,100 slot and video games, 128 blackjack tables ($3 to $1,000), using 4- to 8-deck shoes, and a 1,200-seat bingo palace. The casino also offers no-smoking sections throughout the complex.

The casino's Four Seasons buffet is consistently top-rated. There's also the High Steaks Ranch House for meat-and-potatoes fans and the Minnehaha Cafe for lighter fare.

No liquor is served anywhere in the casino, but you'll find a wide selection of nonalcoholic cocktails and near-beers in Wild Bill's Saloon.

For entertainment, the stage at Wild Bill's Saloon spotlights country bands every night and the Celebrity Palace presents headliner acts.

Photo: Joe Oden, Pioneer Press

*Mystic Lake Casino in Prior Lake run by the Skakopee Mdewakanton Sioux tribe.*

The complex offers a shopping mall of mainly American Indian arts and crafts.

Mystic Lake is open 24 hours daily.

Location: From the Twin Cities, take I-35W south to County Highway 42. Take 42 west to Highway 83. Turn south and go a mile to the complex. Alternative: Take Highway 13 west from I-35W, continuing when it becomes Highway 101. Turn south on Highway 83 and go 5 miles.

### TREASURE ISLAND CASINO
*Red Wing* **(800) 222-7077**

This casino began in 1984 as the Prairie Island Bingo Hall and has since been greatly expanded to offer 1,250 slot and video games, 52 blackjack tables ($3 to $500), using 2- to 6-deck shoes, plus matinee and evening bingo sessions.

The complex features a recent-

ly built, lovely domed atrium with palm trees and the colorful Toucan Harry's bar, built to look like the bow of a wrecked pirate ship.

The older section of the casino, however, is made up of less-appealing, crowded gaming rooms.

Liquor is served in the casino and bar. Generous portions are offered up at the buffet. Child care is available at the Children's Center of Prairie Island located across the street (reservations are required: (800) 554-5473 or 385-0351).

The casino books stand-up comics and name acts every week as free entertainment. Treasure Island is open 24 hours daily. An RV park and a marina on the Mississippi are on the property.

Location: Take Highway 61 south from the Twin Cities and follow the signs to the casino, which is located about 35 miles south of St. Paul and 8 miles north of Red Wing.

## Outstate Casinos

Here's a listing of other casinos in the area, those that are too distant for comfortable weekend trips but may make an enjoyable stop during a longer vacation.

### FORTUNE BAY CASINO

| Tower, Wis. | (218) 753-6400 |
| | (800) 992-7529 |

### GRAND PORTAGE
### LODGE & CASINO GRAND

| Portage, Wis. | (218) 475-2441 |
| Hotel only | (800) 543-1384 |

### LAKE OF THE WOODS CASINO

1012 E. Lake St., Warroad (218) 386-3381

### NORTHERN LIGHTS CASINO

| Walker, Wis. | (218) 547-2744 |
| | (800) 252-7529 |

### PALACE BINGO AND CASINO

| Cass Lake, Wis. | (218) 335-6787 |
| | (800) 228-6676 |

### RED LAKE CASINO

| Red Lake, Wis. | (218) 679-2500 |

### RIVER ROAD CASINO

| Thief River Falls, Wis. | (218) 681-4062 |

### SHOOTING STAR CASINO

| Mahnomen, Wis. | (218) 935-2701 |
| Hotel only | (800) 453-7827 |

# BUILDING HOMES FOR FAMILIES AND NEIGHBORHOODS WITH PRESENCE.

At LANDICO we build simple elegance ... deliciously comfortable.
Custom crafted for your family on the site of your choice.

# Inside
# **Neighborhoods**

From uptown penthouses to quaint Victorian homes nestled on shady city streets, from palatial lakeshore estates to "Leave it to Beaver" suburban ramblers, the greater Twin Cities area offers an amazing array of housing — for rent or for sale — to suit all personalities and pocketbooks.

At first glance, Minneapolis and St. Paul may look like one sprawling metropolis sliced by a river, but, in reality, the two cities are very different.

Even though it has its share of old, stately neighborhoods, Minneapolis, with a population of roughly 368,000, exudes a big, brash, modern image with its cutting-edge music scene, pro sports teams and bustling industry. St. Paul, with a population of approximately 272,000, possesses more of a small-town, traditional, old-monied, intellectual atmosphere — after all, seven colleges are located within its boundaries.

Minneapolis is, for the most part, laid out logically in a flat grid-like pattern, its streets sensibly patterned. St. Paul is a map maker's nightmare: Its roadways dance willy-nilly over hills and river bluffs. The Mighty Mississippi curves defiantly through its urban core, making the waterway a more dramatic presence in the Saintly City than in its sister city to the west.

While not immune to big-city problems of unemployment and crime, both cities, nonetheless, have relatively healthy economies, cultural treasures and extensive park land and lakes — qualities that greatly enhance their livability.

There's a park every eight blocks in Minneapolis — one acre of green for every 43 residents. While homes along Twin Cities lakefront boulevards command a hefty price, it is possible to find surprisingly affordable housing just a few blocks away, within walking distance of the water. It's devilish good fun to merrily jog around Lake Calhoun, wave at passersby and just pretend that the pink 20-room Tudor mansion over there — the one with the Ferrari in the driveway — is your home sweet home. Who's to know the difference, except you and your pocketbook?

In 1991, *USA Today* named the Minneapolis-St. Paul area 24th among the sample of the most-affordable U.S. housing markets. This ranking was achieved by matching housing costs to average incomes. According to a National Association of Realtors report published in

*The Kenwood neighborhood house where Mary Richards from the "Mary Tyler Moore" show lived.*

February 1993, the median price of housing in the greater Twin Cities metro area is $94,200. With that as a reference point, Twin Cities home prices vary greatly depending on the neighborhood and, of course, living space and amenities.

For perspective, let's compare the Twin Cities' median housing price of $94,200 with those of other metropolitan areas: Denver, $95,800; Chicago, $135,900; Dallas, $91,300; Los Angeles, $213,800; and New York, $172,600. For those wishing to rent, the average monthly price of a rental unit in the metropolitan area is $534.26. And within the city limits of either Minneapolis or St. Paul, rental housing is even more affordable, at $476 and $490, respectively.

Still, finding the just-right home or apartment in the Twin Cities metropolitan area can be a daunting task, to say the least. After all, more than 2.3 million people make their home in this greater metropolitan area. Unless you're already familiar with the Twin Cities' neighborhoods and suburbs, you may wish to utilize the services of a good Realtor or apartment-search firm.

Two huge companies — Edina Realty and Burnet Realty — dominate the local real-estate scene. Yet there are many smaller realty firms with enough hustle and initiative to give the big guys a run for their money. See our Real Estate Resources chapter, following, for more information.

The housing industry is thriving in the Twin Cities, with new housing developments sprouting in suburbs, old warehouses being transformed into lofts and condos, and quaint Victorian homes undergoing restoration to their original splendor. Despite — or maybe because of — our dramatic climate of subzero winters and blistering summers, the Twin Cities is a sublimely livable locale. According to *Mpls. St. Paul Magazine*, about 75 percent of Minnesotans are natives who wouldn't think of living anywhere else, and more than half the state's 4.4 million population has not moved in the last five years. Thousands have come reluctantly and remained contentedly. Watch out, it could happen to you.

What follows is a brief overview of both cities, their neighborhoods and suburbs.

## Minneapolis Neighborhoods

The Mississippi River is a good reference point for both cities. Minneapolis is located on both the east and west banks of the Mighty Mississippi as it rolls southeast toward St. Paul. The western and southern parts of the city are much larger, spreading over lake-dotted rolling landscape to join the suburbs of Brooklyn Center, Robbinsdale, Golden Valley, St. Louis Park, Edina and Richfield. Beyond lie the second-tier suburbs of Bloomington, Eden Prairie, Minnetonka, Maple Grove and Plymouth.

On the eastern side of the Mississippi are found the communities of Northeast Minneapolis and the neighborhoods surrounding the University of Minnesota to the southeast.

Spreading out from Northeast Minneapolis are the suburbs of Fridley, Columbia Heights and St. Anthony.

Here's a look at some of Minneapolis' most colorful neighborhoods. Keep in mind that the average home sale price in Minneapolis proper is a very affordable $84,610, but there are great variations, depending on location, square footage and amenities.

### BRYN MAWR, KENWOOD AND CALHOUN-ISLES

On the western edges of Minneapolis are the areas of Bryn Mawr, Calhoun-Isles and Kenwood, hilly neighborhoods of tree-lined streets and large, stately old and new homes. Bryn Mawr is bordered on the north by Glenwood Avenue and expansive Theodore Wirth Park, 957 acres of gardens and greenery encompassing Theodore Wirth Lake. On its southern end, it veers southwest to encompass the genteel neighborhoods on the north and west shores of Cedar Lake.

Just south and southeast of Bryn Mawr are the areas of Kenwood and Calhoun-Isles, prestigious neighborhoods surrounding Lake of the Isles and Cedar Lake. Kenwood is the home of the famous "Mary Tyler Moore" house from the popular TV sitcom of the 1970s. (It's at 2104 Kenwood Parkway.) Some of the old Kenwood homes have been divided into apartments, and the community has a lively population of old families and young professionals, many of whom can be seen jogging around the lakes.

### LOWRY HILL

Just east of Kenwood are the Lowry Hill, Lowry Hill East and East Isles neighborhoods, straddling Hennepin Avenue. This interesting area offers a pleasant mix of 19th-century mansions and old and new apartment buildings. Residents range from the very wealthy to struggling young professionals and bohemians. It's a choice locale containing the renowned Guthrie Theater, Walker Art Center, the Minneapolis Sculpture Garden, plenty of interesting restaurants and video stores. Lovely Loring Park and downtown are just a 5-minute walk away.

### UPTOWN

At the southern edge of Lowry Hill East and centered at Hennepin Avenue and Lake Street, is the bustling Uptown area, a popular draw for young sophisticates and raging individualists. Conveniently close to the frenetic outdoor social scene at Lake of the Isles and Lake Calhoun, Uptown also is home to a variety of comedy clubs, bars, ethnic restaurants, coffee shops, boutiques and two movie theaters, one of which, the Uptown, specializes in the latest foreign films. Calhoun Square, right at Hennepin and Lake, is a popular shopping complex featuring one-of-a-kind shops and restaurants.

The Uptown Art Fair, held one weekend in August every year, is one of the most popular summer events in the cities.

Housing in Uptown includes affordable apartments and interesting big and small older homes.

Many of the larger homes have been divided into apartments and condos.

### SOUTHWEST NEIGHBORHOODS

Elegant homes, sprawling yards and lake views typify southwest neighborhoods, fanning out around the south shore of Lake Calhoun and picturesque Lake Harriet. Here you'll find the neighborhoods of Linden Hills, Fulton, Lynnhurst and East Harriet. This is gentrified living, and many of its spacious and moderately sized homes have been in the same families for years.

The area of 43rd Street and Upton Avenue has a collection of charming little shops and ice cream stores. It's a great place to visit on Saturday afternoons.

### NOKOMIS NEIGHBORHOODS

The residential areas surrounding Lake Nokomis and along Minnehaha Parkway in South Minneapolis are quiet, stable communities with an interesting mix of large and small homes. Lake Nokomis and Minnehaha Park are popular destinations for fishing, picnicking, walking and biking. The housing here ranges from pricey to surprisingly affordable, anywhere from $70,000 to $150,000 and more.

### POWDERHORN PARK

Many young families who want to settle in the inner city find their first home in this old south-central city district. At its center is the lovely Powderhorn Park, a historic 65-acre park containing a small lake and a popular children's playground. The park is the scene of a colorful May Day Celebration, an annual event featuring gigantic puppets and banners, as well as the Powderhorn Arts Festival, an "alternative" art fair that coincides with the Uptown Art Fair.

Like any inner-city neighborhood, Powderhorn Park has its share of property crime and occasional drug-related incidences. "But we have a relatively low crime rate for an inner-city neighborhood," says Scott Hawkins, executive director of the Powderhorn Park Neighborhood Association. "People are very active in the neighborhoods. We have a lot of block clubs.

"We have a lot of younger families, senior citizens who've lived here 40 to 50 years and lots of youngsters. So there's lot of vitality. Homes here sell fast, especially on the south side," according to Hawkins.

North of Powderhorn is the Phillips neighborhood, bounded by I-35W to the west, Hiawatha Avenue to the east, Franklin Avenue to the north and Lake Street to the south. The site of some of the highest poverty and infant mortality rates in the city, Phillips faces many challenges. Fueled by a strong neighborhood association, however, the community is working to fight the demons of crime and unemployment. Positive strides have been made. A former porn theater has been transformed into a youth art center. Children are painting colorful murals in the neighborhood park. An annual celebration, Phillips Power, Phillips Pride, com- memorates the closing of a troublesome neighborhood liquor store. A series of weekly outdoor concerts celebrates the community's cultural diversity.

### SEWARD NEIGHBORHOOD

The Seward neighborhood, located just south of the University of Minnesota's West Bank campus, south of I-94 and west of the Mississippi, is a stable mix of college intellectuals, professionals and working-class folk, plus a few leftover '60s activists who run a successful food cooperative and inhabit the egalitarian and colorful Seward Cafe on Franklin Avenue. The homes here are well-maintained older two-stories and bungalows.

### CAMPUS COMMUNITIES

University of Minnesota campus communities of Dinkytown and Stadium Village dominate southeast Minneapolis on the east bank of the river. This area also includes Prospect Park, a cozy residential area of winding streets whose landmark — the "Witch's Hat" tower — can be seen as you drive I-94 east over the Mississippi. This is one of the quieter neighborhoods in Minneapolis.

### NORTHEAST NEIGHBORHOODS

Northeast Minneapolis, located on the northeast bank of the Mississippi, is a traditional, working-class ethnic district with roots in the Polish and Eastern and Southern European heritages. Several northeast landmarks served as settings in the movie *Untamed Heart*.

This old address suddenly has a new cachet. Many young families and couples — plus some artist types — are migrating northeast, attracted by its stability, affordable housing and proximity to downtown.

### NORTH MINNEAPOLIS

While it has a troublesome crime problem, North Minneapolis nonetheless claims a rich, colorful history, some great old houses, distressed projects, an ethnically diverse population (34 percent African American, 10 percent American Indian and Asian American), and easy accessibility to downtown Minneapolis.

"Half of our housing stock is over 100 years old, and it's well-maintained," said Paula Saunders, director of the Jordan Neighborhood Association on the near north side.

At one time, North Minneapolis was a prestigious address, harboring thriving communities of Jewish and Eastern European heritage, and its schools were considered among the best in the city. Today, crime and poverty pose major challenges. Yet Saunders believes the challenges are being overcome because of a strong program of block clubs and neighborhood activism.

A four-bedroom home in North Minneapolis can be had for as little as $50,000.

### DOWNTOWN

There are 81 distinct neighborhoods in Minneapolis, and we've only touched on a few. Not to be overlooked is downtown Minneapolis itself, which claims 24,000 residents living in apartments, condos and townhouses. Here the advantages are obvious — convenience, convenience, convenience! Within walking distance are major commercial centers, retail stores, restaurants and the warehouse nightlife scene and concert halls.

## St. Paul Neighborhoods

We begin with downtown St. Paul, where around 5,000 people make their homes in high-rises and charming warehouses-turned-lofts, all within walking distance (in enclosed skyways, no less) to theaters, concert halls, churches, stores and a lively urban farmers market. The downtown district is, in fact, St. Paul's fastest-growing neighborhood.

Many neighborhoods in St. Paul draw home buyers like magnets because they offer a strong sense of community, stability, value and unique advantages. Here's a look at a few of these "hot" locales.

## WESTERN ST. PAUL

Well-maintained, interesting homes, stable, safe neighborhoods and the convenience of city living attract many buyers to the St. Anthony Park, Macalester-Groveland, Highland Park, Summit Hill and Crocus Hill areas of St. Paul.

Houses in these areas range in value from $50,000 to several hundred thousand dollars. In these neighborhoods are found good homes of all sizes and styles — from inexpensive bungalows to stately Victorians.

## SUMMIT HILL

In the highly desirable Summit Hill neighborhood, west of downtown St. Paul, homes can sell for as much as $1 million. This area includes magnificent Summit Avenue with a breathtaking span of historically preserved 19th-century mansions. Today, many of these grand edifices have been divided into townhouses and rental units, yet their stately exteriors remain unchanged. Interspersed among the estates are many charming, but smaller, turn-of-the-century homes inhabited by solidly middle-class folks. Residents cite as advantages the area's charming ambience and its proximity to bustling Grand Avenue and downtown St. Paul. Average home value is $155,656.

## CROCUS HILL

The prestigious Crocus Hill area, bounded roughly by St. Clair Avenue on the south, Lexington Parkway on the west, Grand Avenue on the north and Dale Street on the east, is graced with glorious old Victorian mansions on quiet, shady, lamplit streets. This is where the great industrialists and civic leaders settled in the 1900s and it remains a highly desirable residential area. Homes here can go for as much as $1 million.

## ST. ANTHONY PARK

St. Anthony Park, in the northwest corner of St. Paul, has a strong sense of "small town" community spirit, abundant gardens and stable neighborhoods. Proximity to the University of Minnesota's St. Paul campus is an added plus. Homes here range in price from $60,000 to upwards of $200,000 for more spacious, typical dwellings with old-fashioned woodwork and built-in buffets. St. Anthony is such a "hot" area that many homes sell privately, through word of mouth, without the assistance of a real-estate agent.

## MERRIAM PARK

Merriam Park, located between Hamline Avenue and the Mississippi River and University and Summit avenues to the north and south, was home to many large Irish families in the early 1900s. Mat Hollinshead, editor of the *Merrian Park Post* newspaper, likens the community to an "urban village that retains a lot of the atmosphere of the Victorian railroad and garden suburb it originally was 100 years ago."

The hilly community also affords a scenic panorama of the Mississippi River. This stable, predominantly middle-class district of single-family homes and apartments

Photo: Richard Marshall, Pioneer Press

*One of several beautiful homes on Summit Avenue.*

has an enviable reputation as one of St. Paul's safest neighborhoods. Homes range from cozy to luxurious and the median value here is $88,350. One real-estate agent says this is where many larger Victorian homes can be found.

### MACALESTER-GROVELAND

The Macalester-Groveland area, home to Macalester College, the University of St. Thomas and the College of St. Catherine, has a quiet, traditional "East Coast" ambience with its housing stock dating back to the 1920s and '30s. This area is bounded by Summit Avenue on the north, Ayd Mill Road on the east, the river on the west and Randolph Avenue on the south. Its safe, stable neighborhoods are within walking distance to movie theaters, markets and the ever-popular Grand Avenue, with its arty boutiques and ethnic restaurants. Houses range from small two- or three-bedroom homes selling for as low as $50,000 on the east end to luxurious $400,000 estates on the Mississippi River. Realtors say homes in the "Mac-Groveland" area have the best resale value in all of St. Paul.

### HIGHLAND PARK

Highland Park, to the southwest, is home to a thriving Jewish community, as well as many non-Jewish residents. A major employer here is the Ford Motor Plant. This mature neighborhood contains quality housing that ranges from small homes to estate-like mansions and distinctive apartment buildings. Most were built in the

1940s and '50s. Amenities include well-maintained neighborhoods, distinctive recreational facilities such as a public golf course, sprawling Highland Park with its spacious swimming pool and new community recreation center, and high-quality schools. Disadvantages include an increasing — but manageable — crime problem.

### COMO AREA

There are many handsome bungalows and two-story homes with quality touches such as built-in buffets and extensive woodwork in the residential areas surrounding lovely Lake Como and Como Park and extending directly eastward to I-35E. While much of the housing stock dates from the 1920s, some homes were built as early as the 1880s. They range from charming bungalows to Queen Anne-style mansions along the southern shore of Lake Como.

### HAMLINE-MIDWAY

South and slightly west of the Como area is the Hamline-Midway district, bounded by University Avenue to the south, Cleveland to the west, Lexington to the east and Burlington Railroad tracks to the north.

Hamline-Midway is a safe area with stable, middle-class neighborhoods, where housing is affordable and of good quality. The majority of homes were built between 1890 and 1940, and some hold such surprises as leaded and stained-glass windows and rich woodwork. Amenities include several parks, a neighborhood recreation center and proximity to both Minneapolis and downtown St. Paul. There's a concentration of Southeast Asian grocery markets and businesses in the eastern part of the Hamline-Midway area, just one of many cultures represented in this neighborhood. This area is also heavily commercial/retail, and there's a growing community of artists who've moved their studios into many of the old converted warehouses here.

### PAYNE PHALEN

The Payne Phalen district, located northeast of downtown St. Paul and west of I-35E, was, for the most part, developed around the same time as Highland Park — from the late 1930s through the '50s. There are some charming neighborhoods here, especially in the area around and north of Maryland Avenue. Housing ranges from ramblers to one-and-a-half stories to larger homes. Amenities include proximity to downtown St. Paul and recreational areas such as Lake Phalen and Keller Golf Course.

### RECLAIMING THE CITY: THE WEST SIDE, DAYTON'S BLUFF AND WEST SEVENTH STREET AREAS

Across the river, just south of downtown, is the West Side (so named because it's on the "west" bank of the river), a vibrant community that prides itself on its cultural diversity. The predominantly Anglo population mingles with a strong Hispanic element (20 percent), ever-growing numbers of Asian Americans, and some African Americans. This cultural stew is seen in the array of ethnic markets that dot the West Side — Mexican, Filipino, Asian-American grocery stores and even a Lebanese-Mexican deli. The community's Cinco de Mayo celebration annually draws thousands of spectators.

Housing is reflective of residents' economic profiles, ranging from rather well-off to stolidly middle class to the poor. There are some real finds here for enterprising individuals: Recently, a four-bedroom Victorian with stained-glass windows sold for $57,000!

Despite its stable families and cultural ties, the West Side has its share of joblessness, poverty and crime, concerns the community is addressing through social agencies and neighborhood groups.

### DAYTON'S BLUFF

The picturesque Dayton's Bluff neighborhood, located on the east bank bluffs of the Mississippi River and east of downtown St. Paul, is another stressed urban area that is undergoing difficult but hopeful transition. Enterprising individuals are moving into its neglected old houses — many dating to the 1880s — and restoring them to their original splendor. While there's no denying the serious problems of crime and poverty that plague the area, Dayton's Bluff residents possess an incredible community spirit and loyalty to this area. Average value of housing is $59,810, and monthly rent averages $366.

### WEST SEVENTH STREET

This historic, "working-class" neighborhood — site of the birthplace of St. Paul — is located southwest of downtown and north of the river. It, too, is undergoing exciting revitalization. West Seventh was settled by immigrants from Germany, Ireland, Poland, Bohemia and Italy, and, generations later, some of their descendants still make their homes in the neighborhood. Homes here, some circa 1880s, are being renovated, putting a fresh face on the community. And real "finds" can be had at very affordable prices.

A highlight of the area is the Irvine Park neighborhood, once St. Paul's finest residential community. Neglected for years, it was rediscovered in the '70s, and many of its elegant homes have been lovingly restored. The centerpiece park is located at Walnut Street and Ryan Avenue.

## The Suburbs

In the wake of World War II, when thousands of Johnnys came marching home again, they and their families set their sights on the new, idyllic suburban Camelots, just beyond the city limits. Ideally suited to the postwar mood of prosperity and family togetherness, these semi-rural havens promised peace and contentment, affordable housing, double-car garages and barbecue grills — far away from the urban madness. What more could one want?

Like every major metropolitan area, the Twin Cities experienced a painful flight to the suburbs in the 1950s and '60s. In 1950, Minneapolis' population numbered 500,000 — today, it ranges around 368,400.

The following is a brief look at these outer-limit Camelots today, their characteristics, charms and faults. We'll begin with the western suburbs.

### LAKE MINNETONKA AREA

Just 12 miles west of Minneapolis is the renowned Lake Minnetonka. With its myriad bays and inlets, Minnetonka possesses the most shoreline of any lake in the state.

Lake Minnetonka's long tradition as a resort and recreation center dates back into the 1800s, when people from throughout the country would vacation on its shores.

Today, Lake Minnetonka is a residence of choice for Minneapolis' movers and shakers, some of whom live in the charming city of Wayzata along the lake's northwestern shore. Others reside in rambling estates in the Lake Minnetonka communities of Orono, Navarre, Excelsior, Deephaven, Minnetrista, Minnetonka Beach, Shorewood, Mound or Tonka Bay.

Lake Minnetonka living offers the best of both worlds, especially in summer. Minneapolis, with its employment and cultural offerings, is just 30 minutes away. And evenings and weekends can be spent in your own private laid-back, sand-in-the-toes world of sailing, boating, lake sunsets and waterfront dining.

Such pleasures have their price — and, unless you're independently wealthy or a fast-track exec, Lake Minnetonka communities may be out of your reach. For example, in

1993 the average home price in Wayzata was $217,993. Occasionally, one may chance upon a real "find" — a modestly priced fixer-upper or older "cabin" situated a few blocks from the water that won't dent the pocketbook.

For renters, there are more options, including attractive waterfront apartment complexes in Wayzata and Excelsior, plus some apartments in private homes.

Both Wayzata, on the lake's north shore, and Excelsior, on its southeast shore, are picturesque cities whose main streets offer lovely vistas of the legendary lake. Both possess a small-town ambience with bustling main streets that have changed little over the past 50 years. Excelsior even has a soda fountain in its local drugstore, not to mention antique shops galore.

For a taste of lake living, stop by Park Tavern in Excelsior on any summer night, choose a table outside on the deck overlooking the lake, and wait for the spectacle to begin. In a short time, boats — big and small — will queue up, ferrying their scantily clad, tanned occupants to choice outside tables for a round of merrymaking.

### THE GREAT SOUTHWEST

The suburbs of Chanhassen, Eden Prairie and Chaska, located along the Minnesota River southwest of Minneapolis, are hot areas of residential growth and economic development. Residents are attracted by the gently rolling landscape, well-planned neighborhoods of upper-bracket housing, plentiful lakes and relative proximity to Minneapolis.

Chaska is home to the Hazeltine National Golf Course (site of the 1991 U.S. Open) and a state-of-the-art, city-owned indoor water park. The average home sale price is $96,853.

Chanhassen claims the Minnesota Landscape Arboretum, a beautiful 500-acre preserve owned by the University of Minnesota, and Chanhassen Dinner Theatres, an award-winning entertainment complex. New upper-bracket developments are sprouting in this rural, lake-studded setting. The average home sale price here is $141,471.

Eden Prairie continues to draw residents with its lovely mix of parks, lakes, creeks and wooded areas amid well-planned upper-bracket neighborhoods. Average home sale price here is $142,317.

As the state's third-largest city and home to Mall of America, the southern suburb of Bloomington is a hopping, happening place these days! Many well-designed neighborhoods of moderate to expensive homes on large, wooded lots dot the rolling landscape of this attractive older suburb. Bloomington's eastern area was developed between 1945 and 1960 and features moderately sized and smaller homes; its western regions are relatively new and still growing. Bloomington's most desirable residential areas border the expansive Hyland Lake Park Reserve, a popular recreational area. Average home sale price here is $112,721.

Just to the north are the prestigious homes and gardens of Edina, "la creme de la creme" of suburbia. Edina offers scenic, winding neighborhoods of upper-bracket housing, plus pockets of moderately priced housing, a first-class school system, plentiful parks and tasteful commercial centers. Average home sale price is $176,086.

### NORTHWEST

As the metro area pops its buttons, outer-edge north and northwestern suburbs such as Maple Grove, Anoka, Plymouth, Coon Rapids and Brooklyn Park experience burgeoning waves of new residents. Maple Grove and Plymouth especially are growing rapidly, with new housing developments sprouting in formerly open fields and woodlands.

Plymouth is bisected by I-494, promoting easy accessibility to other metro communities and businesses. Also within its borders are walking paths, several lakes and handsomely designed parks, such as French Regional Park on Medicine Lake and the swimming beach and park at Parkers Lake. The west-

ern edges of Plymouth are home to exclusive "country manor" estates on sprawling acreage with horse barns and pastures. The Luce Line bike trail begins in Plymouth and continues westward to Winsted. Ridgedale shopping center is close by.

Maple Grove offers a solid mix of single-family homes, townhouses and condos, surrounded by several lakes, parks and biking paths, attracting younger families searching for a rural setting and relatively affordable housing.

Anoka possesses a charming "small-town" atmosphere with a thriving city center, many Victorian homes on well-maintained streets, plus some new homes and apartments. After all, former Miss America Gretchen Carlson and writer Garrison Keillor were once residents, so it must be "above average"!

Coon Rapids, located along the Mississippi River northeast of Brooklyn Park, is also gaining in new residents and industry. Amenities include plentiful parks, such as Coon Rapids Dam Regional Park (site of the annual Carp Festival) and Bunker Hills Park Reserve. Its population (56,493) is youthful; the average age of residents is 28.

Brooklyn Park has grown steadily to become the state's sixth-largest city, and nearly half of its land is still undeveloped. Planners have painstakingly designed neighborhoods with generous room for parks and nature areas. Very attractive executive housing surrounds the recently built Edinburgh USA Golf Course.

Average home sale prices in the above communities are as follows: Plymouth, $134,546; Maple Grove, $106,093; Anoka, $80,708; Brooklyn Park, $88,206; and Coon Rapids, $85,107.

Inner-ring suburban areas offer affordable housing dating from the 1950s and '60s, cultural and age diversity, proximity to the cities and many individual charms. Plus, they're virtually totally developed with schools and utilities already in place, so property taxes aren't unreasonably high.

St. Louis Park, New Hope, Robbinsdale and Crystal to the west and Richfield to the south all contain housing that ranges from rows of standardized post-WWII homes to large, handsome homes in safe, tree-lined neighborhoods to myriad apartment complexes. You'll find a strong sense of community and stability in these fully developed suburbs and many long-standing residents.

Golden Valley to the west has many attractive larger homes in woodsy neighborhoods. Part of Theodore Wirth Park is found in this community.

Not to be forgotten is the western suburb of Hopkins, with its old-fashioned thriving Main Street, quiet tree-lined city neighborhoods of moderate housing and secluded upper-bracket woodland properties. It's almost like a small town that's been plopped right down in the middle of suburbia.

### NORTH BY NORTHEAST

St. Paul has more than its share of upper-bracket, country-club suburbs, especially in the north, notably the private community of North Oaks, as well as parts of Shoreview, White Bear Township, Gem Lake, Mahtomedi, Dellwood Grant Township and the St. Croix River Valley. In these areas of rolling countryside and secluded lakes, property can and does sell for a million dollars or more. Exclusive neighborhoods also are found to the south around Sunfish Lake, as well as parts of Mendota Heights.

North Oaks, a private planned city of 3,516 residents, offers handsome homes on estate-sized lots in a beautiful natural setting. Former Vice President Walter Mondale lived here; retired basketball great Kevin McHale is a current resident.

White Bear Lake also offers a mix of modest, mid-priced homes, as well as expensive homes, and then there's that spectacular lake, which has an intriguing history all its own. Like Minnetonka, it was once a popular summer resort locale.

Closer to St. Paul and more down to earth are the inner-ring suburbs of Roseville, Falcon Heights, Little Canada, Maplewood and North St. Paul, offering solid neighborhoods and a range of affordable housing.

### STILLWATER AND ENVIRONS

Situated on the hills and bluffs overlooking the St. Croix River 20 miles northeast of downtown St. Paul, Stillwater is as pretty as a Victorian picture. The historic rivertown offers a colorful Main Street, rambling, old Victorian homes, a friendly, small-town atmosphere, and easy availability to the Twin Cities. In fact, many Stillwater residents work in the St. Paul area. The area is fully developed, and houses sell rather briskly, many by word of mouth. Average home sale price is $102,679.

### EASTERN AND SOUTHERN SUBURBS

Woodbury, a suburb just east of St. Paul, is growing like corn in July — its population almost doubled between 1980 and 1990, and there's no signs of it slowing. Here you'll find a mainly white-collar, professional community housed in upper-bracket homes ranging anywhere from $125,000 to $250,000 and more. A magnificent natural setting of rolling hills, lakes and woods lends a "country" feel to this suburb.

Cottage Grove, located near the confluence of the Mississippi and St. Croix rivers, is an older suburb that is experiencing renewed popularity, with developers adding new upper-bracket homes to the mix of moderately priced older homes.

West St. Paul, located south of St. Paul's West Side, and South St. Paul, located east of West St. Paul (we know, the directions are screwy!), are inner-ring suburbs with stable neighborhoods and nice, affordable homes. Because they are in Dakota County, rather than Ramsey County, their property taxes are significantly lower. Average home sale prices are: West St. Paul, $94,171; and South St. Paul, $79,890.

Inver Grove Heights to the south offers a full range of housing on large lots and a "country-living" atmosphere. The average home sale price here is $100,024.

Eagan, located directly south of St. Paul, is a booming suburb attracting young families and singles with a mix of modest to upper-bracket housing, duplexes and fourplexes. The median age of residents is 30. The average home sale price is $111,317.

The south suburbs in general, especially Burnsville, Apple Valley and Rosemount, seem to be growing with an influx of young families who are attracted by their new affordable housing, plentiful parks and freeway access.

# Inside
# Real Estate Resources

To the delight of local real estate agents and builders, the Twin Cities really do sell themselves.

Minneapolis and St. Paul's natural beauty, vital economy and highly rated quality of life make them very desirable places to live. Our bustling local real estate market is one indication that the rest of the country is rediscovering us. We're actually becoming a downright trendy destination!

In this chapter, we'll offer some practical information to help you in your search for a new home — be it an apartment or a custom-built house. Included are listings of real estate firms, relocation companies, apartment locators, tenant unions, senior housing resources, builders and mortgage companies.

## Realtors

The local real estate scene is dominated by two giants, Edina Realty and Burnet Realty, both with offices scattered throughout the cities. They are joined by hundreds of other smaller companies who manage to grab a fair share of the market. When seeking out a real estate company to help you in your home search, don't shortchange the smaller firms. What they lack in size, they many times make up for in innovation, experience and good old-fashioned hustle.

Overall, the real estate scene in Minnesota is aboveboard and well-regulated, thanks, in part, to new laws that encourage openness between agents and potential clients — be they buyers or sellers.

The following listing is a representative sampling of real estate firms in the Twin Cities. It is by no means comprehensive. For a more extensive listing, check the Yellow Pages or call the Realtor Associations listed below.

**BURNET REALTY**
*(at least 37 offices)*
*Corporate office*
*7550 France Ave. S., Edina*            844-6400

**CENTURY 21**
*(at least 22 independent offices)*
*Minneapolis office*
*4536 France Ave. S., Edina*            925-3901

**COLDWELL BANKER**
*(about 20 offices)*
*St. Paul office*
*604 Snelling Ave. S., St. Paul*        699-6666

**COLDWELL BANKER JAMBOR**
*604 Snelling Ave. S., St. Paul*        699-6666

## COUNSELOR REALTY
*(six offices)*
*Edina/Bloomington office*
*5810 W. 78th St., Edina*          921-0911

## EDINA REALTY
*(at least 50 offices)*
*Administrative office*
*4015 W. 65th St., Edina*          927-1100

## ERA REAL ESTATE
*(nine independent offices)*
*Minneapolis office*
*2719 E. 42nd St., Minneapolis*     729-7346

## ROGER FAZENDIN REALTORS
*1421 E. Wayzata Blvd., Wayzata* 473-7000

## GRIFFIN REAL ESTATE CO.
*(3 offices)*
*Bloomington office*
*3800 W. 80th St., Bloomington*     893-6300

## RE/MAX REALTY
*(at least 17 independent offices)*
*Minneapolis office*
*3915 Hwy. 7, Minneapolis*          929-7050

## REALTY WORLD
*(at least 7 offices)*
*Northeast office*
*3800 Apache Lane, St. Anthony*     781-7484

To receive more information on the real estate market in the Twin Cities, call one of the following associations:

## MINNEAPOLIS AREA ASSOCIATION OF REALTORS
                                    933-9020

## ST. PAUL AREA ASSOCIATION OF REALTORS
                                    774-5206

## CONSUMER CREDIT COUNSELING SERVICES
*1111 Third Ave. S., Ste. 336*
*Minneapolis*                      349-6953

This agency can counsel consumers before home-purchase or rental decisions are made and help in cases of loan delinquency or financial mismanagement. Charges are based on ability to pay.

## DIVISION OF ENFORCEMENT AND LICENSING
*State Department of Commerce*
*133 E. Seventh St., St. Paul*     296-6694

This office investigates complaints about real estate agents, lenders, building contractors and appraisers. It also provides information on home-owners insurance and tips on buying real estate.

## COMMUNITY ASSOCIATIONS INSTITUTE
*4248 Park Glen Rd.*
*St. Louis Park*                   927-9220

This national, nonprofit organization can provide information on individual condominium, co-op or home-owners associations, plus general information on issues pertinent to community associations.

## BLACK RELOCATION ASSOCIATION
*P.O. Box 582201*
*Minneapolis 55458*                623-4362

This is a business, professional and social relocation service tailored to meet the needs of African Americans new to the Twin Cities. It works with many local corporations, providing a newcomer's connection from a black perspective.

## Relocation Assistance
Buying a home is one of the

Photo: John Doman, Pioneer Press

*A view of downtown St. Paul with the Mississippi River in the foreground.*

# AMERICA'S LARGEST HOME BUILDER

## Building the best of the Twin Cities
## (612) 936-7833

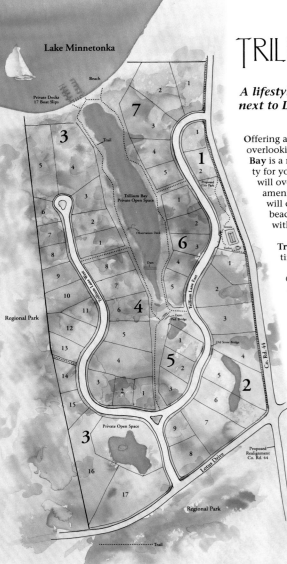

# TRILLIUM BAY

### *A lifestyle dream coming true next to Lake Minnetonka*

Offering a beautiful private enclave overlooking Halstead's Bay, **Trillium Bay** is a new, one-of-a-kind opportunity for your next home. Your home will overlook park-like natural amenities and the whole family will enjoy private trails, a private beach on the Lake and dock space with limited availability.

**Trillium Bay**...the perfect setting for your next home.

*Custom homes from $300,000 Select one of the Twin Cities' premier builders:*
- Bruce Bren Homes 475-0918
- James Bruce Homes 475-3026
- Robert H. Mason Homes 935-3486
- George C. Maurer Construction 894-8904
- Smuckler & Breezee 828-1908

*Homesites from $85,000 to $370,000 by:*
- **The Pemtom Land Company 937-0716**

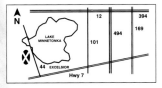

Community plan and maps are artist's conception and subject to change
© 1994 The Pemtom Land Company

# WELCOME HOME

R elocating to a new city is exciting, but it can also be very unsettling, especially for children. Moving into a beautiful new home in a safe and friendly neighborhood can make a lot of difference.

At Lundgren Bros. we've been helping newcomers settle in for a quarter-of-a-century. Our reputation as one of the area's top builders has been hard won and carefully preserved.

You'll find our homes are innovative. They're designed for the way today's families want to live. And our construction is of the highest caliber. We're skilled at working over long distances with our clients. And for those who need to move-in in short order, you'll find we'll often have a home under construction that may be just right.

We carefully site all our homes in naturally-beautiful and environmentally-sensitive neighborhoods. Easy access, nearby shopping and services, plus abundant parks and recreation are always of first priority.

We know you'll discover that the Twin Cities is a wonderful place to live and work, and to call home.

**WELCOME HOME!**

*Please call for more information about Lundgren Bros.' new neighborhoods and homes priced from $180,000 to $800,000*

**LUNDGREN BROS.** CONSTRUCTION INC.

## 612/473-1231

*935 East Wayzata Blvd. • Wayzata, MN 55391*
*Builder Lic. #0001413*

# Nothing Else Compares.

Only Wedgewood offers the advantages of master planned living in Woodbury, the Twin Cities' fastest growing suburb, including:

• Eight of the area's finest builders • Championship 18-hole golf course • Neighborhood parks • Colby Lake recreation area • Miles of hiking and biking trails • Country landscapes • Easy access to both downtowns and the airport • Homes from the $170s, townhomes from the $240s.

*A master planned community by Minnesota Mutual, represented by LCA Marketing, Inc. Sales and Information Center open Monday-Thursday 10-6, Friday-Sunday 1-5, or call 731-4588. Models open daily. From I94, travel south on Woodbury Drive 2-1/2 miles.*

REALTOR®

Equal Housing Opportunity

St Paul  94

Valley Creek Road

494

Woodbury Drive

Bailey Road

WEDGEWOOD™

Designed For Living

A Minnesota Mutual community represented by LCA Marketing, Inc.

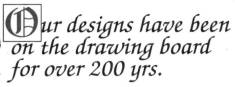 ur designs have been on the drawing board for over 200 yrs.

*Specializing in reproductions of 17th & 18th Century New England homes & furniture, adapted for a 20th Century lifestyle.*

For
Immediate
Information
Call or fax now at:
**612-535-5225**

☐ *Yes! I would like more information about your vintage homes & furnishings.*

Name _____

Address _____

City _____ State _____ Zip _____

(Phone) _____

### Vintage Builders, Inc.

8401 73rd Ave. N.
Suit 90
Minneapolis, MN 55428

---

Name _____

Address _____

City, State, Zip _____

We're moving in: ☐ 1-3 months
☐ 6 months plus

Telephone

( ) _____ Home

( ) _____ Work

Best time to call: _____

# TEMPLE-INLAND MORTGAGE CORPORATION
## Attn: Dominic Silvestri
## 7760 France Ave. S.
## Suite 210
## Minneapolis, MN 55435

most important — and most stressful — milestones of your life.

The process becomes even more challenging if you are relocating across the country instead of merely across town. Transplanted into a totally new city, you may feel like a 20th-century explorer, searching out everything from the right neighborhood school for your child to the nearest hardware store. Depending on your attitude, it's either a grand adventure or a royal pain.

This is where relocation specialists can help. Many of the larger real estate firms have these specialists who, at a moment's notice, can provide prospective newcomers with a plethora of information on schools, churches, newcomers associations, neighborhood housing costs and other concerns.

Relocation departments at many of the larger realty companies can accelerate the sale or purchase of property around the country by plugging into national marketing networks.

Here are come very busy relocation offices in the Twin Cities:

**EDINA REALTY**
*Relocation Department*
1400 S. Hwy. 100, Golden Valley 591-6400

**BURNET REALTY**
*Relocation Services*
7550 France Ave. S., Edina     844-6500

**ROGER FAZENDIN REALTORS**
1421 E. Wayzata Blvd., Wayzata 473-7000

## Apartments

For those in the market for apartments, there are apartment-search companies that do the legwork for you. Here are some helpful resources for apartment hunters.

**APARTMENT SEARCH**
7200 France Ave. S.
Edina     830-0500, (800) 989-8780
This company will help find the

# Builders
# of the
# Twin Cities

## CENTEX HOMES

The strengths Centex Homes has developed — geographic diversity, well-designed homes in excellent locations, thoroughly-trained and experienced management at all levels, and superior service and dedication to our customers — positioned Centex as the nation's number one home builder for the fourth consecutive year.

Each year, Centex's four head architects provide our customers with several hundred new first-time, move-up, and in certain markets, custom home designs. They do this by traveling to each Home Building division and working with the local division management to determine the ideal product for a particular market segment and neighborhood.

A driving force in recent years has been to differentiate Centex Homes from our competition by improving the execution of the entire home building process in the eyes of our customers. The focus of all our efforts is complete customer satisfaction — recommendation of a Centex home to family and friends without reservation.

## PEMTOM BUILDERS

Pemtom was formed in 1963 with the goal of creating neighborhoods sensitive to trees, wetlands, and topography, and to blend this sensitivity to the housing consumers' need for privacy, individuality and value. After developing more than 4,000 homes, lots, and numerous unique neighborhoods. Pemtom's current focus has been to create neighborhoods such as Windfield, Kingston Ridge, St. Edward's Field, Crimson Bay, Green Woods on the Lake, Brynmawr Place and Trillium Bay and to leave building homes to the custom builder. All of these neighborhoods have won acceptance by consumers acquiring home sites in these communities at a rapid rate. It is equally important to insure each home is placed accurately on the site and to work with home designers, builders and consumers in creating an appropriate home on each site. The final result not only provides an outstanding place to live but creates an atmosphere for a long term Real Estate investment.

## BREAM BUILDERS INC.

Bream Builders Inc. creates comfort and elegance as an experienced designer, developer, and builder of quality townhomes, condominiums, and custom single-family dwellings. An old-line family firm with a tradition of excellence, Bream Builders Inc. offers not only extensive experience in development but complete in-house design capabilities as well. Their professional staff can work closely with you in creating the kinds of special living spaces that are a reflection of your individualism, personality, and lifestyle. Custom features and out-of-the-ordinary quality are specialties of Bream Builders Inc.

They offer uncompromising quality and craftsmanship in such custom-design features as gourmet kitchens, solariums, luxury baths, and beautiful fireplaces.

Bream Builders Inc. has specialized in homes of distinction for the past 30 years. For an elegant modern or traditional home, be sure to call on the experts at Bream Builders Inc.

# Builders
# of the
# Twin Cities

## PULTE HOMES OF MINNESOTA

Since 1950, the Pulte Home Corporation has maintained its founding philosophy of giving the customer "the most house for the money." This philosophy, combined with a commitment to quality, affordability and design, along with the best features in the most preferred locations, has earned Pulte Homes the reputation of one of the nation's largest and most quality-driven home builders.

A Focus on Quality Living

Ranked by the Builders Association of Minnesota as one of the top five Twin Cities builders in 1993, and a member of the American Society for Quality Control, Pulte Homes of Minnesota maintains a focus toward bringing quality to a broad range of home buyers. It is Pulte Homes of Minnesota's belief that the quality of your home is the most important factor in affecting the quality of your life. That's why every Pulte home is equipped with the most desirable features, modern conveniences and fine workmanship to fit the needs and lifestyles of today's home buyers. Club, Court and Single Family homes range in price from the mid $60's to the mid $200's. Pulte provides a level of luxury you would expect in homes costing much more.

Buying With Confidence

When you choose a Pulte Home, you can buy with confidence, knowing your purchase is backed by one of the top companies in the United States. With divisions from coast to coast, Pulte's geo-graphic diversification provides added stability. This buying power puts more strength and value into every home which is built. And this reputation for excellence guarantees that only the best professionals and finest materials in the industry have gone into your new home.

## PRATT HOMES

Home is a place where family traditions are born, and where these traditions make memories to last a lifetime. Your home is much more than boards and nails. It is an expression of your taste, a showcase of your self-image . . . a reflection of the best you have hoped for.

Since the founding of Pratt Homes in 1973, Len and Lowell Pratt have developed a business philosophy that reflects an understanding of these ideals. This understanding is the common thread you will find throughout the Pratt Homes organization. Care, concern and attention to detail have established Pratt's reputation for excellence in homebuilding.

From the first meeting with your builder representative, through the building process and Pratt's follow-up customer service program, we are committed to your satisfaction. The building industry and local communities have recognized this dedication to excellence for both design and construction. We've built our reputation over time . . . home by home, family by family, dream by dream. At Pratt Homes, we know you have the final word on our success.

# Builders
# of the
# Twin Cities

## LUNDGREN BROS. CONSTRUCTION INC.

Lundgren Bros. is a Twin Cities' land development and homebuilding company with a 25-year track record of excellence in creating residential neighborhoods, designing and building homes, and serving over 2,000 homebuyers.

Our customers, many of whom are buying their second and third Lundgren Bros.' home, like the synergy of Lundgren Bros. in the role of both developer and homebuilder. Over the years our homes have been advertised and resold as Lundgren Bros. homes because our name has become a symbol of quality and long-term value. This synergy between a new home and its community is what sets us apart from most other homebuilders in the Twin Cities.

Our team effort to find land, design, and develop neighborhoods means that we rely on financial resources beyond those of the average homebuilder. This stability provides us the staying power which is symbolized by our 25 years in business. Rather than resting on our laurels we are continuously improving our homes, neighborhoods, and delivery systems to better serve our customers, many of whom are moving from out of town to begin a new life in Minnesota.

## VINTAGE BUILDERS INC.

Don and Yvonne of Vintage Builders Inc. like to build homes that "reach out and give you a big hug," and that they do. They specialize in reproductions of 17th and 18th century New England homes, tailored for a 20th century lifestyle.

"We collected out first antique 27 years ago," says Yvonne, "and after a while, we just naturally progressed into housing. Over the years, we've taken many trips together to New England, collecting and taking classes on antiques and Early American housing."

All of their homes include many authentic items that truly make these homes unique. "We also discovered that many of those small things, you can't get here in the Midwest." As a result, "we started establishing our network of suppliers from all over the world."

The Kutzes have found many people share their interest in authentic reproductions. "Lots of people like to collect antiques," says Don, "and when they put that interest into a home, they're automatically the kind of people we'll end up building for."

# Builders
# of the
# Twin Cities

## WEDGEWOOD

The Wedgewood community in Woodbury is a 1500-acre planned community made up of neighborhoods which offer amenities and price ranges to meet a variety of lifestyles. This allows for consistent high quality. Through the master plan and architectural review Wedgewood's developer attempts to retain and enhance the community's value. Architectural review, currently provided by the developer, will be assumed in the future by the Wedgewood homeowners' association.

This type of community provides many recreational and scenic amenities. Wedgewood's championship golf course, city parks and trails, acres of open space and lakeside neighborhoods offer residents year-round recreational opportunities and a backdrop of lasting beauty for their distinctive homes.

Quality builders are chosen by the developer to maintain Wedgewood's strict quality standards. A variety of builders ensures a variety of design choices and competitive pricing. The Wedgewood sales staff can provide more information about individual builders and the neighborhoods in which they build.

## LANDICO INC.

Our design philosophy is based on the involvement of the homeowner in the planning process, giving careful consideration to the personality and lifestyle of our clients. Landico's expertise and professionalism can transform your ideas and dreams into an original and exciting home that is perfect for the location. We're proud of the fact that our homes reflect the individual tastes, energies and lifestyles of our clients.

Building simple elegance . . . deliciously comfortable. Custom crafted for your family on the site of your choice. It's a basic premise we believe in . . . designing and building homes that express your lifestyle, your originality! Blending the space with a unique use of sunlight, filtered through elegant glasswork, warming the natural stones, and fine hardwoods.

With quality workmanship and design unparalleled. Involving you in every step of the process, design through construction. Whether you're looking for the strong details in a contemporary home or the gracious spaces and finite detail in a traditional home, we will create it for you. Simple elegance . . . true comfort.

right apartment for you. There are 11 branch offices in the Twin Cities. No fees are charged.

### APARTMENT RENTER'S CHOICE
*1935 W. County Rd. B21, Roseville 636-5414*
This company has three offices in the Twin Cities.

### APARTMENT RENTAL SERVICES
*8100 Penn Ave. S., Bloomington 884-1225*
This firm specializes in the rental of privately owned townhouses and condos.

The following free apartment directories are available at grocery stores, libraries and shopping centers throughout the Twin Cities: *Apartment Living Guide*, 884-2980, and *For Rent* magazine, 830-0515.

## Tenants Unions

These organizations help resolve disputes between landlords and tenants. Volunteers offer advice and make referrals to legal services, housing or reconciliation courts. Membership fees are minimal, ranging from $10 to $15 a year. A *Tenants Rights Handbook* is available for $5.35 ($6.85 by mail) from either the Minneapolis or St. Paul tenants union or from the Minnesota Public Interest Research Group (MPIRG), 2512 S.E. Delaware Street, Minneapolis 55414.

### MINNEAPOLIS TENANTS UNION
*1513 E. Franklin Ave.*
*Minneapolis 871-7485*
This is also known as the Minnesota Tenants Union. If you're in desperate need of a quick answer,

you can call its pay-per-call hotline number, (612) 976-8888.

### ST. PAUL TENANTS UNION
*500 Laurel Ave., St. Paul 221-0501*
This organization answers tenants' inquiries from 9 AM to 5 PM weekdays.

### ST. PAUL HOUSING
### INFORMATION OFFICE
*21 W. Fourth St., St. Paul 266-6000*
This office provides free information on all sorts of housing issues — from mortgage programs to rehabilitation loans.

### MINNESOTA
### MULTI-HOUSING ASSOCIATION
*4250 Park Glen Rd.*
*St. Louis Park 927-8602*
This nonprofit organization offers information and assistance to both landlords and tenants. Its free hotline number is 858-8222 and operates between 2 and 5 PM Monday through Friday.

## Builders

The Minneapolis and St. Paul greater metropolitan area is one of the largest, most active home-building communities in the nation.

There are a whopping 1,200 members in the Builders Association of the Twin Cities, with 600 members comprising 75 percent of the local building marketplace. To help you begin your search for the builder that will be a good match for you, we've listed some Twin Cities home-construction companies below. Here, too, are a few guidelines on how to select a good builder.

• Ask friends or acquaintances who've recently built their own homes for recommendations.

• Drive by a builder's construction site. If the work area is orderly and neat, that's one indication of a good builder.

• Inspect one of the builder's model homes. Are ceramic tiles evenly spaced? Does the wood trim along floors, windows and doors fit snugly against the walls? Are the floors quiet?

• Call the Builders Association of the Twin Cities and ask whether your prospective builder is licensed or has been the subject of any consumer complaints.

• Ask builders for references and make follow-up calls.

Each fall, the Builders Association sponsors a new-home showcase called the Parade of Homes. More than 500 new homes in a variety of price ranges are showcased during this two-week event. Parade of Homes directories are distributed in the *Star Tribune* and the *St. Paul Pioneer Press* newspapers.

If you haven't been bitten by the remodeling bug yet, you will be once you've visited International Market Square in Minneapolis. Located in the Warehouse District at the corner of Glendale and Lynwood avenues, the IMS is a showplace of building products and home furnishings. Housed in the historic Munsingwear — yep, we're talking underwear, folks — Building, the IMS is filled with attractive displays of furniture and appliances from traditional to ultramodern. The building is open to the general public, but purchases must be made through an interior designer.

**BREAM BUILDERS INC.**
*961 Grand Ave., St. Paul*       298-1044

**CENTREX HOMES**
*12400 Whitewater Dr., Suite 120
Minnetonka*       936-7833

*A home in the Prospect Park neighborhood of Minneapolis.*

### CHARLES CUDD CO.
*1802 Wooddale Dr., Woodbury   731-3153*

### COUNTRY HOME BUILDERS
*800 Ivy Lane, Eagan             452-0336*

### GOOD VALUE HOMES
*9445 East River Rd.*
*Coon Rapids                   780-HOME*

### HANS HAGEN HOMES
*941 N.E. Hillwind Rd., Fridley   572-9455*

### LANDICO
*7835 Telegraph Rd.*
*Bloomington                   829-0555*

### LUNDGREN BROS. CONSTRUCTION INC.
*935 E. Wayzata Blvd., Wayzata   473-1231*

### ORRIN THOMPSON HOMES
*8421 Wayzata Blvd.*
*Golden Valley                 544-7333*

### PEMTOM LAND CO.
*14180 Hwy. 5, Eden Prairie   937-0716*

### PRATT HOMES
*4225 White Bear Pkwy., Suite 100*
*Vadnais Heights               429-8032*

### PULTE HOMES CORP.
*1355 Mendota Heights Rd., #300*
*Mendota Heights               452-5200*

### ROTTLUND HOMES
*2681 Long Lake Rd., Roseville   638-0500*

### SHAMROCK BUILDERS INC.
*3200 N.W. Main St., Coon Rapids   421-3500*

**TOWN & COUNTRY HOMES**
*6800 France Ave. S., Edina* 925-3899

**VINTAGE BUILDERS**
*8401 73rd Ave. N., Suite 90*
*Minneapolis* 535-5225

**WEDGEWOOD CUSTOM HOMES**
*3040 Woodbury Dr., Woodbury* 731-4588

For more information on building, contact the associations:

**BUILDERS ASSOCIATION OF MINNESOTA**
646-7959

**BUILDERS ASSOCIATION OF THE TWIN CITIES**
851-9242

**BUILDING CODE DIVISION**
*State Administration Department*
*Metro Square Building*
*St. Paul* 296-4639

This division establishes the State Building Code and can provide free information on all types of building codes.

## Mortgage Companies

Once you find that perfect lot or home, you'll need to arrange financing. Here are some companies with good local reputations to get you started on your search for the mortgage lender that best suits your needs.

**CHEMICAL MORTGAGE**
4105 Lexington Ave. N.
Arden Hills                    482-1991

**EASTERN HEIGHTS STATE BANK**
7525 Currell Blvd., Woodbury    736-9959

**FIRSTAR MORTGAGE**
3900 Sibley Memorial Hwy.
Eagan                          454-3301

**FLEET MORTGAGE**
7760 France Ave. S., Edina     921-0330

**HOMESTEAD MORTGAGE CORP.**
4105 Lexington Ave. N.
Arden Hills                    490-5555

**MARQUETTE MORTGAGE**
55 E. Fifth St., St. Paul      291-2288

**TEMPLE-INLAND**
1811 Weir Dr., Woodbury        730-7950

## Seniors Housing

There are many retirement apartment complexes in the Twin Cities offering such assisted-living amenities as meal service, on-site nursing services, housekeeping and activity programs. Some may be listed with the previously mentioned apartment-referral firms. Here are other helpful resources.

**EBENEZER SOCIETY**
15 locations                   879-2200

**EDINA PARK PLAZA**
3330 Edinborough Way, Edina    831-4084

**FRIENDSHIP VILLAGE**
8100 Highwood Dr., Bloomington 831-7500

**REMBRANDT RETIREMENT COMMUNITY**
3434 Heritage Dr., Edina       920-9145

**ROSEPOINTE**
2555 Hamline Ave. N., Roseville 639-1000

**WALKER METHODIST**
13 locations
Call ElderLine for information  827-8310

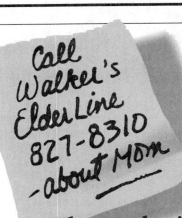

Other helpful groups include:

### SENIOR RESOURCES INC.

2021 Hennepin Ave. E.
Minneapolis                    331-4063

This organization can provide information on senior housing, volunteer programs, transportation services and other issues.

### MINNESOTA SENIOR FEDERATION

1885 University Ave. W.
St. Paul                       645-0261

This advocacy organization also provides information on retirement living.

# *Inside*
# Schools and Child Care

Minnesota is justifiably proud of its public school system. The state has the highest commencement rate — 91 percent — in the nation. And a whopping 90 percent of Minnesota's high-school graduates go on to receive some form of post-secondary education.

The North Star State has a long tradition of academic excellence, from preschool through college, in both the public and private sectors. This is especially true in the greater Twin Cities, where per-pupil funding is, on average, higher than it is in other areas of the state and the nation.

Although Minneapolis and St. Paul proper have their share of big city problems, their public schools are among the nation's best urban schools. In addition to traditional neighborhood schools, both districts have a range of magnet schools offering specialized study areas along with the basics. Such programs promote desegregation by attracting students from diverse neighborhoods. Both city school districts pride themselves in their solid academics and allow motivated students the option of taking university-level courses while attending high school.

"Choice" is the keyword in Min-nesota's innovative open-enrollment program, which has garnered national attention. The open-enrollment policy allows students in kindergarten through 12th grade to apply to attend any public school district in the state. The district to which the student is applying may approve or reject the application, based on available space. In Minneapolis and St. Paul, students also must receive permission from their home districts to leave, and such permission may be denied if the departure would harm desegregation.

Of course, it's always best for parents and students to visit several districts personally before making any enrollment decisions. For more information on open enrollment, call the Enrollment Options Hotline at (800) 657-3990 or, in the Twin Cities, 296-1261.

Minnesota also is in the process of adopting new graduation standards to ensure that every high-school graduate possesses the knowledge and skills necessary to succeed in the global economy.

Another innovative program is the above-mentioned "post-secondary option," a program that allows students to take college courses while still in high school. This gives them a valuable head start on their higher education.

In the area of special needs, Minnesota schools offer students with disabilities a full range of services to create the least-restrictive learning environment. For more information on these services, contact local school districts or call the state Department of Education at 297-2843. Also, virtually all school districts offer enrichment programs for the gifted and talented.

In all, the greater Twin Cities are home to 48 independent public-school districts offering K through 12 education and more than 250 private elementary and secondary schools. The following is an overview of public and private K through 12 educational offerings in the Twin Cities. Space limitations prohibit listing *all* public and private schools. A great resource for more complete information is *Schoolhouse Magazine*, an annual directory of Twin Cities public and private schools. Here's vital information on this valuable publication:

*Schoolhouse Magazine*, ($7.95 a copy), Advertising Sales Inc., 35 W. Water Street, Suite 201, St. Paul, Minnesota 55107, 227-1519.

Also, recognizing the vital importance of early childhood education and quality child care, we've also included important information for parents of preschoolers. You'll find it at the end of this chapter.

# Public Schools

## St. Paul Public Schools
*360 Colborne St., St. Paul    293-5208*

There are 46 elementary schools, five middle schools (grades 6 through 8), three junior highs (grades 7 and 8), five high schools (grades 9 through 12), one secondary complex (grades 7 through 12), three alternative secondary schools, a K through 12 open school and a technical college within the St. Paul Independent School District.

Student population numbers around 39,000; of that, 49 percent are students of color, primarily Asian Americans (22 percent), African Americans (19 percent) and Hispanics (6 percent).

St. Paul offers 24 magnet schools at the elementary level and 15 specialty schools at the secondary level, in addition to traditional neighborhood schools. While all St. Paul schools offer the basic subjects, the magnets and specialty schools have special emphases in certain areas. One of St. Paul's most unusual is the American Indian Magnet School, which focuses on the history and culture of the American Indian, especially the Ojibwa, Lakota and Winnebago tribes, and stresses such values as racial harmony, environmentalism and cooperation rather than competition.

Another is the Jackson Preparatory Magnet School, emphasizing strong reading, math, computer and thinking skills. Other magnets concentrate on the environment, outcome-based education,

Spanish and other languages, gifted programming, science, math and technology, humanities and creative arts. Students also have an option to attend neighborhood schools, which, in some cases, may also be magnets.

St. Paul secondary schools also vary in format and subject focus. Students may choose from a number of specialty options, including media/communications, business/ math/science, graphic communications (printing), performing arts, Chinese language and the International Baccalaureate program. The latter is a rigorous two-year, pre-university program for motivated students.

Overall, the district promotes a "High Five" set of goals: higher readiness, higher achievement, higher graduation rate, higher parent participation and higher adult literacy. For information on the various school options, call the Student Placement Center at 293-5413.

### MINNEAPOLIS PUBLIC SCHOOLS
*807 N.E. Broadway, Minneapolis 627-2929*

In 1993, Minneapolis Public School District took a bold step and selected as its superintendent Peter Hutchinson, the head of a management consulting firm with virtually no formal training in education. It's just one example of the district's no-holds-barred approach to education.

There are 57 elementary school programs, seven middle schools (grades 6 through 8) and seven senior highs, serving a total of 44,500 students, in the Minneapolis School District. Class size is limited as follows: 19 in grades K through 2, 25 in grades 3 through 8, and 26 in grades 9 through 12.

At the elementary level, parents and students are offered a plethora of educational alternatives, ranging from the traditional classrooms to "continuous-progress" programs (ungraded multi-age classrooms with team teachers) to Montessori-style schools. There also are several learning centers focusing on specific curriculum themes: for example, international and fine arts; math, science and technology; urban/environmental; Spanish immersion; American Indian immersion; and French immersion. Ninety-three percent of students applying for specific programs receive their first choice.

Middle schools offer such innovations as team teaching and an interdisciplinary approach. Students also may specialize in areas such as urban/environmental; math, science and technology; and a pre-International Baccalaureate. All seven high schools offer the traditional curriculum plus one or more magnet programs, such as American Indian, arts and communication, automotive, aviation and aerospace, health careers/medical, and international studies.

High-schoolers may choose from among eight foreign languages, including Chinese, Japanese, Latin, Ojibwa and Russian.

### ANOKA-HENNEPIN PUBLIC SCHOOLS
*11299 N.W. Hanson Blvd.*
*Coon Rapids*               422-5521

This large north-suburban district serves a student population of about 36,500, with 27 elementary schools, six middle schools, four high schools, an alternative secondary program and a technical college. The district encompasses all or parts of Andover, Anoka, Blaine, Brooklyn Center, Brooklyn Park, Burns Township, Champlin, Coon Rapids, Dayton, Frid-

ley, Ham Lake, Oak Grove and Ramsey.

The elementary level is characterized by self-contained classrooms with limited team teaching. A strong writing program is emphasized in all grades. (After all, radio personality/writer Garrison Keillor is a graduate of the Anoka school system.)

The district is proud of its strong emphasis on basic skills, while offering a wide choice in elective subjects. Language choices include Spanish, French and German, beginning in seventh grade. It has received state recognition for its discipline-based elementary art program.

### ARTS HIGH SCHOOL OF MINNESOTA
*6125 Olson Memorial Hwy.*
*Golden Valley*             591-4700

The Arts High School, established in 1989, is a tuition-free, statewide public high school for 11th- and 12th-graders who are selected through a competitive application and review process. Enrollment numbers 250. Arts offerings include dance, literary arts, media, music, theater and visual arts. These are taught in addition to a full range of academics, and special emphasis is placed on creative and analytical thinking, problem-solving and decision-making. Two-thirds of students live on campus in dormitories.

### BLOOMINGTON PUBLIC SCHOOLS
*8900 Portland Ave. S.*
*Bloomington*              885-8454

This sprawling southern suburban district boasts nine elementary schools (K through 4), an intermediate school (5 through 6), Hillcrest Community School (an elective K through 6 school with multi-age instruction), a junior high, a Bravo school (an alternative for grades 7 and 8), and two senior highs. Enrollment is around 11,500.

While the elementary level emphasizes self-contained classrooms and team teaching, intermediate-level students are clustered in groups of about 160, working with teams of six teachers. The alternative programs — Hillcrest and Bravo — feature small groups, interdisciplinary study and multi-age grouping.

At the senior-high level, French, German, Japanese, Latin, Russian and Spanish are taught. Computers are used in all subject areas, and all schools have computer labs.

Three Bloomington schools have been named National Schools of Excellence by the U.S. Department of Education. The district also was recently recognized by an Ohio school-selection consulting firm for offering a "parent-pleasing" curriculum.

### BROOKLYN CENTER PUBLIC SCHOOLS
*6500 Humboldt Ave. N.*
*Brooklyn Center*　　　　*561-2120*

This district, comprising 2.8 square miles of Brooklyn Center and surrounding areas, serves 1,728 students with an elementary school and one high school. The high school (grades 7 through 12) offers four years of French and Spanish with independent learning enhanced by a language lab.

The elementary school has two computer labs; the high school offers four. A College in the Schools program offers advanced courses in writing and modern fiction. The staff-student ratio at the elementary level is 1 to 19.

### BURNSVILLE-EAGAN-SAVAGE PUBLIC SCHOOLS
*100 River Ridge Ct., Burnsville　　895-7212*

This district serves 10,500 students in Burnsville, Eagan, Savage, Apple Valley and Shakopee with nine elementary schools, two junior highs, a traditional and an alternative senior high. The district boasts a strong, wide-ranging curriculum, including French, German, Spanish, Latin and Russian, plus a highly-lauded computer-literacy program. Its elementary computer program has been replicated worldwide. Apple Computers has named the district a "Classroom of Tomorrow" consulting site.

### CHASKA PUBLIC SCHOOLS
*110600 Village Rd., Chaska　　368-3607*

With a student population of 5,350 and growing fast, this district in the burgeoning southwestern suburbs serves Chanhassen, Carver, Chaska, East Union and Victoria with an early childhood center, four elementary schools, a middle school (grades 6 through 8) and a high school. An additional elementary school will open in the fall of 1995, and another high school will open in the fall of 1996.

Basic skills are stressed at the elementary level, and in the middle schools, these skills are reinforced in a supportive setting where students meet daily with advisors. The high school offers more than 250 courses in 14 departments. In 1993 Chaska placed second in the nation in the High School Quiz Bowl, and, over the last decade, its debate team has competed seven times at the national level.

### COLUMBIA HEIGHTS PUBLIC SCHOOLS
*1400 49th Ave. N.E.*
*Columbia Heights*          574-650

This district serves more than 3,000 students in Columbia Heights, southern Fridley and Hilltop with three elementary schools, a middle school (grades 6 through 8) and a high school. A variety of teaching methods — team teaching, multi-age classrooms and self-contained classes — is used in the elementary grades. Four years of French, German and Spanish are offered in high school. Computers are used throughout all grades, and a fully equipped TV studio allows students to explore the world of broadcasting.

### EDEN PRAIRIE PUBLIC SCHOOLS
*8100 School Rd., Eden Prairie*      937-3648

This district, located in the upscale southwestern suburb by the same name, serves 7,500 students with a kindergarten center, four elementary schools (grades 1 through 4), an intermediate school (grades 5 and 6), middle school (grades 7 and 8), and a high school.

Foreign-language instruction is offered on an exploratory basis in the intermediate school, and five years of French, German and Spanish are offered in the higher grades. Additional courses in Chinese, Japanese and Russian are available via interactive cable TV. Computer literacy is stressed at all levels.

The intermediate school groups children into "neighborhood clusters," allowing them to circulate among small groupings of classrooms. In the middle school, students are grouped into eight teams of approximately 150 students each. The high school was recently remodeled and expanded to include a new football/track stadium. Typically, 88 percent of graduates go on to college or technical school.

### EDINA PUBLIC SCHOOLS
*5701 Normandale Rd., Edina*      920-2980

This district, located in an affluent suburb just south of Minneapolis, boasts a long tradition of academic excellence. It serves 5,500 students with a kindergarten center, five elementary schools (grades 1 through 5), two middle schools (grades 6 through 9) and a senior high.

Its middle and high schools have received excellence awards from the U.S. Department of Education. The high school especially has been named among the nation's top schools in such magazines as *Money*, *People*, *Parade* and *Town and Country*.

A French-immersion program is available in the elementary grades and an array of languages — German, French, Latin, Spanish, Russian, Japanese and Chinese — is offered in high school.

The high school has been recognized for its literary magazine, choir, concert band and athletics.

# We don't teach kids what to think. We teach them how.

Mounds Park kids don't just memorize facts; they learn to think for themselves. To find out more about a fully accredited college preparatory school (K-12) that cares about kids, call (612) 777-2555.

**Mounds Park Academy**

### FRIDLEY PUBLIC SCHOOLS
*6000 N.E. West Moore Lake Dr.*
*Fridley* 571-6000

With two elementary schools (K through 5), a middle school (grades 6 through 8) and a high school, the Fridley district, north of Minneapolis, serves a student population of around 2,500. One of its elementary schools and its middle school have been named National Schools of Excellence by the U.S. Department of Education. Fridley High School was a recent finalist for the honor.

In addition to offering an extensive college-preparatory curriculum, Fridley High School also boasts of a strong vocational education program, including state-of-the-art technology and a greenhouse.

### HOPKINS PUBLIC SCHOOLS
*1001 Hwy. 7, Hopkins* 933-9107

Serving a student enrollment of about 7,700 in Hopkins and Minnetonka, this west-suburban district

has seven elementary schools, two junior highs and a senior high. French, German and Spanish are taught to students in grades 4 through 6; in high school, the choices expand to include Chinese, Japanese and Russian. The high school also offers accelerated college-level courses.

The high school and middle schools have been named National Schools of Excellence, and the district has been designated a National Technology Lighthouse.

### INVER GROVE HEIGHTS PUBLIC SCHOOLS
*9875 Inver Grove Tr.*
*Inver Grove Heights* 457-7210

This district, located in a southeastern suburb of St. Paul, serves 4,000 students with five elementary schools, a middle school and a senior high.

With its classes among the smallest in the Twin Cities, the IGH elementary schools feature self-contained classrooms with an emphasis on individualized learning. In the middle school, interdisciplinary classes merge social studies, English, math and science. An innovative program, Quest, is used in the seventh grade to help build student self-esteem and decision-making skills.

All schools boast computer labs, and computer literacy is a high priority.

### MAHTOMEDI PUBLIC SCHOOLS
*1620 Mahtomedi Ave.*
*Mahtomedi*            426-3224

Serving 2,500 students in the northeastern suburbs of St. Paul, this district has two elementary schools, a middle school and a senior high.

At the elementary level, whole language, mathematics, technology and critical thinking skills are emphasized. Following the Carnegie Commission Report on Middle Level Education, the middle school incorporates daily advisor sessions, team teaching, flexible scheduling and interdisciplinary units. A broad academic curriculum and extensive extracurricular opportunities are offered at the high-school level.

Mahtomedi stresses "individual attention with a world view."

### MINNETONKA PUBLIC SCHOOLS
*261 School Ave., Excelsior*       470-3406

This award-winning district in the western suburbs serves 6,900 students with six elementary schools (K through 5), two middle schools (grades 6 through 8), and a high school.

Elementary schools emphasize basic skills, including a fourth "R": responsibility. The elementary schools recently introduced a world-language program, offering two 30-minute weekly classes in French, Spanish or German (depending on the school). The high school is a National School of Excellence.

### MOUNDS VIEW PUBLIC SCHOOLS
*2959 Hamline Ave., Roseville*       636-3650

There are eight elementary schools (K through 5), three middle schools (grades 6 through 8), two traditional senior highs and two alternative senior highs, all serving a student population of 12,000, in this suburban district north of St. Paul.

The district stresses site-based management with each of its schools choosing its own organizational structure and curriculum teaching methods. Parents are active participants in school advisory committees.

Technology is a high priority in Mounds View, whose schools have interactive cable TV and computer labs.

The secondary schools offer advanced-placement classes and College in the Schools courses. Students perform above national averages in standardized tests.

### NORTH ST. PAUL-MAPLEWOOD-OAKDALE PUBLIC SCHOOLS
*2055 Larpenteur Ave. E.*
*Maplewood*            770-4600

Schools in this district include two kindergarten centers, nine elementary schools (K through 5), two middle schools (grades 6 through 8), and two high schools — serving a total enrollment of 10,200 students.

This district pioneered the concept of "outcome-based education," requiring that all of its students meet a certain level of competency in the basics.

Foreign languages offered at the secondary level include: French, German, Russian and Spanish. In addition to a strong college-prep curriculum, secondary students are also offered a vocational education program and an opportunity to attend a nearby technical college.

### ORONO PUBLIC SCHOOLS
*685 N. Old Crystal Bay Rd., Orono 449-8300*

Serving 2,500 students in the western communities of Independence, Maple Plain, Medina, Long Lake, Orono and Minnetonka Beach, this district has a primary school (early childhood, K and 1), an elementary school (grades 2 through 4), a middle school (grades 5 through 8), and a high school.

At the elementary level, self-contained and multi-age classrooms are educational options. Foreign languages include Spanish, German and Japanese (the latter offered via TV).

Computer-literacy is stressed at all grade levels, and Orono students have pioneered keyboarding units that are replicated around the country.

### OSSEO PUBLIC SCHOOLS
*11200 93rd Ave. N., Maple Grove 425-4131*

The fifth-largest school district in the state, Osseo serves 21,000 students in the growing northwestern suburbs. The district has 20 elementary schools, four junior highs and two senior highs. A third high school will open in 1996, and two present elementary schools will be relocated to new buildings in the near future.

Osseo's Cedar Island School has been named a National School of Excellence. And Northview Junior High is a National Drug-Free School. Osseo is a solid contender in the Odyssey of the Mind competition, placing in the Top 10 in international competition.

### RICHFIELD PUBLIC SCHOOLS
*7001 Harriet Ave. S., Richfield     861-8244*

Four elementary schools, a junior high and a senior high serve a student population of 4,400 in the Richfield district, one of six districts in the nation to participate in the Quality Districts Project of the National Center for Outcome-Based Education.

Reinforcement in basic skills is stressed in the elementary grades. Environmental study is enhanced by frequent use of the nearby city nature center. Also, sixth-graders spend a week at an environmental camp in northern Minnesota.

Computer literacy begins in kindergarten and is reinforced throughout all grades. Other highlights of the district include strong journalism and writing programs in the senior high and extensive interscholastic athletic programs.

### ROBBINSDALE PUBLIC SCHOOLS
*4148 Winnetka Ave. N.*
*New Hope                    533-2781*

With 12 elementary schools,

*Students in St. Paul's Walkabout Summer School Program get out of the classroom to combine learning with community service.*

four middle schools, two high schools and an alternative high school, Robbinsdale serves a student population of 14,000 in the northwestern inner-ring suburbs. Linda Powell, Minnesota state commissioner of education, is a former Robbinsdale principal.

Strengths of this district include a commitment to outcome-based education, a belief that every child can succeed, and innovative teaching methods such as language immersion and continuous progress/applied skills program.

The middle schools offer adviser relationships and interdisciplinary learning teams. One middle school is devoted to technology and its uses in all subject areas. The high school offers extensive courses, including Japanese.

Three district schools have been named National Schools of Excellence.

### ROSEMOUNT-APPLE VALLEY-EAGAN PUBLIC SCHOOLS
*14445 Diamond Path, Rosemount 423-7775*

This sprawling southern district serves 23,000 students in 17 elementary schools, five middle schools, three high schools and an alternative secondary program.

Each school has a computer lab with extensive instruction in technology. Foreign languages include Spanish, French, German, Russian and Japanese.

The district prides itself on a comprehensive curriculum, committed teachers and a supportive community. Two of its high schools and one middle school have been named National Schools of Excellence. Three schools have received awards for excellence in the arts.

## ROSEVILLE PUBLIC SCHOOLS

*1251 W. County Rd. B2, Roseville 635-1600*

Seven elementary schools, a middle school and a senior high serve 6,500 students in the Roseville district, which prides itself on its grass-roots community involvement and cooperative-learning methods.

The middle school groups students into "houses," small comfortable learning units. The high school offers a strong college prep and vocational education programs.

## ST. ANTHONY-NEW BRIGHTON PUBLIC SCHOOLS

*3303 33rd Ave. N.E., St. Anthony 782-1000*

With 1,050 students, this district is one of the area's smallest, a factor that enhances individualized learning and teacher-student rapport. The district has one elementary school, a middle school (grades 6 through 8) and a high school.

A unique feature at the elementary level is the extended-day program on certain weekdays and Saturdays, offering more learning opportunities for students and parents. The high school offers four years of French and Spanish.

The district boasts strong community involvement, high learner expectations and an emphasis on emotional growth as well as academic learning.

## ST. LOUIS PARK PUBLIC SCHOOLS

*6425 W. 33rd St., St. Louis Park 928-6064*

This district, located in the inner-ring western suburb of St. Louis Park, has four elementary schools (two K through 3, two 3 through 6), a junior high (grades 7 through 8) and a senior high, all serving a student population of more than 4,000.

In 1993, the district jumped aboard the information superhighway with a state-of-the-art telecommunications program that linked its schools to a worldwide network. St. Louis Park has recently remodeled its school libraries to incorporate the latest video and computer equipment.

In addition to stressing the basics, the district strives to help students develop critical thinking and research skills and a familiarity with a broad range of technology. Highlights at the elementary level include multi-age classroom alternatives, whole language and a new foreign language (French and Spanish) program.

St. Louis Park alumni include *New York Times* journalist Thomas Friedman and Hollywood filmmakers Ethan and Joel Coen (*Raising Arizona, Miller's Crossing, The Hudsucker Proxy*).

All of St. Louis Park's schools have been named National Schools of Excellence by the U.S. Department of Education.

## SOUTH ST. PAUL PUBLIC SCHOOLS

*700 N. Second St., South St. Paul 457-9400*

With a student population of 3,500, South St. Paul district has two elementary schools and a high school.

At the elementary level, options include student groupings, team teaching and cooperative learning. The district places special emphasis on developing writing skills. French, German, Spanish and Russian are offered, and the district participates in the International Baccalaureate program.

## SOUTH WASHINGTON COUNTY SCHOOLS

*8040 S. 80th St., Cottage Grove  458-4200*

This mushrooming district in the rural, southeastern suburbs of St. Paul encompasses all or parts of Newport, St. Paul Park, Cottage Grove, Afton, Denmark, Grey Cloud and Woodbury, serving a student population of around 13,000.

The district has 11 elementary schools, two junior highs (7 and 8), two senior highs and a secondary alternative learning program.

The district is a showcase of outcome-based education, providing written learner outcomes for all subjects taught. Other highlights include: an extensive gifted program, accelerated and advanced-placement classes in many subjects, intensive computer and keyboard training, Junior Air Force ROTC programs in the high schools and an academic awards program that gives out school letters to high achievers.

Voters here approved a $43.5 million bond issue in December 1992, enabling the district to plan for two additional junior highs and improve its existing high schools.

Of course, strong community support for schools is not surprising in Washington County, which was recently listed among the top 20 fastest-growing, wealthiest and most educated areas in the country by the *Wall Street Journal*. It shares the distinction with nearby Dakota County.

## SPRING LAKE PARK SCHOOLS

*8000 N.E. Hwy. 65*
*Spring Lake Park*          786-5570

Serving the northern 'burb of Spring Lake Park and parts of Blaine and Fridley, this district of just over 4,000 students has four elementary schools, a middle school and a senior high.

The basics of reading, writing, language, spelling and math are stressed at the elementary level, where students often are grouped according to ability. In middle school, highlights include a seven-period day, two sophisticated computer labs, exploratory courses in a range of subjects and a strong advisory program.

The high school has distinguished itself in the areas of chemistry, math, physics, music and advanced college placement opportunities.

Computer literacy is stressed throughout all grades.

## WAYZATA PUBLIC SCHOOLS

*210 N. County Rd. 101, Wayzata 476-3100*

This western suburban district serves a student population of 7,500 with seven elementary schools, two junior highs (grades 7 through 9) and a high school.

Fourteen 1993 Wayzata graduates were named National Merit semifinalists, the highest number of any school in the state.

At the elementary level, self-contained classrooms — with limited team teaching — are the norm. Reading is taught through a literature-based program. The district places a high emphasis on com-

puter literacy and all schools have computer labs.

Three of its schools have been named National Schools of Excellence, and one of its elementary schools was named a Minnesota School of Excellence.

### WEST ST. PAUL PUBLIC SCHOOLS
1897 Delaware Ave.
West St. Paul                     681-2300

There are five elementary schools, a junior high and a senior high serving 4,700 students in the West St. Paul district, which encompasses Lilydale, Mendota, Mendota Heights, Sunfish Lake, West St. Paul and parts of Eagan and Inver Grove Heights.

At the elementary level, the basics are stressed with special emphasis on math. Environmental education is enhanced by frequent visits to a nearby nature center. Science and math are emphasized in junior high, enhanced by a Macintosh computer lab. College prep and vocational courses are offered in high school, which boasts a new IBM computer lab along with Macintosh technology. Foreign-language instruction is offered in French, German, Russian and Spanish.

The high school fine-arts program has won national recognition.

### WHITE BEAR LAKE PUBLIC SCHOOLS
2399 Cedar Ave.
White Bear Lake                    773-6000

This large northeastern district serves about 9,500 students in 10 elementary schools, two middle schools and a senior high, which is divided into two campuses.

In addition to the traditional self-contained classroom model, an elementary alternative features individualized instruction and flexible curriculum. A multi-year technology-acquisition program is in place to expand students' computer skills.

The district stresses education in the basic skills and higher-order thinking skills, and an innovative community program links schools with local business and industry.

## Private Schools

More than 250 private elementary and secondary schools — many with a religious affiliation — are found in the greater Minneapolis and St. Paul area. Here's a brief overview of some of the area's finest.

### ACADEMY OF THE HOLY ANGELS

*6600 Nicollet Ave. Richfield      866-8762*
*Tuition:                $2,350-$3,950*

Founded in 1931 as a Catholic girls school, the academy today is coeducational — football team and all — providing quality academic instruction in a Christian environment.

The academy comprises grades 7 through 12 and boasts an enrollment of about 730 students. At the middle school level, the student-teacher ratio is 17-to-1. Holy Angels has a modern computer lab and offers an array of computing courses. The academy offers five years of French and German and four years of Spanish and Russian.

It boasts a range of sports for boys and girls, including soccer, track, football, hockey, basketball and tennis, and its extracurricular activities range from dance line and cheerleading to math league and speech.

### BENILDE-ST. MARGARET'S

*2501 S. Hwy. 100, St. Louis Park 927-4176*
*Tuition:                $3,350 - $4,250*

This coeducational Catholic school is the happy result of a 1974 merger of two well-respected parochial schools, Benilde Catholic boys school and St. Margaret's Catholic girls school.

With a junior high and high school, Benilde-St. Margaret's has an enrollment of 810 students. Religious affiliation is not a factor in the admission process; however, religion classes are required as part of the curriculum.

Emphasizing academic excellence in a Christian environment, Benilde-St. Margaret's in the 1992-93 school year had the largest number of National Merit semifinalists of any private school in the state. A full range of college-prep academic courses is offered. Foreign languages include French, German and Spanish. Computers are found in labs and classrooms.

Benilde-St. Margaret's recently completed a $1.8 million physical education center with a gym, weight room and locker rooms.

### BLAKE SCHOOL

*511 Kenwood Pkwy.*
*Minneapolis                338-2586*
*Tuition:            $5,185-$10,180*

This highly regarded nonsectarian private school offers a strong program of academics in a supportive environment. Approximately 1,100 students are enrolled in preschool through 12th grade at Blake, which has been named a National School of Excellence by the U.S. Department of Education.

Blake is divided into three separate campuses in Minneapolis, Hopkins and Wayzata. At the elementary level, the emphasis is on small classes, student-teacher interaction, cooperative learning and positive self-esteem. French, German and Spanish are offered in the in the lower grades. Blake Lower School was included in *Child* magazine's 1991 listing of the "10 best schools in America."

In the middle school grades of 6 through 8, students are grouped into supportive "families," and classes stress the academics, independent learning and critical thinking. In high school, several advanced courses in math and the sciences, as well as the humanities, are offered. Teacher-to-student ratio in high school is 1-to-10.

### BRECK SCHOOL
*123 Ottawa Ave. N., Golden Valley      377-5000*
*Tuition:                $4,905-$7,660*

Located on a rolling 47-acre campus in Golden Valley, just west of Minneapolis, Breck School is an Episcopal, coeducational, college-preparatory day school encompassing preschool through 12th grades.

With a student population numbering 1,105, Breck considers its strengths to be solid academics taught in a nurturing environment. Breck has been recognized as a National School of Excellence, and in 1991 two of its seniors were among 13 students nationally to achieve a perfect SAT score.

At the elementary level, a whole-language approach to reading and writing is stressed. Foreign languages include French, Chinese, German, Spanish.

A unique feature at the middle school level (grades 5 through 8) is Project Adventure, a course of physical, emotional and moral challenges that includes games, problem-solving and high- and low-rope obstacle courses.

### CONCORDIA ACADEMY
*2400 N. Dale St., Roseville      484-8429*
*Tuition:                $2,406-$4,355*

This coed Lutheran high school is attended by 225 students in grades 9 through 12.

The school offers an Apple computer lab, German and Spanish and optional vocational courses at nearby Northeast Metro Technical School for those who choose not to go on to college.

Concordia lists its strengths as a small teacher-to-student ratio, commitment to academic excellence and a Christian environment.

### CONVENT OF THE VISITATION
*2455 Visitation Dr.*
*Mendota Heights              454-6474*
*Tuition:                $2,350-$5,670*

Founded by the Sisters of the Visitation in 1873, this Catholic day-school enrolls 500 students in lower, middle and upper levels. While the lower and middle schools are coed, the upper school is girls only, the only all-girls secondary school in Minnesota.

Ninety-nine percent of upper-school graduates continue on to college. Self-esteem and leadership are nurtured in a family-like environment.

### CRETIN-DERHAM HALL
*550 S. Albert St., St. Paul      690-2443*
*Tuition:                $4,150*

This coed Catholic high school has a student enrollment of 1,150 and offers a varied curriculum at honors, advanced, college-prep and basic levels. Languages include German, French and Spanish.

The school is equipped with two computer labs. Emphasis is on the academic, spiritual and emotional education of the "total person."

### DE LA SALLE
*25 W. Island Ave., Minneapolis    379-1105*
*Tuition:                    $3,850*

Administered by the Christian Brothers, De La Salle is the only coed Catholic high school in Minneapolis proper. Its enrollment is 350.

Features include two computer labs (in both Apple and IBM), computer-assisted design programs, college-prep academics, small classes, campus ministry and a culturally diverse student population. The school recently conducted a major fund-raising campaign to renovate buildings and build scholarships.

### FIRST BAPTIST SCHOOL
*14400 Diamond Path, Rosemount 423-2271*
*Tuition:                    $1,750*

Affiliated with the First Baptist Church of Rosemount, this K through 12 school enrolls 195 students in a rigorous academic program presented within a Christian environment.

Self-contained classrooms are the norm at the elementary level, which also boasts art and science specialists. At the secondary level, there are eight daily class periods. The 20-year-old school has won awards for its band and choir.

### FOURTH BAPTIST CHRISTIAN SCHOOL
*1250 W. Broadway, Minneapolis 522-3620*
*Tuition:                    $1,680*

This 27-year-old school enrolls

510 students in kindergarten through 12th grade. Emphasis is on self-contained classrooms, individualized attention, solid academics, a strong volunteer program and parental involvement. The school recently rebuilt its computer lab to provide one computer for every four students. An in-house FM radio station helps augment students' speech skills.

### HILL-MURRAY HIGH SCHOOL AND MIDDLE SCHOOL
*2625 Larpenteur Ave. E.*
*Maplewood                  777-1376*
*Tuition:            $3,200-$4,250*

This coed Catholic school is the result of the 1971 merger of Archbishop Murray Memorial High School for girls and Hill High School for boys. Guided by its Benedictine and LaSallian roots, the school emphasizes "work, prayer, service, hospitality and love that acts justly."

Serving 700 students in grades 7 through 12, Hill-Murray offers a college-prep, interdisciplinary curriculum, fully equipped computer labs, technology education (engines, plastics, woodworking), plus a full range of sports. Its hockey team is a serious contender in state tournaments.

More than 96 percent of Hill-Murray grads go on to college.

### INTERNATIONAL SCHOOL
*6384 Beach Rd., Eden Prairie    941-3500*
*Tuition:                    $6,350*

This nonsectarian school, part of a worldwide school system founded in 1886, serves 330 students in preschool through grade 12. Befitting its global outlook, the school offers daily instruction in French and Spanish for all ages. It also emphasizes math, science and computer literacy.

Other features include a gym, pool, tennis courts, soccer field, playgrounds and nature trails.

### MEADOW CREEK CHRISTIAN SCHOOL
*3037 N.W. Bunker Lake Blvd.*
Andover                                    427-4595
*Tuition:*                            *$1,224-$2,484*

This coed, K through 12 private school is housed in the interdenominational, evangelical Meadow Creek Church and has an enrollment of 590 students.

The school strives to offer a quality education based on Biblical principles. Other features include a computer lab for secondary levels, Spanish (beginning at grade 7) and a strong music program. The staff includes a full-time special-education teacher.

### MINNEAPOLIS JEWISH DAY SCHOOL
*4330 Cedar Lake Rd.*
St. Louis Park                             374-5650
*Tuition:*                         Approx. *$4,000*

Located within the Jewish Community Center, this 10-year-old private elementary school offers a high-quality academic program that includes a healthy dose of Hebrew studies. Enrollment is around 140 in grades kindergarten through 6.

### MINNEHAHA ACADEMY
*32nd St. and West River Pkwy.*
*Minneapolis*                              729-8326
*Tuition:*                       *$4,250-$4,950*

Founded in 1913 by the Northwest Conference of the Evangelical Covenant Church, this coed private school enrolls 900 students on two campuses: Upper School (grades 9 through 12), at 32nd Street and W. River Parkway, and Middle and Lower Schools, at 4200 W. River Parkway.

The school welcomes students of many denominations and offers quality academics in a strong spiritual setting. A high percentage of its graduates go on to college. Foreign languages include French, German, Latin and Spanish. Computer literacy is encouraged in all grades.

The school's well-rounded athletic program includes 21 sports, three gyms, three fields, tennis courts and an indoor ice arena.

### MINNESOTA WALDORF SCHOOL
*2129 Fairview Ave. N., Roseville  636-6577*
*Tuition:*                    *$3,885-$5,200*

This school is one of more than 500 worldwide following the Waldorf system, which relies heavily on imagination, play, art, mythology, song and nature to help children develop their full potential in body, mind and spirit. The school encompasses kindergarten through eighth grade.

Children begin each day with a two-hour main lesson, concentrating on one subject for a period of three to four weeks. Lessons are imaginatively presented; for example, music and movement may enhance the teaching of math.

Students remain with the same teacher from first grade through eighth grade. Classes are small, ranging from 10 to 20 students. Foreign languages include French and German. The City of Lakes Waldorf School, at 3450 Irving Avenue S., Minneapolis, offers a similar program. Its telephone number is 822-1092.

### MOUNDS PARK ACADEMY
*2051 E. Larpenteur Ave., St. Paul  777-6788*
*Tuition:*                    *$6,500-$7,700*

This coed, college-prep school enrolls 600 students in grades K through 12. Mounds Park emphasizes individualized learning through small classes, creative teachers, extensive fine arts offerings in addition to a challenging core curriculum and foreign languages (French and Spanish) in all grades.

### NEW LIFE ACADEMY
*6758 Bailey Rd., Woodbury  459-4121*
*Tuition:*                    *$1,925-$3,168*

This Christian school (preK through 12) has an enrollment of 502. Features include a computer lab, career center with computers and guidance software, German and Spanish instruction, small classes and a high-quality music program, all provided in a Biblically based program.

### ST. AGNES SCHOOL
*530 Lafond Ave., St. Paul  227-1886*
*Tuition:*                    *$3,400*

This coed K through 12 Catholic school encourages academic and spiritual development in a Christian setting. The school offers courses in Latin, German and Spanish and a range of math (including calculus), as well as advanced-placement courses for the gifted. Both IBM and Apple computers are available for use by students. Enrollment is around 500.

### ST. BERNARD'S HIGH SCHOOL
*170 Rose Ave., West St. Paul  489-1338*
*Tuition:*                    *$3,450*

This Catholic high school offers four years of French, German and Spanish, advanced math and religion courses, as well as the usual secondary-level curriculum. The school considers its strengths to be its Christian emphasis, small classes and individualized learning. Enrollment is around 350.

### St. Croix Lutheran High School
*1200 Oakdale Ave., West St. Paul* 455-1521
*Tuition:* $2,500-$4,000

Established in 1958, this high school stresses intellectual, spiritual and physical development in a caring Christian community. Spanish, German and Latin are offered, as is computer training. The school is known for its high standards, small classes and individualized instruction. Enrollment is around 220.

### St. Paul Academy and Summit School
*1712 Randolph Ave., St. Paul* 698-2451
*Tuition:* $6,360-$9,790

This nondenominational, coed school enrolls 859 students in grades K through 12.

Summit School, the lower school, is located at on a separate campus at 1150 Goodrich Avenue, St. Paul. Summit offers both self-contained classes and multi-age groupings.

The Academy boasts a traditional college-prep curriculum, taught in a flexible, interdisciplinary setting. The teacher-student ratio is 1-to-9, and the average class size is 15. Foreign languages include German, French, Latin and Spanish. Seventh-graders participate in a week-long environmental education course in northern Minnesota.

Typically, one-fourth to one-third of SPA seniors earn recognition in the National Merit program. In recent years, 100 percent of graduates have gone on to college.

### St. Thomas Academy
*949 Mendota Heights Rd.*
*Mendota Heights* 454-4570
*Tuition:* $4,600-$5,500

The only all-male high school in the Twin Cities, St. Thomas Academy has an enrollment of 525 in grades 7 through 12 and offers a rigorous college-prep academic and religious curriculum. The student-to-teacher ratio is 1-to-13.

A full 100 percent of the 1992 graduating class went on to college. Students may earn advanced-placement college credit through a program with local colleges. Every student is required to take a Junior Reserve Officers Training Corps course. Strengths include small classes, challenging academics and emphases on leadership and self-discipline.

### Talmud Torah Day School
*636 S. Mississippi River Blvd.*
*St. Paul* 698-8807
*Tuition:* $4,900

This private elementary school (K through 6) offers an academic program that encourages students to explore various subject areas via a multidisciplinary approach that integrates math, science, history, writing and art. Students are from all Jewish backgrounds: affiliated, unaffiliated and secular. Hebrew is used throughout the day. The enrollment is around 160. Talmud Torah also offers an afternoon school for youth in grades 2 through 7, as well as a Midrasha educational program for teens in grades 8 through 12. There is also a preschool program on premises.

### TESSERACT SCHOOL

*3800 Tesseract Place, Eagan        454-0604*
*Tuition (for K through grade 8;*
*preschool rates vary):            $6,290*

This private, nondenominational school offers instruction in preschool through eighth grade. Strengths include a 12-to-1 student-teacher ratio, rigorous academic curriculum, Spanish instruction and an active parent-teacher relationship.

With its philosophy based on research gathered by Control Data Corp., Tesseract stresses individualized, active learning and strong parental involvement. At Tesseract, no student is labeled as a failure; instead, instruction is customized to each student's needs.

Oh, yes, that strange name. "Tesseract" was inspired by Madeline L'Engle's classic children's book, *A Wrinkle in Time*, where it describes a fifth-dimensional corridor for traveling to otherwise unreachable destinations.

### TORAH ACADEMY

*2800 Joppa Ave. S., St. Louis Park 920-6630*
*Tuition:              Approx. $5,000*

This full-day Jewish school provides secular and Jewish studies coursework for 260 students in grades pre-kindergarten through 8. While the school is based on Orthodox principles, its students come from all types of Jewish backgrounds.

### TOTINO-GRACE HIGH SCHOOL

*1350 Gardena Ave. N.E., Fridley  571-4675*
*Tuition:              $4,600*

This coed Catholic high school (grades 9 through 12) offers a challenging curriculum in a Christian community. Enrollment is 860. Foreign languages include German, French and Spanish. Computers are found in each classroom and in a lab.

A recent remodeling project added a second gym, art rooms, choir and band facilities, and an industrial arts room. A campus ministry program offers worship, retreats and social-justice projects.

## *The Early Years*

Education doesn't begin at the kindergarten door. The preschool years are a time of bold discoveries, grand adventures and blossoming friendships. More and more, we're discovering just how smart babies are and how they absolutely thrive on mental, emotional and physical stimulation — delivered, of course, in a loving, secure setting.

To address this educational challenge, the state of Minnesota has funded an extensive educational program called Early Childhood Family Education (ECFE) for children from birth through age 4 and their parents. Administered locally through almost every one of Minnesota's 380 school districts, ECFE consists of weekly parent/child classes that incorporate creative play, adult discussion and peer support. More than 213,000 parents and children participate in the ECFE

*Photo: John Doman, Pioneer Press*

*Outside Mounds Park All-Nations Magnet School in St. Paul.*

program. Information about local ECFE programs may be obtained by calling your local school district or the state Department of Education at (612) 296-8414.

## Options in Child Care

Finding good child care is a never-ending challenge for working parents. Where's June Cleaver when you need her? Hello. Wake-up call. It's the '90s, and today's June is chasing a paycheck and chauffeuring "the Beav" to the nearest day-care center.

There are many options in child care today. Some parents seek out licensed home-care providers, because they prefer a more family-like setting. Others opt for licensed commercial child-care centers, finding security in the professional staff and standardized "no-surprises" setting.

Whatever your choice, do your homework. Contact a local child-care referral agency or your city or county offices for guidance and a listing of licensed centers and home-based providers (see the contact numbers listed below). Also, friends, relatives and neighbors are great sources for child-care referrals. Another place to turn is your neighborhood public school. It usu-ally can provide a list of reliable child-care providers.

Call ahead and schedule your first visit to a prospective child-care provider, and then stop by again unannounced during hours of operation to see her/him in action. Ask questions. What is the adult-to-child ratio? What is the staff members' turnover rate? Educational training? Check out the play areas, bathrooms, kitchen and the supply of age-appropriate toys. Ask to see an up-to-date license, immunization records and emergency cards. Observe how the provider interacts with her/his young clients. And trust your instincts. If something just doesn't seem right, it probably isn't. Move on to the next facility.

Perhaps the most comfortable arrangement of all is to hire a nanny or an "au pair" (a foreign nanny who comes to the United States on a one-year visa). While the latter live with the host family and earn an average stipend of $100 a week, in addition to room and board, nannies may be hired on either a live-in or day-care basis. There are many referral agencies for both nannies and au pairs. For more information, look in the Yellow Pages under Nannies.

An option for the older pre-schooler is nursery school or pre-school. The drawback here is that these programs usually are only partial-day programs — but that may be just the ticket for the part-time worker who only requires a few hours of child care a day.

As children age, child-care needs naturally lessen. School-age children often require only before-and after- school care. Fortunately, more and more schools are offering these extended-day services. They're worth looking into. In most cases, the staff is well-qualified, and your child will feel right at home in the comfortable school setting among his or her peers. As another plus, many extended-day programs also offer care during school-release days and summer vacations.

Increasingly, Minnesota employers are getting into the act and supporting harried parents in a number of ways — from opening child-care centers at the job site to offering such benefits as flextime and job sharing. Some Minnesota companies — actually only 1 percent of state employers, according to a study conducted in 1990 — are forward-thinking enough to offer child care at the work site. A leader in this area is the St. Paul Companies, which in 1991 built a $1.6 million child-care facility at its headquarters in downtown St. Paul.

Other companies offer working parents such benefits as flextime, job sharing, work-at-home telecommuting options, tax-exempt child-care savings plans, liberal sick-day

and parental-leave policies, and re-source and referral services.

Despite such innovative policies, finding the "just right" child-care provider remains a major dilemma for most working parents — and a major investment. In the Twin Cities, child-care costs vary, according to the age of your child and whether you use an in-home provider or a center. Centers may charge anywhere from $101 a week for preschoolers to $141 a week for infants. Licensed in-home care providers charge an average of $81.80 a week for preschoolers and $95 a week for infants.

Because of the high cost of quality day care, Minnesota has established a Child Care Fund to provide child-care assistance to eligible families. Parents are required to pay a portion of the child-care costs while receiving assistance through the fund.

The following are child-care referral and information services for various geographic areas of the greater Twin Cities.

Greater Minneapolis Day
  Care Association     341-1177, 341-2066
Resources for Child Caring
  (serving Ramsey County)       641-0332
Community Action Council
  (serving Dakota County)       431-2424
Anoka County Community Health
  and Social Services 422-7146, 422-7153
Carver County Licensing
  Department       448-3661
Scott County Child Care
  Resource and Referral       431-7752
Washington County Community
  Social Services       439-6901

## Parent Hotlines

Here are helpful numbers for parents who need emotional support or just some good advice:

### FIRST CALL FOR HELP

| | |
|---|---|
| *Minneapolis* | *335-5000* |
| *St. Paul* | *224-1133* |

First Call for Help is a United Way service that offers crisis counseling and referrals to parents.

### CRISIS NURSERY

This service provides temporary child care for parents in crisis who need a respite from their children. Here are the numbers of various crisis nurseries in the Twin Cities (most limit service to children younger than 12):

| | |
|---|---|
| *Crisis Nursery of Ramsey and* | |
| *Washington counties* | *641-1300* |
| *Minneapolis Crisis Nursery* | *824-8000* |
| *Crisis Nursery of Anoka* | *785-1181* |
| *Crisis Nursery of Dakota County* | *432-5578* |

# Inside
# Higher Education

In a region where kids graduate from high school at an extraordinarily high percentage and people of all ages are notoriously heavy users of the library systems and area book stores, is it any wonder that institutions of higher learning are everywhere you look? The Twin Cities boasts an enormous range of opportunities in higher education, from two-year community colleges to renowned private institutions to one of the nation's largest public universities.

Among the educational choices are one of the largest public universities in the nation (the University of Minnesota); the liberal-arts college with the second-highest endowment in the nation (Macalester College); a school that blazed a trail in allowing working people to attain college degrees (Metropolitan State University); an institution with a program in jewelry-making (Minneapolis Technical Institute); and one of the country's best-known art schools (Minneapolis College of Art and Design). Some are old, some new, some tiny and others sprawling. They all, however, offer proof that Twin Citians love to learn — whether for fun or for profit.

In addition to the institutions listed here, dozens of professional schools give training in careers that include accounting, acupuncture, electronics and radio broadcasting, veterinary medicine, acting and modeling, and truck driving. You can find them in the Yellow Pages under Schools and Instruction — Business and Vocational.

## Four-Year Colleges and Universities

### AUGSBURG COLLEGE
*731 21st Ave.S., Minneapolis     330-1000*

It's easy to inattentively drive by this Lutheran-affiliated liberal arts college, whose compact 25-acre campus is squeezed between the sprawl of the University of Minnesota and the rush of I-94. Founded in 1869, Augsburg is primarily an undergraduate residential college, with only about a third of the 2,900 students living off-campus or commuting. The college offers pre-professional programs in such fields as medicine, law, veterinary science and theology, and the most popular majors are business, education and communication.

### BETHEL COLLEGE AND SEMINARY
*3900 Bethel Dr., St. Paul     638-6400*

About 1,800 students attend this

Northrop Auditorium on the University of Minnesota's Minneapolis campus.

124-year-old private college, located about a 20-minute drive from both downtowns and affiliated with the Baptist General Conference. Despite Bethel's vintage, its campus is the newest in the state, with up-to-date academic, recreational and housing facilities. Business, nursing, education and psychology number among the most popular majors. Christian spiritual development receives much emphasis in the form of chapel services, Bible study groups and on- and off-campus ministry activities. The adjacent Bethel Seminary has a 70,000-volume theological library.

### COLLEGE OF ASSOCIATED ARTS
*344 Summit Ave., St. Paul          224-3416*

There are no sports teams or dormitories for the 150 students enrolled in this private art school ensconced within one of America's greatest neighborhoods of turn-of-the-century Victorian residences. The college offers majors and a Bachelor of Fine Arts in communication design, fine arts and illustration, as well as study-abroad opportunities in Australia, Ireland and England. The college is not accessible to physically disabled students.

### COLLEGE OF ST. CATHERINE
*2004 Randolph Ave., St. Paul        690-6000*
*2500 S. 6th St., Minneapolis        332-5521*

St. Cate's, as the institution is affectionately nicknamed, is a Catholic-affiliated college with 3,900 students who attend classes at campuses in St. Paul and Minneapolis. Founded as an undergraduate institution for women in 1905 by the Sisters of St. Joseph of Carondelet, the college was the first Catholic school in the United States to be awarded a Phi Beta Kappa chapter. Students at the well-groomed St. Paul campus, all women, focus on liberal-arts and professional programs. The bachelor's degree is offered in more than 30 disciplines.

At the Minneapolis campus (formerly known as the St. Mary's campus), a coeducational student body pursues associate degrees and certificates in such health-related fields as holistic therapy, medical transcription, nursing, respiratory therapy, and chemical dependency family treatment. St. Catherine's also offers master's degree programs in education, library science, nursing, theology and other areas, and a Weekend College program for women who want to continue working as they learn.

### CONCORDIA COLLEGE
*275 N. Syndicate St., St. Paul      641-8278*

Concordia, a private college affiliated with the Lutheran Church (Missouri Synod), recently celebrated its centennial. It has a tidy 26-acre urban campus that serves as academic home for approximately 1,200 students. Nearly half the students study business, with others majoring in such fields as education, social sciences and humanities.

### HAMLINE UNIVERSITY
*1536 Hewitt Ave., St. Paul          641-2800*

Hamline is Minnesota's oldest private institution of higher education, having been established in 1854 as a college affiliated with the

United Methodist Church. Its 50-acre campus, conveniently close to the state fairgrounds and the Midway district of St. Paul, bridges a business/retail district and a quiet residential neighborhood. The atmosphere of the university is progressive, and its 2,500 students (who include about 1,000 in graduate programs — quite a few of them 35 and older) are considered a pretty sharp bunch. Undergraduates primarily major in social sciences, arts and humanities and business.

### MACALESTER COLLEGE
*1600 Grand Ave., St. Paul       696-6000*

Long before it added hundreds of millions of dollars to its endowment several years ago due to a windfall from the estate of alumnus DeWitt Wallace (the founder of *Reader's Digest*), Macalester was a college worthy of attention. Academically strong and home to international students from some 75 nations during a typical year, Macalester boasts a spirited appreciation of diversity and dissent. Walter Mondale went to school there, and Hubert Humphrey taught there. Founded in 1874 by the Presbyterian church (although today the church connection is nominal), this liberal-arts college has the necessary financial strength, academic rigor and multicultural orientation to keep it prominent for a long time. About 1,700 students, all undergraduates, attend.

### METROPOLITAN STATE UNIVERSITY
*121 Metro Square Bldg.*
*Seventh and Robert Sts., St. Paul   296-3875*

When the Minnesota State University system created this institution in 1971, the school was leading a pack of universities grappling with the needs of working adults who wanted to further their education. Initially marketed as a "college without walls," it continues to offer programs for students unable to find a comfortable place within other post-secondary schools. Today the median age of its 5,000 students is in the mid-30s, and classes meet throughout the Twin Cities area in a variety of locations. Popular majors are an individualized study program and nursing.

### MINNEAPOLIS COLLEGE OF ART & DESIGN
*2501 Stevens Ave. S., Minneapolis 874-3700*

Everyone calls this fine-arts college MCAD (pronounced "emcad"), and its location next to the extensive museum holdings of the Minneapolis Institute of Arts places the works of Rembrandt, Titian, O'Keeffe and Grant Wood within easy reach. Founded in 1886 (the renowned children's book illustrator and author Wanda Gág was an early alumna), the college now has 600 students seeking degrees at the bachelor's level. Many members of the faculty — the student-faculty ratio is a tiny 12:1 — are prominent practitioners of such disciplines as sculpture, architecture, painting, animation, video and clothing design. Well-known visiting artists teach as well. The MCAD Gallery, located in the main building,

mounts outstanding exhibitions of artworks from around the world.

### WILLIAM MITCHELL COLLEGE OF LAW
*875 Summit Ave., St. Paul    290-6326*

This law school's noted alumni include retired U.S. Supreme Court Chief Justice Warren Burger, former Minnesota Supreme Court Chief Justices Douglas Amdahl and Peter Popovich, and nearly one-third of Minnesota's current judges. Ranging in age from 20 to 60, William Mitchell's 1,150 students benefit from the school's renowned legal writing program, a highly respected clinical law program, the availability of an unusual Master of Laws in Taxation degree, and the recently added Warren E. Burger Library. Forty-four percent of the students are women.

### NATIONAL COLLEGE — ST. PAUL CAMPUS
*1380 Energy Ln., St. Paul    644-1265*

National College, one of the newest (founded in 1975) and smallest of the Twin Cities' post-secondary schools, has an open admission policy. Its 240 students primarily study business administration and management, and all are commuters.

### NORTH CENTRAL BIBLE COLLEGE
*1410 Elliot Ave. S., Minneapolis    332-3491*

Affiliated with the Assemblies of

God, North Central Bible College has about 1,000 students pursuing studies in such areas as pastoral studies, youth ministries and elementary education. Other fields of academic focus include Biblical languages, broadcasting, children's ministries, church business administration, urban studies, drama and journalism. Most students live on campus, and two-thirds are from outside Minnesota. The campus is small and close to downtown Minneapolis.

### NORTHWESTERN COLLEGE
*3003 N. Snelling Ave., Roseville    631-5100*
Northwestern, a nondenominational Christian liberal-arts college founded in 1902, offers a full range of majors, from accounting to youth ministries. Most of its 1,300 students, however, focus on education, arts and humanities, business and social sciences. The 95-acre campus is close to the Rosedale shopping mall. Students desiring to venture further afield can take advantage of study-abroad opportunities in Greece, Israel, Japan and England.

### ST. MARY'S COLLEGE OF MINNESOTA
*2510 Park Ave., Minneapolis    874-9877*
St. Mary's is the graduate-level branch of a liberal-arts college in Winona, Minnesota. Affiliated with the Catholic Church, it serves more than 2,000 adult students who take part in 11 master's degree programs in day, evening and weekend classes.

### UNIVERSITY OF MINNESOTA
*Minneapolis    625-5000*
*St. Paul    625-5000*
Truly a city within a city, the Twin Cities branch of the University of Minnesota almost defies description. It's big: Nearly 45,000 students (undergrads and grad students) scatter their studies throughout a 1,730-acre campus that spans the Mississippi River and leapfrogs to the north edge of St. Paul. It's venerable: Founded in 1851, it includes a central mall originally conceived by Cass Gilbert (later much altered in design) that now typifies the Big 10 university look. It's academically distinguished: Only half of the undergrad applicants are offered admission (and it says a lot for academic quality that 40 percent of the entering students come from out of state), the libraries contain some 8 million items, and the graduate programs include a nationally renowned medical school, a law school, the Hubert Humphrey Institute of Public Affairs and the Carlson School of Management.

Among the newest buildings are an eye-popping art museum and the ear-pleasing Ted Mann Concert Hall. As a Big 10 university, of course, the U of M boasts plenty of pennant-waving intercollegiate athletics — the women's and men's Gopher basketball teams have done particularly well lately (see the Spectator Sports chapter).

### UNIVERSITY OF ST. THOMAS
*2115 Summit Ave., St. Paul    962-5000*
St. Thomas, a coeducational liberal-arts university established in 1885 by the Roman Catholic Church, enrolls about 10,000 students — a group evenly divided between undergrads and graduate

*Photo: Joe Oden, Pioneer Press*

*University of Saint Thomas, Minneapolis campus.*

students. The 78-acre main campus sits squarely within a residential area that constitutes St. Paul's "college belt"; the College of St. Catherine and Macalester are close at hand, and even Hamline is not too distant. The university offers a kaleidoscopic range of academic majors, although more than a third of the undergrads opt to concentrate on business. Graduate students also frequently pursue M.B.A.s and other business-related advanced degrees. Even among undergrads, living off campus or commuting is the norm (which, in the past, has contributed to conflicts with neighborhood residents over parking congestion). St. Thomas has two branch campuses: one in Chaska and a recently constructed facility in downtown Minneapolis that contains one of the largest fresco paintings in North America,

a work (on the ceiling) by Minnesota-born artist Mark Balma.

## Community Colleges

These public two-year institutions are enormously important in the grand scheme of the Twin Cities' higher educational offerings. For some students, the community colleges provide a way to learn and improve career skills at night and on weekends, outside the boundaries of the normal work day. For others, these schools pave the way for enrollment in four-year institutions. And some students simply use the colleges as a non-intimidating route to a subject of interest. All of these colleges offer three different two-year degrees: the Associate of Applied Science, providing career-related skills; the Associate of Arts, which transfers to four-year schools; and the Associate of

Science, which transfers to technical programs.

### ANOKA-RAMSEY COMMUNITY COLLEGE
11200 Mississippi Blvd. N.W.
Coon Rapids                    427-2600

### INVER HILLS COMMUNITY COLLEGE
8845 College Tr.
Inver Grove Heights           450-8500

### LAKEWOOD COMMUNITY COLLEGE
3401 N. Century Ave.
White Bear Lake               779-3200

### MINNEAPOLIS COMMUNITY COLLEGE
1501 Hennepin Ave.
Minneapolis                   341-7000

### NORMANDALE COMMUNITY COLLEGE
9700 France Ave. S.
Bloomington                   832-6000

### NORTH HENNEPIN COMMUNITY COLLEGE
7411 N. 85th St.
Brooklyn Park                 424-0702

## Public Technical Colleges

The area's many technical colleges emphasize career skills, offering such majors as accounting, apparel and upholstery, aviation mechanics, barbering, cosmetology, child development, culinary skills, commercial art, retail sales and machine tool technologies. At a technical college you can learn how to overhaul an engine, use airline reservation software, manage a small business, construct necklaces and bracelets, edit videos, practice reflexology or tailor clothing. Tuition fees are moderate, and virtually anyone older than 18 can enroll. People 62 or older receive special discounts.

### ANOKA-HENNEPIN TECHNICAL COLLEGE
1355 W. Hwy. 10
Anoka                         427-1880

### HENNEPIN TECHNICAL COLLEGE
Suburban Technical Institute
1820 N. Xenium Ln.
Plymouth                      559-3535
#### SOUTH CAMPUS
9200 Flying Cloud Dr.
Eden Prairie                  944-2222
#### NORTH CAMPUS
9000 Brooklyn Blvd.
Brooklyn Park                 425-3800

### MINNEAPOLIS TECHNICAL COLLEGE
1415 Hennepin Ave.
Minneapolis                   370-9400

### NORTHEAST METRO TECHNICAL COLLEGE
3300 Century Ave. N.
White Bear Lake               770-2351

Insiders' Tips

Although a charter for the University of Minnesota was drawn up and approved by the legislature in 1851, the school did not offer its first college-level classes until 18 years later.

**ROSEMOUNT-DAKOTA
COUNTY TECHNICAL COLLEGE**
*145th St. and Akron Rd.*
*Rosemount* 423-2281

**ST. PAUL TECHNICAL COLLEGE**
*235 Marshall Ave., St. Paul* 221-1370

## Adult Continuing Education

Most of the public school districts in the Twin Cities area offer a wide variety of low-cost continuing education classes for adults. Courses range from the esoteric (How to Review a Movie) to the practical (How to Make Your Will). In between lie classes in foreign languages, sports instruction, yoga, writing, music, financial planning, self-defense, cooking and computers. The instructors can be genuinely knowledgeable or merely enthusiastic. For more information, contact your local school district.

**MACPHAIL CENTER FOR THE ARTS**
*1128 LaSalle Ave., Minneapolis* 321-0100

After 28 years as part of the University of Minnesota's Continuing Education program, MacPhail became in 1994 an independent, nonprofit arts education institution serving both adults and children. Founded in 1907 by violinist William S. MacPhail, the school had been a degree-granting institution for decades. Now MacPhail offers a huge choice of instrumental and vocal music instruction, as well as sponsoring master classes, music ensembles and music history and theory classes. The children's Suzuki programs and adult class-piano courses are especially highly regarded. MacPhail, located in downtown Minneapolis near Orchestra Hall, is one of the nation's largest community arts schools.

**OPEN U**
*706 N. First St., Minneapolis* 349-9273

Open U is a private and for-profit provider of continuing education classes, which are held at locations around the area. Prices tend to be a bit steeper than the courses that school districts offer but are still reasonable. Open U is particularly strong in classes about relationships, intimacy, career development, local history, the film business, the arts and travel, and it often flies in nationally known experts to teach.

Photo: Neale Van Ness, Pioneer Press

*Barges travel the Mississippi River near downtown St. Paul.*

# *Inside*
# **Business**

For years, despite the occasional defection of some local manufacturer to low-tax South Dakota, the Twin Cities have consistently been ranked among the nation's healthiest business centers. Seventeen of the Fortune 500 industrial companies are based in the area, along with several of the nation's largest privately held firms.

Several ingredients contribute to the region's robust commercial climate: a diversified business base, a skilled and well-educated workforce, an unemployment rate that consistently remains about 2.5 percentage points below the national average and a healthy per capita income. Residents of the Twin Cities enjoyed a per capita personal income of $23,284 in 1992, which was 16 percent above the U.S. average.

Deep in the past are the days when three businesses — railroads, lumber and flour — dominated the Twin Cities economy. Since the end of the 19th century, the railroads have declined in power, the timber has vanished and most of the flour has been milled elsewhere, but a great many other industries have stepped in to fill the void.

Starting in the 1950s, for example, computers became big business in the Twin Cities. At the same time that Minneapolis-based Control Data went through a spectacular rise (and eventual decline), such other local high-technology companies as Univac and Cray Research were making their mark. The Twin Cities also carried technology into the medical-devices business, providing a home for Medtronic, St. Jude Medical, Cardiac Pacemakers and other companies.

The Twin Cities' placement in the heart of a rich agricultural region ensures that food processing remains an important commercial activity here. The former milling giants General Mills and Pillsbury are still going strong, although they have extended their reach into such areas as yogurt, frozen meals, ready-to-eat breakfast cereals and restaurants. (And Pillsbury is owned by a corporate entity in the United Kingdom.)

Two other regional industrial behemoths, 3M and Honeywell, have weathered defense cuts by strengthening their international business and stressing innovation. 3M received more than 1,250 patents in 1993.

Probably the most distinctive aspect of business in the Twin Cities has been a remarkable commitment to community involvement. Scores of firms, large and small, annually give 2 or 5 percent of their pre-tax income to charitable arts and social service organizations, and the area is nationally renowned for the number of big-business families that have endowed foundations to annually give money to community causes and nonprofit groups. Corporate-sponsored employee volunteerism is a powerful force, as well, and the Points of Light Foundation recently gave three of its six national community involvement awards to Twin Cities companies: Dayton Hudson, Honeywell and General Mills.

## Profiles of Twin Cities Corporations

### AMERICAN EXPRESS FINANCIAL ADVISORS INC.
*IDS Tower, Minneapolis*       671-3131

This is the new name of an old Twin Cities firm long known as IDS Financial Services. Owned by American Express Company, it commissioned the area's most famous skyscraper, the IDS Tower (although it no longer owns the building). American Express Financial Advisors provides financial planning services throughout the country and offers several types of insurance, mutual funds, investment certificates and other investments. It employs more than 3,000 people in Minnesota. Annual earnings are $3.2 billion.

### CARGILL INC.
*15407 McGinty Rd.*
*Minnetonka*       475-7575

Many Twin Citians are surprised when they learn that this low-profile giant is the world's largest privately held company, with revenues approaching $50 billion. Its business is the trading of such commodities as wheat, vegetable oil, corn, meat, animal feeds, fertilizers, salt, steel and resins. Founded in 1865, it employs more than 3,000 people in Minnesota and about 60,000 worldwide.

### CARLSON COMPANIES INC.
*Carlson Pkwy., Minnetonka*       540-5000

Founded in 1938, this diversified and privately-held firm has made its chairman and CEO, Curtis L. Carlson, one of the wealthiest men in the Upper Midwest. It employs about 33,000 people (10 percent of them in Minnesota) and operates Carlson and Nieman Marcus travel agencies, corporate incentive programs, the Radisson Hotels, Colony Hotels and Resorts, and TGI Friday's and Country

Kitchen restaurants. Company revenues top $2 billion annually.

### DAYTON HUDSON CORPORATION

*777 Nicollet Mall, Minneapolis   370-6948*

One of the nation's largest retailers, Dayton Hudson operates three store groups: Target, the upscale discounter; Mervyn's, which concentrates on mid-price apparel and linens; and a department store division that includes Dayton's, Hudson's and Marshall Field's stores scattered throughout the nation's midsection. The company began in 1902 when George Draper Dayton opened his first Dayton's store at the corner of Seventh and Nicollet in Minneapolis (the store is still there, albeit much enlarged), but Marshall Field's and Hudson's corporate roots are even older. Minnesotans fondly think of the company as strictly a local product, but only a small fraction of Dayton Hudson's 800-plus stores are in the state. With $18 billion in sales, it is the state's largest publicly held company. Dayton Hudson's charitable largesse is legendary — since 1946 it has donated 5 percent of its pre-tax earnings to community organizations through the Dayton Hudson Foundation and funds administered by each store group.

### GENERAL MILLS INC.

*1 General Mills Blvd.*
*Golden Valley                      540-2311*

Much more than Cheerios and Betty Crocker mixes come out of this place. General Mills also produces Bisquick, Yoplait yogurt and Gold Medal flour (a very old Twin Cities product), as well as operating Red Lobster and Olive Garden restaurants. Everyone knows that Big G is one of the three heavy hitters in the highly competitive breakfast cereal market, but fewer realize that the corporate headquarters in Golden Valley is the site of some great outdoor sculptures; Jonathan Borofsky's "Man with a Briefcase" is a fine example. General Mills is a prominent (and progressive) donor to charitable causes; in recent years it has been named by various publications and organizations as one of the nation's best workplaces for African-American employees, one of the most admired food companies and one of the country's best equal-opportunity employers. Annual sales are more than $8 billion.

### HONEYWELL INC.

*Honeywell Plaza, Minneapolis     951-1000*

Once a major defense contractor, Honeywell has in recent years focused on building its international business in developing and building control systems of various kinds for many markets. There's a good chance that your home thermostat or security system is a Honeywell product, and the company also markets gas valves, sensors of all kinds and energy management devices. A space and aviation systems division manufactures guidance systems and controls for use in military and commercial aircraft and spacecraft. Honeywell's annual revenues of $6.2 billion make it the fifth-largest publicly held company in Minnesota.

### NORWEST CORPORATION
*Sixth St. and Marquette Ave.*
*Minneapolis*                667-1234

Norwest, headquartered in downtown Minneapolis' beautiful Norwest Tower (see Architecture and Historic Sites), is the state's largest banking institution, providing mortgage, trust and investment services. With annual revenues of $4.5 billion, it owns banks in a dozen states stretching from Arizona to Indiana and has been aggressive in acquiring new banks and savings and loans.

### NWA INC.
*5101 Northwest Dr., Eagan*    726-2111

NWA, the parent company of Northwest Airlines and several other travel-related businesses, was the second-largest privately held company in Minnesota until it recently went public. It now seems solidly in the black after a few financially disastrous years in which bankruptcy appeared possible. Northwest Airlines uses the Twin Cities as its home base and one of its hubs, giving the community unusually good air access to other cities around the world. About 18,000 Minnesotans work for NWA.

### PILLSBURY
*Pillsbury Center, Minneapolis*    330-4966

Founded in 1869 and originally known as Pillsbury Flour Mills, this $4 billion company has been owned since 1988 by London-based Grand Metropolitan, a multinational giant. It produces some of the best-known brand names in the food business: Green Giant, Hungry Jack, Totino's, Jeno's and Joan of Arc, not to mention the Pillsbury line of cake mixes and dough products. Pillsbury also provides restaurants and other commercial food services with baked and frozen products. About 3,400 Minnesotans work for the company.

### THE ST. PAUL COMPANIES
*385 Washington St., St. Paul*    221-7911

The occupant of one of the newest and flashiest business headquarters in St. Paul happens to be the state's oldest corporation. One of the most amazing features of the St. Paul Companies' facilities is a palatial in-house child care center for employees' kids — which promptly earned the company kudos in *Working Mother* Magazine. Founded in 1853 as St. Paul Fire and Marine Insurance Company, the company is the nation's biggest underwriter of medical liability insurance and also handles property liability insurance, reinsurance and insurance brokerage services. Its annual revenues are $4.5 billion.

**Insiders' Tips**

J. Paul Getty, who accumulated a fortune of $4 billion by the time of his death in 1976, was born in Minneapolis.

*Corporate headquarters for the 3M Company is located in Maplewood,
a suburb of St. Paul.*

# Made or Invented in the Twin Cities

Every day, whether they know it or not, people around the world use products or services that come from the Twin Cities. Going back to the 19th century, Twin Cities businesses and inventors have developed more than their share of neat and innovative stuff. Here's a sampling.

### ARMORED CARS

In 1919, a Minneapolis factory turned out the nation's first.

### BETTER BUSINESS BUREAU

This organization traces its origins to an effort to crack down on deceptive advertising in Minneapolis in 1911.

### BETTY CROCKER

Way back in 1921, when it was still called the Washburn-Crosby Company, General Mills invented Ms. Crocker to respond to people's baking questions. She's since graced countless food packages, appeared on the radio and undergone a half-dozen facial updates.

### BREATHE RIGHT

That hot-selling bandage-like thing that helps people breathe easier while they sleep was developed by CNS Inc. of Chanhassen.

### BROADCAST SATELLITE

In 1993, United States Satellite Broadcasting, of the Twin Cities, launched the world's first high-power direct-broadcast satellite. Subscribers with satellite dishes can receive 150 TV channels.

### BURMA-SHAVE

Minneapolis was long the home of Burma-Shave, and all those highway signs were cooked up in the Twin Cities.

### CARAMEL APPLES

A food vendor at the 1916 Minnesota State Fair introduced them.

### CHEERIOS

Along with dozens of other cereals, this is one of General Mills' key contributions to America's morningtime culture. It first hit the store shelves in 1941 under the brand name "Cheerioats." Thirteen years later, General Mills introduced Trix, one of the first presweetened cereals. (The Trix Rabbit came later, in 1960.)

## COOTIE

Minneapolis postal worker Herb Schaper invented this louse-inspired game in 1948, and his firm, Schaper Manufacturing Company, went on to develop such other toys as Stadium Checkers, Ants in the Pants and Inch Worm.

## CORTLAND, HARALSON AND WEALTHY APPLES

They were all developed by Twin Cities apple specialists between 1885 and 1935.

## CRAY SUPERCOMPUTERS

Used all over the globe, they're manufactured in Eagan.

## CREAMETTES MACARONI

You can bet your noodle that this pasta originated in Minneapolis.

## DELUXE CHECKS

A goodly number of the personal checks we write are printed by Deluxe Corp., which is based in Shoreview.

## ENCLOSED SHOPPING CENTER

Southdale, which opened in Edina in 1956, was the country's first indoor shopping center.

## GLASS MEATCASE

A now-forgotten Minneapolis butcher installed in his shop the country's first glass case for meats, around 1897.

## GRAIN BELT, LANDMARK, PIG'S EYE AND SUMMIT BEERS

Twin Cities breweries produce all of them.

## HAMM'S BEAR

Hamm's, purveyors of the brew made in "the land of sky blue waters," turned a white-bellied cartoon bear into a national celebrity with its ads in the 1950s and '60s.

## HAPPY TO BE ME DOLL

The doll that raises the self-esteem of girls comes from High Self Esteem Toys in Woodbury.

### HEART-LUNG MACHINE
University of Minnesota scientists built the first one in 1955. Twenty-two years later, they followed up with the first total-body computer tomagraphy scanner.

### HEART PACEMAKER
Medtronic, based in Minneapolis, became the first company to market wearable, battery-operated heart pacemakers in 1957. It later followed with the first implantable pacemakers. St. Jude Medical in Little Canada has built its international business on mechanical heart valves.

### HOME THERMOSTAT
You can thank the tinkerers at Honeywell in Minneapolis for developing the first ones (c. 1885).

### HYDROELECTRICITY
The western hemisphere's first hydroelectric generating plant was built in 1882 at Minneapolis' Falls of St. Anthony.

### LAND O'LAKES BUTTER
And cheese, too — they're both the bread and butter of the Arden Hills dairy cooperative.

### LOG CABIN SYRUP
It first dripped out of the Twin Cities around 1920.

### MINI DONUTS
Lil' Orbits Doughnut Machines in Plymouth manufactures the gizmos that make them.

### MALT-O-MEAL
More than 75 years ago, Malt-O-Meal began producing its cereals in Minneapolis.

### MMPI
Now used as an employment screening tool around the country, the Minnesota Multiphasic Personality Inventory was invented by University of Minnesota psychologists in 1939.

### MUNSINGWEAR UNDERWEAR
Now they market everything from kitchenware to household novelties, but Munsingwear in Minneapolis once produced the clothes that were close to everyone's skin.

### NORDICTRACK

If Americans have grown more fit in the past decade, Nordictrack in Chaska is partly responsible.

### NUT GOODIE

Something of a cult following keeps this candy alive.

### PEANUT BUTTER PARFAIT

Along with Slurpees and other Dairy Queen treats, they're prepared everywhere, but Dairy Queen International is based in Bloomington.

### PILLSBURY DOUGHBOY

That pudgy little dude, invented in 1965 by an ad agency for Minneapolis-based Pillsbury, has endured countless pokes in the belly.

### POST-IT NOTES

3M scientist Art Fry invented them in 1974, and they first reached the market four years later. Now they're stuck all over.

### PUFFED RICE

University of Minnesota professor Alexander Anderson invented the puffing process in 1901.

### ROLLERBLADES

Blame your strong ankles and bruised knees on Scott Olson and Brennan Olson of Minneapolis, who invented Rollerblades in 1980. The company they founded is now based in Minnetonka.

### SATELLITE TOILETS

No construction site or outdoor event would be complete without them. Satellite is headquartered in Plymouth.

### SCOTCH TAPE

3M developed the first cellophane tape in 1928. Not by coincidence, the first rolls of masking tape also came out of 3M's labs in 1925.

### SHOPPING BAG

St. Paul grocer Walter Duebner invented the nation's first commercially produced shopping bag with handles in 1916.

### THINSULATE

It's another 3M invention.

> ### TOASTER
> In 1926, McGraw Electric Company of Minneapolis began marketing the first electric toaster for use in the home.
>
> ### TONKA TRUCKS
> They were developed and long manufactured in Minnetonka.
>
> ### YEARBOOKS AND CLASS RINGS
> Odds are that Jostens in Bloomington produced your class ring, and there's a good chance they printed your school yearbook, too.

### SUPERVALU INC.
*11840 Valley View Rd.*
*Eden Prairie*              828-4000

Supervalu is one of the nation's biggest food wholesalers, serving more than 2,500 independently operated supermarkets around the country — stores that use the Supervalu, Cub Foods, NewMarket, IGA and County Market names, among others — and 100-plus corporate-owned food marts. With $12.6 billion in revenues, it ranks as Minnesota's third-largest publicly held company

### 3M COMPANY
*3M Center, Maplewood*        733-1110

Formerly known as Minnesota Mining and Manufacturing, 3M is Minnesota's most profitable publicly held business, reporting a 1993 income of $1.26 billion on sales of $14 billion. Perhaps not by coincidence, it outspends all other U.S. manufacturers in research and development, a practice that resulted in 167 new products in 1993. (Since its founding in 1902, 3M has developed more than 60,000 products.) The company's goal is to generate 30 percent of its sales from products that are less than 5 years old. Scotch Tape, Post-it Notes and other adhesives still make up a big part of the company's sales, but 3M is also into electronic pain blockers used by dentists, fingerprint identification systems and other high-tech devices. Half of its business is overseas. The company employs 23,000 people in Minnesota.

## Business Organizations

Need to know more about a Twin Cities business? Want to check out its record with consumers? These organizations can help.

### IMPORTANT PHONE NUMBERS

| | |
|---|---|
| Better Business Bureau | 699-1111 |
| Chambers of Commerce: | |
| Greater Minneapolis | 370-9132 |
| Minnesota African American | 374-5787 |
| Minnesota American Indian | 222-8623 |
| Minnesota Hispanic | 222-0569 |
| Northern Dakota County | 452-9872 |
| St. Paul Area | 223-5000 |
| Suburban Area (St. Paul suburbs) | 483-1313 |
| Twin West (western suburbs) | 540-0234 |

# *Inside*
# Worship

Even more than the determination of where to eat, shop or find entertainment, the decision of where to worship is personal and often based on intangibles. We each seek out places of worship (or choose not to go to them) in accordance with our upbringing, moral positions, craving for a particular spiritual atmosphere, habits, family situation, ethnic background and even political beliefs.

In the Twin Cities, the choices seem virtually unlimited. The region has a national reputation as a bulwark of Lutheranism, and indeed the dominantly German and Scandinavian ethnic makeup of the population has made the Twin Cities one of North America's largest communities of Lutherans. Religious membership figures (which are notoriously unreliable when it comes to reporting true religious affiliation) actually point to Roman Catholics as the state's largest religious group, followed (in order of descending numbers) by members of the Evangelical Lutheran Church of America, Missouri Synod Lutherans, Methodists, Presbyterians, Lutherans in the Wisconsin Evangelical Synod, Assemblies of God church members, Baptists, Jews, Episcopalians and Black Baptists. The number of agnostics and atheists is unknown.

There are many notable places of worship in the Twin Cities, and not all of them are in buildings. Many people, of course, worship at home and outdoors. Consider what follows as the sketchiest outline of places of worship in the area — a thumbnail guided tour that requires your own spiritual investigation and participation to become genuinely helpful.

## African Methodist Episcopal

### St. Peter's A.M.E. Church
*401 E. 41st St., Minneapolis    825-9750*

St. Peter's congregation can trace its roots back to the 1880s, when it broke away from St. James A.M.E. Church, which had been founded in 1869. The long history of the church is immediately apparent — in front of the building sits a two-foot-square foundation stone from the congregation's first home.

## Baptist

### Zion Baptist Church
*621 Elwood Ave. N.*
*Minneapolis    377-5436*

This church provides religious

support and social programs for the African-American Baptist community in Minneapolis.

## Buddhist

### TWIN CITIES BUDDHIST ASSOCIATION
*No address*                    *545-2211*

This organization sponsors English-language Buddhist services several times each year, with a minister from the Chicago Midwest Buddhist Temple presiding, at First Universalist Church, 3400 Dupont Avenue S., Minneapolis.

## Congregational

### PLYMOUTH CONGREGATIONAL CHURCH
*1900 Nicollet Ave.*
*Minneapolis*                   *871-7400*

Built in 1908 in the English Gothic style, this church has a socially active congregation and a fine performing arts center that hosts theater performances and concerts of all kinds. The Plymouth Music Series uses the church as its home base.

## Episcopal

### CATHEDRAL CHURCH OF SAINT MARK
*519 Oak Grove St.*
*Minneapolis*                   *870-7800*

Since 1908, this Gothic Revival fortress has faced Loring Park in Minneapolis. The church is filled with stately art: a detailed carving of John the Baptist by Isaac Kirchmeyer; stone carvings by Twin Cities artist John Rood; lovely carved wood throughout; and vibrant Renaissance-style stained-glass windows by Charles J. Connick. Following the plan of many English churches, it has a long nave, side aisles and a deep choir space. The square crenellated tower, recently damaged by a lightning strike, has been repaired. The church is the home of an Episcopal congregation that was founded in 1852.

## Greek Orthodox

### SAINT GEORGE GREEK ORTHODOX CHURCH
*1111 Summit Ave., St. Paul*        *222-6220*

St. Paul's Greek Orthodox community receives religious, educational and cultural benefits from this spiritual bulwark, which sponsors classes in the Greek language, dance and music as well as conducts spiritual services.

### SAINT MARY'S GREEK ORTHODOX CHURCH
*3450 Irving Ave. S.*
*Minneapolis*                   *825-2247*

Walkers and bikers circumnavigating Lake Calhoun can see the gold dome of this Byzantine church peeking above the trees. St. Mary's, which was built in 1957, serves as the heart and soul of the Greek Orthodox community in Minneapolis.

## Islam

### ISLAMIC CENTER OF MINNESOTA
*1401 Garden Ave. N.E.*
*Fridley*                       *571-5604*

Islamic people of all backgrounds come to this center for worship, cultural programs, exhibits and other activities.

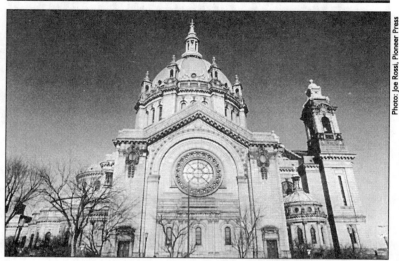

*St. Paul Cathedral in St. Paul.*

Photo: Joe Rossi, Pioneer Press

## Jewish

### MOUNT ZION TEMPLE
*1300 Summit Ave., St. Paul*     *698-3881*

This Reform synagogue houses Minnesota's oldest Jewish congregation, which was established in the 1850s. The temple itself dates from 1955 and was designed by Eric Mendelsohn. Other St. Paul area synagogues include Temple of Aaron (Conservative), 698-8874, and Adath Israel Orthodox, 698-8300.

### TEMPLE ISRAEL
*2324 Hennepin Ave.*
*Minneapolis*     *377-8680*

Temple Israel, completed in 1928, is the third Minneapolis home of this congregation and the largest Reform synagogue in the state. Outside, the building is a stately example of the columned Classical Revival style, but the interior betrays the theatrical leanings of its architect, Jack Liebenberg, who designed movie theaters throughout the Upper Midwest. There's a wide balcony, great sight-lines and incredible acoustics that make the synagogue a favored venue for such ensembles as the Saint Paul Chamber Orchestra. There are eight other synagogues in Minneapolis and its suburbs: Among them are Adath Jeshurun Congregation (Conservative), 545-2424; Beth El Synagogue (Conservative), 920-3512; Bet Shalom Reform Congregation, 933-8525; and Kenesseth Israel Congregation (Orthodox), 920-2183.

## Lutheran

### CENTRAL LUTHERAN CHURCH
*333 12th St. S., Minneapolis*     *870-4416*

Before the growth of the sub-

MOUNT OLIVET
LUTHERAN CHURCH
5025 Knox Avenue South
Minneapolis, MN 55419-1095

**Sunday Morning Worship:**
9:00 10:00, 11:00 and 12:00 noon

Pastor Paul M. Youngdahl, D.D.
Senior Pastor

*Attend as a visitor...Leave as a friend.*

urbs, Central was the dominant Lutheran church in the Minneapolis area. Located downtown and affiliated with the Evangelical Lutheran Church of America, it still draws many people, is a well-liked concert venue and has a large membership.

### LA IGLESIA LUTERANA DE CRISTO EL REDENTOR
*784 Jackson St., St. Paul          291-2757*
Services and classes are mainly in Spanish at this St. Paul Lutheran church in the Hispanic community.

### MOUNT OLIVET LUTHERAN CHURCH
*5025 Knox Ave. S.*
*Minneapolis          926-7651*
The size of this southwest Min-

neapolis church's parking lot testifies to the enormity of its congregation. Mount Olivet, in fact, boasts one of the largest memberships of any Lutheran church on the continent. Practically every weekend includes several weddings at the church, and services at Christmas and other peak times create traffic jams along 50th Street.

### NORWEGIAN LUTHERAN MEMORIAL CHURCH ("MINDEKIRKE")
*10th Ave. S. and E. 21st St.*
*Minneapolis          874-0716*
This Norwegian church offers Sunday services, social and cultural programs and an annual festival paying tribute to the accomplishments of Leif Eriksson.

Minnesota's first church, raised by French priest Lucian Galtier, was completed in St. Paul in 1841.

Insiders' Tips

## Maronite Catholic

### ST. MARON'S
### MARONITE CATHOLIC CHURCH
*219 Sixth Ave. N.E.*
*Minneapolis*                    379-7647

This church, which offers weekly services in the Maronite Catholic tradition and an Aramaic mass, primarily serves people of Lebanese descent. It sponsors classes in Arabic studies as well as English courses for recent immigrants. There is at least one other Maronite Catholic Church in the Twin Cities: Holy Family Maronite Catholic Church in St. Paul, 291-1116.

## Metropolitan Community

### ALL GOD'S CHILDREN
### METROPOLITAN COMMUNITY CHURCH
*3100 Park Ave. S., Minneapolis*   824-2673

The name of this church tells a lot about it. Located in a solidly urban south Minneapolis neighborhood, it opens its doors to people regardless of their economic status, ethnic background or sexual persuasion. Most of its members, in fact, are gay and lesbian, and for the past 20 years the church has been the site of countless holy unions among same-sex couples. In most respects, however, the services at All God's Children are no different from those at many other conservative Christian houses of worship in the Twin Cities, and visitors are often surprised to discover that.

## Presbyterian

### CENTRAL PRESBYTERIAN CHURCH
*500 Cedar St., St. Paul*         224-4728

Central Presbyterian dates back to 1889, when St. Paul's downtown was considerably less built up than it is today. Nowadays, commercial buildings butt right up to the church, but the rustic and spacious interior is a welcome sanctuary from the bustle of the city.

### WESTMINSTER PRESBYTERIAN CHURCH
*1201 Nicollet Mall*
*Minneapolis*                     332-3421

The Paul Granlund sculpture at the front of this Nicollet Mall church, "Birth of Freedom," provides a soaring statement that this is a church that reaches out to the community. Erected in 1897 in the English Gothic style, the church boasts active public programming that includes the Westminster Town Hall Forum, a series of noontime lectures by speakers of national reputation on topics of current interest. The talks are free, open to the public and broadcast on radio nationwide.

## Roman Catholic

### ASSUMPTION CATHOLIC CHURCH
*51 W. Ninth St., St. Paul*       224-7536

Built in 1873 for a German-speaking congregation and modeled after the Ludwigskirche in Munich, this downtown church — the oldest Catholic house of worship in St. Paul — raises twin towers that have long been a city landmark. Viewed from the outside, its

# ST. LAWRENCE CATHOLIC CHURCH
## A MINISTRY OF THE PAULIST FATHERS

**If you've been away from the Church for a while, we'd like to hear from you...**

Mass Schedule: Sunday 8 & 10 am & 8 pm
Monday, Wednesday, Friday 12:10 pm
Tuesday, Thursday 5:10 pm, Saturday 9 am

Reconciliation: Tuesday, Thursday 5:30 pm,
Saturday 9:30 am

## CATHOLIC FAITH INSTRUCTIONS OFFERED
### 1201 SE 5th St. • 331-7941

German Romanesque Revival face appears almost plain, but inside is a gorgeous sanctuary full of murals, statues and a sea of votive candles in richly colored holders. Its designer was Joseph Reidl, who served as architect to the King of Bavaria.

### BASILICA OF SAINT MARY
*88 N. Seventh St., Minneapolis    333-1381*

The Vatican has designated only 31 basilicas in the United States, and this was the first, achieving that rank from Pope Pius XI in 1926. (A basilica is a church that has been singled out for its special religious or historical significance. You can recognize them by the pavilion and silver-belled standard located in the sanctuary.) When construction began in 1907, the nave was reputed to be the widest of any church in the world. The neo-Baroque church, which took 18 years to build, has greatly benefited from a recent renovation that

brightened up the copper dome and from a rerouting of roads that makes the approach to the building much more attractive. A statue of Father Louis Hennepin stands in front of the basilica, placed there in 1930 to celebrate the 250th anniversary of the missionary's visit to Minnesota.

### CATHEDRAL OF SAINT PAUL
*239 Selby Ave., St. Paul    228-1766*

This great cathedral, a domed structure situated on a hill overlooking downtown St. Paul, is certainly the most famous house of worship in the Twin Cities. Completed in 1915 after nine years of construction, through the dedicated fund-raising and vision of Archbishop John Ireland, it was designed in the Renaissance style by the Parisian architect E.L. Masqueray. It seats 3,000 people and draws crowds not only for religious services but also for organ recitals and choral concerts (avoid the seats behind the pillars). The dome is 175 feet high and 96 feet in diameter.

## OUR LADY OF GUADALUPE CHURCH
*401 Concord St., St. Paul 228-0506*

St. Paul's Hispanic community and Our Lady of Guadalupe are inextricably intertwined, and the church has long been a mainstay of the city's Mexican and Mexican-American people.

## OUR LADY OF LOURDES CHURCH
*1 Lourdes Pl. S.E., Minneapolis 379-2259*

Located in the heart of old St. Anthony, the birthplace of Minneapolis, this is the oldest continuously operated church in the city. It was built in 1854 as a Universalist church and purchased 23 years later by a French-Canadian Catholic congregation, who came to town to mill logs and grain, and now is recognized as a U.S. Historic Landmark. You can still hear French carols there at Christmas, and the church offers guided tours that showcase the original tapestries, stained-glass windows and statues. The church also prepares and sells tourieres, a type of French meat pie.

## SAINT LAWRENCE CATHOLIC CHURCH
*1201 Fifth St. S.E., Minneapolis 331-7941*

Serving southeast Minneapolis for more than 100 years, Saint Lawrence Catholic Church is located in Dinkytown, near the University of Minnesota. Its Paulist Fathers focus on reconciliation, evangelization and ecumenism, and they are particularly interested in reaching out to people who feel separated from the Church. Known for its good preaching and spirited music, the church is home to a parish enrollment of about 1,200 diverse people who include many young families, college students and young adults.

## SAINT LOUIS CATHOLIC CHURCH
*506 Cedar St., St. Paul 224-3379*

St. Paul's French Catholics built this church in 1909, and it has always operated in the shadow of the magnificent Cathedral of Saint Paul less than a mile away. (Emmanuel Masqueray designed both buildings, as well as the Basilica of Saint Mary in Minneapolis.) Nevertheless, it is a venerable parish church built of limestone and brick, with a cruciform interior plan and a pair of beloved towers.

## SAINT OLAF CATHOLIC CHURCH
*215 S. Eighth St., Minneapolis 332-7471*

This church, raised by Scandinavian Catholics in the 1950s, maintains a strong community presence in downtown Minneapolis. Its subdued architecture also presents an interesting contrast to the older and

**Insiders' Tips**

In 1888, Russian Orthodox followers built the first church in the 48 states for the members of their faith in Minneapolis.

# BASILICA OF SAINT MARY

## *A Traditional Church with a Modern Message!*

### HENNEPIN AT SIXTEENTH
#### DOWNTOWN MINNEAPOLIS
#### OPEN DAILY 6:30 AM -5 PM ✦ HOLIDAYS 9-12 PM

### *Welcome Visitors! (612) 333-1381*

*America's First Basilica and National Historic Landmark!*

**Saturday:** 5:00 pm ...........Vigil Eucharist
**Sunday:** 7:30 am ..........Sunrise Eucharist
9:30 am .........*Choral Eucharist
11:30 am* & 6:15 pm ....Folk Eucharist
**M - F:** 7:00 am & 12:00 pm .........Eucharist
**Legal Holidays:** 10:00 am .........Eucharist
*Nursery Available

more ornate churches that German, Irish and French Catholics erected elsewhere in the Twin Cities. A Chapel on the Street along Second Avenue S. was added in 1972.

## Romanian Orthodox

### SAINT MARY'S
### ROMANIAN ORTHODOX CHURCH
*854 Woodbridge St., St. Paul    488-5669*

This historic house of worship, built in 1913 and since designated a historic landmark, is modeled after the church of Sanicolaul Mare in Romania. In addition to a striking carved iconostasis and altar, the church contains archives and old books of church liturgies.

## Russian Orthodox

### RUSSIAN ORTHODOX CHURCH
### OF THE RESURRECTION OF CHRIST
*1201 Hathaway Ln. N.E.*
*Fridley                    574-1001*

A focal point of the Twin Cities'

Christian Russian community, this church offers language classes and cultural programs as well as worship opportunities.

## Ukrainian Catholic

### SAINT CONSTANTINE
### UKRAINIAN CATHOLIC CHURCH
*515 University Ave. N.E.*
*Minneapolis            379-2394*

Ukrainians and Ukrainian Americans have lived for generations in northeast Minneapolis, and this church is an active member of that ethnic community. Offering Byzantine Ukrainian rites, Saint Constantine's also sponsors Ukrainian social and cultural events and has a sizable and historic collection of Ukrainian art.

## Ukrainian Orthodox

### SAINT MICHAEL'S
### UKRAINIAN ORTHODOX CHURCH
*505 N.E. Fourth St.*
*Minneapolis* 379-2695

With nearly 200 families in its congregation, this is one of several Ukrainian Orthodox churches in the Twin Cities. It supplements its worship services with the sponsorship of music groups and other cultural organizations.

## Unitarian-Universalists

### THE FIRST UNITARIAN
### SOCIETY OF MINNEAPOLIS
*900 Mount Curve Ave.*
*Minneapolis* 377-6608

Founded in 1881, the First Unitarian Society occupies a handsome building two blocks south of Walker Art Center and the Guthrie Theater. It offers Sunday Assemblies renowned for their music featuring the First Unitarian Orchestra and Chorus, Sunday Morning Forums covering a wide range of current events and topics, children's programs, and religious education for kids and young adults, as well as social activities, support for the Twin Cities' Tibetan community, and transgenerational events. The Twin Cities has one of the largest concentrations of UUs outside of Boston, and many prominent figures in Minneapolis' history were Universalists.

## United Church of Christ

### SPIRIT OF THE LAKES
### UNITED CHURCH OF CHRIST
*2930 13th Ave. S.*
*Minneapolis* 724-2313

This is one of a small number of openly gay and lesbian churches in the Twin Cities. Spirit of the Lakes celebrates holy unions and involves itself in efforts to help people with AIDS, combat homophobia and provide a spiritual home for people who have been cast out of other churches.

## United Methodist

### HENNEPIN AVENUE
### UNITED METHODIST CHURCH
*511 Groveland Ave.*
*Minneapolis* 871-5303

At night you can see a slender, dramatically illuminated spire reaching for the sky near downtown Minneapolis. The spire, 238 feet high, belongs to this Gothic-style church, erected in 1916. The church seats 1,000 people, with an octagonal sanctuary design inspired by the central core of the Cathedral at Ely, England. Charles J. Connick of Boston, who also created the windows at the Cathedral of Saint Mark just down the block, designed this church's fine stained-glass art. In a second floor art gallery is one of America's largest collections of religious paintings owned by a church. Spanning the 16th through 19th centuries and donated early in this century by a church member, the lumber baron (and founder of Walker Art Center) T.B. Walker, the collection includes "Ecce Homo" by Antonio Ciseri, "The Annunciation" by Juan Correa de Vivar and "Abraham and the Three Angels" by Pieter Pourbus. The gallery also hosts temporary exhibitions.

## Wicca

**MINNESOTA CHURCH OF WICCA**
*No address*                                827-4474

Wicca adherents are numerous in the Twin Cities, and some of them do not like the pejoratively intended "pagan" or "witch" labels that others try to slap upon them. But other Wicca people wear those badges with pride. Falling cleanly outside the Judeo-Christian tradition, Wicca believers follow nature-based practices that have existed in various cultures for millennia.

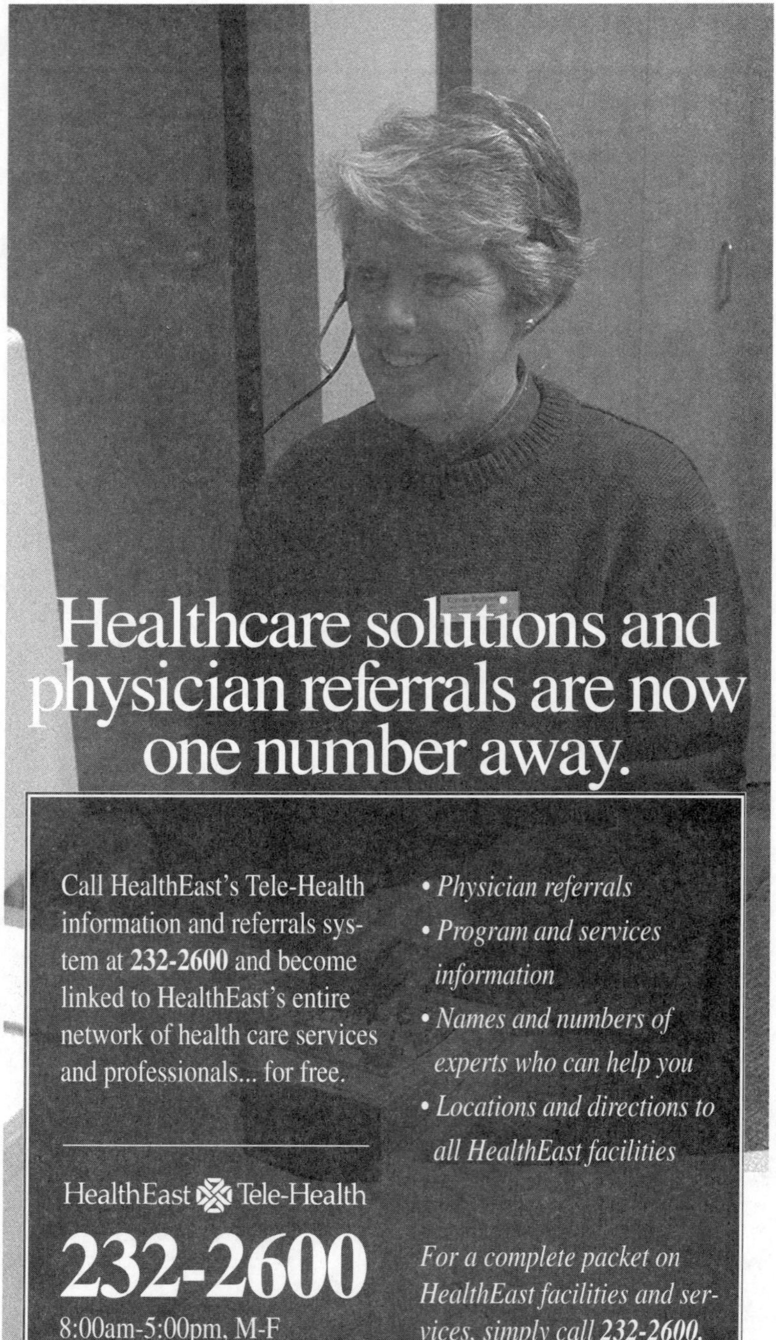
Healthcare solutions and physician referrals are now one number away.
Call HealthEast's Tele-Health information and referrals system at 232-2600 and become linked to HealthEast's entire network of health care services and professionals... for free.
• Physician referrals
• Program and services information
• Names and numbers of experts who can help you
• Locations and directions to all HealthEast facilities
HealthEast Tele-Health
232-2600
8:00am-5:00pm, M-F
For a complete packet on HealthEast facilities and services, simply call 232-2600.

# *Inside*
# **Health Care**

Not quite at the top of the list of things that people associate with Minnesota, but somewhere in the Top 10 — behind the cold weather, Garrison Keillor, lakes, loons, wild rice and mosquitoes — is great health care. More than a century ago, people with tuberculosis, cholera and other diseases headed here because they believed the climate would help them recover. At the same time, the birth of the celebrated Mayo Clinic in Rochester (about 80 miles south of the Twin Cities) contributed to our healthy image, but it is the statewide excellence of the health care system that makes headlines these days. After all, Minnesota boasts the second-highest life expectancy of all the 50 states (behind Hawaii and its warm weather — try to explain it), and the Mayo Clinic can't take credit for all that.

Reduced to its essentials, good health in Minnesota probably boils down to skilled health care providers, creative health care organizations and government agencies, and few local opportunities for the population to engage in such hazardous activities as cliff diving, oil rig work, and eating fresh shellfish.

Overall, if you're sick, this is a good place to be, and if you're well, it's a good place to stay well. A recent *Money Magazine* study placed two of the Twin Cities' health maintenance organizations, Group Health and MedCenters, among the Top 10 nationwide. In addition, *U.S. News and World Report's* annual survey of the nation's top hospitals included the University of Minnesota Hospital and Clinic as well as the Mayo Clinic.

For a medical emergency anywhere in Minnesota, call 911. For non-emergency information or help, check out the Twin Cities hospitals and organizations listed here. Remember that the quality of a hospital or HMO (Health Maintenance Organization), in particular, can be difficult to gauge. The best way to determine how well a health care organization will meet your particular needs is to ask doctors, ex-patients and the people who work there. The *Twin Cities Hospitals' Community Service Directory*, which contains information on hospital hotlines, primary care programs, community services, and charity care policies, can also help; to receive a copy call 641-1121.

# Hospitals

### ABBOTT-NORTHWESTERN HOSPITAL/ SISTER KENNY INSTITUTE
*2727 Chicago Ave. S.*
*Minneapolis* 863-4000

Among the Twin Cities' private hospitals, the 960-bed Abbott-Northwestern is by far the largest. It offers 24-hour emergency care, inpatient and outpatient treatment, chronic care rehabilitation and cardiac care. Behavioral health programs are a particular strength, with inpatient, residential and outpatient care available for children, adolescents and adults needing treatment for chemical dependency and mental health problems. The Sister Kenny Institute is a specialized acute care facility that has programs for people with brain injuries, strokes, spinal cord injuries and chronic pain; its phone number is 863-4400.

### BETHESDA LUTHERAN MEDICAL CENTER
*559 Capitol Blvd., St. Paul* 232-2000

A member of the HealthEast hospitals group (the largest such health-care aggregate in St. Paul), Bethesda Lutheran, located near the State Capitol, is a chronic and rehabilitative acute care facility that provides general medical, respiratory and transitional care services.

### CHILDREN'S HOSPITAL
*345 N. Smith Ave., St. Paul* 220-6000

Children's Hospital offers a range of specialized services for kids, as well as pediatric emergency services and a physician referral service.

### CHILDREN'S MEDICAL CENTER OF MINNEAPOLIS
*2525 Chicago Ave. S.*
*Minneapolis* 863-6100
*TTY* 863-5165

This is another highly regarded hospital for kids, with a sudden infant death center, behavioral services, teenage medical services and a physician referral line.

### DIVINE REDEEMER MEMORIAL HOSPITAL
*724 19th Ave. N., South St. Paul* 232-6000

Another HealthEast institution, Divine Redeemer has around-the-clock emergency services, 130 hospital beds, maternity care, outpatient services and full medical and surgical care.

### FAIRVIEW RIDGES HOSPITAL
*201 E. Nicollet Blvd.*
*Burnsville* 892-2000
*TTY* 892-2077

One of three Fairview hospitals in the Minneapolis area, this one offers adult chemical dependency treatment, pediatric services, prenatal care and 24-hour emergency care. It is located just north of the I-35W/I-35E fork off County Road 42.

### FAIRVIEW RIVERSIDE MEDICAL CENTER
*2450 Riverside Ave.*
*Minneapolis* 672-6000
*TTY* 672-6273

The most centrally located of the Fairview facilities (with easy access from I-94), it has an institute for athletic medicine, a multiple sclerosis clinic, chemical dependency services for adults and adolescents, MS services, obstetrics, senior care and mental health treatment.

### FAIRVIEW SOUTHDALE HOSPITAL

6401 France Ave., Edina     924-5000
TTY     924-5066

Fairview Southdale, with a high reputation for the quality of its treatment, is an acute short-term hospital that provides adult mental health services, adult chemical dependency treatment, senior services, a wound care center, a spine care center, an eating disorders program, preventive cardiology treatment, maternity care and a sleep center.

### GILLETTE CHILDREN'S HOSPITAL

200 University Ave. E., St. Paul    291-2848
TDD     229-3928

Gillette offers treatment, rehabilitation and family counseling — as well as customized braces, breathing ventilators and wheelchairs — for kids and teens with brain and spinal cord injuries, cerebral palsy, epilepsy, scoliosis and orthopedic problems and spina bifida.

### HENNEPIN COUNTY MEDICAL CENTER

701 Park Ave., Minneapolis    347-2913
TTY     347-6219

A virtual microcosm of the Twin Cities and its people, HCMC, located in downtown Minneapolis, is a bustling and pulsing facility, the site of both family pain and personal triumph. As a Level 1 trauma center and burn center, it receives many of the area's most serious and violent emergency cases, and its emergency room plays out drama, tragedy and comedy. Among HCMC's best known facilities are a regional sleep disorders center, a regional kidney disease program, nurse and midwife services, a head injury program, and an arthritis and orthopedic specialty center. A full range of outpatient services includes allergy, endocrine, eye, infectious disease, pediatrics, plastic surgery, psychiatry and speech treatment.

### MERCY HOSPITAL

4050 Coon Rapids Blvd.
Coon Rapids     421-8888

Mercy is part of the HealthSpan organization, offering 24-hour emergency care, general medical and surgical treatment, and behavioral health care in the northern suburbs.

### METHODIST HOSPITAL

6500 Excelsior Blvd.
St. Louis Park     932-5500

Minneapolis' western suburbs are well-served by Methodist Hospital, which has 24-hour emergency service, ReadyCare treatment for minor injuries, a Parkinson's Disease clinic, hospice care, a sleep disorders center, a back and neck clinic, and a good reputation for treating cardiac cases.

### MIDWAY HOSPITAL

1700 University Ave., St. Paul   232-5000

Midwest, the most westerly of HealthEast's hospitals, is an acute-care institution that offers full medical and surgical, maternity with special care nurseries, pediatrics, emergency, diagnostic and lab services.

Photo: Chris Polydoroff, Pioneer Press

Hazelden Treatment Center for alcohol and drug rehabilitation near Center City.

## NORTH MEMORIAL MEDICAL CENTER

*3300 Oakdale Ave. N.*
*Robbinsdale*                        *520-5200*
*TTY*                                *520-5775*

The largest hospital in the northern suburbs of Minneapolis, North Memorial has 24-hour emergency services, a cancer center, a hospice program, a pain institute, perinatal treatment, speech pathology services and an institute for athletic medicine.

## ST. FRANCIS REGIONAL MEDICAL CENTER

*325 Fifth Ave., Shakopee        445-2322*

For the far western end of the metropolitan area, St. Francis provides about 100 hospital beds and a full range of services.

## ST. JOHN'S NORTHEAST HOSPITAL

*1575 Bream Ave., Maplewood      232-7000*

St. John's, located near the intersection of I-694 and Highway 61, is a 140-bed hospital that offers acute care in a wide range of areas: pediatrics, maternity, surgical, and general medical, as well as a variety of outpatient services.

## ST. JOSEPH'S HOSPITAL

*69 W. Exchange St., St. Paul      232-3000*

Now a HealthEast institution, St. Joseph's is the state's oldest hospital. It sprang into being suddenly in 1853 when a cholera epidemic ravaged St. Paul, then a hamlet of barely 1,000 people. Four nuns, sisters in the order of St. Joseph of Carondelet, shouldered the burden of helping the sick. They established their first infirmary in a log church built in 1841, near today's intersection of Minnesota Street and Kellogg Boulevard. Within a year, the facility moved to its current location at Ninth and Exchange (then the outskirts of town) and built several structures on the block. St. Joseph's began St. Paul's first ambulance service and, in 1886, was the site of America's first successful gall bladder removal. Now, after much new construction in the 1970s, the oldest part of the medical complex dates from 1922. St. Joseph's is an acute-care hospital offering a broad range of inpatient and outpatient services.

## ST. PAUL-RAMSEY MEDICAL CENTER

*640 Jackson St., St. Paul        221-3456*

Renowned for its emergency services, St. Paul-Ramsey is a teaching hospital with physicians in almost every field of medicine. The only Level 1 trauma center of the Twin Cities' eastern area, it is home to a burn center and participates in the LifeLink III network for local, regional and national medical emergency transport. A ReadyCare clinic treats minor illnesses and injuries as well. The hospital's main building is located in downtown St. Paul, with easy access from I-35E and I-94.

## SHRINERS HOSPITAL

*2025 E. River Rd., Minneapolis    335-5300*

Shriners Hospital is a philanthropic rarity: an institution that provides — usually at no charge — pediatric and orthopedic care for kids from qualified families. The money for treatment comes from Shriners fraternal organizations and their fund-raising efforts.

## UNITED HOSPITALS

*333 N. Smith Ave., St. Paul* 220-8000
*TDD/TTY* 220-8757

Located just a block from Children's Hospital of St. Paul, close to downtown, United provides all-day/all-night emergency services, prenatal care, and full medical and surgical treatment. It also operates smaller Urgent Care Centers in Eagan, 454-7809, and Roseville, 488-9815.

## UNITY HOSPITAL

*550 Osborne Rd., Fridley* 421-4222

A hospital in the HealthSpan network, Unity provides a full range of medical services, including behavioral health treatment and around-the-clock emergency care.

## UNIVERSITY OF MINNESOTA HOSPITAL AND CLINIC

*412 Union St. S.E., Minneapolis* 626-6000
*TDD* 626-0990

Whoa, this place is big! With 700 beds and top-flight teaching, research and technological resources, the U of M Hospital is one of the best medical centers in the country. Well-known for its cancer center, heart and lung institute, transplant center and children's hospital, it also has more than 150 other specialty clinics dealing with a wide range of medical problems in audiology, dermatology, ophthalmology, hemophilia, HIV treatment, psychiatry and psychology, women's health, and oncology, to name a few. There are also special clinics for women's cancer, teens at risk, sports medicine and hand rehabilitation, spinal cord injuries,

and therapeutic radiology. It's located on the U of M campus.

## VETERANS MEDICAL CENTER

*I Veterans Dr., Minneapolis* 725-2000

Serving a half-million vets in the entire Upper Midwest region, the Veterans Medical Center offers short-term and extended care, chemical dependency treatment, cardiac care, and many other types of services. If you're a veteran, you probably already know all about it.

# *Chemical Dependency Programs*

Around the world, Minnesota has a reputation as a center of chemical dependency treatment — and the tongue-in-cheek "Land of 10,000 Treatment Centers" label is probably not too far off the mark. Actors, politicians, authors, artists and plenty of people in other occupations have flocked here from far and wide for short- and long-term dependency care.

There are literally dozens of dependency treatment centers scattered throughout the region, and the decision of which to use should be based on such factors as doctors' recommendations, cost, location, treatment philosophy and reputation. Because of its size and fame, however, one treatment provider merits individual mention.

## HAZELDEN

*P.O. Box 11*
*Center City, MN 55012* (612) 257-4010
(800) 257-7800

Hazelden, founded in 1949, is a nonprofit organization that offers many techniques to assist people in recovering from chemical dependency. It provides rehabilitation care for adolescents and adults, aftercare and family services, dependency counseling training, and a variety of publications and educational materials.

The main campus is in Center City, a community about a 45-minute drive north of the Twin Cities, but there is another local Hazelden facility in Plymouth (a Center for Youth and Families). The organization's rehabilitation program — based on the Twelve Steps of Alcoholics Anonymous — typically requires a stay of 10 to 40 days, using individual counseling, group treatment techniques and aftercare. Hazelden's publishing department produces and distributes 1,500 books, videos and audio cassettes for chemically dependent and non-dependent people. Many of these materials are available in area bookstores.

## Health Maintenance Organizations (HMOs)

The Twin Cities have been fertile ground for the HMO, a prepaid system of health care involving physicians and other health care providers working in a group practice in conjunction with the services of affiliated hospitals, pharmacies, opticians and other providers. Group Health, now part of the hefty HealthPartners organization, was one of the nation's first HMO groups when it began in 1957. Since then, many other HMOs have sprouted locally, and some experts have lauded HMOs as being partly responsible for the high quality and relatively low cost increases of medical care in the state.

Most Twin Citians who receive services from HMOs gain their membership as an employee or retiree benefit. Typically they'll select their HMO from a limited choice that the employer offers. The location of the HMO clinics and costs are often important factors in the enrollment selection.

The Twin Cities area is also out front in the creation of new types of managed medical care organizations. ChoicePlus, an HMO built from scratch in 1992 by some of the region's largest private employers, seems to be succeeding in lowering costs while giving members good care. It includes employees from such businesses as General Mills, 3M, Honeywell, Dayton's and Target stores, and First Bank Systems.

Often, though, it is difficult to evaluate and compare HMO services. A consortium of public and private organizations is currently working on gathering comparable data from HMOs in preparation for the creation of an ambitious guide that will allow consumers to really measure one organization's quality and services against another's. Until that information is available, however, consumers can do some of their own comparison shopping by checking out two publications. One is a free report on HMO operations in Minnesota, published by the HMO division of Minnesota Department of Health. It includes some basic statistics and performance indicators and can be ordered by calling 282-5649. The second publication is *Minnesota Managed Care Review*, published by the Citizens League, which compares the enrollments, expenses and services of HMOs. It costs $20 and is available by calling 337-5919.

The largest HMO group in the Twin Cities is HealthPartners, whose Group Health and MedCenters plans together have 574,000 enrollees. Next in size is Medica, which arose from the merger of Physicians Health Plan (now Medica Choice) and Share (now Medica Primary). Medica has 482,000 enrollees.

| | |
|---|---|
| Blue Plus | 456-8000 |
| HealthPartners | |
|    Group Health | 883-6000 |
|    MedCenters | 883-6000 |
| Medica | 936-1200 |
| NWNL Health Network | 672-8510 |

## Community and Government Health Organizations and Services

### AIDS EMERGENCY FUND
*P.O. Box 582943, Minneapolis   331-7733*
When people living with AIDS encounter financial problems, they can turn to this community fund for assistance.

### ALIVENESS PROJECT
*730 E. 38th St., Minneapolis   822-7946*
People with AIDS or who are HIV-positive can take advantage of the Aliveness Project's massage and chiropractic services and support groups.

### AMERICAN CANCER SOCIETY
*3316 W. 66th St., Edina   925-2772*
This is the Twin Cities chapter of the national health organization focused on eliminating cancer through education, research, services, and preventive measures.

### CHILDREN'S HEALTH PLAN
*444 Lafayette Rd., St. Paul   297-3862*
This plan provides outpatient medical and dental care for children from low-income families.

### COMMUNITY CLINIC CONSORTIUM
*450 N. Syndicate St., St. Paul   644-6555*
Sixteen clinics in Ramsey, Hennepin and Washington counties fall under the umbrella of this consortium, each offering health services on a sliding scale of fees. People of all ages can take advantage of the services. The physicians and other health care professionals are often volunteers treating their patients out of a dedication to community service.

### COMMUNITY HEALTH PLAN
*2414 Park Ave. S., Minneapolis   879-5277*
Through this plan, eligible unemployed and in-transition people from the entire seven-county metro area can purchase one or two years

of health insurance, including HMO-provided outpatient care and hospital inpatient treatment.

### COMMUNITY UNIVERSITY HEALTH CARE CENTER

*2016 16th Ave. S., Minneapolis    627-4774*

This clinic offers medical, dental and mental health services, along with access to treatment at the University of Minnesota Hospitals, all on a sliding fee scale. Often the program is fully subscribed and can take no newcomers.

### HENNEPIN COUNTY BUREAU OF HEALTH ASSURED CARE PROGRAM

*525 Portland Ave., Minneapolis    348-6141*

Assured Care provides discounted, income-based access to services offered by the Hennepin County Bureau of Health: medical clinic treatment, dental care, mental health services, eye care, pharmacy, emergency room treatment and others. The renewal membership is for a year, and it costs nothing to apply.

### INDIAN HEALTH BOARD

*1315 E. 24th St., Minneapolis    721-9800*

Anyone — not only Native Americans — can use the Indian Health Board's medical care, dental care, and counseling services, as well as the special programs for diabetics, smokers trying to stop, and pregnant women. It bases its fees on the patient's income.

### MEDICAL ASSISTANCE

*Hennepin County*
*400 S. Fifth St., Minneapolis    348-2722*
*Ramsey County*
*160 E. Kellogg Blvd., St. Paul    298-5446*

You must come in person to apply for Medical Assistance, Minnesota's program for people on low incomes.

### MINNEAPOLIS HEALTH DEPARTMENT

*250 S. Fourth St., Minneapolis    673-2301*

The Health Department provides a variety of low-cost services for people in need of nutrition and health education, immunizations, prenatal care and child health care.

### MINNESOTA AIDS PROJECT

*2025 Nicollet Ave. S.*
*Minneapolis    870-7773*

An AIDS organization that's been around a while now, Minnesota AIDS Project helps HIV-positive people and those with AIDS in such areas as housing, support groups, referrals, legal services and more.

### MNCARE

*297-3862*

A couple of years ago, Minnesota beat the Clintons to the draw and made U.S. history by becoming the first state to create a comprehensive health coverage package for uninsured and underinsured people. Inpatient and outpatient coverage is available for lower and moderate income individuals and families. The program bases its charges on a sliding scale in accordance with the insured's income, and the processing time is supposed to be quick. Call for current rates and qualifications.

### MINNESOTA COMPREHENSIVE HEALTH ASSOCIATION

*P.O. Box 64566, St. Paul    456-5290*

People whom other insurers

turn down as "uninsurable" can receive medical coverage through this organization's plan, even those with pre-existing conditions and in high-risk occupations. The rates are not cheap (about 25 percent higher than other forms of health insurance), but low-income people receive some breaks.

### PILOT CITY HEALTH CENTER
*1349 Penn Ave. N., Minneapolis  348-4600*
Charging fees based on a sliding scale, this health clinic offers medical, dental, mental health, and social service assistance to people in the community.

### PLANNED PARENTHOOD OF MINNESOTA
*1965 Ford Pkwy., St. Paul          698-2406*
Five Planned Parenthood clinics in the Twin Cities provide women with a variety of health care, counseling and reproductive health services.

### RED DOOR CLINIC
*525 Portland Ave., Minneapolis   348-6363*
Operated by Hennepin County, this clinic specializes in the detection of sexually transmitted diseases and in health counseling.

### WOMEN'S AND CHILDREN'S HEALTH PROGRAMS
*6601 Shingle Creek Pkwy.*
*Brooklyn Center               569-2670*
Services available for women here include family planning, prenatal care and delivery, Pap and pelvic exams, nutrition and health information and pregnancy test-

ing. For kids, developmental, vision, hearing and speech screenings are offered, as well as immunizations, referrals and exams. Patients pay fees based on their income and family size.

## Health Care Phone and Referral Services

These phone lines provide information on specific health problems or give out referrals to doctors — usually physicians on the staff of the sponsoring hospital or part of a group practice or professional group. If you're looking for a physician, don't hesitate to ask friends and co-workers for referrals, as well.

| | |
|---|---|
| *American Board of Medical Specialties* | *(800) 776-2378* |
| *Children's Hospital of St. Paul Physician Referral Service* | *220-6880* |
| *Fairview HealthWise Connection* | *672-7272* |
| *HealthEast Tele-Health* | *232-2600* |
| *Hennepin County Medical Center Poison Control* | *347-3141* |
| *Methodist Hospital Health Directions* | *932-5500* |
| *North Memorial Medical Center's The Professionals* | *520-5555* |
| *Ramsey County Medical Society Doctors Referral Service* | *291-1209* |
| *Ramsey Poison Center* | *221-2113* |
| *Ramsey Tel-Med* | *221-8686* |
| *United Hospital Medformation* | *863-3333* |
| *University of Minnesota Hospital and Clinic Cancer Line* | *626-5555* |
| *University of Minnesota Hospital and Clinic Physician Referral* | *626-6000* |
| *Women's Cancer Resource Center* | *331-6403* |

Photo: John Doman, Pioneer Press

The Mayo Clinic at Rochester.

# Inside
# Community Service and Volunteerism

Minnesotans may have cold noses and frostbitten fingers (at least six months a year), but our hearts are warm and giving.

Volunteerism is thriving in the Twin Cities area, where thousands of individuals pull up their shirt sleeves and lend a helping hand to social service agencies, charities and arts organizations. They organize high-falutin' symphony balls, walk their soles bare for AIDS, read to the blind, befriend troubled teens, deliver meals and smiles to shut-ins, shepherd third-graders on field trips and even clean the kennels at the animal shelters. Hey, somebody's got to do it!

Perhaps the impulse to reach out and help is partly a natural response to our living conditions. The truth is, our winters can be life-threatening and cruel. Just ask anyone who's been stalled on a desolate Minnesota highway on a 30-below night. Minnesotans think nothing of pulling over to share jumper cables or push a car out of a snowbank. Heck, those are considered social events in January!

Likewise, when tornadoes threaten and occasionally strike entire communities, neighbors help neighbors without a second thought. During the cataclysmic Mississippi River floods of spring 1993, hundreds of Twin Citians flocked to the aid of stressed-out Iowa river towns. Boarding bus caravans and free Northwest Airlines flights, they headed south to pack sandbags, clean up mud-laden homes and console residents.

Superbowl 1992 — held in Minneapolis during a frigid January — was a surprising success mainly because of the hearty goodwill and ebullience of thousands of local residents who volunteered as guides, greeters and hosts to the thousands of visitors.

Officially, 60 percent of Minnesotans regularly donate their time in volunteer pursuits. As Garrison Keillor would say, "We are above average."

"Minnesota is recognized as a place where people volunteer at a higher rate than the national average," says Bruce Glasrud, special programs coordinator for the Voluntary Action Center of St. Paul.

As the adage goes, when you volunteer, you help yourself as well as helping others. In addition to the peace of mind and satisfaction that comes from giving of yourself, volunteering is a way to make new friends, learn about your community and develop valuable leadership and people skills. Especially for the young, those volunteer hours lead to important social and professional contacts that prove beneficial later on in life.

To find the volunteer slot that's right for you, call around to local hospitals, nursing homes, social service agencies, churches, senior citizens centers and schools. They're all crying for help. Nature centers and parks, too, always need volunteer tour guides, hosts and clean-up crews in the summer and cross-country trail guides in the winter. Or, if you're feeling overwhelmed by it all and need a little guidance, call one of the following agencies that can refer you to the right organization.

### THE UNITED WAY VOLUNTEER CENTER
*404 S. Eighth St., Minneapolis    340-7621*

This referral service matches individuals to more than 5,000 volunteer opportunities in 600 Twin Cities agencies and charities. It predominantly serves the Minneapolis/west metro area. The Volunteer Center also regularly publishes lists of specific volunteer opportunities in the Minneapolis-based *Star Tribune*, as well as in several suburban newspapers. In 1993, according to the center, more than 9,000 people were referred to volunteer opportunities.

### THE VOLUNTARY ACTION CENTER OF ST. PAUL
*251 Starkey St., St. Paul    227-3938*

Like its counterpart in Minneapolis, this center also refers individuals to volunteer opportunities — predominantly in the St. Paul/

east metro area. Its database includes more than 4,000 opportunities in 600 agencies. The Voluntary Action Center also publishes lists of volunteer opportunities in the *St. Paul Pioneer Press* and east-metro suburban newspapers.

## Other Volunteer Resources

### COMMUNITY VOLUNTEER SERVICE
*2300 Orleans St. W., Stillwater    439-7434*

This agency refers volunteers to agencies and charities throughout Washington County. It also operates a senior center and a bureau for holiday volunteering.

### NATIONAL RETIREE VOLUNTEER COALITION
*607 Marquette Ave., Minneapolis    341-2689*

This organization links retirees to volunteer opportunities that best utilize their skills. Placements include hospital and school positions, as well as a program that supports parents of inner-city school children.

### MINNESOTA OFFICE ON VOLUNTEER SERVICES
*Department of Administration*
*117 University Ave., St. Paul    296-4731*

This state organization promotes volunteerism by publishing a quarterly newsletter and conducting training programs for persons in the volunteer field.

## Brother, Can You Spare a Dime?

For some, community service may simply take the form of signing a check or making a financial pledge. In the Twin Cities, 25 percent of all employees contribute funds to charities. The generosity doesn't stop at the office, but continues at home. *NonProfit Times*, a publication on nonprofit management, has rated the Twin Cities the nation's most responsive area for telemarketing appeals for charity. The magazine also ranks the area ninth nationally in terms of its overall fund-raising climate. The following is a good source of information for those who are faced with financial requests from charities.

## THE MINNESOTA CHARITIES REVIEW COUNCIL

*122 Franklin Ave. W., Minneapolis   870-0657*
*(800) 733-4483*

This private, nonprofit organization serves as an independent source of information about national and local charities. It can be a real help for consumers who are inundated by telephone solicitors and confused about where their valuable dollars are going. The council's database contains information on more than 3,000 charities.

# *Inside*
# Media

You may not realize it, but the Twin Cities is a media powerhouse of sorts. Skeptical? For starters, it's one of the few metropolitan areas of its size that still has competing daily newspapers. It also has competing alternative weeklies and a pair of battling city magazines. The area boasts the nation's largest public-radio system and is the headquarters of a public-radio network that out-distributes National Public Radio. And in the realm of moving images, more than 50 million people during the past year have rushed to the theaters to see such made-in-Minnesota movies as *Untamed Heart, The Mighty Ducks, Grumpy Old Men, Iron Will* and *Little Big League*.

What do you expect from a city where winter sets in for a five-month stay starting in November — that people will sit outside and revel in the chill? (Well, some do — see the chapter on Winter.) Instead, Twin Citians are prodigious readers, listeners and viewers, and this town offers plenty to engage their eyes and ears.

## Daily Newspapers

### ST. PAUL PIONEER PRESS
*345 Cedar St., St. Paul* 222-5011
*Home delivery* 222-1234

This paper, the morning daily that is a publisher of this *Insiders' Guide*, can trace its origins to some of the earliest ink spilled in Minnesota Territory. Among its direct ancestors are the *Minnesota Pioneer*, the state's first newspaper, founded in 1849; the *St. Paul Daily Democrat*, which arrived on the scene soon afterward; and the *St. Paul Daily Press*, spawned by the Civil War. Nowadays the *Pioneer Press* is part of the Knight-Ridder newspaper group, sports a daily circulation of more than 200,000 (nearly 300,000 on Sundays) and is the primary paper serving the 40 percent of the Twin Cities that lies in the east metropolitan area — Ramsey, Washington and Dakota counties — along with parts of western Wisconsin. (There is currently no home delivery to most addresses in Minneapolis and points west, although the *Pioneer Press* is widely available at newsstands and vending machines throughout the Twin Cities.) The paper is best-known for its thorough and award-winning sports coverage, its high-quality and wide-ranging feature writing (which earned the paper two Pulitzer Prizes during the 1980s), and its attractive, reader-friendly design.

Another popular feature of the *Pioneer Press* is its Bulletin Board section, an indescribable collection of reader-supplied gossip, rant, cute kid stories, and general observations of life displaying varying levels of couth and intelligence. It has proven so popular that the paper has published two anthologies, *The Best of Bulletin Board* and *The Simple Pleasures* (Andrews and McMeel). Also take note of The Line, the newspaper's telephone audiotext service, which supplies movie reviews, stock prices, sports scores, historical sound clips and, perhaps uniquely, bird calls; the number is 222-1000. Subscribers to America Online can get access to the newspaper's back issues via their computer screens as well.

## STAR TRIBUNE
*425 Portland Ave. S.*
*Minneapolis*                     673-4000

The sole survivor of 130 years of journalistic wars, cannibalism and mergers in Minneapolis, this morning daily is one of the nation's only metropolitan papers lacking the name of a city on its masthead. The reason is that the *Star Tribune* publishes separate editions for Minneapolis, St. Paul and outstate Minnesota, generating a daily circulation of more than 400,000 (nearly 700,000 on Sundays). Consequently, home delivery is available throughout the Twin Cities area. Owned by the Cowles publishing empire, the paper has dour columnists (excepting the deliciously irreverent C.J., the purveyor of gossip), solid entertainment and business reporting, spirited food writing, a page called News with a View that mixes journalism and personal essay and enough syndicated advice columnists to satisfy the cravings of the worst addict. The paper's Minnesota Poll has taken important opinion samplings of the state's residents for many decades, and the *Star Tribune* earned a Pulitzer Prize in 1990 for investigative reporting. Like its crosstown rival, the paper offers several services to readers over the phone, including stock prices, music clips, movie reviews, late-breaking news updates and fax-on-demand information. The *Star Tribune* has also announced plans to launch a complete newspaper and backfile service for on-line subscribers.

## Other Newspapers

### THE AMERICAN JEWISH WORLD
*4509 Minnetonka Blvd.*
*Minneapolis*                     920-7000

The World is an award-winning weekly publication that has served as the voice of Minnesota's Jewry for decades. It includes local news, international news with a local slant, religious reports, profiles, events listings and commentary.

### ASIAN AMERICAN PRESS
*422 University Ave., St. Paul*      224-6570

Members of Minnesota's Asian and Pacific Islander community are the audience of this weekly newspaper, which boasts a surprisingly high number of news stories from

# TALK

## For Conservatives 24 Hours A Day

## KSTP AM 1500

the international realm. Topics include business, the arts, politics and education.

### ASIAN PAGES
*P.O. Box 11932, St. Paul 55111*     *869-1232*

With readers throughout Minnesota, Iowa and Wisconsin, the biweekly *Asian Pages* features "softer" news than *Asian American Press*, serving as a resource in the areas of immigration, personal finance, the arts, cooking and education.

### CITY PAGES
*401 N. Third St., Ste. 550*
*Minneapolis*     *375-1015*

One of two alternative news weeklies in the Twin Cities, *City Pages* is a bit more of a muckraker than its rival, *Twin Cities Reader*, more often featuring exposés and investigative reporting. *City Pages* also seems aimed at a somewhat younger audience, with strong coverage of the arts (especially music) and sports, along with good cartoons. Free, it's available throughout the area in racks.

### FINANCE AND COMMERCE
*615 S. Seventh St., Minneapolis*   *333-4244*

This weekly newspaper is the place to look for legal notices and lists of real estate transactions, bankruptcy petitions, legal judgments, liens and new business

openings. Each issue also contains several news stories, mainly wire service articles.

### INSIGHT NEWS
*422 University Ave. W., Ste. 8*
*St. Paul*     *227-8968*

In-depth stories, sports news, arts coverage and commentary are the strengths of this weekly newspaper for the African-American community. Insight also features business and employment news, health stories and a community calendar. It is available free at points throughout the Twin Cities.

### MINNEAPOLIS ST. PAUL CITYBUSINESS
*5500 Wayzata Blvd., Ste. 500*
*Minneapolis*     *591-2701*

CityBusiness presents a thorough weekly roundup of the business news of the Twin Cities, with a sprinkling of humor, company profiles, opinion and commercial statistics, along with an every-issue top-25 list sketching the movers and shakers in a variety of business endeavors. It's available at newsstands and by subscription.

### MINNEAPOLIS SPOKESMAN/ ST. PAUL RECORDER
*3744 Fourth Ave. S., Minneapolis*   *827-4021*
*909B Selby Ave., St. Paul*     *224-4886*

These weekly papers for the

Twin Cities' African-American community, produced by the area's oldest black publishing firm (founded in 1935), offer local and national news, business stories, sports reports, a church directory and the opinions of several columnists.

### MINNESOTA CHRISTIAN CHRONICLE
*1619 Portland Ave. S.*
*Minneapolis*          *339-9579*

Established in 1978, this weekly newspaper presents local and national Christian news, pro-life commentary and an extensive events calendar.

### THE MINNESOTA WOMEN'S PRESS
*771 Raymond Ave., St. Paul       646-3968*

This thoughtful and well-written biweekly newspaper aims to approach the news through personal perspectives, relating the diversity as well as the shared experiences of women. Many of the stories focus on individual women and their work, and there are also articles on finance, the arts, politics and lifestyles. Some of the most provocative writing is in columns and first-person pieces. The *Women's Press* is distributed free at more than 350 locations throughout the area.

### THE NATIVE AMERICAN PRESS
*422 University Ave. W.*
*St. Paul*          *224-0098*

Heavy with local and national news about Native Americans and their communities, the weekly *Press* packs a lot of information into each issue. It includes opinion pieces and the writings of columnists as well. It's free and available at several locations in the area.

### SKYWAY NEWS/FREEWAY NEWS
*15 S. Fifth St., Minneapolis       375-9222*

These free weeklies, available in racks in downtown and suburban Minneapolis and downtown St. Paul, serve a readership mostly made up of commuter office workers. They consider themselves the community papers of their areas, and their coverage of business, retail and development issues within their geographic realms is good. Downtown arts and entertainment coverage is also commendable. Special issues each year devoted the the St. Paul Winter Carnival and the Minneapolis Aquatennial are great introductions to these big events and often offer historical perspective as well. Each of the Minneapolis and St. Paul *Skyway News* prints useful maps of its city's skyway system in each issue.

### TWIN CITIES READER
*10 S. Fifth St., Ste. 200*
*Minneapolis*          *321-7300*

The *Reader* is a long-time staple of consumers of so-called alternative news, although the publication has grown more respectable with age. Long gone are the explicit ads seeking sexual encounters; they've been replaced by the area's biggest selection of tastefully written "eligibles" ads, along with an editorial emphasis on city and state politics, media coverage and the arts. The paper (available free at racks in office buildings, restaurants and places of entertainment) also contains good events listings.

## Magazines and Other Publications

### COLORS
2608 Blaisdell Ave. S.
Minneapolis                    874-0494

Self-described as a "journal of opinion by writers of color" in Minnesota, *Colors* is skillfully written, attractively designed and always interesting to read. Recent issues have presented interviews, first-person essays, examinations of social issues, a lively letters page and a calendar of events.

### COMPUTERUSER
220 S. Sixth St., Ste. 500
Minneapolis                    339-7571

Once strictly a Twin Cities publication, the monthly *ComputerUser* now boasts distribution in several other areas of the country. The tabloid covers computer technology, software and office equipment with grace and wit, allowing even non-nerds to gain something from reading it. Its listings of user groups and BBS linkups are especially useful. *ComputerUser* is free, available at public libraries, computer stores and other pick-up points.

### CORPORATE REPORT MINNESOTA
5500 Wayzata Blvd., Ste. 500
Minneapolis                    591-2701

Often subdued in tone and quite corporate-looking, this monthly magazine profiles CEOs, provides in-depth examinations of Minnesota industries and keeps up with business trends throughout the state. It is well-written, though not often explosive. Each year it publishes an encyclopedic and highly successful directory of Minnesota's public and privately held businesses.

### FAMILY TIMES
2912 Xenwood Ave. S.
St. Louis Park                 922-6186

*Family Times*, a monthly tabloid focusing on issues concerning Minnesota's families, has a circulation of 65,000 and is distributed free at stores, restaurants, medical offices and clinics, libraries and other public facilities. It covers such topics as foster parenting, child rearing, children's education, family medicine, entertainment and new products and services.

### GAZE MAGAZINE
2344 Nicollet Ave. S., Ste. 30
Minneapolis                    871-7472

With the demise of the newspaper *Equal Times* in 1994, *Gaze Magazine* became the Twin Cities' most influential publication for gay men and lesbians. A bi-monthly, it offers personality profiles and coverage of the arts, sports, astrology, community events, social issues and popular culture. It's free and available at racks around the region.

# TALK

## For Liberals
## 24 Hours A Day

## KSTP
## AM
## 1500

### MINNESOTA HISTORY
*345 Kellogg Blvd. W., St. Paul*    296-6126

A quarterly magazine published by the Minnesota Historical Society, *Minnesota History* presents longish and satisfying explorations into the state's past, covering everything from architecture, politics, ethnic history, popular culture and transportation to new books and prominent personalities. The photos and maps, largely drawn from the Society's own collection, are gorgeous.

### MINNESOTA MONTHLY
*15 S. Ninth St., Ste. 320*
*Minneapolis*    371-5800

Award-winning in its design and distinguished in its writing, *Minnesota Monthly* covers the state's (primarily the Twin Cities') lifestyle, venturing into the arts, home design and planning, politics, current affairs and profiles, with occasional forays into semi-investigative reporting. Each year, the magazine sponsors a writing competition and a photography contest. Available on newsstands, *Minnesota Monthly* is also sent free to members of Minnesota Public Radio, and the network's radio schedule occupies the last quarter of the magazine.

### MINNESOTA PARENT
*401 N. Third St., Ste. 550*
*Minneapolis*    375-1203

Each month, *Minnesota Parent* serves up an assortment of articles on living with kids. No facet of the family experience seems unturned: Food, entertainment, shopping, books and software, health, art and travel are all present in abundance.

The free tabloid publication is distributed throughout the region.

### MINNESOTA SPORTS
*15 S. Fifth St., Ste. 800*
*Minneapolis*    375-9045

If you run, bike, golf, swim, lift weights, ski, skate or camp, you should check out this monthly publication full of events listings, nutrition advice, gear reviews, motivational techniques and sports news. It's crammed with information and is available free at pick-up points throughout the area.

### MINNESOTA'S JOURNAL OF LAW AND POLITICS
*10 S. Fifth St., Ste. 415*
*Minneapolis*    338-3828

This is a brash, smart, funny and irreverent magazine about attorneys and politicians, and you should find a copy even if you normally have no interest in the machinations that take place in the capitol or in our legal system. Its writing is great and its covers are often outrageous.

### MPLS.ST.PAUL
*220 S. Sixth St., Ste. 500*
*Minneapolis*    339-7571

With a long string of national city-magazine awards and a hefty circulation, *Mpls.St.Paul* is influential, often-quoted and well-read. Its directories of the best in everything from doctors to restaurants to schools are sensible and accurate, and the magazine also delivers good celebrity coverage, travel reporting and profiles.

For folks out there in radio land who might want a complete listing of where to tune to meet their up-to-the-minute radio mood, here's a handy one for you:

**AM Stations**

| | | |
|---|---|---|
| KTCJ | 690 | Adult album music |
| WMIN | 740 | Hits of the '40s, '50s and '60s |
| KUOM | 770 | College alternative |
| WCCO | 830 | News, general interest |
| KTIS | 900 | Inspirational music, talk |
| KJJO | 950 | Country music |
| KMZZ | 980 | Hard rock |
| WCTS | 1030 | Religious music, news |
| KFAN | 1130 | Sports |
| WIMN | 1220 | Nostalgia |
| WWTC | 1280 | For children |
| KNOW | 1330 | News, information |
| KLBB | 1400 | Big Band music |
| KQRS | 1440 | Album-oriented rock |
| KDWA | 1460 | '50s and '60s music |
| KBCW | 1470 | Country music |
| KSTP | 1500 | News, talk |
| KKCM | 1530 | Christian music |
| KYCR | 1570 | Religious programming |
| WIXK | 1590 | Country music |

**FM Stations**

| | | |
|---|---|---|
| KBEM | 88.5 | Jazz |
| WCAL | 89.3 | Classical music, news |
| KMOJ | 89.9 | Soul, blues, gospel, reggae, jazz |
| KFAI | 90.3 | Music, news, talk shows |
| KNOW | 91.1 | News, information |
| KQRS | 92.5 | Album-oriented rock |
| KEGE | 93.7 | Modern rock |
| KSTP | 94.5 | Adult contemporary music |
| KNOF | 95.3 | Religious programming, music |
| WLKX | 95.9 | Country music |
| KTCZ | 97.1 | Adult album music |
| KTIS | 98.5 | Religious programming, news |
| KSJN | 99.5 | Classical music |
| WBOB | 100.3 | Country music |
| KDWB | 101.3 | Contemporary hit music |
| KEEY | 102.1 | Country music |
| WLTE | 102.9 | Light rock |
| KJJO | 104.1 | Country music |
| WREV | 105.1/105.3 | Alternative |
| KCFE | 105.7 | New adult contemporary |
| WIXK | 107.1 | Country music |
| KQQL | 107.9 | Golden oldies |

## Twin Cities Business Monthly

220 S. Sixth St., Ste. 500
*Minneapolis*                    *339-7571*

A newcomer in the area's crowded field of business publications, this one has made its mark by offering snazzy design and an emphasis on the people in business. Its regular columns, however, are devoted to such topics as personal finance, home businesses and (no kidding) the prostate gland. The feature articles are long, but they'll generally hold your interest.

---

## TV Stations

### KARE (Channel 11)
*546-1111*

This station is the local NBC affiliate. Its news department, traditionally strong in weather (which is by no means a topic of peripheral interest in temperature-challenged Minnesota) and seemingly aimed at a slightly younger viewership than some other stations, sometimes tends toward the sensationalistic but offers strong on-air talent.

### KLGT (Channel 23)
*646-2300*

KLGT, an independent station, is the rerun capital of the TV dial. It airs "Hill Street Blues," "St. Elsewhere," "Perry Mason," "I Love Lucy," "Little House on the Prairie" and almost any other old show you may need to get your nostalgic heart pounding. It carries some pretty good old movies late at night, too.

### KMSP (Channel 9)
*944-9999*

KMSP is the biggie among the area's independents. Its weekday evening schedule is dominated by an hour-long 9 PM newscast, giving the station added time to present local stories in more detail. Because of KMSP's limited resources in the past, its reporters had the reputation of often being the last to arrive at a news scene, but this may be changing.

### KSTP (Channel 5)
*645-5555*

KSTP, the ABC affiliate, has a distinguished history of innovation. During the 1940s, it became the first TV station in the Midwest to air a daily newscast and later was the first full-color station in the world. In reporting, its strength has traditionally been its quick response to spot news — disasters, fires and other emergencies. KSTP was also the only station in the state to keep complete archives of its news stories going all the way back to 1948, and this valuable collection was recently donated to the Minnesota Historical Society for public access.

## TWIN CITIES PUBLIC TELEVISION
### KTCA (CHANNEL 2)
### KTCI (CHANNEL 17)
#### 222-1717

Headquartered since 1989 in a new television center in downtown St. Paul, Twin Cities Public Television is an active producer of programming and enjoys a devoted following. Its self-produced shows include "Newton's Apple," "Arts on 2," "Almanac," "Tape's Rolling!" and "NewsNight Minnesota" — the latter a news show introduced in 1994 that aims to explore meaty issues and avoid fluff. Channel 2, which usually goes off the air at 1 AM, airs the bulk of the programming, while Channel 17, shut down at midnight, broadcasts a continuous radar weather summary during the day and repeats KTCA airings at night.

## KXLI (CHANNEL 41)
#### (612) 262-8666

Broadcasting from the St. Cloud area, KXLI is an independent station with programming that includes movies, reruns and Christian shows.

## WCCO (CHANNEL 4)
#### 339-4444

The Twin Cities' long-time CBS affiliate, WCCO has evolved into a community-oriented station with a news department strong in in-depth reporting, crime stories and sports. In 1994, it introduced "family sensitive" newscasts, in ad-dition to its regular news shows. The innovation gained national attention.

## WFTC (CHANNEL 29)
#### 424-2929

The region's FOX affiliate, WFTC also airs Twins baseball, morning cartoons and "Gilligan's Island," "Brady Bunch," "Batman" and "Twilight Zone" reruns.

## Cable Television

Several cable TV firms serve the Twin Cities' various municipalities. Rather surprisingly, considering the long winter in these parts and the need to burrow in, the Twin Cities has one of the nation's lowest cable TV subscription percentages — fewer than half the households.

### AMERICAN WIRELESS SYSTEMS
#### 452-8010

This small, upstart company offers cable services within 30 miles of downtown Minneapolis.

### MEREDITH CABLE
#### 483-9999

This company serves the northern suburbs of Roseville, Columbia Heights and Anoka.

### MIDWEST SPORTS CHANNEL
#### 330-2678

This is a local all-sports channel.

### PARAGON CABLE TV
#### 522-2000

Paragon serves Minneapolis and many of the western suburbs.

### CONTINENTAL CABLEVISION
*222-3333*

Continental is the cable company for St. Paul and suburbs.

## Radio Stations

With a few notable exceptions, radio stations in the Twin Cities are much like they are any place else in the United States. At last count, we have 42 places to park on the AM and FM dials, and listeners have the usual choices of formats: country-western (shop around among five stations), album-oriented rock, classic rock, top 40, alternative rock, oldies, urban contemporary, adult contemporary, gospel, contemporary Christian, classical, jazz, news and sports/talk.

A few of the stations, however, do stand out as distinctive, either for historical, cultural or program-related reasons.

### KBEM 88.5 FM
*627-2833*

If not for this little noncommercial station that broadcasts from studios in Minneapolis' North High School (the station is operated by the Minneapolis Board of Education), we'd have precious little jazz to hear on the radio. The station also airs a fine bluegrass show on

Saturday mornings and is the absolute best source of traffic information, courtesy of reports from the Minnesota Department of Transportation.

### KFAI 90.3 FM
*341-3144*

The "fresh air" slogan of this community supported station is no lie — you can pick up French, African, urban folk, bluegrass, Greek and Russian music off its airwaves, along with tunes from many other parts of the globe. Its signal doesn't always carry far, and its on-air folks are sometimes discombobulated, but a generous spirit and appreciation for diversity is apparent in its broadcasting.

### KMOJ 89.9 FM
*377-0594*

Though frequently beset by organizational troubles, this noncommercial station has successfully served as the voice of the Twin Cities' African-American community for many years. Frequently described as "urban contemporary" in format, its programming actually ranges from gospel to rap, with some very savvy DJs calling the shots.

# TALK

**For Those
In-Between
24 Hours A Day**

**KSTP
AM
1500**

Photo: Joe Oden, Pioneer Press

Garrison Keillor's radio program "A Prairie Home Companion" is
broadcast from St. Paul's Fitzgerald Theater.

## MINNESOTA PUBLIC RADIO
### KNOW 91.1 FM
### KSJN 99.5 FM
### KNOW 1330 AM
*290-1500*

Who would have thought that public radio — formerly the bastion of ill-clothed techno-geeks, classical music eggheads and paroled campus radicals — could evolve into an efficient, well-organized, financially strong and popular medium? To everyone's surprise, it happened years ago in Minnesota.

Minnesota Public Radio, a network of 27 stations scattered throughout the Upper Midwest (there's even one in Idaho!), has grown into the nation's biggest producer of shows, gatherers of listeners and raisers of money among the nation's public radio enterprises. Its nationally distributed programs include "St. Paul Sunday Morning," Garrison Keillor's "A Prairie Home Companion," "Sound Money," "Pipedreams" and broadcasts of Minnesota Orchestra and Saint Paul Chamber Orchestra concerts.

It's also a founder of Public Radio International (headquartered in Minneapolis and formerly called American Public Radio), a program distributor whose shows match (and perhaps surpass) the listenership of National Public Radio's programs. In the Twin Cities, MPR operates three stations: KSJN (99.5 FM), a primarily classical music station that dabbles in eccentric popular-music programming during the morning drive time; KNOW (91.1 FM), whose all-news format, international programming and intelligent, award-winning reporting make it one of the best sources of information among all the choices in the Twin Cities media; and KNOW-AM, a canned all-news station.

### WCAL 89.3 FM
*(800) 222-9225*

An improved signal now makes WCAL accessible to most Twin Cities radios. Broadcasting from St. Olaf College in Northfield, this public radio station (which is not part of the Minnesota Public Radio network) is a great place to tune in to hear amiable voices and the relaxing complexities of baroque fugues. Founded more than 75 years ago, WCAL is the nation's first publicly supported station — so you can blame them for every listener support drive that's ever been broadcast.

### WCCO 830 AM
*370-0611*

Although its legendary Arbitron

Twin Citians LOVE to hate sports curmudgeon Sid Hartman on WCCO-AM Radio and in the *Star Tribune*.

Insiders' Tips

ratings have slipped some over the years, WCCO remains one of the most dominant stations in any radio market in the nation. When a blizzard threatens, you can bet that nearly 100 percent of the parents in the Twin Cities tune in to hear about district school closings. And when folks anywhere in the Upper Midwest want to find out Minnesota's take on an issue (the station's signal really carries), they tune in as well.

On the air since 1922, WCCO has had plenty of time to perfect its approach: Its on-air talent conveys a warm and neighborly persona — not too intellectual and not too cynical. Its talk shows sometimes sound more like family re-

unions than the cutting, ego-powered exercises that can take place elsewhere on the dial. In recent years, the "Good Neighbor" has become more like other stations, but folks still tune in for weather and Twins baseball.

## WWTC 1280 AM
### 926-1280

This spot on the dial is reserved for kids. The home of Radio AAHS, this station delivers children's music, commentary and other programming, and 25 percent of the kids in the Twin Cities listen to it. Satellites carry its signal to 16 other full-time children's radio stations around the country.

# Inside
# Public Services

If you're just moving to the Twin Cities, you'll need to get your phone and electric service started. If you've lived here a while, you may want to complain about a dog on the loose, find out where to register to vote, or learn the location of the nearest public library. Whatever the crisis or reason, and for better or worse, we rely on those indispensable services of government and utility companies to help us get through the day.

Especially in the Twin Cities, where two large metropolises lie side by side, the different responsibilities of each level of government can be confusing. In addition to the federal-state-county-city hierarchy that exists all over the country, we can boast an additional layer of metropolitan councils, multi-county agencies that oversee certain government services for the whole metropolitan area. You'll find more about that later in this chapter.

One important thing to remember: for any fire, police or medical emergency, call 911 from anywhere in Minnesota. That's the fastest way to receive help in life-threatening situations.

Government junkies will find the Citizens League's frequently updat-ed *Public Affairs Directory* a useful resource. Call 338-0791 for more information.

A final note on one Minnesota political peculiarity: our Democratic Party is called the Democrat-Farmer Labor Party (DFL; it reflects the Democrats' merger with the left-leaning Farmer Labor Party a half-century ago), and the Republicans are here called the Independent Republicans (IR; the name, originally intended to distance Minnesota Republicans from the national Republican party, is a souvenir of the Republican-bashing days of the late '70s).

## Federal Government Services

Uncle Sam maintains Federal Courts Buildings at 110 S. Fourth Street, Minneapolis, and 316 N. Robert Street, St. Paul. For general information on any aspect of U.S. government services, call the Federal Information Center at (800) 366-2998.

| | |
|---|---|
| *Consumer Product Safety* | |
| *Commission* | 290-3781 |
| *Immigration and Naturalization* | |
| *Service* | 854-7754 |
| *Internal Revenue Service* | 291-1422 |

### PASSPORTS
Several different facilities in the

area accept applications for U.S. passports. They include the Hennepin County Government Center, 348-8240, and the main Minneapolis Post Office, 349-4736.

### SOCIAL SECURITY ADMINISTRATION
*(800) 772-1213*

### UNITED STATES POSTAL SERVICE
*349-9100, 293-3777*
These numbers connect you to Postal Answer Line, an automated postal information service that requires you to use a touch-tone phone. To speak with a real live person, call 349-4711. For ZIP code information, call 349-3535.

### VETERANS ADMINISTRATION
*(800) 368-5899*

## State Government Services

St. Paul is the state capital, making access to state services, or at least to state workers, relatively easy for most in the Twin Cities. The center of state government activity is the Capitol complex, a prominent grouping of buildings at the north edge of downtown St. Paul. Call 296-6013 for general information on state services.

| | |
|---|---|
| Arts Board | 297-2603 |
| Health Department | 623-5000 |
| Human Rights Department | 296-5663 |
| Job Service | 296-3644 |

### MINNESOTA STATE LOTTERY
*635-8100*
If you dream of effortlessly striking it rich, the state lottery might be one of the government "services" you'll enjoy the most. After voters authorized a state lottery in 1988, the Minnesota Legislature approved lottery legislation a year later. Now, we have two kinds of lottery games to play: instant (or scratch-off) games and computerized number games. Some 4,000 retailers throughout Minnesota sell instant or on-line tickets, so you should have no problem finding someone willing to take your wager. Winning numbers are announced on TV, radio and in newspapers, or you can call the 24-hour Player Hotline at 297-7371. About 55 percent of players' wagers are returned to lottery winners, with the rest of the money going to the state's general fund and an environment and natural resources trust fund. The state's proceeds from the lottery annually amount to about $70 million.

### MOTOR VEHICLE SERVICES
*296-6911*
If you have a car, the Driver and Vehicle Services Division of the Department of Public Safety wants to know about you and your auto. To get a driver's license, you must take an exam at one of the many exam stations located throughout the Twin Cities area. If you're a new Minnesota resident, you must register your car within 60 days of your arrival. In the Twin Cities, registering your car, and renewing your registration annually, requires you to take the vehicle to an emissions test station, many of which are scattered around the area. The emissions checkers tend to get swamped toward the end of the month, when last-minute renewers all rush in at once, so the

# Other Libraries That Speak Volumes

In addition to the dozens of public libraries in the Twin Cities, other libraries in the region have valuable holdings in a multitude of fields. Every college and university, for example, has a library of some kind, and most are open to the public (with school alums often retaining borrowing privileges). The holdings of the University of Minnesota are particularly impressive, with special collections devoted to African-American literature, World War I, architectural history, ballooning, the YMCA of the U.S.A. archives, mathematical astronomy, and Greek literature, to name a few.

Here are some Twin Cities libraries especially worthy of checking out:

### AMERICAN SWEDISH INSTITUTE

*2600 Park Ave. S., Minneapolis    871-4907*

The institute's library is a large repository of historic information on Swedish immigration to the United States. Much of it, of course, is written in Swedish.

### ANDERSON HORTICULTURAL LIBRARY

*Minnesota Landscape Arboretum*
*Chanhassen                         443-2440*

Come and root out all the information you need on plants and horticulture. This collection of books, magazines and seed and nursery catalogs is the only horticultural library in the Upper Midwest.

### BAKKEN LIBRARY

*3537 Zenith Ave. S., Minneapolis 927-6508*

Here's a truly one-of-a-kind collection of materials about the history of electricity and magnetism in the life sciences. It includes a fascinating selection of publications on quack electric cures.

### GOLDSTEIN GALLERY
### FASHION PHOTOGRAPHY AND ILLUSTRATIONS COLLECTION

*University of Minnesota*
*St. Paul Campus              625-2737*

This is a horde of fashion magazines, illustrations, photos, catalogs and costumes, deep but not too large. It's used by writers, fashion designers, historians and theater costumers.

### JAMES J. HILL REFERENCE LIBRARY

*Fourth and Market Sts., St. Paul   227-9531*

Sharing a building with St. Paul's Central Library, this is an exceptionally user-friendly (and privately funded) facility for people who seek business information. Here you can find business periodicals, annual reports, electronic databases and books, along with some of the most helpful librarians in town.

## KERLAN AND HESS COLLECTIONS

*University of Minnesota*
*Minneapolis Campus*          624-4576

These children's literature research collections, containing more than 120,000 kids' picture books, story books, manuscripts, photos, drawings and press proofs for all types of children's volumes, constitute one of the world's finest accumulations of its kind.

## MINNESOTA HISTORICAL SOCIETY

*345 Kellogg Blvd. W., St. Paul*   296-2143

The Society's Minnesota History Center — palatial in all other respects, as well — contains a beautiful Research Center that sets historians' mouths watering. People researching genealogy and house histories like it, too. It contains vast holdings of manuscripts, books, maps, business records, photographs, periodicals and oral-history tapes, along with just about every newspaper ever printed in Minnesota (on 70,000 reels of microfilm). To avoid crowds, the best time to go is on weekdays.

## MINNESOTA LIBRARY FOR THE
## BLIND AND PHYSICALLY HANDICAPPED

*Minnesota State Academy for the Blind*
*Faribault (507) 332-3279, (800) 722-0550*

Although this library is located in southern Minnesota, well outside the Twin Cities area, it distributes its materials via the U.S. Mail to patrons throughout the state who can't read conventional printed materials because of blindness or other disabilities. Its collection includes cassette tapes, computer disks, Braille books and large-print books.

## QUATREFOIL

*1619 Dayton Ave., St. Paul*      641-0969

Materials about gay men, lesbians and other sexual minorities are the focus of this lending library, which also sponsors book discussions and art shows.

## REPRODUCTIVE HEALTH LIBRARY

*Planned Parenthood, 1965 Ford Pkwy.*
*St. Paul*                698-2401

Open by appointment only, this collection includes materials on birth control, reproduction, sexually transmitted diseases, infertility, abortion and sexual assault.

## SMALL-PRESS LIBRARY

The Loft, 66 Malcolm Ave. S.E.
Minneapolis            379-8999

The Loft, one of the nation's foremost organizations for writers, maintains a substantial small-press library that includes literary journals, poetry chapbooks and works of fiction and criticism, all issued by publishers not catering to the mass market.

## WOMEN'S HEALTH LIBRARY

Melpomene Institute for Women's
Health Research
1010 University Ave., St. Paul     642-1951

Materials in this collection cover all aspects of women's health: fitness, aging, pregnancy, body image and osteoporosis, for example.

least crowded time to go is in the first half of the month, especially on weekdays.

| | |
|---|---|
| Revenue Department | 296-3403 |
| Road Condition Information | 296-3076 |
| Veterans Affairs | 296-2562 |

## Metropolitan Services

Because the Twin Cities metropolitan area now embraces seven different counties, several metrowide agencies provide services that cross county lines. For general information on metropolitan services, call 291-6359.

| | |
|---|---|
| Metro Airports Commission | 726-8100 |
| Metro Mosquito Control District | 645-9149 |
| Metro Parks and Open Space Commission | 291-6333 |
| Regional Transit Board | 229-2700 |

## County Government Services

Here's where things start to get complicated. We have seven different counties in the Twin Cities, each providing the same basic services to its residents.

### ANOKA COUNTY

| | |
|---|---|
| General Information | 421-4760 |
| County Commissioners | 323-5680 |
| Highway Department | 323-5519 |
| Job Training Center | 784-1800 |
| Parks and Recreation | 757-3920 |
| Sheriff | 323-5021 |

### CARVER COUNTY

| | |
|---|---|
| General Information | 361-1500 |
| Community Health Services | 446-1722 |
| Community Social Services | 361-1600 |
| Highway Department | 446-1722 |
| Parks | 467-3145 |
| Sheriff | 361-1231 |

### DAKOTA COUNTY

| | |
|---|---|
| General information | 437-3191 |
| Community Services | 450-2742 |
| Employment and Economic Assistance | 450-2611 |
| Highway Department | 891-7101 |
| Job Training | 450-2748 |
| Parks | 437-6608 |
| Public Health | 552-3100 |
| Sheriff | 438-4700 |

### HENNEPIN COUNTY

| | |
|---|---|
| General Information | 348-3000 |
| Children and Family Services | 348-2102 |

| Child Protection Services | 348-9020 |
|---|---|
| Community Health | 348-3925 |
| County Commissioners | 348-3081 |
| Economic Assistance | 348-5198 |
| Licenses | 348-8240 |
| Parks | 559-9000 |
| Sheriff | 348-3744 |
| Social Services | 348-4806 |
| Voter Registration Information | 348-5151 |

### RAMSEY COUNTY

| General Information | 266-8500 |
|---|---|
| Auto Impound Lot | 482-5212 |
| Community Human Services | 298-5351 |
| County Commissioners | 266-8350 |
| Garbage | 292-7900 |
| Job Training Program | 770-8900 |
| Parks and Recreation | 777-1707 |
| Public Health | 266-2400 |
| Public Works | 266-2600 |

### SCOTT COUNTY

| General Information | 445-7750 |
|---|---|
| Highway Engineer | 496-8346 |
| Human Services | 455-7751 |
| License Bureau | 496-8448 |
| Sheriff | 496-8300 |

### WASHINGTON COUNTY

| General Information | 439-3220 |
|---|---|
| Community Services | 439-6901 |
| Parks | 430-6230 |
| Public Works | 430-4300 |
| Sheriff | 430-7600 |

## City Government Services

The municipal governments of Minneapolis and St. Paul provide the most comprehensive city ser-vices in the Twin Cities, but every suburb and town does its own part. Here's a sampling.

### MINNEAPOLIS

Minneapolis city government is led by Sharon Sayles Belton, the first African-American and first woman mayor in the city's history. The 13-member city council meets every two calendar weeks in Room 317 of City Hall, 350 S. Fifth Street.

| General Information | 673-3000 |
|---|---|
| Animal Control | 348-4250 |
| Animal Licenses | 673-2050 |
| Auto Impound Lot | 673-5777 |
| City Council information | 673-2215 |
| Civil Rights | 673-2144 |
| Elections and Voter Registration | 673-2070 |
| Fire Department Emergencies | 911 |
| Fire Department Non-emergencies | 673-2890 |
| Garbage Collection | 522-6644 |
| Health Department | 673-2301 |
| Housing Complaints | 673-5858 |
| Mayor's Office | 673-2100 |
| Park and Recreation Board | 661-4800 |
| Police Department Emergencies | 911 |
| Police Department Non-emergencies | 673-2853 |
| Public Works | 673-2352 |
| Recycling | 673-2917 |
| Snow Emergency Information | 348-SNOW |
| Water Works | 673-1098 |

### ST. PAUL

St. Paul's mayor, Norm Cole-man, presides over a seven-mem-ber City Council that meets on

Tuesdays and Thursdays in the Council Chambers, Third Floor, City Hall.

| | |
|---|---|
| General Information | 266-8989 |
| Animal Control | 645-3953 |
| Animal Licenses | 645-5451 |
| Child Care Information | 266-8505 |
| Employment and Training Center | 228-3283 |
| Fire Department Emergencies | 911 |
| Fire Department Non-emergencies | 224-7811 |
| Health Center | 292-7721 |
| Housing Information | 266-6000 |
| Human Rights | 266-8966 |
| Mayor's Office | 266-8510 |
| Parks and Recreation | 266-6400 |
| Police Department Emergencies | 911 |
| Police Department Non-emergencies | 291-1111 |
| Public Works | 266-6070 |
| Voter Registration | 266-2717 |
| Water Utility | 298-4237 |

There are scores of other cities and towns in the Twin Cities area; consult your phone book to find out more about municipal services outside of Minneapolis and St. Paul.

## Public Libraries

Minnesota is blessed with good and heavily used public library systems (some county libraries are even open on Sundays!), and the best part is that if you have a library card from any of the state's 101 public library systems, you can check out materials from any other public system in Minnesota. (By the same token, you can return most materials to any library, regardless of where you checked them out.) So whip out your St. Paul library card in Minneapolis, your Dakota County card in Anoka County, or your Hennepin County card in Duluth!

A warning for the computer-phobic: Not one of these library systems maintains a "card catalog" system any more. All instead use on-line computer catalogs or microfiche catalog listings. Don't be afraid of those computer terminals — they make it a lot easier to find materials.

### MINNEAPOLIS PUBLIC LIBRARIES
*Central Library*
*300 Nicollet Ave., Minneapolis    372-6500*

The 15 libraries in the Minneapolis Public Library System, evenly scattered throughout the city, hold nearly 2.5 million items. More than 1.6 million of those items are housed in the Central Library, a four-floor, 1960s-vintage downtown building that is becoming increasingly crowded — so crammed, in fact, that only 16 percent of its books and other materials are visible on open shelves. (You have to request the rest from closed stacks.) Despite the lack of space, the Central Library remains the best public library in the Twin Cities to do most kinds of research, and the librarians who staff the reference desks in the library's 10 departments know their areas of the collection inside out. Departments of especially notable strength are business and economics, children's books, and history and travel. Certainly the most heavily circulated part of the collection is the movie videos, which you can borrow for a week at a time for free. Most departments also have InfoTrack periodical search terminals that have

Photo: Joe Rossi, Pioneer Press

*Minnesota State Capitol in St. Paul.*

made the old and unwieldy *Reader's Guide to Periodical Literature* a relic of the past.

The third floor of the Central Library contains the valuable Minneapolis Collection, an aggregation of books, clippings, photos, maps and other materials covering the city's history, and special book collections that focus on North American Indians, natural history, travel and exploration, fables, World War II, the antislavery movement, and Mark Twain's works.

During the summer of 1994, the library inaugurated InfoLine, a free telephone reference service that answers callers' inquiries about everything from addresses to weather facts. You can reach InfoLine at 372-6633.

Library users with computers and modems can access the Minneapolis Public Library's on-line cata-

log by calling 332-5135 (1200 bps) or 332-5223 (2400 bps).

### St. Paul Public Libraries
*Central Library*
*90 W. Fourth St., St. Paul        292-6311*

Of all the public libraries in the Twin Cities, the St. Paul Public Libraries' downtown Central Library is the greatest architectural gem. Constructed in 1916 with slabs of pink Tennessee marble and blocks of Kettle River sandstone, it's an Italian Renaissance palace that rises at the edge of Rice Park. (The St. Paul Library shares the building with the James J. Hill Reference Library; see the sidebar for more information.) Inside is a wonderful marble staircase that most patrons apparently eschew in favor of the elevators.

As a place to read and do research, the 99,000-square-foot Central Library leaves much to be desired: It is cramped, poorly signed and cold, and the collection (or what little of the collection is available on open shelves) is confusingly organized in far-flung rooms. A baffling on-line catalog doesn't make it easy for patrons to find materials. While an access-minded renovation succeeded in making the building simpler for people with disabilities to navigate, the interior redesign also closed off the splendid original entrance and replaced it with an uninspiring ground-floor reception area.

With a collection significantly smaller than Minneapolis', the 400,000-volume Central Library's greatest strength is its librarians, who meet patrons' needs even while working under an obviously tight budget. There is a good audiovisual department, Children's Room, and literature collection, as well.

Twelve other branch libraries make up the St. Paul system, whose total collection contains about 700,000 items. People with computers and modems can access the on-line catalog by calling 292-6376.

## County Libraries

For Twin Citians in suburban or outlying areas, the seven county library systems place books, audiovisual materials and information within easy reach. Many of the county libraries are very heavily used — just go inside the recently enlarged Southdale-Hennepin Area Library in Edina on a typical weeknight during the school year, and you'll see what a busy library really looks like. (The Dakota County Libraries, in fact, have the Twin Cities' highest per-capita circulation despite the relatively small size of their collection.)

### ANOKA COUNTY LIBRARIES
*Central Library*
*707 Hwy. 10 N.E., Blaine*          784-1100
There are 10 branches in this system and a collection of more than 500,000 items. Remote access to the on-line catalog is available at 784-8950.

### CARVER COUNTY LIBRARIES
                           *448-9395*
This diminutive system, serving the southwest part of the Twin Cities, has fewer than 100,000 items in its collection. Computer/modem access to the catalog is shared with the Scott County Libraries, 496-8235.

### DAKOTA COUNTY LIBRARIES
                           *452-9600*
The five Dakota County libraries serve neighborhoods in West St. Paul, Eagan, Burnsville, Farmington, and Apple Valley. Com-

puter/modem access to the on-line catalog is available at 452-6008.

### HENNEPIN COUNTY LIBRARIES
*540-8200*

The Hennepin County Library system includes 26 facilities with 1.4 million items and an annual circulation of 8.9 million — the highest of any public library system in the region. Access the dial-in catalog by calling the number above.

### RAMSEY COUNTY LIBRARIES
*631-9435*

The seven libraries in this well-trafficked system — holding some 600,000 items — are located in the non-St. Paul areas of the county. Call 486-2222 for dial-in catalog access.

### SCOTT COUNTY LIBRARIES
*873-6767*

Second-smallest of the metro-area library systems, Scott County's has seven branches. Dial-in access to the catalog is at 496-8235.

### WASHINGTON COUNTY LIBRARIES
*459-2040*

The Washington County system has 300,000 items in its collection. Call 739-9647 for dial-in access.

## Utility Services

In general, Twin Cities area water and sewer service is provided by local municipalities. But if you want natural gas, electricity and phone service, you'll have to deal with these guys.

### MINNEGASCO
*372-4727*

Minnegasco is the utility that supplies natural gas to Minneapolis and its surrounding suburbs. Call 372-5050 to report gas leaks or emergencies.

### NORTHERN STATES POWER (NSP)
*282-1234*

They've got the volts, and they also provide the natural gas to St. Paul and its suburbs. Call 221-4411 for electric emergencies and 221-4421 if you smell gas.

### U S WEST COMMUNICATIONS
*(800) 244-1111*

For 99 percent of the Twin Cities area, call U S West if you want to order new home phone service, to ask billing questions, or to change existing home phone service. The person you'll speak with will probably be in Englewood, Colorado, which is where U S West is headquartered. For home phone repairs, call (800) 573-1311. To receive copies of the White or Yellow Pages call (800) 422-8793.

# *Inside*
# Service Directory

The following is a list of useful Minneapolis and St. Paul telephone numbers for both the traveler and new resident.

Keep in mind, however, that despite our best efforts to be up-to-date, some of these organizations and businesses are staffed by volunteers and/or are just testing the waters to try and fill a need so may have ceased efforts by the time of this volume's publication. For complete listings, check the Yellow Pages. And don't forget that sometimes the best information comes via word of mouth — from neighbors, hotel concierges and taxi drivers.

Businesses, services and organizations are listed alphabetically. At the end of the chapter, you'll find a special listing of emergency and crisis hotline numbers. See our Public Services chapter for other helpful numbers.

## *Animal Services*

### Humane Societies

**ANIMAL HUMANE SOCIETY
OF HENNEPIN COUNTY**
*522-4325*

**HUMANE SOCIETY OF RAMSEY COUNTY**
*645-7387*

### Kennels and Pet Sitters

(For information on other kennels and pet sitters in the Twin Cities, check the Yellow Pages or consult your veterinarian.)

**PETS ARE INN**

| | |
|---|---|
| North Minneapolis suburbs | 544-4104 |
| South Minneapolis and suburbs | 888-3545 |
| St. Paul and suburbs | 292-8933 |

**HOME AND PET SITTERS**
*459-6091*

**PAWS PLUS**
*537-6159*

**ANIMAL INN BOARDING KENNEL**
*777-0255*

**DOG HOUSE BOARDING KENNELS**
*473-9026*

**KOLSTAD'S K-9 ACRES**
*934-3884*

**CAMP COMFORT KENNEL**
*462-4614*

### Veterinarian Referral

**MINNESOTA VETERINARY
MEDICAL ASSOCIATION**
*645-7533*

## Banks

Here we are listing the larger banks, those with convenient locations throughout the Twin Cities. But remember, it's not size, but service, that counts.

### FIRST BANK
*(40 locations)*      973-1111

### FIRSTAR BANK
*(24 locations)*      784-5100

### INVESTORS BANK
*(13 locations)*      475-8500

### MARQUETTE BANK
*(17 locations)*      661-4000

### METROPOLITAN FEDERAL BANK
*(20 locations)*      225-7000

### NORWEST BANKS
*(61 locations)*      667-9378

### TCF BANK
*(40 locations)*      823-2265

## Child Care

### GREATER MINNEAPOLIS DAY CARE ASSOCIATION
*341-1177 or 341-2066*

### RESOURCES FOR CHILD CARING
*(Serving Ramsey County)*    641-0332

### COMMUNITY ACTION COUNCIL
*(Serving Dakota County)* 431-2424

## Services for the Disabled

### MINNESOTA STATE COUNCIL ON DISABILITY
*296-6785 or (800) 652-9747*

This state office serves as a general referral agency for people with disabilities, providing information on everything from housing to employment training to financial assistance.

### METRO MOBILITY
*221-0015*

This company provides transportation for the handicapped in converted vans and buses.

### ARC MINNESOTA
*827-5641*

With 55 chapters in Minnesota, this organization provides education and support to people with developmental disabilities.

### COURAGE CENTER
*520-0520*

This is a Golden Valley-based rehabilitation center for people with physical disabilities.

### METROPOLITAN CENTER FOR INDEPENDENT LIVING
*783-4722*

This organization promotes independent living for people with disabilities.

## Newcomer Services

### SUBURBAN WEST AREA NEWCOMERS CLUB
*473-8588 or 449-0038*

### WELCOME WAGON
*General number*      332-6231

**WELCOME WAGON**
**OF THE SOUTHWEST SUBURBS**
*934-7995*

## Road-Condition Information

**DEPARTMENT OF TRANSPORTATION**
**ROAD-CONDITION HOTLINE**
*296-3076*

## Transportation

### LOCAL BUSES

**METROPOLITAN COUNCIL**
**TRANSIT OPERATIONS**
*373-3333*

### CARPOOLING

**MINNESOTA RIDESHARE**
*349-RIDE*

### TAXICABS

**AIRPORT TAXI**
*721-0000*

**SUBURBAN TAXI**

|  |  |
|---|---|
|  | *884-8888* |
| *(south)* | *545-1234* |
| *(west)* | *781-1111* |
| *(north — Minneapolis)* | *349-9999* |

**ST. PAUL YELLOW CAB**
*222-4433*

### TRAINS

**AMTRAK**
*(800) 872-7245*

## AIRLINES

**NORTHWEST**
*726-1234*

### TWA
*333-6543*

**AMERICAN**
*(800) 433-7300*

**CONTINENTAL**
*332-1471*

**DELTA**
*339-7477*

**UNITED**
*339-3671*

**US AIR**
*(800) 428-4322*

## Trip Planning

**MINNESOTA TOURISM DEPARTMENT**
*296-5029 or (800) 657-3700*
These folks can give you information about every area of the state.

**DEPARTMENT OF NATURAL RESOURCES**
*296-6157*
The DNR provides information on outdoors issues, including Minnesota hunting seasons and laws.

**CANADIAN CONSULATE**
*332-4314*
The Canadian Consulate provides information on traveling in Canada.

## Volunteer Centers

**UNITED WAY'S VOLUNTEER CENTER OF MINNEAPOLIS**
*340-7621*

**VOLUNTARY ACTION CENTER OF ST. PAUL**
*227-3938*

**NATIONAL RETIREE VOLUNTEER COALITION**
*341-2689*

## Weather Information

**TIME AND WEATHER**
*452-2323*

**NATIONAL WEATHER SERVICE**
*725-6090*

## ZIP Codes

*Information*     *452-3800*

## Crisis Numbers

**AMBULANCE, FIRE AND POLICE**
*911*

## AIDS Information

**AIDS HOTLINE**
*373-AIDS*

## Child Abuse

**HENNEPIN COUNTY CHILD PROTECTION**
*348-3552*

**MINNESOTA COMMITTEE FOR THE PREVENTION OF CHILD ABUSE**
*641-1568*

**RAMSEY COUNTY SOCIAL SERVICES**
*298-5655*

## Parent Helplines

**MINNESOTA CRISIS INTERVENTION CENTER**
*347-3161*

**METRO CRISIS NURSERY PROGRAM**
*646-4033*

## Crime Victims

**CITIZENS COUNCIL VICTIM SERVICES**
*340-5400*

## Domestic Abuse, Rape and Sexual Assault

**FIRST CALL FOR HELP**
*Minneapolis*     *335-5000*
*St. Paul*     *224-1133*

**MINNESOTA COALITION FOR BATTERED WOMEN CRISIS LINE**
*646-0994*

**RAPE AND SEXUAL ASSAULT CENTER**
*825-4357*

## Family Planning

**MINNESOTA FAMILY PLANNING HOTLINE**
*(800) 783-2287*

## Drugs and Alcohol

**COCAINE HOTLINE**
*(800) 262-2463*

**ALCOHOL, DRUG AND**
**PREGNANCY HELPLINE**
*(800) 638-2229*

**CENTER FOR SUBSTANCE**
**ABUSE TREATMENT**
*(800) 662-4357*

**AL-ANON**
*(For families of alcoholics)* 920-3961

**ALCOHOLICS ANONYMOUS**
*Minneapolis* 922-0880
*St. Paul* 227-5502

## Gambling Addiction

**MINNESOTA COMPULSIVE**
**GAMBLING HOTLINE**
*(800) 437-3641*

## Gay, Lesbian Issues

**GAY AND LESBIAN HELP LINE**
822-8661

## Poison Control

**MINNESOTA REGIONAL POISON CENTER**
*St. Paul* 221-2113
*Hennepin County* 347-3141

## Suicide Hotlines

**HENNEPIN COUNTY**
347-2222

**RAMSEY COUNTY**
641-1300

**DAKOTA COUNTY**
891-1414

## General Crisis Hotlines

**MINNESOTA CRISIS**
**INTERVENTION CENTER**
347-3161

**CRISIS CONNECTION**
379-6363

**UNITED WAY'S FIRST CALL FOR HELP**
*(General referral services)*
*St. Paul* 224-1133
*Minneapolis* 335-5000
*Anoka* 783-4880

# Index of Advertisers

# Index

# ORDER FORM
## Fast and Simple!

**Mail to:**
**Insiders Guides®, Inc.**
**P.O. Drawer 2057**
**Manteo, NC 27954**

**Or:**
**for VISA or**
**Mastercard orders call**
**1-800-765-BOOK**

Name _____

Address _____

City/State/Zip _____

| Qty. | Title/Price | Shipping | Amount |
|---|---|---|---|
| | Insiders' Guide to Richmond/$12.95 | $2.50 | |
| | Insiders' Guide to Williamsburg/$14.95 | $2.50 | |
| | Insiders' Guide to Virginia's Blue Ridge/$12.95 | $2.50 | |
| | Insiders' Guide to Virginia's Chesapeake Bay/$12.95 | $2.50 | |
| | Insiders' Guide to Washington, DC/$12.95 | $2.50 | |
| | Insiders' Guide to North Carolina's Outer Banks/$12.95 | $2.50 | |
| | Insiders' Guide to Wilmington, NC/$12.95 | $2.50 | |
| | Insiders' Guide to North Carolina's Crystal Coast/$12.95 | $2.50 | |
| | Insiders' Guide to Charleston, SC/$12.95 | $2.50 | |
| | Insiders' Guide to Myrtle Beach/$12.95 | $2.50 | |
| | Insiders' Guide to Mississippi/$12.95 | $2.50 | |
| | Insiders' Guide to Boca Raton & the Palm Beaches/$14.95 (8/95) | $2.50 | |
| | Insiders' Guide to Sarasota/Bradenton/$12.95 | $2.50 | |
| | Insiders' Guide to Northwest Florida/$12.95 | $2.50 | |
| | Insiders' Guide to Lexington, KY/$12.95 | $2.50 | |
| | Insiders' Guide to Louisville/$14.95 | $2.50 | |
| | Insiders' Guide to the Twin Cities/$12.95 | $2.50 | |
| | Insiders' Guide to Boulder/$12.95 | $2.50 | |
| | Insiders' Guide to Denver/$12.95 | $2.50 | |
| | Insiders' Guide to The Civil War (Eastern Theater)/$14.95 | $2.50 | |
| | Insiders' Guide to North Carolina's Mountains/$14.95 (2/95) | $2.50 | |
| | Insiders' Guide to Atlanta/$14.95 (4/95) | $2.50 | |
| | Insiders' Guide to Branson/$14.95 (7/95) | $2.50 | |
| | Insiders' Guide to Cincinnati/$14.95 (9/95) | $2.50 | |

Payment in full (check or money order) must
accompany this order form.
Please allow 2 weeks for delivery.

N.C. residents add 6% sales tax _____

Total _____